Perón

Perón

AND THE ENIGMAS OF ARGENTINA

Robert D. Crassweller

W · W · NORTON & COMPANY

NEW YORK · LONDON

FIRST EDITION

*The text of this book is composed in Baskerville, with display type set in Centaur and Egiziano.
Composition and manufacturing by the Maple-Vail Book Manufacturing Group. Book design by
Marjorie J. Flock.*

Library of Congress Cataloging in Publication Data
Crassweller, Robert D.
  Perón and the enigmas of Argentina.

  Includes index.
  1. Argentina—History—1943– . 2. Perón, Juan
Domingo, 1895–1974. 3. Argentina—History. I. Title.
F2849.P48C73 1986   982'.062'0924   86–5298

ISBN 0-393-02381-8

W. W. Norton & Company, Inc., 500 Fifth Avenue, New York, N.Y. 10110
W. W. Norton &— Company ltd., 37 Great Russell Street, London WC1B 3NU

1 2 3 4 5 6 7 8 9 0

To Molly and
to Peter and Claudia, Karen and Steven,
and Pamela for their interest,
understanding, and patience

Photographs follow pages 143 and 291.

Contents

Acknowledgments   ix
Prologue   1

I   *THE ENIGMAS*

The Enigmas of Argentina   7
The Enigmas of Perón   11

II   *THE CRUCIBLE OF TIME, 1516–1943*

1. The Land   17
2. From Colony to Modern Nation, 1516–1880   22
3. Argentina in the Years of Triumph, 1880–1930   45
4. The Conservative Restoration, 1930–1943   71

III   *THE PERONATO, 1943–1955*

5. Perón's Rise to Power, 1943–1945   97
6. Peronism Ascendant, 1945–1946   136
7. Peronism in Power, 1946–1950   183

8. Peronism at High Tide   220

9. The Ebb Tide of Peronism, 1950–1955   234

IV *EXILE AND RETURN, 1955–1974*

10. The Caribbean Exile, 1955–1960   287

11. The Spanish Exile, 1961–1973   314

12. The Return of the Phoenix   340

Postscript: Peronism as Memory and Legend   369

Appendix: Presidents of Argentina   377

Notes   379

Sources   403

Bibliography   406

Index   421

Acknowledgments

MANY BOOKS OF this kind represent a greater venture in collaboration than the name of a single author would suggest, and the present instance is no exception.

I have been assisted at all times and on many levels by the skill, intuition, and devotion of Mrs. Elsa C. Waller, whose work as Research Assistant has been outstanding. She conducted many interviews on my behalf in her native Buenos Aires with an empathy born of rapport with the Argentine civilization that I have attempted to interpret in this book. Her help has been invaluable throughout.

Friends and strangers alike have contributed significant insights into the principal themes of this volume. I am thus much in debt to Alphonse De Rosso of Washington, D.C., well versed in Latin American affairs and a source of sensitive insights, and to his wife, Joan De Rosso, who volunteered assistance in archival aspects; Professor Walter Bateman of Rochester Community College in Rochester, Minnesota, my good friend of very long standing who opened up productive vistas into cultural anthropology; Professor Claudio Véliz of La Trobe University, Bundoora, Victoria, Australia, who is very knowledgeable in the sociology and culture of Latin America; Professor Rollie E. Poppino of the University of California, Davis, who graciously shared with me his understanding of Brazilian history and culture as they relate to Southern Cone realities; and Yenny Nun of Los Angeles, who commented on Southern Cone value patterns.

To my friend and colleague, Ricardo Lifsic of Buenos Aires, I express deep thanks for assistance that ranged widely over so many phases of the Argentine panorama, and for the knowledge of his country and society that he shared with me so willingly.

Many individuals, out of friendship or goodness of heart, have helped in specific ways, often at considerable personal inconvenience. My deep thanks therefore go to the following: Grace Darling Griffin, for her guidance and efforts that were instrumental in the initial launching of this project; my close friend Frank Vos, for helpful editorial advice at an important juncture; Professor Robert Alexander of Rutgers University, for access to interviews and research materials referred to more fully in the Bibliography; my fellow lawyer, Dr. Guillermo Walter Klein of Buenos Aires, for local assistance of various kinds; my good friend Tomás (Jimmy) Pastoriza of Santo Domingo, Dominican Republic, for his help in obtaining local information concerning Perón in that country; the historian, Maria Cecilia Ribas Carneiro, vice-director of the Centro de Memória Social Brasileira in Rio de Janeiro, for significant information concerning Brazilian foreign policy and the role of Getulio Vargas in Argentine relations; Bonifacio del Carril of Buenos Aires, for his analysis of Argentine political life; Heldo Borzaga for substantial assistance in regard to interviews and arrangements in Buenos Aires; Ralph Farbman, of Los Angeles, and his Argentine relatives, with regard to interviews in Buenos Aires; William Corthorn of Santiago, Chile, for help in obtaining materials; Professor Reuben E. Reina of the University of Pennsylvania, for his reply to my request for information; New York free-lance editor Carol Kahn for a very helpful editorial suggestion; my friends and one-time colleagues, José González and Pablo D'Onofrio, for generous assistance with respect to arrangements in Buenos Aires; Torcuato S. Di Tella of Buenos Aires, for his help with local sources of information; my former colleague, George McKinnis, and Professor Ronald G. Hellman of the Bildner Center for Western Hemisphere Studies at the City University of New York Graduate Center, for suggestions concerning interviews; and James D. Theberge, recently United States Ambassador to Chile, and Joshua Powers of New York City, for help regarding sources.

And, of course, libraries and official archival sources were essential. The staff of the National Archives and Records Service in Washington, D.C., provided broad support, and the courteous and efficient cooperation of Sally M. Marks, Archivist, was outstanding. My requests under the Federal Freedom of Information Act were well handled by the Information and Privacy Staff at the United States Department of State, whose representative, Georgene S. Cassels, went out of her way to be helpful. The staff and fellow members of the Council on Foreign Relations were constantly helpful, including the remarkably competent and generous Helena Stalson; the editorially skilled Robert Valkenier; and the librarians who contributed so much, in particular Janet Rigney and Virginia Etheridge. The staff at the Ferguson Library in Stamford, Connecticut, provided continuous help, and its Interlibrary Loan Service deserves much credit.

Needless to say, I bear full responsibility for the contents of this book, including its themes, concepts, and possible errors and omissions, and no blame on any score should be imputed to the aforementioned persons and institutions.

Robert D. Crassweller

Perón

BOLIVIA

PARAGUAY

JUJUY
Jujuy ★
Salta ★

FORMOSA

● Asunción

SALTA

CATAMARCA

San Miguel de Tucumán
TUCUMÁN ★

SANTIAGO
DEL

CHACO

Catamarca ★
Catamarca

Santiago del Estero ★

ESTERO

La Rioja ★
LA
RIOJA

SAN
JUAN

San Juan ★

Córdoba
●

CÓRDOBA

SANTA
FE

Esperanza ●
Santa Fe ★

CORRIENTES

Corrientes ●

MISIONES

BRAZIL

ENTRE
Paraná ★

URUGUAY

RÍOS

Mendoza ★

San Luis ●

SAN
LUIS

Rosario ●
San Nicholás ●

Santiago ⊙

MENDOZA

Junín ●
Chivilcoy ●

Fed.
Dist. ⊙

Buenos Aires

La Plata ★

Montevideo ⊙

Río de la Plata

C H I L E

LA PAMPA

BUENOS
AIRES

Bahía Blanca ●

Mar del Plata ●

NEUQUÉN

Neuquén ★

RÍO NEGRO

San Carlos
de Bariloche ●

PACIFIC OCEAN

42° ———————————————— 42°

Rawson ★

CHUBUT

ATLANTIC OCEAN

Comodoro
Rivadavia ●

SANTA

CRUZ

Argentina

⊙ National Capitals
★ Provincial Capitals

Río Gallegos ★

TIERRA
DEL
FUEGO

Ushuaia ★

MALVINAS
(FALKLAND ISLANDS)

MILES
0   100   200   300   400   500

CHAZAUD

Prologue

Time present and time past
Are both perhaps present in time future,
And time future contained in time past.
If all time is eternally present
All time is unredeemable.

—T. S. Eliot, *Burnt Norton*

O N THE EVENING OF June 21, 1978, an enthusiastic audience at the Prince Edward Theatre in London applauded the opening of a new musical, based on the life and early death of the second wife of a president of Argentina. Those present, and thousands of audiences to come, were commemorating a legend and in so doing were themselves participating in the unfolding of another legend, for the worldwide success of *Evita* has come to mirror the mythology of its heroine.

Dreams seem to attend it, among them one that runs somewhat counter to the main themes of the musical and emerges almost fortuitously, a longing of the times caught in the cadence of the most memorable of the songs and held there in tonal amber:

Don't cry for me Argentina.
The truth is I shall not leave you
Though it may get harder
For you to see me
I'm Argentina
And always will be.[1]

There, perhaps, is the key: the promise of community and devotion in the fragmented Argentina that the real Evita knew and in the worlds beyond Argentina that the audiences have experienced, worlds of anomie and apartness seeking unity and support, searching like Browning's Abt Vogler for the perfect round in a creation of broken arcs.

Whatever truth is inherent in this view applies as well to Juan Domingo Perón, the husband of the mythic Evita. For it is the first theme of this study of Perón and Argentina that his success and his failure and his ascent into legendry were in part the consequences of a similar intuitive identity and community that united the leader and a majority of the nation in a tenacious relationship of quite unusual loyalty.

There is a second theme: To an important extent, Perón's achievements flowed from his personification of Argentina's Hispanic and Creole civilization. From that civilization and from its lodging within himself came his failures as well; thus, in the end, the hint of tragedy that lingers around his memory.

An explanation is in order here. The word "civilization" is used, for the experiences of Perón and of Argentina indicate that we are dealing not merely with a particular polity or economy or social structure, but with a distinctive ethos, a civilization in the sense that Octavio Paz has used the term: ". . . that fluid zone of imprecise contours in which are fused and confused ideas and beliefs, institutions and technologies, styles and morals, fashions and churches, the material culture and that evasive reality that we rather inaccurately call *le genre de peuples.*" Or, further, "A civilization is not only a system of values, it is a world of forms and codes of behavior, principles and customs, rules and exceptions. It is a table of commandments and a ritual of transgressions and expiations. It is society's visible side—institutions monuments, ideas, works, things—but it is especially society's submerged, invisible side—beliefs, desires, fears, repressions, dreams."[2]

Despite superficial similarities and language carelessly used, this Argentine civilization is quite different from the civilization of those who view Argentina from the outside, expecting to find patterns of life and development similar to those of northern Europe and the United States. Perón's civilization is a culmination of cultures and values bequeathed by Rome, by the Moors who dominated the Iberian peninsula for many centuries, and by Castile in old Spain, all revised and reinforced during four centuries of New World history.

Inevitably, there is much that is enigmatic and generally misunderstood in the tale of Perón, his country, and his civilization. To provide a kind of view from Olympus and a framework for the narrative history that follows, Part I of this book contains brief sketches of what are seen as the enigmas of Argentina and of Perón.

The enigmas are, of course, rooted in the past, and the story, intensely human and historical, thus becomes an adventure in time and its interactions in which the past (and the future as well in Eliot's concept) is summoned to elucidate the present.

> Go, go, go, said the bird: human kind
> Cannot bear very much reality.
> Time past and time future
> What might have been and what has been
> Point to one end, which is always present.
>
> — T. S. Eliot, *Burnt Norton*

I

THE ENIGMAS

The failure of Argentina as a nation is the biggest political mystery of this century.

— *The New Statesman*, 1978

The Enigmas of Argentina

VISCOUNT BRYCE, one of those urbane British citizens of the world who combine with easy grace the vocation of diplomacy and the avocation of letters, visited Argentina during the buoyant period at the end of the first decade of this century. Observing the progress that was one of the marvels of the world, Bryce predicted that within the time of men then living, Argentina could take its place beside France, Italy, and Spain, becoming the "head and champion" of the Latin races in the New World. It was already "the United States of the southern hemisphere."[1]

Argentina was then being compared favorably with Canada and Australia. Its political stability was as widely lauded as its splendid economic achievement. A British scholar, contrasting Argentina with its turbulent neighbors, wrote in August 1929 that revolution in Argentina was as improbable as it was in England.[2] His timing was unfortunate, preceding by only ten months the military revolution that signified the great turning point, the end of a long era of success and the approach of more than half a century of Argentine misfortune.

Since 1930, twenty-five governments have risen to power, fourteen of them by coup d'etat or by less overt forms of military persuasion, in a country that before 1930 had looked back upon seventy years of unbroken civilian supremacy. Representative government was twice abandoned for years at a time.

Riots and strikes, assassinations, and waves of guerrilla insurgency and official counterviolence have roiled society on every level. After the possibilities of political mismanagement had been almost exhausted, a military government in 1982 led the country into its first shooting war in more than a century, and lost it in seventy-four days. Elections in 1983 brought encouraging developments, but as of 1986, the prospect contains much that is familiar. Precedents that lighted the way to disillusion for decades have lost their monopoly but not their vitality.

The economy fared little better. In 1928, the Argentine per capita gross national product ranked eighth in the world; now it is forty-third. There were some showings of health, more than the Argentines, who compared them unfavorably with higher growth rates in the United States and elsewhere, would admit, but crises and burnt-out ministers of economy were familiar landmarks.

A sour mood settled over the land in the 1930s and during most of the years that followed, mingling alienation, apathy, outrage, cynicism, hostility, and pure bewilderment, When the dark spirit lifted for a time, as it did during the first two Perón administrations, it was replaced by bitter contention over social purposes that divided classes, friends, families. The fall from grace was seen to be almost biblical in its sweep, as if a judgment had been rendered. But throughout all this, the basic sources of Argentine success remained unchanged. Why, then, the fall, from which redemption is still uncertain? That is the first great enigma.

But other enigmas complicate its solution, for it is expressed here in the customary ethnocentric terms, which assume Argentine political and social values to be identical with those of western Europe and the United States. They are not, and Argentine objectives and performance must be judged accordingly. Even the language in general use takes on the aspect of enigma. "Democracy," with its related vocabulary, has become a universal currency of discussion, invoked by all, but the connotations so familiar in North America and in parts of Europe that they are taken for granted do not prevail in the same way in the very different context and background of Argentina: the usages of language reflect the civilization.[3] Thus Perón could be elected under traditional democratic rules and then turn at times to repressions that he insisted were also "democratic"; thus his opponents who admired traditional democracy could implement it by depriving the Perónists of the right to vote on the ground that they were "antidemocratic," although they were the largest political group in the country and had invariably come to office through the ballot.

There are many lesser enigmas of this most interesting country, illuminating the scene and providing material for speculation. In a land substantially supported by pastoral and agricultural resources, why is there no true agrarian consciousness? Why do neighborhood relationships in urban settings often stop short of true friendship, resulting, instead, in correct but impersonal social distance? What does the proximity of one's burial lot to the cemetery entrance in provincial towns have in common with the distance of one's house from the town's central plaza?

The enigmas have attracted enormous speculation from specialists who have provided explanations based in every discipline. Many of the conclusions are persuasive, but they often seem incomplete because there is usually something in the background sensed but not fully brought forth, a hint of chambers beyond chambers, as if the courier in Kafka's tale were trying once more to advance beyond the Great Wall of China. The missing element in the explanations often seems to be an understanding of the motivation and conduct of the individuals who form the priesthood of public life, and of those who follow them inarticulately.

The search for the mainsprings of human conduct as the keys to the enigmas leads to values and beliefs and the institutional patterns in which they are expressed, and to the origins of these in civilization and heritage. For there is, in fact, a distinctive constellation of traditional Hispanic and Creole values, attitudes, and practices, glimpsed in every interstice and interplay of Argentine life, often subtle and touched with a bit of mystery, like distant lights in the darkness of night.

The perennial rebirth of this intricate inheritance in the lives of the great Argentine leaders, and in their society, is a fascination. This is true of Juan Perón above all, for he was the most important political leader in his nation's history, and it is clear that the Creole values of time past and time present were fundamental to his formation.

The story goes that, before or after he died, he found himself before God, and he said: "I, who have been so many men in vain, want to be one man: myself." The voice of God replied from a whirlwind: "Neither am I one self; I dreamed the world as you dreamed your work, my Shakespeare, and among the shapes of my dreams are you, who, like me, are many persons—and none."

— Jorge Luis Borges, *Everything and Nothing*

The Enigmas of Perón

THE MAN WHO EMERGED to cope with the enigmas of Argentina at a critical moment was himself a repository of endless enigmas. There were so many of them, and they pointed in so many directions, that one is tempted to conclude that, like Borges's Shakespeare who beseached God for his identity, he was many persons—and therefore none.[1] He in fact suggested that he was a "double"—one being who acted and another who observed himself from afar.[2]

There was the Perón of balcony bombast, the populist orator above, with the shouting multitude below. There was the Perón of sober pragmatism. There was occasionally a reckless Perón, and one who was a stranger to temerity, holding back at the moment of crisis. One of the Peróns was cultured in speech and in writing; another could hold forth in picturesque *lunfardo,* the colorful argot of the Buenos Aires slums. Among the Peróns was one who spoke the truth, and his opposite who spoke as if he had never heard of it. There was a military Perón and a very different political Perón. Was the Perón who assailed "imperialistic" foreign corporations the same Perón who negotiated privately with Standard Oil?

The parade of Peróns is endless. There was one who was devious and labyrinthine, matched by a simple and straightforward counterpart. A histrionic Perón and one of plain facade. The Perón who sometimes condoned violence when it was done on his behalf and an opposite who was mild in action. The Perón who lived his life among multitudes, never alone, and the one who was solitary at the heart of a throng. The Perón who revered order and organic principles, and the one who elevated improvisation to the level of high art. The Perón who pursued political objectives openly and directly, and the Perón whose economic tactics were indirect.[3]

His relations with women abound in enigma. He found much happiness with his first wife, a very private homebody. Was he the same husband whose second wife, an actress, wrought changes in the entire political and social order? Was either of these husbands the one who made his third wife, a nonpolitical dancer of minor public skills, the vice-president of Argentina and, as his successor, the first female president in the Western Hemisphere? One Perón valued women more for their company than for their bodies, and another at the age of fifty-eight took a fourteen-year-old mistress, perhaps in subconscious search of the child he never fathered. One part of him was traditional male and another part defied the mores of a male-dominated society.

Other enigmas arise from a cursory view of Perón's life. He left a permanent mark upon his society, changing Argentina forever. But how many leaders of such a stamp advance routinely well into middle age before power even beckons at a distance? Until Perón was forty-eight, there was no indication whatever that he would even have a political career, let alone that he would be elected president when he was fifty. He fell from high office, departed into distant exile, and still remained the hub around which the public process rotated. After eighteen years, being then an old man on the verge of death, he returned to the presidency by way of a smashing victory in free balloting. What other authoritarian leader did any of these things?

On the surface it is not easy to discern how Perón accomplished what he did. What was visible in him was very impressive, but hardly enough to account for the extraordinary phenomenon of his career. He was tall, handsome in a masculine way, wore his uniform well, and was generally charming and ingratiating; and his smile was a splendor. He worked hard and he possessed the discipline and the physical vitality necessary for political performance at the highest level. Although he was not an intellectual in the most profound sense of the word, he had a superb intelligence, inquiring and absorptive. He read widely, learned rapidly, wrote with facility, and was the author of numerous books and a stream of pamphlets, newspaper columns (published under the pseudonym of "Descartes"), and lesser works. He had taught at the War Academy, and to the very end he retained among his personalities the didactic persona of the would-be professor: a strange union of the man of arms, the man of politics, and the man of letters. Late in his life, when he was worn down by the abrasions of politics, he dreamed of a retreat to the Hudson Institute in Croton-on-Hudson, New York, where he would indulge his curiosity and live in the more tranquil world of concepts. Yet even in this area of his personality there was duality and enigma. Was the Perón who traced his political movement back to Lycurgus and who drew upon Plato and the *Philosophes* the Perón who closed universities when their opposition became too boisterous?

Guile was as natural to Perón as breath. He was a man out of the *cinquecento* who found his political mentor and spiritual guide in Machiavelli, for he had inherited from the great Florentine both the noble and the pragmatic: the love of patriotism and unity and the genius for opportunistic maneuver. But yet there was often a kind of open, bluff heartiness about him that dissolved the darker residues of deceit, as if he were Falstaff laughing at his sins and those of the world and calling for another tankard. He was a sincere patriot and he wished the best for his country, but beyond that his exact relationship to principles must be charted from the ground up by anyone who wishes to study the man, for no received wisdom on this point can withstand the ferocious disagreements of those who admit no good in Perón and those who admit nothing else. It is possible to spend hours perusing the enormous literature on Perónism and talking with Perón's friends and enemies without encountering more than a few inches of common ground. His enemies saw him as a tyrant, a robber, and the focus of evil. But a close friend, a hard-headed and successful man of affairs, said of him, "Perón for many of us, above all for the most humble people, is an idol, a God. I have no doubt that within a hundred or two hundred years . . . the people will address themselves to God, and not to the saints but to God and to Perón. I am certain it will be so."

To account for Perón's remarkable achievements, one must understand his abstract and invisible qualities, which did not lend themselves to quick stereotype or caricature. Among them were his intuition, his almost preternatural understanding of the popular psyche and his emotional rapport with the Argentine civilization.

Summoning a vision of a new order, he attempted to impose it, and he succeeded to some extent. He redressed the social balance, thereby changing the dynamics of Argentine society for all time, and for many he represented the sense of community and social cohesion hinted at in *Evita*. But his achievements fell far short of his hopes for the nation, and he died no stranger to disillusion.

Thus arose the central enigma of Perón's relationship with Argentina: how was it that he did so much and yet did no more? Nemesis appeared toward the end in the form of physical decline, but in the years that had gone before, Perón's principles had been resisted as stoutly as they had been sustained, and the enigma of mingled success and failure remains.

II

THE CRUCIBLE OF TIME
1516~1943

> . . . what impressions must be made upon the inhabitant of the Argentine Republic by the simple fact of fixing his eyes upon the horizon, and seeing nothing?—for the deeper his gaze sinks into that shifting, hazy, undefined horizon, the further it withdraws from him, the more it fascinates and confuses him . . .
>
> — Domingo F. Sarmiento, *Facundo*

1. The Land

THE LAND IS IMMENSE, a bazaar of opposites, a tribute to improbability. Its tiny base in the remotest south, amid antarctic wind and current, is Tierra del Fuego, an island surrounded by frightful waters made famous by Magellan, by Drake, and by Darwin. From there it thrusts northward for some 2,200 miles, an elongated and irregular triangle wildly various. The Andes, the second highest mountains in the world, lie along the west, and on the east is the world's second largest ocean. The Argentine north is rimmed by the hot scrubby lowlands of Paraguay and Brazil and the rising highland approaches to moonlike Bolivia. There are 1,084,359 square miles of this strangely positioned land—the makings, almost, for four states of Texas.

The natural approach to Argentina is through its great capital, Buenos Aires, the metropolis rising and sprawling on the low, flat western bank of the Rió de la Plata, the River of Silver, 150 miles inland from the river's outlet in the Atlantic and thirty miles from neighboring Uruguay, across the water. "Silver" is a strangely inappropriate name to apply to this shallow, coffee-hued river. It reflects the first of the chimeras of the early Spanish explorers, convinced that the Plata would lead them upstream northwesterly to the silver that legend had already certified in Bolivia. It is really the broad estuary of two other rivers, the Uruguay and the Paraná, which flow into it at a common point just above Buenos Aires.

The city by the great river, with its formless metropolitan area and its ten million *porteños,* is a place of sumptuous boulevards, opera, and women of high fashion, a distillation of France and Italy and continental elegance. Like Washington, it forms a Federal District. It also forms a gigantic monopoly, for government and finance and trade and politics and communication all exert here the strongest of tidal attractions, the rest of the nation flowing in willy-nilly.

Surrounding Buenos Aires on all its landward sides is the important province of the same name. City and province and the adjacent areas that share the same remarkable topography make up the first of the five major regions into which the country may be divided. Here is the feature for which Argentina is famed, the pampas, the perfectly flat grassy plains without perceived limit extending like an intimation of eternity toward a horizon as elusive as the river's silver, almost unbroken, unrelieved, and unmarked under a sky so vast as to suggest a pronouncement by an archaic god. The horizon has fascinated the Argentine mind and entered into the Argentine soul, the horizon that, as a famous Argentine writer expressed it, ". . . always looks the same as we advance, as if the whole plain moved along with us . . . here prairie is expanse, and expanse seems to be nothing more than the unfolding of the infinite within, a colloquy of the traveler with God."[1]

It is the pampas that have produced the gaucho of legend, and the horses, the cattle, and later the wheat that have made Argentina a colossus of export. The imagination is coerced by stark immensity. Here and there, as if discerning the smallest of islands in the largest of seas, the eye is caught by clumps of eucalyptus and lombardy pine that surround some *estancia,* breaking the rush of the wind. Apart from these there is only the occasional solitary ombú, the single tree indigenous to the area, the symbol of Argentina, unique among trees as the pampas are unique among landscapes. The ombú has a huge trunk and widely spreading branches, but its distinction lies in its roots and in its obstinacy. The roots, knotted and gnarled, rise out of the ground and spread out in strange forms and shapes, profuse and weedlike. Its obstinacy fits it for its life as the emblem of a tumultuous land and culture. No cyclone has ever leveled an ombú, no drought has ever killed one, no fire can burn one. It cannot be cut by customary means and so has no utility as lumber. But it can enter into the national life in its symbolic way, since it attracts men and events as the only plausible stopping point in a world almost undifferentiated. Thus General José de San Martín, the liberator of the southern portion of the continent and the Argentine national hero, once tarried with two other leaders of independence, the three of them sitting on the roots of a massive ombú while they exchanged vows of perseverence, after which the tree became known as the Ombú of Hope. Other ombús have been named for treaties signed in their shade during times of civil strife.

The metaphor of the lighthouse has often been applied to these grand and lonely trees, and the analogy of the sea is apt. The pampas indeed reflect the great oceans, the grasses and the flowing miles of grain undulating wavelike in the wind, the flaming sorcery of dawn and sunset glowing as at sea.[2]

Buenos Aires is the constantly encroaching center of a dominating littoral. To its southeast are the provincial capital, the coastal city of La Plata, once known as Eva Perón, and a famous resort city, Mar del Plata. To its northwest, on the banks of the Paraná River, is Rosario, important in the industrial belt that stretches along the Plata-Paraná. Farther up the river is the significant city of Santa Fe, and inland to the northwest, but still on the outer verge of the pampas, is Córdoba, the second city. The statistics are dry, but not without relevance: in this first region of Argentina are 22 percent of the country's land area, 65 percent of its population, 70 percent of the railroad trackage, and 85 percent of industrial production.[3]

In the northeast, and between the Paraná and the Uruguay rivers, are the provinces of Entre Ríos, Corrientes, and remote Misiones. This is the second of the five national regions, an area humid and subtropical, where rolling plains deep in grass alternate with forested valleys. The largest city is Paraná, the capital of Entre Ríos, a river town almost across from Santa Fe. Misiones is the far northeastern tip of Argentina, thrusting up in the shape of a rhinoceros horn to the tremendous Iguazú Falls, where Brazil, Paraguay, and Argentina come together.

To the west and north begins the third of the Argentine regions, the lowland plain called the Chaco, a kingdom among wastelands, the haunt of scrub growth, of spine and thorn and hostile thicket resistant to humankind, a place that knows some of the highest temperatures on the continent.

The fourth Argentine zone is the far northwest and west, the earliest settled region. Some of it resembles the adjacent areas of Bolivia, or High Peru as it was called in colonial times, with mountains and foothills and piedmont oases rising to elevations of from 11,000 to 13,000 feet and peaks and isolated ranges that exceed 19,000 feet. The northernmost Argentine community is Jujuy, a verdant spot lying green along the Río Grande, with some of the Indian flavor and nuance of Bolivia. Not far to the south is the old colonial center, Salta, a dim and remote spot with no hint of its once-great importance as the economic center of the entire northwestern region, which then greatly overshadowed the eastern part of the country.[4]

Farther to the south is Tucumán, an active old colonial town that marks the center of Argentine sugar cultivation. Directly behind the city to the west, peaks soar imperiously above 17,000 feet without the preliminary bother of foothills or lesser frontal ranges. Further down the western border and past the isolated and underdeveloped provinces of Catamarca and La Rioja, is the ancient town and province of Mendoza, where vineyards and wine production predominate. The vineyard provinces, including all of Mendoza and parts of neighboring San Juan and San Luis, are known collectively as the Cuyo. The titanic and otherworldly bastions of the Andes seem to rise almost at the edge of Mendoza, masking behind them the peak of Aconcagua, at almost 23,000 feet the highest point in the New World.

About six hundred miles south from Mendoza, still shadowed by the spine of the Andes, is a high, cool, Alpine lake district centering around Lake Nahuel Huapí and the small city of San Carlos de Bariloche, a country of crags and fjords and mighty peaks within a national park of more than 3,000 square miles that is not diminished by comparison to the Rockies and the Alps.

Extending east from the lake district and far to the south, occupying the narrowing southern end of the long national triangle, is Patagonia. This is the fifth region and the largest. Below it there is only the Strait of Magellan, the island of Tierra del Fuego, which is shared by Chile and Argentina, the Beagle Channel, Cape Horn, and grim cold waters. Patagonia covers 25 percent of the national territory and contributes about 1 percent of the population; one person per square mile is a respectable figure in these parts. Patagonia is mostly a vast, cool desert plateau, the largest desert area in the Americas, dry and hard, bullied by clamorous winds carrying with them so much fine dirt and dust that haze often obstructs even near-range vision. Patagonia's relationship to time seems ambiguous, for its aspect is older even than time past, something precedent to time yet fated to outlive time future. Remoteness and isolation become almost tangible here, crushing realities that dominate life and perception. The tiny immigration that has had the hardihood to penetrate Patagonia includes, in addition to Chileans, a high proportion of arrivals from England, Germany, Scotland, and particularly Wales. "If God made the earth," an old Welsh settler wrote in the early, hard years, "the devil made Patagonia and he made it as like his own special home as two pies."[5]

There is ample legendry here, the inevitable yield of a land of almost unique geography, climate, and emptiness. The strange and the marvelous are generated spontaneously here where no witness discourages the imagination. It was in Patagonian waters that the albatross appeared to Coleridge's Ancient Mariner. The Tehuelche Indians who once lived in Patagonia were models for the giants with whom Swift populated his Brobdingnag. Caliban and the god Setebos, from *The Tempest* and from Browning's poem, trace back to Patagonia and to Magellan's voyage of discovery.

> And so, though Spanish-American civilization is to
> be admired on many counts, it reminds us of a con-
> struction of great solidity—at once convent, fortress,
> and palace—built to last, not to change. In the long
> run, that construction became a confine, a prison.
>
> — Octavio Paz, in *Mexico*, Tommie Sue Montgomery, Ed.

2. From Colony to Modern Nation, 1516-1880

The Heritage of Castile

AT THE FIRST MOMENT of Argentine history, a paradox
arose. The Río de la Plata, the highway to Argentina, is on the western
rim of the Atlantic, and Spain is on the eastern rim. How natural to
colonize the Plata area through direct crossings. But nothing in
Argentine history was ever that simple. Instead, the colonizing effort
proceeded by way of the west coast of South America, and the Atlantic shore was reached from the Pacific, an eloquent and not untypical
commentary on the hardly credible vitality of the great wave of explo-
ration, conquest, and settlement that brought Castile to the New World
in the sixteenth century.

The first sightings of what is now Argentina did indeed come from
the Atlantic approaches, but these were ephemeral. The river route
to the interior by way of the Paraná was discovered, but it led to little
more than a handful of gold and silver trinkets filtered down from
Peru and some wishful myths. In 1536, an expedition arrived under
the command of Pedro de Mendoza, and a settlement was established
along the banks of a small tributary to the estuary, the Riachuelo.
Thus Buenos Aires was born, but prematurely. Harried by privations
and hostilities, it was abandoned in 1541. The survivors retreated
upstream to Asunción, leaving, however, an informal memorial in the

form of seven horses and five mares turned loose on the adjoining pampas. Doubling their population every three years, the animals laid one of the foundations for the Argentine sociology of the future.

When Buenos Aires was founded for the second time, and permanently, it was done by Juan de Garay from Asunción as a base. In the Spanish colonies, cities did not appear spontaneously, as they did in the English possessions; rather, they were founded in the most official way by the joint action of Crown and Church, with documents, plans, and ritual. These formalities occurred on June 11, 1580, and the city whose name has been winnowed down in the air age to "B.A." was dedicated as *Ciudad de la Santísima Trinidad y Puerto de Santa María de Buenos Aires*. The design of the city, as of all others, followed the forms and dimensions laid down in Book IV, paragraphs 7 and 8 of the Laws of the Indies, a good example of early centralized government.[1]

But in a sense Garay was too late. The focus of settlement had already been established in the northwest and in the interior. Coming out of Peru and what was later Bolivia, and from Chile as well, small streams of settlers continued their efforts after founding Santiago del Estero in 1551–52. San Juan, Tucumán, Córdoba, Salta, and Jujuy were all established between 1561 and 1592.

The discovery of a magnificent silver mountain, a great cone rising high above the surrounding plateau in present-day Bolivia, and the founding in 1545 of the town of Potosí at its base, deeply affected the course of empire in South America. One consequence was the predominance of a mining economy and the strengthening of the commercial and political interests that quickly formed around the burdensome but already established lifeline of empire from Spain to Peru by way of the Isthmus of Panama. It was now clear that the destiny of tiny reborn Buenos Aires would long remain that of an outpost, an afterthought, a drab collection of primitive structures balanced precariously between the ocean and the edge of nowhere.

Thus the incongruous sequence of original settlement was confirmed. For two centuries all communications and trade flows to the future Argentina would proceed by sea from Spain to the Atlantic coast of Panama; would there be shipped by mule train across the peaks and jungles of the arduous Isthmus to the Pacific shore; would there be reshipped and sent by sea down the coast to a Peruvian port; would there be unloaded and sent by wagon train to the high, cold plateau where the mines provided the economic focus of the continent; would there be reloaded for the land voyage by mule train to some point on the upper Paraná; would there be unloaded again and reshipped on river craft down perhaps 1,500 miles on the Paraná to Buenos Aires. Or the goods might go by mule train from Potosí all the way through the interior to the Plata. If all went well, the trip from Spain to Buenos Aires could be made in approximately eight months.[2]

A strange undertaking. If travel between England and the early North American colonies had proceeded up the St. Lawrence River, across to Georgian Bay, down Lake Huron, across to Lake Erie, and overland from the site of Cleveland to Massachusetts Bay or Jamestown, the distance would have been less than half that of the Spanish route.

The early settlements in the Argentine northwest and in the interior, followed later by the developments on the Atlantic littoral, brought the timeless Spanish civilization and values. These formed one basis, and an exceedingly important one, of the future Argentine nation. To understand the latter, and to comprehend Juan Perón as an Argentine phenomenon, one must proceed as indirectly as did the early colonists and consider first the traditional civilization of Peninsular Spain.

Its crowded origins are difficult to untangle, but Rome is prominent among them. From Rome came the Spanish spirit, Spanish law, Spanish esthetics, and the ideal of the public man, the magistrate, the legislator.[3] Another great source began to appear in 710, when Moorish invaders from North Africa pushed northward from Gibraltar and soon brought much of the Peninsula under their control, keeping it there for centuries. The Spaniards fought back, bit by bit, in the process known as the Reconquest. The crusades became for the Iberian Peninsula an entire national history, ending only on that January day in 1492 when the last Moorish king rode forth from Grenada, the final stronghold, to surrender the keys of the city.

By that time, the separate crowns that had shared the Peninsula had become unified under the leadership of Castile, which was fortunate in having a succession of remarkable monarchs: Isabella and Ferdinand, known as the Catholic Kings; the famous emperor, Charles V; and his son, Philip II.

Spain might be Castile, but Castile was still the Reconquest. That long and arduous crusade had deeply marked Castilian character and personality. Society was pastoral and had lived by war for centuries, disdaining lesser and demeaning pursuits such as commerce. A powerful and authoritarian state emerged, energized by effective government. The parliament of Castile, the Cortes, lacked the power of the purse and soon languished. Royal power, resolutely exercised, curtailed any political role for the aristocracy, which contented itself with social privilege, and there was no significant challenge from below.

Freedom in the Anglo-Saxon sense of the word was not a product of these tendencies, but that implies neither tyranny nor misrule. All the monarchs of the age were popular and intuitively sensitive to public moods and aspirations. Thus royal authority was willingly accepted and viewed as consistent with freedom and liberty. Absolutism, tied to religious values, was not seen as tyranny, since individual rights and dignity were protected.[4]

Side by side with the State stood the centralized and authoritarian Church. The passionate nature of life during the Reconquest, and the need for a symbol and focus in the long struggle against the infidel, had given enormous strength to the Church. Profoundly identified with the people and associated with national causes, the Church was firm on the strongest of foundations. The political and religious heritages of the Reconquest were brought to unity in that most fascinating of architectural monuments, the Escorial. Built on the Castilian plateau some twenty miles north of Madrid by Philip II, the Escorial is part palace, part monastery, and part something more than palace and monastery combined. Rarely has architecture bespoken so truly the ethos within which it was created. Anyone interested in penetrating the deeper layers of Spanish civilization would do well to spend a day contemplating the Habsburg portions of this extraordinary structure, so austere, so measured, so steeped in somber dignity, so powerful, so joyless, so suggestive of dark brooding. The spirit of the Spain that was transmitted to the Indies resides not in flamenco and guitar but in the Escorial, rising out of the flint-hard soil of Castile like an incarnation.

The authoritarian State and the authoritarian Church shared one historical reality in particular: neither had any experience with shared or diffused power. The State had never known feudalism in the northern European sense of a system with centers of political power apart from, and often in opposition to, the royal authority. There had been no Magna Carta in Spain, no warlike barons jealously and successfully protecting their local powers, no system of courts enforcing laws that did not originate with the king's justice. The Church was the Church of the Counter-Reformation, necessarily broad and pluralistic in many respects, a palace of many chambers, but nowhere in it had there been any experience in the sharing of the power that was tightly consolidated in the successors of St. Peter.

Thus neither Crown nor Church could contribute to the traditions, the techniques, and the psychological attitudes that are essential for adjusting successfully the claims of competing power centers in a society containing many such. The arts of compromise and conciliation, and the habits of mind necessary for their appreciation, were dormant and undeveloped.

But what the State and the Church could do effectively was to serve as a core around which lesser institutions, philosophy, and political thought could coalesce. The intellectual thrust of the age, drawing heavily on Aquinas, Aristotle, and the medieval schoolmen, was embodied in Renaissance Scholasticism. Its great spokesmen were Francisco de Vitoria in the first half of the sixteenth century and Francisco Suárez in the second half.[5] It was at once a body of thought and a style of life, fitting well with the monoliths of State and Church and providing their conceptual basis. It had little to do with social contract theory in the northern sense, in the sense of Rousseau, Locke, and Hobbes. Rather, it was a powerful stimulus to an organic theory of life and of the State, a theory of natural harmony in which every human and every institution had a purpose, a station, ordained and secure. And it was also a powerful support for the prevailing Mediterranean and Iberian corporatism, defined in the broad sense of a "sociopolitical organization that is . . . hierarchical, elitist, authoritarian, bureaucratic, Catholic, patrimonialist . . ."[6]

This society, molded by the Reconquest, by Crown and Church, and by the teachings of Renaissance Scholasticism, was quite distinct in essential respects from those that were then emerging to the north of the Alps and the Pyrenees, where commercial, industrial, and scientific progress was in the bud and new secular and religious concepts were under debate.[7] Spain, in contrast, firmly maintained the old values.

Castilian society exalted courage and honor and defined them in an exclusive and stringent code as ideals appropriate for the man of rank, the gentleman, the *hidalgo*. For such a man and such an ideal, ". . . work did not redeem and had no value in itself. Manual work was servile. There was little or no interest in science and its fluid experimentation, or in technology and technique in general, or in any kind of economic activity. The superior man neither worked nor traded: he made war, he commanded, he legislated. He also thought, contemplated, loved, wooed, and enjoyed himself. Leisure was noble."[8]

Through various chains of causation, compelling in their subtlety and interplay but beyond the scope of this volume, numerous consequences of the Castilian value systems came to be ordained in the Hispanic civilization: a tremendous individualism, resistant to every form of compromise and delegation;[9] the exaltation of "being" over "doing"; dislike of the machine, intuitively sensed as dehumanizing;[10] an enormous preoccupation with dignity, not as decorum or anything else external but as the distinctive spiritual possession of every human, almost an aspect of soul, and first cousin to honor and pride;[11] the importance of social rank and ostentation; the absence of a bourgeoisie class, since society was determined to ignore economic activity; the emergence of the *pícaro* as an accepted social type, with all his tricky manipulations that eventually came to be known in Argentina as *viveza* or *viveza criolla;* the emphasis and reliance upon personal pull and favoritism; a system of huge landholdings, fostering a pastoral life and values as opposed to agricultural commitment; the Moorish style in private life, with the macho male, the secluded female, and the inwardly oriented house with blind facade on the street and cordial patio in the farthest interior.

A final quality of the civilization, difficult to express persuasively because it is antithetical to the northern perception and sensibility, should be understood. This is the concept of extremes, or of polarization. All Hispanic life seemed to be concentrated in a series of distant opposites, held in very uneasy tension: the vastly rich and the totally poor; the highest religious ideals and the lowest of conniving practices; unquestioning loyalty and foul treachery. But no person and no thing, no group, no practice, no value, occupied much of any middle ground. It was as if the society could not embrace anything without driving it to an extreme and could not tolerate existence in any centrally located space. A civilization of disjointed dualisms, lacking any continuum.

One reality stands forth clearly: in this Hispanic civilization, the many parts of the whole were mutually reinforcing. All movements and influences followed not linear but circular and centripetal courses, for the civilization was an organic whole, a natural symbiosis, a garden whose blooms were complementary to one another in form and hue and whose roots were deeply entwined. Thus the extraordinary tenacity of the social organism and its triumph over time, its sturdy resistance to significant change, and the ease of its transfer to South America in the great outflowing of creative vitality from sixteenth-century Castile.

Life and Culture in Colonial Times

After the founding of the first towns in the land that became Argentina, a slow development began in the interior. Several different social orders gradually emerged, with their related social psychologies. In the northwest, small centers of specialized agriculture and their associated handicraft industries began to appear. Tucumán developed its flair for sugar; vines were introduced into benign Mendoza and San Juan; Córdoba grew as a strategically located transit point on the route between the Atlantic littoral and the Peruvian uplands. There in the northwest, under the influences that flowed from High Peru and from Lima, always the most Spanish and Castilian city in South America, the heirs of the original *conquistadores* and friars had introduced the Spanish view of life in its purest form in a settled and traditional class-based society that would have seemed familiar in Castile. The well-born Creole, the closest to the Peninsular line of descent, and the whitest, formed the capstone of hierarchy. The mestizo, combining the heritage of a Spanish father and an Indian mother, filled the middle and lower ranks. The base was provided by Indians, who sustained what agriculture there was, and by imported Negro slaves, whose numbers, however, did not approximate those in tropical colonies.

In portions of the interior, and in the adjacent pampas, a rougher and more primitive mestizo way of life predominated, based on livestock and leather and resentment. "The casual unions between the invader and the women he enslaved left their irredeemable consequences in the mestizo, who would turn against society and the past when his hour came. Out of them would burst forth the civil wars and the political convulsions that followed them, with mestizo chieftains almost always at their head."[12]

Out of mestizo mixtures came the famous gaucho, the cowboy of the pampas. In those early times, before he had graduated into mythology, the gaucho was not an object of wide veneration. From his Spanish father came his anarchic individualism and his Moorish fatalism. From his Indian mother, whose life gave little cause for celebration, came his feeling for the land and his brooding sense of grievance. He was swarthy, lean, with black hair long and matted, and he was dressed in a collection of garments seemingly assembled at random: cotton drawers, a long diaper called a *chiripá* over the drawers and belted at the waist, a shirt, a jacket, a felt *chambergo* on his head, featuring a crown and a brim but no shape, perhaps a handkerchief knotting together his long hair, and boots made from the partially intact hide that had once covered the hind leg of a colt. Later the *chiripá* gave way to the cossack trousers known as *bombachas*. Everything was loose, semi-divorced from everything else, and in the opinion of some, reminiscent of Arabic attire.

The gaucho's possessions were as spare as his physique. They

included the horses that were for him the basis of everything, his di-
shevelled clothing, his knife or other weapons, his poncho, his *bolea-
dores* (the balls linked by leather cord, used as a kind of lariat to bring
down an animal), and a few pots and utensils if he was married. His
habitation was a filthy hovel of mud and thatch, furnished with an ox
skull or two for seating. His diet was beef and little else, since even
bread did not reach the pampas for a long time to come. His habits
and tastes were chaotic and violent. He respected physical skill and
courage; he detested learning, weakness, restraint, rules, work, settled society, and order in general, as well as almost everything else
that was not associated with life on horseback. His sense of honor
consisted of loyalty to the chief who was strong enough to control
him, and a hatred of thievery. For lesser offenses, such as homicide,
he was inclined to forgiveness. He was the repository of important
elements of the Castilian heritage, he was one of the founders of the
Argentina yet to come, and he was not a favorable portent for stability. "The psychology of the gaucho will never be fully understood,
nor will the soul of the anarchic Argentine multitudes unless one thinks
about the psychology of the humiliated son and dwells upon the results
that may come about through an inferiority complex irritated by
ignorance in an environment favorable to violence and whim."[13] The
words hint of time long past, but they were written in 1933.

There were connections of sorts between the interior and the
northwest, and even between the region of the Plata and the northwest, but they were hardly intimate, consisting mostly of the traffic in
hides and horses destined for Peru. For more than a century the mode
of travel consisted of the long mule train. By the mid-eighteenth century, the *carreta* was being developed. This was a covered wagon surmounting two enormous wheels, perhaps eight feet in diameter, and
drawn by six oxen. Traveling in caravans, the *carretas* could make a
round trip between Buenos Aires and Salta in about a year.[14]

Life in Buenos Aires and in the littoral nearby resembled neither
the pattern of the northwest nor that of the pampas. Although legal
commerce was forbidden to the Río de la Plata area for almost two
hundred years, smuggling was a way of life, bringing many foreigners
to resident status and multiplying every kind of foreign contact.[15]
Buenos Aires therefore developed from the beginning a more flexible
social order, more directed to the world outside, less parochial.

Although the inherited civilization thus received a differing stamp
from one area to another and was everywhere subjected to modifying
influences peculiar to Argentina, it retained its identity undiluted
because the modifying influences generally had the effect of intensi-

fying rather than weakening the legacy.

The most conspicuous of the new influences were those that reinforced individualism and encouraged its always latent tendency toward
anarchy. They arose from the facts of geography and distance. The
Spanish state had been sustained by relatively efficient administration
within a rather small physical area. But when its principles were
extended across the ocean and through a huge and largely trackless
continent, they could not be sustained in fact as opposed to theory. In
an empire whose communications between home and periphery took
eight months or more, the instructions of a central bureaucracy had
to yield to local initiative. But not for a moment was this seen as a
negation of the Crown's rule. No theory of divided power ever emerged.
Everything that unavoidably conflicted with some inappropriate
instruction from Spain was handled ad hoc, as an exception, or as a
compliance with the assumed true intent of the Crown, or as a special
interpretation, or in whatever way could be plausibly argued.

The same factor of distance applied within the colony. Given the
total absence of roads, the paucity of river transport, the perils of
travel posed by marauding Indians, and the agonizing slowness of the
occasional *carreta* lumbering across the landscape, distances were
immense. Towns hundreds of miles apart, with nothing in between,
lived as separate principalities. Acknowledging no de facto authority
but that of the local leader, the *caudillo,* or that of the local landowner,
the *estanciero,* whose acreage might extend from horizon to horizon,
they became crucibles of individualism.

It was the most legalistic of societies on the surface, full of procedures and forms, but none of this really tamed the individual will or
conditioned its possessor to forego something desired. Force and
authority alone could do that. The internal, voluntary restraints did
not function effectively. "This came to mean that as long as some
symbol of authority did not expressly prevent an action, that action
was permissible . . . the emphasis on individualism also encouraged
vociferous and explosive defense of one's position unless adequate
authority or force were present."[16]

The customs and values of old Castile fitted into the new Argentine environment with remarkable congruence. Since local autonomy
was guaranteed in practice by geography, there was no reason to
question the dogma of supreme royal power. No one thought of questioning the Church. The class system of Spain could be implanted
with little or no change, with mestizos, Indians, and slaves substituted
for the traditional lower classes. The Castilian pastoral tradition was
beautifully appropriate for the pampas. Life on horseback was a familiar

carryover from the Peninsula. The Castilian aversion to settled agriculture, to technical enterprise, to commerce, and to manual labor was gratified by an environment that generated a low demand for these. The Spanish passion for leisure was indulged by an irregular way of life that rested on the labor of horses and the easy fecundity of cattle and sheep. Protected by distance and insularity, Castilian individualism could expand almost infinitely. The Peninsular pattern of polarization and extremes almost seemed designed for a land vast, primitive, and sparsely peopled, in which "middle spaces" of any kind, whether of geography or of society, hardly existed. The failure of the mother culture to develop bonds of community would hardly be held against it in a new land in which space itself stood ready to destroy community. Moorish elements in society and personality fitted naturally into an ambiance that in many ways replicated that in which Islam had been born. And the homogeneity of the early settlers supported the prevailing values and beliefs, since there were no varying political and religious legacies that had to be adjusted and compromised.[17]

The adaptation of the old culture to the new land, if not perfect, was thus made under an unusually propitious star. The early and firm rooting of the culture determined the direction the social order would take. The Argentina of Perón was adumbrated in the colonial wilderness of the late sixteenth century.

Thus shaped, colonial society began to expand, slowly rather than rapidly, governed from a great distance as a part of the viceroyalty of Peru. Gradually the Indians, never numerous, were assimilated into the mestizo peasant class. There was a modest overseas immigration from the beginning, consisting mostly of Spaniards, and these frequently merged into the lower or middle class in Buenos Aires. Agriculture remained the specialty of the Indian underclass, and it remained weak and spasmodic.

Out on the great pampas, everything revolved around cattle and horses. The production of salted meat became significant around the beginning of the nineteenth century. Hides remained the dominant element in this economy of leather, which was employed for almost everything imaginable, for furniture, for roofing material, for containers, for curtains, for wagon springs. And there were abundant secondary products from the empire of the horse and the steer—bones, lard, tallow. By 1850, almost 50,000 tons of cattle horns were shipped annually to England alone.[18]

The pampas also witnessed an early development that later history never much ameliorated, the extreme concentration of land holdings into gigantic tracts that left little room for the small, independent owner.

To some extent these huge agglomerations served an economic purpose, for the carrying capacity of the land was then so limited. To obtain a minimum yield of ninety hides a year, a herd of nine hundred cattle was necessary. To support that number, 4,500 acres, almost seven square miles, would be required. That was a minimum. Given the many adversities that usually prevailed, it would have been a reckless landowner who would have challenged fate with fewer than one hundred square miles,[19] and holdings in the thousands of square miles were not unknown. Obtained from the Crown by grant or purchase, these gigantic tracts and the *estancieros* to whom they belonged became the early, firm base for a small but very powerful landowner class, often resident in Buenos Aires, a class that eventually emerged as probably the single most important element in the economy and sociology bequeathed by colonial to modern times.

As the realities of colonial trade and geography and the impracticality of the old Pacific shipping route and of the old prohibition of Atlantic commerce became apparent toward the end of the eighteenth century, the declining exports of silver began to be made through Buenos Aires rather than Lima, and other concessions to trade became necessary. In 1776, the viceroyalty of the Río de la Plata was formed, based in Buenos Aires and comprising the territory that is now Argentina, Bolivia, Paraguay, and Uruguay. Two years later, complete freedom of import and export through Buenos Aires was decreed; the city still had a population of only 24,000.[20] With the stimulus of these changes, the way was cleared for Buenos Aires to grasp its future.

At the turn of the eighteenth century, the Spanish monarchy was well advanced into bad times. The old empire bequeathed by the Catholic Kings, Charles V, and Philip II was dying of inward decay and outward pressure. As Spain stumbled into wars with France from 1793 to 1795, and with England from 1796 to 1802, its effective control in the Río de la Plata became enfeebled. Another war with England broke out in 1804, lasting until 1807. This was just long enough for the British to mount two invasions of Buenos Aires, in 1806 and 1807. Both of these were rather extemporaneous affairs, launched from Cape Town in South Africa, but they were real enough: 1,700 troops and a squadron of ships in 1806 and reinforcements in 1807, under a top military command.[21]

The admiral and general in charge, eminent men both, quite misunderstood the social, political, and psychological realities of the community they intended to overturn. Their pragmatic Anglo-Saxon assumption that the citizenry would rally to a new flag if economic betterment for the colony could be credibly predicted proved wildly inaccurate.[22] The two invasions brought glory only to the Creole leadership in Buenos Aires. The viceroy, the Crown's appointee, fled with most of the colony's bullion treasure, leaving others to defend the city. The British mismanaged a large part of their effort, but the Creole defenders who took over marshalled a magnificent defense. The city's architecture lent itself to heroics, for the narrow streets and the blank facades of the houses simultaneously channeled and menaced the invaders, and every first-story roof surrounded by a low parapet was a little fort, sheltering everyone who could handle a gun or hurl down lethal objects. The British could have prevailed only by blowing each house in the city into rubble, but they lacked the resources, and probably the desire, for so strenuous a commitment. They surrendered instead, and sailed off.

These rousing events, so consistent with the confusions now loose in Napoleonic Europe, were soon followed by the Corsican's invasion of Spain (1808–13), the abdication of the Spanish King, Ferdinand VII, and the coronation of Napoleon's younger brother, Joseph, in his place. Spanish control in the Plata was by now nonexistent, and the governing Creoles in Buenos Aires, greatly inspired and emboldened by their rout of the British, recognized the scent of self-government in the air.[23]

The Era of Independence

Appropriately, the enigmas of Argentina extend even to its national independence. It is impossible to settle upon a clear-cut date for the creation of the nation in its present form since much depends on definitions. The formal stages of independence clearly began on May 25, 1810. There was then no de facto connection between the colony and any Spanish government, and the Creole citizenry had been agitating forcefully for full administrative control. Peninsular rule simple disappeared. The viceroy and the city government handed over authority to a Creole junta described as a "Provisional Junta of the Provinces of the Río de la Plata, governing for Ferdinand VII." Thus technical independence was neither achieved nor attempted, although in effect the old viceroyalty had cut itself clear of the empire through the format of local rule.

The first date identified with formal independence was July 9, 1816, when a congress consisting of thirty-two representatives of a limited number of provinces met at Tucumán and declared the existence of the United Provinces of South America, a name that owed more to aspiration than to reality.

The two decades that followed brought an extraordinary succession of furious events. The original Provisional Junta of 1810 was followed by two Triumvirates, five Supreme Directors, the collapse of central authority, a first dissolution of the United Provinces, seven governors of Buenos Aires Province during a seven-month period in 1820, a president of a revived United Provinces, two failed constitutions that never went into effect, and a constituent congress that handed over power to an appointed governor before it dissolved the central government for the second time and adjourned sine die.

One of the greatest men of Argentina, Bernardino Rivadavia, was both the product and the victim of these catastrophic times. In the 1820s he served as minister of government in Buenos Aires and as foreign minister during a period when that province represented the United Provinces abroad. In 1826, he was chosen president of the Provinces and suffered during a brief tenure, unable to implement his preference for a centralized government of the political elite. Short, dark, small of arm, and big of belly, he was hardly the archetypical romantic Latin, but his French manners and his charm captivated women, and his capacious mind and even more capacious curiosity set him apart. He was a typical Latin American Renaissance Man, knowing something about everything, with the sole exception of the Argentine back country, which he never visited. His views were liberal in the nineteenth-century manner, his measures were salutary and covered an immense range, and in a very short time they aroused violent opposition.

Rivadavia's hopes for the country were honorable. He abhorred the gaucho class, as did his Europeanizing liberal associates. And he sincerely desired a land in which small holders joined in cooperation would predominate. To that end he devised a program of land leases, but he had miscalculated the realities, and the leases ended up in the hands of speculators and large land holders. After his fall, the titles passed from the government to the private holders; and the immense problem of land ownership, the bequest of Peninsular and colonial precedents, was worse than ever.

Like so many well-intentioned men in advance of their time, Rivadavia could not cope with determined opponents who were of their own time or behind it. His presidency lasted seventeen months and he resigned in the face of a general revolt.

The indignities and disasters that were visited upon Rivadavia and the others of his era attest to such a lack of internal unity that "'anarchy" seems the only appropriate term. Its causes bear examination, because of its virulence and depth and because many of the most important developments in later Argentine history, including Perón and Peronism, descended from it directly or more remotely.

The Great Rift

The eighteenth century brought first the intimations and then the reality of cleavages in the national life of such magnitude that time never healed them. One may speak of a Great Rift, but with care, for the Rift is not a single phenomenon but, rather, multiple versions of one. It appears in the social geography of Argentina like one of those long and deep rifts that geologists trace in the land, winding, changing form and character, at times disappearing entirely under cover of vegetation and rocky overlay, reappearing in new directions, dividing and subdividing, always different and yet in a larger sense the same. The many guises of the Rift would include such divisions as those between the liberal-democratic and the corporatist traditions, center and periphery, modernism and traditionalism, nationalism and internationalism, democratic techniques of rule and authoritarian practices, the enlargement and the diminution of the Church's functions in public and private life, and in recent times, liberalism and national populism.[24] Each new manifestation would seem novel and distinct, but time present would blend into time past and the new profile of the Rift would develop a family resemblance to the old.

Although the Rift was much more than a simple dichotomy of haves and have-nots, its principal continuing effect was to separate in one way or another those who were included from those who were excluded; those who were empowered from those who were not; those above from those below; the elite from the disinherited.[25]

Perhaps the first appearance of the Rift was the hot colonial rivalry between the native-born Creoles and the Peninsular Spaniards, a division of much consequence. There were gradations of disdain in the colonial social system as a whole, the worst being reserved for the Indians, the blacks, and the mixtures that resulted from their union with other elements, including the rough, half-wild gauchos in particular, but a less abrasive disdain came to be extended also to the Creoles in the original sense of that word, meaning the native-born offspring of pure white Spanish blood. As racial intermixture continued and Creoles of the original definition mingled with mestizos, the term "Creole" broadened to include all mixtures and all native-born stock, leaving only the Peninsular Spaniards with their claims of exclusivity. The establishment of the viceroyalty brought this social contention to a head, because with the new importance of Buenos

Aires the distant Crown thought it necessary, in accordance with custom in other colonies, to entrust local government to Spanish officials.
The supplanted Creoles, who had acquired economic influence, were
now soured by political frustration. "Kept out of public office, rele-
gated to lowly social tasks, the ambitious and capable Creoles, whether
they were white, or, as was more frequent, mestizo, preferred a rural
existence in which they did not have to bear constant witness to their
inferiority."[26]

In its second manifestation, the Great Rift expressed the master
theme of nineteenth-century Argentina: the rivalry and brooding ill-
will that set the interior apart from Buenos Aires. The city-country-
side schema is not a complete polarity, but it is a useful generalization.
This evolution had long been under way. The countryside at the end
of the eighteenth century still claimed the great majority of the population, but the coastal towns, and Buenos Aires in particular, had
acquired disporportionate power that was enhanced by the creation
of the viceroyalty.

This division was based partly on geography and partly on deep
differences in values and beliefs. Geography was involved in the rising eminence of Buenos Aires as the representative of the region to
the world, as the locus of the customs offices and the revenue they
generated, and as the only important commercial center in a time of
rapidly increasing trade. Cultural differences were involved in the
striking disparity of the expectations with which the port city and the
interior had viewed the movement of May 1810.

The expectations of the Men of May were relatively clear. These
leaders were all *porteños*, a small band of liberally oriented intellectuals
based in the professions, in the bureaucracy, or in commerce. Cosmopolitan in outlook, they were devoted to Europe and to the latest
theories out of France, particularly those of Rousseau, the least rigorous and most chaotic of romantics. They were eager reformers gen-
uinely devoted to the general welfare, but naive and rigid, uninformed
concerning social psychology outside their narrow group, and most
of all the psychology of their own hinterland. They had assumed all
along that Buenos Aires had a right to lead, bringing enlightenment
to the interior masses who would surely be happy to follow. They had
also assumed that this process would be effected through a centralized government reflecting their own liberal and high-minded principles. Outside of Buenos Aires, however, the expectations were less
focussed but nevertheless clear on one point: the rejection of the pre-
sumptions (as they were regarded) of the *porteño* elite. It was not that
the interior opposed independence. On the contrary, it supported the

change and its own version of formless local rule. But it was emotionally opposed to the alien and visionary tone of the *porteños* and to the centralization that would confirm the strange new doctrines. As antagonism deepened, the men of the interior began to rally around their local leaders, the *caudillos*, who were suddenly everywhere, rising from the ranks of the people whom they mirrored with fidelity and whom they understood on an intuitive level that had much to do with emotion and little with formal doctrine.

In opposing the Buenos Aires reformers, the men of the interior thus evolved less a coherent philosophy than an attitude, an emotion, a way of thinking about life. Various elements, all of them subdivisions of the Great Rift, were fused in this: country values as opposed to city values; the common man in preference to the aristocrat; jealousy of the capital; opposition to the current speculations of the elitists concerning a liberal monarchy; sympathy for the ignorant and the uninformed as against the enlightened theorists. Out of these passions and resentments, and augmented by the extremism that was everywhere, emerged the doctrine of free states united in some loose national organization—federalism, as its proponents called it. The *porteño* reformers, soon to be known as *Unitarios*, or Unitarians, fought tooth and nail for a centralized political structure that would reflect their own desires and preeminence.[27]

Thus the social order was divided into two intolerant groupings whose disputes were brought to white heat by the uncompromising heritage they shared. The Great Rift was fully formed.

Rivadavia fell in July 1827, unable to bridge the Rift. Argentina, by whatever name, was in tatters. The time was prepared for the strongest of strongmen, a tyrant, a *caudillo* of *caudillos*. Such a man happened to be ready and waiting, the first of the two famous leaders who were in some respects forerunners of Juan Perón. His name was Juan Manuel de Rosas.

The Classic Caudillo—Juan Manuel de Rosas

Rosas was the most complete and undiluted example of the *caudillo*, the provincial leader of the common people who ruled by physical and psychological prowess. In a society that lived by equestrian skills, the *caudillo* had to be brave, enduring, audacious, stronger of arm and will than the rest. But even more important was the *caudillo*'s born talent for command and his psychological identity with those he represented, since his rule was entirely de facto and owed nothing to law or election. He was simply accepted as the natural leader in his area, fully supported because he was seen as the embodiment of the emotions, traditions, and values of his society. If, as was sometimes the case, he was also seen as the repository of mythic and supernatural powers, all the better.

Rosas was a remarkable man, a wealthy and powerful *estanciero,* all will and sense of command, who excelled both in the violent pursuits of the gauchos and in the refinements of city life.[28] These qualities he now exerted to the fullest in support of those existing on the far side of the Great Rift, who were now to be exalted for the first time in Argentine memory. In a strange anticipation of Juan Perón, he married a woman, Doña Encarnación, who shared his political skills and his social leveling. His sure touch brought the first recruitment of common people as elements in a political machine, in the form of an espionage network of domestic servants in upper-class households and through the first political overtures to the Argentine blacks, then proportionately much more numerous, who lived in their groupings of black nations. Doña Encarnación was active in all of this. In 1831, she wrote to her husband, telling him, "I have called together the *paisanos,* I have spoken to them, as well as to the presidents of all the black nations." Rosas wrote to her in the same vein: "You have already seen what the friendship of the poor is worth, and how important it is to nurture it and not miss ways to attract and cultivate their allegiance . . . write them frequently, send them gifts, and don't worry about the expense . . ."[29]

Mixed motives were doubtless at work in these novel purposes. Certainly the participation of elements from the bottom of the hierarchy served an innovative political purpose, but there is no reason to conclude that it was all facade and playacting. There were enough complications in Rosas to accommodate all kinds of overlappings. Idolized by many, he nevertheless felt more attachment to things and to animals than to humans. Although he personified hardness and rebellion against all rules but his own, he still had a soft side, a strain of mysticism that sometimes brought him to the lonely pampas at night for solitary meditation.

By 1835, the confusions in Buenos Aires Province were so desperate that Rosas, who had ruled during a previous term, was recalled to power on his own conditions, as expressed in the simple phrases of his formal investiture: "The entire public power of the Province, for as long as he thinks necessary." Not content even with this, Rosas further insisted that he be confirmed by popular plebiscite. When the votes were counted, he was finally content: 9,315 ayes and five noes. Assuming the title of Restorer of the Laws, he set out on the path of total rule for seventeen years.

During this period, Rosas was Argentina. He represented, and symbolized, the other side of the Rift, the nativist and Creole side that scorned whatever was modern or foreign.[30] Scarlet was his color, and the red ribbon worn by all—by priests, by legislators, by fine ladies— was the pledge of loyalty and the price of survival. Ruling nominally as a Federalist, he persecuted the centralizing *Unitarios* into destruction or exile. There was no exaggeration in his famous exhortation, "Death to the Unitarian savages!" He had neither plan nor desire for the organization of a national state. Instead, what he wanted and attained was a loose federation of local authorities headed by their own *caudillos*, who in turn would be brought under his own de facto power. A system of alliances was thus achieved, guided and controlled by the formless extension of the personal power of Rosas. Those from abroad who viewed the strange despotism tended to be impressed by the aspect of tyranny. The U.S. Chargé d'Affaires in Buenos Aires thus wrote to President Buchanan in 1846: "Such is the terror—the crushing fear—which is inspired by one man over that multitude, which now submits to his decrees with a zeal, apparently as ardent, as it is certainly abject and submissive . . . not a breath of free thought or manly speech . . . yet Gen'l. Rosas is the only man who could keep them together for twenty-four hours . . ."[31]

This was a just appraisal, although not a complete one. It should be rounded with the acknowledgement of the man's remarkable gifts in presenting himself, and being accepted, as the defender of beloved traditions and patterns of life, the apostle of Creole values, the man of the people who personified popular virtues.[32]

By 1852, the time of Rosas had passed. His order was crumbling, his old supporters had lost their intensity of faith, and he was overthrown in battle by General Justo José de Urquiza, who inaugurated a new order. Rosas found safety in England, where he lived for another quarter of a century, writing tracts and pinching pennies. No monument in Argentina bears his name.

Rosas had served a purpose. Under him, the confederation had survived as perhaps the only kind of union then possible, and he had preserved what could be sustained out of a cyclone of centrifugal forces. Despot he was, and also the emotional expression of a social order. His influence upon Juan Perón is easy to trace, and like Perón he left a disputed inheritance to be debated by a divided nation.

A Nation is Organized, 1852–1880

With the fall of Rosas, the movement toward national unity so long sought by his opponents could proceed. The format for a confederation was established in the constitution of 1853, a document that reflected the forms of the unsuccessful early charters of the postin-dependence period, various political concepts then in vogue in Europe, and some of the structure and content of the United States constitution. Awareness of the northern power and its attainment of independence, which had hardly existed in Argentina in the era in which the latter's colonial ties had been severed, had since been ignited by the spectacle of rapid progress in the United States.[33]

But one clause, in practice, undercut the entire concept of federalism. This was the short, rather bland Article 6, stating that "The Federal Government intervenes in the territory of the Provinces to guarantee the republican form of government, or to repel foreign invasions . . ." From these words came the theory and habit of intervention by which the central government can assume control of provincial governments or other instrumentalities of the political system, including such bodies as universities and labor unions. Under the guise of a federal division of power, the supremacy of the central government was thus decreed in the purest Castilian form.

This much was necessary, it can be plausibly argued, to protect the system itself against the ravages of local *caudillo* uprisings, for a classical federal system along North American lines would certainly have gone up in smoke at an early moment. But even with this concession to the realities, the constitution of 1853, modified slightly in 1860, was rather an ill-fitting garment. It survived, but only through the wasting away of local powers.

The years from 1862 to 1880 brought the consolidation of the country and the beginning of vast economic surges. These years also brought the beginnings of what may be termed the Liberal System, the organizational pattern that defined in a broad way the political, economic, and social structure of Argentina for the next seventy years. The term "liberal" in this context did not refer to the practices of democracy, or to social reforms, or to the thrust for equality. Rather, it denoted the principles upon which the state and the economy were organized. These included republican institutions, however small and select the electorate might be; free trade and an international orientation; full freedom of religion; and laissez faire in economics.

Power and influence now recrossed the Great Rift. Three memorable presidents, representing tendencies and values generally opposed to those of the Rosas epoch but moderated by the memory of the idealistic and failed Men of May, dominated public affairs during the critical years of the Liberal System's creation. All of them had unusual vision and competence and even more unusual honesty and devotion to the public good.

The first of these exemplary presidents was Bartolomé Mitre, who was elected in 1862. A *porteño* who never lost the ideal of national union, Mitre was another Renaissance Man, a politician, general, orator, writer, patriot, whose crowded life still left time for translations of Dante and Horace. Austere and devoted, he confronted the task of binding the nation, in practice, into the union defined in theory by the constitution. The question of the national capital was the single remaining important political issue, and Mitre proposed the solution that no one was able to implement until 1880, the federalization of Buenos Aires as the capital of Argentina and the construction of a new capital city for Buenos Aires Province.

Mitre was immersed in nation-building and in an unfortunate war with Paraguay, whose conclusion fell to Mitre's successor, Domingo Faustino Sarmiento, yet another Renaissance type who held the presidency from 1868 to 1874. He was so remarkable a man that his accomplishments bear examination for the light they throw upon national thought and psychology.

A native of San Juan Province in the northwest, Sarmiento had, like Mitre, spent much of his life in exile, mostly in Chile. His careers were diverse—he was a writer, journalist, clerk, teacher, lecturer, mine foreman, poet, politician, diplomat, and, along with whatever else he was doing, always the born educator. He was immensely precocious. As a child, he had been acclaimed as a prodigy in reading, a fact that may account for his subsequent egotism, a vanity sufficient to overflow the million square miles of Argentina. He was a compulsive learner who at one time paid half his tiny wages as a clerk to a teacher who would rouse him at two o'clock in the morning for English lessons. He traveled widely, investigating systems of public education in Europe and in the United States. He enjoyed writing, and his complete works were published in an edition of fifty-three volumes before his death in 1888.

One of these works is particularly significant. *Life in the Argentine Republic in the Days of the Tyrants,* subtitled *Civilization and Barbarism* and sometimes called merely *Facundo,* is one of the monuments of Argentine literature. It is an easy book to praise but an impossible one to define. It is a history that is not fully historical; a novel that is more like a long essay, except that it is not an essay either; an unprecedented kind of epic that dissolves into political and sociological overviews. Whatever it is, it is as good an approach to the national traditions and cultural heritage as any. Written in exile as an attack on Facundo Quiroga, a *caudillo* second in power and significance only to Rosas, and indirectly as an attack on Rosas, this eloquent book gives systematic formulation to the theory of an entire generation of liberals and

intellectuals that the gaucho and the countryside represented barbarism, whereas the city represented civilization. It is a long plea for
urban values, for the culture of Europe, for the rejection of the Hispanic past, for the redemption of life on the primitive pampas, for
education everywhere. As formless and as unstructured as a novel by
Thomas Wolfe and written with the same breathless rush, filled with
profound insights and lyric eloquence, immensely colorful, it is a
remarkable work. It is also a memorial to a mind that, despite all its
repudiation of Spanish antecedents, was deeply imbued with Hispanic characteristics. Like the civilization itself, Sarmiento is all
extremes: what seems good to him receives a reverence worthy of the
synoptic gospels; what seems bad has been summoned out of hell. An
acute and very ardent intelligence was at work here, naive and idealistic yet realistic when the dreams temporarily receded; quite divorced
from balance; and, one might judge, writing with passion during midnight hours in a lonely study through which a high wind was blowing.

Sarmiento's presidency was a crescendo of works initiated and
pursued. There were major achievements—the end of the Paraguayan war and the final liquidation of the old *caudillos* as a military
force. The first national census was taken in 1869, revealing a population of 1,800,000, of whom 500,000 lived in Buenos Aires Province
and 178,000 in the city itself.

Over the protests of Mitre, Sarmiento promoted Nicolás Avellaneda as his successor in 1874 and insured his election by means that
were less than theoretically pure. Progress continued. Avellaneda
completed the tasks of his two great predecessors, and in 1879–80
took the further step of settling, once and for all, the Indian problem
on the southern reaches of effective settlement. For this an army containing gaucho elements was formed under General Julio Roca. It
penetrated to the deep south, to the Río Negro, from whose banks
Roca could look across to the cold, dry plateau of Patagonia, then
almost the end of the known Argentine world. The expedition exterminated some of the Indians and captured others, moving them elsewhere and liquidating their society. It was also the last hurrah for the
traditional gauchos. With the wild border pacified, their military *caudillos* toppled from power, and civilization encroaching, they had
nowhere to go but to the army barracks or the great *estancias,* where
they could linger on in the diminished role of cattle hands.

Two facts should be noted concerning this period. The first is the
prevalence and acceptance of fraud and electoral coercion. The victory of Sarmiento in 1868 had been relatively free of improper pressures of any kind, but the next election of which that could be said

occurred only in 1916. The second fact, significant as a commentary on the civilization, concerns the inability of these three great presidents to override their personal dislike for one another. Sarmiento had a prickly sense of honor and slight. Drafted into the militia at the age of sixteen, he had preferred to go to jail rather than tip his hat to his military superiors. The strong acid of his egotism and pride of self can be sensed in one of his comments concerning General Urquiza, with whom he had worked briefly: "It was necessary to reduce oneself to zero in his presence . . . no one knows, no one can ever appreciate the tortures I suffered, the self-control I had to impose upon myself to reconcile my will with that man's. It cost me an effort to speak to him . . ."[34] Sarmiento did not like Mitre; Mitre did not like him; Mitre did not like Avellaneda and ran against him when Sarmiento backed the latter in 1874. Having lost, Mitre accused Sarmineto of fraud and raised a military revolt, the failure of which put him in jail. Other political leaders of the era, just below the three presidents in rank, disliked all of them.

It seems surprising at first. The men of this period had all shared the privations of exile under Rosas; they were all serving in a comparatively mellow time when the nation wanted peace and unity; the country was prospering remarkably. And yet they were so quick to disagree, so testy in the face of opposition, so unable to compromise. Much of it was old Spain, the Spain of the Moors, whose traits Sarmiento (when he visited Algiers) had been quick to attribute to the gauchos he despised. They were great men in many ways, all of them, but political harmony was beyond them.

Good government brought enormous progress. Schools and enrollments were nearly doubled under Sarmiento. Libraries, books, hospitals, scientific societies, bridges, the National Bank, city beautification, port facilities, lighthouses—nothing seemed too small to justify the attention and restless energy of Sarmiento and the other presidents of the era. In economic matters, the small currents of development that were to combine into a rising flood after 1880 were gathering volume. Railroads were begun with governmental patronage of British capital. The first six miles were laid in 1857, and by 1880 there were almost 2,400 miles of track in place. Sheep-raising expanded dramatically. The coming revolution in the livestock economy was presaged in the 1870s by the invention of barbed wire and the refrigerator ship.

Finally, this period before the frantic expansion of the 1880s brought the rise and, unfortunately for the future, the potential decline of something that could have made a great difference in Argentine

life: agricultural colonization. Agriculture, as opposed to pastoral
pursuits, had from the beginning been trivial in the Argentine scale
of things. As late as 1865, all of Argentine agriculture occupied a
mere 373 square miles out of one million.[35] But in the 1860s and 1870s
the policies of the government and the efforts of private companies
in Europe had produced a strong ripple of farm colonization on lands
marginal to the prevailing pastoralism. The contributions of the
industrious European settlers who had brought traditions of local
government with them were too limited to alter the prevailing social
structure. And like so many other aspects of Argentine life, they were
overtaken by the relentless surge of growth that came with the 1880s,
transforming the nation beyond recognition.

The Snopes sprang untarnished from a long line of
shiftless tenant farmers—a race that is of the land
and yet rootless, like mistletoe; owing nothing to the
soil, giving nothing to it and getting nothing of it in
return; using the land as a harlot . . .

— William Faulkner, *Father Abraham*

3. Argentina in the Years of Triumph, 1880-1930

The Deceptive Sociology of Wealth

So MANY THINGS came together in or around 1880 that it
can be taken as a watershed point. The federalization of Buenos Aires
as the capital completed the process of national organization. General
Roca's War of the Desert against the Indians had greatly increased
the effective size of the national domain. Various technological advances
in refrigeration, transportation, cattle breeding, meat packing, and
other areas transformed the economy and brought an outpouring of
foreign capital, mostly British. An immense flood of immigration began
to obliterate or threaten most of the social landmarks. The new Generation of '80 rose to influence, determined to bring about expansion,
progress, and greatness, within the familiar structure of the Liberal
System.[1] The Generation of '80 went directly against the grain of the
traditional civilization, for the proponents of modernization and outreach to the world now prevailed over those on the other side of the
Rift who favored the old ways of the interior. The justification for this
turn of events, and its boundary line as well, was the success that lasted
for several decades.[2]

These developments were all interrelated, but they began with the
transformation of the pastoral economy. Improved strains of cattle
were introduced, and these required alfalfa; but alfalfa requires plowed

land and regular cultivation by agricultural labor on a very large scale.[3] There was no such labor in sufficient amounts, and there was only one way to get it: immigrants, and lots of them.

The call for immigrants had been the great theme of Juan Batista Alberdi, Argentina's foremost political thinker, who had been influential in the drafting of the constitution of 1853, and of Mitre and Sarmiento. It was enshrined in the constitution as a national priority. The intellectuals, influenced by the social philosophy of positivism, had joined in the cry, contending that immigrants were necessary not only for economic reasons but also to bring life and change to a stagnant culture and order to a chaotic political process. The intellectual vogue at this time was strongly opposed to Creole values, so this Europeanizing viewpoint flourished, reaching its climax about 1905. The consequences were dramatic. Between 1880 and 1905, net immigration was 2,827,800, in a country whose entire population in 1869 had been 1,800,000.[4]

In 1914, the peak year of immigrant impact, 30 percent of all Argentines were foreign-born, a percentage twice the highest figure ever reached in the United States.[5] Italian immigrants considerably outnumbered all other nationalities, with the Spaniards next, followed by the French, "Russians" (meaning Slavs in general), and "Turks," which included Middle Eastern peoples. The British component was small, but very influential.

The swarming immigration coincided with an equally sudden expansion of the railway system under the auspices of British investors. The 2,400 miles of 1880 became the 22,200 miles of 1915, by which time Argentine railway mileage ranked eighth in the world, and third in the Western Hemisphere, behind the United States and Canada. The period was one almost of coronation for British investment, for it now went well beyond railroads and the processing and exporting of pastoral production to such other enterprises as tramways, utilities, waterworks, gas plants, insurance, banking, shipping, public services, and importing. Education and sports were other areas in which the British influence put a permanent mark upon Argentina. The British community in Argentina was the largest outside the physical bounds of the British Empire. The British came to administer the works their technicians had installed and they remained into the third generation, but usually no longer, never assimilating into the Argentine social order, forever alien to Argentine public life, ". . . an army of those honest, unimaginative empire builders who drank gin and bitters between ten-thirty and noon and wore their dinner jackets when dining alone at night, that they might not 'go native.' "[6]

The gigantic tracts of land now opening up wherever the railroads penetrated brought into high relief one of the tragic mistakes of Argentine national development, the pattern of land ownership and use. The early emergence of concentrated, enormous landholdings has been noted; later history was all of a piece. In the 1820s, 21 million acres of public land were awarded to approximately 500 owners in lieu of monetary compensation for military and political services rendered.[7] Seventy million acres in Patagonia were given to a settlement company in 1877 before Patagonia had been fully explored, let alone surveyed. One hundred and fifty million more acres became available with General Roca's defeat of the Indians, but the war had been financed by mortgaging the land in advance. Bonds redeemable in minimum lots of 25,000 acres had been sold, the cost working out to six cents per acre. But this was only the beginning of concentration, for these holdings were bought up by speculators, and 541 of these feisty plungers presented claims for more than 11 million acres.[8] Again, in 1889, 150 million acres in the farther parts of Patagonia and in scarcely better explored areas of the far north were earmarked for sale through European agents, with great advantage to speculators. These tracts, too, were unsurveyed and their location was a bit of a mystery.[9] Legislative efforts to control these practices were utterly ineffective. When a Ministry of Agriculture was created in 1898, it discovered that so much land had been given away that there was no record of what public lands were left or where they might be located. By the end of the century, a national land policy that could have helped the immigrant or the local small farmer was, quite literally, no longer possible.

It is interesting that 12,000 of the rather mysterious, unlocated acres in Patagonia came to have a connection with the North American film industry more than half a century later. In 1902 a tract of that size was granted to two well-known fugitives named Butch Cassidy and the Sundance Kid, whose flight from the law took them to Patagonia—but not to Bolivia. The movie version owes more to Hollywood imagination than to historical fact.[10]

Vast holdings were now commercially practical, and the price of land rose steadily. Colonizers were simply bought out and no successors appeared because the new price levels precluded small would-be purchasers. But the landowners had contributed very little to their own well-being. Their livestock multiplied on its own initiative, immigrants and sharecroppers did the basic work, the government cleared away the Indians, the British constructed the railways, daily administration came usually from foreign managers. The owners typically sat by while rapidly rising land values made them wealthy. There was, in fact, competent and devoted pastoral leadership in the very upper-class *Sociedad Rural,* but it could not change the system in time, and the pattern remained one of indifference and under-development sustained by easy, almost inevitable, wealth that was routed to Buenos Aires and to Europe. It was thus confirmed that tenancy, sharecropping, and land speculation would be the agricultural destiny of Argentina.[11] It was also thus confirmed that there would never be any close connection between people and land. Everything would be temporary, migratory, tentative, half-hearted. The consequences for social psychology were enormous,[12] and half a century later Perón would be the beneficiary.

After 1890, there began to appear in large numbers a kind of immigrant who had even less permanent effect on the rural order, the *golondrina,* the swallow, whose migratory customs recalled the birds he emulated. The *golondrina,* usually from Italy, arrived from Europe during the winter months in his homeland, spent three or four months harvesting during the Argentine summer, and recrossed the Atlantic, leaving nothing of himself behind.

Wheat and maize rose rapidly in significance, and in 1903, for the first time the combined value of wheat, maize, and linseed exceeded the value of animal products.[13] But not even this evolution sufficed to develop the "multiplier effects" that might have been expected. Elsewhere, as in the North American wheat belt, a flourishing agriculture brought local commercial activity, stores, servicing facilities, and processing industries. But on the pampas and in adjacent areas, negative elements in society, in the economy, and in heritage were too strong to confront. Among these was frequently active persecution by provincial and local officials, often greedy and illiterate small tyrants who knew how to extort and receive bribes, and little else. There was no stable class to provide consumers, no wide interest or concern at any level.

This is to say, with a different emphasis, that a frontier in the North American social sense described by Frederick Jackson Turner in his famous thesis never developed in Argentina. Despite the abundant land, the Argentine frontier emerged in bits and pieces in a centrifugal rather than a centripetal process, a settlement here and an *estancia* there. It was not, as it was in North America, a band of integrated settlement that performed as a social cutting edge, giving rebirth to settled areas behind it, inculcating democratic values, a pragmatic spirit, and the cult of optimism, and providing a unifying national ideology with a myth to match. The differing values and emphases of the contrasting civilizations thus wrought surprisingly different consequences in areas of physical similarity.[14]

Even the sugar industry was captured by the gravitational pull of the capital. Centered in far-distant Tucumán, that industry should have attained a strong regional base if ever such a thing were possible. This occurred, but very briefly; before long the political and economic management of the sugar sector had migrated to the familiar destination that was sought by all.[15]

By 1914, the economic side of the Liberal System had been established in a form that was unique to the area of the Río de la Plata. Nothing else in Latin America even approximated it. Its fabulous success and the growing conviction in the governing classes that both the pattern and its success were inherent in the very nature of Argentina, a work not of man but of destiny, gave it enormous tenacity in the public mind. The pattern, a natural symbiosis, was one of almost total economic specialization. Argentina would have an export economy producing pastoral and agricultural products for Europe and, principally, for England. In turn, Argentina would buy from Europe and, principally, from England its requirements in coal and manufactured goods, and would obtain from its trading partners capital investment and human labor. To produce locally too large a part of Argentina's requirements would disrupt the smooth balance and discourage foreign purchases of Argentina's produce of the land. Such manufacturing activity as did develop locally was limited largely to the processing of agricultural and pastoral output, or to supporting it in such sectors as meat packing. Commerce, likewise, evolved mainly as the handmaiden to the export economy.[16]

A new social order developed. It had been assumed by the governing classes that society would remain much the same, except that the immigrants would add the necessary new productive capacity, mainly on the land. But there were two surprises. The first concerned an unsuspected economic attitude on the part of the immigrants that was in the sharpest contrast to that of the great landowners. The immigrant was motivated only by money, and by short-term money at that. If he found poor pickings in the countryside, he would forsake his agricultural ambitions and try his luck in the cities of the littoral, usually Buenos Aires. Many immigrants, in fact, never penetrated beyond the capital in the first place. The enormous construction under way there, the opportunities in the factories devoted to processing, the endless requirements of the service occupations, and the need for

artisans, craftsmen, and tradesmen, all insured outlets for energy and
ambition.

The second surprise concerned an unsuspected entrepreneurial
talent. The diligence of the immigrants astounded the Creoles. Their
willingness to save money astounded them even more. As early as the
1860s, Europeans, 12 percent of the population, had provided 82
percent of the savings deposits in the Banco de Buenos Aires.[17] They
were innovative and energetic, they adhered to values alien to those
of the Creoles, and they prospered. By 1914, as 30 percent of the
population, they owned 72 percent of all commercial firms. They held
full control of both wholesale and retail commerce everywhere in the
country except in the deepest interior. In the capital, they owned 82
percent of all commercial establishments, and almost 65 percent of
the existing industrial capacity.[18]

The immigrants and their first-generation descendents soon began
to alter the old social structure, with its two classes separated by very
small middle sectors. Economic expansion was now creating a new
urban middle class of teachers, professionals, merchants, soldiers, and
into this the immigrants and their children began to penetrate, showing themselves more successful than the native-born lower classes. Only
the governmental bureaucracy remained unattainable to the thriving
newcomers.

This rapid progress, which filled the oligarchy with all manner of
fear and dread, was accompanied by pressures for a more open and
democratically organized social order. The numbers of this new class
were indeed intimidating for the Creole elites. By 1914, there were
more than 1,200 fraternal and mutual-benefit societies, with more than
half a million members, offering membership to first- and second-
generation ethnic groups. The elites knew that the incredible development of the last quarter of a century had been due to the new
arrivals in larger part than they readily admitted, and that continuing
prosperity required more of the same. And yet the tide would in time
surely swamp the traditional social order, beginning with the elites.

It is quite understandable that immigration now came to be viewed
with very different emotions than the rapture that accompanied its
first days. Now it was begrudged, its past contributions minimized and
its future hedged about with protective devices, chief among which
was a new cultural nationalism aimed at assimilation of the newcomers. The old values would be indoctrinated, and the hateful materialism of the new middle-class aspirants would be combatted as firmly as
possible. The ruling intellectuals abandoned the once-stylish positivism, and their devotion to Herbert Spencer and the international ori-

entation of the Liberal System, and embraced the old Creole ways of life and the Hispanic past that Sarmiento and his allies had consigned to darkness. The first manifestations of this, enhanced by the native pride aroused by the centenary of independence in 1910, were seen in Ricardo Rojas, Manuel Gálvez, and Leopoldo Lugones in the years just before the First World War.[19]

Cultural nationalism, with its overlap into economic and political nationalism and with assiduous cultivation by the intellectuals, caught on quickly. The gaucho, no longer despised as a barbarian, was now brought forward as the epitome of the national character, the symbol of national greatness. He had already been immortalized for posterity by the poet José Hernández in *Martín Fierro,* an epic poem of rural social protest, published in two parts in the 1870s, whose protagonist was a gaucho who struggled against the official order of things. In 1913, Lugones gave a series of lectures that were a highlight of the social season, glittering affairs patronized by all who counted, including the president. The gaucho, according to Lugones, who had forgotten the traditional intellectual disdain of the "barbaric" countryside, was the source of the principal Argentine character traits, which he identified as compassion, elegance, honor, loyalty, and generosity. Other intellectuals discovered in *Martín Fierro* the finest expression of the Argentine spirit.[20] Another writer, Carlos Bunge, who in 1903 had defined the mestizo as morose, arrogant, and shiftless, discovered in 1914 that he was loyal, courageous, and patriotic.[21]

Beneath the surface, this rehabilitation was, in effect, an effort to redefine the national character, identifying it with old Castilian ideals of hierarchy, elite dominance, and a timeless social order. The pain felt by those who believed in the traditional order must have been intense, to issue forth in so unreal a mythology.

There were physical changes to match. The numbers that attested growth would have been unimaginable only a few years before. From the seat of the old Spanish viceroyalty, with its 24,000 inhabitants, and the city of 178,000 in the census of 1869, Buenos Aires now had 300,000 inhabitants in the mid-1880s, and was on its way to 1,500,000 by 1914.[22]

With these figures came the beginning of changes in residential and working patterns that would affect Argentine values and personality, helping to open the way for Juan Perón. One set of patterns characterized the *gente decente,* the upper 5 percent of the population, and another marked the remaining 95 percent, the *gente de pueblo.*

The *gente decente,* relatively united in group and clan consciousness, were the principal gainers from the public construction then transforming Buenos Aires into a great city with a continental European image.[23] Theirs were the magnificent new palaces with the foyers that imaged Paris and the exterior ornamentation reminiscent of Italian baroque. Theirs to enjoy were the spaciousness of the new Plaza de Mayo and the splendor of the new Avenida de Mayo, connecting the Congress and the Casa Rosada (the executive office building, the Argentine White House) with a grandeur worthy of the city by the Seine. Theirs was the commerce that was turning the muddy silver estuary into a marine highway. They lived in the center of town, near the plaza that symbolized the central state, near the cathedral and the *cabildo* that spoke of the Two Kingdoms. After the plague of 1871, the elite had resettled just to the north of the Plaza, and even today the *Barrio Norte,* so despised by Evita Perón, remains the center of upper class prestige. For them, these areas were the city and the capital and the country as well, an assurance to its inhabitants that they were the natural rulers, as they thought they should be.[24]

With the *gente de pueblo* it was different. Although many of them found rudimentary shelter downtown in the immense and labrynthine *conventillos,* or apartments, they increasingly expanded outward into the neighborhoods and suburbs that today characterize the far-flung city. Here identity followed the *cuadra* and the *barrio,* the former being the area comprising the two facing sides of a city block, and the latter being a neighborhood with several *cuadras.* The local store, which was the social and political center of the *barrio,* and the local cafe served each such area and helped to define it. Here the family "belonged"; they were residents of a certain *barrio,* and within it, a certain *cuadra.* Only secondarily and vaguely were they residents of the city, and even less of the nation.[25] Social life was civil and amiable, but limited basically to the quick smile and greeting on the sidewalk, or to the casual visiting that was briefly possible at the corner store and the sidewalk cafe or at Mass. One's home was for the family only.

Fragmented and dispersed by the diffuse geography of the city, having no focus other than the *barrio,* unused to collaborative civic activity, and devoid of connections and common interests, the manual laborers and the blue- and white-collar groups that would later coalesce into the lower class and the middle class were free to pursue their personal interests in ways that further promoted the individualism already so pronounced. The upper fringes of these groups imitated the *gente decente* and might or might not gain eventual admittance to their ranks, depending on their economic performance. The lower and middle ranks entrusted whatever outside chances they might dream of for social advancement to luck or to some slick coup, to *viveza,* as it was called.

In time, wider horizons succeeded the limited vision of *barrio* and *cuadra*. But the evolution came gradually. The old order retained much of its importance down to the time of Perón and beyond, and it lived on in the mental attitudes and psychological values of individualism, fragmentation, tenuous personal relationships beyond the family, and a lack of social cohesion.

It was much the same in the lesser towns, whether in the littoral or in the interior. There, too, it was a lifelong struggle of fragmented men and women trying to accomplish through economic achievement what was closed off to them in politics and society. Nor did the struggle end with life itself, for what had been defined by the calculus of possibilities for the living remained so defined in death: the location of one's burial place in the cemetery, whether near the entrance, where the elite were at rest or toward the remote sections at the rear, where the lowliest of the *gente de pueblo* were interred, was a faithful mirror of one's station in life. Hierarchy and disjunction ruled from the grave.

With the growing success of the Liberal System, the old upper class was gradually transformed. In the time of Mitre and Sarmiento, the elite had been liberal in the sense that it sought reforms that would unify and benefit the country. It had been relatively austere in morality and conduct. Bribery in either public or private life was not the norm. After the watershed of the 1880s, however, some of the elite, pushed from below by immigrants and corrupted by easy riches from unprecedented land values, evolved into a wealthy oligarchy, no longer austere, no longer interested in reform. Bribery appeared and began to reach upward.[26] Some elements of the oligarchy remained responsibly active in finance and public service, but more of them concentrated on the defense of privilege.

The potentials of public ostentation now came to be fully realized by those who were qualified to sustain it and by many who were not. Again it was the heritage coming forth, with the old belief that men of quality played public roles, reinforced by public display. It was not the money per se that counted; it was the display that the money made possible, since that confirmed the leadership and status credentials of the person or class concerned. These were the years that diverted the wealth of the pampas to the banks of the Seine and the coast of the Riviera, the years that witnessed the arrival of the squandering Argentine playboys, *les sauvages argentins*.[27] Money began increasingly to make up for deficiencies in rank, ancestry, and education, fueling the upward social mobility that became a conspicuous aspect of the second generation of immigrant stock. The change was not absolute, merely one of degree. Interestingly, the new materialism was one of the few Argentine social characteristics, if not the sole one, that does not trace back to Hispanic origins.[28]

Social tensions were inseparable from the new developments in immigration and in the economy. The frightened Creoles reacted defensively by giving ever more fervent loyalty to the old customs, to the disdain for labor and economic progress, to the devotion to leisure, and to the easy elegance of the old life on the *estancias* with its natural hierarchies. These values remained as the most sure passport to heightened social status. The immigrants, on the wrong side of formidable social ramparts, threw their energies into money-making, hoping that it might be the road to some kind of advance. The oligarchy, beleaguered and haughty, huddled in the Jockey Club, the *Circulo de Armas,* and the *Club del Progreso;* social and political power was strangely divorced from economic power. The oligarchy was detached in every way from the now-teeming urban multitudes and could exert no leadership because there simply was not enough connection for informal mechanisms of control or influence to be established. The oligarchy's tendency was therefore to exclude, to restrict, to keep the upstarts out of politics and to withhold assistance or participation in economic matters. The members of the existing middle class were equally unhelpful, since they followed the lead of the oligarchy, still supported the Liberal System, devoted themselves to service activities in law, education, and the government, and gave not a fig for the usual activity of the urban bourgeoisie elsewhere.[29]

An interesting relationship evolved between the traditional Hispanic value system and the immigrant multitudes. It might have been expected that the old Peninsular civilization, as reinforced in Argentina, would have given way before such an astonishing influx, much of it from non-Peninsular sources. But this did not occur. The newcomers brought mostly Mediterranean values that differed only in degree from those they now encountered. Absorption rather than conflict or reciprocal acculturation was the result, although inevitably some alteration of social identity took place.[30]

The explanation is generational. The first generation had little effect upon public life. Its member almost never became naturalized citizens and hence did not vote or participate in politics. This was no accident; the proceedings for naturalization were easy in theory but difficult in practice, in ways that can be best understood by those who have dealt at first hand with Latin American bureaucracies. And there was no real incentive for naturalization, since the constitution and laws guaranteed the immigrant all rights and benefits available to citizens, and, in addition, exempted him, after 1902, from military duty. Even if he did become a citizen, the immigrant generally came from a background that had provided him with little or no tradition of electoral politics and he rarely had any developed system of public values to contrast to the Argentine pattern, had he wished to do so. Those who did have such values found the Argentine patterns distasteful, and for that reason, in addition to others, they abstained from becoming citizens. German immigrants reserved their most severe strictures for what they saw as the corruption and frivolity of government and the flouting of the rule of law.[31] Many could neither understand nor accept the prevalence, and indeed the approval, of *viveza criolla*.

But the second generation was in a very different position. Citizens by birth, speaking the language as natives, and having at least a possibility of advancing socially, its members became very intense Argentines, partly in reaction against their parents' continuing foreignness, partly out of strong ambition, and partly out of fear of ridicule, a *porteño* phenomenon that became increasingly conspicuous.[32] It was clear to them that there was no hope of real arrival, either in society or in the economy, without emulation and full acceptance of the entire environment. So the values, customs and practices all around them were adopted with a vengeance by every generation after the first, and were thus strengthened and further extended.[33]

With the coming of economic riches and social complications, political power came to be seen as more imperative than ever; the executive branch of the government became more absolute, and while the constitutional norms were ostensibly observed, it was easy to subvert them by fraud or by occasional violence. One-party rule thus arose in the 1880s. This was one cause of the turmoil in politics that marked the 1890s. Another cause was the economic decline in those years that resulted from mismanagement during the wild bonanza of the 1880s. Financial policies had been misguided, inflation had become destructive, speculation had undermined stability, and corruption had taken on the open horizon of the pampas.

The Radicals and the Rise of Yrigoyen

The time had come for political protest. It now found serious expression in the abortive revolution of 1890 and in two other urban-based revolts, both likewise snuffed out, in 1893 and 1895. The most significant inheritance of these unquiet years was the creation of what has remained, despite numberless splits and divisions, the only Argentine political party with a continuous institutional history, the *Unión Cívica Radical,* or Radical Party. ("Radical" in the Argentine usage

has no necessary connection with violent or excessive change.) Its fig-
urehead was the great old president, Bartolomé Mitre, now in his
seventies, white-haired, his gaunt frame and aquiline face as distinguished as ever. But the real leader was Leandro N. Alem, a lawyer
and politician hitherto outstanding in neither calling, his face sad and
brooding above an incredibly long gray beard, a man marked from
childhood as too sensitive and feeling for the tumult of Argentine
politics. His father had been a follower of Rosas and was suspected of
membership in the Mazorca, the dictator's secret police. When Rosas
fell, the father was hanged, and the son's life was never the same
again. He was persecuted at the university: "I was the son of the man
who was hanged. In my examination a rotten vengeance was taken on
me. Many of the professors had come back from exile in a blind rage
against all that smelled of Rosas. I was the son of the hanged man."

Alem held control of the Radical Party for several years, long
enough to bring his nephew, Hipólito Yrigoyen, to the forefront of
the movement, long enough to see the failure of the third uprising,
in 1895, long enough to sense that the nephew he had favored had
chosen to betray his leadership, long enough to pen some final words
assumed to refer to Yrigoyen: "A viper feeds at my breast, biting at
my heart . . . It is preferable to die rather than to live a life of sterility,
uselessness, and humiliation. Yes, a man may break, but he must not
bend."[34] So writing, he reached for his pistol and shot himself.

It was a time of rough dissention and labor strife, barely veiled by
lush prosperity. Anarchism had taken early root in Argentina and it
provided most of what leadership labor then possessed. Social upheaval
was the goal of anarchism, direct action its style, and the general strike
its preferred instrument. There were nineteen major strikes in 1895
and sixteen in the following year. Twelve thousand railroad workers,
whose connection was not to the anarchists but to the socialists, walked
out for several weeks in the same year. The national economy staggered for a time in November 1902, when the anarchists mounted
another general strike. A state of siege was proclaimed, and legislation was adopted that permitted expulsion of foreign-born persons
who were found by the president to be disturbing public order. In
1907, another general strike called out 150,000 workers. Two years
later, 200,000 struck to protest police violence. The national Chief of
Police was assassinated in 1909. In 1910, there was further legislation
aimed at immigrants, amid signs that resentments and even hatred
based on the cleavages of class were a serious reality.[35] The Great Rift
was there for all to see, if they had wished to do so.

It was also a time that brought many leaders of the next half century to their political baptism. In 1896, the Socialist Partly was formally established by a distinguished Buenos Aires physician and disenchanted radical, Juan B. Justo, who would remain its leader for decades to come. In 1904, the Socialists elected their first member in the Chamber of Deputies, the subsequently famous Alfredo Palacios, an original if there ever was one. Short and slight, he disguised his lack of physical stature by high-heeled boots and an immense black moustache shaped like the letter "W," so striking an adornment that the viewer ignored everything else. A natty dresser and a ferocious swordsman, he fought at least six duels in defense of his prickly honor. How prickly it was, and the intensity of which individualism is capable, can be gauged from his response to an invitation to join the Socialist Party: "I am a Socialist, but I am not disposed to submit myself to any discipline."[36] He was expelled from the party in 1915, ostensibly because of one of his duels but in reality because of his weakening internationalism, and he founded his own Argentine Socialist Party. In 1918, the Socialists split again.[37]

And there was the brilliant and caustic Lisandro de la Torre, the senator from Santa Fe, a blue-eyed, coiled spring of passion and intensity, perhaps the most intelligent and almost certainly the most intransigent of them all, honest and idealistic, a concentrated flame of rectitude. There were others similar to all these, less highly marked, but all the children of the same value system. They had most of the requirements for political success of the kind that might have stabilized the country over a period of time, except for balance and the ability to compromise, to delegate, and to work together effectively.

The greatest interest, however, lies with one of the emerging public men of the 1890s who was to become before long the most popular leader in Argentine history until the rise of Juan Perón. This was Hipólito Yrigoyen, the nephew of the self-destroyed Leandro Alem, who inherited the Radical Party in 1896. Like Rosas, he was to have a strong influence upon Perón. His career, like that of Rosas, is rich in instruction for those who would understand Argentine politics, and as with Rosas and Perón, his personality and intuition were basic to his achievements.

In terms of personality, he was certainly one of the strangest public men in the history of Argentina. The descriptions of him by his contemporaries leave one in doubt as to whether they apply to the same person. Lisandro de la Torre, who disliked Yrigoyen with his habitual emotional intensity, wrote that "Underneath his black clothes and taciturn manner, underneath his repeated disclaimers of all ambition, underneath even his easy and frequent tears, he was intriguing, deceitful, ambitious."[38] On the other hand, a supporter wrote in rapture of Yrigoyen ". . . the true head of a Roman emperor rests magnificently by means of a well-proportioned, robust neck, on shoulders that are wide, cyclopean, made to bear the weight of a great nation. His glance is piercing like the eagle's . . . to see at great distances where the sight of mortals cannot reach . . . forehead wide and high like the mountain summit . . . like the granite deep in the Andes, the ideas are firm, well rooted."[39] Observers less partial, if they had managed to see him at all, would have noted a large, dark-skinned, heavy-set man, rather shambling, with a bowler hat atop a large head, and a heavy, squarish face bearing a vaguely Indian cast.

Yrigoyen was the product of a lonely and unfortunate childhood. His illiterate father had been a stable hand for Rosas. His mother had both Indian and Oriental blood and was given to tears, as was his grandmother, for Yrigoyen's grandfather had been shot in the triumph of the anti-Rosas forces. Yrigoyen's maternal aunt was forced to leave both home and family because of an unpardonable illicit liaison with a priest that produced two children. Surviving these desolate experiences, the future leader became a *comisario* of the local police in Buenos Aires Province, a position somewhat like that of a precinct captain in American politics, a splendid introduction to intrigue and real life. A modest inheritance in the form of an *estancia* freed him from want, but his requirements in any case were as simple as those of a monk. He never married, but a daughter, the issue of an affair with an Indian woman, devoted her life to him.

For a brief time, Yrigoyen taught philosophy and history in a provincial school, and there he was exposed to the thought, then in vogue, of the German philosopher, Karl Christian Friedrich Krause. Krause preached a rather vague metaphysical doctrine in which God was the universe, with man forming an integral part of the divine organism; the inner self, in contact with God, is the source of all knowledge. These dogmas deeply affected Yrigoyen. Adopting the Krausian preference for somber clothes and turning his life inward, he embarked upon the career for which he was ideally fitted, that of a political conspirator and organizer.

As a man of intrigue, Yrigoyen developed a secretive, molelike style for which no precedent seems available. He was soon known as "The *Peludo*," after a burrowing species of armadillo whose underground life resembled Yrigoyen's. He gave no speeches. His entire history before he became president in 1916 reveals only one public talk, and that was a very short one given at a very early stage of his career. For many years no pictures of him were available. He talked with many followers, but always with one at a time, meeting the solitary coworker in a small, darkened office and consulting with him in hushed tones. Even at a political convention he would not make an appearance, but would direct events from a tiny, hidden office nearby, sending his instructions by one courier at a time. He lived in Spartan obscurity in a small house as badly in need of refurbishing as was his meager wardrobe of rumpled clothing, it being his habit to give away the suits he was not wearing, which in any case had been tailored in the style of twenty years before.

To this furtive manner was joined the mystical element derived from his obscure religious dogmas. He viewed the Radical Party as a moral movement, a state of mind or spirit. He viewed his own role in terms of apostleship. Visitors admitted to his darkened chamber would hear from him, as from an oracle, metaphysical utterances so impressive and so incomprehensible that they left with the sure conviction of his sainthood. Amid the fascination and the soaring spiritual ideals that were thus communicated in the softest of tones and in the most unintelligible of rhetoric and syntax, something akin to a cult began to grow. Soon Yrigoyen was the undisputed political *caudillo* of Buenos Aires Province, and the Radical Party was beginning to take on a national dimension. His particular crusade was electoral honesty. For the rest, he favored equality and social programs in general and whatever else could be done for the middle classes and the downtrodden; but in no sense did these woolly aspirations ever coalesce into programs fleshed out with details. For decades, the Radical Party, in fact, never lost its character as a movement, as a gigantic spiritual exercise in a mundane, dangerous, and dirty world, and it never stooped to a platform.[40]

Yrigoyen had little education and a mediocre intellect. He cared nothing for the arts, the theater, and literature. He read one novel in all his life. Honest, naive in important respects despite the skill of his intrigues, and devoid of ideas beyond his murmured philosophical abstractions, he knew little of the larger aspects of affairs and nothing at all about the world beyond Argentina. His extraordinary success and the almost mad devotion he aroused were a tribute solely to the one quality in which he was supreme: moral force, moral prestige.

Two men less capable of working together than Yrigoyen and Lisandro de la Torre could not have been found in the entire Argentine Republic. Their inevitable early parting occurred in 1897, when de la Torre bitterly attacked Yrigoyen at a convention of the Radical Party, describing him as ". . . a negative but terrible influence, that with cold premeditation made the revolutionary plans of 1892 and

1893 come to nothing." In the brittle personalism of Argentine politics this was a fatal slur, and Yrigoyen challenged de la Torre to a
duel. They fought with sabres and cut each other, parting without a
reconciliation, de la Torre to found his own party in Santa Fe.[41]

There was another attempted revolution in 1905, promoted by
Yrigoyen and the Radicals, who enlisted army elements as its means.
Again it was abortive, and Yrigoyen now developed the doctrine that
was to define the Radicals far into the future: abstention. Convinced
that Radicalism could never win an election because of the corruption
of the system, and that it could succeed only by revolution, Yrigoyen
now refused to participate in any election and forbade party members
to vote for candidates of any party.

But a change was at hand. The governing class had been shaken
by the unsuccessful attempts at revolt in the 1890s and 1905 and by
the working class violence that the anarchists had generated. There
was genuine concern that the Radicals might find the key to a successful revolutionary coup.[42] And by 1910, the Radicals had come to be
seen as rather less threatening in an electoral context, less Jacobin,
and with closer links to elements of the oligarchy, than was first thought.
Might not the middle-class Radicals, viewed in this new light, stand
together with the oligarcy as a dike against the swarming masses below?[43]
The centennial of the May revolution was a notable event of the year,
with dazzling spectacles and visiting dignitaries, and the time was one
of relative calm, when pride had crested and conflict had ebbed for a
moment.

It happened also that in 1910 an enlightened and honest conservative, Roque Sáenz Peña, had come to the presidency speaking of reform
and meaning what he said. The consequence was the famous Sáenz
Peña law of 1912, establishing universal, private, and compulsory male
suffrage, and creating a system in which legislative representation would
be divided between the two parties with the highest total vote, in the
proportion of two to one. The door was now open for Yrigoyen in
national elections in 1916.

The events of that electoral season were dramatic. The Radical
Party convention, in a storm of emotion, with wild cries and streaming
tears, nominated Yrigoyen by acclamation. Typically, he was not present, having remained in his stark little home, alone. He now communicated with the convention by letter, refusing the nomination. He
had never wanted office, he said; his life work, his apostleship, was
now complete. The convention rejected the letter and renewed its
insistence. Again he refused. The delegates now threatened to dissolve the Party if he remained adamant. His voice trembling, he finally

gave in: "Do with me what you will." But he relented in his own manner, took no part in the campaign, and retreated to his *estancia,* where he refused to receive visitors or even to open his mail. He won a narrow victory when Lisandro do la Torre, who had run as a candidate of his personal party, overcame his hatred for the moment and threw his crucial support to Yrigoyen, whose conservative opposition he hated even more.

Yrigoyen's conduct in victory was consistent with what had gone before. He appeared for the oath of office and for what was assumed would be a statement of his plans, since he had remained in seclusion after his election, saying nothing of any program. But at the moment of triumph he placed his hand on the Bible and the cruficix, repeated the oath of office, made a half turn, stepped through the heavy curtains behind the rostrum, and disappeared.[44] When he was found, and directed to the horse-drawn coach that was to take him to the Casa Rosada, he saw that men in the street had unhitched the horses and were fighting with one another for the honor of pulling his coach themselves. Appalled, he asked the captain of the guards why they allowed such a display of inequality. "Sir," came the answer, "we could avoid it only by using our swords." Half a million people were in the streets that day. Mass psychology as an element in politics and public life had come to Argentina.[45]

Yrigoyen in power was reminiscent of Yrigoyen in opposition. He tried to run the government as he had run the party, as if it were a part of his household. He had no grasp whatever of the need for delegating any power; it was as if the thought had never entered his mind. Nor did he ever really understand that the constitution gave Congress, and Congress alone, the power to vote appropriations, for he spent money as he deemed necessary, whether authorized or not. He had no program precise enough to find its way into legislation, and fine generalities produced little. His cabinet consisted of nonentities whose virtues, in his eyes, were anonymity and acquiescence in the intense personalism of the administration. De la Torre pronounced a fair verdict: "A more absolute rule, or a more personal work, have never been seen. He decides, he orders, he makes and unmakes. He is President, Treasurer, and Secretary, all at once. He surrounds himself only with men who obey him and whom he can manage at will."[46]

Ironically, too, much that he had criticized in his conservative predecessors—their excessively centralized governments and the graft and illegality of their administrations—now came to pass under the great reformer. Not since Urquiza, in the first uncertain days of the new

Republic, had any president intervened in the provinces on the scale of Yrigoyen. His first administration produced twenty interventions in the fourteen provinces. Yrigoyen himself retained his anchorite's simplicity and his disinterest in money, but those around him all too often forgot the spirit of the earlier times, when they had planned in darkened rooms for a more pure future, and they indulged in graft and political spoils in the familiar old immoderate way.

One event of Yrigoyen's first administration was notable for the direction in which it pointed and for its implications for the years to come. The first weeks of January 1919 were a time of labor strife and increasing tension in the government. A general strike was in progress, and nasty violence had broken out in the streets. The *Semana Tragica,* the Tragic Week, had come. Yrigoyen had been following a policy of conciliation. Then on the afternoon of January 9, an event occurred for which there had been no precedent since the beginning of constitutional government in the 1850s: General Dellepiane, the commander of the important Campo de Mayo garrison outside of Buenos Aires, appeared at the Casa Rosada with a well-armed battalion of troops. The army, he announced, would no longer continue its support of the government unless strong measures were taken to suppress the strike. Yrigoyen instantly reversed his policy. Order was restored by firm action and the administration joined in the search for the perpetrators of the confusion, or at least for those who could be so accused. It was the first direct intervention of the armed forces in the process of government. A small portent, perhaps, but a vivid and significant one.[47]

When Yrigoyen's first administration ended in 1922, he was succeeded by his fellow Radical, Marcelo T. de Alvear, a very different kind of personality. Alvear came from the top of the elite and was a familiar figure in the Paris he loved. Large, bald, amiable, he had long been respected in public life and he made a good, if not spectacular, president. Yrigoyen had believed that he would continue to rule in the manner he liked best, out of the limelight, by guiding his successor. But Alvear had his own sense of independence, and a split developed. From the mid-1920s on, the Yrigoyen Radicals were known as the Personalists, and the followers of Alvear, opposing the concentration of all authority in the leader, called themselves the Antipersonalists.

Yrigoyen's first administration had not impaired the popularity of the strange old patriach of the Party, and he was elected again in 1928 by a large margin. But he was now seventy-six and verging on senility. He was anxious to avoid the excesses and venal betrayals of his first government and so refused to trust even those whose help was necessary for the daily mechanics of government, thus redoubling his own personalism and dragging the government down to the level of immobility. He would sign nothing that he had not personally read and analyzed. Great heaps of papers accumulated, awaiting his depleted energies, while he indulged feminine admirers with bits of philosophical conversation. He signed two or three state papers a day, while ministers waited in his anterooms and creditors of the State poked around in the bureaucracy trying to find someone who would initial an invoice. The spoils system flourished, undeterred by the old president's feeble precautions. A later investigation of the Customs Service found 3,500 employees unauthorized by any law. Every bureaucrat seemed to be an actual or a potential thief. The entire environment in which the administration operated had by now taken a turn for the worse. It was clear that the government was unlikely to live out its term, and that portentous changes were imminent.

The Young Perón and His Family

In 1827, in the very pit of the miseries of the dying and disunited United Provinces, a young man named Tomás Mario Perron arrived in Buenos Aires, bearing a passport issued by the Kingdom of Sardinia. Six years later he married a woman named Ana Hughes, the daughter of a London carpenter, whose family had preceded Tomás Perron to Buenos Aires by two years. The young couple continued to live in Buenos Aires where Tomás Mario Perron (later known as Perón) followed a business career as a shopkeeper. If his great-grandson's account is accurate, he owned several shoe stores and imported boots and footware from Italy.[48]

Seven children resulted from this marriage, one of them a son destined to fame within Argentina. This was Tomás Liberato Perón, who became one of the most eminent Argentine physicians of his time, the foremost national authority on public hygiene, and a distinguished professor of chemistry and clinical medicine, widely acclaimed for his brilliance and for the nobility of his character. A photograph of him has survived, revealing lineaments of striking beauty and sensitivity, the face and the haunting blue eyes of a poet or a saint. An esthetic tendency in such a man is to be expected, and it is not surprising to learn that he had assembled in his garden the finest collection of roses in South America, with 500 varieties.[49] Tomás Liberato Perón married Dominga Dutey, a native of Paysandu, a town in the interior of Uruguay. Her parents had come from Savoy, in southeast-

ern France, and thus Dominga contributed yet another national strain
to the heritage of the eventual grandson who was given her name.
The elder of the two sons of Tomás Liberato Perón and Dominga
Dutey, born in 1867, during the presidency of the great Bartolomé
Mitre and named Mario Tomás, reflected in pale light some of the
interests and values of his distinguished parent, including the latter's
indifference to material success.

Tall, well built, chestnut-haired, and swarthy of complexion in the
Creole mold, young Mario Tomás studied medicine for a few years
and then struck out in new directions, geographically and otherwise.
He had inherited some land in the vicinity of Lobos, a small town on
the pampas about sixty miles southwest of Buenos Aires, where the
tone of the frontier still lingered undiminished. The change probably
represented the emergence of his true self, for Mario Tomás Perón
was a true man of the countryside. Juan Perón years later characterized him as a *horaciano,* a latter-day Horace, who treasured bucolic
values and beauties. Now he acquired by rent or purchase other tracts
in the area around Lobos and settled in. He was soon serving as an
alguacil, a kind of constable, as a sideline to his administration of his
ranch lands.

Mario Tomás soon found a mate who shared many of his qualities,
although not his intellectual interests. Juana Sosa Toledo, heavy-set
and solid, was pure Creole in descent and in temperament. Her parents' families, the Sosas and the Toledos, had long been established
on the pampas, humble country families stolidly impervious to isolation, danger, and adversity. Her mother contributed yet another ethnic strand to the complex fabric of Juan Domingo Perón's heritage,
for her Spanish blood had been mixed with that of the Mapuche Indians from the south of Chile.

A first son, Mario Avelino, was born to Mario Tomás and Juana
Perón in 1891. Four years later, on October 8, 1895, a second son was
born and was given the name of Juan Domingo. Although the union
of Mario Tomás Perón and Juana Sosa was stable and continuous,
they were apparently not married at this time. Juan Perón's birth certificate is lacking, but the declaration of the father, made on October
8 to the local registrar of documents, describes himself as unmarried
and refers to the infant Juan Domingo as a natural child. The subsequent marriage of the parents is referred to in a certification of the
original entry, made at a later date.[50] The family was now living in the
house in Lobos that is pictured as Juan Perón's birthplace, a typical
row house in the Latin American style with the few windows on the
street side, and its interior patio where family life centered, a middle-

class house in a small town, no part of which was very far from the open pampas.

Here Juan Domingo received his first impressions of the virtues of the country folk, the horsemen, the *paisanos,* whose merits he was to extol all his life. His principal mentor was a ranch hand named Sixto Magallanes, whose special skill was breaking in horses, but the young Perón appears to have had very warm childhood experiences with all these untutored men of the pampas. "They were like family to me, and I treated them like uncles. I never considered them peons in the pejorative sense that the word is often used . . . they are magnificent people; in their infinite humility they achieved a grandeur that it was not easy to find later among more developed people."[51]

It happened, of course, that this empathy so often annotated by Perón coincided perfectly with the political and social policies for which he was idolized, but his sincerity in this need not be questioned. The requirements of strategy and tactics are not necessarily antithetical to one's true preferences and values and indeed may benefit from a nat- ural congruence. Whatever later exaggerations Perón committed, verbally and otherwise, the evidence indicates rather clearly that his identification with the underpriviliged was sincere and that its origins traced back to his early years.

The restless father, yearning for yet more empty space and not tied down by any outstanding success in Lobos, soon began to think of Patagonia. In 1899, he established a connection with a company that owned huge tracts around Río Gallegos at the farthest point in Patagonia, moved his family in with relatives in Lobos, and took ship alone for the remote south. In a gesture of almost feudal paternalism, the family retainers, the ranch hands, the *peones,* were assembled into a small caravan of mule-drawn wagons and sent to Río Gallegos under the direction of the versatile Sixto Magallanes, whose only solid infor- mation was that he was supposed to head for that destination, and that it lay far to the south, about 1,200 miles in fact. More precise directions would hardly have helped much on the roadless and untracked pampas. The caravan arrived with all hands intact several months after Mario Tomás Perón had reached his destination. The family followed by sea a year later.

Life at their new ranch, devoted to sheep raising, was a constant struggle with the gritty environment, with the frightful cold of winter, with the spectral winds that blew forever. It was suited to Mario Tomás's interests as an amateur scientist, for there was much to study in the the way of geology, the sparse but interesting botany of the region, and archaeology in the form of early Indian tombs. He maintained a flourishing correspondence with scholars in Buenos Aires, sending them samples of various items, inquiring, and commenting. He also served, once more, as an unpaid minor public official, using the ranch home as an office.

Doña Juana was equal to the new rigors, riding a horse like the men, curing the ill with folk remedies, participating with her husband and sons when they rode forth to hunt guanaco and wild ostrich, comforting the sons with a bit of understanding and a coin or two on the side. Their instruction was provided by a tutor and monitored closely by Mario Tomás, whose small library was Juan Perón's first introduction to the world of scholarship: "From a very early age I acquired the habit of reading good books, especially those about philosophy, science, botany, religion and mineralogy, mostly because those were the only ones I had at hand."[52]

But the most important contribution of Mario Tomás to the education of Juan Domingo seems to have taken the form of moral example. The father was rather austere, as his son remembered him, but notable for his human sympathies and for his sense of dignity. Several examples have been handed down from the period in Patagonia, including the incident of the destitute Indian who came seeking help from the father. Mario Tomás received him with grave courtesy, addressed him in the Indian dialect, gave him a pair of goats and space on the ranch to build a little hut. Juan Domingo asked him why he had been so good to an Indian. "Didn't you see the dignity of that man?" Mario Tomás replied. "It's the only heritage he has received from his ancestors. We call the Indians thieves and we forget that we're the ones who have robbed them of everything."[53]

The anecdote is illustrative. Here was the class structure in profile, the hierarchy, the *patrón* at the top and the peon below. Here was the sense of mutual obligation that is part of the concept of the organic society. Here was the fierce stress on the dignity of each individual, creating a plane of equality that compensated in part for the extreme material disparities. It was all very Creole, and it was bred into Juan Perón's being.

By the age of nine, the young Perón had outgrown the available educational facilities, and he was enrolled in school in Buenos Aires, returning to Patagonia thereafter only for his summer vacations. But that remote land had been a tremendous formative experience. ". . . I believe that the whole family received a lesson in character from Patagonia. I give thanks to God for that; I have always thought that those five years in which my subconscious was formed exercised a favorable influence over the rest of my life."[54]

Although he was in contact with his grandmother Dominga and her family in Buenos Aires, he noted years later how difficult the change had been from absolute freedom in Patagonia to the strict discipline and routine of school. He was a mediocre student, but applied himself more actively and effectively to sports, for which he had already developed the passion that never left him. The principal legacy of the first five years he spent away from home seems to have been his sense of independence and self-sufficiency, the product of complete separation from parents and the experience of traveling alone back and forth over the twelve hundred miles of his vacation trips. It was reinforced by the absence of any father figure in Buenos Aires, so that Juan Domingo came to consider himself much more mature than his years indicated. "Because my grandmother was already elderly, I could take the place of the head of the family. It was a great influence in my life, because I began to be independent, to think and to decide for myself."[55]

His first important decision, taken in 1910, was to change his intended career. He had begun to prepare for medical school, but now he turned to the army, influenced, as he claimed later, by several companions who were about to enroll in the *Colegio Militar de la Nación*, the national military academy. In March 1911, Perón began his courses in that institution, from which he graduated in December 1913. The decision had not been without its pangs, however, for Perón had suppressed a secret aspiration for another kind of career for which he had already prepared application papers: he had wanted to be an engineer, attracted as he said by "mathematical exactitude and rigor."[56] It is curious that a man who developed a genius for politics, the most inexact and intuitive of arts, would harbor a secret urge for such an exact and objective calling. Another enigma of Perón.

In the strict environment of the *Colegio Militar* there was no place for the indulgent, the faint of heart, or the dilettante.[57] His fellow cadets would remember Perón more for his personality and for amiability and good will than for intellectual distinction. His marks were creditable but not remarkable. He was also remembered for athletic skill, for good behavior, and for his youthful age and appearance. The average age of graduates was between twenty and twenty-one, but Perón graduated at eighteen, the youngest of the 128 cadets in his class, with the rank of sublieutenant.

Some aspects of the years in the *Colegio Militar* were pleasant for him, particularly the friendships he developed, many of which he kept for life. What he missed most was intimacy and familial warmth, for old relationships were now attenuated, and there was certainly little of either warmth or intimacy in his first relations with women, which were with prostitutes. "In the epoch in which we were boys, we weren't accustomed to go to social parties, and it would not have occurred to us to go to a home and make love to a family girl."[58]

On the whole, Perón's remembrances of the *Colegio Militar* were less favorable than one might expect. In his views expressed late in life, he may well have incorporated many accretions deposited during the years, and the technique of adapting old memory to new political requirements was one that he acquired early and never forgot. But nevertheless, his later appraisals, although self-serving, sound essentially convincing and consistent with his basic convictions. Thus he objected to the repressive environment of his classes. "It was a barbaric kind of teaching . . . it seemed to be aimed only at falsifying the true nature of each one of us." And he objected to the military mentality, a ". . . deformed mentality. The humanistic mentality which the cadet had acquired in his home gave way to an education that was a pure imposture . . ."[59]

There was always in Perón a certain ambivalence about the military. He spoke of its mission in high tones, he counted many friends among its members, and he valued his rank and wore the uniform with pride, yet he was often quick to disparage the armed forces. He often found their political and other views benighted and he had a low opinion of the abilities of a large proportion of the officer corps. The genesis of this odd mixture of devotion and hostile skepticism appears to have gone back to the beginnings of his career.

Something equally enduring in the formation of his values came to Perón as a present from his father on the day of his graduation from the *Colegio Militar* on December 18, 1913, in the form of three books, neither casually given nor casually received. Perón always kept them on his night table, and he said of them years later, ". . . I have never been separated from these three teachings that ruled my life." Each book came with his father's inscription. The first was Hernández's classic, *Martín Fierro,* with the words "So that you will never forget that above all other things you are a Creole." The second was Plutarch's *Lives* with the injunction "So that you may always be inspired by them." The third was Lord Chesterfield's *Letters* to his son, with the inscription "So that you may learn how to comport yourself among people."[60] Each parental selection and each dedication was a tribute to values enshrined in the Argentine civilization. The Creole nationalism and sense of cultural identity invoked by the legendry of pastoral life, the individualism taught by essays that looked to heroes rather than to impersonal historical processes for explanations of events, and a book of manners defining form, deportment, and display deemed appropriate for men pursuing public roles: such elements, among others, were the stuff of which public leadership was compounded in the tradition that the young Perón was absorbing.[61]

The new sublieutenant was assigned to the Twelfth Infantry Regiment, in Paraná, and given a section of eighty soldiers and ten noncommissioned officers. It was illuminating for him. "In a country with fifty million cattle, thirty percent of the army conscripts were rejected for physical weakness, and those that were accepted came there half naked . . ."[62] There seemed to be signs of misery everywhere in the countryside, and Perón traced a vivid broadening of his social consciousness to this stimulus.

He learned his trade well, developing excellent relations with his men by ignoring the tradition of authoritative command, by sharing with them, by his readiness to assist, and by recognition of their dignity and individuality. In 1916, now a second lieutenant, he was transferred to Santa Fe. Here labor disputes intersected with Perón's military career when he was sent with detachments to preserve order. He became deeply involved, particularly in 1919 in San Cristóbal, a small town in Santa Fe, where railway workers were on strike. Perón stayed two months in San Cristóbal, having long discussions with a strike leader named Oscar Aldrey who later wrote about the episode.[63] Perón's thinking on labor relations and social justice as it emerged in 1943 was much influenced by the experience in San Cristóbal.

In 1920, he was transferred to the *Escuela de Suboficiales*, the School for Noncommissioned Officers at the big Campo de Mayo base. He was at this post, with brief absences, from January 1920 to March 1926, instructing noncoms and administering programs of the school. This was another productive link in Perón's career because, again, it brought him into contact with the lives and problems of those whose circumstances suggested the political themes he would later adopt. The school was attended by young men aged sixteen to twenty-one from undistinguished backgrounds all over the country who were seeking lesser careers in the military. A few of them might qualify at the end of their two years for entry into the *Colegio Militar*, but their social and intellectual limitations made this exceptional.

Perón was an excellent instructor in these years, demanding of himself, demanding of others to the extent necessary to handle the task in hand, understanding but firm, and seeking a kind of equilibrium (a word and a concept that he favored even then) in approach and performance that was based on respect for authority. He continued his own individual participation in athletics, winning his first army championship in fencing in 1918 and repeating the feat several times in the 1920s. He was promoted to first lieutenant in 1919, and to captain in 1924.

In 1924 and 1925 came the first intimations of Perón's activity as a writer. He edited two chapters of the *Manual del Aspirante,* a compilation of instructions for military personnel, including an analysis of will and of military leadership that foretold clearly some of the significant themes that would inform Perón's most important book, *Conducción política,* in 1952.

Assignment to the *Escuela Superior de Guerra,* the War Academy, followed on March 12, 1926. This was a school that prepared middle-level officers for advancement to high command. The requirements were exacting. Perón had prepared for the entrance examinations with almost monastic concentration and persistence and was admitted to a three-year program for captains. His record at the War Academy was very good, and the years there were pleasant, darkened only by the death of his father in 1928, at the age of sixty-one.

On January 26, 1929, Perón graduated from the War Academy and was assigned to general staff duty. He continued his historical researches and his prowling in the National Archives, for these were congenial to him and fitted well with his part-time appointment to the faculty of the War Academy. This was in January 1930. Perón did not know it, but great changes were about to overtake the army and the nation. The event that would foretell the new order was just over the horizon. The fall of Yrigoyen was imminent.

> To meet the crisis that began in 1930, several dif-
> ferent approaches were attempted, which finally
> reduced to two: one was typically fascist; the other
> we may call fraudulent democracy.
>
> — José Luis Romero, *A History of Argentine Political Thought*

4. The Conservative Restoration 1930-1943

The Fall of Yrigoyen: 1930

THE WORST OF the difficulties that overcame President Yrigoyen came from abroad in the form of the worldwide depression of 1929–30 and of reduced income from British purchases of Argentine exports. But the long-range effects were even more ominous, for the depression implied that the era of free international trade might be ending, a victim of new systems of bilateral trade and regional preferences. Other difficulties were internal, some of them representing political fallout from the loss of export revenues. Those revenues had financed not only the economic sectors concerned but the government as well, and the Radical Party in particular. Oddly, for a moral movement, that party was an immense patronage machine benefitting hordes of middle-class aspirants in and to the bureaucracy. These could no longer be accommodated, even as their numbers increased with the hardships of the early 1930s. Student opposition to the bungling of the government soon became another factor. The wrangling of the Yrigoyen supporters and their opponents continued the feud that had split the party. Both sides were now assisted by organized small bands and groups that were committed to direct action in the streets, thus heralding a new tendency to unofficial violence. Worse, the armed forces had now become disaffected.[1] The military policies of Yrigoyen were unfortunate, for he had used the army indiscriminately in his interventions in the provinces and he had granted special favors, disregarded regulations, and openly favored the reincorporation of retired officers who had sided with him in early domestic conflicts, thus upsetting what the majority of the military saw as the order, discipline, and balance of a hierarchical institution.

By the spring of 1930, all of these sources of opposition had coalesced into two concurrent military plots.[2] The leader of one of the movements was General José Uriburu, an officer of great prestige with substantial relationships in business, society, and politics, and a man of strongly traditional and austere views. The leader of the other plot was General Agustín P. Justo, formerly war minister under Alvear. Justo, who also had a large following among the military, was a portly and avuncular man whose benign demeanor obscured great ambition, and potent political skills in support of it, not excluding a talent for devious manipulation.[3]

The objectives of the two men were different. General Uriburu sought an eventual reshaping of political and social life, with a turn to corporatist principles, discipline and hierarchy.[4] His was the more thoroughgoing program, since Justo and his followers had no basic revisions in mind. They merely sought power within what they saw as a crumbling situation, to be followed by a return to civilian government.[5] The two movements were reconciled on September 5, 1930, under General Uriburu, and the next day he led the military column that took over the state. It was an easy operation, hardly more than a parade-ground exercise, a mere 900 soldiers and 600 cadets comprising the column. President Yrigoyen was simply ordered out, and so badly had affairs deteriorated that even his popular following deserted him completely. A mob invaded his simple home and threw his few possessions into the street, books, papers, and all, where they were burned. Where men had once come to blows for the honor of pulling his coach, the cry of "Death to the *peludo!*" now echoed grotesquely. He was removed as a prisoner to Martín García Island in the estuary, and there he spent the next fifteen months, alone with his daughter and a secretary, doing nothing, sitting all day. He died in July 1933 at the age of eighty-one, in a cheap iron bed in a cheap upstairs flat. By then, when it was too late, fickle public opinion had swung around to another of its extremes, and his casket was followed to the grave by hundred of thousands of mourners.

It was an ironic destiny for Yrigoyen. He had flirted with the armed forces and enticed them with intrigues in his early years,[6] and in the end he had to stand by helplessly, a feeble old sorcerer, while the most formidable of apprentices began to change the very structure of the nation.

The Troubled Decade

The revolution of 1930 marked a qualitative change, the end of a long era and the beginning of something new that probably has not yet fully run its course. Historically, military power in Argentina had always been subordinated to the civil. Now there began a shift in the relationship of these fundamental forces.[7] The sentiments of those who were primarily concerned are worthy of note, for it is easy to assume that the men who overthrow governments in Latin America respond only to greed or to hunger for power. On the contrary, a fierce idealism is often the motive, coupled with a naive optimism whose historical memory has failed. An important military supporter of General Uriburu, usually given to restrained prose, wrote: "The people and the army together were writing a new and shining page in the annals of democracy. A deep joy filled our hearts." Another supporter found the September coup "superior in every respect" to the French Revolution.[8]

What General Uriburu intended was not a mere shuffling of the top command in the Casa Rosada, but a deep change in social structure, with power vested in a hierarchical system in which the armed forces would participate significantly.[9] If in the decades to come the military would sometimes be on the sidelines while some civilian government elected with their approval formed the official lineup, they would henceforth remain close enough to the playing field to halt the game whenever they wished, and to substitute an entire new squad.[10]

Two generalizations about the military forces are in order as they arrived at this stage. The first is that references to "the military," or to "the armed forces," are in a sense misleading, since they imply a monolithic entity, an unbroken uniformity of belief and sentiment. The farther the point of observation from the men themselves, the greater becomes the impression of this unity. As Potash has pointed out, factors long considered to have exerted a steady, unvarying influence on the officer corps, such as the impact of German military precepts, or social class relationships, or generational factors, did not in fact have the assumed consistency of effect.[11] The officer class was in fact deeply divided on basic questions of foreign and domestic policy, for it responded, as did all other classes, to a complex calculus of motivations in which public and private elements and professional and personal considerations were integrated.[12]

The second generalization concerns the long-range effects of the 1930 revolution upon the military. Although these were varied, there was a consistent tendency: politics was opened up to the men of the barracks as never before. Issues formerly deemed the exclusive and arcane responsibility of civilians were now a familiar subject of debate between colonels and majors. With familiarity often came a bit of contempt. The shufflings of the politicians came to be seen as tawdry in comparison to the presumed nobility and patriotism of the military calling, and the political function itself began to lose some of its legitimacy for the disillusioned officers. But, correspondingly, the armed forces had come to lose some of their own legitimacy in the view of the public, since they were now seen as contenders on the political battleground rather than as guardians well above it. The result of all this was an increase in general skepticism on all sides, the last thing Argentine society needed.[13]

The new consciousness of the military now focused on foreign policy, with a trend toward nationalism, often with civilian prompting. This accorded with changes in Europe. Charles Maurras in France, Primo de Rivera in Spain, Benito Mussolini in Italy, and Generalissimo Francisco Franco in Spain all exerted an influence. The spectacular early triumphs of Hitler capped the process by which nationalist movements in Argentina, with strong right-wing coloration, were accepted in various quarters as the direction of the future.

General Uriburu was more an ideologue than a politician, and he and his largely civilian administration were unable to gain much support for his basic revisions. Military insurrections and civil strife broke out, and Uriburu was pressured to step down. National elections in 1932 were played under the old rules of fraud. Every kind of trickery and deceit was employed as graves opened and the dead rose up and proceeded unerringly to the nearest polling place.[14] General Justo was the winner, and he served his six-year term. His electoral machine, a coalition of the conservatives, the anti-Yrigoyen Radicals, and the Independent Socialist Party[15] was called the *Concordancia,* and it remained the dominant political power during the decade.

The Radicals continued their decline, having opted again for abstention, and did not contest the next elections, at the end of 1937, among the most fraudulent in Argentine history. Justo manipulated the victory of his chosen successor, Roberto Ortiz, a lawyer from the Antipersonalist wing of the Radicals,[16] and was doubtless surprised when Ortiz emerged as a throwback to Roque Sáenz Peña and established his administration squarely on the base of honest elections. But fate took a hand, and not for the better. Ortiz had advanced diabetes when he came to office and soon became almost blind. By 1940 he had to step aside while the vice-president took over in all but name. This brought to the fore Ramón Castillo, a typical Creole of the old school, shrewd rather than profound, a bit cynical even for a man in a cynical calling, given to the facade of an amiable and slightly fuddled character sucking his gourd of yerba mate, the Argentine native tea, through the traditional silver straw. But he was not nicknamed "The Fox" for nothing. He was from Catamarca, a backward spot that had never been favored with an honest election, and he was a true product of its political culture.[17]

The political performance during the years from 1930 to 1943 was almost entirely unfortunate. It was a time of cynicism and corruption, a time of resignation and disillusion, a time in which all the political parties seemed to be in terminal decline. The conservative elements, lacking a real party, could offer little more than ad hoc improvisations; even in this they were at a disadvantage, because the oligarchy had little contact with the industrial power centers and hardly any leverage that could have sustained a strong party operation. The Radicals, leaderless after the death of Alvear in 1942, were in little better condition.[18] The very nature of the party as a moral, almost mystic, movement had limited its ability to develop programs with specific content, and after the Sáenz Peña Law of 1912 had implemented the Party's great theme of universal and honest suffrage, it seemed to have little momentum left.[19] The Socialists, too, had exhausted their inspiration. Their forty-five representatives in Congress in 1932 had declined to seventeen by 1943, most of them in office as the constitutionally mandated minority representation.[20] Their intellectual distinction and legislative innovation had brought forth innumerable ideas in advance of their time, but they had little effective relationship with the masses whose name they invoked. They had never succumbed to nationalism, for their old tradition of world outreach was too rigid to bend, as were the fine old men who enunciated it, sectarians all, a generation of vintage patriarchs who would soon leave a vacuum rather than successors.

The legislature was equally stultified. The record of the Congress in 1937, admittedly worse than usual, was spectacular in a negative sense, that body managing to pass only three laws in the entire year, one authorizing itself to spend more money and two authorizing the president to leave Buenos Aires for vacations.[21]

Enormous economic and social forces were revising the political agenda. The big old issue from the time of Sarmiento, the balance between Buenos Aires and the provinces, the problem of federalism and centralism, was fading away; the city had triumphed. The Great Rift was now quietly being refashioned as the division between "haves" and "have-nots" in city and country alike.[22] No one paid any attention.

The economic performance in the years between 1930 and 1943 mingled the positive and the negative, but always in a context in which ambiguity, tension, and social strain provided a dominant coloration. The decline and fall of the Liberal System was the central phenomenon. Premonitions of this had been sensed as far back as the First World War by a few perceptive observers who argued that the conditions supporting the export economy were gone forever.[23] These prophets may or may not have been premature, but they were solidly confirmed by the adoption of a system of imperial trade preferences at a Commonwealth Conference held at Ottawa in 1932,[24] bringing the acute threat that Argentina might be replaced by Canada, Australia, and other Commonwealth sources as the prime supplier of foodstuffs to Britain. The Argentines were therefore forced to negotiate from a weak position.

The result was a famous trade agreement, the Roca-Runciman Pact, in 1933. In return for continued purchases of foodstuffs and wool, the British obtained an Argentine commitment to "Buy British," even at the expense of domestic sources, to leave imported coal on the free list, and to grant other concessions.[25] The renewal of the pact in 1936 even required Argentina to close down private bus lines in Buenos Aires that competed with the tramway system owned by British interests. There was much resistance to these harsh terms, but it is difficult to see what else the government could have done. Nor is there much plausibility in the familiar contention that the Roca-Runciman Pact benefitted the export-oriented oligarchy and no one else; it seems clear enough that its effects were national.[26] But that was not the general perception, and the pact gave much fervor to the nationalistic view that Argentina was bound in thralldom and that the national ills originated overseas. By 1937, other bilateral arrangements had been concluded between Argentina and most of the continental European nations, as well as with Brazil, Uruguay, and Peru.[27]

The basic problem was that Argentina and Britain were no longer complementary in their economic requirements. Argentina continued to need a market for its large pastoral and agricultural exports and a source of investment capital, but the war and the imperial preference system did not permit these to the extent necessary. England needed a source for its imports of food, but within the sterling area, and it now wanted tangible support in its war effort, and Argentina could meet neither of these conditions. For Argentina, the old technique of balancing its trade deficit with the United States against its surplus with England was no longer possible in a world of bilateral trade relations.[28] And efforts to achieve a trade agreement with the United States failed in the face of opposition by American agricultural interests.[29]

The landed oligarchy itself was suffering. Land values were no longer rising, and the strings of polo ponies and the villas scattered in a golden shower between Cannes and Monaco were threatened. Mortgages had to be looked in the face. Bankruptcies intruded into old families whose names had been familiar to Rosas, and many a gentleman of former wealth was now to be found working in some ministry where his connections had been put to good use.[30]

The export economy and the landowners suffered the most from the depression. In other sectors, recovery was relatively rapid. Against the pressures of the British Government, President Justo presided over the first substantial program of road building in the nation's history, and he introduced the income tax.[31] By 1936, the depression was a thing of the past. Economic management under the *Concordancia*, in a technical sense, was very professional, and industrial modernization flourished in the thirties, assisted by foreign investment, exchange controls, and restrictions on imports. The process had been shocked into life by the dislocations of the First World War, whose effects were profound in Argentina; it had deepened since then, and now new products, industries, and techniques came on the scene, particularly in the fields of metallurgy and textiles. Forty-three important enterprises entered Argentina from overseas during the decade. By 1940, the industrial economy was no longer seen as a stopgap, or as a limited response to an aberration originating in the outside world, but rather as something permanent, a new element in the national life.[32] There was something self-perpetuating about the new trend: the more that import substitution and industrialization flourished, the more important became the Argentine economic and political interests associated with them, and the more detached from the traditional sources and objectives the decision-making became.[33] But several negative factors persisted in the evolving economy. There was still almost no capital-goods industry, technology lagged, electric power usage was low, and small companies remained the norm.

The growing nontraditional economy and the unchanged hardships of rural life produced extensive internal migrations between 1930 and 1943. By the mid-thirties, the tide running from country to city reached the figure of 80,000 annually and a few years later it passed 95,000,[34] a further element of upheaval.

Nationalists and Intellectuals in Discontent

As the world view of the Liberal System began to fade, the 1930s brought a strong upsurge of nationalism.[35] By the 1920s, the momentum of the movement was quite apparent. In 1924, Leopoldo Lugones, the poet, made a famous speech in which he hailed the coming of "the hour of the sword," the arrival of authoritarian and hierarchic rule under the guiding hand of Church and State. Lugones had been part of the intellectual force behind General Uriburu. Another part of that force was Carlos Ibarguren, the politician and writer, who drafted what he called the Statute of the Nationalist State, outlining broad purposes and policies. Ibarguren, who was another of the many precursors of Perón, has been seen as one of the Argentine originators of "enlightened fascism."[36]

But this was also a traditional nationalism, the aristocratic variety congenial to the right wing.[37] Hispanicist and based on the landowners, the army and the Church, it was bitterly anti-Yrigoyen and sweetly nostalgic, looking back to the 1860s and 1870s as a golden time of civic virtue, a time innocent of corruptions and immigrant hordes and the gross antics of those to whom wealth now came too easily. These perpetuators of old rural values now sought to defend their dreams by some kind of corporate representation. The intellectual linkage between their various desires, which included national dominion over the increasing foreign investment, was provided by Lugones, but no political leader was at hand to channel their demands into realistic party activity. As always, there were fringe elements on the right of the right wing; these had none of the intellectual respectability of Lugones and Ibarguren and they attacked everything in sight, reviving the old crusading mentality of the "Sword and Cross" persuasion.

But there was also another nationalism, a new variety whose stridency would have been quite out of place in the Jockey Club and the *Circulo Militar,* and whose advocates despised the genteel patricians pledged to the memory of Mitre. This was the nationalism of the left wing, a popular nationalism that spoke of power to the people, meaning the middle class. Its accent was Jacobin and firmly antiforeign. Its strongest institutional base was in FORJA, the Radical Orientation Force of Young Argentina, an offshoot of Yrigoyen Radicalism, given to pamphlets and street meetings assailing colonialism and other ills.[38]

The old nationalism and the new kind happened to converge in the 1930s, driven to alignment not by fundamental affinity of purpose but by their shared dislike of liberalism, democracy, capitalism, and foreign domination.[39]

Nationalism provided a philosophical spur to the growing industrialization that was now widely seen as the correct economic replacement for the departing Liberal System, as the means for achieving economic sovereignty by breaking the grip of England, and as a national security objective. In one of the most emotional and sensitive sectors of all, the Radicals had founded in 1922 a state petroleum agency, the YPF, and General Enrique Mosconi, its first director, labored for years to achieve Yrigoyen's goal of a monopoly. The theme and mood of "petroleum nationalism" developed rapidly.[40] Other military proponents of nationalism argued for industrialization within the state-owned sector, a clear anticipation of Perón.[41]

Nationalism became a dominant influence on foreign policy, which had always been a reflection of economic interests. The nation's relationships with the countries that bought Argentine products, the soundness of the export/import tie with England, the freedom of action that could secure economic survival in an uncertain future—these had always been the things that mattered. Everything else connected with foreign policy had been marginal.

Even thus limited and defined, however, foreign policy was being put to the test. The absolute primacy of the English economic connection had faded, and although elements of the old order remained in the continuing but reduced trade, in the British investments now more or less dead in the water, in the old social artifacts like the Hurlinham Club with its polo field and cricket green and the Pipers' Band of the St. Andrew's Society of the River Plate and the Burns' Night Supper, it was not the same.[42] New uncertainties created insecurity and insecurity generated resentment, and all of these encouraged economic nationalism. So did disillusion with the United States, which would not buy beef, wheat, and flax. Against this background, the neutrality policy of the wartime years is more understandable in retrospect than it was to others in the hemisphere at the time.

It was this policy that the military forces adopted with increasing enthusiasm, but with shadings of their own. Pro-Axis sympathy had surfaced among many officers. This does not indicate, however, a desire for the introduction of the Nazi system into Argentina or for the incorporation of the country into the German orbit. It does say that many officers admired the German military machine for its professional excellence, that they would have been happy to see Britain brought down, and that the German ideology of the time was not troublesome to a majority of them[43]

Writers and intellectuals added their varying analyses to those of the politicians, the economists, and the nationalists, redoubling the voices of discontent. Many of the reigning prophets and teachers among the intellectuals were Europeans of a pessimistic orientation, among them Oswald Spengler, José Ortega y Gasset, and Count Keyserling.

There were more than enough Argentine intellectuals, and they took up the European themes and added others of their own, no less disheartening. Raúl Scalabrini Ortiz wrote two books of concerted attacks on British imperialism and remained an inspiration to all good nationalists. Eduardo Mallea provided an analysis of the Argentine personality in varying tones of gray in his *Historia de una pasión argentina* in 1937. Jorge Luis Borges was coming into his maturity in the late 1930s, and his introspective genius reached outward to Europe and backward to a presumably better Argentina. Manuel Gálvez, the novelist, plumbed the depths of loneliness in modern Argentina and likewise turned to the culture of Europe. Roberto Arlt, in a series of realistic novels and plays, wrote of the frustrations that had succeeded hope for the middle classes.

All of these writers were grim enough, inclined to the dark vision, but one of the earliest of their number outdid them all in the probing of despair. They had written in depressing and muted tones, but Ezequiel Martínez Estrada, in his *Radiografía de la Pampa,* wrote in a color that, until stronger language can be found, must be termed pure black. The beautifully written book is an absolutely exhaustive analysis of the national ills, presented without hope of redemption or betterment. The land itself, with its malignant telluric influence, is implicated in the general ruination. Combining anger and resignation in a strange harmony, Martínez Estrada struck a note consistent with the intellectual discord of the time. In 1933, his bleak book won the national book prize for literature.

It is not surprising that analysts soon began to probe the past, to determine when and how it all had begun to go wrong.[44] Revisionists came to the fore, and soon a cult devoted to the resurrection of Rosas emerged. Carlos Ibarguren defended Rosas as a man of hierarchy, property, and religion, and Manuel Gálvez in another biography of the tyrant merged the economic nationalist and the man of order with the democratic leader who reflected mass opinion by mystic means. A few now even remembered Rosas as an agrarian reformer, a feat of recollection that is hard to imagine.

With the intellectuals in such form, the mass culture reflected similar impulses. As it developed in the 1930s, that culture began to represent something new, a melding of two distinct heritages, that of the old Creole social order and that of the immigrants.[45] Anger and disillusionment were in the soul of it.

The tango and the motion picture were the principal vehicles of the popular culture.[46] The individual who participated in both of them and who contributed a personal legend as well as his artistry was Car-

los Gardel, the dominant figure in Argentine entertainment until his
death in 1935. Gardel was a tremendous success, and the manner in
which he imaged it brought one of the few golden touches to his time.
Doubtless, as often alleged, the mass public saw him as the avenger of
its own inadequacy, the symbol of dreams fulfilled for those who would
dream forever in vain.[47]

The tango became the authentic voice of the age. Nostalgic and
forlorn, viewing time present as a misfortune, the tango reflected a
total style of life, a psychology, a creative sensibility that nevertheless
expressed the viewpoint of the loser with a fatalism recalling the
Moorish strain in the Creole heritage. Martínez Estrada saw it as ". . .
the dance of pessimism, of everyone's sorrow: a dance of the never-
changing, enormous plains and of a subjugated race that crisscrosses
them without end and without destiny, in the eternity of a forever-
repeating present." And he spoke of the slow movement, ". . . with
the feet dragging and with the pace of a grazing ox . . . it has the
seriousness of the human during procreation . . . the fixed earnest-
ness of copulation because it seems to engender without pleasure."[48]

Certainly in the tangos of Enrique Santos Discépolo, the most profound of the composers who added social commentary to this art form,
the cynical refrains of the age were bitterly clear:

> Don't you see, you poor fool,
> That whoever's got the most dough is right?
> That honor's sold for cash, and morals for pennies?
> That no truth can withstand two bucks?[49]

Teacher and Writer

Perón was not involved in the earliest stages of the plotting for the
coup in 1930. Then a friend, Major Angel Solari, introduced him to
Uruburu. On the basis of this private exposure, Perón formed a very
favorable view of the general and was happy to throw in his lot with
the conspirators. "I saw in him a pure man, well-intended, determined at this final stage to play the bravest card of his life."[50]

Perón wrote an account of the revolution from his angle of vision
in 1931. It was later published as the first section of his *Tres revoluciónes militares*, Three Military Revolutions, and it makes very clear the
confusions and ineptitude that dogged the whole episode. What it
fails to illuminate is Perón's state of mind when he first became actively
involved. He reveals no soul-searching as to the propriety of a military
revolution. Could some other means have been found to salvage the
situation? He does not speculate, or even mention the possibility. It
apparently sufficed for him that a trusted colleague in the general

staff, superior in rank, invited his participation.

Soul-searching there was, but it arose from his almost immediate distrust of some of Uriburu's closest associates and from his even greater distrust of the abilities of those managing the coup. A shadow general staff was formed on paper, with Perón's participation on a level below the top, since his rank of captain made him relatively junior in this movement of colonels, lieutenant colonels, and majors. He was increasingly dismayed by the incompetence all around. "Never in my life will I see a more disorganized or worse directed affair, nor a chaos so terrible . . ."[51] He withdrew briefly, but he came aboard again at the urging of his old chief at the War College, Lieutenant Colonel Bartolomé Descalzo, this time with the Justo group. He was thus a participant when the coup took place on September 6, serving in an armored car, helping to maintain order and performing liaison duties.

The interesting aspect of Perón's account of the Uriburu coup of 1930 is the light it throws upon his views concerning the importance of the entire general public in political life, a significance that would have seemed silly to many politicians and military men of that period. Throughout his later career he made innumerable comments indicating high regard for the masses of the public, their virtues, and their vital place in the public process; but almost always he spoke or wrote with an immediate motive, so that it is difficult to separate the real from the expedient. But in 1931, Perón as yet had no political agenda or hopes, and if he did not alter his words from 1931, they are indicative. In the June discussions among the conspirators, it was clear that General Uriburu favored constitutional changes of a basic character. It was pointed out that public opinion would not support a military movement that was directed from the beginning against the Constitution. Uriburu was unconvinced and the question was never fully settled. Perón, whose status would not permit a strong stand, nevertheless wrote of his fear that the revolution would lose the "principle of the mass" that he thought indispensable for its success.[52] His opinions at this time, in opposition to those of a leader as prestigious as General Uriburu, foretold his assertions a decade later that he would never accept the presidency except through elections.

Perón returned briefly to the general staff after the fall of Yrigoyen but was soon assigned to the War Academy, following a thorough two-month reconnaissance of the Argentine borders with Bolivia and Paraguay. His promotion to the rank of major came on schedule at the end of 1931.

The five-year period on the faculty of the War College that now began was a productive and pleasant time for Perón, engendering his works on military history for which he became noted in the army: *El*

Frente Oriental de la Guerra Mundial in 1914, The Eastern Front in the
World War in 1914, in 1931, based on the theories of Marshal von
der Goltz concerning the nation in arms; the more important *Apuntes
de historia militar,* Notes on Military History, in 1932, reflecting the
same theories, which was used for instructional purposes for many
years; and three volumes of a third book in 1933 and 1934, devoted
to the history of the Russo-Japanese war. In 1935 came one of the
most unusual publications ever produced by a military writer, a small
work on Patagonian place names of Araucanian origin. Araucanian
was the name of the indigenous Indian tribes in the Andes of the far
south.

But it was Perón's work on the War Academy faculty during these
five years that helped to mold his talents in ways basic to his success.
His conspicuous ability to communicate, both orally and in writing,
ranked well toward the top of his skills. To his fellow officers, and
particularly to those in lower ranks, his ability to extemporize on any
subject at any moment was almost phenomenal. His breadth of background knowledge and his ability to expound it so easily were almost
unprecedented among military leaders and found few counterparts
among civilians. These were the skills that were honed to a fine edge
by the years of professorship in the War Academy.[53]

The pleasures of Perón's life in the 1930s owed much to his marriage, that was almost coterminous with the decade. He had first met
Aurelia Tizón, nicknamed Potota, at a social affair in September 1926
while he was studying at the War Academy. She was seventeen and
had just been accredited as a teacher. She was small and attractive,
with wide-set eyes and an expression faintly melancholy or wistful.
Her parents lived in comfortable circumstances; her father was involved
in several businesses, including rural real estate.

For two years, Perón and Potota were *novios,* a relationship somewhat comparable to an engagement. The marriage was celebrated on
January 5, 1929, two months after the death of Perón's father. Potota
had simple tastes and domestic managerial skills, and the couple got
by on Perón's salary. She helped Perón with his research and teaching
materials, put aside what money she could, and found pleasure in
domesticity. And in music, for she was a pianist and an excellent per-
former on the guitar, with Perón contributing his gusto for Italian
songs. Sometimes he would cook, particularly when colleagues or
friends came to the apartment for study sessions and the cook happened to be off duty. Soups were his specialty, and *puchero* and tortil-
las Spanish style.

The marriage lacked only children. Some who knew Perón well
have believed that of his three wives, Potota was the only one he truly

and deeply loved.[54] It was all the more sorrowful, therefore, that the marriage was destined to end after nine years and nine months, with the premature death of Potota. And it is all the more puzzling to read the standard Argentine biography of Perón, written with his cooperation, that omits even a mention of Potota. One can only surmise the pressures that were brought to bear.[55]

Service in Chile

In January 1936, a new stage began. Perón was designated Military Attaché to the Argentine embassy in Santiago, Chile. It was an important step in his career, more so than he probably realized at the time, for the relationship between the two countries was vital to both, and a knowledge of history and nuance in this field was important for any Argentine who might enter upon high office. It was a relationship that richly illustrated both the factors that may bring nations together and those that keep them apart.

A boundary dispute embittered the two neighboring nations as early as 1843, when Chile occupied Tierra del Fuego in the extreme south and laid claim to southern Patagonia. War had threatened, but in 1881 this disagreement was settled. Tierra del Fuego was divided, and a newly defined and rather vague boundary in the south kept most of Patagonia in Argentine hands. These and other boundary settlements were completed in 1899 and 1902 through arbitration sponsored by the American and the British governments. The famous statue of the Christ of the Andes, an immense, towering construction erected on the border close to the highest peak in the New World, commemorates the agreements with the dramatic inscription, "The firmament will crumble before Chileans and Argentines break the peace sworn at the feet of Christ the Redeemer."[56] But serious contention still remained concerning the ownership of islands in the Beagle Channel, near the Strait of Magellan.

The geographical border shared by Chile and Argentina thus was a traditional factor in their separation. They had many other similarities, and these too sometimes worked against compatibility—witnesses of brotherhood that contributed to a simmering rivalry. The military power balance began to turn against Chile around the turn of the century, and the Argentine economy was outdistancing the Chilean. As a generalization, Chileans often found Argentines unpleasant, and the latter not infrequently felt a certain disdain for their western neighbors.

Perón from his earliest days was familiar with the general reso-

nance of the Chilean relationship, for the area of his boyhood was
Chileanized to some extent in the social sense. He had studied the
Araucanian Indians in the border zones, explored large areas by foot
during vacations and several of his tours of duty, and he had read
extensively in the fields of Chilean history and folklore. He was a natural choice for the post he now undertook.

Perón and Potota drove to Santiago, following the historic route
of San Martín and his army in the heroic crossing of the Andes in
1817. Perón settled easily into his duties, traveling extensively in the
difficult geography of Chile and particularly in the southern strategic
border zones, in a labor of mingled love and duty. The collection of
military and related intelligence is a natural function of the military
attaché, which is to say that he serves as a genteel spy when he can.
Perón was no exception. He established a small network that included
a former Chilean military officer, and arranged to procure the alleged
Chilean War Department contingency plans for war with Argentina.
Delivery had not yet been made when Perón's tour of duty ended in
March 1938. He may or may not have known that he had come under
the surveillance of Chilean intelligence. If he did know, he said nothing of it to his successor, Major Eduardo Lonardi. The latter picked
up the strings of the plotting just in time to be apprehended while he
was in the act of photographing the documents, with the payoff money
in plain sight on a table nearby.[57] He was promptly declared persona
non grata, a fact that he most certainly remembered seventeen years
later, when he headed the army coup that overthrew Perón.

Potota's health became a problem by the time the couple left Santiago. Symptoms of uterine cancer appeared in June, and an operation was performed. It was not successful, and on September 10 she
died, at the age of twenty-nine. Perón grieved deeply, for his loss was
genuine.

In Europe

Perón, now a lieutenant colonel, was on the threshold of an even
more important period in his career, the twenty-two months of his
service in Europe. It was significant in his development for two reasons. It provided him for the first time with exposure to the culture
of a wider scene that differed from his Creole environment, giving
him a deepened understanding of international affairs and the variations that exist among men and institutions. And it came to be a
marvelous lever for moving the admiration of others in his political
career to come: He had seen the world, he could refer with familiar

ease to men and events scarcely known to his political circles at home, and he could awe military colleagues and subordinates with information and sophistication that set him apart.

Many aspects of Perón's period in Europe are still open to question. Others have been deliberately confused or misstated, out of Perón's desire to rewrite history or biography, or out of his frequent easy indifference to precision and literal accuracy. Four basic sources exist for the months in Europe. In descending order of credibility (and probably accuracy as well) they are: his official army dossier, by all odds the most solid of the sources; the "official" biography of Perón written in collaboration with him by Enrique Pavón Pereyra; Perón's short written *Memorias,* published in 1970; and his taped reminiscences, published in 1976. The alchemy that could transmute these accounts into a single truth does not exist.

The difficulties begin with the nature of the assignment given to Perón, even before he left by ship for Italy on February 17, 1939. His own descriptions invest his journey with high and mysterious statecraft. He claimed that the war minister called him in, told him that he was one of the most capable officers available, and that he wanted Perón to go to Europe to observe the situation: study the Italian army, including its Alpine divisions, visit Germany, talk with friends and officers, decide who would win the war that was expected to break out in the near future, and what Argentina's policy toward it should be. Pavón Pereyra, on the other hand, although hinting at some hidden objective, identified the purpose of the mission as the completion of Perón's studies in an international setting.[58] Pavón Pereyra has much the better of this disagreement. If political analysis of the wide European scene had been the purpose, the war minister would hardly have sent Perón to serve with Alpine units of the Italian army in the remotest mountain recesses, but that is where he went for most of his time in Italy. Nor would Perón, who spoke no German and little French and English, and who had no European background or experience, be a likely candidate for such an assignment in the field of international political intelligence.

Perón's dossier marks July 1, 1939, as the beginning of his assignment to the "Tridentina" Alpine Division, headquartered at Merano, near the Brenner Pass and the Austrian border; the Pavón Pereyra biography places him there within a few days of his arrival in Italy, presumably in March. The chronology of his subsequent assignments is remarkably fuzzy although there is no disagreement on the basic activity he pursued. He himself, in the Pavón Pereyra study, is quoted as claiming that he served in Merano for six months; that he put in five months with another Italian army division in Chieti, in the Abruzzi mountains; and that for seven months he was with Alpine units in Aosta and in Courmayeur, both near the French border.[59] That accounts for eighteen months. But even assuming that these assignments began as early as March, it is clear from the army dossier that Perón had finished his tour of duty with Italian mountain divisions by June 1, 1940, when he went to Rome for a brief period of service with the Argentine embassy there, and that maximum period covers only fifteen months.

To make it worse, in the same book in which Perón listed his eighteen-month tour of duty, he also asserted, four pages later, that upon his arrival in Italy he enrolled in a course in public organization and administration in Turin; the distance from Merano to Turin, for a diligent crow, is about 220 miles, so the two undertakings were entirely incompatible. Continuing, Perón then referred to another course he completed during a second eighteen-month period at Milan.[60] The same crow, weary by now, would have to fly ninety miles to get to Milan from Aosta, 110 miles from Courmayeur, and 330 miles from Chieti.

The discrepancies do not abate after Perón reached Rome about June 1, 1940. The Pavón Pereyra biography notes that Perón, who admired Mussolini, was an "anonymous witness" to Italy's declaration of war, which occurred on June 10, and that he was in the Piazza Venezia when the Italian leader spoke from the famous balcony. In his taped memoirs, however, Perón elevated this encounter into an interview with Mussolini in the latter's office.[61] Such a meeting is in the highest degree unlikely; Perón then had no unusual credentials that would have required such a diversion of the time of a head of state who had just taken his country into the greatest of all wars. Nor is it any more likely that Perón entered Paris with the German troops when that capital fell, as he also claimed in the taped memoirs.[62] That date was June 14, and Perón, in Rome and without direct access to German military or political headquarters, could not have made the necessary complicated arrangements for so unusual a venture in the few days available after his arrival in the Eternal City; nor would the Germans have had any reason to indulge so unprecedented a request from an unknown South American; nor would the Argentine authorities in Rome have countenanced it, for obvious political reasons.

Argentine nationals in Italy were ordered home immediately after the Italian declaration of war, in June. The exact date of Perón's departure from Rome along with thirty-seven other Argentines is not known, but according to Pavón Pereyra he spent a week in Spain and then a month and a half in Lisbon waiting for a ship bound for Buenos Aires; and although it was a long sea voyage by way of Brazil, he still arrived home around the end of the year.

The trip produced yet another serious discrepancy in the accounts. The editors of Perón's taped memoirs learned from "indirect sources" that Perón was stranded in Barcelona for several months waiting for a ship; that during this period Perón met and lived with an Italian actress; that when the actress eventually returned to Italy she was pregnant; that Perón in his later exile in Spain sent his close friend, Jorge Antonio, to Italy to discover if a child had been born; and that Antonio could find no trace of either child or mother. But Pavón Pereyra's biography is clear that Perón was in Barcelona for only "brief hours" before departing "immediately" for Madrid and that the homeward-bound ship sailed from Lisbon.[63]

These divergences certainly preclude a firm conclusion, but some version or variation of the story has plausibility. It is unlikely that Perón was in Barcelona for more than a very brief time, but he was in Spain longer than a week, at the least, and a liaison was entirely possible. The woman in question was not an actress, as rumored, but a teacher. Years later, while he was in exile, Perón did send an intimate emissary to trace the woman, but unsuccessfully, and he would hardly have done so without cause. His motive in so forlorn an enterprise was doubtless a final flare-up of his never-forgotten desire for a child.[64]

Despite the ambiguities, several important facts and generalizations about the period in Europe seem clearly established. Perón spent most of his time in Italy serving with Italian army Alpine units, learning about mountain and winter warfare. Some of his remaining time was passed in Rome, working out of the embassy there. He traveled extensively in the interstices of his program, visiting Germany, France, Hungary, Albania, and the Dalmatian coast of the Adriatic. He explored Italy in depth, driving a tiny Fiat. He was much affected by many things he encountered, including the nature of the Italian state under Mussolini, with its hint of corporatism and its public pageantry. He was impressed in a different sense by Germany, where he had ". . . the sensation of an enormous machine which functioned with marvelous perfection, where not even a small screw failed." He was impressed in a still different way by Spain, then still bleeding from the raw wounds of civil war, where he was appalled by the awful desolation of the destroyed University City in Madrid, remarking, "Only God knows who won here!"[65]

Above all, perhaps, he was moved by the sensation of being in the midst of vast movements and evolutions: "I studied the social and political phenomenon in depth. They had a great crucible there where something new was being born . . . In the American continent, and particularly in North America, there are many superficial people who go to Germany, take notes, snap their photos and later, when they return to their country, they exclaim, 'Uf, fascism and national socialism are systems of tyranny,' and everybody agrees with that, without penetrating into the social phenomenon there in which something is incubating."[66] This was a master impression that would inspire, in part, and reinforce the distinctly pro-Axis coloration of Perón's views concerning the war and Argentina's relationship to it.

Immediately upon his return from Europe, and so rapidly that he could do little more in Buenos Aires than attend to his laundry, Perón was sent to a post that followed naturally from his experience in Italy. On January 8, 1941, he was assigned to Mendoza as a professor at an instruction center for mountain troops, another indication that the purpose of the interlude in Europe had been educational rather than high-political.

During this quiet period in his life, at the end of 1941, he was promoted to colonel and became chief of the "Mendoza" Mountain Detachment. The location was fortunate for him, for he loved the mountains, flourished in cool and cold weather, and was exposed at close range to the scenes and legendry of his hero, San Martín.

Perón continued his studies of social organization, carrying forward the interest developed in Europe. Again, Mendoza was a likely spot, for the Cuyo was the home base of two populist adumbrations that had preceded Peronism, in the time of Yrigoyen and thereafter. One of these was *Lencinismo,* taking its name from its founder, José Nestor Lencinas, and his son, Carlos Washington Lencinas. The movement represented a radical and populist variant of Yrigoyenist Radicalism, as did the other of the movements, known as *Bloquismo* in the neighboring province of San Juan. The founder of this breakaway movement, destined to remain a small but vigorous and shaggy regional specialty for many years, was Frederico Cantoni, who shared with the older and younger Lencinas the customs and style of the traditional Creole *caudillos. Lencinismo,* now in feeble condition as an independent political force, was still represented by the brothers of Carlos Washington Lencinas, and Perón had frequent discussions with one of them about the social questions and the populist agendas that were a staple of political fare in the region. And he read copiously, absorbing works of such unlikely authors as Harold Laski and Lord Beveridge, whose famous Beveridge Report concerning English social conditions was issued in 1942.[67]

In terms of Perón's future political career, undoubtedly the most significant development of the Mendoza period was the deepening of his relationship with two colleagues who would assist him in his rise to power. One was General Edelmiro Farrell, with whom Perón had been in contact before his departure for Italy. Then they corresponded until Perón's return brought him under the direct supervision of Farrell, who was serving as the director of the military center in Mendoza. Perón was following precisely in the career steps of Farrell,[68] and part of Farrell's later complacency in the face of Perón's ambitious thrust for power may be traced to this succession of similar stages; the older man may have seen the younger as a kind of son and successor. But certainly much of the famous Farrell unconcern and lethargy must be attributed to innate character. The term *laid-back* was certainly not invented with Farrell in mind, but it might well have been. He was popular, socially amiable, musical, given to festivity and a happy drink, and quite uninterested in serious questions.

The other important relationship was Perón's developing friendship with Lieutenant Colonel Domingo Mercante, a fellow student from the early army years and a capable officer, who was also serving under Farrell. By 1942, Farrell was serving on the general staff in Buenos Aires, and Perón followed in March, still under Farrell, as did Mercante soon after.

But all these activities, familiar and almost routine, were soon to be superceded. Perón had been correct in his overarching impression of Europe: it was a time and a place of great change in the making. But not only in Europe, for similar movements, less visible because they were buried in the subsurface of social and political life, were also under way in Argentina, and Perón would find in them an extraordinary new career.

Argentina on the Eve of the Peronato—1943

On the surface, the Argentina of 1943 reflected the many hues and variations of success. It led the continent of South America in wealth, in culture, and in progress, seemingly a sumptuous panoply of high achievement. But this was the thinnest of veneers. Just beneath were immense problems in political life, the economy, and social organization and psychology.

In politics the great reality was the highly centralized state whose importance in the scheme of things was beyond anything imagined in North America, for in Argentina it was the state that inspired, created, and directed, while individual enterprise followed. The power of the state was still held tightly by a small ruling class that shared lineage, interests, policies, clubs, gossip, and links to the City in London. But this exercise of authority was ad hoc and almost informal, for the political system whose function was to define and manage and allocate public power had broken down almost completely. The federal polity glimpsed in the constitution had long since subsided into theory, if indeed it had ever come to life at all. The powers of the provinces in any significant aspect were hardly more than an amiable fiction; between 1852 and 1940, provincial governments had been displaced through interventions by the central authorities on 135 occasions.[69] The political parties were close to nullity or disintegration, none of them providing representation worthy of the name for labor, or for most of the business sector, or for rural interests. The art of effective political participation was in atrophy.

As for the new locally owned industrial economy, the substantial increase in establishments between 1935 and 1941 has been seen.[70] The value of manufactured products during those years increased from 3.5 billion pesos to 6.3 billion. Of the one hundred highest-income taxpayers in 1941, no fewer than forty-six came from manufacturing and only ten from pastoral and agricultural enterprise. In 1941, 829,000 workers were employed in industry as against 462,000 only six years before. The principal industries, ranked by value of production, were meat-packing, construction, power, petroleum refining, milling, and textiles, but there was also by this time a rainbow spectrum of consumer products.[71]

But the basic economic issues confronting Argentina in 1943 were still those left behind by the retreating Liberal System. Argentine dependence on Britain remained impervious to remedy: even now, Britain bought between 30 and 40 percent of everything Argentina sold, and 90 percent of its meat exports.[72] But the compensating elements of the old liberal equation remained out of joint. The rise of industrialization put a sharp edge on this issue, for if the new production continued, it would deeply change Argentina's master design in economics: with manufactured goods no longer being imported on a major scale, who would buy the Argentine agricultural and pastoral production? There can be no exports without reciprocal imports or some other form of balancing. To ask the question was to invite yet another internal conflict between the landholding interests and the new men of industry.

Another interesting question still remained, the raising of which may seem quixotic in the face of the success that industrialization was attaining in 1943. That success, however, to some degree at least, was born of wartime imperatives. In a sense, the society was being driven to these unfamiliar expedients rather than embracing them out of true affection. With some exceptions, it still remained true in 1943 that fundamental Argentine values worked against, rather than reinforced, the basic concepts and attitudes of business enterprise. Further progress in industry would certainly be made, but not as much, or as easily, as if the social chemistry favored it. Indeed, it has been argued that psychological conflict resulting from conscious imitation of business values unconsciously abhorred resulted in social malaise, in rage, anxiety, and apathy.[73]

In 1943, substantial place still remained for foreign capital, 60 percent of which was now owned by British interests. This was about four times the amount of the United States capital. British direct investment, as opposed to the broadly based British economic leverage, was concentrated largely in public utilities and services, but these dated mostly from the last century and were aged and frequently feeble: tramways rattled and gasped as they clung tenaciously to life. The combined British investments had yielded just under 5 percent annually in 1914, but they were returning only 2.4 percent in 1942.[74] The foreign investment of the United States, although much smaller, was increasing and quite profitable. In the early 1940s, it was centered in meat-packing, banking, and manufacturing, and its profit levels ranged from a low of 7.8 percent for Standard Oil to almost 93 percent for General Motors.[75] The ability of the British to apply pressure for the survival of their investments through their leverage over Argentine exports, and the new extent and muscular profitability of the United States investments, were combining to raise both qualms and resentment.

The relationship of city and countryside was among the most urgent of the national issues in 1943, as it had been from the beginning. The problem had become mostly economic and social, rather than political, and its source was the great and always growing disparity between center and periphery. For these were still distinct worlds, increasingly linked and yet by strange circumstances increasingly separated. The wealth still came from the pampas, and it still left them quickly and never returned. The railroads still tied the provinces to the capital but not to each other. The new industries still bloomed mostly in Buenos Aires and the nearby littoral. The modernization that had come to pass in those places served as a reproach as well, further emphasizing the backwardness of the provinces, rather than correcting it.

In much of the interior the mode of life had hardly changed at all from what it had been in the prime of the gauchos.[76] Huts of adobe or branches, with bare floors; rampant disease; children living on a concoction of corn and mutton grease called *tulpo;* lack of running water; an illegitimacy rate of over 50 percent; peons jammed into cattle cars and transported to work over long distances: a desolation by contrast with the gracious capital. Eduardo Mallea, the novelist, risked an overnight trip to Santa Fe and was so disillusioned that out of the experience he wrought his masterpiece, *Historia de una pasión argentina*. A federal interventor who was dispatched to Jujuy Province in 1942 by President Castillo to take over the local government was so appalled that he could stand it only three months, resigning in despair.[77] The farmer was a small world apart, having little contact with his neighbors. Roads in 1943 remained few, as were automobiles, to say nothing of organizations through which the farmers' needs might have been expressed. Even language was sometimes still a barrier. An awareness among farmers of the deeply ingrained values of a social order that limited the rural populace to the tail end of every ranking of prestige insured that subjective and psychological obstacles would complicate those provided by the environment.[78]

The small towns of the interior were a bit more advanced than the rural areas, since the pampas still had no settlements or commercial facilities of any significance. There would be a small church in the village, a school, a few little stores, unpaved streets, a priest, a police chief: in all, hardly enough to ruffle the surface of the geography. Countryside and small town had little in common except resentment of Buenos Aires, for humble as they were, the little towns lacked meaningful connections with the rural scene in which they were hardly more than intrusions. The small town and the bare rural environment around it shared no common social community and no cultural traffic. The knowledge and thought of the one were not those of the other. Social distance prevailed over social intercourse in this microcosm of the general fragmentation.[79] From small town and countryside alike the dispossessed and the disillusioned were flooding into the cities, into the capital above all, bringing with them either the political culture of the rural *caudillo* society that remained a monument to Rosas, or no political culture at all.[80]

The cause of the countryside had now fallen to the new nationalists. On emotional and nostalgic grounds, nationalism had always looked back to a legendary Creole past based on traditional provincial values. Now, with the problems so conspicuous, the grievances of provincial Argentina found their way into the agendas of nationalism, providing further vitality for that complicated movement.

Other social problems were not lacking in 1943. The disparities between classes, once tolerable, had become more offensive with the economic and sociological changes of the last sixty years, and nothing had been done, or even proposed, to mitigate them. The efforts of mass interests to gain a bit of place in the sun, mostly through socialist leaders, had been thoroughly rebuffed.[81] Argentina almost completely lacked, in practice, the social legislation now commonplace elsewhere, for new laws did not exist, and the old ones were still uninforced. The labor movement was small and weak. The concept of labor, and the underprivileged in general, as possible repositories of power had occurred to no one.[82]

Most women ventured only tentatively beyond patio and threshold, emerging to attend a charitable event, to shop, or to patronize an art exhibit. With initiative and pluck they might, like the widely admired Victoria Ocampo, preside over a literary salon, edit a literary journal, or rally the avant-garde.[83] But they had as yet shown little solid interest in obtaining the right to vote. Nevertheless, sensitive observers were beginning to hear the first rustlings of a movement toward increased participation. An Eva Perón was still over the horizon, but by now something more than total rejection was awaiting her.[84]

On the level of social psychology, most phenomena remained largely in the form in which the civilization had created them. Castile and the world of the gaucho had disappeared, but only in the narrow literal sense. The interior remained Creole, both deep down and on the surface. The capital was European on the surface, but Creole at heart in spite of easy denials. All in all, for the country as a whole, ". . . the influence of that civilization that came over the altiplano from High Peru in the sixteenth century is still much stronger than *porteños* themselves believe."[85]

But the familiar social psychology was making no headway against perceived troubles. With the multiplication of problems and the subtraction of solutions, the public spirit was by now one of strong disillusion that would figure prominently among the obstacles with which new leadership would have to contend. Individualism and community were not, in the splendid phrase of James Oliver Robertson, "bound together in agonizing symbiosis."[86] Rather, they were at swords' points. Disunity was everywhere, responding to some unknown principle that seemed to force all elements farther and farther apart. The armed forces, labor, the social classes, and the old and the new nationalists all reflected this sundering. "The nearest approach to a consensus that remained seems to have been in the wide-spread belief that the times were out of joint, and that sooner or later, and whether one wanted it or not, a drastic change was bound to come . . ."[87]

The Great Rift had never been so wide and so deep. It had never assumed so many forms and had never spawned so many subrifts. Few efforts at bridging had been made and none had succeeded.

In short, Argentina in 1943 was a country drifting beyond the control of any helmsman who had yet appeared, officers and crew alike struggling helplessly against wind and tide. The time had come for a new course, and a new pilot.

III

THE PERONATO
1943-1955

I have always thought that above all material values
are the permanent values of spirit, which are the
only eternal things.

— Juan Domingo Perón, *Memorias de Juan Perón 1895–1945*

5. Perón's Rise to Power 1943-1945

The Revolution of June 4, 1943

NINETEEN FORTY-THREE would be the year of the emergence of Perón as the strongman of Argentina, and the year of the beginning of the Peronato, as the period of his domination may be termed.

The administration of President Castillo was beginning to crumble, in part because of the growing resentment of the armed forces at his involvement of them in partisan activity. As 1943 began, a specific fear emerged, concerning the president's choice of a successor. It was rumored that this would be Robustiano Patrón Costas, a senator from Catamarca. Not only did the armed forces almost unanimously oppose Patrón Costas, but they were also in a mood to repudiate the massive fraud that was the only means by which he could be elected. Military sensitivity on this point had heightened since the forces had accepted the fraudulent election of General Justo in 1932. They had approved the abortive efforts of President Ortiz to cleanse the electoral process, and now they found repugnant the prospect of corruption on a scale sufficient to elect one of the most unpopular men in the country.[1]

There could be no doubt about the depth of the sentiment arrayed against Patrón Costas. An influential conservative, he was also the political boss of the northwest, one of the largest landowners in the country, and a foremost figure in the sugar industry. His mills flourished on something akin to slave labor that was fortunate if it did not succumb to the leprosy, the malaria, the trachoma, the tuberculosis and the mange that were endemic in the senator's primitive home base. Perón reflected the general sentiment when he stated, years later, "That great exploiter had a mill in San Martín de Tabacal, where he issued his own currency and had his private police. A form of feudalism. Those feudal estates are no longer conceivable in the times we live in . . . that was the reason for the revolution."[2]

The indignation felt by Perón and by so many others was not, in his case, a novelty of the moment, inspired by Patrón Costas alone. Since his return from Mendoza in March 1942, Perón had been nurturing plans in which concern for the welfare of the armed forces and his own personal ambition were blended in a mixed motivation that he himself would have been unable to untangle. Kindred spirits were at hand, and Perón now associated himself with a small group of officers, including his old classmate at the Military Academy, Miguel Montes.

The organizational device conceived by Perón and adopted by the group was a familiar one in the Argentine military tradition, and yet mysterious: a logia, a secret society of officers banded together as a nucleus within the army to work for certain shared objectives.[3] Such a body had been discussed in slowly widening circles during the last half of 1942 as Perón and his colleagues cautiously approached other officers who were likely to have some concern or grievance, of which there was no lack. Whatever the discontent, Perón and his core colleagues were ready with inducements and patriotic appeals. These were reinforced by the apparent abnegation of Perón and his fellows, who renounced all personal ambition and even the concept of a leader of the group, relying instead on an executive board.

The details of the group's clandestine life remain obscure, including the precise activity of Perón. Colonel Mercante, his close friend and associate for years to come, has attributed to Perón the leading role in the formation of the logia and the definition of its objective as a revolution.[4] It is known that in February 1943, Perón approached a general with the outline of the statutes for the proposed group, the name of which (after several other titles with the same initials had been discarded) was the *Grupo de Oficiales Unidos,* the Group of United Officers, or the GOU, as it was generally termed.[5] Several events hastened the creation of the GOU at this moment. On February 17 came an announcement that removed any possible doubt about the identity of the presidential succession: it was to be Patrón Costas. In February, also, the army general staff recommended to the president a policy of rapprochement with the United States so that Argentina could qualify for military purchases under the wartime lend-lease program. President Castillo rejected the idea, but nevertheless it gave immediate concern to the logia-to-be, which was unanimously proneutrality and partially pro-Axis.

Matters were therefore brought swiftly to a head. The GOU was formally established on March 10 through the adoption, with some changes, of a charter prepared by Perón. A directive body of twenty officers, including Perón, was soon designated. An oath of secrecy was sworn by all. Meetings of the directive body were held thereafter perhaps twice a month, each time in a different place. The first emphasis was on recruitment; Perón was particularly intent on enlisting junior officers, for the populist politician-to-be was already developing his technique of working from the bottom up rather than from the top down.[6] From the beginning he was one of the two leaders of the GOU, the other being his friend, Lieutenant Colonel Enrique P. González, nicknamed "Gonzalito."

By May, the Patrón Costas candidacy had become an urgent problem. It was Gonzalito and not Perón who now took the lead, probing the sentiments of officers and political leaders alike. The bridge to the latter was Juan I. Cooke, formerly a deputy in the Congress, who was soon to become a loyal *Peronista*. The political approach was to certain leaders among the Radicals, although other parties were sounded out. Again a fundamental tactic of Perón stands forth, his reluctance to be out in front, to be on the cutting edge of any dangerous undertaking. His language in later times, often excessive, has not infrequently given him the image of a latter-day Hotspur, but beneath the words there was generally a cool caution, even a careful hanging back.

The GOU inquiries in May led to a decision to mount a revolution in September if the president's plans for the succession remained firm. This schedule was known to the Radical Party leaders who had been in contact with Gonzalito. Oddly enough, it was also known to the war minister, General Pedro Ramírez.

A competent officer but a poor politician, Ramírez was to be a key figure in the coming revolution, through the unlikely medium of his ambiguity and equivocation during the last week in May. Late in that month he was asked by several Radical Party leaders if he would accept the presidential nomination on the Radical ticket. It was a remarkable question for opposition elements to put to the war minister of an incumbent government, but they apparently knew their man. The general's answer, mired down in conflict of interest, was delphic rather than intelligible. President Castillo was informed of the secret meeting and of his war minister's dishonorable hemming and hawing. Outraged, he called him in for an explanation. General Remírez replied that he had not agreed to any candidacy, which was true enough technically, but he retreated into his shell when the president prodded him for more information. A statement to the press by the general was as murky as his other utterances and merely marked his rupture with the president. The latter now expected a resignation, but in vain. On the morning of June 3, therefore, he ordered the preparation of a decree that would relieve General Ramírez of his office. The news leaked instantly, and within a few more instants became the catalyst for what must surely have been one of the most rapidly constructed revolutions in history.

The entire operation was assembled during the late morning, afternoon, and evening hours of June 3.[7] If the groundwork had not been thoroughly prepared by events and by public opinion, it would have been quite impossible. Plans were rushed to completion in a blur that obliterated everything but the operational military aspects. Gonzalito told General Ramírez that the decree was being issued, stressing that the removal of Ramírez would certainly impede the GOU scheme to thwart the election of Patrón Costas; and he asked to be released from his military obligations so that he could organize a counter-stroke to save the situation. General Ramírez, in another remarkable demonstration of two-faced dexterity, released Gonzalito so that the latter could undermine the government of which Ramírez was a principal minister, saying at the same time that he himself would remain neutral. As a part of this neutrality, he even had the gall to suggest that the conspirators find a general to head the movement.[8]

Within a few hours Gonzalito enlisted his former commanding officer, General Arturo Rawson, then the army chief of cavalry. The two men spoke only of the immediate issue of intervention by the army, for there was a notable lack of candor on both sides. Gonzalito did not reveal the existence of the GOU and Rawson did not disclose a circumstance that gave the entire movement an aspect of farce, namely, that Rawson himself, at the head of a group of officers, was plotting his own revolution. This is the stuff of which serious disagreements are made. Gonzalito thought he was asking Rawson to join the GOU movement, without so referring to it; Rawson thought he was being asked to take over the movement Gonzalito mentioned, and in his mind he merged it with his own still-undisclosed operation, seeing himself as the leader in fact as well as in name. Political questions were ignored.

The next urgency was to round up enough troop commanders to put soldiers in the streets. Here the GOU leaders, including Perón, could contribute little more than their considerable powers of persuasion, since the GOU directorate consisted almost entirely of staff officers, and staff officers do not have direct unit or troop command. But unit commanders were amenable, the most important being Colonel Elbio Anaya, the garrison commander at the Campo de Mayo base. He arranged for a meeting of regimental chiefs at the Cavalry School, at ten o'clock that night. Meanwhile, Perón, Gonzalito, and Montes beat the bushes for more unit commanders who could assist, and General Rawson tried, without success, to bring aboard other generals.

At the decisive ten o'clock gathering of regimental chiefs, fourteen officers met and decided that the troops would move in the morning. A manifesto, composed earlier in the evening by Perón and Colonel Montes, was adopted. Their joint authorship is clear, although Perón would later insist that he alone had composed the document, and in fewer than fifteen minutes.[9]

The flexible and disloyal General Ramírez came to Campo de Mayo during the night, having been directed by the president to head off the uprising whose existence was by now generally known. Ramírez requested a twenty-four-hour delay on behalf of the president. He noted that there were troops that were still loyal and urged Colonel Anaya to avoid bloodshed. But that was all. His posture of neutrality was seen for what it really was by President Castillo on the morning of June 4, when he confronted Ramírez, ordered his arrest as a traitor and demanded his resignation. But it was too late. The troops, ten thousand of them in three columns, were on the march from Campo de Mayo.

There was only one violent episode en route, at a naval installation. A misunderstanding arose between one of the troop commanders, Colonel Eduardo Avalos, and the naval officer in charge, and in the confusion gunfire broke out. There were about seventy fatalities, a few of them civilian. This was significant for the future, if psychological interpretations are accurate, for destiny was to bring Avalos and Perón into confrontation two years later at the most critical moment of Perón's career.[10]

By the middle of the afternoon on the 4th, Buenos Aires was in the control of the revolutionary forces. President Castillo took refuge on a naval minesweeper in the estuary, submitting his resignation the next day at La Plata, as Yrigoyen had done before him. By that time,

General Rawson had appeared and without any fanfare had simply walked into the president's office and sat down at the presidential desk.

Three aspects of this remarkable uprising are particularly interesting. The first concerns the technique of Perón at the climactic hour. The meeting of the fourteen troop commanders at Campo de Mayo on the night of June 3 should have been a meeting of fifteen, for Perón had been requested to attend. But after he and Colonel Montes had composed their manifesto earlier in the evening, he disappeared. Nor was he in evidence the next morning, when the troops marched. Colonel Montes and a political colleague stopped at Perón's apartment at dawn on the 4th and found him absent. They could not reach him by telephone and they concluded that he was deliberately out of touch. In his autobiographical notes, which are quite sparse when it comes to the GOU and the 1943 revolution, Perón claimed that he was one of several colonels who went to the First and Second Infantry Divisions early in the morning to insure that they would follow their revolutionary officers,[11] but no contemporary account confirms this. Perón, in fact, did not surface until most of the afternoon had passed and it was clear that the uprising was successful. Once more, prudent restraint.

The second interesting aspect is the total chaos of the uprising on the political level. Some of the fourteen officers were democratically inclined. Some were nationalists of one stripe or another. This one favored the Allies in the war. That one was pro-Axis. Several were leaders of the GOU. Others had never heard of the GOU. Gonzalito, who had Axis sympathies, recruited General Rawson, who favored the Allies. Political orientations were simply irrelevant at this moment of action, so great was the preoccupation with pulling down President Castillo.[12] It seems incredible, but a government was overthrown by officers who had not even discussed, let alone decided, either the policies to be followed if they succeeded or the identity of the person or group that should replace the president. Some had the idea that General Rawson would be designated; others assumed that General Ramírez of the easy conscience would be in charge; still others had vague notions about a triumvirate. But these were mere impressions.[13]

Thus follows the third interesting aspect. A movement so unformed in every detail except the marching orders was without much significance with regard to Argentina's international posture. Observers abroad were as baffled by what was going on as were those who cheered the troops in the Plaza de Mayo. Allied sympathizers, noting the pro-Axis sentiments of Perón and some others, concluded that the revolution had been incubated in the German embassy. In turn, that embassy was so confident that it was all a United States manipulation that it burned its secret files on June 5.[14]

The conclusion that the revolution lacked significant international implications is seemingly contradicted by the famous incident of the purported GOU Circular of June 3. This was a sensational document outlining the purposes and geopolitics of the GOU in wild, pro-Axis language, hailing Hitler and the German precedent and committing Argentina to the objective of a broad regional hegemony. The circular was widely disseminated and it entered into the harsh dispute between Argentina and the United States in late 1945 and early 1946. But there is good reason to doubt the authenticity of the circular as an official GOU document. It has proved impossible to verify it through the means by which other GOU statements, some of them quite controversial, have been established. And there are textual reasons suggesting that it may have been written originally in another language.[15]

With confusions so vast as these, it was certain then that the revolution of June 4 would be a very unstable compound and that the melee sure to come would exalt those who had a clear vision of their goal and manipulative talents to match. It was a prescription written for Juan Perón.

Perón and the Ramírez Administration

The unruly prospects of the revolution were fulfilled immediately. Perón and his allies were instantly antagonistic to General Rawson, partly because of his stated preference for the abandonment of the neutrality policy but probably even more, in Perón's case, because of personal ambition and lack of respect for the general. Perón's autobiographical account oozes with dislike: "He was a sort of outsider, he had nothing to do with it, he knew nothing. . . . He saw his opportunity and he said 'I'm the head of this revolution because I'm a general' . . . He proclaimed himself President. He did it without consulting us."[16]

The unfortunate general, a political innocent, played into the hands of his enemies. On the night of June 4, after blithely occupying the presidential office, he dined with friends at the Jockey Club and proceeded in the most insouciant way to offer two of them cabinet posts in the government he would be forming. The positions so casually handed out were important, and the recipients, of the old school of the overthrown Castillo, were quite unacceptable to the GOU men. Perón and Gonzalito were anxious to be rid of Rawson in any case, but others in the GOU hierarchy wanted to support him if he would only disavow the two cabinet choices. This he refused to do, maintaining a rigid and impracticable punctilio. He had given his word, he said, and he could not renege. His allies gave up and joined the Perón group, which then forced the resignation. He had been in office for forty-eight hours.

By consensus, General Ramírez was now installed as provisional president. Perón later was asked why one of the colonels, presumably himself, had not been selected, and his answer was a commentary on his sagacity, his caution, and his sense of timing. "No, no. It wasn't advantageous for me. I knew that revolutions begin with these little episodes that burn themselves out, foolishness, political things. In the first stages you have to stay out of the line of fire."[17] This was not a whim but a settled psychological orientation. In February 1953, at a conference at the University of Chile, he said pretty much the same thing: "Sometimes I was in disagreement with 95% of their decisions, but it was necessary to fight from within. Revolutions always need a crowned head who reigns but doesn't rule. The government is always in the back room of the revolution."[18]

Perón now had broad, new opportunities, although they were the kind that had to be cultivated rather than harvested immediately. And it would be a difficult road, with many obvious obstacles. The first necessity was dominant influence in the army. Circumventing President Ramírez was among the lesser problems, for that officer's experience, courage, and skills were entirely military rather than civilian. He was hopelessly out of his element in the Casa Rosada, and he developed at once a fatal defect: a great readiness to follow advice, provided that it was advice given by the person who had most recently spoken to him on that subject. But the GOU connections would have to be nurtured and mobilized. In this, Perón was favored by his alliance with Gonzalito, who had the ear and the confidence of Ramírez. In particular, the selection of General Farrell as the war minister on June 7 was propitious for Perón; on June 8, Farrell appointed him to the number two position in the ministry, chief of its Secretariat, equivalent to the rank of undersecretary.

The GOU came off especially well in the allocation of influential posts just below the top level. Gonzalito became head of the presidential Secretariat; the new chief of police was a strong GOU man; Perón's close friends, Mercante and Montes, became deputy undersecretaries in the war and interior Ministries; important troop commands went to GOU men.

The next step was to cultivate a large following among younger officers who could be deployed for useful assignments and shaped into an informal network. For this, a certain tinkering with history would be necessary. Although probably half of the fourteen troop commanders assembled on the night of June 3 would not have recognized the name of the GOU, that body was now portrayed in its bulletins and in the writings of cooperative journalists as the supreme, sometimes even the sole, source of the June 4 revolution.[19] Perón was tireless and vastly persuasive in addressing these junior officers, and they had no experience to the contrary and no reason to disbelieve. Once they became members they constituted a most useful network of informers, reporting to Perón. This was the consequence of the GOU rules, which required recruits to pledge themselves to support General Farrell as war minister and to accept his directives absolutely, as well as to inform on other officers who were opposed to the activities of the GOU. As a further demonstration of loyalty, recruits were also required to sign undated requests for retirement from military service.[20]

Other tactics were necessary for the extension of Perón's influence in the top reaches of the government. There the power of military appointment, centered in the war ministry, was a mighty lever. Ramírez' supporters were enticed away by the offer of appointments as military attachés abroad, positions dripping with perquisites and opportunities, and replaced by GOU members. If lures did not succeed, a vindictive policy might. Grumblers and opponents could be reassigned to posts deep in Patagonia and the remotest northwest.

Still a different approach was required with senior officers, one properly respectful of their rank and status. Colonel Avalos, the important commander of the Campo de Mayo garrison, had been instrumental in the events of June 4, but had not been a GOU member. In midsummer he became one. Perón converted him with arguments and enticements that have not been fully described, although it is possible that an immediate top position in the GOU may have been the attraction. At any rate, Avalos began at once to preside over weekly sessions of the logia.[21]

President Ramírez had frequently been pressed by advisers, and even by his wife, to take steps against Perón, whose fast climb was already conspicuous, but he had equivocated throughout the summer. In October, in an uncharacteristic display of fortitude, he ordered General Santos Rossi to take over the war ministry by force the next morning and to arrest Farrell and Perón. These instructions were passed to General Rossi in mid-afternoon. By two o'clock the next morning President Ramírez had changed his mind. The order to Rossi was countermanded, Rossi was told that the original order had never been issued, and he was discharged from his command.

It was clear that events were flowing in the direction of Perón. The trends of summer and early autumn were favorable to these hard-line and nationalistic views. The State of Siege proclaimed on June 4 still remained in effect. Important political appointments in the provincial governments, which were all under federal intervention, had begun to go to right-wing, nationalistically oriented antidemocrats. The elections scheduled for September had been cancelled. The press was under new restrictions, and it began to look like a long haul for the military government rather than a sweetly reasonable interlude.

During these months foreign affairs continued to pose problems. The big issue, as always since 1941, remained the neutrality policy and its interaction with the Good Neighbor Policy of the United States, the cornerstone of the Roosevelt administration's approach to Latin American affairs. Wilsonian in its principles and aimed at countering the historic Latin American fear of encroachment from the north, the policy stressed the juridical equality of states and nonintervention by any country in the affairs of another.

In the first half of the 1930s, the Good Neighbor had the kind of success that comes in easy times. Then the American government became increasingly preoccupied with Hitler and other totalitarian movements in Europe. Preoccupation bred concern, fear, and the desire for a secure Western Hemisphere. That, in turn, required diplomatic agreements for defensive links. From Washington's point of view, it seemed so clear and so desirable, but the attempt to achieve that purpose embittered the better part of a decade. For the United States, the crux of the problem was Argentina.

As has been noted, freedom of action in regard to European nations was the oldest of Argentine objectives and traditions in foreign policy. There were also other factors. President Yrigoyen's neutrality policy during the First World War had been widely popular and therefore constituted a precedent. The Argentine military feared any steps that might lead to hostilities in the South Atlantic, far from any military reinforcement. The nationalism of the prewar years, now widely disseminated throughout Argentina, saw neutrality as the best means of paying off old grudges against England and clearing a space in which Argentina could flourish by pursuing an independent course.[22] And finally, through nationalistic impulse and psychological heritage, Argentina had come to see itself as the counterweight in the south to the United States in the north and as the natural leader of the Latin American nations.

All this suggested a stormy encounter with the American push for close-knit security measures. Owing principally to Argentine resistance, hemispheric conferences in 1936, 1938, and 1939 had stopped well short of adopting the joint arrangements the United States had advocated, creating in Secretary of State Cordell Hull the conviction, destined never to leave him, that Argentina was by its very nature obdurate beyond all reason.[23] A fourth conference, in 1940, in Havana, resulted in Argentine agreement that an outside attack on any American state would be deemed an act of aggression against all signatories, but it did not define a required response, and it was the highwater point of Argentine cooperation.[24]

Then came Pearl Harbor. The United States at once invoked the Havana Resolutions that called for consultation. This was the origin of the Río Conference, which assembled in January 1942. The United States urged the hemispheric nations to break their relations with the Axis countries, but had to be content with a recommendation rather than a binding decision, due to Argentine opposition.[25] In the aftermath of Río, all the Latin American nations, except for Chile and Argentina, either broke relations or declared war; and Chile finally took both steps in January 1943.

The basic Argentine posture toward the war, from Pearl Harbor almost to V–E Day, really changed very little, and relations with the United States during this period of three and a half years were therefore determined largely by the American response; and this in turn depended on the balance of power from time to time between two contending factions in the Department of State.[26] One was a group of old Latin American hands led by Undersecretary of State Sumner Welles. The other, whose members were more widely oriented internationally and tended to see Latin America in relation to other critical world issues, was led by the Secretary of State, Cordell Hull. Both groups were Wilsonian in derivation, but the internationalists were far more sympathetic than the Latin Americanists to the moralistic Wilsonian belief in the mission of the United States to promote democracy worldwide and to compel enlightened behavior.

The bureaucratic struggle in Washington was greatly complicated by the presence of other would-be decision makers. Secretary of the Treasury Henry Morgenthau, Vice-President Henry Wallace and his Board of Economic Warfare, the Reconstruction Finance Corporation under the conservative Jesse Jones, the United States armed forces, and the British allies who feared for their food supplies, all stirred a large pot of mutual contention. It was quite a complicated mix of interests and personalities, and it must have been baffling to Perón and his colleagues, just as the intricacies of the Argentine government were well beyond the American power of analysis.

The Latin Americanists in the State Department carried the day at the Río Conference, and the United States therefore signed the watered-down Río Declaration that recommended rather than mandated rupture with the Axis. For them, unity was paramount and Argentina had to be accommodated. But the victory came at a price, won only by the direct intervention of the president, who overruled Secretary Hull. The latter was embittered. With the backing of American public opinion, which was still resentful of what was seen as Argentine sympathy (or worse) for the enemy in a life-and-death combat, Hull and the internationalists maintained steady pressure on the Latin Americanists to produce the changes in Argentine policy that all desired. This they were unable to do; Welles admitted defeat, and the internationalists soon took over.

Hull and his followers were sorely disappointed by the revolution of June 4, which they had first interpreted as a reaction by anti-Axis elements who favored a change in foreign policy. In the period that followed June 4, the American embassy substantially misconstrued Argentine opinion, believing for some reason that there was a strong ground swell of sentiment among the public in support of the Allies, that only a few military types at the head of the government held this in check, that strong military desire for access to arms would force a sharp turn in policy, and that only a short time and a bit of restraint would suffice to usher in a return to democracy and to the hemispheric consensus and to many other good things. All of this reflected the embassy's penchant for optimism and its close relations with various Radical Party politicians. But it erred in good company. Much of the United States press was even more persuaded of these things, and the embassy's bureaucratic rivals in the economic field held similar views. These illusions soon dissolved. It was apparent within a month that there would be no immediate return to constitutional life, whereupon the indignation of the State Department, and that of most sectors of American public opinion as well, reached a peak.

Secretary Hull was by now well into the development of a devil theory that would link Argentine neutralism with a pro-Axis sympathy, and Argentine authoritarianism with both of these. With this kind of conviction, United States-Argentine relations in the balance of 1943 and during all of 1944 sank into a hostile and frigid stalemate.

In the face of such pressures from abroad and the counter-pressures from turbulent Argentine factions at home, President Ramírez was blown about from one side to the other, sometimes almost concurrently. In his wavering, it was never too late to advance a tentative position and never too early to repudiate it. But the neutrality question was becoming further complicated by the issue of arms supplies. Brazil, which had not only broken relations with the Axis but declared war as well, was receiving substantial assistance from the United States, and the former approximate balance between Brazil and Argentina was rapidly tilting toward Brazil. This had been the reason for the stillborn recommendation of the Army General Staff in February 1943 for a rapprochement with the United States.

It was clear that nothing would come from the north until Argentina broke relations with the Axis, but could something be done with Germany? President Ramírez was ready to test the water slightly, and with the urging of Gonzalito, he participated in several contacts during the summer with German representatives.

At this point there was a final effort by the Argentines to reach an agreement with the United States without compromising neutrality. The foreign minister, Admiral Storni, who was sympathetic to the Allies, addressed a strange letter to Cordell Hull on August 5. It contained a request for military assistance, but on the diplomatically unprecedented ground of restoration of "the position of equilibrium to which [Argentina] is entitled with respect to other South American countries."[27] Its original form had represented Storni's own composition, but then it was edited by the president, by Gonzalito, and, presumably, by Perón. It has been suggested, but not documented, that the latter two played the part of *agents provocateurs,* inserting the unorthodox language in the hope of drawing a strong rejection.[28] In any case, that is what they got. Hull's reply was blistering. The Argentine government, in violation of custom, allowed publication of the exchange of letters, strengthening the view that the Storni letter may have been a deliberate provocation which the ostensible author never intended. A political storm blew up. "Never has our country suffered a humiliation like this . . . the entire nation was sensitized by the episode."[29] Admiral Storni gallantly took the blame and resigned.

The last chance for survival of the pro-Allied elements in the Argentine government was now destroyed. The GOU immediately disavowed the Storni initiative and delighted in the new proof that no assistance could be expected from the United States.

It was now easier to proceed with an outreach to the Germans. In September, President Ramírez agreed to the dispatch of a one-man mission to Germany to see what could be obtained there. It would be the most secret of undertakings, and the only Argentines who knew of it were the president, Gonzalito, the acting foreign minister, and the navy minister, Admiral Sueyro. The man chosen for the delicate assignment was an Argentine reserve officer named Osmar Helmuth. He was associated with Johann Harnisch, a Buenos Aires businessman of German extraction, who was, if his word was good, the personal representative of Hitler in Argentina. Helmuth was given the title of Argentine Consul in Barcelona in order to provide credibility, and he carried letters of introduction signed by Gonzalito and Sueyro and addressed to the appropriate German officials. He sailed on October 2, scheduled for Bilbao, happily unaware that he was heading not for Bilbao but for disaster.

While Helmuth was at sea on the first leg of his unfortunate voyage, events in Argentina further strengthened Perón. The resignation of Foreign Minister Storni had exacerbated the simmering conflict between liberal elements and the right wing nationalists pushing for an authoritarian state. Just at this moment, in October, came the fiasco of General Rossi, who had been asked to arrest Farrell and Perón and then was left high and dry by another presidential change of mind. Perón and the GOU faction saw the opportunity and made an immediate move for real as opposed to nominal control. Out went the cabinet moderates and in came the new vice-president, General Farrell.[30]

The replacements for the cabinet moderates were all strongly authoritarian types attuned to Fascist movements abroad. The most influential among them was the new minister of the interior, General Luis Perlinger, pro-German and rigidly reactionary. The press was further restricted, and dismissals of dissenting officials and academics became commonplace. On the last day of the year came three iron decrees. The first dissolved all the political parties. The second, breaking with Argentine precedent, established compulsory religious instruction in all schools. The third was a set of rules governing the functioning of the press.[31]

By the end of 1943 the GOU leadership had been concentrated in four colonels: Juan Perón; Enrique González (Gonzalito); Emilio Ramírez, the Chief of the Federal Police; and Eduardo Avalos, the Garrison Commander at Campo de Mayo. But all was not serene, even within this core group. There was a perception among many officers that Perón was using the GOU for his own political advancement, as he of course was, despite the pledge that he and all the other GOU members had taken to refrain from any pursuit of public office. In particular, a split was developing between Perón and Gonzalito, whose position as chief of the presidential Secretariat had recently been elevated to cabinet status.

Gonzalito, more than Perón, looked to the day of return to traditional civilian activity, and he decided to prepare a statute that would govern the functioning of the parties when the hour of their rebirth came. About this time, Perón approached Gonzalito with a deal. Using an intermediary, he proposed that Gonzalito run with him on the same ticket when presidential elections were next held. Gonzalito refused the offer and continued with his drafting, adding a provision that would prohibit any member of the military from being a candidate in the next election, whenever held. Perón was now persuaded that he would have to move against Gonzalito.

The crisis that made this possible for Perón soon arrived, in the form of explosive developments in foreign relations. Two quite separate undertakings came together and reached a sorry denouement in November and December of this eventful year, 1943. The first concerned the attempts of the Argentine government to subvert neighboring governments that had come down on the Allied side of the neutrality question. The effort was successful in Bolivia in December. Other governments in the southern part of the continent began to worry, because the Argentine responsibility for the coup, which was beyond all doubt, was soon widely known on a confidential basis.[32] The United States now became actively concerned. The subversion in Bolivia fitted in nicely with the conviction, now fully developed, that Nazis and Fascists operating a Berlin-Buenos Aires axis were trying to take over the continent. Wider plots were rumored, and in the atmosphere of the day they soon took on the solidity of certifications. The State Department let it be known that the details of the Argentine involvement in Bolivia would soon appear in a published memorandum.

The second undertaking that backfired at the same time was the mission of Helmuth to Germany. His ship called at Trinidad early in November, and the British authorities in Port of Spain, alerted by a leak in German intelligence, put Helmuth under arrest and began to interrogate him. The bad news came to Gonzalito and Perón by a secret transmission from the Argentine ambassador in Caracas on November 5.

The Argentine government did not at first share the instant realization of the German Foreign Office that if the documents Helmuth was carrying were discovered by the British, or if he broke down, the consequences might well be fatal for the Ramírez regime.[33] The worst did indeed happen. At the end of December, the British authorities notified the Argentine government that they had Helmuth's confession that he was a German agent. This unveiling of a German espionage web in Argentina, the existence of which violated the understanding with Germany that formed a basis for the neutrality policy, made firm action by Argentina inevitable. On January 24, 1944, the foreign minister, General Gilbert, advised the United States ambassador that a diplomatic break with Germany was imminent, and he asked that the United States refrain from further pressure and from publication of the Bolivian materials. This was agreed to, and relations were broken on January 26. Only two officials, President Ramírez and General Gilbert, signed the decree.

There was good reason for this reticence on the part of the other ministers who would normally have signed. The facts that had generated overpowering pressure on the government were known only to a handful of men in the Casa Rosada, and they could not be revealed. The end of the neutrality policy in so sudden and mysterious a manner after its long life blew up a storm of protest in the GOU and elsewhere. Many refused to believe the published explanation that the break had been caused by the discovery of a German spy network, attributing it instead to capitulation in the face of United States pressure. The GOU was badly split on the issue and the entire officer corps was agitated and confused.

Perón himself, at the height of the controversy just before the break was announced, reverted to the policy he generally reserved for conflicts in which there was no way to win. That is, he lay low. Gonzalito, whose back was approaching the wall, asked Perón to defend the government's policy aggressively, but Perón chose the quiet and unhelpful course. He had, he said, given his word to the foreign minister that he would support the move, and he would live up to his word. But that was all that he said. In one sense, Perón was on the defensive, for the extreme nationalists in the GOU were attacking him for what they considered his lack of forcefulness on their behalf. General Perlinger, the hard-liner who could pose a threat to Perón's ascendency, was in a position to outflank him on the right. But in another and more important sense, the break in relations and the way it was handled presented Perón with a marvelous opportunity to move against Gonzalito and Foreign Minister Gilbert, and ultimately against President Ramírez. It would take some imagination, and a good bit of nimble deception, and an absence of shame. But it could be done.

The basis for such new intrigues was the continuing resentment of many officers at the rupture with Germany. But more was necessary, and it soon appeared in the form of rumors that the president, under pressure from Gonzalito and Foreign Minister Gilbert, was about to issue several decrees that would have the gravest effects, decrees that would proclaim martial law, mobilization of the armed forces, and

war against Germany. Perón instantly began to oppose these purported steps, managing simultaneously to clear himself and to build
strong pressure against Gonzalito and Gilbert. Both men resigned on
February 15, 1944, unable to find sufficient support. Perón was the
clear victor, but not by accident, for the rumors so helpful to his efforts
when he repudiated them appear to have originated within Farrell's
and Perón's war ministry itself, and that could not have happened if
Perón had not instigated them, or at least approved their circulation.[34]

The other loser in this plotting was President Ramírez. He had
failed to move strongly against the ouster of his two cabinet ministers,
and he immediately began to come under the same pressure. The
rumors continued. He denied them in the most absolute language in
addresses to officers, but the audiences were disillusioned by his
seemingly inexplicable abandonment of the neutrality policy, which
he could not defend with the truth, and they chose not to believe his
disclaimers.

But a problem remained as the president's hour of peril approached.
Perón and the other GOU officers had all taken oaths to support
Ramírez, and military honor was involved. So they found a way. Not
a very good way, but it sufficed: they simply dissolved the GOU, on a
pretext that was almost comical, saying with a straight face that the
GOU might otherwise have become "an obstacle to the normal march
of government."[35]

The president now resolved to take the offensive, and on the
morning of February 24 he asked for Farrell's resignation. Farrell
rounded up his supporters. The navy minister, Admiral Sueyro, advised
the president to arrest Farrell and Perón, offering military support if
necessary. But the true nature of Ramírez got the better of him and
again he refused confrontation. That night the War Ministry forces,
headed by Farrell and Perón, took over the government. Ramírez
resigned, then withdrew his resignation at the request of the military,
who feared problems of recognition abroad, and delegated his powers instead. Civilian leaders began to organize a movement around
him, but the fickle weakling left them in the lurch with a final resignation on March 9. As vice president, General Farrell succeeded to
the presidency.

The United States was quite upset by this development, attributing
it to retribution on the part of pro-Axis officers headed by Perón. All
sorts of misunderstandings were current in the United States. The
New York Times, in an editorial on February 25, advanced the quaint
notion, divorced from all reality, that the fall of the president was
occasioned by his intention to form a liberal government. Opinion in

the press and in Congress, diverse and misinformed as it was, had a common denominator, the desire to see the end of the Argentine regime and its replacement by something democratic and pro-Allied. It was a mood that favored the missionary drive of Secretary Hull, a throwback to the tactics that had preceded the Good Neighbor Policy. This viewpoint prevailed, and on March 4, the United States suspended official relations with Argentina, thus embarking on a policy of nonrecognition that lasted until April 1945.

The Social Revolution Begins

The ascension of General Farrell to the presidency put Perón himself within striking distance of that objective, given his domination over his mentor. During all his demanding and even perilous activity on the level of military politics, Perón was simultaneously engaged in erecting another structure of power that would incorporate the underprivileged classes as a base, combining them with the armed forces as the twin foundation stones of a political movement. It is impossible to say with assurance when such a concept first occurred to Perón. Perhaps it went back to the days in the School for Non-Commissioned officers, or to some other early military experience, when the reality of the shoeless and illiterate conscripts first struck home. Perhaps it germinated so slowly that it had no definable genesis.

What is apparent, however, is that none of the political parties in Argentina, apart from sectarian fringe groups and the Socialists, provided inspiration for so heterodox a notion. It also seems reasonably clear that Perón had the thought well in mind before June 1943. At least he said so in his autobiographical recollections, and his conduct on various occasions was consistent with that view.[36]

The issue rose directly to the surface after October 11, 1943, when General Farrell assumed the vice presidency. Perón immediately took advantage of this favorable development that he had nurtured so long and hard, but he did so in a strange way that concealed his real purpose from his rivals: he asked Ramírez to appoint him president of the National Labor Department. It was an astonishing choice in the view of every observer who paid any attention. The National Labor Department was a nothing, a feeble body theoretically charged with certain regulatory responsibilities, but in fact it was largely dormant, except for the collection of labor statistics. The appointment was effective on October 27, 1943. It was clear to Perón, if to no one else, that this rickety stepchild of the bureaucracy had great possibilities if it could be broken loose from the interior ministry to which it then belonged and given independent status and a serious purpose. It was easy to gain such a favor from the impressionable President Ramírez, and a month later, on November 27, the department was transformed into the independent secretariat of labor and welfare, reporting directly to the president.[37] On the next day, Perón was appointed secretary of labor and welfare, retaining at the same time his position as chief of the war ministry secretariat. It was clear what his direction would be. "One of our assumptions dominates all the others because of its importance: social justice," he announced when he arrived at his new office.[38]

It was also clear that Perón would approach this enormous undertaking in the manner in which he approached many other things, that is, in the manner of two quite different men acting out their unalike psychologies. There was now to be seen the Perón for whom "testing your luck" was a guiding principle. "You have to try your luck, to see if you can hit it, because someone who doesn't risk anything never wins anything."[39] It was the test-your-luck Perón who found the courage to override laws and regulations when they seemed inconvenient. "Colonel," an aide would say to him, "what you're doing is contrary to the regulations." And Perón would reply, "First we'll solve the problem and afterwards we'll change the text of the regulations."[40] But this Perón was never out of the sight of the prudent Perón, who favored quiet persuasion and who never forgot that he was acting in the name of the president. Shortly after Farrell was inaugurated on March 11, 1944, Perón went to him.

"Look," he recalled having said to Farrell, "There have been lots of political revolutions here but no social ones. And the problem with Argentina isn't political, it's social. It's the discontent of the workers that produces all the disturbances, and that has to be attended to if we're going to avoid all these conflicts and revolutions. I think we have to give this revolution a social content and the only way to do that is to bring the masses into the national life."

"Go ahead, do it," was the reply that Perón remembered.[41]

The conversation may or may not have been what Perón reported, but its essence was true to Perón's beliefs and to the relationship of the two men.

"Doing it" at that time was tantamount to exploring an empty landscape, so little was there of effective, implemented social legislation. Nothing in the first months of the 1943 revolution, between June and November, had changed this picture materially. There had been several actions that favored the urban lower classes, but the Ramírez government had done these things in the traditional strong-arm way, dominating the labor organizations, ignoring or breaking them as it wished, and giving a bit here and there for the body but nothing for the spirit.

But now, operating in this unaccustomed field with almost carte blanche ("I had at that time absolute freedom to proceed with the idea that had been accepted, and I began to implement it"),[42] Perón called upon still another of his personalities, that of the communicator. This Perón realized by intuition that he would have to reach out beyond the corridors and musty offices of the bureaucracy, beyond the necessary meetings with small groups of experts and officials, and beyond the limited contacts that can be made face to face.

Fortunately for Perón, an instrument was at hand. It was not brand new, but in its relatively short life it had never yet been used in Argentina in a serious way for political purposes, and it was ideally suited to Perón's strengths. This was the radio. It could reach millions, it smiled upon an assured speaker whose forte was eloquence, and it blessed the possessor of a voice that was an incantation. The radio was meant for Perón and he for it. Their symbiosis began on December 2, only five days after Perón took the oath as secretary of labor and welfare. Addressing the country on the national network, he proclaimed the coming of a new age: "With the creation of the Department of Labor and Welfare, the era of Argentine social policy has begun."[43]

Perón could not take on this agenda unaided. Helpers with the appropriate skills and versatility would be required, and in this he was fortunate. Four men were available to help, each in a distinctive capacity, each ideally suited to his task.

The first was General Farrell, whose contribution in his successive roles of war minister, vice president, and president was the provision of shelter and protection, or "cover" as Perón once put it. That convivial officer was happy to enjoy the functions and the fruits of high office as long as someone like Perón was around to do the thinking and the acting without claiming all the credit, and he could be counted on to provide loyalty to his nominal subordinate in return for the satisfactions of the status quo.

The second core colleague was the intellectual and the technician, José Figuerola, a man of immense knowledge and experience in the field of social legislation on both sides of the Atlantic. An exiled Spaniard, he was in charge of the statistical work in the moribund national labor department, where Perón inherited him.[44]

The third colleague was Cipriano Reyes, the tough guy, the rough head of the rough meatpackers' union in the rough suburb of Berisso.

Years later, Perón gave his view of Reyes: "He was short in stature and crude in his manners. But at that moment he was the necessary man. In the beginning it worked out very well. He was the kind of man who lacks direction, who could turn out well or badly. No principles, but a man of action . . ."[45]

The fourth colleague was the familiar friend from the Mendoza days, Domingo Mercante, three years younger than Perón and now his informal ambassador to the labor movement. Aided by the prestige of his father, a respected member of *La Fraternidad,* the union that represented the railroad engineers, Mercante presided over an ad hoc network of contacts in the house of labor, overcoming as best he could the endemic suspicion of union members for all things military.

Thus the social revolution was launched, in the lee of General Farrell. Even with that protection, Perón's seductions of labor were regarded with suspicion or worse in various military quarters. They had been an element in the break with Gonzalito by early 1944. Those who objected were mostly senior officers who found Perón's entire conduct undignified, contrary to military tradition, and unnecessary. The only way to mollify them was invoke the menace of communism. Younger officers, always particularly attracted to Perón, generally took a more tolerant view.[46] But with or without full approval, Perón pressed ahead. Sometimes there was a particularly innovative and therefore particularly upsetting initiative on his part. Thus in December 1943, a friend of Perón who was the subdirector of the military academy arranged for the graduating class of that year to visit, en masse, the secretariat of labor and welfare, where Perón was ready with an address. A small scandal resulted.[47] On occasions like this Perón was at his best. His easy, unprompted eloquence radiated warmth and sophistication. He would refer to the larger picture in the world beyond Argentina, giving impressions and opinions about matters that were unfathomed mysteries to his audience, and he connected these with unfailing intuition to the immediate concerns of those before him, selecting just the right mood and language and intonation for that group. It was not entirely spontaneous, for he knew at least a day in advance which groups would be coming and he had ordered the research necessary for *ad hominem* approaches. But it was enormously impressive, and all the more so because on a typical day it was done three, four, or five times, occasionally as often as eight times, without any diminution of technique or energy.[48]

The work of the social revolution proceeded rapidly. Figuerola delved into the existing labor laws, many of which had been preserved in amber since their enactment, without enforcement. Regulations began to flow from the new Secretariat, putting life into old writ and opening up new approaches, and if this happened to be done in a manner suggesting that entirely new measures created by Perón were involved, so much the better. And, in fact, numerous new laws did begin to appear, each issued by decree bearing the flowing signature of Colonel Perón. Social security was extended outward to the farthest fringes of labor where health insurance and retirement benefits had never been heard of. Dismissals of workers were now subject to sharp restrictions. Holidays and vacations were no longer payless intervals.[49]

A more forceful approach was needed in some conspicuous situations, such as that which prevailed in the packinghouse industry, where unions had come under the domination of a tough Communist named Peter. This called for the skills of Cipriano Reyes. As Perón put it, "We had to break this Communist dictatorship, and for that, since they were gangsters, we had to use other gangsters. Reyes fired the shots in the unions against the Communists, and thus we gained the influence we needed."[50]

In his use of his colleagues, and in particular the strong-arm types like Cipriano Reyes, Perón gave full rein to his intuition and his comfortable pragmatism: "In politics you have to do it that way. You have to use everything. You can't choose only the good things because then you'd be left with three or four elements and you can't form a political movement with those. It's like building a house. You can't stop to reflect that the brick contains dirt and mud. With all those elements you build a wall, a house, and afterward it's a home, full of private values. In politics it's the same, and anyone who wants to get into politics has to build with the materials at hand, using this for one purpose and that for another. Each one helps to build the structure. The skill, the art, of politics lies in knowing how to combine all the forces."[51]

The Communists were overcome, their union was dissolved, and a replacement was created. A strike in the Armour plant brought the intervention of Perón in the form of a proposed settlement. Management refused it and Perón ended the strike by decree, giving the workers what they wanted.[52] Such imposed settlements, invariably partial to labor, soon became commonplace.

Not content with forcing employers to bargain with unions and to give pretty much what the unions demanded, Perón took to forming entirely new unions on a massive scale. Some of these soon numbered members in the hundreds of thousands, and they were not limited to Buenos Aires and the cities of the littoral.[53] The vineyard workers in

Mendoza were not overlooked, nor were the laborers in the hitherto semi-feudal sugar industry in Tucumán and the far northwest, nor even the rural types who represented what was left of the gaucho tradition on the cattle ranches, or those sowers and harvesters of alfalfa and wheat who had enough permanency in their lives to justify signing up. For these, the Statute of the Peon was enacted. If the leaders were under control, once the members were signed up they benefitted from open and democratic union administration. This local autonomy within a framework of firm government control was a prime reason for Perón's success with labor.[54]

But Perón's concept of the proper role for labor went beyond these measures. He wanted to organize it from above into a unified movement responsive to the central power of government. He was a true inheritor of his traditions: if something is good, it will be even better when it is centralized. There was no precedent for this in Argentine industrial history because the Socialists, who were predominant in labor politics before Perón, had followed a different theory, one less responsive to Argentine psychological reality; they had refrained from manipulation of the labor movement for their own purposes, or from proselytizing the unions on behalf of socialism.[55] It followed that the *Confederación General del Trabajo,* or CGT, the one important central labor organization, formed in 1930, had never acquired electoral significance or real strength. On the contrary, shortly before the revolution of June 4 it had split into two bodies, reflecting the destiny of everything touched by the Socialist parties. CGT-1 consisted of the two large railroad unions and a few others and was led by Socialists. CGT-2 contained unions led both by Socialists and by Communists. Perón viewed the situation with distaste. He decreed the dissolution of CGT-2, intervened the two big railroad unions of CGT-1 (naming Mercante as interventor), and proceeded to rebuild the CGT to his own taste.[56]

But he wanted still more. "I thought that the unions should not only represent the professional interests of the members but should have their own politics too. . . . All right, then, I called the unions in and said, 'You ought to have an organization for the unions, directed by a central source, by the CGT, and develop and have your own political policy. Why shouldn't you have representation so you can defend your interests in the government, and in national legislation? Go ahead then, unite, form yourselves' . . . this way I was preaching to the masses. . . . If ten people came in to my office, or a hundred or a thousand, I talked to them. I think I talked with everyone in those months. Bit by bit, as they say. And if they said to me that this was a

long job, I would reply, 'Don't forget that the parrot, eating one ker-
nel of corn after another, will consume the cornfield.' . . . And that's
the way I politicized the Argentine masses."[57] That was hardly the
whole story of how it was done, but it was an important part of the
astonishing achievement. And it was vintage Perón.

In all of this Perón was true to another of the traditional values.
Everything he did was personalized, as it never had been under the
Socialists, who responded to a more typically European value pattern.
If a law was to be proposed, Perón made the announcement. When
delegations came to discuss the matter, Perón addressed them. When
the law was signed, it was his hand that held the pen. If there was a
ceremony that could be worked up, it was held in his office. If a gesture was desired to tilt a strike negotiation to the side of labor, it was
Perón who would visit the premises and be photographed chatting
with the strikers. If union leaders had to be coaxed, it was to Perón's
office that they were invited. Whenever massive publicity would help,
and that was often, it was Perón's picture and Perón's words that dominated the press. If radio was indicated, it was Perón's voice that was
heard. As time went on, the entire novel movement came to be seen
as the personal and sole achievement of Perón, a movement in which
Perón led and the labor leaders struggled to maintain his pace. He
was using them, not the reverse. This was not the way that the labor
leaders had originally planned it when they were first recruited by the
beguiling minister of labor and welfare, but that is the way it turned
out and the way the nation observed it. The culmination of this process, although the labor leaders still didn't fully realize it, came with
the law of professional associations in October 1945, establishing a
limit of one union to each industry and requiring their prior approval
by the government.[58]

Perón Reaches for Power

Perón pursued the social revolution with furious determination
throughout 1944, but in tandem with political objectives of equal significance. General Farrell's elevation to the presidency necessarily left
the position of war minister vacant, and Perón wanted it. His enemies
were now coalescing around nationalist elements on the right, but
Perón's bond with Farrell held tight and he received an interim
appointment on February 26.

This new position was now the crucial element, for Perón was
beginning to face more concentrated opposition from several points
within the armed forces. The nationalists were pointing to Perón's

half-hearted stance in the rupture of relations with Germany and his failure to support nationalist positions more aggressively as betrayals and they were aligning themselves around the interior minister, General Perlinger. These forces included some who were not nationalists at all but who shared the disillusionment with the old politics and hoped for some kind of nontotalitarian new order. Among them were the young men, mostly upper class, banded together in a renovation movement headed by Bonifacio del Carril, with whom Perón flirted briefly for support.[59] At the end of February, there was an abortive coup by dissident officers. Various generals were applying pressure to President Farrell to mandate the withdrawal of all officers from politics.[60]

Perón counterattacked with various devices, including the bureaucratic tactics of carrot and stick. And he recalled the device that had worked well in the GOU, the use of formal oaths to bind officers to certain objectives. An emissary acting on his behalf began early in March to collect signatures on a new pledge, which, as usual, invoked the name of General Farrell. The oath required officers to serve unconditionally the solidarity of the armed forces, to repress every form of dissention or conspiracy, and to yield their position without resistance when called upon to do so. Continuing, it stated: ". . . I will fulfill the orders of his [General Farrell's] Interim War Minister, Colonel Juan D. Perón. If I should at any time renege on this solemn obligation of honor, may God, the Fatherland, and my comrades demand fulfillment."[61] Within a week he had received several hundred signatures.

Developments in the navy also aided Perón. This was hostile country, the officer ranks being almost solidly against him. There were a few possibilities, however, mostly young officers, and one senior, Admiral Alberto Teisaire. Perón, as usual, was happy to reach out to the young officers. For several months he held regular meetings with a group of captains, and these were now cooperative enough to visit President Farrell in support of the appointment of Admiral Teisaire as head of the navy ministry. Farrell was his customary compliant self.[62]

This appointment brought into prominence a relatively new figure. Alberto Teisaire was the least charismatic of men and superficially one of the most unlikely to achieve distinction in the passionate political life of Argentina. He was very tall, overweight, stoop-shouldered, long of face, and impassive of expression. He was noted for his fixed gaze and for the cautious silence that enabled him easily to melt into the background. His professional career had been distinguished, but nothing in it pointed to a political destiny. There was one clue, however. His father had been elected deputy in the National Congress, but that body for some reason refused to recognize his credentials and would not seat him. The son appears to have suffered from this affront for years and sometimes spoke of vindicating his parent. If this was his motivation for seeking office now, he was a likely recruit for Peronism, that house under whose wide roof the outsiders, the wounded, the impotent, the resentful, and the others on the distant side of the Great Rift were beginning to congregate. As a politician, he proved to have one of the rarest of talents, the ability to recognize his own limitations and to adjust his ambitions accordingly. He therefore remained afloat in waters that capsized so many others, content to be the useful advisor and collaborator in the forefront of the second rank.

In July, Perón forced the issue of the rising power of General Perlinger. The vice presidency had been vacant since March, and it was a rich prize that both Perón and Perlinger desired. Perón convened an assembly of army officers for the purpose of making a choice and was supported over General Perlinger, although the vote was very close.[63] Perón now was free to move against Perlinger. With the cooperation of Teisaire, he asked for Perlinger's resignation on the ground that both the army and the navy wanted it. President Farrell was also in Perón's corner, and Perlinger, having no support in reserve, resigned. The decree confirming Perón as vice president was issued on July 7. He retained his posts as minister of war and secretary of labor and welfare, and with these three positions his dominance of the government was unquestioned. At the same time, Teisaire was designated acting minister of the interior while retaining his office of Navy Minister.[64]

It was more than clear that Perón had his heart and mind set on the presidency, presumably by electoral means. Yet he resolutely denied it or dissembled the issue, as events required. In so doing, he was very aware of the strong feelings against electoral participation by officers that obtained in many quarters of the armed forces, and in the higher ranks in particular. Among these, Perón was even more discreet than usual, and no murmurings of ambition were heard. In public, he was silence itself.

It is impossible to say when the thought of election to the presidency, as a realistic possibility, first entered his mind. He was too guarded to leave firm indications in sensitive matters and when he appeared to do so, the indications were often a deception. But certainly the thought must have preoccupied him since the revolution of June 4. And certainly it must have been immensely stimulated by the exhibitions of military incompetence in political life that he saw on all sides and that led to the low esteem in which he had come to hold the abilities of the armed forces in general, much as he respected them in the abstract: the rather ridiculous impracticability of General Rawson, the wan irresolution of General Ramírez, the easygoing indulgence of General Farrell, and the ineptitude of so many others he had already outmaneuvered.

It seems clear, however, that at least by December 1943, Perón had formulated a plan for achieving the presidency by the use of the Radical Party as a vehicle, together with the mass base of labor. On December 8, Perón conferred with Bonifacio del Carril, and he was surprisingly candid. "In this country you're born a Radical or a Conservative. I was born an *orejudo* [a nickname for a conservative]. My father was an *orejudo* and my grandfather was an *orejudo*. But I'm not going to be an *orejudo*, who are fewer; I'm going to be a Radical, there are more of them." Then he spoke of separating the labor masses from their leaders and combining the former with the Radicals. Del Carril suggested it might be difficult to gain the adherence of the new labor leaders who would have to replace the old ones. Perón smiled. "That's the easiest thing. Put the cheese on the table, begin to cut it, and you'll see how they adhere."[65]

When the first acknowledgement of presidential ambition did surface outside private circles, it was in the strangest place imaginable: in the United States embassy. On March 2, 1944, one of Perón's representatives sought an interview in which he disclosed to an embassy official, quite without hesitation, the hopes that Perón nurtured for his election, which he foresaw coming about with the help of the Radical Party.[66] The timing of the disclosure was important. It was an attempt to head off the nonrecognition of the Farrell government that was threatened in the aftermath of the fall of Ramírez at the end of February, and that did indeed come to pass on March 4. In the embassy meeting, Perón's representative attributed the fall of Ramírez to an internal power struggle in the government, an explanation that the embassy found unconvincing.

It is ironic that in this instance, Perón, who had so often succeeded when he was arguably in the wrong, failed when he was in the right. He had been telling the truth, for the overthrow of Ramírez and the entire chain of complicated events that preceded and followed it were attributable more to internal political struggles than to ideology and foreign policy. Perón did indeed favor the Axis powers in this war, but he favored his own rise to the top much more, and if those two objectives should collide, there was no real question as to which one he would be faithful to. His prudent departure from center stage when the controversial break with Germany was being debated was entirely consistent with his priorities, and with his tactics as well.

The embassy's conclusion about the pro-Axis motivations of the coup that unseated President Ramírez was an error of a kind that was not uncommon in those years. It was an error that is easy for diplomats to make, and the truth that would gainsay it is hard to come by. From the point of view of the embassy and the State Department, the only thing that had really mattered for the last three years had been the world war and the policies of various nations toward it. Everything was analyzed and appraised from that central point of reference. Given such a mind-set, it was psychologically easy, perhaps inevitable, to leap to the conclusion that events within Argentina reflected the same monolithic priority. The difficulty thus created was enormously complicated by the opaqueness of the true state of affairs; few people in Argentina, let alone the embassy, could have unraveled the intrigues that Perón and a handful of others had woven. But the fact remains that the United States policy of nonrecognition that was adopted in March 1944 was based in substantial part upon a faulty analysis of Argentine reality.

In any case, the policy led to a strange situation. In the following months, American pressure was exerted constantly, but in a kind of vacuum, in that the real reason for it and the kinds of response that might end it were never communicated to the Argentine government, and could not be, for the real reason was the Argentine government itself and its very nature.[67]

Perón had also been forthright in his assertions to the embassy on March 2 that he would seek the support of the Radical Party in his bid for the presidency. In April and May, approaches were made to its intransigent wing. Perón was in a mellow mood at this time in regard to the merits of the politicians, or at least those of them who might be brought to his side. This contrasted strongly with his general stance of contempt for the political leaders, whom he usually viewed as obsolete and selfish representatives of decadent movements now outflanked by history. But in these April and May days, with their requirement of support from whatever source, the practical Perón took charge and found immediate worth in the Radicals. On May 9, in a talk given at the Campo de Mayo, he described the party as a great force, still powerful, and likely to collaborate with the military government.[68]

The Radicals, however, had never been long on collaboration with anyone, including each other, and now they were mostly obstinate. At least they would not give Perón everything he wanted on his own terms. The pragmatic Perón was disillusioned. The hard-edged Perón entered, and the embassy noted a sudden difference. Now the politicians were denigrated, denounced as the bearers of "sinful insinuations" and "unworthy seductions."[69]

This return to a firm position marked the abandonment of Perón's effort to recruit assistance from new sources, but at least it had the benefit of strengthening his position with his more plausible bases of possible support, such as the nationalists who had been cool or even freezing cold to him in his rivalry with General Perlinger. If nothing could be gained from the Radicals, perhaps a gesture to the right could produce benefits.

And so Perón went down to La Plata on June 10. The university there had created a chair of national defense studies and Perón had been asked to give the inaugural address. The speech that resulted has sometimes been described as the most important of his career, a judgment that may be questioned. If one were to accept the speech at full face value, it might be entitled to such an appraisal, since it spelled out unequivocally an international posture for Argentina that harmonized with almost every possible nationalist theme, a posture that seemed to rest upon a totalitarian regime at home.

Perón made three principal points in the speech. The first was the inevitability of war as a social phenomenon. The second was the insistance "that so-called pacifist nations, such as ours, must prepare for war if they want peace." Here he again invoked the theme of the nation in arms that he had expressed in *Apuntes de historia militar,* in derivation from Von der Golz.

The third point was an elaboration of the second: "The national defense of the nation is an integral problem which involves all the activities of the state . . . all the best minds of the nation, each one in the field relating to its activity, should strive to know war, to study and to understand it as the only way of reaching a complete solution of the problem that may be presented to us and which we shall have to resolve if some day God should decide that the clarion call of war must resound on the banks of the Río de la Plata."[70]

This discourse was received abroad with alarm, particularly in the United States, where it soon assumed a prominent position among the arguments supporting the nonrecognition policy. It confirmed the worst fears of those who saw the current Argentine government as an Axis outpost in the New World, girding for aggressive onslaughts abroad and firm tyranny at home. To be sure, a selective reading of the speech was required for these doomsday views. Perón had included his country among the satisfied rather than the dissatisfied nations and he disclaimed every kind of conquest, demand, or hegemony. But these were less conspicuous parts of the whole, and the Hull group in the U.S. State Department found it easy to analyze the speech as the handiwork of the plotters who had helped to topple the government in La Paz six months before.

The great significance of the speech might therefore be argued on the basis of its practical effect on foreign policy, intended or otherwise. But if the speech is evaluated on the basis of its immediate purpose, it is more difficult to sustain its singular importance, for it appears to have been another move in the contention between Perón and General Perlinger, another effort to consolidate military and right wing support behind Perón less than a month before their showdown. There are indications that the furor over the La Plata pronouncements surprised Perón.[71] The speech was well received in Argentina, even in circles unsympathetic to Perón and partial to the Allies in the war.[72]

In another aspect, the address at La Plata was the first conspicuous example of a phenomenon that would recur many times in the future, that is, a speech or an article in the controlled press generating resentment or alarm abroad and explained by Perón as being intended for local consumption only. Some of the most bitter misunderstandings between the United States and Argentina during the years of the Peronato arose in this manner, and the difficulties of interpretation and the loss of mutual comprehension that resulted, although mitigated at times and papered over, were never fully overcome.

Military issues continued prominently on Perón's agenda during the balance of 1944. Pay and promotions were liberalized. The officer corps was expanded, particularly in the upper grades, thus opening avenues for promotions. More troops were called for service. A separate Air Force was created in October, with bureaucratic opportunities for many.

On a different front, Perón increased the war ministry's contributions to the general directorate of military factories, the DFGM, which supervised war-related industries, arsenals, and factories providing small military equipment. Mixed enterprises were being contemplated at this time for arms production, and Perón was happy to allocate funds. Military production was a subdivision of the effort being made at the time to build up industrial production in general. In April, two new instrumentalities had been created, the *Banco de Crédito Industrial*, the first of its kind and soon to provide financing for new industries of "national interest"; and the secretariat of industry and commerce, reporting directly to the president. The first secretary was a general, emphasizing the close connection between industrial and military circles in the management of both the bank and the new secretariat.[73]

A larger question still remained in this military area. The need for arms purchases was now becoming serious. Perón kept on with German negotiations through September of 1944, conducted through the Argentine military attaché in Madrid despite the break in relations in January. With Allied forces advancing toward the Rhine, a lesser realist than Perón would have known long since that the Axis, heading for defeat, could spare nothing and had no time or motive for such peripheral matters. It was almost certainly shadow play aimed at sustaining Perón's credentials with pro-Axis nationalists, while the necessity for the inevitable turn to the United States as a supplier sank in.

Such a rapprochement would have to wait upon external events, for the hostility born in 1943 had steadily hardened in 1944 until in the aftermath of the La Plata address it had attained the texture of granite. In August, the United States froze more than $400 million in Argentine gold reserves, and export licenses were cut back in October.[74] But opinion in the hemisphere began to coalesce in favor of an inter-American meeting of some kind to prepare the New World nations for the postwar reorganization of the world and to clear the slate of the Argentine imbroglio. Hull and his colleagues, losing power in the Roosevelt administration and isolated by growing skepticism concerning the Argentine policy, hung on with weary tenacity. But as autumn declined into early winter in Washington, a change of direction was almost at hand.

Although 1945 was to be a time of triumph for Perón, 1944, now concluding, had its own distinction as an historic watershed. Probably by the middle of the year, and certainly by its end, an evolution had been completed and the agenda of public life had been created in the form in which it would exist for the next forty years. That agenda is simply stated: it was Perón. The traditional issues and conflicts that had absorbed energies and emotions since the time of independence had now faded. In 1944, one was for Perón or against him and everything else was subordinate. His immense capacity not only to mobilize opinion but also to divide it was now a reality in every corner of society, in every institutional and private context. This is not to say that there was as yet general recognition or agreement as to his precise purposes and policies; but he had become the central issue in Argentine public life, the most recent and startling form of the Great Rift.

This was the principal legacy of 1944, to be given definitive shaping in 1945. Yet there was another legacy, too, marking the beginning of a new era or phase, a legacy that would combine with the emergence of Perón to change the face and the soul of Argentina forever, for 1944 was also the year of the coming of Evita.

Evita

It is symbolically appropriate that the first meeting of Perón and Evita should come as the direct result of an earthquake.[75]

On Saturday, January 15, 1944, a small but distinct tremor rippled briefly in the tranquil summer heat of Buenos Aires, just enough to rattle a window here and there. But 600 miles away, in the Andean northwest, the ancient town of San Juan that had been the birthplace of the great Sarmiento had just been destroyed. The old cathedral still stood, badly damaged, but hardly another structure remained. Ten thousand people lay dead in the ruins.

A major relief effort was mounted immediately, and the government, needing someone with a sense of command, organizational ability, and enough magnetism to rally the country, selected Perón to head the effort. Perón immediately announced the taking of a national collection, beginning with 200,000 pesos that represented the current salaries of military members of the government, and sought the collaboration of commercial and industrial circles, artists, and the entire nation. As part of this outreach, Perón immediately called a group of artists to his office. A young woman unknown to Perón spoke, and he recalled the moment many years later:

I remember that she wasn't seated in the first row; that she was wearing a very simple dress; that she was thin, that she had blonde hair, and that she had a little hat, like they wore in those days. "We don't need festivals," she replied to proposals that had been made, "we should go directly to ask, without offering anything. At this moment we don't have to organize any spectacles, or any tea, or anything like that, because those are old hat, out of style. Let's go to the streets, to the public places, to the hippodrome, to the theatre, to all the important places, and say to the people, 'our brothers are striken, we have to help them!' We have to get money from those that have it, because those that don't have it can't give it."

I liked the way this woman thought and worked. I thought she wasn't like the others. She had something very superior to the others in the way she talked and in her suggestions. She was practical and had new ideas.

"Good, very well," I said to her then, "it's your idea, organize it." And that's the way it was. She organized everything.[76]

In another recollection, set down at some undated moment in his exile, Perón recalled her fragility on that day, her strong voice, her feverish eyes, and the long blonde hair cascading over her shoulders. "I looked at her and felt that her words were overpowering me; I was almost overcome by the power of her voice and her look. Eva was pale, but when she spoke her face was touched with flame. Her hands were red with tension, her fingers were interlocked, she was a bundle of nerves. . . . I saw in Evita an exceptional woman. A true passion, animated by will and by a faith comparable to that of any of the early Christians."[77]

These accounts, written long after that dramatic January, are accurate in essence, although many of the details suffered from loss of memory or from abundance of imagination. Evita's hair was still dark at that time; it was bleached later for a movie role. She did not organize the collection campaign, although she participated in it, as did Perón, who wore a white jacket and black boots, promenading with artists and other officers in dress uniform in the Calle Florida, bearing his money box. At the end of the week, on January 22, there was the charity festival that Evita was said to have spoken against, held at the stadium in Luna Park. Evita attended with a friend, wearing a black dress, a white hat replete with feathers, and long gloves. The president spoke, as did Perón. When he had finished, Evita and her friend went to greet him. Perón was first paired with the friend, and Evita with another man, presumably Colonel Aníbal Imbert, but in the postmidnight hours the couples switched. In any case, Perón and Evita talked at length and as the night wore on they went home together.[78]

She was born on May 7, 1919 in Los Toldos, a forlorn little village lost in the great pampas. There was not much of it: the inevitable church, a few unimpressive stores, the equally unimpressive plaza, some low brick houses along unpaved streets that formed the usual grid. A few blocks in any direction and the infinite pampas took over. Buenos Aires lay an endless 150 miles to the east.

She was the fifth and last child of Juana Ibarguren and Juan Duarte. In their names lies, in all probability, the clue to the intense consciousness of injustice that was to trigger the extraordinary sensitivity of their unique fifth child, for Evita, like her brother and her three sisters, was illegitimate. Her baptized name was Ibarguren, but neither her mother nor any of the other children ever used it, preferring Duarte. The arrangement was not unusual in that time and place. Duarte had his legal family in Chivilcoy, a town twenty miles distant, but he worked as an estate manager in the area around Los Toldos and lived there with his second family. This pattern had gone on for eighteen years, and life for the second family, although lacking in social acceptance, was not one of deprivation as long as Duarte remained there. But in 1920 he returned to Chivilcoy and his legal family, and Doña Juana, deprived of other support, had to provide for the six of them on her small earnings as a seamstress. They moved to a lesser home in a poor section of the poor village, still afflicted with the image of illegitimacy and social disrepute.

In 1926 came the blow that, one suspects, was decisive in Evita's evolution. Juan Duarte died in Chivilcoy. Doña Juana, a determined and self-reliant woman, decided her family should attend the funeral, a presumption that ran counter to all the customs of the day, a minor scandal. They arrived late and were turned away at the door, being admitted only upon the intercession of the mayor. They were allowed to view the body briefly while the guests stood aside, and then they had to wait outside in the dusty heat until they were permitted to follow the hearse to the cemetery, at a respectable distance so as not to disgrace the legal family at the head of the procession. All her life, Evita, like her siblings, was blighted by the issue of her illegitimacy, so dramatically highlighted by the cruelty of her family's rejection in the hour of death. It was her first venture into the world beyond Los Toldos.

In 1930, the family moved to Junín, a larger town twenty miles away. Here the older children found work, and Doña Juana, now known as the Widow Duarte, served meals in the home to guests; there was no restaurant in the town. Evita went to school here, ". . . a self-absorbed child with an intense inner life, great sensitivity and great vulnerability," in the assessment of one of her teachers,[79] still suffering the rejection of classmates because of an unfair perception of her mother's reputation, which seemed impossible to shake. Junín was the quintessential Argentine small town of Manuel Puig's *Betrayed by Rita Hayworth,* a town whose escape from tedium and dusty reality was the movies. Evita's early idol was Norma Shearer, the poor girl who rose to stardom.[80]

In 1935, when she was still short of sixteen, Evita left Junín forever and sought her future in Buenos Aires. The most frequently told tale of her departure links it to her seduction of Agustín Magaldi, a tango-singer second in fame only to Carlos Gardel. This is the verson perpetuated in the musical *Evita.* It is not a story that invites easy credence. Magaldi was happily married and traveled with his wife, and there is no record of his appearance in Junín during 1935. Another version has Doña Juana accompanying her daughter to the big city and returning home soon after. The facts are quite obscure, and every variation of every version can be supported by this or that witness.[81]

But arrive in Buenos Aires she did, still little more than a child, without funds, without friends, and totally devoid of either experience or prospects.

Then began the years of cheap, gloomy little rooms in dismal down-at-the-heels lodging houses, bit parts with theatrical companies whose ties to solvency were tenuous even in the best of days, predatory directors whose habit was to sleep and forget ("In an hour half a dozen girls would come to his table and he would pinch their asses.")[82], extended unemployment, the trickle of money sent back to the family in Junín, and the struggle against rumor and humiliation. There was a six-month period of living with a young actor who spoke of marriage but opted instead for an unheralded departure, cleaning out the apartment as he went. Some remembered her in these years as hard and ruthless; more recalled her gentleness.

By 1939, Evita was toughened a bit by the rough road upward, but she had found her metier: soap operas, broadcast on the radio. She emerged in 1939 as the codirector of a leading company that produced these dramas. At some point in 1940, her brother, Juan Duarte, took a hand in her career and arranged for the sponsorship of her programs by, appropriately enough, a soap company. In 1941, she moved with her group to Radio El Mundo, the leading station in Argentina. By 1943, she had reached the top of her specialty and was among the best paid radio actresses in the country. She made forays into the movies and the stage but in neither did she advance beyond the bit-part stage until after she had met Perón. She once told her confessor, at the end of her acting career, that her work had been "bad in the cinema, mediocre on the stage, and passable on the radio."[83] It was a fair judgment and did her credit.

At this point, the San Juan earthquake intervened. Everything changed, but not simultaneously. Her personal life was affected first. Perón had been living with a young mistress nicknamed Piraña, an adolescent of sixteen from Mendoza who was said to be silent, plain in appearance, and sometimes bored with her secluded role as Perón's "daughter." There are two explanations of the way Perón and Evita met this problem. The first, attributed to a close friend of Perón, is the more colorful; Evita loaded a truck with her own belongings and had it unloaded at Perón's apartment, simply ordering Piraña back to Mendoza and thus presenting Perón with a fait accompli when he returned later in the day.[84] The other explanation, less dramatic but more plausible, holds that Perón handled the matter himself. In any case, Evita soon acquired the apartment next to Perón's, and they used them as one.

Evita's acting career changed, too, but more slowly. She continued with her radio work, now for Radio Belgrano. Her new contract broke all records in this field, doubtless due to her relationship with the powerful colonel. In a tradition so devoted to the use of influence, a *palanca*, a lever, as magnificent as this would open any door. A movie studio now announced a contract for Evita, and a role in a new production about to begin. Again the *palanca* revealed its power, for Perón had helped the studio obtain an allocation of scarce film stock.

In May 1944, Perón's labor policies crossed with Evita's radio career, forming a happy juncture. A new union for broadcasting performers was announced, presumably at Perón's suggestion, and it would be the only one permitted in the industry. Here he had the advantage of a built-in relationship with the new union's officialdom, since the performers, who were not unobservant, had elected Evita president of the organization. Faithful to appearances, Perón received her in his office with her petition for union recognition, which she presented formally and he accepted with the usual protocol.

The radio broadcasts continued, now at the rate of three a day. Evita's health gave way in September, for she had never been robust, and she was obliged to take a rest. But she continued with appearances and meetings and interviews, the latter being dedicated to the image of a simple woman devoted to simple routines, the home-lover, the seeker after the quiet life, the reader of the classics, and a great deal of other nonsense.

The change in her life that was the slowest to materialize was her transformation into a woman of public affairs. Perón, looking back, forgot various things or chose to distort them, deliberately erasing the female reality and laboring the image of the coworker linked with him in an immediate and spontaneous dedication that was almost monastic in its demands. "When I first knew Evita what attracted me in her was not the beautiful woman but the good woman. It's true that she combined those two things: beauty and goodness. Instinctively I perceived that the collaboration of a woman of this kind would be invaluable for the social task I had in mind. . . . I had to prepare a woman who would be the feminine *leader* of my political movement: a capable woman with enough basic culture, natural talents of intuition, with dedication . . ."[85]

There was myth-building as well as history here, for Perón was concentrating on the concept of their mutual abnegation in the name of public service. And, at times, another element appeared, a kind of cool, detached appraisal of Evita's physical appeal in those early times, as if he were determined that history would remember only the abnegation. ". . . our private life as totally subordinated to the political and social calling . . . a veritable tyranny to which we submitted ourselves as if it were a mission. Evita, in those first days, didn't care much about her appearance, or want to be taken for an elegant woman. She went to work, and working all day didn't leave much time to care for herself or to attend to her clothes."[86]

Perón's account of an instant transformation of the actress into the dedicated public servant had little basis in fact. It is accurate in its reference to a joint endeavor such as the world had rarely if ever seen before, but it is quite incorrect in its time sequence. The Evita of blind dedication to a mission did not appear until 1947–48. During 1944 and approximately the first half of 1945, Evita remained what she had been, the actress who was also the mistress of the high official.

But this, too, must be qualified, because for Perón keeping a mistress was not the almost exclusive undertaking of passion that it would be for many others. The fact is, the sexual drive was not highly developed in Perón. His physical demands were entirely orthodox, but they were relatively mild. His urgent need, on the other hand, was for domesticity, for company, for a listener, for a woman hovering about. The same low level of physical passion seems to have been true of Evita. Arturo Jauretche, who as writer, historian, and intellectual knew both Perón and Evita from a point of view more favorable to Peronism than was typical of his type, concluded, "Eva, in spite of her fancy for the theatre, was a very unsexual girl. She didn't have that much interest in it. . . . And that was her affinity with Juan Perón, because he too was not a sexual type. In that marriage two wills were united, two passions for power. It was not a marriage of love."[87]

In the very early days of the relationship Perón said somewhat the same thing, but on the more idealistic plane of high principle. "I'm firmly convinced you shouldn't marry a woman who pleases you physically, but one who has the other qualities. Follow what Plato said, 'Everything in its measure, and harmoniously.' That's what you have to take into account in love. Because physical beauty is only for a time, later comes spiritual beauty which lasts longer, and the intellectual, that lasts longest of all. The man who doesn't think of this . . . has a woman for a short time!"[88]

They were living together openly, and this itself was a symbol of the novelty that was afoot. For an army officer to have a mistress was almost routine, and society would not fret. But to share living quarters and the public eye with a mistress was a scandal. The mistress would customarily have her separate small apartment where she could be visited and from which she could be brought forth for discreet appearances. Or she could be introduced as a daughter, as Piraña had been. But this was a bewilderment to which others did not know how to respond: here was this woman, an actress in soap operas, hardly respectable anyway, sharing the living room with politicians and officials and army officers, listening to the babble of talk, helping out with the refreshments but failing to remove herself as even a wife would have done. Perón's friends, called upon for explanations, sometimes replied with more macho resentment than accuracy: a nobody, a folly of the colonel's, "one of those tiresome girls who screw all over the place in the hope that someone will give them a part."[89]

As Perón's influence grew and as the relationship with Evita became more conspicuous, it inevitably served as a point of attack against them, individually and jointly.[90] Evita's image as a prostitute, strongly held in some quarters, was one consequence although it had no basis in fact. But it served well the sense of class antipathy and division that was growing up around Perón, and in a society so deeply fragmented and so hotly personalized any weapon that came to hand was welcome. Perón's posture in the face of the growing public reaction is more difficult to assess. He certainly must have understood the depth of the feelings arrayed against the relationship, since some of the strongest among them were centered in the army officer corps and could threaten him directly. They, in fact, did exactly that only a year hence, when they formed a prominent motive for the army movement that briefly forced Perón from power. It has been suggested that because Perón had come to politics so late he simply never realized what was acceptable and what was unacceptable in that Byzantine calling.[91] It is probably more likely that Perón felt he could hold the line against army resentments, and for the rest, the relationship would hurt him only in circles that were by definition hostile to his political cause, and not in the social spheres to which he was appealing, thus leaving him free to follow his instincts, which were quite open and tolerant in such matters.

There was irony in the situation, and a bit of further enigma. One of the Peróns appeared to enjoy dissimulation, even in situations in which it seemed needless; and now, in a situation in which that unpleasant quality would appear to serve a necessary purpose, the dissimulating Perón vanished and was replaced by the straightforward Perón, who introduced his mistress all around as if he were presenting a virginal younger sister.

For her part, Evita was learning. Her education was primitive and entirely unequal to the demands of this new life in the center of power. "She viewed me with respect, but she didn't like me," Arturo Jauretche remarked. "Poor child, she had a very large distrust of intellectuals."[92] But she was a quick learner. Her technique at the beginning was simple. She listened to Perón, absorbed everything he said, and then infused it with her own passionate emotion. Perón was not inaccurate in his recollection of her discipleship when he said, "Evita adopted my political and social ideas, imbuing them with a feminine sensibility, to the point of creating within herself a second 'I'."[93]

Even as Evita was adapting to new requirements, and as Perón was struggling to prevail in the political world now defined and divided by his rising power, events were hurrying to the dramatic denouement that would give 1945 its almost sacred symbolism in the Peronist calendar.

6. Peronism Ascendant 1945-1946

The Miraculous Year, 1945

THE YEAR BEGAN with a sudden change of policy by the
United States. The hard line toward Argentina that had prevailed for
two years, and now seen as harmful to prospects for a viable United
Nations, was overtaken by the planning for the postwar period.[1] Secretary Hull, enfeebled by age, resigned in December and was succeeded by Edward Stettinius. The latter, a Wilsonian like Hull, was
nevertheless flexible and realistic. If he was not the man to launch
large crusades, neither was he one to go very far down a dead-end
road.

Nelson Rockefeller now came to office in the new position of assistant secretary for Latin American affairs, hoping to resurrect the Good
Neighbor, with a greater economic emphasis. This view was strongly
supported by the United States military and by American business
interests, and it received a boost, also, from a less predictable source,
Juan Perón. As early as October 1944, the embassy in Buenos Aires
had reported that Perón's influence in the government was being
exerted against the hard-line elements, that a cooperative turn in
Argentine policy was now possible, and even an evolution toward constitutional government. Perón, having worked on the hard-liners in
his La Plata speech and in other ways, was now quietly courting civil-

ian opinion in political circles. In addition to his other motivations, he had the powerful incentive of access to military equipment and supplies.[2]

Although public opinion in the United States had not made the transition from hostility to cautious rapprochement as rapidly as the diplomats had, President Roosevelt approved a policy of recognition if Argentina would take appropriate steps, including a plan for elections, a declaration of war, termination of Axis organizations and influence, and the ending of the State of Siege. The forthcoming Mexico City conference, in February, would provide the appropriate theater for action. Perón, meanwhile, was working at his end of the lever, combining economic and political enticements. He had used a political device with an economic carrot, the creation of a national council on postwar planning in September 1944, which he would head. His officials spoke of bountiful contracts that could follow repair of the broken relations, and the American press took up the cry.[3]

The way was clear for two diplomatic initiatives aimed at a reconciliation. Both took place in February. In the first, emissaries of Perón met with officials on the staff of Adolf Berle, now ambassador to Brazil, but still a power in policy circles.[4] The second took the form of a secret United States mission to Argentina in mid-February, for which the account of Sumner Welles is the best available evidence.[5]

On March 8, the Mexico City conference produced the Act of Chapultepec, which defined common procedures in case of aggression against any hemispheric state from within or without, and which looked to postwar treaty arrangements on these points. Argentina's readmission to the regional system was not settled, since Perón rejected the United States proposal based on Argentina's declaration of war, but it was left on the basis of hope, with an invitation to Argentina to align itself with the others.[6] It wasn't what the State Department had wanted, but it did remove the taint of noncooperation from the United States and put it on Argentina.

Perón knew that little time remained for the decision on a declaration of war. Among other factors, Argentine admission to the proposed United Nations depended on the action, and that wouldn't wait. Accordingly, Decree No. 6945 was issued on March 27, covering all requirements: Argentina was at war with Germany and Japan; Argentina now adhered to the Act of Chapultepec; various security measures were adopted.

Latin American opinion was delighted. In the United States, opinion was divided. In Argentina itself, no one was really happy with developments. The American embassy summarized the reactions: "The declaration of war was greeted in general with an attitude ranging from apathetic to resentful and has brought the government, particularly Perón, to its lowest level of prestige within the country. The pro-Nazis, anti-Yankees, anti-British, ultra-nationalists, etc., do not want war against Germany. The democratic-minded are ashamed at Argentina's having fallen so low as to declare war on a beaten nation, and many, furthermore, are convinced that recognition is about to follow and will serve only to solidify the dictatorial government in its position. This fear emerges in editorials urging the calling of elections."[7]

As part of Perón's juggling of public opinion during this confused and tense period, he decided upon a brief outreach to liberals. On February 10, professors and teachers who had been dismissed for their participation in a democratic manifesto in October 1943, were advised that they would be reinstated, although without back compensation. But the enthusiasm of those thus benefitted was fitful at best. Still in a querulous mood, they pointed out the deficiencies of the remedial legislation. Perón won few middle-class and intellectual converts through this means.[8]

He was, in fact, winning no converts in any direction at this time. The collapse of Germany, now easily visible, seemed to be sensitizing all the elements of the opposition. Students remained recalcitrant, like their professors. Politicians, unable to speak for their outlawed parties, were agitated. Army officers of pro-Allied tendency were inching toward resistance. Exiles across the water in Montevideo kept up a ceaseless recrimination. It was a period of sour public opinion in general, and the immediate cause for alarm on Perón's part was the day, surely almost at hand, when Berlin would fall. Given the weight of symbolism, that event could hardly fail to ignite demonstrations or worse. It was time to reverse course. Repression would now be in style.

A suitable justification was available. A group of liberal army officers partial to the Allies and led by a retired general, Adolfo Espindola, had been conspiring for some time. Their precise purposes are not clear in retrospect, and probably never were. On April 20, General Espindola was arrested, along with seven other officers, on suspicion of conspiracy. Soon more than 400 others were arrested, civilians and military alike, but mostly the former. A week later, the press was given a long explanation, a mélange of inconsistent references to communism, fascism, civil war, terrorism, executions, and the like. But included among these absurdities were several allegations that deserve reluctant admiration for their psychological insight into the fears and concerns of the lower-grade officers and noncoms to whom they were addressed. The commissioned and noncommissioned officer corps, said the announcement, were to have been reduced by the Espindola forces by 30 percent; all army schools were to have been shut down for ten years; and the police were to have been dissolved and their duties assigned to the entire army, a thought calculated to make a junior officer's blood run cold. There is nothing to connect Perón personally with this creative and imaginative press announcement, but it could hardly have been issued without his approval, and in its catering to insecurity it was pure Perón.[9]

The Espindola affair could not have come at a worse time for Perón, and one must conclude that however grossly he permitted it to be warped and exaggerated, he must surely have acted out of the fear, whether justified or not, that something very real was in the making. Otherwise he would hardly have accepted the high price the episode and its natural consequences entailed.

Part of that price, a small part, was the awkward surfacing of the rumors of Perón's presidential ambitions. These had been circulating quietly but there had been little public speculation as yet. Now, with the Espindola affair, it became urgent for Perón that military support remain steadfast. That, in turn, required credibility for Perón, and credibility required that he clarify the presidential rumors. Earlier in April he had faced the issue privately by calling a huge assembly of officers. With more than a thousand in attendance, Perón had taken an unequivocal stand: "I will not accept a candidacy of any sort and much less that of president, even if they come and ask me on their knees."[10] But the rumors persisted, and in the heat of the Espindola repressions more was required, this time in public. And so the Argentine people were treated to a most unusual and mystifying tactic on April 23; without having heard of the arrests because of censorship (the guileful press statement referred to above did not come until four days later) and knowing nothing whatsoever of the context, they were informed by a press release at the bizarre hour of 2 A.M. that Perón was expressly denying any presidential aspirations. ". . . I do not aspire to be president of the Republic and I will oppose energetically all efforts which may be made to advance my candidacy."[11]

A larger part of the price was the difficulty surrounding Argentina's admission to the United Nations, then in formation at San Francisco. With strong Russian opposition, it took a tremendous effort by the other hemisphere nations, particularly the United States. A still larger price was exacted by the deterioration in United States-Argentine relations. The so-called Warren Mission had just produced an agreement in Buenos Aires concerning military supplies, and this was now in some jeopardy.[12]

Luck now intervened for Perón. Whether that luck was good or bad for him is an interesting question, but in any case the deteriorating climate of United States relations happened to coincide with the coming of an ambassador from Washington, implementing the renewal of diplomatic relations. The ambassador arrived on May 19. He departed from Buenos Aires on September 23 to become assistant secretary for Latin America, in replacement of Nelson Rockefeller. In the intervening eighteen weeks, he gave the coup de grace to the entire Argentine policy of the United States as it had evolved since the end of 1944. His name was Spruille Braden.

He was an unusual man and an even more unusual diplomat. Short, powerfully built, his large head thrusting forward from strong shoulders and neck, he reminded some of a bulldog, while to others he projected the image of a buffalo. His background had been in the mining industry; his father had founded the Braden Copper Company, an important producer in Chile. The son no longer retained any interest in that venture, but it was the first of his credentials as a man of affairs in a Latin American context. He had later turned to public life and had been a decisive influence in the peace conference that ended the horrible Chaco war, serving as chairman of the United States delegation. During the last five years he had been ambassador to Colombia and to Cuba. He had many connections and friendships in South America, knew the area intimately, and spoke fluent Spanish. He was competent, forceful, and exceedingly energetic. He was also honest and totally dedicated to democratic principles, holding all variants of totalitarianism, whether of the right or of the left, in equal abomination.

These conspicuous merits were offset by deficiencies that can easily be fatal to a diplomat. Braden lacked wide empathy. He could know all about the externals of a culture and completely miss its internal realities. Subtleties usually escaped him. He preferred to go through obstacles rather than around them, and all shades of gray were absent from his color spectrum. He was blunt and direct and very rigid. His courage, unrestrained by his temperament, often lapsed into something unpleasantly like arrogance.

Superficially, the timing of Braden's arrival was unfortunate for Perón. Argentine compliance with the war decree of March 27 was lackluster and feeble.[13] The repressions occasioned by General Espindola and his failed plot were still conspicuous. General Rawson, of the forty-eight-hour presidency, was among those arrested in the continuing turbulence. Press censorship had been instituted. Public meetings were banned. The new ambassador, witnessing dictatorial practices all around, was confirmed in his worse expectations. Doubtless he had known from the moment of his appointment that his true mission would be to force the government to return to constitutional forms; in any event, he acquired that conviction, or that obsession, very early on and never allowed realities to dilute it. He thus found himself in a situation that he construed as begging for action, and he immediately began to lay about him on all sides.

In little more than a week he had scuttled the agreements of the Warren Mission; on May 29, the State Department announced that performance of the Chapultepec agreements would be a precondition of military assistance.[14] Several meetings between Braden and Perón, some of them bordering on the explosive, merely served to harden their natural antipathy. This new turn was damaging to Perón in regard to the military aspect, but Braden's other activity was on the whole helpful, although certainly not so intended. He began to intervene openly, giving speeches to cheering audiences of Perón's opponents, criticizing the government for its slow motion toward anti-Axis objectives and for its totalitarian domestic policies. This was offensive not only to Peronist and nationalist opinion but also to the sentiments of many who were in the middle of the road, including the Yrigoyen Radicals, for Yrigoyen, too, had been not only a neutralist but also something of a nationalist at home.[15] All of this was lost on Braden, for his friendships and contacts were limited to oligarchic and solidly anti-Peronist circles that cheered him to the rafters, and he never understood that they did not speak for all the nation.

The basis for Braden's vehement partisanship was his conviction, very sincerely held, that Perón personally, and the government he headed in fact if not in title, represented little other than a replication of fascism, inspired by Hitler and Mussolini and devoted to the same violent tactics and ends. It brought him to a perverse and drastically incorrect misreading of history, raising for him a vision of apocalypse. Two months after the German surrender, he sent a telegram to the State Department that reads strangely in retrospect: ". . . we must ever bear in mind that present regime is a foreign inspired and supported movement resting on and taking full advantage of the underlying xenophobia, vanity and and ambitions of Argentine people. I have arrived at following conclusions: It was not merely accidental that so-called June 4 [1943] revolution occurred almost immediately after tide of war turned decisively at Stalingrad and in North Africa. Apparent paradox of Fascist regime rising in Argentina when Fascism began to recognize its doom in Europe was, on the contrary, a logical development. Argentine Fascists remained in shade so long as victory of Nazi Germany appeared possible since that victory would have automatically placed them in power without risk or effort. So soon as German defeat appeared certain, they and their German Nazi advisors realized that Argentine fascism had to seize power openly and positively in order to preserve this country as a base for winning the ideological war which would follow the ending of armed conflict in Europe and thus to insure fascism's survival."[16]

Braden's illusion that the coup of June 4, 1943 was the direct result of events in the Soviet Union and North Africa is particularly upsetting as an illustration of how far from the mark an ambassador's analysis can be. If the fourteen officers who huddled at the Campo de Mayo on the night of June 3 produced a revolution so impromptu that they didn't know whom they would install as president the next morning, we can be very sure that they were not thinking deep thoughts about Stalingrad and Tripoli.

Wrong as Braden was, he did act in the spirit of the crusading psychology of the war years. The universal Allied view of the war as a Manichean conflict of good and evil had thoroughly penetrated both the perception and the analytical powers of almost all who had to exercise leadership. In Argentina, the resentment, loathing, or sheer panic with which opponents of Perón variously observed his rise were naturally translated into the symbolism of anti-Nazi rhetoric. It was all the easier because there was then no forum or format in which opposition could function rationally, and because Perón himself, in his sympathies and in his flirtations with pro-Axis causes and personalities, had laid a basis that could easily be built upon by his enemies. These postwar months were thus a prolific period for the circulation of rumors dedicated to the Nazi–Fascist perception. Two of these rumors in particular proved to be marvelously durable in their attachment to Perón over the remainder of his life.

The first was the set of purported revelations in a book written by Silvano Santander and published in Montevideo in 1953, after the substance of the accusations had circulated for years as rumor. Santander, a furious anti-Peronist politician, alleged that both Perón and Evita had for a long time operated as paid Nazi agents, establishing a German outpost directly responsive to orders from Berlin. There were photostats of all sorts of official-looking documents said to come from Nazi archives, complete with seals and file numbers and the usual illegible bureaucratic notations. But the substance, not the form, of the charade gave it away. There were various impossibilities set down as hard facts; several checks payable to Perón and to Evita, identified by date and number, were said to have been delivered to them two and a half years before they met. Large sums were said to have been paid to Evita at times when she was still immersed in soap operas, without a political thought in her head. The German government in 1954 confirmed the absolute falsity of several of the key documents in the Santander volume.[17]

The second presumed exposé was also larger than life, a wildly inventive tale of the creation in Argentina of a "Fourth Reich," which would carry on the work of the Third Reich. The founders of this remarkable kingdom, according to the subsequently forged documents that were its only source, were Perón, Evita, and Martin Bormann, Hitler's close associate, whose ambiguous end in the death bunker in Berlin, or elsewhere, was ideally suited to a resurrection across the ocean. The noted Nazi hunter, Ladislas Farago, contributed to the obfuscation in a book written decades later.

The spirit in which Braden acted was also the spirit of the Latin American liberal leaders of that era, although their tactics were usually more refined. Liberal opinion in the United States, and to some extent south of the border, tended to take its cue from Romulo Betancourt, then president of the governing junta in Venezuela. His word carried enormous weight in liberal circles, and he considered Perón a ruthless rabble-rouser of Fascist tendencies and a menace to the continent. He made it quite clear to the American ambassador in Caracas shortly after Braden returned to Washington that he was all on the latter's side in the dispute with Perón. Betancourt, of course, had his own agenda in all this, since he was embattled with Perón's allies in the Caribbean area, inluding, above all, Rafael Trujillo in the Dominican Republic, whose hatred of Betancourt would lead a decade later to an attempted assassination. Betancourt's voice, however, was all the more influential for that reason, since his enemies were widely unpopular in the United States, and he helped to solidify the American stance.[18] Pepe Figueres, the president of Costa Rica, who was another trusted figure in the United States, held similar views, as did various lesser Caribbean leaders.

It was also true that Braden's course was abetted by considerable provocation, for Perón in the winter of 1945 was embattled on almost every side and at times said things that were chosen for their shock value rather than for rational dialogue. Thus on July 2, sixteen days before Braden's telegram, quoted above, Perón had given an interview to Pedro Cue, the editor of a leading paper in Havana, Cuba, in

Entrance to a typical ranch in Patagonia. Credit: AP/Wide World Photo.

Hipólito Yrigoyen, influential
political leader and twice
president of Argentina.

Domingo Faustino Sarmiento, distinguished author and
scholar and twice president of Argentina.

Juan Domingo Perón (left) with his brother Mario
Avelino and their mother, Juana Sosa Toledo de
Perón, ca. 1900. Credit: The Bettmann Archive, Inc.

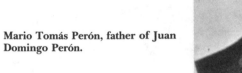

Mario Tomás Perón, father of Juan
Domingo Perón.

Juan Domingo Perón as a military cadet, 1911.

Perón at his inauguration for his first term as president, 1946.

An early stage of the huge mass meeting in the Plaza de Mayo in the afternoon and evening of the famous October 17, 1945. The Casa Rosada is to the left.

Perón, his second wife, Eva María Duarte de Perón ("Evita"), and a llama at Perón's country house at San Vicente, near Buenos Aires, October 1950. Credit: AP/Wide World Photos.

Perón and Evita before attending a gala celebration at the Colon Opera House, June 1951. Credit: AP/Wide World Photos.

Evita greeting the crowd at the Loyalty Day celebration in the Plaza de Mayo, October 17, 1951. Credit: AP/Wide World Photo.

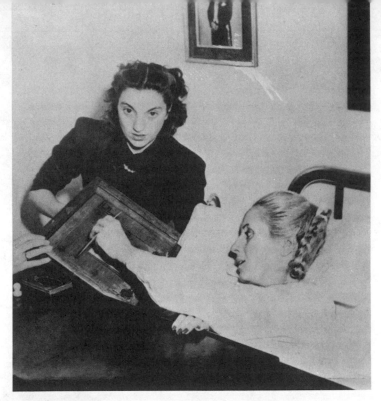

Evita casting her presidential ballot from her hospital bed, November 1951. Credit: AP/Wide World Photos.

Perón and Evita at Perón's inauguration for his second presidential term, May 1, 1952. At the left, Héctor Cámpora, president of the Chamber of Deputies and subsequently president of Argentina. Credit: AP/Wide World Photos.

Evita's funeral cortege, August 9, 1952. Soldiers salute as the gun carriage bearing the casket passes. Credit: AP/Wide World Photos.

which he had loosed a real blast, complete with references to civil war, "corpses in the streets," "workers armed with clubs," and his own preference for bloodshed.[19] There was much excess of this kind for Braden to contemplate during the winter months, and unfortunately his temperament reinforced his views rather than disciplining them, and he had little defense against the confusions around him.

It was an exceedingly complicated time for Perón, since his requirements all pointed in different directions. On the one hand, as he saw it, the internal unrest spreading on all sides required strong controls. Yet, on the other hand, there had to be liberal concessions to defuse the most urgent pressures. But the concessions should not be of a kind that would offend the necessary labor support or the nationalists, who were already very suspicious of Perón. Braden's attacks had to be countered, but, too, there should not be needless damage to the recent new relationship with the United States.

So the greatest delicacy of maneuver was called for, and the unceasing use of intuition and political instinct. The State of Siege that had smothered political life for the last three years was lifted on August 6.[20] Braden was assailed as an imperialist intruder, but in a controlled way that stopped short of raucous abuse. Provocative speeches to labor groups, dripping with class conflict, continued on a daily basis, but the oligarchy was not directly harmed. National elections were announced on July 6, to be held by the end of the year, with the clear statement of President Farrell that they would be completely free. There was something for everyone.

By July, there was another complication large enough to swallow all the others. Perón's presidential aspirations emerged as a clear fact of life, whatever verbal camouflage might still carry out the function of the fig leaf.

There was, of course, nothing so explicit as an announcement of Perón's candidacy, but it was apparent enough. Only six days after Farrell's announcement of forthcoming elections, a very large labor rally in downtown Buenos Aires featured the slogans and blown-up photographs and familiar shouts that are all part of a political campaign.[21] Twelve days after that, on July 24, Perón's followers introduced the theme of Perón as the successor of Yrigoyen, at a huge dinner in the Parque Retiro attended by some 2,000 to 3,000 " true soldiers of Yrigoyenism." A small core group interrupted the proceedings at an appropriate moment and insisted that the entire gathering proceed en masse to Perón's residence to pay their respects. Many hundreds did set off, escorted by mounted police who just happened to be on hand, waiting to be helpful. Around midnight, the walking column reached Perón's apartment on Posadas Street, and the reiterated cries of "Pe-rón, Pe-rón" brought the coy candidate to his balcony on the ninth floor. He had a microphone, by coincidence, and this had already been connected in the most spontaneous manner to a sound truck on the street, the vehicle bearing, again by pure coincidence, an illuminated sign reading, "Grand Act of Impartial and Valiant Democratic Reaffirmation of Yrigoyenism." A short address followed, indicating Peron's intention to follow the example of Yrigoyen.[22] Day by day, gatherings of all kinds now began to hasten this activity.

This kind of indirect campaigning went hand in hand with efforts, previously initiated and abandoned, to bring elements of the Radical Party into the fold. There were some successes, albeit modest ones. On August 2, J. Hortensio Quijano, a Radical of the second rank, was appointed to head the important interior ministry. At the end of the month, a more significant Radical, Juan Cooke, came aboard as Foreign Minister. A third Radical was brought into the Ministry of Finance. At the very least, these breakaways represented further fissures in the party, and the trend suggested to some that Perón might be trying to create a new version of the Radical Party, headed by himself.[23]

As excitement mounted, violence broke out in the streets, with riots, hundreds of injuries, the deaths of four students, and some 12,000 arrests. The police returned on August 17 and resumed their practice of breaking up unauthorized meetings as if the State of Siege were still in effect.[24]

In the midst of the turbulence that was confirming his worst fears and convictions, Ambassador Braden was recalled to Washington, but not before he had been honored by a mammoth banquet sponsored by the Argentine–American Cultural Institute at the elite Plaza Hotel on August 12. It was a memorable affair, gleaming and glittering, with the flags of the hemisphere, the cream of public and private life and the diplomatic corps, and a copy of George Washington's Farewell Address specially printed in Argentine and American colors at every plate. Eighteen hundred guests crowded into the great ballroom, the balcony that circled it, and the corridors adjacent. More than a thousand people were turned away for lack of space. Waves of emotion surged and reverberated as Braden assailed the government without mentioning it by name, employing every resource of sardonic contempt. Cries and shouts interrupted him. Women whose public roles had been limited to attendance at charity teas leaped to their feet, fanning the hot enthusiasm as if they were cheerleaders at a football game. It may well have been, as an Argentine historian has asserted, ". . . one of the most aggressive and insolent speeches that has ever been given by a diplomat in any country."[25]

Braden saw it differently. In a remarkable demonstration of illusion, he would write later, ". . . I should say that never, while in Argentina, did I criticize the government or any Argentine official. I did defend our record in World War II, and constitutional representative government."[26]

The ambassador's recall was related to yet another lurch in American policy. Stettinius and Rockefeller had both resigned. The new secretary of state, James Byrnes, announced immediately that he would entrust Latin American policy to Rockefeller's successor as assistant secretary and he appointed Spruille Braden to that position. Braden was eager to continue his struggle with Perón from the new vantage point. No ambassador was appointed to replace him in Buenos Aires, the embassy there being headed until further notice by the counsellor, John Moors Cabot.

A Brahmin from the famous Boston family, Cabot was tall, distinguished in appearance, and, along with Dean Acheson, would have been selected by any casting director as the archetypical diplomat. He was competent and levelheaded and much more balanced than Braden. But he, too, was caught up in the strong moods and shared convictions of the time. Some of the views presented to and passed on by the embassy were surely the undiscounted product of quite biased sources. The truth was confined to a handful far from the embassy, and Cabot had the uncomfortable assignment of reporting to Braden. Nevertheless, some of the embassy's conclusions during this period lead one to wonder. An analysis dated August 29 and based on a report submitted by a "qualified observer," but apparently adopted by the embassy, begins with the statement that "The 'civil war' threatened by Perón is on, although it is not as violent as expected. It has been precipitated by those politicians, workmen, students and intellectuals who have opposed Perón's policies and his presidential candidacy." It ends with the pronouncement that "Everything that has happened lately, including the defamatory campaign against Mr. Braden, strikes, demonstrations, et cetera, should be considered a chain of agitation instigated by Perón and his supporters." It would have taken some marvelously close reasoning to reconcile these conclusions, but the space between them contained only polemics such as "an S.S. corps in the Nazi manner . . . ," "fake labor unions . . . ," "Hitler style 'arbeitsfront' . . . ," "Perón and his mafia . . ."; the opinion of sane Argentines . . ." and so on, including the remarkable statement that although 30 percent of the army could be persuaded to rise against

Perón, their leaders are ". . . tied down under surveillance of the Federal Police, so that any attempt against the present dictatorship would be a failure, . . ." thus implying that the police had somehow taken over the country.[27]

On the same day, Cabot forwarded a long review that at least had the merit of candor: "Political currents have been so conflicting during this period [the last few weeks], many seeming to indicate that the position of Colonel Perón and his military regime has been weakened and others seeming to indicate the direct opposite, that perhaps the most serviceable manner of presenting a review of this nature will be to divide it into two sections expounding the two different points of view." Unfortunately, both sections of this remarkable document remain a memorial to the treachery of prophecy. Perón's greatest strength was said to be the absence of any serious opposition within the military, whereas, in fact, this was Perón's greatest weakness, it being the military that would come within a half inch of sending him into oblivion only six weeks later. His greatest strength, which was his appeal for the broad, anonymous labor masses, was entirely overlooked, and his standing with labor was listed as one of his greatest weaknesses. The hatred of the oligarchy, which was certainly part of his appeal to the general electorate, was indicated as a significant and surprising weakness.[28] A revolution in the political culture of Argentina was far along in gestation, and the embassy and the Department of State were responding with almost complete incomprehension.

One of the battlegrounds on which Perón was now engaged was, unlike many of the others, fully exposed to public view since the disputants carried on their conflicts by written and published charges and appeals. This was a running conflict with students and university groups, which mounted demonstrations and an appeal to the Supreme Court to withdraw recognition of the government and assume the executive power itself, pending elections. Perón spoke to the students on radio, but for once badly misjudged his rhetoric, receiving in turn from his audience a storm of colorful vituperation.[29]

The public agitation was so extreme as the winter wore on that it brought a development almost unprecedented, a spontaneous evolution toward a united front of most opposition elements. A democratic coordinating board was formed, headed by small groups of leading citizens, none of them politicians. The parties were generally cooperative, although no formulas for electoral ends were adopted. The Radicals, in their usual manner, debated the matter furiously and then limited the extent of their cooperation, specifically rejecting any thought of so infamous a thing as an electoral pact and vowing that they would never cooperate with those who were responsible for the corruptions between 1930 and 1943, meaning the conservatives. Despite the grudging response of the Radicals, whose intransigent wing never did join in, the concept of the board prevailed. Business interests, civic groups, students and prominent individuals from every class and sector flocked to the cause.[30]

The high point of the board's life was a gigantic demonstration held on September 19 and known as the "March of the Constitution and Liberty," in which several hundred thousand citizens paraded in opposition to Perón and to the government, their demands centering on early elections following the assumption of power by the Supreme Court.[31] Civilian elements had gone about as far as they could on their own, and they now began to collaborate with military leaders.

Everything would depend on the willingness of the armed forces to take a strong lead, and on their competence in doing so, and there was serious cause for concern on both points. As to the willingness to act, in the most basic sense it was present, but it was diluted by fundamental disagreement concerning the locus of state power in the period between the overthrow of Perón and the elections to follow. The civilian opposition had been arguing and demonstrating for some time in favor of a transfer of power to the Supreme Court during the interim period. A minority of military officers agreed. The great majority of the officer corps, on the other hand, wanted President Farrell to remain in office until his elected successor qualified. The basis for this latter view was largely psychological and intangible, since recourse to the Supreme Court in this unprecedented manner would imply an offense to military honor and dignity. It was almost impossible to fashion a coordinated movement when opinion was so divided on so important an immediate objective. Since the army officers who counted, that is, the officers who held the guns in the form of troop commands, were almost entirely in favor of retaining President Farrell and felt strongly about it, common sense would have seemed to indicate a concession on this point by the supporters of the Supreme Court.

The competence of the army in anything so ticklish as the overthrow of a well-defended regime was also dubious. There was no leader of conspicuous stature. Despite the variety of factions, and of voices to lead them, no one commanded the prestige to make them pull together. And there was ineptitude, pure and simple. Time and again, as events would soon demonstrate, officers who had spent years flirting with intrigue and cabal turned out to be careless, ingenuous, superficial, wretched judges of events, and indulgently over-optimistic in the moment of performance.

Much of this indictment is applicable to General Rawson, who began the sequence of events that rushed to the point of watershed in October. Rawson had strong connections with the Fourth Infantry Division, headquartered in Córdoba, and with its sympathetic commander, General Osvoldo Martín. Rawson's confidence extended to his belief in the support of the regimental commanders, and in the likelihood of a rising by other military centers, among which the great Campo de Mayo base would be the most significant. Rawson arrived at Córdoba on September 20[32] and was working out the final details of a coup on the night of the 24th. A proclamation was ready, inviting the president of the Supreme Court to take over the government. But the four-day interval had testified to a more cautious spirit at Córdoba than Rawson had anticipated and it was helpful to loyalist officers whose sentiments were apparently unsuspected by Rawson and Martín. Thus, during that climactic evening of the 24th, they voiced neither objection nor suspicion when a colonel and a lieutenant colonel asked permission to leave the meeting, explaining that they wanted time "to think things over." The two officers had already alerted and deployed the troops under their command; the two careless generals had not; and a bit later, when the former reappeared, they simply told the latter that they were under arrest. The Córdoba coup deflated like an untied baloon.[33]

Perón had feared an attempt of this kind at Córdoba and had intended to replace General Martín in any case. A new commanding general could therefore be dispatched within hours. Other officers were now put under arrest as the prelude to a major effort by Perón at political repression. The State of Siege was brought back on September 26, and under its umbrella arrests of hundreds of civilian leaders and opponents of Perón were carried out. They covered the full gamut—politicians, intellectuals, engineers, educators, lawyers, journalists, doctors. For the most part, they were held in very brief detention, particularly if they were prominent or influential, but the implications were clear enough, and not a few, fearing for the future, soon left Argentina lest they become seriously entangled in this novel authoritarianism. The universities, closed at first by strikes and then by official action, were the scenes of several thousand arrests. A rather imaginative penalty was invented for the women involved: there was no brutality, but their place of detention was the *Asilo San Miguel,* a prison for female moral delinquents, following the release of all the current inmates.[34]

When the military opposition was faced, it was the conciliatory Perón who did it. A military judge absolved Generals Rawson and Martín of any involvement in a revolutionary movement on the picturesque ground of "lack of evidence."[35] A bit of humor is always welcome in difficult times. But the placatory gesture was blown away in the stormy wind, and plotting within the armed forces accelerated. It was brought to the edge of mutiny by a rather implausible event in early October that seemed superficially less inflammatory than tedious.

On October 5, the appointment of a bureaucrat named Oscar Nicolini as director of postal services and telecommunications was announced. Nicolini was known to be a friend of Evita and of her family and his designation was widely perceived as a recompense for past favors. The army had a candidate of its own for the position and supported him strongly. The appointment was thus taken not only as a challenge to the army but also as a demeaning slap in the face. A popular army candidate was seen as victimized by a low boudoir intrigue. All of the simmering resentment of Evita and of Perón's flaunting of her began to boil.[36]

General Avalos, who had generally favored rather than resisted Perón, and who still retained his powerful position as commander of the Campo de Mayo garrison, took the lead in the confrontation that followed. He saw Perón on Saturday, the 6th, at the War Ministry and conveyed the army's distress. He saw Perón on the afternoon of the same day, at the Posadas Street apartment, with Evita present. The latter intervened in the discussion in a manner certain to given further offense. Perón refused to budge. There are various explanations for the conduct that brought him to this apparently needless conflict, but it is probable that he merely miscalculated. He now got his back up, as the army was doing. On Sunday, the agitation at Campo de Mayo ran so high that the base was put on alert, ready to march. Avalos did not back down, but he was clearly seeking a solution short of the ultimate one.[37]

On Monday the 8th, Perón's fiftieth birthday, the principal actors in the seething drama assembled in the War Ministry. Perón attacked the military interference in a governmental decision and was backed by his supporters. Avalos made some references to his own retirement, and repeated this at Campo de Mayo in the evening, but hotheads rejected the idea and urged an immediate march by the troops. Avalos, playing for time, delayed his decision.

His final maneuver, on Tuesday, October 9, took the form of an invitation to President Farrell to come to Campo de Mayo to judge the situation firsthand. At the War Ministry, Perón's aides developed contingency plans for armed resistance if the garrison should march. Perón refused to sign them.[38] What he wanted was not a solution by force, and certainly not a possibly bloody encounter, but rather a settlement that would open the way to an electoral triumph. Meanwhile, the president arrived at Campo de Mayo and was given the full treatment by a large assembly of officers that filled the dining room. Farrell gave ground slowly, suggested various solutions short of the complete resignation by Perón of all his offices that was now being demanded, but he was shouted down. Reluctantly, he gave way.

It was decided to send a small committee to take the news to Perón; this group included his old friend, General Juan Pistarini, and the interior minister, Dr. Horacio Quijano, who had been the only civilian at the Campo do Mayo gathering. The group left the base at half past three, with the understanding that if they did not return by eight in the evening, the restless garrison would put its columns on the road to Buenos Aires. General Pistarini volunteered to put the ultimatum to Perón alone, and it was done very quickly, at 5 P.M. As Perón recalled in an interview four years later, Pistarini began with some circumlocution, and Perón, interested only in Farrell's verdict, cut him off:

"What is the General's decision?

"He feels it advisable that you should resign."

Perón thereupon called his aide-de-camp and said, "Tell the officer in charge of the operation to stop all troop movements and order them back to their barracks. Bring me a sheet of paper on which to write out my resignation."

This was done. Perón wrote out in his own hand a short resignation of all his positions, signed it, and handed it to General Pistarini with the comment that he had written the document personally so that it would be clear that his hand had not trembled as he did so.[39]

Perón described his reaction later, in a mood doubtless more philosophical than the one that oppressed him on that famous 9th of October: "That chapter of my life was thus closed and I gave thanks to God that this had been permitted without the sacrifice of one single human life . . . I called the members of my staff and embraced every one of these noble friends of mind, and then left quietly to enter upon what I imagined would be a bright and smiling future."[40]

Perón's fortune on this bitter day might have been worse, and very nearly was. He had been scheduled to visit the War Academy that morning but was diverted by the rush of dramatic events at the War Ministry. If he had kept to his schedule, he would have encountered at the War Academy a group of more than thirty captains with drawn pistols, waiting to assassinate him.[41]

At the Posadas Street apartment that night the chill of defeat was palpable. Evita was in tears. Perón had changed into a seedy, red smoking jacket that contrasted oddly with his army pants, and did little to lighten the funereal atmosphere that had closed in around the hosts and the visitors who came and went. Everything seemed lost. And no wonder, for an objective appraisal of the situation was bleak indeed. The opposition to Perón that was now triumphant included the most powerful military center in the country, many other army officers, all of the navy, the university students and the educational hierarchies, the intellectuals, the political left in the form of the Socialists and the Communists, the political right embodied in the conservatives and the strong nationalists, the political center that encompassed the Radicals and lesser party leaders, the business community, the oligarchy, and the vast majority of the press. In this crushing front of opposition, it was hard to discern any possible sources of support apart from the CGT and labor. The police still supported him in Buenos Aires and in the provinces, and various army officers spotted here and there remained loyal, but all of these could be annulled in seconds by the signature of a decree or order. What Perón really had in his favor was the devotion of anonymous hundreds of thousands on a psychological level whose depth was still quite uncomprehended; and the equally profound devotion of his small band of allies, including Evita and Mercante; and his own will and ability. And one thing more: he had the marvelous advantage of being one, while his incompetent enemies were many.

What was soon to become a full countereffort by Perón was heralded by Quijano, the interior minister, less than an hour after Perón wrote out his resignation. Quijano released an announcement at six o'clock that was promptly carried on national radio, an adroit distortion that turned black into white and defeat into a noble gesture. He began by stating that the cabinet had that morning decided to call for elections next April, and he continued:

"The vice president of the Republic, Colonel Perón, . . . entered into a commitment with himself, signifying as well a commitment to the people of the Republic and to the armed forces, to resign all his current functions as soon as the Executive Power decided to call for elections. Anticipating that the decree will be issued in two days, Colonel Perón has given his resignation as vice president, as Minister of War, and as Secretary of Labor and Welfare. I leave to the opinion of the press and to public sentiment any commentary on his attitude, which in a civic sense dignifies the country because it is an expression of his own dignity; and dignifies the army because it is also an expression of its finest virtues."[42]

It was outrageous to the officers at Campo de Mayo, but it was very effective, in large part because it mirrored the values of the ethos.

It would be inconceivable for such an announcement in an Anglo-Saxon society to appeal to dignity in this direct and almost romantic manner, but the invocation here was of the Hispanic dignity that is a spiritual force on its own high plane, and the entire tone of the announcement was Creole to the core. It was cut from the same cloth as the equally successful (and, to a foreigner, equally curious) phrase that became highly visible in later years under the Peronato: "Perón Performs: Evita Dignifies."

On this same night, Perón rallied sufficiently amid the dolor and the untasted cold buffet in his apartment to consult with Mercante concerning demonstrations or a general strike that might be called. These discussions continued on Wednesday, with the inclusion of other labor leaders, as General Avalos was being sworn in as war minister. In the afternoon, Perón, with a flash of presumption and genius, called President Farrell to ask permission to address his staff and followers at the secretariat of labor and welfare and to have his remarks carried on the national radio network. Farrell had no desire to alter the willing compliance that never seemed to fail him, and he agreed.[43] The speech was given at seven o'clock in the evening to a mass assembly of about 70,000 workers and others who overflowed the streets in front of the Secretariat, an impressive performance on very short notice by obviously well-organized labor leaders.

Perón was all himself on this crucial occasion. The speech was one of his best. For the most part it was calm rather than belligerent, and he followed the lead of Quijano's press release in explaining what had happened. He reviewed the work of his Ministry, referred to pending measures for wage and salary increases and profit sharing that he was leaving incomplete, and invoked broad visions of the future: "And now, as a citizen, departing from public duties and leaving this building which has such pleasant memories for me, I want to express once more the firmness of my faith in a perfect democracy, such as we understand here. Within that democratic faith we have taken our indomitable and incorruptible position against the oligarchy. We believe that the workers should rely upon themselves, and we affirm that the emancipation of the working classes lies in the individual worker. We are pledged to a battle that we will win because history is advancing in that direction. One must have faith . . . we will prevail in one year or in ten, but we will prevail. For that task, which is sacred for me, I place myself as of today at the service of the people."

And he combined the plea for order and the hint of force in a manner worthy of one in whom many personalities coexist: "I ask for order, that we may continue on our triumphant march: but if it is necessary, some day I will ask for war." And he added the sentimental touches. "I am not going to say good-by . . . because from now on I will be among you, closer than ever." In sum it was, as the United States embassy noted, ". . . not a swan song but his first address as a presidential candidate."[44]

The effects of this agile performance were substantial, both on the general public and on the armed forces, which responded with rage. Furious debates resounded at the *Circulo Militar* the next day, October 11. Delegations came and went, groups and committees met and dissolved. A similar high, brittle tension suffused a long meeting of the democratic coordinating board, where folly prevailed. The board could not rid itself of its obsession with a transfer of power to the Supreme Court. Never mind that all the dominant forces in the army, beginning with Avalos, rejected this alternative more firmly than ever; never mind that the court was seen as a hostile and reactionary body by the labor elements that would have to be placated; never mind that by law the court could serve only as a short bridge to elections that were already scheduled; never mind that the power of the court would have to be exercised by its president, a respected jurist whose entire life had been spent amid bone-dry opinions and footnotes, a man whose knowledge of political crisis management was that of a well-chaperoned schoolgirl. Never mind reality. The board insisted on the Supreme Court. So it lost everything.

October 17

As the intensity of public agitation increased, threats on Perón's life began to be rumored. He had no peace, in any case, in the Posadas Street apartment, with the endless comings and goings, and he thought it time now to leave the city. Toward midnight, accompanied by Evita and Juan Duarte and by the son of his long-time friend, Ludwig Freude, he drove off at the wheel of Freude's car. Mercante bid him an anxious farewell. Among the suggestions that had bubbled up during the last few days was the idea that Perón might leave the country. Now, Mercante asked, "You're not going to go, are you? We're going to keep on with the game?"

"We sure are," Perón responded.

The group spent the night at the home of a friend. The next day, the 12th, was the *Día de la Raza*, the Day of the Race, the Hispanic race, a holiday that corresponds to Columbus Day in the United States. Perón celebrated it by moving with Evita to a rather romantic destination. Several miles northwest of Buenos Aires, near the point where the Paraná River meets the Uruguay River to form the Río de la Plata, there is a cluster of small islets reached by boat from the town of Tigre, on a small tributary. These little islands, green and mysterious in their dense foliage, quiet and otherworldly, hushed in the shimmering heat of midday, are linked one to another by an almost impenetrable labyrinth of narrow waterways, as if the forms of Venice had been superimposed on the Garden of Eden. Here Ludwig Freude had a summer cottage, rustic and alone, and here Perón and Evita came by launch in the early morning hours of the *Día de la Raza*.

In Buenos Aires there was no such bucolic scene. The public fever rose. Mercante met with several score labor leaders to urge the calling of a general strike. The police clashed with civilian demonstrators. General Avalos and President Farrell, sensitive to the tumult and the demands that were issuing from the unending debates at the *Circulo Militar,* decided that the cabinet should resign and that Perón should be put under arrest, for his own protection if for no other reason. The order went to the new Chief of Police, Colonel Mittelbach, basically a supporter of Perón but unable to help him much at this moment. Mittelbach learned from Mercante where he could find Perón and took a launch from Tigre to the little island in the fading light of late day. Perón was near the dock, embracing Evita, as he approached.

Mittelbach explained the reason for the arrest and for his request that Perón accompany him back to Buenos Aires. Perón asked where he would be taken and responded with disgust when Mittelbach replied that he would be held on a naval ship, or possibly on Martín García, the island in the estuary where Yrigoyen had been incarcerated fifteen years before. Naval custody was bad news, and Perón asked for army detention. It would be up to Farrell. They all returned to Perón's apartment, arriving after midnight, Evita struggling with her tears. Farrell refused to change the custody arrangements, and an officer arrived to take Perón to a naval vessel. He was given time to shave, while Mercante brought him up to date on the latest labor developments. Then the men left, about three in the morning, Perón literally breaking Evita's fierce hold as he entered the elevator, leaving her sobbing in the hallway.[45]

Perón boarded the ship, a gunboat, in the rainy predawn. Mercante was there, and Perón's last word to him was a request that he look after Evita. Mercante remembered years later that a young sailor had been standing guard nearby, with tears running down his face, and he remembered his own sense of relief: "At that moment I felt a great tranquility, for I knew then with perfect clarity that we were going to win the game."[46]

The ship headed for Martín García Island, where Perón would have a few days of anxious respite. But there would be no break in the tortured political process in Buenos Aires. Avalos and Farrell struggled with the government, one of their efforts being a request to Juan Alvarez, a respected and traditional figure then serving as Attorney General, that he put together an interim government.[47] Meanwhile, the country remained without a cabinet; the executive authority consisted of General Avalos as war minister and acting interior minister together with Admiral Vernengo Lima as navy minister. Even this abbreviated authority was exercised with a restraint that seems heedless in retrospect, marked by the failure to move rapidly and effectively against Peronist elements that remained.

On October 13, also, Mercante continued to rally the labor leaders as best he could, but he was put under arrest in the afternoon and confined to Campo de Mayo. The liaison that he had been maintaining with the CGT labor leaders became the responsibility of a few colleagues in the middle and lower levels of the labor ministry's bureaucracy.

On the 13th and 14th, Perón wrote several letters from his captivity on the island. One was to Avalos, inquiring as to the offense for which he had been arrested and asking to be tried in accordance with the law or to be set free. Another was to President Farrell, requesting prompt action on his retirement application and a transfer to Buenos Aires on the ground of health. A third letter, to Evita, has been lost. The fourth and fifth letters, to Mercante and to Evita, are of unusual interest, since they were written for hand delivery in the most private of contexts, without any posturing or political stage setting, and without any expectation of publication. If there is any path to be traced through the forest of Peron's enigmas and complexities, it must be with the aid of such guideposts as these.

To Mercante he indicated his indignation at the naval detention imposed on him, for he thought he had Mittelbach's promise that he would be put under army arrest when he returned from Freude's island. If Mittelbach had promised, he could not deliver, since Farrell had refused to intervene. "When I arrived here," Perón wrote, "I knew what value to place on the word of honor of those men. Nevertheless, I have what they don't have: a loyal friend and a woman who loves me and whom I adore. I command more than they do, because I live in many humble hearts." And a little later, with more than a touch of self-sympathy, he wrote, "Ingratitude is the luxuriant flower of our times. It is overcome by the eternal values, and God has distributed those only as a tiny proportion of the vices. Virtue increases with suffering, and sorrow is its teacher, we hope that God will compensate it, since men are perfidious and traitorously unjust."

There was very little about the workers and their agitations, merely a passing sentence. He obviously had no expectation of any massive demonstration just over the horizon. In some passages he was philosophical: "Everything considered, I'm content that not a single man was killed on my account, and with having avoided violence. Now they've lost all possibility of avoiding it, and I have the greatest fears that something serious will come about."

There were glimpses of his mental pressures. "What's troubling me is that I can't sleep. My nerves have been in crisis during those last two years of such intense sensations, and I'm beginning today to get rid of all the tensions . . . I'm calming down bit by bit." And there was concern about Evita. "I entrust Evita to you, very much, because the poor little thing has broken nerves and I'm preoccupied by her health. As soon as they give me my retirement I'm going to get married and everything else can go to the devil."

The letter to Evita, except for a few references to the possibility of legal steps to be taken, was a long declaration of love.

My adored treasure:
Only when we are separated from loved ones can we measure our affection. From the day that I left you there with the greatest sorrow that can be imagined, I haven't been able to soothe my troubled heart. Today I know how much I love you and that I can't live without you. This immense solitude is filled with your memory.
I've written today to Farrell asking him to hurry up my retirement, as soon as I get out we'll get married and we'll go somewhere else and live quietly . . . please tell Mercante to speak to Farrell to see if they'll let me alone and the two of us will go to Chubut.
You ought to be quiet and take care of your health while I'm away . . . I'll be tranquil if I know that you're not in any danger and that you feel well . . . if the retirement comes through, we'll get married the next day and if it doesn't come I'll arrange things in some other way, but we'll end this unprotected situation you're in now.
Little sweetheart of my soul, I have your little pictures in my room and I look at them all day, with tears in my eyes. Nothing must happen to you because then my life would end. Take good care of yourself and don't worry about me, but love me lots because now I need it more than ever . . . my treasure, keep calm and learn to hope. All this will end and life will be ours. With what I have done I am justified before history, and I know that time will prove me right.
My last words in this letter are that I want you to stay calm and tranquil. Many, many kisses and remembrances for my beloved chinita.[48]

Most of these letters were delivered through Perón's personal physician, Captain Mazza, who was free to visit him on the island and who served as the only means of communication during the four days that Perón spent on Martín García.

While Perón was thus on the sidelines, Evita did what she could, which was not much; She looked for legal assistance, with no success. The romantic imagination of Peronists later attributed to her the ordering of events and the resurrection of the political Perón as she roamed the great city, preaching, exhorting, begging, rallying the dubious, holding the cause aloft single-handedly. Perón himself contributed his nostalgia to this version,[49] but it is a leaky vessel. The Evita of three or four years later could have done much of it, but the Evita of 1945 was untested, known to the gritty labor leaders and to most others only as the disrespected mistress of a military adventurer who had overreached himself. Her clout can be estimated from the fact that when Perón had resigned on the 9th, she had been fired by Radio Belgrano within hours, even though she was then in the middle of a role.[50]

Captain Mazza continued his lobbying to have Perón returned to the mainland. Labor agitation increased inexorably and was cropping up in the interior cities. The CGT leadership met on the 16th and called a strike for midnight on the 18th. Cipriano Reyes took the lead for the Peronist forces at the moment, visiting factories and labor centers in the industrial belt between Buenos Aires and La Plata and urging a march on Buenos Aires. On the 16th, the first signs of such a movement were discerned; workers bypassed or filtered through police lines and entered the city in small numbers, demonstrating here and there.[51]

Much as the government and the private sector wished to avoid any confrontation of the kind now looming, they both helped materially to bring it about. The new secretary of labor and welfare took to the air on the 13th to outline the labor policies that would now prevail. His evenhandedness and certain assurances to employers more than offset his insistence that labor's recent gains would be maintained. The speech was all very fine in the abstract, but it was the work of a political innocent who failed to realize that his words would be judged against a background of rumors, now widespread, that labor would lose everything because Perón had fallen. Even the *Día de la Raza* had contributed to this impression; Perón had recently signed a measure that would provide full pay on such a holiday, but the workers lining up at the pay windows after the 12th found that various employers had a ready reply when the workers requested the day's pay: "Go and ask Perón for it."[52]

And so, on the 16th, the little trickles of marchers began very slowly to grow and coalesce. Captain Mazza, too, did his part. He had by now convinced Farrell, on the basis of an out-of-date X-ray, that Perón had a health problem that required his removal to Buenos Aires. Two doctors were sent to Martín García to verify the claim, and Perón, tipped off by Mazza, refused to be examined. The tactic prevailed, and in the evening the order came to transfer Perón to the Military Hospital in Buenos Aires. He was taken there by boat at half past two on the morning on the 17th, arriving at the hospital four hours later. A thousand workers were soon demonstrating in front, a small sampling of the throngs that by now were at large in the city seeking him. Perón was given the chaplain's suite and relaxed in his blue pajamas while the Argentine world changed around him.

He talked with Evita by telephone, but did not ask her to come to his suite, which was the center of continuing consultations and calls, for a policy and program had to be improvised on the edge of the moment. Mercante was released at noon from his arrest and went to join Perón. It was the strangest of hours. By now the city was paralyzed. In the shops the iron shutters had been lowered, and the trains had ceased to flow in from the pampas and the littoral. A great quiet prevailed, mysterious, almost eerie, as if fate were holding its hand for a brief time. To Ernesto Sábato, the writer, it was as if "an enormous and silent force, almost subterranean, had been put in motion."[53] In the background, hour after hour, the great city heard only the shuffle and murmur of the columns of marching workers, coming together, breaking apart, seeking information, moving restlessly, penetrating every interstice, probing, looking for Perón. By bridge, by boat, by wading they crossed the Riachuelo, the little stream turned drainage ditch that separates the city from the industrial suburbs and towns to the south. They offered no challenge or ill will to the police and received none. They simply moved on, like a force of nature, until gravity or happenstance brought them to a focus in the Plaza de Mayo, facing the Casa Rosada. There they remained, uncounted, unkempt thousands, milling about peacefully, shouting their demand to see Perón, wading occasionally in the elegant fountains and pools for relief from the heat of the humid spring day, now pressing together, now flowing outward as more thousands were deposited by strange tidal forces.

The military commanders at Campo de Mayo felt an urgency that contrasted oddly with the bemusement prevailing at the Casa Rosada. The commanders wanted to take steps of some kind, of any kind, and they knew that time was vital, but they would do nothing without the approval of General Avalos, and he could not be reached. And when he could be, he was indecisive, the picture of a man hoping that a solution would descend from above, meanwhile rejecting violence above all else. He had believed all along that the sentiment for Perón would crest and decline, and when it did not, it was too late. In any case, no violence was being perpetrated and therefore none could be rationalized as a defense; and he would not shed blood without extreme provocation. So he chose to preside over the end of an era and the termination of his career.

Late in the afternoon, Perón's representatives and Avalos were approaching agreement. Avalos asked Perón to speak to the multitude, to insure calm, but Perón refused, judging the time premature for his purposes because he knew that more thousands were quietly arriving at the mighty rendezvous. Farrell had by now entered the discussions and by 9 P.M. an agreement was reached: Perón's terms were accepted, including the resignation of the present partial cabinet and the formation of an interim government consisting entirely of his supporters. And Perón would speak from the balcony of the Casa Rosada. The triumph was sealed at a conference between Farrell and Perón at the presidential residence, at 9:45. Mercante, who deserved to be in at the final victory, had just been hospitalized by a stomach ulcer. And a triumph it certainly was, for now Perón had what he had sought for two years: not the top position, but a chance to achieve the presidency in an election, and a favorable context for that election in the form of sufficient influence over a government basically loyal to him.

And just now, at the moment an epoch was passing, its epitaph was traced in a symbolism that combined irony and pathos. Juan Alvarez, the attorney general who had been asked to propose a civilian cabinet, emerged from his study after several days of intense labor with a list of names resurrected from the 1930s, apparently unaware that the world personified by the list had disappeared while he was conferring. Now, at 8:30 P.M., he had his secretary deliver it to the Casa Rosada, where it was received with polite incredulity.[54] A passenger on the *Titanic* was requesting a return reservation at the exact moment the iceberg was glimpsed.

At eleven o'clock, Perón and Farrell stepped onto the balcony, setting off an ovation and a frenzy that lasted fifteen minutes. The crowd by this time had acquired immense but unmeasurable dimensions. It was all around in the dim light of the plaza, seen and unseen, bounded here and there by flickering torches, shaped by palm tree and fountain, choking side streets that could barely be discerned, stretching into the darkness far beyond eyesight, apprehended only through sound. Half a million people were there, some have said. Perhaps there were between 250,000 and 300,000.

Farrell moved to the microphone to quiet the roaring sound so that Perón could speak, but Perón stopped him. "No, let them shout . . ." Farrell eventually introduced him, and Perón began by asking that the national anthem be sung, a suitable device that gave him time to collect his thoughts, for he had no prepared text and no notes on this most impromptu and spontaneous of all nights. When he spoke, it was not at great length. He noted that his resignation from the army had been accepted that day, and he made a moving reference to the values and ideals of the military life. He would now don civil attire and join with "that suffering and sweaty mass that creates with its work the greatness of the nation." He asked for an indestructible brotherhood of the workers, the army, and the police, "a spiritual unity of the true and authentic forces of nationality and order." He spoke of peace and construction, of faith in the future, of dignity. He spoke of patriotism, linking it to brotherhood, "because to love one's country is not to love its fields and houses but to love one's brothers." He spoke of his love for the workers, his desire to mingle with them and press them to his breast as he would his mother, and his injunction to them to unite: "Upon the brotherhood of those who labor we must construct in this beautiful land the unity of all Argentines." He remembered to greet the workers in the interior, and to remind the mass in the plaza to protect the women workers present when the occasion ended.

Even these excerpts, however, give a sense of continuity to the speech that it lacked in life, because it was a speech only in part. It was also to some extent a dialogue, for Perón was interrupted by shouts of "Where were you?" and the like, and the immense assembly took on the unlikely aspect of a town meeting.[55]

The spontaneous, living-room quality of this extraordinary event was in fact one of the keys to its real significance. It was not a typical political harangue, with loud and easy promises handed out to an audience clamoring for more. It was not a mass uprising aimed at taking over the state. There was nothing revolutionary or threatening about it. Neither Perón nor those who heard him mentioned tangible benefits for the workers. The essence of the day and of its unique culmination was not political and certainly not economic, but in a sense religious. The workers traipsing the streets were looking not for trouble but, literally, for Perón. They wanted to see him, and to be reassured. At the vast night assembly in the plaza, they were passionately concerned with Perón's presence but only incidentally interested in his speech. Hence the many questions uttered from the darkness were not ideological or political but personal. The speech itself was, for the most part, abstract, appealing to idealism and to the large themes like brotherhood that verge upon the religious. The event was an act of public and almost mystic communion between leader and followers, on a scale whose equal does not come to mind.

Although the night of October 17 was a political event of the first magnitude, certifying Peronism as the predominant political faith in Argentina for many years to come, it was thus in its essence less a political phenomenon than a spiritual one. What was political in it was made possible by what was in a broad sense religious. It was a night of epiphany.

It is therefore perhaps fortunate that the night was attended by a strange incongruity. Here was a supreme moment in the national history, the most critical in Perón's life. He spoke to hundreds of thousands in person and to millions over the radio network. Yet there is no text or written transcript of his exact speech, no recording of it, and no photograph of him or of his audience as he gave it. Several versions of the speech exist, from one of which the quotations given above were taken, but they all date from after the event. Thus the words and the night were freed of literal constraint and ascended all the more easily into the realm of faith, where they have remained to this day.[56]

The reasons for the enormous success of October 17, both at the time and subsequently in the Argentine collective memory and imagination, are easy to discern. The events that began on October 9, with Perón's temporary fall were inherently dramatic, irresistably so to a nation in which politics are so preeminent. But an important facet in the legendry of October 17 must surely be the accord between those events and the Argentine civilization. So many of the Creole values and sentiments were embedded in the scenario of October. There was the *caudillo* theme, for Perón no less than Rosas and Yrigoyen was in the *caudillo* tradition of the leader who embodies the popular aspirations and leads his people by force or strength and by psychological identification with them. There was all the personalism of Hispanic inheritance, for the tale of that night was of a complete and exclusive personal affinity. The mystic overtones were a reminder of the quasi-religious style of Yrigoyen. The format of the assembly, with its aspect

of dialogue or open questioning, was a many-times-magnified variation of one of the oldest of Spanish colonial customs, the *cabildo abierto,*
the ancient, open town meeting bringing together municipal authorities and parts of the citizenry. The emphasis upon idealism in Perón's
words was in the tradition of Creole political discourse. The theme of
brotherhood that he stressed was reminiscent of organic social visions
from the sixteenth century. The guidance that he gave to the workers
in some of his sentences was tutelary in spirit, patronal and even
patriarchal, and could have been addressed equally well to an audience of peasants in old Castile. His care and concern for the dignity
of the workers touched one of the mainsprings of the civilization. It
was all very Hispanic, very Argentine, quintessentially Creole. And
effective beyond measure.

The Presidency Attained

After the epiphany, the direct route to the elections of 1946 was
open. But only after marriage. Perón sincerely desired this, and it
would have been necessary even if he had not. Even a politician with
his indifference to social convention could not face an election in
Argentina while living openly with a mistress.

The ceremony was celebrated on October 23 at the Posadas Street
apartment, sheltered by the kind of privacy that usually attends a conspiracy. Other than Perón and Evita and the clerk who came from
Junín with his documents, only three persons were present: Mercante, Juan Duarte, and a friend of Evita. There was no publicity of
any kind. What there was, instead, was a bit of tampering with the
official documents, since many of the statements in the marriage record
were at variance with known facts. The most serious of these misde-
meanors had been committed by Evita earlier in 1945, in a caper that
revealed her sensitivity and insecurity: she had caused the documents
in the registry at Los Toldos to be falsified so that she could now
claim, in her marriage contract, to have been born in 1922, rather
than in 1919.

But her reason for such a drastic step had nothing to do with her
age. Rather, it was her desire to appear in the records as having been
born legitimately. For this purpose an elaborate scheme was con-
cocted that must have come with a price tag. Her birth certificate was
torn out of the Los Toldos register and destroyed. Then a child had
to be found who had been born about the same time and had died
soon after. Such a child was identified, in the listings for 1922, and
Evita's name and statistics were substituted in the record by an elabo-

rate forgery. But a problem remained. The records referred to the marriage date of the infant's parents, and there was no way around this but to invent a marriage certificate for Doña Juana and her lover, Juan Duarte, under a number that would have come (if it had ever existed) at the end of a volume, so that it might be assumed to have fallen out during binding. All this required that a large register of records be disassembled, doctored by forgery, and reassembled and rebound, and that a back-up volume filed in La Plata be destroyed. Thus the illegitimate Eva Ibarguren, born in 1919, metamorphosed into the legitimate Eva Duarte, born in 1922.[57] It is an interesting revelation of an intense private agony. And an interesting commentary on the sometimes uneasy relationship between *viveza* and the formalisms of the most legalistic of societies. Some years later the town clerk at Los Toldos, who had not been involved, found out about the tampering and protested. Although Evita was no longer living, he was removed from his job by the Peronist government that spoke of social justice.[58]

The religious ceremony was held at a church in La Plata on December 10. Again there was no publicity and no time for a honeymoon. "Politics was the romance of our honeymoon."[59] This was the definitive date of the rebirth of Evita. The actress was now gone forever. Her pictures and publicity materials were recalled from the studios. Photographers yielded their negatives. Her last movie, still unreleased, was handed over to her as a present and was never shown. A pervasive obscurity that was to deepen with time began to enfold the facts and the memories of her early days. She was now the wife of a presidential candidate.[60]

For Perón, who had no previous political machinery to reactivate, everything had to be constructed from the ground up. Even the labor support, which would obviously have to form the foundation of his campaign, would have to be handled with organizational delicacy, for the adoration of the working rank and file was not yet unanimously reflected among union officials. This seems strange in retrospect, but it reflects the reality in 1945 that most of the union leaders, while appreciative of Perón and friendly to his cause, were not yet unconditionally committed to him and still expected to use him, rather than the reverse.

This was illustrated by the circumstances surrounding the birth of the Labor Party, which appeared in time for the elections. The decision to form it was taken on October 6, only four days after the decree that legitimized such an effort. Although the twenty-four leaders who attended the founding meeting, held at the Labor and Welfare Secretariat, were supportive of Perón, they did not inform him of their meeting or their purpose, and twenty-two of them vowed to proceed with their new party along the lines of the Labour Party in Britain, with or without Perón. They shared a lingering suspicion that Perón, who was known to have been negotiating with members of the Sabattini wing of the Radical Party, might yet make some deal behind their backs. Then came October 17 and new impetus for a permanent labor party in national politics. The initiative of October 6 was absorbed into a broader effort.[61] The result was a meeting of about fifty labor leaders on October 24 and the formal creation of the Labor Party.[62] The president of its governing committee was Luis Gay, a longtime labor leader sympathetic to Perón, and the vice president was Cipriano Reyes, who was, of course, more than sympathetic. The United States embassy, still believing that the Socialist and Communist leaders spoke for labor, referred to the committee members as ". . . collaborationist labor leaders of relatively little prestige in their own circles and of no political prestige whatever."[63]

The Labor Party would provide one base of support, but another would be necessary to appeal to more traditional elements. Perón found this in the small band of Radicals that had come over with Hortensio Quijano. The strategy here was to retain as much as possible of the Radical Party's name and mystique. The breakaway elements now gone over to Perón could not hope to capture the party, for the mainstream of Radicalism, embodied in the orthodox national committee that derived from the old Alvear wing, was too firmly anti-Peronist. So was the Sabattini, or intransigent, wing that derived from Yrigoyen. But even though Perón's negotiations with the latter had not been fruitful, it might be possible to make inroads through the narrow breach that Quijano had opened up.

The Quijano forces organized under the name of *Unión Cívica Radical Junta Reorganizadora,* the UCR Renovating Board, or UCRJR.[64] Quijano headed the organization, which attempted to duplicate to the extent possible the structure of the Radical Party itself. Its principles, advanced in the name of Yrigoyen and his ideals, were those of social justice as defined by Peronism.

The Labor Party and the UCRJR were very uneasy partners, separated by traditions, by social class, by speech and customs, by almost everything, in fact, except by support of the man who headed their respective electoral tickets. United on Perón and on the broad principles of Peronism, they disagreed heartily on all the nuts and bolts, and particularly on the selection of joint candidates for the various provincial offices. Perón was wise to keep these two unlikely collaborators as distinct from each other as possible, rather than uniting them in a formal structure. He reserved for himself the arbitration of their many differences.

There were several other sources of support for Perón. FORJA, the left-leaning group of young activists, had already disbanded, but many of its leaders and enthusiasts now became Peronists. The ardent nationalists, often rebuffed by Perón and often hostile, now drifted in his direction for want of any other appealing destination, and because they were against many of the things that Perón opposed. Their hot-headed cutting edge, the Nationalist Liberation Alliance, or ALN, joined in now with a kind of paramilitary zeal.

But these forces available to Perón were dwarfed by those massed in opposition to him. The United States embassy reported correctly that "It is simple to say 'the opposition'; it is difficult to describe it. On paper it is impressive: all of the old-line political parties, the over-whelming majority of financial, industrial, commercial, and agricul-tural interests, practically all professional men, most of the intellectuals, a great majority of the middle class, practically all of the responsible press, etc." But, the embassy added, ". . . the opposition is fatally lack-ing in leadership, organization and cohesion."[65]

The vehicle that was set up to coordinate and unite this aggrega-tion was the *Unión Democratica,* or Democratic Union, the UD, a team of marvelously strange bedfellows headed by the Radical Party, and particularly by its main wing. The Radicals recruited into this alliance the Socialists, the Communists, and the small Progressive Democratic Party. The Conservatives and the Radicals were too deeply mired in ancient feuds to permit any formal cooperation now.

Leadership was a serious problem for the UD. The Radicals insisted on José Tamborini as the presidential candidate, and the other parties had to concur. Tamborini had long experience in government but little general appeal and no magnetism whatsoever. The United States Embassy, in one of its strange assessments, described him as having ". . . the general appearance and rather less than the intelligence of a tame teddy bear."[66] This was unfair to his mentality, for he was a very cultivated man, devoted to literature and the arts, and an accom-plished public servant. Nor was it entirely accurate as to his physical qualities. He was rather too large and rough-hewn for a teddy-bear, with a face that has been described as coarse and bloated, and yet possessed of ". . . a certain beautiful ugliness."[67] Beauty of spirit he certainly had, together with a high-pitched, reedy voice that seemed in strange contrast to his craggy bulk.

But Tamborini's main problem was neither mental nor physical; it

was his dullness, his lack of excitement and charisma, and the stale-
ness of the themes that the UD developed. Nevertheless, looking at
the disparity of the forces mustered behind the two candidates, it was
difficult to avoid the conclusion that the victory of the UD was almost
inevitable.

Much would depend on the course adopted by the interim government, and that seemed almost schizophrenic.[68] On the one hand, the
army itself, as an institution, played no partisan role in the events
about to unfold, and the interior ministry, which was in charge of the
police and the federal interventors in the provinces and hence had
the major responsibilities, was as scrupulously impartial as could be
expected. The army officers who headed this ministry imposed a cri-
terion of strict official neutrality and free and honest balloting. The
federal interventors were called in and given strict instructions to permit no political activity by provincial employees.[69]

On the other hand, the ministry of labor and welfare under Mercante was a stronghold of vivid partisanship. Under this strident
direction, the ministry placed at the service of the Peronist campaign
all the considerable resources of its national network of offices and
agents and all the skill of its political policy-making.

It was generally appreciated that this election would be a landmark, that it would point a course as few elections do. Coming after a
long period of either false ballots or none at all, and in a world setting
that had been remade by war, and amid internal developments and
pressures that were entirely novel, the choice now before the nation
was clearly of unusual significance. Time past and time future were
being fused into time present.

It was inevitable that the campaign would be emotional, intense,
and brittle, and all the more so because the psychic waves generated
on October 17 continued to reverberate. The tone that pervaded
Buenos Aires was best interpreted by a visitor, Jorge Mañach, a Cuban
writer, journalist and one-time minister, who interviewed Perón on
November 6. Mañach, a man of exquisite insight and perception,
approached the Argentina of late 1945 with admirable detachment
and fairness of mind, but noted the fears palpable in the press, the
political parties, the universities, and in the upper and middle classes,
"who felt themselves circumvented and beaten . . . these days the air
of Buenos Aires is full of the tang of civil strife; the atmosphere is
charged with rancor and forbodings . . . a state of the highest tension."[70]

For the stakes and the passions were immense, and between
Peronists and anti-Peronists there were differences and mutual

imcomprehensions of almost infinite depth, as if the Great Rift extended down to the center of the globe. Each side believed that its survival was in some way at issue. Each side fought for its principles in the spirit of Armageddon, for idealism of almost religious intensity was as much involved as was self-interest. Strangely, the principles were the same on each side—liberty and freedom—but they were defined in such different terms that they were unrecognizable to each other. For the anti-Peronists, freedom and liberty meant the traditional and constitutional civil rights, unhampered by the State of Siege and by political persecution and abuse, and the right to follow the familiar social and political customs. For the Peronists, freedom and liberty meant social and economic justice and a broad redistribution of opportunity and reward.[71] With such a setting, it was fortunate that the election proceeded with no more violence and repression than it did.

On November 12, the government, after discussion with the parties, announced February 24 as the new date for balloting. Perón's campaign was launched in a spirit of frugality and informality and was conducted from the Posadas Street apartments and from another office shared with Tessaire. Perón appeared frequently in more sporty attire than customary in so formal a society, wearing a red cardigan over a blue jersey. He radiated amiability and an optimism that suffused the entire staff, now so swollen that it almost overflowed into the street. No one knew just how Perón would win, but there was no doubt at all about victory.[72]

This period marked the beginning of the undistinguished and eventually tragic public career of Evita's brother, Juan Duarte, who served now as Perón's personal secretary. More significantly, the symbolic theme of the *descamisado* arose in these days following October 17.[73] "Shirtless," in its literal meaning, the term was first employed by the better-born as a denigration of the rough-bred types who milled about on that famous day with happy indecorum. The word was loaded with class disdain, for proper attire in public was one of the deep and hitherto unchallenged values of the Argentine civilization. Anyone appearing in public in less than tie and jacket, regardless of heat, was at the very least a boor and a clod. As for cooling one's feet in a public fountain, it was unthinkable, worthy of a *descamisado*. Perón, with his lack of convention and his intuition, saw the possibilities in a word that so clearly drew the line between his followers and the establishment, a word that could by itself give birth to an overpowering mystique. Thus he would conclude his campaign speeches from then on by taking off his jacket and rolling up his sleeves; thus when a staff bearing the Argentine flag and a worker's shirt nailed in place beneath it was handed up to him at a massive political rally on December 14, he was happy to wave it aloft, a gesture for which the opposition accused him of desecration.

There were three campaign trips, in the familiar style. What was new was the presence of Evita, for no wife of an Argentine presidential candidate had ever appeared with her husband in a campaign setting. Evita's name and growing legend had preceded her, as had her aura of mystery, and her appearance at Perón's side, discretely silent, a rather fragile beauty beneath massed blonde hair, was for many the coming of a romantic apparition out of a fairy tale.

The selection of a running mate, which was deferred until January 23, brought a painful dilemma for Perón. Mercante had previously suggested to the Labor Party his own nomination for vice president; and the party was delighted to comply. But two military men on the same ticket, Perón thought, would be one too many. He preferred, Dr. Hortensio Quijano, the choice of the UCRJR, on obvious political grounds. Difficult as it was in personal terms, Perón persuaded Mercante to reverse his acceptance and to stand instead for the governorship of Buenos Aires Province on the Labor slate. Quijano was a wise selection, bringing a balancing stability of image. Elderly, rotund, white-haired and impressively wax-moustached, grandfatherly, he might have stepped out of some movie about a politician from Edwardian times. And he was totally loyal.

Although violence marred the campaign, it was not massive and it was not, with some exceptions, an expression of governmental policy. The United States embassy, hardly indulgent to Perón, reported on January 9, 1946, "Although in a good many instances Government acts have clearly been partial to Perón, I am inclined to believe that Governmental aid to Perón has not been wholly disproportionate to the aid which an administration candidate normally receives in an election in the United States . . . The same emphatically cannot be said with regard to governmental acts against the opposition. Despite fair-sounding words . . . it is quite clear that Peronist officials (notably the Peronist police under Velazco), with the acquiescence, if not the connivance, of the Government, are subjecting the opposition to a widespread if covert campaign of intimidation . . . The effect of this campaign so far, however, does not appear to have vitally prejudiced the opposition . . . The opposition also complains bitterly about the State of Siege, restrictions on meetings, petty attacks on opposition organs, etc., but taking the record as a whole they do not appear so far to be very important . . . coercion of the opposition has not played a vital role in the campaign so far, even though its importance must not be disregarded."[74]

Nor was the UD at a serious disadvantage concerning access to the radio. There was some discrimination with respect to use of the official network, but it was not serious. Privately owned radio facilities were freely available. With regard to the press, the UD had a great advantage, for the leading papers, *La Prensa* in particular, were solidly anti-Peronist. The meetings and the speeches of UD candidates received enormous coverage, but accounts of Perón's activities were brutally condensed and hustled off to inconspicuous back pages. The much smaller Peronist press was equally partisan, indulging in slander and abuse.[75]

The masterstroke of the Peronist campaign was a decree issued by Mercante's ministry on December 20, providing a Christmas tree of good things for labor. Perón had mentioned in his last public speech, before his brief fall in October, a decree he was preparing that would institute profit sharing. Like Perón himself, the decree had only a temporary eclipse, and here it was. Although it postponed for further study the question of profit sharing, its gifts were luscious nevertheless: a wage increase, an annual year-end bonus effective immediately, vacation pay, sick pay, and severance pay. This bounty had several effects in addition to the obvious one. It was so basic that employers could not take it in stride on the spur of the moment. They therefore opposed it. Labor unrest followed at once. The employers finally capitulated, but by this time their intransigence had made it clear to the workers what the consequences of a Perón defeat would be. And for the UD, the decree was an agony. It forced the Socialists and the Communists into the most difficult of choices, and they ended up opposing both the decree and the visible, immediate interests of their alleged constituencies.[76]

Events originating outside the government added two other windfalls for Perón. The first was the release on November 17 of a pastoral letter by the Catholic hierarchy that was widely seen as supportive of Perón, although it was undoubtedly motivated less by a specific design to help him than by defensive concern for the existing role of the Church in the social areas that were its concern; the higher levels of the hierarchy tended to distrust Perón and abhorred his open way with Evita. The pastoral letter did not mention him by name, but it did state that no Catholic might join a party or vote in favor of candidates whose programs favored separation of Church and State, legal divorce, lay education, and certain religious usages in public practice. What else was the Church to do? The parties of the UD all supported one or more of these measures. Perón, on the other hand, had been the most influential member of the regime that had decreed compulsory religious education in the public schools at the end of 1943, and he was now indicating his support of the Church's position in general, emphasizing his devotion to the faith on every possible occasion. In the campaign, the lower Catholic ranks centered in proletarian parishes, and the country priests and the members of the preaching orders took to the pastoral letter with enthusiasm, and although the support thus generated cannot be measured, it certainly did not harm Peron.[77]

The second gift presented to Perón from outside came from a very different, and improbable, source. It came from Spruille Braden, who had lost none of his distaste for Peronism. Early in October, on the basis of the extensive Nazi archives that had become available with the Allied victory in Europe, he had ordered an investigation into the connections between Nazi activities in Latin America and the Argentine government and its officials, including Perón. The research was formidable. Several tons of materials were involved. A task force was assembled in the State Department. And by early February a large report was ready. But the question of its release at so delicate a moment raised a fundamental issue of United States policy

Little had changed in that policy since the departure of Braden in September. October 17 had come and gone and had brought a first reaction of incomprehension and incredulity from the embassy. The event had been attributed two days later to ". . . excellent organization of hoodlums on Fascist lines like Brown Shirts and Black Shirts." A long step toward social revolution was foreseen, a development that Cabot thought ". . . in itself is perhaps proper; tragedy is that a Fascist dictator is leading it and using such methods." Cabot and Braden now expressly rejected a policy either of appeasement or of full crackdown and adopted an intermediate course involving steady reaffirmation of democratic values and a firm position against Argentina in hemispheric and world relations.[78]

Subsequent reporting by the embassy began slowly to encompass the reality of Perón's labor support, while clinging tenaciously to the belief that October 17 was also a testimony to organization, to strong-arm methods, and to police collaboration.[79] By the first half of January, Cabot's despatches had come to represent an interesting tapestry in which the old clichés and misconceptions continued to form the warp, while revised conclusions and sometimes very accurate and pertinent insights, both contemporary and historical, provided the woof.[80]

By the first week in February, Cabot's opinions reached a crossroad. He advised against the release of the department's report, but not for entirely correct reasons. He thought at this moment that Perón was losing, an issue on which he had wavered somewhat from week to week; release was therefore not necessary, and risked incalculable consequences. On the other hand, release would probably not harm the UD. The decision was taken in Washington to release the volatile document, an action that was generally understood as an effort to tilt the election against Perón.[81] Braden wrote later that he had assumed Perón would be elected, that he had won three bets to that effect, and that the report had to be brought out before the election because it would be impossible to publish it after a Perón victory.[82]

Released on February 11, the report (known as the Blue Book) made a crashing entry into the electoral campaign, changing its very nature. The disclosures in the Blue Book were mostly reworkings of charges already familiar, directed to the operations of Nazi sympathizers and agents during the war and to the cordial relations between these and various governmental and nationalistic circles in Argentina. Perón was involved, but not to the directly incriminating degree that Braden had doubtless hoped for. Although Perón now assembled a rebuttal volume, called the Blue and White Book, in tribute to the colors of the Argentine flag, he did not bother in his campaign to respond to the charges. With a profound tactical instinct, he simply ignored them and assailed Braden personally for his intervention in an Argentine election. He coined the phrase "Braden or Perón" and made it his rallying cry for the duration of the campaign. "Braden or Perón" echoed in every speech. "Braden or Perón" appeared in painted or whitewash letters on every wall. "Braden or Perón" dominated the posters. "Braden or Perón," said small stickers and large stickers. Indeed, the entire election now seemed to become "Braden or Perón."[83]

This coincided with a more strident evolution in Perón's electioneering techniques, for the campaign was boiling toward its conclusion. On neither side was the level of debate very high in terms of sober discussion directed to the issues. Perón had started out in a low key, stressing the need to retain the social gains already made, the positive, life-supporting mood of his supporters, and the need for broad cooperation. But the theme of the people against the oligarchy rose steadily to the surface, until in the end it was all subsumed in "Braden or Perón."

On the other side, the election motifs of the UD seemed to stress whatever was outside the mainstream of the campaign or whatever was stale and dull. For the most part, the oratory was routine and would not have been out of place in the old struggles for or against Yrigoyen. The basic UD theme was "For liberty against Nazi–Fascism," a proposition hard to disagree with, but it missed the point of the election completely, so that the fundamental issue of the campaign went to Perón by default, to be defined and pursued in his own manner. That question was put to the public in Buenos Aires by Perón in his proclamation speech on February 12, the address that was the summation of his campaign: "Because the real truth is this: in our country there is no debate on a problem between 'liberty' and 'tyranny', between 'Rosas and Urquiza', or between 'democracy' and 'totalitarianism'. What is being debated in the substance of the Argentine drama is simply a championship match between 'social justice' and 'social injustice.' "[84]

On the eve of February 24, both sides exuded total confidence. The embassy reported that "Great majority of observers . . . now expect democratic victory in absence of flagrant fraud and / or intimidation"; for his own part, Cabot was cautious, but "really hopeful" of such an outcome.[85] In the event, whatever the accusations and the irregularities of the campaign, the balloting on February 24 was scrupulously fair and open, under the close supervision of the army. So much so was this the case that, almost miraculously, everyone agreed. The embassy, on the 25th, noted that all press accounts concurred: the elections were the cleanest in Argentine history, they exemplified the high civic culture of the nation. "No case of disorder or intimidation is reported from anywhere . . . Armed forces came in for merited praise for efficient organization of election and impartiality of their supervision. Tamborini is quoted as saying that conduct of elections evidences 'renewed brotherhood between the people and the armed forces.' "[86]

The counting of the vote was a kind of slow torture, extending for weeks. When it was all done, Perón had won with 52.4 percent of the total. Tamborini, trailing him by almost 281,000 votes, had 42.51 percent. Minor parties and blank and unidentified ballots accounted for the rest.[87] The Perón-Quijano ticket had carried all the provinces except Córdoba, Corrientes, San Juan, and San Luis, and the latter three were of marginal national significance. It was not an overpowering victory, but it was clear-cut.

The image of landslide that arose from the election is attributable to the congressional and provincial contests that produced a far more extreme verdict. The Peronist and UCRJR coalition elected all of the national senators except two. In the chamber of deputies, where minority representation was constitutionally ordained, it still won an astonishing two-thirds majority. And in the provinces it won governorships and legislative majorities everywhere except in Corrientes. No such broad mandate had ever been given in Argentina. It was firmly based, however, in the distrust of political compromise that permeated the very fibers of the Argentine civilization. In an electoral context that required more in the way of coalition management and sacrifice than had any other, the parties of the UD had generally been unable to agree on joint tickets for national offices below the presidential level and for provincial offices. They therefore ran separate tickets for these and they lost everything to the Peronist coalition, whose own serious unity problems were less extreme.

The Socialists were in the very epicenter of electoral misfortune. Traditionally assumed by all to speak for much of labor, and historically strong in Buenos Aires, they now found themselves, for the first time since 1912, without a single seat in the national congress. The deep eclipse they were now entering was concurrent with the predominance of Peronism, which had simply appropriated, almost overnight, the base that they (and the Communists and anarchists as well) had laboriously tried to construct among the workers and the dispossessed.

The events of 1945 and their vindication in the election of 1946 together signified a shift of almost revolutionary scope whose importance in the Argentine saga is comparable to that of the independence movement, of the fall of Rosas, of the work of the Generation of '80, and of the triumph of Yrigoyen in 1916. On each of those occasions old landmarks fell like the statue of Ozymandias and new memorials arose. Now, too. The temple stones of the Liberal System, the mightiest structure in its time, lay scattered on the sand. The laboring classes and the inarticulate outsiders were now admitted to the high altar and could join their voices in the choir of the nation, no longer isolated on the distant side of the Great Rift.

Everything seemed new, either joyous and hopeful or problematic and menacing, depending on one's point of view. The old faces and the ancient styles were in almost visible decline. New voters had appeared by the thousands, and new viewpoints and rules of the game. The familiar parties and the men who had directed them time out of mind were ripe for reassessment. Argentine relations with the world outside would respond to a new and more nationalistic impulse in which pride would be one of the driving forces.[88]

But amid the new, one of the oldest Argentine values was being reclaimed. The election and the events preceding it were, among other things, a renunciation of spiritual kinship with Europe and a cry for the truly indigenous, for Creole reality and Creole myth, for the spirit of *Martín Fierro* lost and ever present, living in the pages of the poem on the new leader's nightstand, the poem that bore a father's inscription: "So that you will never forget that you are a Creole."

> . . . Peronism, which perhaps at times doesn't respect
> the forms but which tries to assimilate and comply
> with the principles, is an effective, real, and deep
> way of practicing Christianity . . .
>
> — Juan Domingo Perón, Speech at Rosario, 1950

> Peronism may be a good example of the high cost of
> social reform when it is indulged in a rhetorical and
> at times high-handed and arbitrary way.
>
> — Guido Di Tella, *Perón–Perón 1973–1976*

7. Peronism in Power 1946-1950

Portrait of a Leader

AFTER THE LONG FEVER OF 1945 and the ensuring electoral period, life resumed a more normal tone. Perón accepted success quietly, and the initial stupefaction of the opposition gave way to a grudging acceptance, the pain of which was alleviated for many by the thought that the new Peronist regime was sure to fall of its own weight, and presumably soon.

This, of course, did not happen, for reasons more clear in retrospect than at the time. Perón brought to the presidency several strengths and assets that were not then fully appreciated. Among them was the historical moment itself, unusually propitious for bold new attempts. Also among them was a wife whose remarkable and, indeed, unprecedented qualities no one, including Perón himself, then fully realized. His political inexperience, assumed to be a weakness, was in some ways an advantage, for a new style joined to a new face was a welcome relief to many for whom the old politics had collapsed into disrepute. As Perón himself put it, "In a certain sense, my lack of political antecedents allowed me to attain a politics cleaner than the usual practices."[1] His other and more obvious assets included a native intelligence that deeply impressed almost all but those who hated him fanatically; a sense of patriotism that was equally recognized; and the ability to generate in his supporters the clear conviction that he was dedicated to justice and social welfare rather than to power for its own sake.

Most important of all, perhaps, was Perón's affinity for Creole reality and his ability to embody it to the nation. Cipriano Reyes, the common man incarnate, saw this early on, remarking, "He knew how to get next to the people, to talk with the people, and to think like the people. Why? Because he had the innate qualities of a *caudillo*, and something that was impossible to overlook, the necessary charisma to prevail over his peers."[2]

Part of this ability to commnicate intimately with the broad public certainly lay in Perón's strange ability to combine lofty language with homespun metaphors. A single interview yields examples taken almost at random. On the mistakes of American policy toward Argentina: "I told them, you can take a hen, kill it, pluck the feathers, cook it, and eat it; but what you cannot do with a hen is to oblige it to lay an egg; you must leave it alone and in determined conditions. What you need from Argentina is an egg, not a hen. Then leave the hen in peace and hope that it will lay an egg." On the need of rural producers for better pay: "Don't burn or cut your hair; massage its roots and the hair will not fall out . . . the economy of our country will not be damaged if we strengthen the root, which is the man who extracts the riches." On winning elections: "In our country it is very easy to win an election. It is sufficient to repeat the example of Faust: sell one's soul to the devil. And the election will be won with money. But when the elected candidate starts to govern, it will not be he who governs, but the devil."[3]

The charisma and the charm of Perón's personality were so related to the Creole ambiance that they did not travel easily outside of Argentina, perhaps with the exception of Spain. North Americans and northern Europeans did not feel the full force of a personality so seductive to Argentine sensibilities that both friends and many opponents would agree with the appraisal of a colleague: "I have seen persons opposed to him who had to interview him for the first time, and a few minutes later they would come out transformed, as if they had been touched by true magic."[4]

In the *caudillo* tradition, a bit of mystery has often been a precious ingredient. Rosas had it, and Yrigoyen, too. Perón had no aura of encompassing mystery, but there were hints of it in a certain solitary image that he projected in the midst of multitudes, the lone leader who is in the crowd and much a part of it, but who in another sense preserves a private *persona*. Close associates usually remarked this quality, and there were few who penetrated to the guarded inner citadel of his being. His relations with his father had centered on respect rather than intimacy, and he was not close to his mother, who did not attend his inauguration in 1946. Perón was thought to be displeased with her remarriage, to a Chilean much younger than she was. His reaction was not surprising, for the marriage of an older woman and a younger man was widely perceived in Argentina at that time as humiliating. Perón did attend her funeral in 1953, although the general impression has been otherwise.[5] Nor was Perón close to his brother, Mario Avelino, a man devoted to animals, who was appointed by Perón as director of the Buenos Aires zoo. Perón rarely saw him, however, and he had little relationship with his cousins.

Perón's natural assets were much enhanced by the focus they received from his energy and discipline. "I am a kind of fakir, and I have come to dominate my sentiments. I not only make myself obeyed, but what is more difficult, I obey myself, I submit myself to the most rigid and implacable of disciplines."[6] The words were spoken toward the end of his life, but they were true from the beginning and they suggest the austerity of his daily patterns. He arose at five in the morning, reached his office at six twenty, signed papers until seven, then began to receive visitors. At noon, he had a light lunch, followed by a siesta until four, when he returned to the office and worked until eight, nine, or ten o'clock. Dinner followed, and he would get to bed late. He was proud that during his more than nine years in the presidency he failed only once to arrive at his desk on time; on that occasion, he had hurt himself slightly in a motorcycle accident on the way to work.[7] There was austerity in his other habits as well. He was not a casual womanizer, and he had no taste for liquor, which was never served at official functions or in his home during Perón's presidency; all guests receiving yerba mate instead. Whiskey he abominated, holding his nose when he once had to drink it on his doctor's orders.

The austerity and the self-control are the clues to a nature that was both passionate and controlled. In his political life he was cold and analytical, detached from his other being, the emotional or passionate one that generally prevailed whenever political requirements receded.[8] The emotional nature was the one that gave the quasi-religious or spiritual tilt to Perón's values, and the emphasis on abstractions such as justice, dignity, pride. "Is it true that you represent a new doctrine?" the Associated Press reporter asked Perón after the 1946 election. To which Perón replied, "Yes, in effect, but not so new as forgotten for a long time, because it is already 2,000 years old: Christianity."[9]

Beyond or beneath the coldly calculating Perón, who seemed to spend his life in a convoluted labyrinth, and beyond or beneath the emotional Perón, whose themes would have suited the archangels, was an essentially simple Perón, who was usually overlooked in the excitement and drama. This was the Perón who enjoyed long week-ends whenever possible at his unpretentious rural retreat, San Vicente, where he and Evita would walk and talk and tend to their own wants, alone, he cooking cannelloni and she making the beds. This was the Perón who inclined to the company of the young, working with neigh-borhood boys, corresponding with them from Europe; who detested uniforms and formal attire, preferring a sport shirt; who in spite of his *Hispanidad* greatly disliked bullfights; who loved animals, particu-larly dogs and horses; who astonished his lawyer during a walk together by insisting on fetching a saucer of milk from the house for a kitten they encountered, saying, "God knows where its mother is";[10] who upbraided an Italian restaurant owner by saying, "Never offer horse-meat to an Argentine. It's like offering human flesh . . . we have so great a love for that animal that eating its meat would be like an act of cannibalism."

This was the Perón of the unsophisticated tastes of the common man who knows what he likes, the man who does not usually read Plutarch and Toynbee for pleasure. He liked speed, the thrill of driv-ing fast cars, motorcycles, and boats. As for movies, he liked westerns with lots of shooting, for relaxation after a hard day. His favorite form of music was the tango and whatever was associated with Argen-tine folklore. Rock and roll jangled his nerves. Concerts and the thea-ter took too much time for either Perón or Evita: "Our concerts and our theater were social policy for her and the work of government for me." In art, Perón preferred the Italian painters, particularly Michelangelo and da Vinci, to the Spanish. Among the latter, he liked Murillo and was surprised that in Madrid informed opinion pre-ferred Velázquez, whom Perón could not appreciate. El Greco was also disagreeable to him because of the purposeful distortions. "I am the enemy of deformation in all senses." This was the Perón who pre-ferred the straightforward, the unadulterated, the pure and literal thing: "I like red or blue but not green." It was a strange contrast, as if the pursuit of political nuance and subterfuge had drained him of tolerance for all other subtleties.[11]

The New Order in Politics and Society

The mistaken notion that the new government had a short life expectancy was understandable, given the serious conflict between its Labor Party base and its UCRJR base. They did not even observe a pause in their disputes after the victory at the polls. On the contrary, they now had the spoils to argue over, and it was clear to Perón that organizational steps would be required to bring about order. Therefore on May 23, on the radio, he ordered the dissolution of the existing parties in his coalition and the termination in office of their leaders, and he announced the formation of a committee to reorganize all Peronist forces into a single National Revolutionary Party. This soon emerged under the unhappy name of *Partido Unico de la Revolución,* the Sole Party of the Revolution.[12]

The State of Siege was lifted by the Farrell administration on May 24. A week later, another decree restored Perón's active service status in the army as of October 17 and promoted him to brigadier general as of December 31, 1945. With these loose ends attended to, Perón was ready for his inauguration on June 4, the third anniversary of his mission into high politics.

In his address to the Congress after taking the oath of office, it was the conciliatory and statesmanlike Perón who spoke: "The time of conflict has ended for me, because I am, and I feel myself to be, the president of all Argentines; of my friends and of my opponents; . . . of those who have followed me from the heart and of those who have followed because of circumstances; of those groups represented by the majority of the congress and of those looking to the minority." Never had he taken the high road so conspicuously: "All the passions of combat have left my will, my mind and my heart, and I ask of God only that he grant me the serenity that the work of government requires."

For the rest, he pledged anew the social goals of Peronism. He foretold clearly the strong intervention of public power in the economy on behalf of industrial development and otherwise. He spoke feelingly of land reform and the needs of agriculture. He asked for practical achievements in preference to "Byzantine discussions"—"We need determined achievers rather than good planners." There was much about dignity and honor and worthy intentions and there was a hint of a showdown with the judiciary in the comment that justice, in addition to being independent, must also be effective, dynamic rather than static, and must therefore keep in step with public sentiment.[13]

It was clear in another respect as well that a new era was at hand. By long tradition the dominant elements in Argentina had been attuned to the world overseas. The reassessment of that orientation now emerged as a rapidly quickening inward tendency. As seen in retrospect, "After the war, and for the first time quite voluntarily, Argentina had embarked on a nationalistic course that had kept the country outside the mainstream of world economic and cultural developments. In a way it was a belated reaction to the previously high level of foreign influence."[14]

This was reinforced by Perón's strong evocation of the indigenous Argentina, of the spirit of the aborigines, and of the valued gifts of the civilization that ". . . under the protection of the Cross was brought to us by the cavaliers of Spain. The fusion of the two cultures . . . has given to our people a human sense of life that may well be compared to the classical Greek and Latin, superior to those by reason of having sifted their essences through the magic of Christian redemption."[15]

The cabinet selected by Perón was, in various ways, a departure from precedent. It was much younger than usual, it was preponderantly civilian rather than military, and its members, being innovators instead of comfortable establishmentarians, were little known and lacking in prestige. There was also a conviction among many that most of the cabinet was incompetent. "Perón's cabinet is lamentably weak," the United States embassy reported in June 1948. "So much so that at times the president himself either jokes about it or gives vent to his feelings of despair."[16] But, again, it is difficult to evaluate such comments, since the embassy, like the sectors of public opinion most available to it, was probably guided by different criteria than those of the new ministers. Certainly the foreign minister, Juan Bramuglia, was clearly able. A labor lawyer, he adapted well to new responsibilities and soon acquired a wide reputation in international circles. The war minister, General José Humberto Sosa Molina, was regarded as another strong man in the cabinet. Angel Borlenghi, a trade union leader by career, was beginning his long and faithful association with Perón in the important position of minister of interior. General Juan Velazco retained his position as chief of the federal police and as the cutting edge of nationalist influence in the government. José Figuerola headed the technical secretariat, which functioned below the ministerial level.[17]

The turmoil in labor preoccupied Perón from the first days of his administration. The UCRJR had gone along with its own demise and the creation of the *Partido Unico,* but the reaction of the Labor Party was in firm contrast. Cipriano Reyes, its chief and now a Peronist deputy in Congress, was a rugged customer. With his lack of education, culture, and breadth of knowledge, he could hardly have posed a national challenge to Perón, but he was shrewd, hard, and determined, and he could cause much trouble. Now he got his back up over the tone of the commands issuing from the *Partido Unico.* In July, he resigned from the Peronist bloc in the Chamber of Deputies and took his Labor Party colleagues with him. He did not attack Perón, but reaffirmed his personal support of "the symbol of our movement," although this of course would not save the situation. The *Partido Unico* expelled Reyes, and he went into open opposition with a dwindling band of followers.[18]

Against this backdrop, the organization of the *Partido Unico* advanced haltingly. In August, Perón decided to lend a hand to the discouraged organizers, and he received a delegation of them in the Casa Rosada. He reiterated that the *Partido Unico* was the only revolutionary party and that he would receive committees from no other. Reverting to the tones of the combative Perón, he urged full speed ahead, ". . . but not because the future worries me without the backing of a party, however, because if some one has the idea of making a revolution I shall do it a week in advance; all that is necessary is to supply a few meters of rope to each *descamisado* and then we shall see who hangs whom. I have with me five hundred thousand *descamisados* and with me at their head, as Napoleon said, we shall be a million . . . to govern is not my calling; my calling is to fight; I am better at that."[19] He was whipping up morale, reverting to the old jugular language that had caught the ear and the heart of the Creole masses.

The Labor Party of Reyes and his followers put up a determined rearguard action. Reyes headed a demonstration on October 17, the first anniversary of *the* day, thus slightly diluting the impact of the major mass celebration in the Plaza de Mayo that the Peronists were inaugurating as an annual event of commemoration. In Perón's words, "A year ago in this same historic Plaza de Mayo the humble people paid tribute to my liberation after the flight of the traitors. Therefore the seventeenth of October will, for all time, be the day of the shirtless, the day of those who are hungry and thirsty for justice." He went on to propose the erection of a statue in the Plaza honoring the *descamisado* since ". . . that shirtless one who was cannon fodder in the independence, who was the gaucho of the knives and of the horses . . . and the same one who later erected these buildings and made the fatherland great, and who will carry it to its grand destiny, still does not have a monument to perpetuate him." Concluding, he said, "Since I am a man of the people and wish to go to the people's dance, I will go to the Plaza de la Republica to dance with you."[20]

On February 5, 1947, Perón intervened in this running dispute in an unusual manner, by visiting Congress and speaking off the record to the Peronist deputies. Again, he urged unity and promised radical measures if necessary to create a satisfactory balance in the internal political scene. "If we have to use a knife, we will use it." He noted also, contrary to all the evidence, that he was resolutely opposed to personalism in politics, and that if he had permitted his name to be used in connection with the *Partido Unico* it was only after personal conflict and as a means of insuring that a plebiscite would decide the name the party should have in the future, and also its program.[21]

The personalism, of course, won out. In November 1947, delegates to a Peronist constituent congress were elected, assembling on December 1 and December 2 and adopting an organic charter. Everything had been done in advance. The only disagreement had come regarding the name of the organization; some wanted "Peronista Movement" and some preferred "Peronista Party." The latter prevailed, but this was personalism at its best. There was a touch of corporatism in the structure of the party, in that it was grouped around labor units and ordinary units. Another statute provided that if a party member were president of the nation he would also be the supreme chief of the party, with the power to modify decisions of other party authorities. The principles of centralism were well served in other respects as well. The superior council of the party had power to appoint interventors of local party groups that, in turn, were to choose congressional and other candidates. It was a large but closed circle.[22]

Meanwhile, the policies of the new government were augmenting the well-being of the labor base of support. Real wages increased steadily between 1946 and 1948, reaching a point of 27 percent above the 1943 levels for skilled workers and 37 percent for unskilled labor. Various other benefits proliferated, including expansion of the retirement system, medical assistance, and the provision of low-cost housing assistance. And there were blessings that were not material: there was much internal democracy in the unions for the election of officers and in the conduct of union affairs, strikes were supported rather than discouraged, and the general effect was one of firm governmental patronage for labor. True, the government retained its veto over strikes and the choice of top union officials, but in practice this rarely led to significant conflict.[23]

The breathing space provided in these years was very helpful to Perón, for it much improved the environment in which he chose to take certain steps that he saw either as challenges or as undertakings necessary for his programs. The first of these concerned the federal Supreme Court. That body was the capstone of what had always been an independent judiciary. Now, however, Perón's quest for what he defined as unity signaled a new approach, the background for which was juridical, political, and psychological. Several decisions had been handed down since June 4, 1943 that imposed limitations on some of the innovations of the regime. The court, normally consisting of five justices, now numbered four, and of these, three were considered antiadministration in their judicial philosophy. The determined efforts of Perón's opponents in 1945 to have the government turned over to the Supreme Court pending elections had cast a political coloration over that institution, although the court itself had not sought such a solution and had not been involved in the political scramble.

In any event, the decision was made to seek impeachment of the three uncooperative justices, and charges were brought in October 1946 on two grounds of alleged malfeasance. The first was the recognition by the court of the post-1930 and the post-1943 regimes as de facto governments, a charge that carried a degree of legal logic but that was hardly to be expected from Perón, who had participated in the first of those coups and who was the principal beneficiary of the second. The other ground, the guts of the charges, was the illegality of the recent decisions that had offended the government. But this fitted badly with the first charge. The government was, in effect, simultaneously attacking the court for having recognized the 1943 government and for having invalidated some of its work, as if the regime, but not its legislation, could be illegal.

The Peronist majorities made it easy to obtain approval of impeachment in the Chamber of Deputies and conviction in the Senate; approval of the latter occurred on April 30, 1947. New justices, with a suitably subservient approach in matters political, were appointed. The ripples of the impeachment controversy spread out to the provinces, and in several instances local legislators defended Peronist measures by confronting their provincial courts. Thus the national judiciary was Peronized early on, a process that entailed for the government a loss of credibility outside of Argentina. Domestically, the action was offensive only in circles already in opposition.[24] As with other developments, it was not that Perón's supporters were always unaware of abuses; at times they admitted them but found them justified as a perhaps unavoidable part of a larger social phenomenon that they believed profoundly necessary: ". . . in a revolutionary process, and that *was* a revolution, everything goes."[25]

The surge of Peronism gave no sign of lessening in 1947 and 1948. The labor elements and the ex-Radicals still tussled for position, but this was hardly more than an annoyance, and the superior council was becoming adept at juggling and balancing and soothing. In the congressional balloting on March 7, 1948, the nation gave Peronism a splendid mandate, with 60 percent of the vote. The Peronist majority in the Chamber of Deputies was now above two thirds, and in the Senate the last non-Peronist had disappeared.[26]

Another disappearance was the shell of the Labor Party that Cipriano Reyes had stubbornly maintained around himself as his followers slowly drifted off to Peronism. The party was deprived of legal standing in January 1948 and could not participate in the March elections, with the result that the congressional seat occupied by Reyes represented still another disappearance. He was now isolated, threatened physically, and very close to the wall, but he fought on in his unreasoning manner, describing Perón to the American embassy in the harshest of terms, the most printable of which were "dishonest," "lying," and "egomaniac."[27] It seemed unlikely that he could now represent any threat other than a fictitious one, but Perón was determined to remove him from the scene. The mechanism for this was a fanciful assassination plot dreamed up for the purpose, to which Reyes could be linked. Fortune favored Perón in the effort, for circumstances that would lend it a degree of superficial credibility were available across the estuary, in Montevideo. It all began rather mysteriously on September 8, 1948, at Santa Fe, where Perón made a raging speech, full of threats and defiance, to a large gathering of workers. It was impossible to know at the time what this purported to be about, but it soon became clear.

At two o'clock in the morning of September 24, the federal chief of police called in the press and announced that a dozen arrests had been made in connection with a death plot against Perón and Evita, planned for October 12. The only prominent name among those arrested was Cipriano Reyes, but the case was given a sensational twist by allusions to the involvement of figures in Uruguay, including John Griffiths, the former United States cultural attaché in Buenos Aires, now retired and living as a businessman in Montevideo. The accusations spread around the country with incredible speed. Individuals and groups began to pour into Buenos Aires, heading for the Plaza de Mayo. The CGT called a general strike, to last until midnight. Shutters on stores were instantly put up, and all public transportation ceased. By the time Perón appeared on the balcony at the Casa Rosada, at 6 P.M., a crowd of about 200,000 had assembled and large throngs had gathered in plazas of the other cities. Perón denounced Griffiths as a spy, implied but did not state the responsibility of the United States (although a rousing campaign in the controlled press made this clear), assailed his opposition, and once more pummeled the "contumacious oligarchs," who "had played the clown for forty years . . ."[28]

The role of Griffiths in all this remained a puzzle. In his embassy days in the time of Braden, he had maintained contacts with Perón's opposition and he seemed to have acquired at that time a taste for intrigue, the more operatic the better. After his resignation and his departure to Montevideo, he indulged this by joining the conspiratorial world of the Argentine exiles who lurked and confided in low voices in the cafés and bars of the Uruguayan capital. He had become entranced with the Martin Bormann legend, and he had taken his enthusiasm and credulity to Washington early in 1948 to enlist the attention of Supreme Court Justice Robert Jackson, the United States prosecutor at the Nuremberg war-criminal trials. Jackson passed the matter to J. Edgar Hoover, who, in turn, passed it to an agent who spent almost two months in Uruguay on the trail of this phantasm before concluding that Griffiths was unreliable and possibly over-inventive.[29]

Reyes fell into the middle of this and was entrapped by military officers who spoke of a coup. He had done nothing overt, and his contacts with Griffiths appear to have been limited to a meal together a long time before. But he did talk to the officers who tried to lure him with the chimera of a plot, and that was enough to bring his arrest. He was given a very hard time and a jail sentence that ended only with the fall of Perón in 1955. The oratorical and press attacks on the United States simmered down, and Griffiths faded away.

But what was behind all this? There were as many answers as questioners. Perón himself explained to the American ambassador that he had done it to maintain labor support, and there was no change in his friendship for the United States.[30]

There was another step that Perón had long pondered, the revision of the federal constitution, which dated from 1853, to reflect the social visions of his government. His enemies insisted that his real motive was the amendment of Article 77, which prohibited consecutive terms for a president, and they were cynically dubious when Perón publicly proclaimed his support for that clause.[31] Whatever his purposes, at his urging the Congress in August convened a constitutional convention for which elections were held on December 5, 1948. The opposition parties were in a disarray now quite familiar, with the Socialists calling for blank votes, the Communists for extreme provisions, the Radical majority voting to fight it out at the polls, and the large Radical minority favoring a boycott of the balloting. It is not surprising that the Peronists triumphed again, this time by 60 percent of the vote. The convention convened on January 24, 1949. José Figuerola had drafted proposals for amendments, but his was now a fading star, and the suggestions that counted were those of Arturo Sampay, a professor of law, who had been chosen by the congressional Peronists to head a study commission. Domingo Mercante, still prospering as the governor of Buenos Aires Province, was the strongest force on the convention floor. Perón stayed in the background.

There were two significant points to argue about. One was the old Article 77, the reelection ban. Perón maintained his opposition to any change in this throughout the convention, so advising Mercante and a delegation of Peronist leaders to their faces at a meeting in the presidential mansion. Mercante and the others were persuaded and returned to the convention prepared to kill the change. Then something happened, and one can take one's choice of explanations. One version, traceable back to Evita, holds that Perón wanted the change all along and expected Mercante and his allies to interpret his no as a yes, and that Evita then had to intervene with the convention leaders to set them straight. The other version, advanced by historian Felix Luna, maintains that Perón was sincere throughout and that Evita, in her passionate fervor, persuaded him to change his mind.[32] Whatever the reason, the article was amended to permit reelection.

The other important controversy concerned Article 40, with regard to expropriation of foreign utilities and payment for them. Sampay and others of a nationalistic persuasion favored replacement of the old provision, which required a law and a fair compensation. They wanted, instead, a provision requiring nationalization of utilities and a price formula that would subtract amortization and any excess profits from previous years, a provision likely to lead to much latitude and excess. In principle, Perón favored the Sampay version, but in practice, with opposition rolling in from every foreign country whose nationals owned Argentine utility interests, he did not want the change. Mercante urged him to reverse himself and thought he had won Perón around. But the next day, Juan Duarte, as Peron's emissary, brought Perón's order to kill the provision. Mercante and Sampay stalled for time until the convention had voted to approve the new article and then told Duarte it was too late. Perón had the task of explaining the mix-up to the embassies that had taken alarm.[33]

Other changes, mostly by way of addition, provide a fine insight into the social thought of Peronism. A new Chapter III enumerated a series of rights inspired by Catholic doctrine and teaching in the field of economic practice. Papal encyclicals—*Rerum Novarum* in 1891 and *Quadragesimo Anno* in 1931—had spoken against abuses in the capitalist system and in favor of their correction by state intervention in the economic sector, in the long tradition of the combined and centralized powers of Church and State that had characterized Mediterranean Catholicism since Constantine. The captions of the new chapter, thus descended, spoke of the audacious idealism now loose in the land: rights of the worker, of the family, of the aged, and the right to education and culture. And the right to work, to acquire skill, to well-being, to economic improvement, and to much else. References abounded throughout to morality and to spiritual aspects of life, and all mention of needs was preceded by "spiritual and material," in that order. "Private property has a social function," another article declared, an oracle's pronouncement heard as if through a veil; and such property was defined as subordinate to the needs of the national economy. The social sweep of the central government touched even so particular a field as education; universities were to establish courses so ". . . that each pupil may know the essence of what is Argentine, the spiritual, economic, social and political reality of the country, the evolution and historical mission of the Argentine Republic."

There were other changes, all testifying to the appetite of the Argentine civilization for government. Subsoil and energy resources were allocated to the State. A new Article 15 provided that "The State does not recognize the freedom to threaten freedom. This is understood to be without prejudice to the individual right to express opinion within the realm of doctrine, subject only to the rulings of the law." The old power of federal intervention, and the old right of the executive to declare a State of Siege with the approval of the Senate, or without it if Congress was in recess, were retained and were now reinforced by the authority of the president to declare a "state of precaution and alarm," a lesser thing but still useful to a leader of spirit and enterprise.

The 1949 document replaced the electoral college with direct election of the president and the Senate, but in other major respects the structure of the old system was unchanged. Thus when the Peronist constitution was approved on March 11, effective on May 1, the old remained to mingle strangely with the new, for much that was new was in its essence old, seeded in the ancient civilization, and much that was old appeared in new guise. It was a festival of time, imaging the civilization.

While Perón was preoccupied with these issues, he was also attentive to the evolution of foreign relations. In Washington, Spruille Braden was in charge of Latin American policy throughout 1946. Although the new ambassador to Argentina, George Messersmith, bore little resemblance to the blunt and formidable Braden, they were alike in having minds of their own. Nothing could overcome their want of mutual purpose and confidence, and conflict between them was inevitable.[34]

Messersmith soon developed a tilt toward Perón, and this reflected the emerging balance of forces in Washington, where there was a growing desire, based on self-interest, for an end to the Argentine imbroglio. An informal coalition of forces had come together in opposition to Braden's policy. The American military wanted to build up the defensive capacity of Latin America, including Argentina. Business interests sensed the fading of British commercial domination in the Plata area and wanted whatever they could get in the new market. Latin Americanists of the old Sumner Welles school had never forgotten their vision of the Good Neighbor. And above all, the drift of events had taken a toll on Braden and his refrain of the Nazi menace. Nothing displaces an old fear so effectively as a new fear, and now there was communism. The Cold War was beginning, and an entire new constituency of anti-Communists had sprung up for which Braden's nagging about the Chapultepec agreements seemed as obsolete as the slogans of the war of 1812. On the Argentine side there were corresponding pressures for accord. In the new scene that Perón's realism was quick to recognize, arms and military assistance and economic collaboration would all have to be sought in the United States, and the Argentine interest would benefit from an end to semi-isolation and dispute.

In recognizing and cultivating anticommunism as the one theme that could most readily harmonize the requirements of the two countries, Perón was at his intuitive best. Anticommunism as a lever for international advantage was merely an extension of domestic policy so Perón could embrace it, never more than when he bargained with the Americans but never so fondly that he sacrificed flexibility and room for maneuver. His private assurances far outran his public statements, but he satisfied the Americans concerning his basic alignment.

To preside over a decisive turn in American policy while at the same time reporting to Braden, who wanted no variation in the old religion, was no easy task, and Messersmith, understandably, developed the curious habit of taking his pulse almost constantly.[35] Under attack from Braden for insubordination, he developed the even more curious habit of going over his chief's head with long written appeals addressed directly to the secretary of state or to other high officials in the department or to the American press or to the president himself. In one of these remarkable displays, on August 16, 1946, Messersmith wrote to Dean Acheson, then acting secretary of state, accusing Braden of undermining him with the press and with his own staff (the same complaint that Braden made of Messersmith): "I am pretty much fed up with some of this stuff that is being given out that I am 'selling out', etc. . . . I am not going to sacrifice any principle, but I am, at the same time, not going to try to perpetuate a quarrel with a country which is important to us and I am not going to recommend that we ask her to do things which we may not have done ourselves and which would go beyond what we have expected of the other American Republics . . . It is enough of a handicap to me to do this job here with Spruille in the Department for I do not know to what degree you are aware of the tremendous feeling there is against him in this country and in most of the other American countries. Little is said, but the feeling is tremendous."[36]

This novel strife could hardly continue, and the decision was made in Washington that both men would have to go. Braden's resignation was effective as of June 30, 1947, several days after the departure of Messersmith. The policy that Washington now favored and that the embattled Messersmith had tried to implement was carried on by a new ambassador, James Bruce. It prospered because of the needs of both countries, and partly because of Perón's conviction, firmly embedded, that the rivalry of east and west in the Cold War years was certain to evolve into open conflict, and soon, and that in the struggle of the titans Argentine resources and supplies would be essential for the United States and the west.

Argentine relations with the United States in the early years of the first administration were therefore relatively serene, suspended in a calm between the storms of Braden's time and those soon to come.[37] Argentina participated constructively in the Río Conference in 1947, whose monument was the Río Treaty for defense against aggression, and in the conference in Bogotá in 1948, where the juridical framework of the hemisphere was crafted in the form of the Organization of American States, the OAS. Thus the American embassy could report in April 1948 that ". . . we feel that the prospects for an understanding with Argentina are certainly as bright as they have been at any time in the past and may possibly be much better."[38]

This was a part of Perón's outreach at this time to the hemisphere and to the world. In July 1947, he addressed the world by radio, calling for an end to "capitalist and totalitarian extremism." His proposal to neighboring countries for bilateral trade agreements received mixed reactions. Argentine labor attachés in Latin America were converted into aggressive missionaries of Peronism.[39]

Repression and the Creole Legacy

These favorable prospects were soon to suffer, however, from a gradual and broad development of great significance. The generous and tolerant sentiments of Perón's inaugural address were giving way, bit by bit in a process of authoritarian accretion, to an ambiance of repression of which the Peronization of the Supreme Court had been only a single example. There was no hint of an unfolding grand design. Rather, it was as if the civilization itself were releasing something from its depths, something out of old times, less a plot than an inevitability.

What is curious in this is not the fact of repression, which is common enough, but rather the absence of any plausible reason for it. Perón and his government, after all, were both very popular in these years and were in office with an admirably legitimate mandate. But instead of reaching out from that secure base toward accommodation, they chose to exacerbate disagreements and to alarm the opposition by taking forcefully what they could have had for the asking. The incongruity of this has struck Argentine observers, including some who are not rabid anti-Peronists: "What is puzzling is that non-democratic practices are usually implemented by minority parties which cannot win in any other way; the Peronists were able to win elections by substantial margins but also thought it necessary to take coercive measures quite unnecessary for electoral success. The democratic values which they mistrusted would have given them a much greater legitimacy; the authoritarian or Fascist ideologies with which they toyed worked against their acceptance."[40] American observers were just as baffled. Assistant Secretary of State Edward Miller asked Perón about it, as did several American ambassadors, but none of them received the kind of answer that indicated true comprehension of the question.[41]

The pattern was the same even on a lesser level than that of real repression, for the style of the Peronist government was becoming one of confrontation, a kind of belligerence in the use of language and symbol, a willingness to antagonize. It is understandable, for example, that Perón would decide not to destroy the landowning elite through land confiscation; but it is less clear what he had to gain by continuing to irritate and threaten an enemy he would not demolish. He was content to remain dependent on landowners and their exports, but he would still alienate them rather than reach out.[42] It would appear to be a prescription for the worst of both worlds. It was certainly psychologically gratifying to his supporters in street and factory to hear the continuing diatribes, but their allegiance had already been secured, and it seemed firm. What more would all this achieve?

It is to the basic division in the civilization that one must look for answers. The limits, laws, and practices to which traditional Argentine democracy of the Liberal System looked for balance and protection were those in favor on the near side of the Great Rift, where they were easily visible to foreign observers, who mistook that element of Argentina for the whole. But those limits, laws, and practices had little appeal and prestige on the far side of the Rift, the side that included the old Creole and gaucho heritage and the spiritual provenance of Juan Perón. There, where Peronists believed they had to defend their gains by counterattack, a different "democracy" served as an ideal and a different sensibility ruled.

There were many signs of this emerging repression. Among them were the withdrawal of legal status from Cipriano Reyes's Labor Party in January 1948 and the imprisonment of Reyes himself in April of the same year. There was Perón's extravagant language in reaction to the alleged assassination plot in September 1948, with its images and metaphors of hanging and lengths of rope to the *descamisados*. On October 10, 1949, the Peronist Congress strengthened the existing law on *desacato*, or disrespect to the dignity of a public official. This concept is familiar in Latin America, despite constitutional guarantees of freedom of speech. Originally there had at least been the consolation that the truth was a defense to a claim of *desacato;* but no longer. The definition of an offense to dignity was vague indeed, but that was part of the trouble, since it permitted extreme leeway to a partisan judiciary. The law was used in March 1950 with ex post facto vengeance against a prominent Radical deputy, Ricardo Balbín, for remarks he made in the 1946 election campaign. He spent ten months in jail, instructing the felons around him in their personal problems, and teaching them hygiene and crafts.[43]

Perón, in fact, seemed more preoccupied with these old scores now, a year or two later, than he had at the time, perhaps because the euphoria of 1946 was now being replaced by the wear and tear of governing. He was beginning to show impatience with the political opposition as early as August 1947, when he defined its proper role in terms associated with sainthood rather than with the hustings. Now, in October 1949, on the day of the decree tightening up *desacato*, another decree also appeared, forbidding electoral coalitions such as the one of 1946 and making more difficult the creation of new political parties. Although the 1946 coalition, the *Unión Democratica*, no longer existed, its former participants were dealt another blow, in November 1949, when a committee of congress went to work investigating the finances and accounts of individuals and organizations that had been connected with it, including contributors such as the Associated Press and the United Press, the Buenos Aires paper, *La Prensa*, banks, the Jockey Club. In December, Perón announced that he would sue *La Prensa* and *La Nación* for having printed references to accusations by an opposition deputy that Perón had enriched himself, allegations that led to the deputy's expulsion from Congress and his flight to Montevideo.

But the most serious manifestations of this process, and certainly the most spectacular in the shaping of world opinion, were those related to freedom of the press. Here again the evolution was piecemeal, sometimes indirect, often a nuance that hardened into an overt act. The government, for more than a year, pointed with pride to its tolerance of the hostile views of several prominent papers, principally *La Prensa* and *La Nación.* At the same time, these were the papers that suffered the most from the government's restrictions on the import of newsprint, because they carried more advertising than other papers. By August 1947, there were also threats of retroactive import duties on newsprint. If enforced, such a claim would have ruined the papers. Other harassments appeared in this early period, some of them serious.[44]

In this period, two other techniques of the government began to be developed for the purpose of coping with the press problem. That a legitimate problem for the government did exist can hardly be denied, for up to this time the press was almost entirely hostile to Perón, and hostile in a partisan spirit not easily imagined in the United States, so hostile that editorial policy lapped over into the news columns, and the government had little opportunity to express its views or even to report its facts. Traditionally, freedom of the press had been divorced from its responsibility. A solution for this problem was found by Perón in the acquisition of newspapers by persons in the government or sympathetic to it. Evita bought *Democracia,* a daily of no great distinction, in 1947 with money advanced by Alberto Dodero, a friendly and wealthy entrepreneur, and made it a Peronist organ. Four other papers, together with magazines and a radio network, were assembled in a company named Alea S.A. under the management of Carlos Aloe, Perón's administrative secretary. This was going rather far in the opposite direction, since the only remaining dailies outside the official orbit were now *La Prensa, La Nación,* and *Clarin,* a lesser paper.[45]

But this was not enough for the Peronist press policy, which wanted relief from press opposition as well as freedom for its own expression. A second technique was employed for this, which was simply a more direct form of assault on the remaining opposition. The well-regarded *Vanguardia,* the organ of the Socialist Party, had been shut down. The pressure against the remaining three papers mounted steadily. Of these,

La Prensa was the most notable, since its circumstances and its relationship to Peronism were unique.

Those who observed Argentina from a distance found it hard to understand why Perón desired, or permitted, the elevation of the *La Prensa* case into the international cause célèbre that it became. Their viewpoint was testimony both to the differences in perception that prevailed within the country and outside and to mutual incomprehension. The paper's reputation abroad always ran well ahead of its standing in Argentina, outside of the small circle for which it was almost a metaphor. It stood for the *Sociedad Rural,* for the landed rich, for the old Liberal System, for the bankers and exporters, for the Argentina whose spirit dwelled in the Faubourg Saint Germain. It had intimate links with international circles, was tied closely to the United Press system to which it paid unusually high fees, and had acquired over many decades a symbolism of lonely journalistic integrity. It was dull reading, a monument to political bias, and unscrupulous in its manipulation of political news coverage. Its personality derived from that of its owners, the Paz family, who lived in the princely home in Buenos Aires, more palace than house, that serves today as the *Círculo Militar.* The head of the family, Alberto Gainza Paz, was a vitriolic anti-Peronist, and Evita believed firmly that in New York he had stated in public, "My country is governed by a whore."[46] Ambassador Messersmith regarded him as the denizen of another age, and as ". . . one of the most arbitrary, selfish and misunderstanding men I know."[47]

The dispute with *La Prensa,* therefore, went far beyond its origins in the issue of freedom of the press and took on the passions of a blood feud. It developed a remarkable power to divide and marshall public opinion in Argentina, in the United States, and in Europe. The bitterness lapped over into attacks on less juicy and conspicuous press opponents. Late in 1949, the Visca-Decker committee of the Argentine Congress, formed to investigate charges of torture and anti-Argentine activity, was diverted to a broad campaign against the press, looking into every aspect of the operations and finances of anti-Peronist papers. Many small journals in the provinces had failed to print in their mastheads a reference to the centennial of San Martín then being celebrated, as a congressional regulation had required, and on this pretext, so silly as to be insulting, they were closed down.[48]

The pressures against *La Prensa* increased. A special session of Congress was convened to consider the matter.[49] Finally, one of the many weapons used against it proved effective. News vendors were encouraged not to handle the paper and to strike in support of their action. Sporadic violence broke out, and the government had its pretext to expropriate the paper, which it did on April 12, 1951, partly on the ground that it was under foreign influence. As a part of the proceedings, the government made a claim for past import duties and not surprisingly found that these exceeded the value of *La Prensa,* so that Gainza Paz was given a huge bill, as well as a short jail sentence, for contempt of Congress in challenging its right to prevent his publishing the paper. But he had already fled to Uruguay.[50]

Perón had won the battle of *La Prensa,* and now decided to turn the publication over to the workers, through the CGT. But his victory came at a terrible price. Gainza Paz in exile, ranging around the hemisphere and receiving the support of journalists and publishers everywhere, was more trouble to the government than he could ever have been in Argentina. The upturn in Argentine relations with the United States that had begun in 1946 soon became a downturn under the ill wind of the press restrictions, and the *La Prensa* case was the hardest blow to those relations since the prime of Braden. The Argentine image suffered similar damage in most of western Europe and in Latin America.

The general drift toward authoritarian principles and practices had its consequences in Perón's relations with Argentine intellectuals, a group of considerable weight in the national balance. Despite his own interest in matters intellectual, Perón had always had an uneasy time with the men of thought. He and they had interests in common but in neither case was the shared ground vital to their essential purposes. Perón was a man of politics and of action who happened to have a natural interest in ideas; the intellectuals were people of ideas who enjoyed dabbling in the world of affairs. Perón's intellectual aspect was quite unusual in a politician, but he was not one of the true academic intellectuals. The latter, like most Argentines, had a continuous simmering romance with public life but could never have become true political actors. Perhaps the terrain they shared with Perón was just spacious enough for each to have a lingering distrust of the other.

In the case of the college students, the acrid hostility of 1945 had abated somewhat, but not much. Perón had formed a student organization along Peronist lines to compete with the traditional Argentine University Federation, and by mid-1947 the new body had the support of perhaps a fifth of the national student enrollment, hardly an impressive number in view of the usual student proclivity for the new thing. Among the university faculties, Perón's support was even less, much less, although here and there an academic in dire need of subsidy had come around. In May, before his inauguaration in 1946, Perón had caused the Farrell government to intervene once again in all six of the universities, in response to a convenient "demand" to that effect on the part of the Labor Party. Between then and mid-1947, what with formal charges and forced resignations, more than twelve hundred professors, 70 percent of the total, had been removed and many courses had necessarily been abandoned. Right-leaning nationalists and the devotees of *Hispanidad* now prevailed in academic governance. A University Law of 1947 abolished the old university autonomy.[51]

The creative intellectuals remained wary and almost none crossed over. The writer, Manuel Gálvez, had allowed himself to be used, ". . . but more as a statue and as a name than as a living and creating intellectual."[52] The one real exception was the respected poet and essayist, Horacio Rega Molina, who adhered to Peronism in 1950 and made a speech invoking *Martín Fierro* and linking it to the Rural Workers' Statute that Perón had authored. "And what had to come has come," Rega Molina concluded. "And what had to be done has been done. And Social Justice was over the Pampa as the light was made over the world in the first chapter of Genesis, when the whole world was one huge Pampa of earth and sky."[53]

Among the intellectuals, the case of Jorge Luis Borges was poignant and striking, throwing a rare light on the two Argentinas that had been thrust into strife by the rise of Perón. The careers of the two men had come to fruition at the same time. Between 1939 and the mid-fifties, Borges published his greatest works. These were the years of *El Aleph, Ficciones,* and *Other Inquisitions,* all of them adversary works written in a spirit of subtle protest and rejection, deep in nostalgia for a mythic Argentina of a century past with its values of primitive hardihood and nobility of spirit, so pure in contrast to a sordid present.[54] "As he crossed the threshold, he felt that to die in a knife fight, under the open sky, and going forward to the attack, would have been a liberation, a joy, and a festive occasion . . . if he had been able to choose, or to dream his death, this would have been the death he would have chosen or dreamt." Thus wrote the sedentary and half-blind Borges in *El Sur,* his favorite among his short stories.[55]

Conflict between Perón and Borges was inevitable, for although the roots of both were leagues deep in the Argentine past, they shared neither values nor historical memory nor cultural inheritance. They were indeed products of differing nations that happened to be juridically a single country. By themselves they constituted a branch of the Great Rift. Perón was the quintessence of Creole Argentina, Hispanic in formation, finely attuned to the grit and dust of daily life. Borges was the quintessence of the cosmopolitan Argentina that looked to France and to England. He believed that Argentine history could be defined as the desire to become separate from Spain—" . . . we Argentines never thought of ourselves as Spanish"—[56], and despite his nostalgia for mythic pampas of the past, he was relatively indifferent to whatever was outside of Buenos Aires, a stranger to all the textures of existence as the multitudes experienced it, a man dedicated to foreign literature and to wondrous visions in which memory and reality lost their identity amid strange transformations. Perón could neither understand nor appreciate. "Men like Borges belong to a human species 'who don't touch the earth', not exactly because of an archangelic vocation but because of their notorious deprecation of mankind."[57]

So conflict came. Borges was working in a branch library as a first assistant, with a second and third assistant below him and a first, a second, and a third official above him: a marvelous example of the civilization's affinity for bureaucracy. As Borges put it, "There were some fifty of us, producing what fifteen could easily have done."[58] In August 1946, the new government devised a humiliation for Borges that revealed a very creative, if perverse, imagination on someone's part. He was "promoted' out of the library to the inspectorship of poultry and rabbits in the public markets, and, of course, resigned from public employment.

It is not known who dreamed up this ingenious ploy. It has been attributed to "some minor bureaucrat with the brain of an insect,"[59] but this will not suffice. If Perón was, in fact, ignorant of the matter at the time, which may have been the case, he could easily have reversed the action and remedied the slight with a simple order that would have done credit to his own stature as a teacher and scholar.

Borges turned to the life of the intellectual, lecturing, teaching, and editing. Although he was not of the oligarchy and had satirized its shortcomings, he continued to despise the Peronist government and what he saw as its demagoguery. His sister and mother, caught up in an unauthorized political demonstration in 1948 in the Calle Florida, were sentenced, respectively, to a month of house detention and a month in jail, a development that did not disabuse him of the belief he maintained to the end that Perón was a Nazi who was married to a whore.

He loved his own Argentina as Perón loved his. They would never comprehend each other and they went their divergent ways, Borges to write and to walk endlessly in his beloved city, his beloved Southside, where in stone-paved street and patio, along walls of pink and pastel, the mournful evocations of old tangos sounded from cluttered bars and cafés. Here for a moment he could escape the somber imaginings that his dreams created out of a past that had never quite been and a present that was not. In the late afternoon in these dim twilight precincts, his hesitant footfall vanishing in the narrow, quiet byways was the symbol of a departing way of life, a lost view of the world, time past flickering in time present.[60]

The Triumph of Evita

These events of the first few years were tightly entwined with Evita's emergence from private into public life, with the maturing of her discipleship, and with her triumph in the sense of her conquest of the political heights. It was a remarkable progression, admitting few if any historical parallels, and a monument to the possibilities of will and passion.

The still-simple young woman who explored with wonder the 283-room presidential residence, the Unzue Palace, and who thought nothing of receiving informal guests while wearing Perón's pajamas with the sleeves and legs rolled up, as yet had barely begun to encounter public affairs. Her public speaking was still awkward and her self-confidence limited. She relied at first upon the almost total attendance of Liliane Guardo as a guide, advisor, and support symbol. Liliane's husband, Ricardo Guardo, a prosperous dentist who had been an early Perón supporter, now found himself designated as president of the Chamber of Deputies in 1946 and he remained a close colleague for almost two years.[61]

Evita had to define and to develop for herself the function she was about to undertake, the role of the intermediary, the visible link, between the president and the millions who were the basis of his political power. There was nothing analytical about it, nothing planned and thought through. That was not Evita's style. She simply hurtled into the perspectives that her new life now opened to her, guided by emotions and ambitions that she would have been unable to define. In the months that followed the inauguration, she began to visit factories and then to dip into labor and social matters. In September, she moved her office to the ministry of labor and welfare, increasing the pace of her consultations with union delegations, her informal givings and bestowals, her role as the people's ambassador to the bureaucracy. Liliane was always there in the background, a personal appellate court in matters of taste, style, and protocol. Was a necklace suitable? Was a gift worthy of its sender? What was the proper protocol for such and such a reception? Liliane would say.

By 1947, Evita was acquiring the status of a genuine celebrity. Her editors at *Democracia*, doing what came naturally, relied heavily on photography that caught the public eye, and particularly on pictures of Evita, for which the market seemed insatiable. When she appeared at gala events at the magnificent Colon Opera House in gowns that were becoming famous in their own right, special issues of *Democracia* had to be printed, devoted largely to pictorial coverage of Evita, and circulation on such days rose from 40,000 to 400,000. She understood what was beginning to happen. "Look, they want to see me beautiful. Poor people don't want someone to protect them who is old and dowdy. They all have their dreams about me and I don't want to let them down."[62] She knew, because she had been there herself. Her emotional rapport was as keen and intimate as Perón's, an intuition developing with remarkable precosity out of hard experience.

Still, some sharpening of definition was needed to confirm her confidence in this new incarnation, and it came in the form of her famous trip to Europe in 1947. Early in the year an invitation had come to Perón from Generalissimo Franco of Spain. The idea was appropriate in a sense, because Argentina and Spain had developed recently a small political and economic axis of their own, and Perón's sense of Hispanic identity was a strong force for affinity. But Franco was controversial, and a trip by Evita, rather than by Perón, extended to other countries as well, would carry less symbolism and yet still garner the benefits. And besides, Evita wanted to go.

She took off on June 6 in a special DC4 provided by Franco, with a large entourage, including her brother Juan and Liliane Guardo. Franco met her at the airport in Madrid. Then began the panoply, the receptions, the slow progressions by automobile through lanes of cheering hordes, the tossed flowers, the speeches from balconies overlooking vast historic plazas, the gifts, the fireworks, the decorations awarded, the visits to cathedral and bullfight and tomb that filled the sixty-four days Evita spent in Europe,[63] in Spain, Italy, Portugal, France, and Switzerland. A visit to England was cancelled; Evita had delayed the visit for two weeks, the queen would be in Scotland on the suggested substitute date, and Evita became huffy, alleging "ill health" as a cover for offended dignity, or vanity.

The royal tour was for the most part a fine success, and it was certainly a distinct element in the shaping and tempering of the new Evita. In the solitude of late nighttime the old Evita remained for a little while, the shadow of the child that had known fear. In the great Prado Palace in Madrid, where the swords of Cortes and Pizarro in the armory and the small army of retainers and guards should have banished any thought of intruders, Evita was ill at ease and insisted that Liliane sleep in the same room with her. The first night, in a surge of insecurity, she asked Liliane to help her push some of the heavy Spanish furniture against the door of their chamber.[64]

Evita returned by way of Río, where the Inter-American conference that produced the Río Treaty on hemispheric defense was hard at work. She spent several days attending functions and speeches, but it could not have been entirely pleasurable for her, since the Argentine delegation was headed by the foreign minister, Juan Bramuglia, probably the most able official of the government, but Evita's *bête noir*. Neither his skills nor his later worldwide fame mattered to Evita. She had been, now was, and continued to be, the implacable enemy of Bramuglia. It all started in October 1945, when Evita had been trying to find legal assistance for Perón during his incarceration on Martín García. Bramuglia, as a leading labor lawyer, was one of the men she had seen. Bramuglia at no time opposed Perón or his program, but on that unfortunate October day in his office he had legal or political reasons for deeming her request unwise and he refused to bring an action on her behalf. Evita, who had a much more tenacious hold on grudges than Perón, never forgot or forgave.

The reason for this single-mindedness, so impracticable in politics, was her personalization of everything that happened. In a civilization notable for the degree to which all activity was personalized, she exceeded all others in this practice. She was not interested in ideas or abstractions, except for loyalty, which she defined narrowly. She was absorbed in people and human relationships within a framework of fanatical devotion to Perón that held dominion over all else. Bramuglia might be competent and famous and Perón might consider him valuable, but it was all immaterial because in her mind he had failed the one imperative test of unreasoning loyalty. Hence his name would never be mentioned in *Democracia*. Hence that paper would never print his picture. Hence, on rare occasions when Bramuglia was included in a photograph that had to be carried, his head was removed by air brushing, leaving an eerie torso to mingle with the group.[65] Evita would pursue him until Perón could be persuaded that he was no longer essential.

The tour and its royal trappings marked a transition for Evita. She would continue to attend to protocol and to observe the rituals of statecraft, but never again, until her death, would these be so conspicuous. Instead, she now turned with greater devotion to her other new career, that of social work and involvement in labor and politics. Perón

indicated the contrary in early September during an unusual informal dinner with the American ambassador and his wife, telling them
that Evita's role in the government had been much exaggerated, "but
that in the future she would confine herself to charitable and benefi-
cent work." On the other hand, the ambassador noted, "When she
arrived from her trip, she was reported to have made a speech from
her boat in which she said that she was going to take a more active
part than ever before. We can only wait to see what the answer will
be."[66] It was not long in coming: Evita's version prevailed, with the
full acquiescence of Perón.

From the first weeks of the administration there had been opposition among many even to the tentative first steps Evita was taking,
just as there had been opposition among the military to her prominence when she was Perón's mistress. The American embassy was always
reporting on her controversial role. She was seen as ". . . a national
Argentine headache . . . a good part of the Cabinet and possibly a
majority of officials and of the Congress heartily disapprove of Mad-
ame Perón and her antics."[67] Although the embassy's contacts were
weighted against Evita, its perception of her emerging career was more
objective than its appraisal of Perón's had been at the comparable
stage, and it carefully rejected as silly rumor almost all of the scandalous stories about her that surfaced during every cocktail hour. The
higher the social circle, the greater the rejection of the novelty she
represented; but many who were not professed oligarchs were unhappy
also.

The reason for this was the belief, which went far back in time,
that the lives of proper women should be private and sheltered from
public view. How deeply this was felt can be gauged from the only
possible precedent in recent Argentine history for Evita's experience.
Marcelo T. de Alvear, the Radical Party leader and president between
1922 and 1928, had social standing as high as any in the land. He had
married Regina Pacini, an opera singer, and it had taken a great effort
on his part to make her acceptable in *porteño* society. As soon as she
became Regina Pacini de Alvear, she disappeared into the protective
privacy of her home, and her husband carefully bought up all the
recordings of her opera performances that were on the market to
minimize this unfortunate stain on her reputation. All this was only
one generation before the emergence of Evita.

It was, in fact, a remarkable evidence of Perón's rapport with his
public and with his civilization that he could bring off successfully
such a sharp break with a previously dominant Argentine tradition.
It was analogous to his and Peronism's unprecedented affirmation of

the dignity of manual labor and to their relative indifference to the old intense stress on formal attire. In part, he could do these things because these particular traditions were at their strongest among his enemies. The wife of some unemployed *frigorifico* worker in Berisso, mother of eleven, who took in washing to survive, and a Peronist to the core, did not have strong views on such matters. In part, he could do it because it fitted with the image of a new day and a new Argentina, so carefully cultivated to suit the psychology of this innovative period. In part, he could do it because he was a *caudillo* to whom much is permitted as long as he is successful. And, in large part, he could do it because there was a need for what Evita was now attempting, and because she immediately demonstrated an astounding talent for this strange activity.

The pace of her involvement quickened. In July 1947, a government announcement had noted that in the first eleven months of the administration, Evita had given away $4,280,000 worth of school-books, clothes, shoes, furniture, toys, and food.[68] This level of activity still relied on her personal efforts and those of a few retainers who would help in handouts to the needy who were now coming directly to the presidential residence or to Evita's office. Or she would drive to the homes of the poor and hand over the merchandise, including sugar that she had personally spooned into packets. But as the news of her intentions got around, the petitioners multiplied wondrously, and so did the sources of supply. She began to receive delegations of workers with substantial gifts in kind for her program, and funds from those who were interested, but disinterested, and from those who were anything but disinterested. By May 1948, she was beginning to receive funds from the ministry of finance out of available surpluses, and letters requesting her help were arriving at the rate of 12,000 a day.[69] But all this was still primitive in relation to what would soon follow.

On July 8, 1948, what would soon be known as the Eva Perón Foundation was created, with a range of social assistance purposes so broad as to give it carte blanche. Evita, its founder, was given sole authority for life in matters of organization, and ". . . the widest powers afforded by the State and the Constitution."[70]

With such singleness of direction, the foundation flourished as none other. By the end of the 1940s it exceeded, in size, in influence, and in general significance, most of the ministries of the government. Its assets exceeded $200 million. It had 14,000 permanent employees, including thousands of construction workers and a staff of priests. It acquired for distribution to the poor fantastic amounts of supplies, such as 200,000 cooking pots, 400,000 pairs of shoes, 500,000 sewing machines. Its flood of revenues came from many sources. Labor unions donated cash and goods made in the factories where members worked. The first few weeks of a pay raise would be donated to the foundation. The CGT contributed three man-days (later reduced to two) of salary for every worker it represented. A tax on lottery and movie tickets and a levy on casino revenues and admissions to horse races were fruitful. The Congress found ways to shift something here and there to the *Señora* without resorting to the direct budget support that Perón opposed. There were also a few cases of contributions that came by way of extortion, and more that were the casual consequence of the foundation's quirky accounting, since its reimbursements were unpredictable. One of the few things that did not interest Evita was this matter of accounting, a subject that she associated with capitalistic coldness of heart.[71]

With such wealth at hand, the foundation's program rapidly outgrew even the massive distribution of mere supplies. Twelve hospitals, with the best equipment available anywhere, were built, A thousand new schools appeared. There were clinics, medical centers, homes for the aged, convalescent centers, a home for girls who had come to Buenos Aires looking for work, transit homes for those needing temporary shelter, student cities, children's homes, including a famous Children's City built to the scale of its inhabitants, with small markets, a church, public buildings, a bank that issued script, streets, houses, and dormitories for four hundred and fifty particularly disadvantaged children. The foundation also built the *Barrio Presidente Perón,* a development with six hundred new houses just west of Buenos Aires, and it built Evita City, a planned community with 15,000 homes. Many of the public structures were notable for a tone of luxury unfamiliar in such places, a touch of brocade and damask and crystal, and this was deliberate, a form of social recompense.[72] Evita was in top command of everything.

The work of the foundation strongly reinforced the personalism that was part and parcel of the authoritarian mystique. Evita herself was careful to preserve her personal and visible connections to the whole immense process. She received delegations of union representatives with their donations, and she held a kind of public court on regular days to greet each of the many suppliants for her assistance. She would be seated at her desk, surrounded by aides who fluttered in and out on errands, bearing memo pads and piles of crisp new bills to be handed out; by secretaries and photographers; by whomever was curious and wanted to come. The suppliants filed by slowly with their inexhaustible requests: an apartment, eye glasses, toys, a bed, a bag of sugar, furniture, redress against a landlord, a job, a dress for a daughter, dentures. It was her practice to give more than was requested because she wished in this public way to emphasize her view, held strongly, that her programs did not represent charity, which she despised almost as much as she did the oligarchs, but, rather, a return to the people of what they were rightfully entitled to.[73]

This personal approach was reflected in everything the foundation did. The names of Perón and Evita were everywhere, as were their pictures, their initials, and the reminders of their virtues. No wall of any foundation building was too small for a Peronist message of some kind, and no shirt too shoddy for a Peronist inscription. The stress on personality brought forth the titles that Evita now bore— The Lady of Hope, the Mother of the Innocents, The Workers' Plenipotentiary, and her favorite, The Bridge of Love.[74] Abroad, such language was seen as excessive, an embarrassment, but in the histrionic and romantic Hispanic spirit it found full sanction. The increasing personalism also brought the endless multiplication of the name of both Perón and Evita throughout the country, on railway stations, parks, aqueducts, schools, plazas, ports, avenues, ships, in city districts, and much else. An astronomer at the University of La Plata who thought he had discovered a new star promptly named it "Evita." The Juan Perón Children's Library was published in twelve volumes, their pages devoted not to Dick and Jane but to Perón and Evita.[75] The domestic opposition to Perón found all of this distressing, and so did general opinion outside of Argentina. Many concluded that it was part of a dictatorial buildup, or a conscious campaign for ego-satisfaction by a pair of leaders thirsting for glory. But this missed the point. Rather, adulation personalized in this manner was another facet of the symbiosis between the leader in the *caudillo*-oriented Creole tradition and his followers, a generally spontaneous response by loyal supporters of a strong ruler.

Strangely, this immense activity of the foundation did not entirely deplete the energies and enthusiasm of Evita, and she was equally active in politics. This did not extend, however, to the issue that has often been identified with her, the attainment of women's suffrage. That question had a long background of attempt and failure, but by the late 1940s, Argentina was ready for it, and various bills were introduced in Congress in 1946 without any initiative by Evita. She, of course, favored the idea and spoke on behalf of one of the bills, but she had little involvement and her role was mostly ceremonial.

Evita, in fact, was not a feminist in the style that is familiar now, forty years later. She had no use for the feminist leaders of her time because they were anti-Peronist. She was not interested in feminist theories. She believed that a women's movement should devote itself to the cause of a man, and that women should not be deprived of their right to a domestic existence. Above all, far above all, the role of women in Argentina was to provide every kind of unceasing support for Perón. And yet she did more to bring women into public life in Argentina than a large army of feminists could have done, and she did it through an instrumentality that was made possible by the suffrage that she had favored but had not brought about: the Peronist Women's Party.

Founded by Evita in July 1949, this new organization was the beneficiary of the enormous registration of women that followed the granting of suffrage in 1947. Very soon the number of voters was more than doubled, and in May 1950, there were more than 807,000 women registered in Buenos Aires, 60,000 more than the number of men.[76] By 1952, Evita's new party had half a million members and 3,600 branches around the country, and it was a mighty factor in Perón's second election.[77] In terms of organization and administration it was miles ahead of the men's party. Within a year or so after the first election, Evita had developed into a highly effective platform speaker, capable of impromptu eloquence and an emotional empathy that ran through crowds like an electric discharge. She did this by ignoring the jargon of politics and speaking instead from her heart, the source of her personality and being. It was effective because it was authentic and reflected the experiences and concerns of her hard formative years, which were the lot of so many of those who listened.

There was no doubt in anyone's mind of the importance she had acquired by 1950, within the government and in the nation. She intervened in labor strikes and labor politics, she dominated the extraordinary foundation, she made and unmade careers in the government, her brother Juan was Perón's private secretary and had much to say about who would get to see the president, and she held the allegiance of millions. There was serious discussion in the United States Department of State as to whether she had less or more power than Perón.[78] Leaders of the army hierarchy, never fully reconciled to the phenomenon of Evita, tried rather cautiously in March 1949 to urge Perón to limit her activity, Perón refused. Instead, he took Evita to a luncheon at Campo de Mayo, where she and the others listened as the war minister, General Sosa Molina, delivered the address that represented the army's strategic retreat. When the American assistant secretary of state, Edward Miller, visited Buenos Aires early in 1951, he was not received by Perón, as he had been in the preceding year, but by Evita and one of her allies, the minister of finance. Miller, who saw Evita as the emerging real power in the state, with tremendous impact, reported that at one point during their discussions Evita told the Minister to "shut up."[79]

With her discovery of vocation and her conquest of power, Evita had reached a lonely eminence by 1950. Surrounded by thousands, she walked among them almost disembodied, a saint-to-be for many, or a beautiful emanation of pure spirit, sexless and serene, or a driven woman at the beck of duties and visions unglimpsed by others. And for her unreconstructed enemies, a combination of scourge, whore, and evil genius.

For she had changed in the three years that followed the royal mission to Europe. No longer was the blonde hair pompadoured in great billows, but pulled back severely into a bun at the back of her neck. Gone were the fabled gowns that had been the talk of Madrid and Rome, and the jewels that had clustered on wrist, bodice, and golden sandals. Now the black suit and the occasional jewelled Peronist emblem spoke not of diplomatic receptions but of duty almost monastic. In plain fact, Evita was working as few monks ever have, working through the day and through much of the night, at a pace the human body cannot long tolerate.

The new vistas had aroused the strain of austerity that was native to her. She did not smoke. She drank no alcohol, only water. She no longer had time to listen to Chopin, her favorite composer. Her only concession to luxury was her continuing love of jewels, but she bought none; friends and unions and ambitious acquaintances provided her with them.[80] The famous publicity photo showed her leaving her office for the day: she was fresh and smiling and waving from the back seat of a modest sedan driven by a fresh and smiling chauffeur; in the background, the illuminated dial of a large tower clock gave the hour as twenty minutes to five in the morning. The caption read, "The day's work is finished." Posed though it was, this tableau was not an exaggeration. Routinely, she would arrive at home just as Perón was about to leave for the Casa Rosada. She would have a hasty meal, sometimes eating only the last course to delude him into believing that she had consumed the first courses as well, and would sleep for two or three hours and then return to her office.[81] It was as if a subconscious intimation of mortality had begun to wrack her, mocking the immense work yet undone.

Thus driven, she abandoned almost all of her private life with Perón, not because of any change of affection but out of sheer time pressure.

They met in public more than in private, and their scant time together was disrupted by incessant distraction. Evita's purposes enlarged as fanaticism deepened, until her crusade almost seemed directed against poverty and injustice per se, not merely against a specific deficiency but against the very idea of social ills. But as purpose expanded and fanaticism intensified, two perceptible evolutions within Evita began apparent.

The first of these changes, which was perhaps merely a new emphasis, concerned an upsurge of harshness and intolerance. She had always found it easy to identify the enemy and she had always felt strongly about almost everything. Hate had therefore always come as easily as devotion. She was proud, she declared in her May Day address of 1950, to have the two greatest distinctions any woman can aspire to, "the love of the humble and the hate of the oligarchs."[82] But now her drives took on a public and political aspect that much affected the direction of national life, for they began to reinforce strongly the tendency of the government toward repression in general. On March 18, 1950, in a formal address, she expressed the wish that the government agencies be purified by elimination of those who were politically indifferent or who failed to realize that "General Perón is burning his life and his hours on the altar of an ideal for the greatness of the Argentine people." Then, very explicitly, she continued, "I ask the workers to denounce the anti-Peronists, because they are traitors, and I also ask their officials to take measures, because if they don't, we shall believe that they too are traitors . . . he who does not feel himself to be a Peronist, cannot feel himself an Argentine."[83] In some jurisdictions within Argentina the failure to obtain Peronista Party membership was already a sufficient cause for dismissal from public employment.[84] Evita had always inclined to view anti-Peronism as something akin to treason, and now, speaking officially, she was extending this extreme concept of treason to those who were merely indifferent.

The second change in Evita as the 1940s ended was the transmutation of her love for Perón into a passion that became a kind of religion. To understand that evolution, one must first comprehend the nature of her feeling for Perón from the early days of their marriage, and then understand how that union created, defined, and limited her power.

Her feelings for Perón were from the very first those of total devotion, enhanced by the intensity of her nature. There are few proofs that have survived, since Evita was not given to letter writing and the recollections of others are partisan and fragile. However, one authentic source does remain, written under circumstances that strongly suggest its sincerity. On the night of June 6, 1947, a short time before her plane took off for Europe, an apprehensive Evita was sitting in her section in the specially equipped plane, fighting her fears. She had never flown; she was frightened of the very thought; she had never been farther from Buenos Aires than across the estuary in Montevideo; she had never been away from Perón since they had met, except for his days on Martín García; she had little experience of the world and none at all of European statecraft; she was about to represent her nation before the world, under conditions that would daunt any young woman of twenty-eight; and she had just received a hurtful blow in the form of some accusation out of her past, which cannot be reconstructed. It was not the moment for playing games. She reached for pen and paper and and with little regard for syntax and punctuation poured out her heart to Perón in a rush of desperation and love:

Dear Juan,

I am very sad to be leaving because I am unable to live away from you, I love you so much that what I feel for you is a kind of idolatry, perhaps I don't know how to show what I feel for you, but I assure you that I fought very hard in my life with the ambition to be someone and I suffered a great deal, but then you came and made me so happy that I thought it was a dream and since I had nothing else to offer you but my heart and my soul I gave it to you wholly but in all these three years of happiness, greater each day, I never ceased to adore you for a single hour or thank heaven for the goodness of God in giving me this reward of your love, and I tried at all times to deserve it by making you happy, I don't know if I achieved that, but I can assure you that nobody has ever loved you or respected you more than I have. I am so faithful to you that if God wished me not to have you in this happiness and took me away I would still be faithful to you in my death and adore you from the skies; Juancito, darling, forgive me for these confessions but you have to know this now I am leaving and I am in the hands of God and do not know if something may happen to me . . . you have purified me, your wife with all her faults, because I live in you, feel for you and think through you . . .[85]

The final words were rich with meaning, for Evita did live in Perón and think through him. This emerges clearly in one of her books, published at the turn of the decade, *Historia del Peronismo*. It contains her lectures at the *Escuela Superior Peronista,* a school where students were trained to go forth and work in Peronist causes. Parts of the lectures were certainly assembled for her, or taken from Perón's *Conducción Política,* but with equal certainty they reflect her true views to which she was lending her name. A selection of her comments about Perón is revealing:

Life for her began on the day she met Perón. It is as difficult to describe him as it is for an artist to paint or describe the sun. He is a true creator who has nothing to envy in the greatest creators of all humanity. He is everything, the soul, the nerves, the hope, and the reality of the Argentine people. He is a genius who has no defects, and if a defect were to be discerned, it would be that of too much heart. He is irreplaceable, and if any unworthy person tried to supplant him, that person would have to be gotten rid of. Perón is the Fatherland, he is work, he is well-being. He is the only locomotive that pulls the nation behind it. "For me Perón, whom I have analyzed deeply, is perfect," "I have said that Perón is my illumination, my sky, that he is the very air, that he is my life. But I have not only said it; I have acted accordingly." And finally, "We then are like sparks from the great meteor of Perón, who is illuminating this Peronist century in national and universal history, because, like the geniuses, Perón is a meteor whose burning enlightens the century."[86]

Such sentiments will seem to many, and particularly to those from another ethos, as extreme to the point of caricature, or even delirium. But there can be little doubt that these feelings are the clue to the real Evita, to her ardent and impassioned nature, and to her union of mind and soul with Perón. Her beliefs thus phrased she held to be true literally, quite literally, and therefore they make clear the central paradox of her power: on the one hand, immense authority and influence in many spheres of the national life, all the more awesome because they were entirely unofficial and entirely undefined; on the other hand, no real power in her own right whatsoever, since everything she was or could do or might become existed (by her own definition and preference) only as a reflection of Perón. He was the source and the limitation, the infinite and the finite. For him, imagination itself could not have created a more serviceable instrumentality, and for her, imagination could not have contrived a higher destiny.

Emotions strung so tautly are likely to take on a religious character. Although Evita was not ostentatious in her practices, she was a believing Roman Catholic. It is not surprising that as her public crusades and her private adorations took on a narrowing intensity after 1946, they simultaneously veered toward the transcendental. It was not that she claimed divinity for Perón, not quite; she had once noted that he was of the earth; but her expressions eventually drew so heavily on metaphors of divinity and Christ that she clearly had come to regard him as a being apart. "Perón is the visage of God in the darkness, and above all in the darkness that afflicts humanity in this moment." Just as the Christians in ancient Rome died for Christ, "We, who love Perón more than anything, are going to die for Perón, because we are not defending a personal thing, but a national cause," since Perón was the nation. The students in her course were sent forth as "apostles of Perón." His greatness of heart was compared to that of Christ who forgave those who crucified him, and ". . . we must hold three things sacred: the Fatherland, the People, and Perón."[87] In her May Day oration in 1950, she described Perón as ". . . that sacred being who is the nation and for whom we would willingly give our lives with pleasure one and a thousand times."[88]

Thus in defining the relationship of Evita to Perón and to Peronism in the years of her triumph, one does well to seek a religious metaphor. And one is at hand: Evita was not the St. Peter of Peronism, not its St. Paul or its Pope Gregory the Great; even less was she its Thomas Aquinas; rather, she was the Ignatius Loyola of Peronism, a one-woman Jesuit Order, the greatest and most God-imbued of the "Grenadier Guards of the Pope." Like Loyola, who had seen the Trinity in Unity on the steps of the Church of the Dominicans in Venice and had wept in wonder at the vision, Evita had seen an Incarnation. And she had become its Bride.

The Economy in the Days of Good Fortune

Evita's social crusade and Perón's policies were swept along by a sustaining current of economic prosperity. Argentina was rich, as if the triangular geography itself were a cornucopia whose tapered end was not yet in sight. The reason for this was simple. During the war, Argentina had exported much more than it was able to import, thus earning immense blocked sterling deposits in London and gold balances in the United States. Its sterling debt was largely repaid or repatriated.[89]

But the ledger had another side. The wartime neutrality policy that had been so attentive to public opinion was a misfortune for the economy. Rejecting the North American effort to mobilize the hemisphere in support of the war effort, Argentina failed to achieve the economic transformations that the war brought to the principal Commonwealth countries and to the larger Latin American nations.[90]

Perón's approach to the new economy that would have to undergird the new nation he proclaimed was immediately clear—it would be a statist policy. On October 21, 1946, he presented to Congress a huge design formulated by José Figuerola and termed The Five-year Plan. It aimed at everything in a spirit of unlimited optimism, all to be achieved through greatly enlarged state ownership, authority, administration, and policy-making. Its core was a new vehicle, the

Instituto Argentina de Promoción del Intercambio, the Argentine Trade
Promotion Institute, or IAPI, a new giant among institutions designed
to dominate the economy, serving as the buffer between foreign and
domestic sellers and purchasers, buying domestic production for a
lower figure and selling it abroad for a higher, and also intervening
actively in the control and purchase of imports through licensing and
otherwise.[91]

To manage this potentially huge bureaucracy, Perón called upon
a new economic man of all skills, Miguel Miranda, a self-confident
entrepreneur equally devoid of doubt and technical training. Perón
was delighted with this iconoclastic high-flyer, and the first stages of
the five-year program, the nationalization of various basic enterprises,
went rapidly and well.[92] But the most important nationalization, that
of the railroads, was more complicated.

The economically pragmatic Perón favored a mixed-company
solution, short of full purchase, but a violent political wind blew up
and the nationalistic Perón flew on its currents. Purchase of the major
foreign holdings was completed on March 1, 1947, accompanied by
an incandescent outburst. A major political coup; but in economic
terms almost certainly a prime mistake, understandable and perhaps
almost inevitable, but a mistake nevertheless. The decomposing railways required capital, but did not generate it. They were not a repro-
ductive industry, did little to stimulate economic growth, provided no
new jobs except through wasteful bureaucratic staffing that became
almost scandalous, and lost money by the bucket. It has been estimated (although the figures are ambiguous) that a single railroad from
1947 to 1951 lost more than half the amount spent to buy the entire
network.[93] And the reserves in London that could have paid for capital goods sorely needed for the ambitious industrialization program
were mostly gone, spent on euphoria.[94]

Meanwhile, IAPI was selling abroad for high prices, but its surpluses could not cover all five-year-plan requirements; what there was
often seemed to be spent haphazardly; the bureaucracy was expensive
and wasteful; business immorality became extensive. Too little was
left for true investment. From this, and from the concentration of
private investment in manufacturing (mostly small-scale, light industry import substitution), came the central problem of Peronist economic administration: investment policy.[95] This, much more than the
rapid increases in wages and social payments that for a time outran
advances in productivity, was the Achilles heel of Peronist economics.
And at the heart of the investment problem was the eternal old lack
of concern in all matters agricultural. Campaign pledges to reform

the patterns of land tenure in favor of small ownerships were put aside, and the great landowners congregated in the rural society were reassured.

The chain of causation seems clear. Capital for imported materials and equipment could come only from exports; that meant the products of the land; and these were declining, with a larger proportion going to internal consumption.[96] The question is not entirely clear, however. Recent economic analysis has tended to give Perón's economic policies higher marks than did early appraisals. It is clear that the land was not being abandoned, and that some of the statistics of declining output fail to reflect an increase in acreage for newer crops and for grazing, a case of changes in investment within the agricultural sector.[97]

The public services continued to soak up manpower, and public expenditures ran well ahead of revenues. The gap between them was covered by monetizing the debt and printing currency. Inflation jumped from 13 percent to 31 percent in 1949. On January 19, Miguel Miranda fell. And an era of optimism and booming good times ended,[98] attesting, among other things, to errors in economic planning and implementation, to the fragility of prophecy (since Perón and Miranda both counted on a Third World War, and soon), and to the preference of the Argentine civilization for political over economic values.

The Third World Priest: "Only an Argentine can understand Peronism. I can talk to you for five years about Peronism, but you will never understand."

— V. S. Naipaul, *The Return of Eva Perón*

8. Peronism at High Tide

The Nature of Peronism

THE WANING YEARS of the first administration represented for Perón and for Peronism a time of transition. The political and social successes of the process that began in 1943 had reached a rather ambiguous plateau whose time boundaries are imprecise. The difficulties of the 1950s, although foreshadowed, were still horizon-distant. The legendry of the man and of the movement had begun to trace the great arc that would extend for decades. Much would alter, but the lineaments of Peronism would retain the essential cast they has assumed by 1950. What, then, was Peronism at this moment in its history?

One should first clear away the inappropriate definitions and parallels. Thus: Peronism was not fascism.[1] Some of Peronism's adherents had a fascist outlook and mentality. Perón himself admired Mussolini and the idea of the corporate state. Some of the trappings of Peronism recalled the ambiance of the Black Shirts. But all this was relatively superficial. No fascist society was ever erected on a mass base of laboring and dispossessed hordes. In its own descriptions of identity, Peronism rejected the Fascist parallel. It was more intimately grounded in the national history and ethos than was any European fascism.[2] The structure of the Peronist state after the constitutional amendments of 1949 remained that of the old Argentine democratic order.

Peronism was not nazism. Again, on the extreme fringes of the nationalist elements collected in the right-wing Nationalist Liberation Alliance (ALN) and among a small number of pro-Axis military officers, there were Nazi sympathizers. And Buenos Aires was a center of German espionage and propaganda activity during parts of the Second World War. But Peronism's main thrust reflected no adherence to Nazi principles. There were occasional minor aggressions against synagogues (and Protestant churches) and the police reaction was not always rigorous, but Peronism as such had no anti-Semitic or other racial bias. As Ambassador Messersmith reported at length in May 1947, "There is not as much social discrimination against Jews here as there is right in New York or in most places at home . . ."[3] In this, Perón did not scramble for the moral high ground in the spirit of a crusader; that was not his style. Practical awareness was always at the forefront of his politics, and in the 1940s there were half a million Jews in Argentina, along with an equal number of Arabs. His private preference was for the Arabs, partly because he believed they assimilated more completely into Argentine society and partly, one may assume, because of the Islamic elements in his beloved Hispanic heritage; but the potential conflict between these ethnic rivals had to be muted in the interests of the organic state, and there was no official anti-Semitism.

Peronism was not communism and it was not socialism. On the contrary, Perón saw these as his principal opposition in the struggle for the allegiance of labor, and the polemics of Peronism vibrate with antipathy for the redoubts of class struggle.[4] Peronism was not Bonapartism, nor was it Nassarism.[5] And it was not a political party. Rather, it was a matter of emotional or spiritual identification; or again, "Peronism is more than a party, it is a mystique."[6]

Peronism was not a movement of the left or of the right. A movement whose founder spends his life combating the economic and social elite, whose great contribution was to bring the anonymous masses into the political and economic mainstream, and whose lifelong electoral base was principally organized labor, can hardly be deemed rightist. On the other hand, a movement that opposed the idea of class struggle, that largely obliterated the old parties of the left, that sought and obtained much industrialization under private ownership, and that preserved the economy of the oligarchy intact is obviously not leftist either. "Indeed, the strength of Peronism reduced many politicians of both left and right to marginal status, thus giving Argentina's political system some of its distinctive features."[7]

Peronism was not a dictatorship. Admittedly, definition is a factor here, but as the American embassy stated in April 1948, ". . . Perón is far from being a dictator in the sense of having absolute authority." This viewpoint was explicitly adopted in the Department of State's Secret Policy Statement of March 21, 1950.[8] The cabinet debated measures at length. The army concerned itself with foreign policy. Totalitarian methods frequently appeared in the operations of the police, or in repression of the press, or in restrictions imposed on the conduct of opposition, but this falls short of a dictatorship. Perón often had to bargain for support, to trim his sails on the timing of initiatives, and to balance interests that could not be overridden. Strong and authoritarian and sometimes oppressive, yes. But not really dictatorial.[9]

Peronism was not a capitalistic or an anticapitalistic movement. Or, perhaps more accurately, it was *simultaneously* capitalistic and anticapitalistic. The "language of words" marks it as anticapitalist, and the "language of facts" points in the opposite direction. In the good times of the 1940s, the surge of small industries was carried on a wave of private ownership. Despite the intrusion of the Peronist state into large areas of the economy, when the economic crisis of the early 1950s had to be met it was confronted with a standard array of capitalistic measures and not by radical restructuring. No attack on rural private ownership was ever made. ". . . Peronism was by no means an *alternative* to capitalism but one of the peculiar forms that capitalism itself may assume in an underindustrialized but modern country with a highly mobilized urban mass."[10]

Peronism was not a working-class or labor movement per se. There were numerous other elements involved in it, and these other elements varied from era to era and between regions in Argentina.[11] Peronism was not a specific class alliance, or a movement definable in class terms, such as bourgeoisie nationalism.[12] The groups and sectors supporting Peronism varied too much over time, and institutions such as the army and the church were too influential to be thus overlooked.

What, then, was Peronism? Any answer must be as complicated as the enumeration of what it was not, but for general purposes Peronism may be seen as a blend, strictly Argentine in its uniqueness, of four component traditions or movements. The first, although not the most important and never fully implemented, was authoritarian corporatism, in the line of descent from the organic community of Suárez and Vitoria. Its homeland was the northern shores of the Mediterranean, and Perón was its spiritual descendent.[13]

The second component, and a very important one, was populism.[14] Functioning on the social and the psychological levels as well as on the purely political, Peronist populism became a tremendously dynamic force for the integration into national life of millions of workers and others who had been on the outside. It is interesting to observe that for reasons related to the failure of middle-class leadership, populism in Argentina arose not in agrarian areas and in bad times as it had in Canada and the United States, but in urban settings and in good times.[15]

The third component, also important, was nationalism; and the fourth, vital indeed, was the *caudillo* element, for it was this that was at the center of Perón's enormous ability to touch the hearts of millions on dimly discerned levels of psychological intimacy. At the time of the great events in 1945, by far the most astute journalist observing Argentina was the correspondent of the *Times* of London, a man who had penetrated deeply into the intangibles of the ethos. "The Argentine masses," he wrote, "have shown a marked preference for a *Caudillo* . . . as against a political party with a doctrine and fixed programme . . . A *Caudillo* is a leader with a personal following. A programme, doctrine, or ideology is not essential; but a *Caudillo* must have great personality and be different from other men. He needs courage, auadacity, good looks, kindness to the poor, understanding of working-class psychology, and an atmosphere of mystery, though not all these qualities are essential. Colonel Perón is a *Caudillo*. There is only one Colonel Perón."[16]

Peronism, then, may be defined roughly as an authoritarian populist movement, strongly colored by Catholic social thought, by nationalism, by organic principles of Mediterranean corporatism, and by the *caudillo* traditions of the Argentine Creole civilization.

The sources of support for this rather complicated and imprecise movement are one of its remarkable facets. It is not surprising that the Peronist coalition was based on organized and urban labor, or that it had the support of many army officers, or that in the beginning it won the allegiance of some of the new industrialists who were seeking innovation and whose support for Perón was helpful in warding off a direct and fatal confrontation of rich against poor,[17] or that some clerical elements favored it. Nor is it surprising that it found support from a minority of the middle class who were clearly disaffected, for Perón in his appeals for broad backing had frequently praised the middle class, even describing it in one of his books as ". . . undoubtedly the source of the most important values of the Argentine people."[18]

But it was unusual that Perón could combine these elements and achieve his essential ends without pursuing any group to the limit, in fact as opposed to rhetoric, and that even the landowners were not expropriated or driven to the point that they had no hope of survival within the system.[19] And it is surprising, indeed, that Peronism could at the same time find a very important power base in the poverty-infested and nonindustrial regions of the interior. Here Peronism developed an unexpected and informal coalition with local *caudillos* and other political leaders, many of them former conservatives. As the urban elements of Perón's coalition, other than labor, tended to dissolve with time, so the breadth and depth of the interior elements tended to increase. Thus Peronism, which by 1946 had almost completely displaced the Socialists and the Communists as the voice of the urban working classes, was doing something quite unusual: it had ". . . consolidated its strength by discarding old power structures over the urban working class and by preserving old power structures over the rural poor."[20]

Simply as a feat of political management, this accommodation of such essentially dissimilar forces is memorable, for different techniques and political formats and institutions were necessary. "The fact that Peronism has managed to provide political expression for two such disparate forces is both its most notable feature and, in the end, the most singular facet of Argentine politics."[21]

Such was Peronism—unique and very much of its time and place. But the uniqueness lay in its totality, and in the specific combination of its elements, and in the emphases and priorities they were given. For almost every single thing that is characteristic of Peronism had precedent in Argentine history. This is no derogation; if it were not so, if Perón had not been able to draw upon the national memory and subconscious, even so sensitive an empathy and intuition as his would not have sufficed. As it was, the mingling of time present and time past was almost spectacular:

In political life, the discontents marshalled in Peronist populism were heralded as far back as the time of Mitre by provincial uprisings that were ended by local *Caudillos* only in 1876.[22] In the time of Yrigoyen, populist political movements in the Cuyo had brought *Lenczismo* and *Bloquismo* to national attention, and they survived into the era of the Peronato; shortly before his death, Peron acknowledged in a letter commemorating *Bloquismo* that the San Juan movement was ". . . a precursor of the postulates of social justice, political sovereignty and economic liberty that nourish the Justicialist Doctrine."[23] Peronism's self-vision as a national movement rather than a party was based squarely on the example of Radicalism under Yrigoyen. The idea of a political organization as a moral, messianic and half-mystic manifestation descended from Alem and Yrigoyen.[24] The first mass spectacle in Argentine politics, foreshadowing so many October 17s and May 1s in the Peronato, occurred under Yrigoyen. The *caudillo*, with his mystique and his intuition, had been exemplified in Rosas, in Yrigoyen, and, in lesser degrees, in scores of figures scattered throughout the Argentine past. The devotion to corporatism was deep in the political culture, and had come to the surface with Uriburu and his political and literary advisers. The Peronist affinity for strong and centralized government had come down from Castile in the great flood of inheritance. Much of the Peronist social legislation was first advocated by the Socialists. Press controls, less thorough than Perón's, had been prominently employed by the governments of the 1930s. Perón's Constitution of 1949 reflected much of a book entitled *La reforma constitucional*, published the year before by Carlos Ibarguren. Perón's neutrality policy in the Second World War followed the example of Yrigoyen in the First World War.

In economics, it was much the same. The changes being made in the economy through state intervention under the Peronato had been proposed in strong and warning terms by an economist, Alejandro Bunge, two decades before Perón rose to power. Argentine industrialization and the import substitution industries now under way were originally proposed by the famous Argentine economist, Raul Prebisch. Perón's IAPI, the keystone of Peronist economics, was the direct descendant of the National Grain Board and of three other boards for meat, milk products, and the wine industry, created a decade before the Peronato by President Justo.[25] Arms industries operated for or by the military, which came into existence with *Fabricaciones Militares*, were proposed originally by then-Colonel Enrique Mosconi in 1929. Exchange controls, among other devices for regulating trade that were embraced and expanded under Perón, dated from the 1930s. Economic nationalism traced its development as far back as the 1880s, when warnings against foreign financing were first heard, and its roots were bundled into a strong mass under Yrigoyen and the YPF.[26]

The social policies of Perón had similar precedents. The theme of the just state was a staple of traditional Catholic social thought. The three master principles of Peronism, always recounted together as "social justice, economic independence, and political sovereignty," had been enunciated in substantially the same language ten years before Perón by Arturo Jauretche, whose militant youth organization, FORJA, had mostly deserted the Radical Party for Perón in 1945. The theme of social justice as the responsibility of the state rather than of the politicians had been contributed to Perón by the influential writer,

Manuel Gálvez, in a 1934 work entitled *Este pueblo necesita*. It was also the program of a group called Argentine Action, organized by pro-democratic and pro-Allied forces in 1940, which attempted to combine nationalism and economic and social reform.[27]

The nationalism so prominent under Perón also had many precedents, some of them much more extreme. There had been the lost *Argentinidad* of Ricardo Rojas early in the century, mellow in comparison to the later urgings of Ibarguren, Leopoldo Lugones, and others; and the preachings of *Hispanidad*. The Radical Party had always assumed things foreign to be things alien.

Even Evita had her precedent, a remote one, in the form of Doña Encarnación, the remarkable wife and political helpmate of Rosas a century back.

And there had been a multitude of foreign precedents, both in Latin America and in Europe, whose examples had filtered into the general consciousness of the times. At the time of the First World War, José Batlle y Ordóñez, in Uruguay, had been the first in Latin America to implant the welfare state and the broad themes of social justice. Getulio Vargas, in Brazil, and Carlos Ibáñez, in Chile, had both brought legislation of a populist character to their countries well before Perón, who was likewise affected by the European examples that he had personally observed in his tour of duty in Italy and in his travels in Germany and Spain. In the latter country, Primo de Rivera had sought to develop labor support for his military government twenty years before Perón.

Justicialismo

Although Perón's views were well settled by 1945, they had not been formulated into a philosophy or ideology. Thus the creation of *Justicialismo* as the formal philosophy of Peronism followed his access to power instead of preceding it, and it was a culmination rather than a beginning. In 1946, such system as his beliefs attained was limited to an historical overview of cycles. In a speech given in December 1945, he stated, "For me the cycle of the French Revolution ends in 1914 and a new historic cycle opens: that of the Russian Revolution. This begins in 1914, triumphs in Russia in 1918 and reaches its apogee in Europe in 1945 . . . The Russian Revolution ends government by the bourgeoisie and gives birth to government by the masses. This is absolutely incontrovertible fact." In his interview with Jorge Mañach in November 1945, he observed that the era of the bourgeoisie had been the era of the rights of man in the sense of the rights of the individual; but starting in 1918, ". . . the period of mass rights has commenced. Everything which has happened since then has tended in that direction: the Russian Revolution, that of Italy, Nazism . . . these are nothing but different aspects of the same historical phenomenon: the transfer of emphasis from the political to the social."[28]

But more than this would be needed if Peronism were to claim a defined ideology. It was not that the men of government during the first, or even the second, administration had major differences of view or policy. Compared to previous regimes, the Peronists were singularly united, without "wings" or "blocs." But they lacked an agreed-upon statement of faith. For the first three years of his government, Perón did not even mention an ordained body of doctrine as such. But by 1949 this had been attended to, with the development of *Justicialismo* as the official ideology, complete with its values and symbols. It immediately acquired, or fell heir to, a near monopoly of political representation, tending to submerge lesser dispensations.[29]

Justicialismo is a term coined from the Spanish words for "social" and "justice," and it translates very uneasily into English. Its official version was articulated in 1951 by Raúl Mende, who had replaced José Figuerola as planning minister. Mende had once been a Jesuit seminarian, and his mind ran to the abstractions that Perón also found congenial. It is not surprising that under Mende's guidance *Justicialismo* reflected the inspiration of *Rerum Novarum* and *Quadragesimo Anno,* together with a whiff of Hegel: "*Justicialismo:* a doctrine whose object is the happiness of man within the society of mankind through the harmonizing of material, spiritual, individual and collective forces, appraised from the Christian standpoint."[30]

Justicialismo divided those forces into two pairs of opposites: spirit and matter, and the individual and the collective. It was nearer to the spiritual extreme than to the material one, and it favored the individual over the collective. But the extremes were to be resisted in favor of the harmonies that would be established at an intermediate point between each pair of them, the location of that point depending on the forces involved in any given situation. If individual interests and collective interests were opposed in some conflict, and the collective interests happened to be more forceful in the ratio of two to one, the point of equilibrium would be two-thirds of the distance along the line from the individual end to the collective extreme.

Thus *Justicialismo* sought to be much more than a political or social doctrine or ideology. It also saw itself as a philosophy seeking to harmonize and reconcile human interests in all spheres. Its goal was the "organized community," in which, under the guidance of the tutelary state, conflicting interests would be brought into harmony. In international affairs, this principle of intermediacy took the form of the "Third Position," an attempt to avoid the extremes of the now-polarized world. The concept, like the other elements of Peronism, had its precedents, in this case an idea advanced by Argentine Action in 1940. Even the phrase itself was familiar, having been employed by Bonifacio del Carril and his Renovation Movement in 1941. As Perón said to him a little later, "You wrote it, but I'm going to achieve it."[31]

All of this lent itself to ambiguity, and even more to flexibility and to improvisation, those two great desiderata of Peronism. Speaking to the Confederation of Intellectuals in September 1940, Perón referred to the Third Position: ". . . [it] is not a middle-of-the-road position. It is an ideological position which is in the center, the left, or the right according to circumstances. We obey the circumstances." In a speech on December 21, 1950, Perón again demonstrated this power of self-definition: ". . . Capitalism calls for maximum profit from the least effort. We call for the maximum production—the amount necessary to meet social needs. That is the important thing. That is *Justicialismo*." On another topic: "It is utopian to want to make communism disappear if exploitation and the abuses of capitalism do not disappear. *Justicialismo* does just that." Or again: "If Russia wants to be communist, all right; everybody can be what he likes in his own country. That is a doctrine of *Justicialismo*."[32] But the improvisation for which it was the outer garment was extremely important, creating a climate of opinion very different from that which results from ideological purity and rigidity. Improvisation is a live-and-let-live approach that avoids, if not confrontation, at least the fatal confrontation of social revolution.[33]

It has been argued that this doctrine that followed and defined action rather than sponsoring it, and that so easily permitted so much room for maneuver and lent itself so cheerfully to whatever was desired from one day to the next, was an esoteric thing limited to a small circle, with tiny impact on political action.[34] But it was very useful, indeed, in legitimizing Peronist policies and in presenting them self-servingly to the public. It gave a certain sheen to Peronism, lent it dignity as it were, and in the Argentine civilization these were high credentials.

The Creole Values of Perón

The basic values of Perón were indicated in the descriptions of Peronism and *Justicialismo*. But a few highlights should be noted, because of their effects on the difficulties that were almost endemic in his relations with the United States.

On April 9, 1949, at Mendoza, Perón gave the principal address at the First National Conference on Philosophy. It was a very long talk, extending to 116 pages in the format in which it was published in 1975 as *La Comunidad Organizada,* The Organized Community. In this work Perón addressed his thoughts about man and community. It would be too much to assume that Perón wrote it, or could have provided many of the references, but the main themes were certainly delineated by him, and it was published with his express approval. Reaching back to Plato and the metaphor of the human body whose functions combine in harmony, he adopted the Greek concept of the just state as one in which each class or element exercises its functions and its special abilities for the benefit of all; and then saw the culmination of that state in Christianity. He followed with the two sets of opposites—man and community, and the physical and the spiritual— that adumbrated *Justicialismo.*[35]

In making these points, and many others related to them, the 116 pages brought forth references to Socrates, Plato, Aristotle, Hesiod, the Rig Veda, Victor Hugo, Spinoza, Descartes, Voltaire, Darwin, Leibniz, Empedocles, Spencer, D'Alembert, Kant, Fichte, Berkeley, Bergson, Schelling, Heidegger, Kierkegaard, Keyserling, Goethe, Grotius, Hobbes, and Rabindranath Tagore. What is remarkable is less the parade of names than the fact that a political leader would wish to present such a persona to the public. It was the pedagogic Perón, the instructor of his people.

The great subject of his instruction, following from the themes referred to, was the ideal of the organic state, which he described best in a speech to a visiting delegation from the CGT on August 9, 1950: ". . . the Argentine Republic can now say that it has a better, finer and more perfectly organized workers' movement here than perhaps anywhere else in the world. It is only logical, therefore, that we should now wish to organize the other communities, the economic forces, the producers, the industrialists, the merchants and the consumers . . . When all this is organized we will have an organized community which will not need to fight, but only to discuss and come to an agreement, like a jig-saw puzzle in which each piece fits into the other and forms a harmonious whole . . ."[36]

Like other ideals, this concept of corporatism in its narrow sense was never achieved.[37] But the ideal was significant nevertheless, for it defined Perón's aspirations, affected his perceptions, and guided him in his selection of policies and alternatives. Thus the pursuit of such

a polity required strong leadership, and this was available by definition in the person of Perón. His responsibility as the *Conductor,* and
the entire process of *conducción,* were presented in exhaustive detail
in his book, *Conducción política,* published in 1952.

The word *conducción* implies leadership, plus the function of the
teacher and, by way of metaphor, that of the leader of the orchestra.
There are three components of the process in Perón's definition: the
Conductor himself, the helpers who work under and with him, and the
mass that is to be led. The *Conductor* must be born for the task, he
must have been anointed, in Perón's favorite phrase, with the Sacred
Oil of Samuel. He is much more than a mere *Caudillo,* for he is a
creator as well as a leader, an artist more than a technician.

The helpers of the *Conductor* are essential, but of a lesser order,
being executors of his work rather than creators. The mass of followers, Peron felt, was to be valued generally not for its intrinsic worth
but for its power of reaction as a mass, in which it is comparable to a
human muscle that responds to the nerve center in the mind.[38] But
an unprepared, ignorant mass must be made organic through moral
and intellectual preparation that teaches it how to be led, yet it must
have some initiative of its own, since every man who is led must also
lead himself.[39]

Given this tutelary grand design, it was inevitable that Perón's concept of democracy would differ widely from that prevailing in western Europe and the United States. It was inevitable that he would be
hostile to the idea of political parties as bases of power, for they were
inconsistent with the functions of the *Conductor.*

It was inevitable that Perón would deprecate the significance of
the Congress, because it, too, came between the *Conductor* and the
mass. He did not attempt to dispense with it, but in his heart he would
follow the old Creole conviction that the Congress existed to ratify the
executive's desires.[40] It was inevitable that Perón's views on freedom
of the press would conflict with those held in the liberal democracies.
In his tradition, freedom of the press is good if it does not go too far,
but it may be subordinate to other social objectives, a desirability but
not an imperative. If opposition of the press becomes strident rather
than muted (and the press in pre-Peronist Argentina was not notable
for fairness or self-control), it becomes offensive to harmony and balance and may be restricted by the executive authority. It is doubtful
that Perón ever really understood, emotionally as well as intellec-
tually, the basis of press operations in Europe and the United States.
When he would cause Argentine press criticism of the United States
to abate, as he did from time to time, he looked for almost immediate

reciprocity, as if his counterpart in the White House had control of the situation.

It was inevitable that Perón would have a concept and a definition of democracy that were widely misunderstood in the northern countries. His references to Peronist democracy were often discounted deeply as humbug and hypocrisy, but it was a matter of definition. He knew, or believed deeply, that ". . . the democracy in the European form, without more, was not applicable in Argentina."[41] For Perón, his regime was democratic because he derived his support from the people. He was in the tradition of the populist from San Juan, Federico Cantoni, who, in 1927, responded on the floor of the Senate to charges that his movement simply took from the few and gave to the many: "That is democracy, to govern for the many."[42] Thus Perón would persuade the many rather than resort to force, insisting on an electoral mandate. "He had a great sense of democracy—probably in his own manner—but he had it."[43] Indeed, he had it to an extent that sometimes seemed a fault to some of his loyalists. He and they believed that the formal variety was a web of forms and abstractions devoid of realities, a manipulation by economic forces and self-serving political parties. In contrast, pure democracy arose from direct contact between *Conductor* and mass and was exemplified by October 17. In his recreated speech on that famous night, Perón said, "This is the true fiesta of democracy, represented by a people who marched for hours on foot to ask its officials to comply with the duty of respecting their authentic rights."[44]

Since Perón regarded government as an exercise in collaboration mediated by a *Conductor,* he had had no experience with the adversarial system of checks and balances that evolved in England in the struggle against Stuart tyranny; and from what he knew, he had no sympathy with it. It is interesting that the historical attributions of which Perón was so fond in his speeches appear to omit the name of the philosopher who was preeminent in the growth of English and American political thought: John Locke, who also formulated the theory of checks and balances. There is no evidence that Perón was familiar with Locke, or that he had read the second "Treatise on Government." He appears to have been less familiar with British thought and practice in general than he was with continental precedents, and he had little feel for British history. He was convinced that the British Labour Party had been created not by the unions but by the British government, presumably because anything of that significance should have an origin in central authority, or perhaps to establish a parallel with his own actions.[45] Hobbes is the one English writer Perón referred to, but

Hobbes was far less representative of British thought than Locke.

In any case, there could have been no room in the Peronato for checks and balances that extended to the judiciary, for Perón viewed justice in the light of populism,[46] and in so doing sometimes reached conclusions that have a strangely contemporary ring: "The equality of the French Revolution consisted in treating all persons in the same manner, while the equality of the present consists in treating them unequally to compensate differences."[47]

Finally, it was inevitable that Peronist Argentina and the United States would find friendship and understanding elusive. Of all the countries that shared the western and Christian traditions, these two were about as far apart as possible in their basic philosophies of government and society. In contrast to the ideal of the Mediterranean organic community, the ideal in the United States was a community maintained by the tension of opposing interests in more or less perpetual but changing conflict that was mediated by compromise, restraint, common sense, and the rule of law as imposed by a deliberately weak government. The heritage was not classical Mediterranean but Anglo-Saxon, and many of its great events such as Magna Carta and the Glorious Revolution were celebrations not of power but of the striking down of power. Peronist Argentina believed that freedom was attained through the exercise of central authority; the United States believed that freedom had to be maintained through opposition to central authority. As Samuel Huntington put it, "The central—and the oldest—theme of the American political tradition is opposition to concentrated power. The revolutionaries of 1776 opposed monarchical power and defined the issue as liberty against power . . . The deeply rooted suspicion of power has been shared by radicals and reactionaries, liberals and conservatives. The extent of this hostility is a distinguishing characteristic of American political culture compared with that of other societies." As if to confirm this view, the Department of State's Secret Policy Statement of March 1950 listed "current interpretations of the function of the state" as one of four sources of basic conflict between Argentina and the United States.[48]

Perón would have replied with one of his classic statements of belief from *Orientación política:* "In my opinion, the world of the future will live in keeping with rules of democracy and respect for individual liberty. Now, the concepts of liberty and democracy are undergoing a rapid evolution. Liberty will be less and less the right of any one to do as he pleases, and will be more and more the obligation to do what is profitable for the community . . . woe to the peoples that . . . persist in establishing an incompatibility between the powers of the State and the ideals of liberty and democracy!"[49]

Still another of Perón's values, almost impossible to overstress, set him apart from the northern societies: his strong Hispanic affinity. "Since the days of our independence we have accepted no other culture than the Spanish culture which we inherited . . . No other culture has entered here; we have been eminently Hispanicists . . . and we continue to be not only Hispanicists but Hispanophiles."[50] It was not entirely accurate, but heartfelt, as was his proclamation of his Spanish descent as his pride and glory. And he did even more, for he elevated Hispanicism into a spiritual value. "To the blind impulse of force and the cold impulse of money, Argentina, one of the heirs of Hispanic spirituality, opposes the life-giving supremacy of the spirit . . . For us the Race is not a biological concept. For us it is something purely spiritual. It constitutes the sum of the imponderables that make us be what we are and impel us to be as we ought to be by reason of our origin and our destiny . . . For ourselves, the Latins, the Race is a style. A style of life that teaches us to live by practicing the Good, and to know how to die with dignity . . . History, religion and the language place us on the map of western and Latin culture, through its Hispanic sources, in which heroism, nobility, asceticism and spirituality reach their most sublime proportions."[51]

Worked into the large fabric of Peronism, these values of Perón united with the social and economic benefits of populism to create for his followers a living enchantment. No one can ever know the order of precedence between spiritual and psychic appeals and those purely materialistic, and many have assumed that Peronist populism was all bread and circus bartered for political support.[52] But this is much too narrow a view of human purpose. A great deal that was religious and quasi-religious went into the enfolded depths of Peronism, and Perón made almost exquisite use of the spiritual themes and ethical values that time long forgotten had contributed to the civilization.

From Esther's Diary, 1947: Now that we poor people
have our newspaper, its many pages the expression
of our leader, in a word the heart of a nation is contained . . . Perón! during the one year you've been
our president there's no room for all the things
you've done for us in the pages of every day of every
month of this year of newspapers . . . and nevertheless in your heart there's room: Toys for your children! all the needy children of the Argentine
Republic, and laws for the workers, not to be humiliated any longer, and welfare for those burdened
with years and with want . . .

— Manuel Puig, *Betrayed by Rita Hayworth*

9. The Ebb Tide of Peronism 1950-1955

Intimations of Autumn

IT IS DIFFICULT to identify a clear watershed in the political topography of the Peronato. Certainly the first two years, through
mid-1948, were a time of triumph and fair wind. The economy fal-
tered in the second half of 1948, with declines in the levels of export
crop production and industrial output,[1] but Peronism itself seemed
little affected. Further deterioration occurred in 1949 and 1950, and
by late in the latter year signs of a troubled economy were fully recognized in the government, although Perón admitted nothing in
public.

Comparable intimations of ills to come appeared in the social sphere.
One of these concerned the relations of the government and the
Church. The original cordiality was probably impossible to sustain
simply because of the nature of the Peronist State, with its increased
activity in areas the Church had traditionally dominated, such as welfare and education. The two great paternalisms were doubtless destined for some disagreement, and in October a more serious symbolic
clash arose.

A week before the October 17 anniversary festivities, a spiritualist conference had been held in Buenos Aires. Perón and Evita were moderate devotees, and had sometimes attended seances organized by the much more ardent Doña Juana, Evita's mother. Perón's view of spiritualism was a blend of interest, mild belief, and gentle skepticism. "In these extra-mundane things, I had been around long enough, and had enough experience, not to deny or affirm anything. I didn't say that it was a lie or that it was true."[2] In this spirit, he sent official greetings to the conference. Catholic opinion was offended and found one outlet in the heckling of the conference by Catholic activists until the streets of the capital rang with shouts of "Christ is King!" The police removed the hecklers with more devotion to duty than the Catholics thought proper, and their resentment increased. Then, on October 18, a papal legate arrived in Buenos Aires to take part in a large eucharistic conference about to open in Rosario. He found that Perón and Evita were at San Vicente, so that Evita could rest, it was said. The snub to the legate was widely resented, and Perón felt obliged to leave San Vicente on the last day of the congress for a personal appearance with Evita.[3]

Another of the signs of the deterioration of Peronism pointed to stress in the vital labor base. The recession of 1949 had given the word: the nationwide prosperity and the visibly rising real incomes of the descamisados, born of the wartime surpluses, would not long outlive their dissipation. Late in 1950, discontent in the railway industry reached the boiling point and in January 1951, a wounding strike broke out. The union leadership was faithful to Peronism and resisted the strike in the name of patriotism and Justicialismo. Every effort was made by the government, by the union leadership, and by Evita in person, all to no avail, and Perón had to play his trump card, issuing a decree that subjected the workers to military mobilization and thus to military law. The strike was broken. But it erupted again in August, and again Perón broke it by drafting the workers.[4]

Still other portents were visible within the armed forces, at least to a discerning eye. There were various reasons, some of them quite general, reflecting the wide influences and motivations at work among the military. Whatever the sources in particular cases, resentments had coalesced sufficiently by 1949 to create various embryonic subversive movements, and 1950 would be a time of watchful waiting, private discussions, and increasing tensions.

Quite another kind of portent had begun to appear in the circle of Perón's and Evita's close advisors. The collaborators with whom Perón had started out were not faring well by 1950. José Figuerola, with his quiet skills and unassuming ways, had been shunted aside at the time of the Constitutional Convention in 1949 and he had not recovered position. His enemies, who had never ceased resenting the influence of this "gallego" from Spain, had managed to insert in the 1949 charter a provision that only native-born Argentines could hold ministerial office. Perón could have used his influence against the change, or he could have found other high-level employment for so competent a man, but the fact is that Figuerola had aroused the ill will of Evita. Figuerola understood, and retired to the sidelines, still loyal. But loyalty alone did not prosper, and his son later had to beseech Jorge Antonio, Perón's financial supporter, for employment for his father, who had been compelled to mortgage his tiny home and pawn some of his clothes. Antonio provided a job.[5] The most useful and wide-ranging of all the early Peronist loyalists had been Domingo Mercante, whose star reached its zenith in 1948–49, when he was elected governor of Buenos Aires Province and presided over the 1949 convention. He was a governor of great competence, moderate and constructive, but when he completed his second term in 1952, his days of intimacy with Perón had already ended, for reasons difficult to clarify. Perhaps he was ambitious, or perhaps Evita thought he was. In 1953, the former "Crown Prince of Peronism" was expelled from the Peronist Party, and he spent the remainder of his life largely in private pursuits. His former collaborator, Juan Bramuglia, had finally succumbed to Evita's enmity in August 1949. Of the early labor leaders of ability, Cipriano Reyes was still in jail and Luis Gay had never recovered from his fall in 1947.

In comparison, the men of the inner circle were now nonentities, or in some cases worse, for some of them sometimes pushed Perón toward extremes.[6] The same mediocrity marked those who surrounded Evita. The man she had promoted to the presidency of the CGT, José Espejo, was so servile an instrument that if the CGT had included a bootlickers union, he would have been elected its president by acclamation. Perón's ardent admirers, of course, saw all of this and deplored it, but they seem not to have sensed the inevitable connection between this phenomenon and Perón's theory and style of government. Loyalty so extreme that it was not deemed loyalty unless it was blind and total was incompatible with the competence and initiative that move a bureaucracy forward.

A single anecdote, often quoted, gives the tone of the inner circle toward the end of the first administration. Alfredo Prada, a champion boxer who was a favorite of Perón, noticed that his name seemed to be disappearing from the media. Puzzled, he went to Perón to see what had happened. Perón was equally nonplussed and ordered an inquiry. The truth emerged. Some weeks before, Perón had been talking in his office with advisors and the subject of the Russian newspaper, *Pravda,* had come up. Perón, using an Argentine idiomatic phrase, remarked in effect, *"Pravda* doesn't count." One of the courtiers present did not understand what *Pravda* was and thought Perón had said "Prada doesn't count." He passed the word to the authorities in charge of information and propaganda, and it rapidly filtered down to the working levels, and before long it was true that "Prada didn't count."[7]

A final sign cast a darker shadow over the Peronato than any of the others. By 1950, it was evident to a few knowledgeable insiders that Evita's health was in serious question. Perón dated Evita's first symptoms of illness to late 1949 and used the term "a strong anemia."[8] It was consistent with the attitude he and everyone close to Evita had taken all along, dismissing her symptoms with almost casual talk of minor maladies. In fact, she had been suffering from vaginal hemorrhages to such an extent that sexual relations had probably been impaired since 1949. And there is some doubt as to how much Perón himself knew, and when, since Evita resisted all discussion of medical matters.[9]

On January 9, 1950, she attended a ceremony for the inauguration of a new headquarters for the Taxi Drivers' Union. While a priest was offering the invocation, she was seized by a strong pain in the groin, and barely managed to hold on until the event ended. She immediately consulted with Dr. Oscar Ivanissevich, the minister of education, who diagnosed acute appendicitis, for which he performed surgery on January 12.

These developments could have direct impact on the highest levels of politics, and the diplomats who knew about them fully understood this. On January 10, the Canadian ambassador had "a very serious conversation" with his American counterpart concerning the guiding factors in Argentine political life in the foreseeable future. These, he believed, were two: the health and continued activity of Evita, and American financial policy in the country. He asserted that Evita was known to have an incurable case of leukemia, which would soon terminate her work in the government.[10] According to Dr. Ivanissevich, in a statement he made years later, he had taken tests at the time of the appendectomy and had discovered uterine cancer. He further insisted that he had thereupon recommended a hysterectomy to Evita, who scorned the advice and attributed it to the machinations of political enemies,[11] a reaction not entirely surprising, since the operation was considered by Argentine women of that day as a disaster and psychologically intolerable. Alberto Dodero, still the close family friend, told the American ambassador that Evita had rejected every doctor who had been sent to examine her.[12] No one knows exactly what Doctor Ivanissevich told Evita or Perón; he never revealed whether he mentioned cancer; the one sure fact is that in May of the same year, he resigned from his ministerial position, under pressure from this incident or from other sources.[13]

It was a sign for Evita, but not as ominous a one as those to come. During the balance of the year and into 1951 she would maintain the pace of frenzy as if she could forever impose will upon matter.

The Reelection of Perón

Despite the signs and the intimations of possible decline, the structure of Peronism was solid. The spring tide might rise and fall with a success here or a failure there, but the beginning of the ebb flow was still not perceived as such. The bid for Perón's reelection could thus go forward with no thought of ill omen.

The work of the new Peronist Womens' Party made such rapid advances that the Radicals began to fear a fate beyond their wildest apprehension a year earlier: the Women's Party, winning the second largest vote, might qualify as the official minority, and the Radicals would almost disappear. It didn't work out that way because the law was soon amended to give the opposition a mandatory one out of fifteen seats in Congress rather than one out of three, but it was a sobering thought and it heralded the role of the Peronist women.[14]

A new concern now began to arise for all elements of opposition, a concern so undreamed of hitherto that it thrust aside almost all the old fears, preempting center stage for itself: it had begun to be rumored that Perón would select Evita as his vice presidential candidate. Unprecedented as were Evita and all her works, this was even more so. There had been no female vice president (let alone president) in any country in the hemisphere, and as her opponents saw it, that norm was under threat from this dreadful woman, a ghastly and intolerable thing. Such views were known to persist in some army sectors, and in July a privately circulated mimeographed document representing the views of one dissident clique stated, "The wife of the president has been imposed on us, she dictates orders, her presence is annoying to military men, she handles two thousand million pesos without control from anyone, she resorts to intrigue with the army, she does not conceal her hatred against army officers and proclaims that the CGT is the real army of the government."[15] The cautious Perón, the Perón who could afford to drift with events for a time, was in charge and the momentum for the strange candidacy was held under control. On April 26, 1951, the Peronist deputies in the Chamber passed a unanimous resolution favoring a Perón–Perón ticket, and although the fact was known and publicized abroad, no announcement was permitted by Perón within Argentina.[16]

Meanwhile, the date of the elections was moved up from 1952 to November 11, 1951. In midsummer, the CGT came out officially for Evita as the running mate, and the Radicals nominated as their candidate Ricardo Balbín, who had spent ten months in jail for disrespect under the *Desacato* law. But the Radicals were in their usual conflict and they had no real prospect of victory, so the principal question raised by the election was the identity of the Peronist vice-presidential nominee.

That issue came to a head at the great *Cabildo Abierto* of August 22, an open town meeting, the second in the nation's history, following the famous event of May 25, 1810, when the *porteños* came together to resolve the end of the tie to Spain. October 17, 1945 had been essentially a *Cabildo Abierto,* but it was spontaneous; the event now unfolding was organized and proclaimed by the CGT in support of the Peronist electoral campaign. It was held on the Avenida 9 de Julio, the widest thoroughfare in the world, fronting two immense posters of Perón and Evita, each the height of a five-story building and connected by a "Bridge of Love." Every effort the state could summon was put at the service of the CGT in its attempt to muster an audience of two million. Free round-trip railway tickets between the provinces and Buenos Aires were handed out to one and all for trains arriving on the 21st and 22nd. Caravans of busses and trucks were organized to flow into the capital. All city transportation, even the taxis, was free on the 22nd.

The size of the crowd, estimates for which range from 175,000 to a million, was impressive, a panorama of spectacle with flags and banners and sky-writing planes overhead. Perón accepted his nomination by saying he would do what the people wanted. Evita was not present, but was sent for and quickly appeared in a prepared maneuver. She spoke in the familiar terms, but made no reference to the vice presidency.

Up to this point all had gone as expected. But now the multitude developed its own dynamic. The scene changed, and Perón and the others on the dias under the gigantic portraits were borne along by a developing swell of emotion that took them all by total surprise. Without plan or preparation for what happened, the entire high command of Peronism now struggled to improvise a response to the staggering sponteneity of the evening and to contain it.

It had begun during Perón's speech. The crowd had taken Evita's very inconclusive remarks as a rejection of the candidacy and it was displeased. There were almost unprecedented interruptions and calls of "Evita" while Perón was still speaking, and after he concluded, the calls escalated into a chant. Espejo tried to quiet the throng and asked Evita to accept. She said she was unable to speak further. The microphone was taken to her, and she began a long and sometimes rambling dialogue with the thousands of ghost-presences now sensed but not seen in shadow and darkness.

"I ask the GCT and I ask you, by the affection which unites us, by the love we feel for one another, that for so overwhelmingly important a decision in the life of this poor woman, you give me at least four days for consideration."

"No, no, now! . . . let's go on strike! General strike!"

"Comrades, comrades." She repeated the word several times, seeking quiet, and began a confused explanation of her past motives, her voice ragged and failing.

"Now! Now!"

She asked for a single day, to consider her reply.

"No! Now!"

"This has taken me by surprise . . . For a long time I had known that my name was being put forward and I did not discourage it; I did it for the people and for Perón . . . Never in my ordinary heart of an Argentine woman did I think I would be able to accept that post . . ."

"Now! Now!"

Finally, she suggested "Tonight."

"No! Now!"

She asked for two hours.

"Now!"

Espejo took the microphone she handed him and announced that they would wait there for her decision. "We shall not move until she gives us a reply in accordance with the desires of the people."

In the background, while she carried on this strange dialogue with the disembodied voices of unknown people almost invisible in the distorting light of flairing torches held high, Perón and the leaders of the Peronato conferred frantically, seeking to improvise. There was a pause while the crowd fell silent. After a time Evita came forward, tears streaming down her face, her voice sunken to a rough whisper: "I will do what the people say."

The meeting was closed, and at nine thirty, all radio stations carried the announcement of the Peronist Party Council that Perón and Evita had been officially nominated.[17] But an uneasy feeling persisted: perhaps the *Cabildo Abierto* was not the final answer. Perhaps the assumptions had been too hasty, something might still be going on. On August 27, Perón and Evita were formally notified of their nominations, but they made no response.

The first published story that Evita would renounce the nomination appeared in Río de Janeiro, in *O Globo,* whose reporter had been told by Perón that this would happen. Then on August 31, Evita announced on the radio her "irrevocable decision" not to accept the nomination. An announcement followed immediately that vice president Quijano had been selected to run again. His illness was almost as far advanced as Evita's, but of this there was no mention.[18]

There was, of course, tremendous reference to Evita's sacrifice. August 31 was designated as Eva Perón Day forever, October 17 would be dedicated to her, and joint resolutions of the Congress paid tribute to her. Perón announced a special medal for her, for her embodiment of ". . . the highest qualities which a true Peronista can demonstrate, those of renunciation and abnegation."[19]

It is impossible to say with confidence what had really happened. It would seem, however, that her decision was made by Perón, based on his judgment of the relative risks and benefits; that she had been serious in seeking the nomination, for otherwise she could have choked off early rumors and shows of support, but that she realized the small likelihood of success; that Perón let the uncertainty go on as long as he did for political reasons difficult to evaluate at this distance; that both of them underestimated the bond between Evita and the *Descamisados* and were taken aback by the spontaneous insistence on her candidacy at the *Cabildo Abierto;* that regardless of motives and tactics, the result would have been the same in any case because her rapidly failing health would have ordained her withdrawal even if she had accepted the nomination; and that the awareness of her serious illness as a conscious or unconscious factor in Perón's decision was doubtless significant, but that the exact degree of its significance must remain a very rough estimate because the detailed knowledge of the illness that they possessed at that moment, and the intuitions they derived from that knowledge, are unknown.

The *Cabildo Abierto* was the meridian point of Evita's career. The emotional outpouring of the public on her behalf was exceeded only by the great demonstration of October 17, 1945, and rivaled only by the public acclaim of Yrigoyen when he was inaugurated and when he died. But at the same time it was also almost the terminal point of her career, for rarely has twilight followed so closely upon high noon. Her tearful and labored remarks at the *Cabildo Abierto* were not her final public words, but the occasion was her last significant participation in high politics.

The campaign season was enlivened by a rather ludicrous military uprising headed by General Benjamín Menéndez, an unbalanced character who pursued revolutions as other men do women, money, and fame. The coup evaporated in a few hours, its pitiful history memorialized by a constitutional curiosity whose shadow would be long. Bypassing a State of Siege and a State of Prevention and Alarm, both of which were available under the Constitution, Perón proclaimed instead, on September 28, a "State of Internal Warfare," for which no legal basis existed. Ratified by Congress, and regardless of its lack of ancestry, it granted broad emergency powers to Perón, comparable to a State of Siege. Its duration was remarkable; except for its suspension on election days, it remained in effect until the day of Perón's fall in 1955, an interesting commentary on the long-term evolution of the government in the direction of repression.

The electoral campaign was not as free and open as it had been in 1946. The press was now as solidly Peronist as it had been anti-Peronist then. Various opposition leaders were still under arrest. There was no access to radio. The *Desacato* law inhibited free comment. And public meetings required a police permit, which was sometimes granted and sometimes denied. This restraint was eased in the last two weeks of the campaign. The balloting itself was free of abuse. Perón received 64 percent of the vote to Balbín's 32 percent.[20] The governorships of all the provinces went to Peronists. The entire Senate was Peronist, and in the Chamber of Deputies the Peronist majority was 135 to fourteen.

The Public Death of Evita

Evita took a turn for the worse immediately after the *Cabildo Abierto*, fainting from weakness and pain the next day. In the middle of September she finally agreed to have tests at home. They were completed on the 24th, and the doctors had the difficult task of telling Perón, in private, that Evita had advanced cancer of the uterus. Evita was not told the truth, but nevertheless was still so resistant to treatment of any kind that she had to be managed by what Father Benítez called "pious lies."

A hysterectomy was necessary, and Evita was receiving preparatory blood transfusions when the Menéndez coup erupted on September 28. Her absence from the balcony when Perón spoke forced the first public announcement of her illness, which was attributed to anemia "of great intensity." The next day, without telling Perón, she sent for the war minister and several members of the CGT executive committee and ordered 5,000 machine pistols and 1,500 machine guns to be stored by the government and distributed to the CGT if another revolution occurred. The Eva Perón Foundation would pay for them. Meanwhile, the earliest of what would be endless public demonstrations of sympathy had begun across the land: masses, altars, votive offerings, prayers in the streets. The full attention of the nation was to be turned on the sickbed of the First Lady in the next eleven months, for her long death was the event of the era, a public dying, a political fact of the highest importance. The foundation and the CGT were now at the heart of the Argentine social order, and if the strong hand that now controlled them were to fail, the consequences might be incalculable.

There was no possibility that these realities could fade from the public awareness, but they were, in fact, now reinforced by the appearance in the bookstores of Evita's autobiography, *La Razón de mi Vida,* translated as *My Mission in Life* in the English-language edition. It was written originally at Evita's direction by a Spanish journalist and it included his favorite theme of the redemptive power of women in politics, as sources of moral insight and leadership. Evita had passed the book on to Perón, who did not like it, and he passed it on to Raúl Mende. Eventually the revised version emerged, much bowdlerized and suffering from the mediocrity that often afflicts texts issued by a committee. But Evita accepted it, and now it was in the stores, a hodgepodge devoid of distinction or originality but bearing the signs of total devotion. It was bought madly—150,000 copies on the first day—and within a month it had outsold every book in Argentine history.

Honors and awards and recognitions of every kind had been pouring in upon Evita for some time, adding to the emotional electricity of the time. A new subway station in Buenos Aires was named for Evita. In July, the Congress had elevated the Chaco and the western area of the pampas known as La Pampa from territorial to provincial status; the Chaco became Presidente Perón Province, and La Pampa became Eva Perón Province.

Surgery had still not been performed by October 17. It was Evita's day this year, with special medals and awards to which she was unable to respond, standing soundless in front of the microphone until she was lifted up and carried to her seat. Then Perón spoke in somber praise of her, as if he were already memorializing her for the ages. Something in this galvanized her, and the spark of love and passion flared briefly again. She struggled to her feet and to his side, embracing him amid sobs and tears. Then she turned again to the microphone and spoke briefly, in a voice hardly audible: "Nothing I have, nothing I am, nothing I think is mine; it all belongs to Perón . . . everything I did, I did out of love for this people . . . All that I have, I have in my heart, it hurts my soul, it hurts my flesh and it burns my nerves, and that is my love for this people and for Perón." And she concluded by asking them for their oath of loyalty, to be given by shouting for a whole minute, "so that our cries will be heard at the end of the earth," the pledge "Our lives for Perón!" It was done, for many minutes, and Evita fell back, in tears again, while Perón held her.[21]

She continued to decline, and it was apparent that surgery could not wait. It was performed on November 5 by Dr. George Pack, of the Memorial Sloan-Kettering Cancer Center in New York, who had been secretly brought to Argentina for that purpose. Evita never knew that the surgeon was not an Argentine.[22] On the 8th he returned to New York, again in secrecy. No announcement of her operation had been made, but on the basis of word of mouth reports, some 20,000 people stood vigil in the streets outside her hospital. The operation seemed successful and Evita thought she might be able to resume some activity. She made a radio speech early in December and distributed some toys at Christmas. But the abdominal pains recurred in February, and further tests confirmed that cancer was present and spreading. This time there was no room for hope. But she was never told the nature of her illness.[23]

Still, she spoke out when her strength permitted. Even now, the power she exercised remained awesome. She held the CGT, the labor movement of the entire nation, in her hand. In March, Espejo came up for reelection as its head, facing real opposition, for he was unpopular. A vote was taken and it went against Espejo by 133 to 132. His followers immediately ordered the police to close all doors to the auditorium and permit no entry or exit. Then they telephoned Evita; she called several of Espejo's opponents to the phone and gave them a piece of her mind. The meeting was then resumed, and a new vote reelected Espejo by 265 to 0.[24]

In public, Evita's words were taking on an even more frantic tinge, for she knew she was dying and she had much to do. Yet she would forego no iota of her hovering concern for Perón. As she lay in bed on a bad day toward the end, more dead than alive, Perón walked by in the corridor beyond her door, coughing as he passed.

"Did you hear that?" she said to her doctor. "General Perón is coughing, because he smokes too much. Please, tell him not to smoke. Examine him. See that he doesn't get sick."[25]

On May Day she revived enough to walk without assistance onto the balcony of the Casa Rosada, and she spoke for the last time to the *descamisados,* with an intensity in which love and hate and frenzy and religious adoration were compressed into the most intense light, a laser beam enveloped in a votive candle. She spoke of traitors and of going out to do justice "with our own hands," and some of her terrible words, losing nothing from her fragility, reverberated like the utterance of an earth-god: "I pray God that He should not allow these madmen to lift their hand against Perón, for on that day, woe to them! I shall go forth with the working people, I shall go forth with the women of the people, I shall go forth with the *descamisados,* and I shall leave no brick standing that is not Peronist."[26]

When she finished, no strength remained, and Perón had to carry her from the balcony. In later times, he wrote of this moment with a kind of awe, for her vitality had so far departed that he could not hear her breathe and the tiny limp body he held in his arms was as that of a dead child.[27] A week later, on her thirty-third birthday, she received from Congress the title of Spiritual Leader of the Nation.

She rallied for a last appearance in public at Perón's inauguration for the second term, on June 4. She now weighed only eighty pounds and could not stand unassisted in the open car that was to take them to the Casa Rosada. A framework of wire and plaster was devised, to prop her up, and with this and a triple dose of a painkiller and a fur coat now so large for her that she was almost lost in it, she made it to the Casa Rosada, where she received another, double, dose of painkiller. She was borne along in the slow procession almost like a sacred icon carried aloft on a pole, a thing of inert sanctity, spirit from which life has fled.

In June, she endured radiotherapy, was burned, and suffered much. Her public dying had by now created a world of its own in Argentina in which strange forces on the psychic level were released to mingle with the religious processions and pilgrimages and the continuous masses. In the interior, many sought out witches and sorcerers and the magic cure.[28] Guilts would out, and submerged fears, and ancestral legends. In the rich *Barrio Norte,* whose people Evita hated so bitterly, rumors warned mothers not to take their children to the doctor's office or to the hospital, because Evita needed new blood every day, young blood, and it was collected for her in those places.[29] Psychiatric disturbances increased. So many superlatives were employed in so many speeches and tributes that language itself fell into contamination. The words of Evita in *My Mission in Life* were compared to those of Christ.

During her last weeks, Evita wrote her final last will, or rather, two wills, one of them in handwriting. This private document was never presented to the public, and was probably merged into the other will, which was read at the Loyalty Day celebrations on October 17, 1952. She also began to write another book, *My Message,* which was never finished, for she was slipping in and out of consciousness. She could therefore hardly appreciate the award she received on July 18, the Collar of the Order of the Liberator General San Martín, a tremendous example of the jeweler's art, with 4,584 elements, composed of gold and platinum and diamonds, emeralds, and rubies.[30]

The end came on July 26, under a gray and heavy winter sky. She entered her final coma at 11 A.M. Four hours later, Father Benítez administered the last rites of the faith, the sacrament of extreme unction. At 8:25 P.M., she died. At 8:26 P.M., the word went forth on radio to the nation, and Argentina entered a new era.

The entire country went into immediate and total mourning. Everything stopped as of the moment of the announcement—movies, restaurant service, theatrical plays in progress, shops, even the usual street and store lights that contended with the darkness. Temporary embalming, the first stage of a long process, was performed during the night and the next day the body was conveyed to the ministry of labor, where it remained on public display until August 9.

The extent of the mourning was unprecedented. The streets around the ministry were almost unpassable for nearly a mile in every direction on Sunday, when the procession bearing the casket inched along toward the ministry. Eight people were killed and more than two thousand injured in the melee. The lines of those seeking to view the casket stretched at times as far as thirty blocks, the mourners silent and stricken along cold streets glistening with tearful rain. On the 9th of August, the coffin was placed on a gun carriage and hauled by thirty-five union members to Congress, where the honors for a head of state were accorded. The next day, the gun-carriage resumed its slow pace through dark streets under lowering skies, past the street lamps shrouded with crepe, while Chopin's funeral march sounded and 17,000 soldiers held back the pressing multitudes, delivering the body to the headquarters of the CGT, where facilities had been readied for permanent embalming.[31]

This was accomplished by an expert, Dr. Pedro Ara, the Spanish

Cultural Attaché, who later wrote a book on the complicated under-taking.[32] It was a laborious process, for Dr. Ara was thinking of a masterpiece for eternity. Meanwhile, the body remained in the CGT headquarters. The original expectation of a gigantic monument in Buenos Aires, either a statue of a *descamisado* or of Evita, within which she would be interred, came to naught. The stupendous size of the structure had bred too many complications. Dr. Ara's final payment came to him only a few days before Perón fell in 1955, and from that moment forward, the disposition of the body became a matter of great political consequence. In 1956, under circumstances that have as many variations as there are narrators, the casket with the fabulous embalmed body simply disappeared, lost in its own legendry.[33]

Evita's public will was read to people during the October 17 cere-monies following her death. Much of the language was vividly remi-niscent of the woman who had been Peronism's great missionary to the people, and for the hour at least, her passions and dreams and hates and loves lived again. It began with her words so often quoted: "I wish to live eternally with Perón and with my people. This is my absolute and permanent desire, and therefore my last will. Where Perón is and where my *descamisados* are, there will my heart ever be, to love them with all the forces of life and all the fanaticism that burns my soul." And a little later, "I will be with them, with Perón, to fight against the traitorous and perfidious oligarchy, against the cursed race of exploiters and the dealers in humanity." She defended her life through the invocation of love: ". . . if I have committed errors, I have committed them out of love and I hope that God, who has always seen into my heart, will judge me not for my errors, nor for my defects, nor for my guilt, but for the love that consumes my life." And in one significant passage she provided the clue to her mystic union with her followers: more than an affinity, more than love, it was an identifica-tion so complete as to be a surrender of the self, an absorption into the mass: "I . . . was born of the people and suffered with them. I have the body and the soul and the blood of the people. I can do nothing other than to surrender myself to my people."[34]

Thus she passed from the scene, this remarkable woman for whom no counterpart can be discerned. She was at once admitted to legend and, indeed, to sacred legend; one of the Argentine trade unions soon petitioned the Vatican to declare her sainthood. Behind her she left an interesting amalgam of grief, guilt, mythology, celebration, and despair as her friends and her enemies sought to adjust to an Argen-tine world devoid of her central presence. Above all, perhaps, she left a large space and no successor.

Almost lost among the memories of Evita that have caught the imagination of the world there was another that has been little noted but whose importance is considerable: the legacy of incomprehension. Her brief and dazzling years were so successful because, in good part, she was so profoundly of the ethos. "I have the body and the soul and the blood of the people." But it was the ethos of the old, Hispanic-Creole tradition, born in the interior out of Lima and nurtured on the pampas. Like Perón, she was wholly indigenous in origin and formation and spirit; like him, she was distrusted and misunderstood in the Argentina of the Liberal System and in the outside world that knew only that Argentina.

Hence the confusions and errors that she provoked. The American embassy recognized her tremendous importance and sincerely tried to come to grips with her mind and personality. On occasion its reports showed insight and understanding. On occasion they were far from the mark. Her tearful performance at the *Cabildo Abierto* in August 1951 was seen as ". . . the climax of a magnificent 'ham' performance . . ."[35] and the entire event, spontaneous in this aspect, was assumed to have been a carefully rehearsed sales job, a "coax me" appeal by Evita. The style and tone of the proceedings were so alien to the North American observers that they simply could not understand, and therefore assumed other motivations.

The same was true with regard to Evita's dramatized death during her last ten months, the dying in public that she sought as the confirmation of her devotion. Such an attitude toward mortality is a variation of the old Hispanic preoccupation with death and with the dignity and splendor associated with it. It had by then faded away in most of the European Catholic societies and it is unknown in the Anglo-Saxon nations. Therefore, many saw her ordeal and the responses of Perón and of the vast public as elements in an essentially political passion play, an attempt to milk some sympathy and benefit out of what should have been a private tragedy. It was simply the legacy of incomprehension, the same legacy that made it impossible for Evita and Perón to grasp fully the emotional intensity of much of the world reaction to the seizure of *La Prensa*, or to other repressions of the Peronato. Thus Evita lived and died, an object of wonder to the world and a memorial to the inability of one ethos truly to understand another.

The Peronoto in the Days of Difficulty

The void that now existed in some of the nerve centers of Peronism had to be filled, and Perón moved quickly. He seated himself behind Evita's desk in the labor ministry, handing out favors and pesos, for just long enough to preempt the function and to assert his heir-

ship of the task before allowing it to fall into desuetude. The Eva
Perón Foundation, with its enormous funds and the political levers it
could move at will, was handled in the same way—Perón had himself
elected its head. There would be no second Evita and no pretender
to that eminence.

It is clear enough that the death of Evita was a major blow to Perón.[36]
He appeared to be surmounting it, but that was for the public to see.
Inwardly, her death led to a process of attrition. He was less able to
confront his many problems, including some that arose within his
immediate circle. Fatigue set in: ". . . he was like a person who has lost
a leg, or something more than that. You could notice the difference,
feel it."[37] And there was another aspect of the loss, not known to the
public. Perón may have felt some responsibility for the failure to
intervene at an earlier moment in Evita's terminal illness. Dr. Pack is
said to have commented that she might have been saved if expert care
had been summoned eight months sooner. Perón did not know the
true state of affairs, for Evita, who herself remained ignorant of the
reality, had said nothing. When he learned the truth, finally, it was a
year after her symptoms were evident to her. But should he have
insisted earlier on his own involvement? Perón's private response to
such a question, assuming that it arose within his consciousness, can
only be conjectured.[38]

Evita's absence was meaningful in yet another sense, for after the
departure of so many old associates who had fallen in the political
wars, she had been almost the sole relief for the solitude in which
Perón found himself: solitude not in the literal sense but in terms of
trusted and competent and honest aides. His close circle was riddled
with mediocrities and plotters and self-seekers. "I feel surrounded by
informers," Perón said to Jorge Antonio, using an almost untranslat-
able and derogatory term rather stronger and broader than the English
word. "It's terrible to be in power and to feel surrounded and not to
be able to break the circle around you."[39]

There had been idle speculation that the passing of Evita would
bring a conflict for influence between the CGT and the armed forces.[40]
This was unrealistic and represented partly a failure to assess the powers
and personalities involved and partly the tendency of those outside
the civilization to overvalue institutions at the expense of those who
led them. The CGT was in no position to launch any crusades for
power. Its head, José Espejo, lost one hundred percent of his influence when Evita died: at the Loyalty Day celebration on October 17,
1952, he had been hissed and jeered by the assembled throng. No
support from Perón could be glimpsed, so he did the obvious thing:
he resigned. His successor, Eduardo Vuletich, bore the same relation-

ship to Perón that Espejo had to Evita. In the unlikely event that these or any other labor leaders aspired to real leadership, Perón had a hundred devices available to thwart them, to say nothing of his ability to go over their heads directly to the CGT membership.

Neither were the armed forces in a position to enter a contest for national supremacy. The collapse of the foolish Menéndez revolt had drained off some of the simmering resentments, and between Perón's reelection and his reinauguration more of them had been vented. The vehicle for this was another ill-executed plot led by another man of perpetual rebellion, Colonel José Francisco Suárez. It included hundreds of civilians, retired officers, and remnants of groups that had survived the confusions associated with Menéndez. This uprising had been scheduled for February 1952, but it came apart when the schemers unwittingly brought an intelligence agent into their fold. The plan had been to seize the principal government buildings and at the same time to batter a way into the presidential residence and kill Perón. Hundreds were arrested, but no word was given to the local press for three months.[41]

This was enough to keep military dissidents off stride for the moment, but it was minor in comparison to other security measures Perón now invoked. One of them was the revocation of pensions received by military plotters or by their families. Another, breaking new and ominous ground, was the organization of counterviolence for use in the event of another attack on Perón, as authorized and directed by a General Order No. 1 and by a document entitled "Plan Politico Año 1952." These documents, which were distributed in secret to officials of the national and the provincial governments, called for the maintenance of lists of enemies to be attacked through personal violence or bombings or arson, and for the formation of squads of enforcers from the Peronist Party and the CGT. The initial lists had the names of more than 300 individuals, fifty foreign businesses, embassies, and individuals, twenty-nine Argentine firms connected with the political opposition, and other data, including the ranking of the individuals on a point basis related to their significance or danger to the government.[42]

It was a strange response, uncharacteristic of Perón, for he was not one to authorize unofficial and extralegal foci of power. It is therefore not surprising that the bands of enforcers were never put to work and that the entire scheme remained in the files of the Peronist officials to whom it was distributed. Perón's motivations for so unruly and illegal a response remain unclear, but it is probable that they included several elements. Perhaps uncertainty as to further mutiny in the army was among them. Perhaps the measures were seen as preliminary to the general tightening of the Peronist political structure being planned for later in 1952, since it was clear from the "Plan Politico Año 1952" that it was intended to inaugurate the replacement of a neutral civil service with one whose members held views satisfactory to the executive power. Perhaps they were designed to smoke out the opposition and those of faint zeal in all ranks of government for possible replacement or for close surveillance, or intended as a political shield to deflect criticism of the economic austerity for which Perón knew he had to prepare opinion in political and public circles.[43]

Such a preparation was already under way, and this period in 1952 therefore represents one of the great divides in Peronism. It separated, once and for all, the bounteous years of 1946–48 and the intermediate years of 1949–51 from the more austere and less innovative period from 1952 to the fall of Perón in 1955. The earlier years were the era of populist outreach and creativity, financed by the reserves built up in the war. In the later years, the money was gone and economic development came to depend on old-fashioned recourses little envisioned in 1946, such as increased rural production, free enterprise, a reluctant acceptance of more foreign capital, and the discouragement of free and easy public demands.[44]

The symbol of the crossing of this divide was announced by Perón in February 1952 in the form of The Economic Plan for 1952, a precursor of the second five-year plan that was presented in December. The economic plan of 1952 appeared amid unhappy signs. Inflation was rising, foreign trade was declining, and industry was merely hanging on. Real wages declined in 1951–53 by more than 20 percent from 1950 and by nearly 30 percent from 1948, but total income declined even more, and labor's share of it remained about the same.[45] The plan centered on austerity and sacrifice, even to the extent of one beefless day a week. Price controls were continued, and wages would be frozen by contract for two years after an initial adjustment. In practice, the wage levels were set basically by the government, after 1952, with a slight bow in the direction of labor-management consultation. But Perón's sense of tactics was never better, for his wage policy was differentiated. Each settlement was unique, crafted to its own requirements, and neither employers as a whole nor workers as a whole were affected in the same way at the same time. Thus divided, they had no reason to present a common front. It was the politics of economic indirection.[46]

Much of the philosophy of this program was carried over into the official blueprint, the second Five-Year Plan, effective as of the new year. It was not a system of state ownership that was envisioned in this design, although, of course, the numerous existing state enterprises would remain, but rather an economy that was planned, organized, and controlled through state power as applied to private ownership and production. Investment priorities were improved and social programs received short shift. Private capital was welcomed, and there were hints that the time of extreme economic nationalism was limited.[47]

Without the slightest diminution of his hostility to the International Monetary Fund, Perón merely preempted its general prescriptions. Between 1950 and 1952, there were annual reductions in hourly real wages ranging from more than 4 percent to 11 percent. Public expenditures rose only slightly after 1950, whereas they had ballooned by 87 percent during the previous five years. Noneconomic public investment and defense expenditures were drastically reduced, while government investment in such basics as energy, fuel, and transport rose substantially. Fixed capital formation grew at very satisfactory rates during these years and industrial output evolved toward diversity and complexity. Cars began to be manufactured rather than merely assembled.[48]

These were all welcome improvements, but they illuminated in stark light the depth of the comparative decline since 1914. The British economist, David Ferns, has illustrated this by reference to the per capita consumption of steel, one of the indicators of a mature and industrialized economy. The level of 1950–52 was little more than one seventh of the level in 1905–14. By 1955, the much-improved figure was still only about 60 percent of the prewar level, a third of the figure in Australia and a quarter of that in Canada.[49]

The Five-Year Plan through which these economic evolutions were focussed also had its political aspect. For some time, Perón had been mulling over the virtues of further "organization" of Argentina and of its political process. The result was Book I of the plan, concerning social action. The themes were familiar: individualism is anarchy, collectivism is dictatorship, and between them is *Justicialismo* and government by *conducción*, which produce a society in which the acts of the government are merely the will of the people, who should now attain organization, with the aid of the government. They are free to organize, provided only that they do so for the consolidation and defense of the three great banners, social justice, economic independence, and political sovereignty. Since these cardinal principles of Peronism were also the fundamental objectives of the plan and the heart of *Justicialismo,* which had already been defined as National Doctrine, it would follow logically that the people would have to organize themselves in support of all of these objectives, and only these. The people so organized would express their will to the government, confirming the Peronist polity, and since the government merely implemented the national will, any disagreement with the government would be contrary to the will of the people. This was Perón's vision of the organized, organic state.[50]

The plan set forth various specific policies within these broad purposes. School programs and books would be revised to conform with national doctrine. A "social code" would be formulated, also in accord with national doctrine. A new culture, "humane and Christian," would be delineated out of classic and modern elements and Argentine tradition, and this, too, would reflect national doctrine. The hold that these dogmas and devotions of Peronism had upon the party loyalists can be sensed from the remark of a Peronist deputy during the legislative discussion of the Plan: "We would rather lose our personalities in Perón's Doctrine, than lose Perón's Doctrine in our personalities."[51] But the deputy was not alone in his satisfaction. The months that followed the presentation of the plan were a time of unusual harmony. The opposition was muted and no plots were rumored. A relaxed Perón decided to allow the opposition to campaign without restrictions in the forthcoming provincial elections in the two new provinces of Eva Perón and Presidente Perón. He even went so far as to receive a group of Argentine and international yachtsmen, hardly *descamisados,* on the occasion of the Buenos Aires–Río race, paying their expenses and lifting the intervention of the sponsoring yacht club, a very oligarchic body, indeed.[52]

But this unaccustomed tranquility did not last long. By April 1953, several upsetting events had converged. Economic discontents came home to roost, catalyzed by the beef shortage. The two-year contracts by which wages been stabilized in 1952 were now a bitterness to labor because of inflation. Perón ordered an investigation into graft and corruption, and it took a sudden nasty turn. It was generally believed that corruption had permeated the administration, including some on the higher levels, although Perón himself was not thought to be involved. In a speech on April 8, he had acknowledged the rumors and announced that all aspects would be investigated. A highly regarded army officer, General Leon Bengoa, took the assignment and began by examining the affairs of Evita's brother-in-law, Orlando Bertolini, a staff official in the Casa Rosada. Bertolini and Evita's brother, Juan Duarte, were widely suspected of major roles in the plundering.

The investigation was punctilious and brief. It began on April 6.

On the 8th, Juan Duarte, who had been suspended as of the 6th from his position as Perón's private secretary, penned a letter to Perón in which he asserted that his health had been undermined and he could no longer find the effort for "the gigantic and patriotic battle which you are now launching . . . inspired by the example of renunciation and disinterestedness that my illustrious and beloved sister gave Peronism, I beg you to accept my irrevocable resignation from the post of private secretary with which you distinguished me . . ."[53]

On the next day, the 9th, Juan Duarte's body was found slumped against his bed, dead from a bullet wound, the gun by his hand. A suicide note next to the body referred to the successful efforts of enemies of Perón to slander him and to his gratitude for Perón's affection, and continued: "I have been HONEST and nobody will be able to prove the contrary. I love you with all my soul and repeat once more that the greatest man I know is Perón . . . I leave this world nauseated with the rabble but happy . . . at having been his loyal friend . . . I beg you to care for my beloved mother and my kindred, and I beg their pardon, I who love them well, I came with Eva, with her I go, shouting Viva Perón . . . My last embrace is for my mother and for you." And there was a postscript: "Forgive the handwriting, forgive everything."[54]

That was the end of the investigation. What did outlive the week was the speculation arising from Duarte's death, for many believed, erroneously, that he was murdered because he knew too much. The people closest to the Peronist inner circle insist that while Duarte may have profited slightly from opportunities available to him, his graft was quite minor; that he died a poor man; that Bertolini, in any case, was far more guilty in this regard; and that there were very persuasive motives for Duarte's suicide.

Among these was the devastation Evita's death had caused him. He was far more afflicted than Perón himself, since the relationship of Duarte and Evita had been so deep as to create a symbiosis more than a mere sibling relationship. At her death, he had fled the room, denying God at the top of his voice. His weakness for carousal had caught up with him, in the form of syphilis, with ataxia; he was having difficulty with his walking. He had recently lost thirty-six pounds, and he was not a large man. He was in deep depression, with little to live for and good reason to die.[55]

But there was yet another twist to the truth of this sad episode, something that was closely guarded and never revealed beyond a tiny inner circle: Duarte did not die in his apartment, where he was found. He died by his own hand in the presidential residence. Staff attendants found him late at night, in the bedroom Evita had used, sprawled on the bed in which she had died. He had apparently been facing her picture on the nightstand when he fired his fatal shot and he died under her gaze.

Instant panic ran like a rogue flame through the attendants who made the discovery, for his death in such circumstances, in Perón's residence, carried a charge of political dynamite. In darkness and stealth they carried him to a car, drove him to his apartment, and placed the body, with gun and suicide note nearby, in a kneeling position against his bed. There he was found in the morning.[56]

A third complication in this hectic month of April occurred on the 15th, during and after a "loyalty demonstration" sponsored by the CGT as a counterbalance to the economic deprivations of the moment. It assembled in the Plaza de Mayo, and while Perón was speaking, two bomb explosions in nearby buildings rocked the Plaza, killing five and wounding many. The men responsible for the act, young men associated with the much-insulted oligarchy, were soon apprehended.

After the explosions, Perón seemed to improvise the rest of his speech, a mixture of routine doctrine and highly inflammatory incitement that spoke of guns in hand, hanging terrorists on trees, a new phase of purge, and recourse to tyranny and repression. But at the end he regained his mellow control, saying, "I beg that you withdraw quietly, confident that I shall know how to deal with things . . . return to your homes . . ."[57]

And return to their homes they did, without disorder, many singing as they went, maintaining the holiday spirit in which they had assembled. But that night terrible deeds were done. Gangs of extremists, led by the right-wing and fiercely nationalistic ALN, broke into the oligarchic Jockey Club and burned it. They had whetted their appetites by first destroying the headquarters of the Socialist Party and damaging those of the Radicals and the Conservatives. The destruction of the buildings was not the worst of it. The Socialist headquarters had contained a unique library, collected over many years, with irreplaceable records and volumes on the history of the Argentine labor movement, and this was burned; and at the Jockey Club the looting and burning included the deliberate destruction of several original paintings by Goya and Velázquez. In all of these cases the police and the firemen were either deliberately slow to respond or refused to act. Violence of this kind and on this scale had not been known under the Peronato.

The violence and destruction elicited neither regret nor contrition among loyal Peronists, and the flames were justified in the adminis-

tration press and in the remarks of Peronist deputies. The Radical
Party received most of the offical blame, although neither the Party
nor its members appear to have been involved in the bombing. Ricardo
Balbín, the Radical candidate in 1951, was jailed, along with other
party leaders. Manhunts and searches for arms were conducted around
the country. Soon after the bombs of April 15, legislation was introduced in Congress to nationalize horseracing, including the Jockey
Club and all its installations; enactment followed in May.[58] Other bombs
were exploded in Buenos Aires during April and May, and in the
sudden wind of crisis that had blown up, political tensions reached a
high point that contrasted abruptly with the relative calm that had
preceded.

Perón continued in his new vein for several months, taking a very
hard line in his May 1 speech to Congress. But even in times of the
clearest commitment to a chosen line of policy, the tactical Perón never
slept. Now, in turbulent May, he provided an illustration of how far
maneuver can be carried, and also a possible glimpse of the new phase
that would begin in July and August. Speaking to the Tailors' Union
in mid-May, he was all populist smoke and fire, brimming with radical
change. The oligarchy would have to be eliminated, preferably through
evolution, but through spoilation or biologic suppression if necessary;
the choice of methods depended on the oligarchy; they had already
been dislodged from the cities and would now have to be driven from
the land, since the plan demanded agrarian reform. A few days later,
Perón spoke at a congress of industrialists in tones of quiet conservatism, as if he were a subsidiary of the International Monetary Fund.
The embassy drew the obvious conclusion: ". . . Perón can be understood better by what he does than by what he says. He may at times
sound like a fascist, communist or even a New England conservative,
depending upon audience and purpose. It is of the utmost importance, therefore, in dealing with Perón, to measure the effect of his
deeds more than his words, and to measure them in terms of how
they affect basic U.S. interests. It would be all too easy to be diverted
by phrases, or to be diverted by domestic actions which, although we
might rightly consider them reprehensible in terms of our own code,
do not bear directly on our own interests."[59]

Against the confused background of April, May, and June 1953,
a new political phase of surprising clarity and consistency emerged in
July and August. It can be defined as the era of conciliation, and it
was destined to endure for almost a year and a half. It began on July
1, with the publication of the first of several petitions by prominent
members of the conservative Democratic Party, addressed to the min-

ister of interior, Angel Borlenghi, suggesting political pacification and peaceful coexistence. Other political parties were heard from almost immediately, approving this approach; the Radicals, the mainline Socialists and the Communist Party opposed it. The government obviously favored the idea, because the petitions of those supporting the concept were printed and those opposed were not, and because political prisoners began to be released.[60]

Soon there was direct evidence of Perón's commitment to this new course. In a series of talks at Santiago del Estero in late August, he made this enthusiastically clear. "Our flag is not one of battle, but rather one of tranquility, peace and work . . . I say to all Argentines to come to us and that in our noble Creole heart—in the usage of the old Creoles—there is room for all loves, even those of our own adversaries."[61]

Three months later, in November, one of the leaders of the conciliation movement, a Conservative, wrote an interesting report concerning the problems and advantages of the outreach. More critical of Perón's inner circle and the party and government officials surrounding him than of Perón himself, it contains good insights into the nature of the Casa Rosada staff and of Perón's psychological patterns. The bureaucracy, seen as determined to retain its position and privileges through the status quo, was cited as a more serious obstacle to conciliation or to any other important change than the CGT and the army. "They [staff and bureaucracy] surround, flatter and deceive him while they appear to defend and exalt him. This is true of 99% of his highest administrative and political collaborators . . . Inasmuch as Perón is not inclined to indulge in after-dinner talks, being a man who leads no social life at all, it is difficult, not to say impossible, to break up the circle of dishonest and disloyal collaborators who are seeing to it that he nourishes distrust for anything that does not suit them personally."

On the subject of Perón's psychology, the report observed that if he could only be reached, "Perón is a very impressionable man; temperamental and emotional, he is acutely sensitive to friendly suggestion, provided he thinks it is sincere. And if whoever makes such a suggestion is above suspicion insofar as the personal interest that may move him is concerned, the suggestion will have the power of fascination. Perón also likes clear, unpolished language. He dislikes circumlocution, he does not enjoy reading between the lines. But he never resists a courageous and rough statement when he is given weighty reasons for it and furnished with proof of the advisability for him to do this or that."[62]

The conciliation policy culminated in an amnesty law adopted a week before Christmas 1953. Civilians benefitted from a full and general amnesty, but something more qualified was offered to military and labor offenders.[63] The question remains, why did Perón embark on this course? And at this time? Various reasons can be discerned, although the weight to be given to each is a subjective assessment. From the most general point of view, a state of quiet and harmony accorded with Perón's vision of the organic and organized community, and this would be his tendency if the circumstances permitted such a luxury. At this moment they appeared to do so. The CGT and labor in general were firmly attached to the government, and while there was discontent among the rank and file with the direction of real income, it did not threaten labor solidarity. The army likewise was quiescent.[64] The political opposition was dispirited, and, like the oligarchy, much of it seemed resigned to the inevitability of Perón until some basic change occurred. It was not that the underlying tensions and resentments of these elements had been dissolved away; it was merely that they were inert and diffused, disposed to coexist for the moment.

If muted internal factors favored conciliation, so did several other circumstances that provided affirmative motivation. Perón at this stage was involved in a series of diplomatic overtures aimed at a degree of economic union in South America, and these would be benefitted if Argentina could bring to the green table the image of a successful and harmonious state. In a more critical area of the economy, Perón was also now devoted to a policy of industrial development through foreign investment, particularly from United States sources, and this required a stable domestic scene and better relations with the northern power. American industry was responding to Perón's signals, and the diplomatic relations that were traditionally so difficult had become surprisingly cordial under the Eisenhower administration. Conciliation was one element, and a very important one, in the new détente with Washington.

So tranquil, in fact, was the first part of 1954 that Perón felt the moment appropriate for an election of a vicepresident, together with the normal voting for half of the congressional membership. The vicepresidency had remained unfilled since that April day two years past when comfortable old Hortensio Quijano had died. Now Admiral Teisaire would be the Peronist candidate, and he had easy pickings. Eight opposition parties appeared in one place or another, most of them split within themselves. The Radicals presented a fascinating picture: the executive committee purported to speak for the Party,

but there were two other factions that recognized neither the committee nor the Radical candidates, who were appointed by the committee, nor the election itself, since they favored abstention. The
Democratic Party of the conservatives was also split on the question
of participation. The campaigning was not entirely free of the usual
constraints that all opponents faced under the Peranato, but it was
relatively open and unimpeded, and the balloting itself was, as usual,
honest. Teisaire won the vicepresidency by almost a two-to-one margin over his nearest opponent, a Radical. Counting all contests, on a
countrywide basis, Peronist candidates won about 69 percent of the
total vote.

The decline of the Radicals was symptomatic of the failure of the
political process to yield any real alternative to Peronism. The party
(or the movement) of Yrigoyen was now divided, like Gaul, into three
parts. The first was the Intransigent wing that possessed the legal credentials, the name, the inheritance, and image of the party. It was
headed by Dr. Arturo Frondizi, later to be known as "The Florentine," in tribute to his endless tactical manipulations. The second was
a dissident Intransigent faction formed around the famous Dr. Amadeo Sabattini, and known therefore as the "Sabattinistas." This group
claimed to speak for all Intransigents and, indeed, for all Radicals.
The third group, the Unionists, had no outstanding leader and were
a bit more conservative.

The Intransigents were characterized by total and blind opposition to everything the Peronists had ever done or proposed, whether
good, bad, or indifferent. As the embassy put it, ". . . while the Intransigents offer negativism, the Unionists offer nothing. Neither offer
has any vitality and neither can hope to revive the political strength
of Radicalism in the face of the positive program of Peronism."[65] Time
and the nature of Radicalism's dynamic had thinned out Yrigoyen's
vagueness and ambiguity even further, to the point that they had now
become almost etherial. Radicals themselves denied the existence of
any doctrine uniting the party, speaking, instead, of abstractions like
"humanistic inspiration," "instinctive character," and the creation of
"a popular soul." The party still had a large following that remembered the glory days, and it still spoke for much of the middle class,
but it gave no sign of descending further in the social hierarchy to
enlarge its base, and no sign therefore of mounting a serious challenge to Perón.

No such challenge, in fact, was visible from any source whatsoever
in this time of conciliation. There was by now a more general acceptance of what was obvious, that is, that Perón commanded a majority

base of support and a willing one. The oligarchy and those associated with it had come to see that the reality of Peronism, although distasteful, was less threatening than its language and that they could probably live with the man, uncomfortably to be sure, whereas if he were to go, who could say? The oligarchy and Perón had come to resemble boxers in their weaving and bobbing and trading of punches, but it was a match in which both contestants sensed that there would be no knockout.[66]

Thus calm prevailed in the Argentine winter and spring of 1954. The economic stabilization program of 1952 had worked well, and 1953 and 1954 were years of rather gentle recovery.[67] There was less arbitrary usage by the government and more confidence on its part, less excitement and propaganda, and much less mass mobilization and frenzy in the Plaza de Mayo. September yielded to October, and on Loyalty Day, the 17th, an assured Perón asked the assembled public in the Plaza the usual question at the end of his address, "Are you satisfied with your government?"

And the shouts came back, in many voices: "Yes."[68]

The general mood of relaxation pervaded what was as organized a community, in the sense that Perón used that term, as Argentina was to achieve during the Peronato or otherwise. The army, the CGT, and the CGE (the General Economic Confederation, which sought with a certain delusion of grandeur to speak for the entire business community) were all closely linked to the government. A third general confederation, Confederación General Professional, known as the CGP, attempted a comparable role for professionals and had the cooperation of Perón. Educational bodies, athletic groups, cultural organizations, and the entire propaganda and communications sectors, with their networks and presses, were likewise embedded in the central State or joined to it in working harmony.[69]

It was fortunate for Perón that politics had attained this unusual tranquility, for he was involved during these same months in economic initiatives that were controversial even in the best of atmospheres. It had been clear for two years that foreign capital would be necessary if the promises of the second Five-Year Plan were to be even approximated. The public sign of the new philosophy, apart form various of Perón's utterances, was the Investment Law of August 21, 1953, favorable to the remittance of profits and capital to foreign investors.[70]

With this impetus, and with the positive mood of the government, new investment from abroad did indeed begin a revival. In addition to the Kaiser initiative for automobile manufacturing, European interests in the same industry appeared in Buenos Aires with their plans. The projected steel mill that the military had taken under its wing, long awaited, began to show signs of life. A mill was purchased in May 1954 in the United States and the blast furnace that was to go with it was committed in March 1955 with the help of a $60 million loan from the Export-Import Bank in Washington, a source of assistance that would have been anathema in the early years of Peronism. Politics soon intervened, of course, and the steel complex did not go into operation until Perón had been in exile almost six years.[71]

But the ghost that sat at the head of the economic table, sensed and invoked in all the discussions surrounding the new foreign investment policy, was petroleum. This subject raised all sorts of problems, one of which was the famous Article 40 of the Peronist constitution, which forbade the transfer of this resource to foreign interests. Perón was determined to make Argentina self-sufficient in oil, and in his earlier presidential years he had maintained the policy of "petroleum nationalism" that had become habitual. But he had a low opinion of YPF, the government-owned and operated oil company. He went so far as to tell the American ambassador in July 1953 that the YPF "had been exploiting the public iniquitously for years."[72] The relatively modest increases in YPF's production in recent years had failed to match even the growth in demand, and foreign exchange was increasingly diverted to oil purchases. Perón therefore faced reality, with his interesting flexibility. He spoke firmly and, one would have thought, persuasively in the last few months of 1953 in defense of a deal with some international oil company. But it was an anxiously delicate topic.

Most of 1954 was devoted to exploring ways and means, and to talks with this or that international oil company. Then came the big development: at the beginning of 1955 Perón announced an agreement. It was with the Standard Oil Company of California, and the contract was approved by Perón in the first week of May and sent to Congress for ratification. The agreement gave Standard an exclusive right to explore and produce oil in a large area in southern Patagonia. The product would be sold to YPF on a price formula until YPF's needs were fully met. Thereafter, Standard could export what was left, dividing the profits half and half with YPF.

Instantly, a vast chorus of opposition raised its many voices. The most conservative sectors disliked the contract, the Communists disliked it, and, as it seemed, so did every individual and party in between those extremes. The armed forces distrusted it. The Radicals in Congress leaped to the attack. The law stuck in the throats of even those most docile of legislators, the Peronist deputies in Congress. The depth of nationalistic sentiment was nakedly revealed, and, in contrast, Perón's reasonable and pragmatic approach. He assailed "comic-opera nationalists" and he insisted that the law did not violate Article 40 because he saw it as a service contract involving no change in title to the oil, but it was impossible to stand against the tide and he soon agreed to seek negotiated revisions. Before anything could come of this, however, political crisis made the subject moot.[73]

The Outward Reach in Foreign Affairs

In terms of Argentine relations with the United States, the first years of the second administration, up to 1953, had been a time of nagging irritation and recrimination on both sides, carried over from 1945 and the first administration. In addition to the usual grounds for abuse, Perón had now settled upon another grievance, the bilateral security discussions and pacts that were being undertaken between the United States and individual countries in Latin America. These were viewed by Perón as divisive intrusions that would tend to freeze out Argentina from the concert of the hemisphere. His views on this sore subject were standard fare in the weekly articles by "Descartes" that were a conspicuous but unacknowledged component of the dialogue between Perón and the United States in these years. Begun in 1950 and published in the Peronist paper, *Democracia,* the short and pithy articles by "Descartes" were assumed to reflect official policy and probably the direct authorship of Perón. The Argentine foreign minister told the embassy that they were written by the editor of *Democracia* and approved by Perón.[74] But they are so true to Perón's idiomatic style that one wonders. In any case, they merit attention, for they were not casual comments dropped inadvertently or emotional outbursts uttered in oratorical heat.

The writings of "Descartes" are an interesting commentary on Perón. Very wide-ranging in content, they reflect the unusual spread of his interests and his didactic personality. All history seemed to be his province in these articles, and all the world his stage. But if there was much breadth, there was often too little depth, for the factual base of the articles was frequently meager or distorted, and an air of rather careless generalization pervaded the writing. Philosophy vied in these paragraphs with momentary economic issues, shrewd insights with paranoia, and large proposals concerning the world order with venomous attacks on the objects of his dislike. The tone and content alike were stridently anti-United States all during the period of 1950 to 1953, and reading them one can easily reach the conclusion that, apart from policy, Perón neither understood nor liked the United States as a country.

This is hardly surprising, but still his perceptions of the northern power will seem strange to Americans. "The history of the United States is the extermination of the Indian, the conquest of Louisiana, Florida, Cuba, Texas, New Mexico, California, Alaska, Puerto Rico, etc. It failed in Canada, but dismembered Columbia and invaded Nicaragua . . . We Latins rose separately but subsequently went to each other's aid . . . They were different men, different peoples. Two distinct worlds which represent two epochs; they, the present, we, the future."[75]

Simple dislike, and anger, appear frequently in the lofty discourse. "North Americans are hated in Asia, the Near and Far East, and in Europe, in addition to the other continents. Now it is Latin America. Are they themselves not to blame? The role of the Messiah adopted by the Yankee leaders has caused them to believe that they are really 'the defenders of liberty,' but it would be opportune to ask on whose authority they have assumed such a role."[76] Perón's perception of the United States government, conditioned by his Creole values, will seem particularly bizarre to Americans: ". . . we observe absolute inefficiency and ineptitude in the government, complete disorganization in the administrative sphere, an enormous degree of disintegration and dishonesty, together with impotency to govern, strikes, disputes between the executive authorities, and contempt for the President and functionaries . . . permanent dislocation of its economy, the fabulous deficits, preparation for war . . . it occurs to us to ask: Why doesn't the United States ask the U.N. for technical aid?"[77]

Although Perón's opinions, emotions, and sensitivities affected his perceptions and judgments to some extent, he was easily capable of overriding them if circumstances required. But from 1951 to 1953, no circumstances so required, and the consequence was a difficult period for the diplomats. The United States had turned to a more cooperative approach with the departure of Ambassador Braden in 1947, but Perón still blew hot and cold. His sense of dignity and his need for recognition seem to have been one of the stumbling blocks. Early in 1953, there was a small revelation for the American ambassador, Albert Nufer, when he happened to read to Perón a sentence of a Department of State communication that referred to Argentina and the United States as recognized leaders of the American community. Nufer reported that Perón flushed with pride, and said to his foreign minister sitting nearby, "See what they think of us!"[78]

Then came the election of General Dwight Eisenhower to the

presidency and, at approximately the same time, the internal factors that pointed Perón in the direction of conciliation, better United States relations, and foreign investment in Argentina. Changes occurred more rapidly than usual.[79] The president's brother, Dr. Milton Eisenhower, appeared in Buenos Aires in July on his South American tour, undertaken at Ike's request, and he was an instant success with Perón. For the first time, Perón felt that the American government was not against him.[80] By November, Secretary of State John Foster Dulles could report to the president that ". . . matters are developing about as favorably as we could reasonably expect." In a memorandum to Ike on November 19, he commented, "I agree that Perón's disinclination to restore the newspaper *La Prensa* to its former owner (whom he considers to symbolize the feudal economic and social structure which he has tried to reform), and the tenacious interest of the U.S. press in this matter will delay any real public acceptance of Perón in this country . . . I fear that this new and, I hope, sincere confidence of Perón in our intentions would be undermined and possibly destroyed if we were to indicate in any way that we considered the *La Prensa* case a fit subject for official U.S. advice or discussions . . ."[81]

Secretary Dulles's comments throw a sharp light upon one of the realities that Perón found hard to accept, that is, that the *La Prensa* case was central to the conflicts between the two countries. His remarks also point to the other great reality, a related one, that Perón could not have really understood because of the differences in the two civilizations: during the entire period after Braden, his problems with the United States were due less to American official policy than to the state of American public opinion. That opinion was dominated by very strong hostility to Perón on the part of two sectors that exerted great influence in American public life. One was the American press. Stanton Griffis, the American ambassador in 1950, reflected the exasperation of the diplomats, referring to the correspondent of the *New York Times* as ". . . obsessed as are all the American correspondents here with the thought that it is their chief mission in life to create freedom of the press in Argentina and that efforts to build good relations between the United States and Argentina are purely secondary considerations."[82]

The other hostile sector was the American labor movement, which was unable to forget that Argentine labor was linked to the government and hence was not free in the American sense. The CIO Committee on Latin American Affairs criticized Perón in the most severe terms to anyone who would listen. Its views were typified by its chairman, the influential Jacob Potofsky, who wrote in May 1950 to Assistant Secretary of State Miller opposing Exim Bank financing for Argentina and expressing "profound concern" for United States moral leadership, since Argentina crushes free labor. A loan would help ". . . to tighten the iron grip of Perón upon the people of Argentina."[83]

The policy that was favored by Dulles prospered, however, despite the domestic criticism, and relations with Argentina became almost mellow.[84]

The years of Perón's second administration found him preoccupied with hemispheric relationships as well as with his American policies. As early as January 1952, "Descartes" was writing in favor of a confederation of Latin American nations, a Latin American Union.[85] This represented a distinctive approach to hemispheric policy by a Latin American country. It would have to contend with the more traditional concept of a Pan American body that included all the Latin nations, and the United States as well, a body that had found its format in the Organization of American States, the OAS, since 1948. Brazil was traditionally associated with this policy and with a close relationship with the United States, as exemplified by Brazilian participation in the Second World War. Perón's suggestion would also have to contend with the apprehensions of his neighbors. Argentina had never embarked on military ventures or sought territorial expansion, but its very size, in comparison to Chile, Uruguay, Paraguay, and Bolivia, and its economic development, gave pause to its neighbors, as did the efforts of Argentine diplomats and labor attachés in South America to spread the gospel of Perón. The concern of the others was also kept alive by the style and personality that Argentina projected. That country saw itself as the head of the Latin American community by reason of size, power, and cultural development. Again, Argentina had by tradition been the most European-oriented and the most isolationist of the Latin American nations in terms of Inter-American collaboration, so that Perón's proposals would have to face considerable residues of skepticism if he chose to advance them seriously.

He did so choose, and the first results, in 1952, were not encouraging. His starting point was a regional pact or union, centered in close economic collaboration, binding together Argentina, Brazil, and Chile. But Brazil indicated its preference for a Pan American solution and its connections with Washington. And in Chile, the president responded angrily to Argentine press attacks on Chile's acceptance of military aid grants from the United States, saying rather bluntly that ". . . the place from which they came indicated in an eloquent manner the urgent necessity of strengthening Chile's defensive might."[86]

Perón persisted, however, and in September 1952, events took his

side when General Carlos Ibáñez was elected president of Chile. Ibáñez was widely known as authoritarian, rightist, nationalistic, and
populistic. He was also known to be a good and like-minded friend of
Perón, to such an extent that he had announced his presidential bid
from Buenos Aires. He was sympathetic to the general tenor of Perón's
Latin American union themes, and he was happy to issue an invitation
to Perón to meet with him in Santiago on February 20, 1953.

On February 10, Perón gave an interview, more bombshell than
journalism, to the director of the official government newspaper in
Santiago. All discussion up to this time had referred to projects of
economic union of some kind, but now Perón said, "I think that Chilean–Argentine union, complete union and not half-way, should be
made totally and immediately. Economic union alone won't be strong
enough ... The Argentine people will open their arms to the Chileans to bring about a complete union."[87] The interview was printed in
Santiago on the 15th, and instantly the trip itself was in jeopardy. But
Perón issued a disavowal of his quoted remarks, and the trip survived.

It must have seemed more nearly an expedition than a trip. Eduardo
Vuletich, the head of the CGT, was there, and Minister of Interior
Borlenghi, and Raúl Mende, minister of technical services, who
upstaged the foreign minister and played a conspicuous and untactful
role. The minister of labor, some Peronist deputies, and a group of
cattlemen attended, to say nothing of ministerial delegations, sports
teams, a dozen aviators, media technicians, and 400 security agents.
The highlight came on February 21, when the Chilean foreign minister appeared on the balcony of the governmental palace and
announced that the Andes were no more. An act had been subscribed
by the two presidents, providing for the signing, within 120 days, of
a Treaty of Economic Union. The minister's faith was evident, but it
was not the kind that moves mountains. The effect on Chilean public
opinion was less than favorable and the government soon realized the
value of foot-dragging.

Ninety days went by, and no headway was made on the treaty. The
Chileans appeared to lose interest. Then on June 3, Raúl Mende
appeared again in Santiago, eighteen days before the deadline, with
a huge document. It proved to be a draft treaty, with sixty-eight articles that went far beyond the economic relations mentioned in the act
on February 21 and intruded into political, military, and cultural affairs.
Again there was consternation in the Chilean government. When
President Ibáñez went to Buenos Aires in July for the signing of the
treaty, he carried with him a much slenderized document of twelve
articles, none of which went beyond the economic sphere. But it was

not very significant, being less a treaty than an agreement to enter into future treaties on a case-by-case basis, with ratification being required for each. Even so, the treaty was never ratified by Chile. Similar undertakings were later entered into by Argentina with Paraguay, Nicaragua, Ecuador, and Bolivia, and these, too, were never fully implemented in practice.

But what of Brazil? Perón had foreseen a union of Brazil, Argentina, and Chile, but no representative from Brazil was either present or heard from in Santiago. Why? Perón's explanation offers an interesting revelation of the darker spaces of his statecraft. The explanation unfolded on November 11, 1953. On that day, Perón delivered a very secret address at the War Academy, preserved by the Defense Ministry in a pamphlet, all copies of which were numbered and registered in the names of the few persons allowed to possess them. In this speech, Perón traced his version of his relationship with President Vargas of Brazil in regard to a union of the three nations. "Getulio Vargas was totally and entirely in agreement with this idea, and in accomplishing it as soon as he would be in office. [He assumed the Presidency, for the second time, on January 31, 1951.] . . . When Vargas came to office he promised me that we would meet in Buenos Aires or in Río and conclude that treaty that I signed with Ibáñez, the same one. That was the formal purpose that we outlined. Even more, we said, 'we're going to abolish the boundaries, if that's necessary.' "

Then, said Perón, Vargas told him that things were very difficult in Río, with the Congress and all, and six months would be helpful to him. Nothing occurred in that period, during which Ibáñez was elected in Chile. Perón then sent a message to Vargas, saying that he wanted to sign the treaty with Chile, but that he had committed himself to Vargas first, and would the latter authorize him to proceed with Chile? The reply, according to Perón, was that Vargas not only authorized him to sign first with Chile, but also empowered Perón to sign the document in Chile on Vargas's behalf. Perón said he did not accept the representation of Vargas, but that he decided to go to Santiago, as he in fact did on February 20. To his amazement and embarrassment, Perón continued, he was met in Chile with the news that the Brazilian foreign minister, Joao Neves da Fontoura, had just made a public declaration that Brazil opposed regional pacts of this kind and, instead, favored the broad Pan American approach. Swallowing his chagrin, Perón said he then signed the act and went home.

Back in Buenos Aires, according to this account, Perón was approached by a Brazilian journalist, Gerardo Rocha, a friend of Vargas, who apologized for the latter. "Vargas ordered me to explain to you what has happened in Brazil. He said that his situation there is very difficult; that politically he's not able to control things; that he has drought in the North and frosts in the South; and that there are uprisings among the politicians; that communism is very dangerous; that he isn't able to do anything; finally, excuse him because he doesn't think that way, and if the Foreign Minister did that, he can't control the Minister either." It was a picturesque evocation of Perón's abandonment and betrayal by a Vargas who had somehow crumbled into silliness.[88]

But none of this was true if one is to believe the infinitely more plausible accounts available in Brazil.[89] The truth seems to be that on four earlier occasions Perón invited Vargas, urgently, to meet with him to discuss some kind of union of the two countries, the first two invitations being sent through the Brazilian ambassador in Buenos Aires, Baptista Luzardo. Perón suggested that they meet at Vargas's farm on the Argentine border, or at the nearby farm of Luzardo, or elsewhere. A third invitation was carried by João Goulart, later president of Brazil. The fourth occurred a few days before Vargas's second inauguration, at the end of January, when Vargas, at his farm, was visited by vice-president Quijano, who was driving with an entourage to a destination on the Argentine side of the border. Quijano descended on Vargas with his party, four cars of them, at eleven o'clock at night, and the two men spent two hours together, alone. Vargas mentioned to Luzardo the next morning that a fourth invitation had been delivered, and that his reply had been the same as it was to the first three, that is, "No." Luzardo pressed him for a reason. With that strain of ambiguity that was so conspicuous in him, Vargas replied merely, "Ah, Luzardo, those military, those military . . ." And he used the word "milicos", a pejorative term, for them.

In fact, Vargas never communicated with Perón, on this subject or on any other, with the sole exception of a telegram of sympathy when Evita died. He never wrote, and the two men never spoke to each other. As for the statement of the Brazilian foreign minister that Brazil would not favor any policy of an ABC block, it was not timed to embarrass Perón in Santiago, but was made in advance of Perón's trip. The Brazilians, however, did employ a symbolism at the time of the Santiago meeting to indicate their disapproval of the proceedings there; while Perón was in Santiago, they revived the proposed Military Security Treaty with the United States that had been in suspension since early 1952, and signed it.[90]

It was a most curious performance, this address by Perón at the War Academy. Much of it was ridiculous on its face, and it could have persuaded only the more naive of the officers. No president of a country would authorize another president to sign on his behalf a treaty with a third country, particularly if the first two countries were Brazil and Argentina. No president would make admissions to a foreign head of state so intimate and potentially so damaging that they could hardly have been uttered aloud in the president's own office. Nor would Vargas have entrusted such humiliating dynamite to Gerardo Rocha of all people, for the latter was at that time merely tolerated by Vargas and was widely believed to be in the pay of Perón. Was the purpose of the strange address to embarrass Vargas for some reason not readily apparent? Or to justify Perón before the army and before history for his inability to bring off his ABC policy of union that he adhered to all his life with genuine tenacity?

Whatever the reason, the speech was leaked and became famous in Brazil. Neves da Fontoura had been replaced as foreign minister in mid-1953 and had broken with Vargas. In April 1954, in a dramatic interview, he accused Vargas of having secretly negotiated with Perón for an ABC block that would be aligned against the United States, and in support of this he cited the speech of Perón, which thus acquired instant notoriety and a place at the center of a political whirlwind. An impeachment proceeding against Vargas was attempted in Congress, but without success.[91] The Argentine government, of course, officially denied that any such speech had ever been given, but as for that, it suffices that Perón included it in his book *Latino América: Ahora o nunca*, first published in 1967 and reprinted in 1973, while he was still alive.

Conflict with the Church

The failure of his designs in foreign policy was a disappointment to Perón, but it had no real effect on the Peronist state, whose internal supports seemed stronger than ever at the time Loyalty Day was celebrated on October 17, 1954. All elements of the opposition appeared to be overcome or seduced or quiescent. From abroad, the view was the same. In the United States, the foremost academic authority on Argentina published a book in December 1954 in which he prophesied that Perón's hold was so strong that he could be expected to complete his term and win reelection or install his choice of successor in 1957. Herbert Matthews of the *New York Times*, a journalist widely experienced in Latin America, announced as late as April 1955, that Perón could not fall and probably could not be overthrown; no element was in a position to act against him.[92]

Nor could Perón himself have suspected that October 17, 1954 would be the last Loyalty Day he would celebrate in Argentina for almost two decades, for the events that led to his fall less than a year later developed with startling suddenness and with little background. Principal among them, although not the sole cause, was a deeply wounding and bitter encounter with the Church.

Of all the improbable causes of an improbable turn of events, a conflict with the Church would seem perhaps the least likely. Perón had always been a believing Catholic. He could say, while in exile years later, "I am a Catholic, but I am not clerical. I believe in the Doctrine: in the word of Christ. But not in the rites, because the rites have been made by men."[93] But that was afterthought, and it did not seem to occur to him that he was thereby defining himself as a Protestant. He had accepted all the teachings of the Church, rites included, without difficulty during all his years.

Church-State relations under the Peronato had always been cordial. Abrasions might occur: Perón's openness to unorthodoxy such as spiritualism; the appearance of an American faith healer in Buenos Aires in 1954; the encroachments of Evita's Foundation upon the Church's domination of charitable activity; and the cult of Evita, which had taken a vague theological turn that had always been implicit in her phenomenon. Images of her were now sometimes rendered in the style reserved for Christ and the Virgin. In 1954, a prayer appeared in which she was addressed in words that parodied the Ave Maria. A woman Peronist senator, in a 1955 parliamentary debate, asserted, "I have seen Eva Perón turn water into wine, because in no other way can you compare the dreams realized by the children, the mothers, the old people."[94]

But problems of this kind, while vexing, had not extended to the large issues upon which the Church–State relationship depended. In regard to those, the record had been quite good. The active support of the Church had been a factor in Perón's victory in 1946, just as Perón had been a factor in the imposition of religious education in the public school system in 1943, contrary to tradition. It was Perón who had symbolized the union of the sword and the cross in the hundreds of rituals and observances that governed civil life. It was Perón who had performed the reverent gesture of laying his general's sword upon the altar of the shrine of the Virgin of Luján. And the position of the Church in Argentine life argued powerfully against the measures upon which Perón now embarked. It was not that all Argentines were pious or that all clerics were esteemed. Argentine men in particular were negligent and even invisible in their attendance at the communion rail. Priests and bishops might be widely disliked for one reason or another. The policies of the Church might be suspect or opposed by many. The number of the truly faithful and ardent might be few, but they did exist and they were powerfully motivated. Most of all, the Church was so pervasive, so intimately a part of historical and communal memory and life, that to attack it on a broad front was to mutilate one's own body. The axioms of geometry did not apply: the whole of the Church was much greater than the sum of its parts; one might disagree with this part or that, or even attack this or that; but an assault on the Whole was almost unthinkable.

Nevertheless, this was what Perón seemed to be attempting in the waning months of 1954. In October, there were occasional unfavorable references to political intrusions by the Church through the creation of a Christian Democratic party or movement. In his address on October 17, Perón classified the enemies of Peronism as the politicians, the Communists, and the wolves in sheep's clothing. The disguised wolves consisted of those who claimed to be nonpolitical and thus had neither good nor bad odor, "like pigeon droppings," and false Peronists. The latter part of this rather oracular avian accusation was generally assumed to indicate vexation at what the government now saw as a politicized Church,[95] and the clergy certainly adopted this interpretation, for the relations of Church and State now deteriorated rapidly as the pulpits took up the challenge.[96]

But the theory that Perón had to oppose the Church because it was a political mover through a Christian Democratic aspiration seems overblown. Whatever a few marginal priests may have said or done, Church policy was firmly against involvement in politics. The activity had been largely among Catholic laymen acting as individuals, political novices already seriously split, who could, at best, take some votes from the Radicals and the Conservatives.[97]

At the same time another explanation came into vogue: the problem was not the entry of the Church into politics, but the reaction of the Church to the entry of the State into religious matters. Here the disagreements swirled around a new organization that had been invented by Perón's minister of education, Armando Méndez San Martín, a man strongly committed to the supremacy of the State and a narrow role for the Church. In 1953, he suggested to Perón the creation of a national organization for students in the secondary school system. Perón was always happy to see another gear of social machinery mesh into place, and the Union of Secondry School Students, the UES, was the result, with its two branches, one for boys and the other for girls. Perón made available various state facilities, including the use of the presidential summer home at Olivos for the girls' branch, beginning in January 1954.

The Church, however, saw this as an invasion of its own field of education and religious influence, since the UES was certain to impress Peronist and lay values upon its adolescent members. A Catholic lay organization, Catholic Action, was already sponsoring youth groups and these came into competition with the UES with the backing of other Catholic adult organizations. On November 10, Perón spoke publicly against Catholic Action and accused several bishops and priests by name of opposing the government.[98] On the 25th, at a mass meeting in Luna Park, Perón and the top echelon of Peronism and of the CGT again lambasted elements of the clergy. Eduardo Vuletich struck the prevailing note by assuring that ". . . if there was ever one man who could practice the doctrines of Perón before Perón, that man was God."[99] Several priests in Córdoba, a center of Catholic sentiment, were arrested soon after. Also, beginning in November, new decrees placed physical education in all schools under state control, with "spiritual counselors" to be appointed by the Eva Perón Foundation to give students advice and "spiritual" instruction in the national doctrine, *Justicialismo*.[100] Tensions continued to increase. December 8 was the celebration of Immaculate Conception, and the services at the cathedral on the Plaza de Mayo attracted an enormous crowd of the faithful, whose numbers, perhaps 200,000, constituted a political rather than a religious statement, and a very strong one.

It was the government's turn, and Perón responded immediately. A Catholic paper was closed, and restrictions were imposed on outdoor meetings. The Congress went to work and with Perón's necessary approval enacted a series of measures infuriating to Catholics: the legalization of divorce, the end of official support for private Catholic schools, the authorization of the houses of prostitution that had been illegal since 1933, and the repeal of the law requiring religious education in the schools. All of these measures were instituted with great rapidity by the end of 1954, and with every evidence of a desire not to conciliate but to win a confrontation. By May 1955, the Congress had approved a measure that advocated an amendment of the constitution to separate Church and State.[101]

This explanation, attributing such a stream of vital events to Perón's desire to protect the government's entry into the field of education and youth-related activities, also seems unpersuasive, at least by itself. Peronist involvement in social matters in a way offensive to the Church could certainly have been adjusted by compromise if the will had been present.

A third explanation was the simple notion of bad advisors luring Perón astray. Bad advisors were certainly present in Perón's entourage at this time, including Méndez San Martín and Raúl Apold, Perón's information and propaganda chief. But Perón had had long experience with bad advice, and it had never gotten the better of him before on the scale now being experienced.

Still another theory postulates that the death of Evita had removed a vital restraining force. But Evita would not seem the most steadying of hands for the kind of crisis that had now arisen. She was much more rigid and hard-edged than Perón in the face of any conflict seen as Armageddon, and such a characterization of disputes came easily to her. Restraint and balancing of interests and subtle maneuver were not her forte, and in the rising war with the Church she would have been out of her element.

A fifth explanation sees the fracas with the Church as a device to divert attention from the Standard Oil proposal already referred to, which came to a head in these months.[102] A sixth explanation asserts that Perón, by reason of his cultural tradition and his innate ambition, could not tolerate any other power center. But in the Iberian concept of the organic state such views applied to control only within the political area, and the corresponding power of the Church in its proper realm was just as fundamental. The themes of Suárez and Vitoria would have required that the matter be settled by conciliation rather than by confrontation.

Each of these individually insufficient explanations[103] does take on significance, however, when considered together with a new factor: Perón's declining abilities. He was simply wearing down from long attrition. There was nothing dramatic about it. It was a slow, downward evolution that affected judgment and will, not uniformly but spasmodically. It is not at all surprising, for in 1955, he was sixty years old and for the past twelve years he had been pouring forth physical and psychic energy in the very vortex of a politics as desperate and intense as any to be found. He had lost two wives to cancer. The nervous tic in the eye that had led one interviewer to wonder if Perón were winking some hidden message was the tiniest of clues to the tension and fatigue that had settled in beneath the surface.

For some time now his writing had come to contain, intermittently, the sort of things that one says casually over cocktails when listeners have their minds elsewhere but refrains from putting on the record. Paranoia was entering here and there into the "Descartes" pronouncements. In the June 19, 1952 article, referring to the destructive work of the two imperialisms and their Argentine allies, he noted, "All is in accordance with a preconceived plan established for the purpose of creating disorder to disrupt unity." It would be quite a "pre-conceived plan" that could link officials in the Soviet Union, the United States, and Argentina in simultaneous collaboration on tactics. The word "Sepoys," in derogation of almost all who had working connections with foreign interests, appeared in his polemics. Something called the "International Synarchy," a nest of intriguers denounced but not defined, lodged in his imagination.

Perón's behavior in Chile during his visit in 1953 had displayed an unexpected obtuseness with regard to local psychology. He had attempted then to mediate a dispute between two groups of Chilean feminine Peronists, and made available to a presumably unified feminine party in Chile a suitcase containing 200,000 Argentine pesos, thus brewing a scandal that had an impact on Chilean politics. He had permitted the tactlessness of Mende and Borlenghi that offended local opinion by cynical references to Chilean realities past and present.[104] This sort of failure is easy and natural, but intuition and empathy had always been Perón's strengths.

The extraordinary speech at the War Academy, in November 1953, concerning Vargas certainly raises the question of Perón's judgment. He would have known, in his better times, that distortions and fabrications on such a scale inevitably come to light, and that what he was saying sounded silly even in the short term.

By 1953, too, his personal conduct had taken a strange turn. More and more he devoted himself to sports and recreation. His old enthusiasm for these had turned to preoccupation. He sought the company of boxers and other athletes. Fast motorboats on the waterways of the estuary and fast motorcycles had a great appeal. Surprised *porteños* would jump aside and watch the leather-jacketed president speed by, with a sports cap perched jauntily on his head.

In this scene of growing indulgence, one facet in particular raised questions of taste and proportion among many Argentines. At the girls' branch of the UES in Olivos, large numbers of young adolescents sported about harmlessly enough, swimming, playing games, taking instruction. But Perón increasingly identified himself with the program, conducting himself almost as a father of a large family. He instructed them, generally had lunch with them, one at a time, and socialized with them as much as possible. Out of this background emerged Nelly Rivas.

She was one among the group until she came to Perón's attention. She was fourteen years old in October of 1953 when she first came to Olivos, the child of a poor worker in a candy factory. Her parents made do with a hundred pesos a month, of which thirty-three went for rent. She slept on a sofa bed at the foot of her parents' bed in the cramped quarters where they struggled for survival. One morning at Olivos she was told she would have lunch with the president that noon, and her legs began to tremble. That lunch led to others, and then she was assigned to take some papers from the UES office at Olivos to Perón at the presidential residence downtown. They spent a long afternoon talking, and she remained there for the night. She spent a second night there after a late sporting event with Perón, and a third night due to a heavy rainstorm, and after that the small sofa bed in her parents' room remained unused.

Now she spent her days watching movies and fending off the efforts of the teachers Perón sent around to instruct her in the rudiments of culture. After a year he gave up. "There won't be another teacher coming here," he said one day. "If you want to remain an ignoramus, away with them." But a few hours later he returned and suggested to her softly, "Why don't you read Plutarch? If you don't understand it very well, I'll help you with a dictionary." Then after a while he conceived the idea of sending her on a trip to Europe to learn about the world. She was terrified: "The very thought of leaving the residence brought me attacks of madness," she wrote later. But she was a comfort to Perón, a companion with whom to share sports and conversation, a simple girl who would listen attentively.[105]

The spectacle of the fifty-eight-year-old president taking a mistress of fourteen years was, of course, a rich tidbit for his opponents, and the suggestive doings at Olivos led to wild speculations and defamatory rumors. Perón was pictured as presiding over quasi-orgies, a Roman emperor running amok among slave girls. It really was not that way at all, although few would believe it. Perón was more fatherly than concupiscent in his activities at Olivos, as now seems clear from the accounts of the women who look back upon that time. In the case of Nelly, Perón certainly took advantage of an inexperienced young adolescent, although he did not see it that way and his conduct was not that of a hit-and-run seducer. And there was certainly a carnal element in the liaison, but it appears to have been secondary to Perón's urge for an undemanding companion. In general, his associations with women remained as they had always been, comfortable rather than exotic, and except for the aberration with Nelly and his slightings of convention with Evita, they would not have been out of place in the England of Trollope's novels.

But that was not the way it appeared to the Church and to those who thought it decadent or, more likely, depraved for the president of a great nation to race around his capital on a motorcycle and to devote hours to fencing lessons for young girls frolicking in their shorts. He had always been a maverick in social decorum, but now, with Nelly Rivas, he was going beyond former levels of offense and giving a moral initiative to his opponents.

All of these instances of declining judgment indicate that the Perón who chose to do battle with the Church in 1954 and 1955 was no longer the leader who had given his name to an age in Argentina. He exaggerated or misconstrued the political challenges, overreacted, enlarged a crevasse into an unbridgeable chasm, and appeared bereft of the uncanny psychological mastery that had brought him to the top.[106]

The battle with the Church accomplished what ten years of political opposition by Perón's enemies had singularly failed to do: it united them for a moment. The Church became a pretext for many who cared nothing for religion or for the clergy, but who could smell a good political opportunity. By the early summer of 1955, the trajectory of this conflict brought it into alignment with another upheaval with which it merged, a military coup that was in an advanced stage. For the fall of Perón was at hand.

The Fall of Perón

The residues of revolution that had survived the failed Menéndez and Suárez revolts smoldered underground until they were revived by the godsend of Perón's break with the Church. Another gift of fortune for Perón's enemies arrived in January 1955, with his announcement that the government had reached general agreement with Standard Oil for the exploitation of Argentine petroleum. Everything now merged into a huge general agitation. The navy, traditionally elitist and traditionally cool, or worse, toward Perón, now took the lead. Admiral Samuel Toranzo Calderón began to organize a movement that reached out to civilian politicians and the army. But the familiar story was to be told yet again. Liaison and general planning were deficient and common sense seems to have abdicated.

But events would not wait. On June 11, there was a great demonstration marking Corpus Christi Day, including the famous incident of the flag that was or was not burned. Activists pulled down the Argentine flag flying above the National Congress and ran up the Vatican flag in its place. The building was stoned, and bronze plaques in memory of Evita were torn out while the crowd cried "Death to Evita!" In the excitement, the government claimed that demonstrators had burned the Argentine flag, and Perón and Borlenghi were photographed inspecting the charred remains. The opposition claimed that the police burned the flag as an incitement. A few others contended that no one had burned a flag. But everyone was quite sure of all the facts.[107]

Whatever the truth, passions outran it. The next day brought an attack on the cathedral in Buenos Aires. On June 13 and 14, Perón heaped abuse and warnings on the clergy, by radio and by strong rhetoric at a large rally. And on the 14th, he took more direct aim at the Church by ordering the discharge and expulsion of two bishops,[108] although his authority for such action was quite debatable. The bishops flew to Rome, and the Vatican was heard from almost immediately, in the form of a decree of excommunication against all persons who had brought about the expulsion of one of the bishops. No names were cited, and that omission was to generate yet another controversy. But that was in the future, and on the 16th, when the decree was issued, the news of it was overwhelmed by the greatest tragedy to occur under the Peronato.

This was Admiral Toranzo Calderón's uprising, too hasty an affair to succeed but too powerful for massive physical damage to be contained, given the reckless master plan. This called for air strikes against the Casa Rosada itself in an attempt to kill Perón, supported by land assaults and by marine contingents, all with supreme disregard for the throngs of civilians who were certain to be in the vicinity. Bad weather upset the timing for the bombing and the land assault, and by the time they occurred Perón had left for the War Ministry. His one active intervention in the details of the defense seems to have resulted from a call by the CGT for workers to proceed to the Plaza de Mayo; Perón immediately gave the word that "not a single worker should go to the Plaza," but by the time his message was received it was too late.[109]

Between the bombs and the attacking marines in the streets, and the crowds of people running about, and the civilian activists dealing out destruction on both sides, death and injury held the day. Bullets and shrapnel and smoke and cries filled the air. But the lack of full preparation told against the naval forces, and by late afternoon the uprising had fallen apart, leaving a thousand casualties, two hundred of them fatal, to be counted in bloody streets and savaged buildings.[110]

With darkness came not peace but the night of the mob and the darting shadow of the looter. Perón's radio appeal at 6:00 P.M. to workers to restrain their anger and commit no offenses—"The struggle should be between soldiers. I don't want even one more member of the public to die"—went unheard or unheeded.[111] A dozen churches were invaded and burned. The headquarters of the archdiocese went up in flame, and with it the archives that went back to colonial times. The interior of the adjacent cathedral was sacked. Sacristy and altar were no match for torch and wrecking bar, and what was sacred was profaned in the fire-lit hour of destruction. The police and the fire fighters for the most part stood aside in their indifference. The evidence concerning Perón's complicity in the violence and in the lassitude of the fire department is, as so often, contradictory. There is indication that although he had tried to avoid the former, he acquiesced in the latter, although on this point the hot passions of the period may have left an imprint. Perón himself denied any personal association with the events.[112] Indeed, in his later taped recollections, he attributed the loss of the churches to fires set from within, by the clergy, in order to advance the Church's campaign against him: "That was an act of provocation toward me."[113] It is difficult to believe that this was advanced as a serious explanation of tragic events, but it throws light upon the unreality that not infrequently attended the extremism of politics under the Peronato, and it throws light as well on Perón's ability to command faith, for his loyalists still assert their belief in this explanation.[114]

Who the thugs and looters were, by whom (if anyone) they were encouraged, and why they were not restrained, are all questions without answers. "The truth was despoiled and incinerated together with the sacred images that burned in that terrible night . . ."[115] But the effects of the day and the night of June 16 upon Argentine consciousness were drastic. The nation had gone to the brink and had looked down into depths that it scarcely knew existed, depths half-remembered from the folklore of Rosas. And the roofless church walls standing bare against the winter sky reminded all that the temples of the common faith, sacred to the gaucho bands of Rosas, had been revered rather than desecrated even in the roughest of old times.

The American embassy caught the mood in a remarkably perceptive and sensitive despatch on July 7:

. . . this sort of thing is entirely foreign to modern Argentine history . . . The bombing of June 16, 1955, burst with cataclysmic force, therefore, upon a population conditioned by a century of peace to the confirmed belief that such things do not happen in Argentina . . . One detects in the people a sense not only of shock, but of shame, that such a slaughter of innocent civilians could have happened in the heart of Buenos Aires. The Argentines are an exceedingly proud and sensitive people, with a high sense of superiority and of civilization. They are men of culture and peace, of a good and plentiful life. They have recoiled with alarm, almost with consternation from this sudden explosion of violence . . . When to this is added the almost simultaneous burning and destruction of the nation's most sacred and ancient religious monuments and churches, the result has been an emotional shock of great disruptive force to the political and social fabric of the nation.[116]

A deeply affected Perón shared in the shock. He had been taken by surprise; an hour before the first bomb dropped on the Casa Rosada, he had told Ambassador Nufer that he expected to win votes from the church dispute.[117] His public utterances after June 16, except for momentary bluster, urged restraint and pacification, truce, "coexistence and life together," and the thought that "only slavery to the law ensures freedom."[118]

But more than words was forthcoming. Cabinet changes followed immediately. Gone now were Angel Borlenghi, who had held the slippery interior ministry since 1946 in a marvelous demonstration of survival, Méndez San Martín, Raúl Apold, Eduardo Vuletich. Gone also was the entire campaign against the Church, for Perón had realized quickly enough his error in overreacting and in underestimating the emotional linkages involved.

In July, the Church issued a pastoral letter calling, in very strong terms, for public order and a wide range of civil rights and liberties. The letter had a profound effect in the aftermath of the tragedies of June,[119] and on July 15, Perón responded with a full-fledged policy of conciliation that changed the political landscape, at least superficially. He admitted that his government had restricted liberties in the past but justified it as necessary for the attainment of the Peronist revolution, whose objectives had now been completed: "There now begins a new era, constitutional in character, without revolutions, because the permanent state of a country cannot be one of revolution. I will cease to be leader of a revolution in order to become president of all Argentines, friends or adversaries . . . I must lift all restrictions imposed in the country with respect to the conduct and procedures of our adversaries . . . pacification is necessary at this time and, in spite of what fools and partisans may say, I will honorably do what I believe is my job: pacify the country.[120]

But the odds against such an effort were considerable. The sheer dynamic of events was against it, for, frightened though it was, the Argentine public was still divided into pro- and anti-Perón elements, both of them seared by June 16 and its aftermath. They remained almost impermeable to reconciliation. And Perón's condition remained somewhat in question, as the American embassy observed: "He is at a point in life where he may lack the recuperative powers, mentally and morally, required to cope with the terrific demands of this crisis and its aftermath."[121]

The mistakes of the American embassy in Buenos Aires from time to time have been commented upon at length. But the embassy was also frequently correct, particularly as the Braden period receded, and now its reporting gave an outstanding example of what can be done with good insight, in the form of a projection that would come to pass almost eerily, both in the short term and in a time frame much longer than anyone could have anticipated. After describing the circumstances prevailing in July, the embassy concluded:

All of the foregoing factors must be weighed in the light of Perón's outstanding political ability. He has for the past decade and more demonstrated a skill and shrewdness in political manipulation much above that of any of his collaborators or opponents . . . He has undoubtedly suffered the greatest shock of his career in the events surrounding June 16, and is weaker than at any time since the abortive military effort to eliminate him in 1945. A less able and agile man would not still be on deck three weeks after a June 16 and even Perón could hardly survive another outbreak of military violence. But having come through to the present moment without any fatal impairment of his position, he may outwit his enemies who were on the point of happily counting him out. By his superior ability and leadership he may achieve another try at perpetuating Peronism.[122]

The pacification movement launched by Perón had a short life, and an unhappy one. It foundered on a basic difference in perception between the opposition and the government. The heart of the problem was the State of Internal Warfare and the various decrees and regulations and practices that flowed from it. The opposition, whose most articulate voice was now that of Arturo Frondizi, viewed this as a fundamental cause of the political strife and therefore insisted that there could be no pacification until these impediments were repealed and until there was a return to constitutional freedoms. The government held to the view that the controversial measures were not the cause of the political conflict but the result of it, and that they could not be repealed until pacification made such action possible.[123]

Both sides really wished to prevail more than they wanted to conciliate; no one would bend very far; and active partisan struggle resumed, except in the area of Church-State relations; Perón and the hierarchy both stepped back from that very deep abyss. But in every other area, the bitterness and incitements that had dominated 1955 refused to fade.

It was against this background that Perón came forth on August 31 with the "resignation" and the famous "five for one" speech that led to a firming of revolutionary resolve in the navy, a determination that had survived the disaster of June 16. The purpose of the "resignation," an elaborate manipulation by Perón, was to regain the initiative, to display public support on a scale that would overawe the opposition, and perhaps to recapture the magic of the original October 17. To that end, he directed a note to the leaders of the Peronist Party, citing its achievements, noting the demands of the opposition for a change, offering to resign in the interest of internal peace, and requesting their permission to do so. This communication, read to the public on the morning of the 31st, had gone to the CGT the night before, where the decision was taken to call a national strike for the 31st, summoning the *descamisados* to the Plaza de Mayo, there to stay until Perón withdrew the resignation offer.[124]

It went off with great precision. The official announcement of Perón's dramatic gesture was made at 9:00 A.M. It was followed by the CGT's call for the work stoppage, and immediately the capital went dead. By 10:00 A.M., no office or store or restaurant remained functioning, and the workers had begun to filter into the Plaza, their numbers increasing hour by hour in the cold and wind. Every preparation had been made for an all-day affair, from the transportation to the food trucks that were sent periodically by the Eva Perón Foundation. By half past six in the afternoon the great plaza was full and overflowing, and Perón rose to speak.

It was a short speech and a fateful one, delivered in fading winter light under skies whose chill was upon the words that were heard: ". . . to violence we will reply with a greater violence. With our excessive tolerance we have won the right to suppress them violently. And from now on we establish as a permanent rule of conduct for our movement: any person who in any place tries to disturb the public order in opposition to the constituted authorities, or contrary to the law or the constitution, may be killed by any Argentine . . . The watchword for all Peronists, whether as individuals or within an organization, is to reply to a violent action with one more violent. And when one of ours falls, five of theirs will fall."[125]

These wild utterances were received with bewilderment by some and with repugnance by many others. They raise, in retrospect, as they did among some intimates at the time, the issue of Perón's mental stability and judgment at so critical a moment. They also raise a question as to what he really intended to say, since he spoke extemporaneously. It would not have been the first time that a more moderate intention had succumbed to passion in the intoxication of playing upon the emotions of massed thousands.[126]

Whatever the combination of reasons, these ill-omened incitements aroused wide consternation, and they insured that the revolutionary plotting that some naval officers had never abandoned would go forward with new zeal. The fall of Perón, in retrospect, probably inevitable sooner or later, would occur sooner. This was hard to see at the time, and the embassy stubbed its toe on the hard stone of prophecy. On September 2, eighteen days before Perón fled, Ambassador Nufer gave his preliminary estimate that the events of August 31 ". . . probably marked the decisive stage in the reconsolidation of Perón's strength. A period of comparative quiet seems likely to follow . . ."[127] Instead, what followed was the rapid consolidation of another rebellion, this time more competent.

Again, the navy was the principal actor in the early stages, with Admiral Isaac Rojas assuming the leading role. The only question was the army, for some of the navy leaders believed that at least a partial participation by the former was necessary. This was difficult because there was less resentment among army officers, and army surveillance made plotting a very dangerous avocation.[128]

A retired general, Eduardo Lonardi, emerged as the head of the overall effort. Lonardi was a man of competence and serious purpose, and his prudence had been demonstrated by his withdrawal from the Menéndez revolt in 1952. It had been Lonardi who had succeeded Perón as military attaché in Chile in 1938, just in time to fall into the trap set by Chilean counterintelligence.

General Lonardi proposed to lead the revolution from the Artillery School in Córdoba, where he knew from his family and other contacts that the general mood was anti-Peronist, as befitted the city's tradition as the center of unyielding conservative Catholic sentiment. He planned his movement for midnight of September 15–16, and received assurances that the navy would rise on the same day. Other supporters in the army pledged their efforts with army installations in the Littoral and in the western provinces. On the 16th, most of these plans began to materialize. General Lonardi was successful, after some fighting, in taking over all elements at Córdoba. Naval units defeated army contingents around Puerto Belgrano and the navy established a blockade of the coast on the 18th and threatened to play the key card: the bombardment of Dock Sud at Buenos Aires, where oil storage facilities were centered, and the YPF refinery at Eva Perón, formerly La Plata. As evidence that this was not mere bluff, a cruiser blew up the oil storage tanks at Mar del Plata on the morning of the 19th. It was a persuasive gesture, and ten minutes before the bombardment of the installations at Eva Perón was to begin at 1:00 P.M.

(following an order to civilians to evacuate the area), General Franklin Lucero went on the air to ask for negotiations and a cease-fire. And he read a letter from Perón that referred to the transfer of his authority to the army in support of a settlement.[129]

The letter represented the last throw of the dice by the master tactician, and it was yet another apple of discord, for it might have been a resignation and, again, it might not have been. The literal meaning of the word Perón employed was "renunciation." A military junta was formed to negotiate with the revolutionary forces and had to grapple with the ambiguous language in order to decide upon its own mandate and purpose. It finally decided that the letter would be considered as Perón's resignation. The junta then proceeded to work out the negotiating stance it would adopt with the leaders of the revolt, but at midnight Perón attempted to summon the junta to his office, a step he could not have taken unless he regarded his letter as less than a resignation. Six generals from the junta went to hear him out in the early hours of September 20, confirming that he now denied his resignation. The word came back from the full junta a bit later that it had unanimously confirmed its previous decision. It considered his letter a resignation. And it would act on its own responsibility as a fully independent body.[130]

A few hours later, at seven in the morning of the 20th, Perón packed a few belongings into a small bag: two shirts, several pairs of socks, toilet articles, a picture of Evita, a small miniature of the Virgin of Luján, and some money.[131] Outside, it was as if this were the day of no dawn, for a dense rain, opaque as a cloth curtain, was falling under the darkest of skies. "The clouds reached to the lower parts of the houses, the way they linger at the foot of the trees in a forest. In that atmosphere blurred with rain and cloud, everything seemed unreal."

The car and the chauffeur and three aides were waiting. Perón got in.

"To the Paraguayan embassy."[132]

IV

EXILE AND RETURN
1955-1974

Of the two of us, Evita is the happier. Though she is
dead and without peace, she is at least in her own
land. I am far away and must live only on hopes,
anxieties and memories.

—Juan Perón, *Del poder al exilio*

10. The Caribbean Exile
1955-1960

Reflections on the Fall

THE FALL OF the Peronato had come with perplexing suddenness, bewildering to all those who had viewed its many battle-
ments and moats and outposts and had judged them impregnable.
But the spectacular speed with which events unfolded in September
1955 should not divert attention from the interesting psychological
and historical factors that were involved, and from the two principal
questions thus raised. Why did Perón act, or fail to act, as he did in
the moment of crisis? And why was there no public outcry, no rallying
of the *descamisados,* when he was mortally threatened?

The first question has puzzled many of Perón's closest friends and
admirers.[1] After all, the balance of forces did not appear to favor the
revolutionary cause. Loyal army units were beginning to converge on
the center of rebellion in Córdoba and on the naval base at Puerto
Belgrano. As Perón himself often pointed out, he could have elected
to stay on and fight, with good prospects of success on both the military and the civilian fronts.[2] But he chose to delegate considerable
authority to General Lucero and to maneuver, instead of leading a
countercharge.

In fact, his conduct on this occasion was not essentially dissimilar
to his technique on the two other decisive moments in his career. In

June 1943, he had done as much as any other person to establish the conditions for the coup that opened the way for the Peronato, and then at the final moment, on the night of June 3, chose to absent himself. In October 1945, he had prepared the ground with marvelous skill for the triumph of his cause, but on the 17th he remained almost on the sidelines, passive in his hospital room, while colleagues and events spoke for him, emerging only to make the address that certified the night as the holy hour of Peronism. In the days that had preceded, in confinement on Martín García, he had written not of crusades but of uncertainty.

The fact, of course, is that despite the occasional oratory of fire and blood and five-for-one, Perón was not temperamentally a man of force,[3] not a revolutionary in any sense, not a gambler who had steeled himself for a desperate draw against the odds. "Blood saves time," he would say, "but it costs a lot."[4] He was a military man, but not a military adventurer, and as much as he admired Napoleon ("Without doubt the greatest and most extraordinary human being . . . in many centuries"),[5] he would not have led the Old Guard into battle at Waterloo. The oratory represented the emotional side of a man who was both emotional and disciplined, as did the campaign against the Church; the discipline simply arrived too late in those instances. Perón was, in his own words, "an herbivorous lion," a pragmatic man of political maneuver to whom the maintenance of options came as second nature. This quality, applied to the events of September, has been interpreted by some as cowardice on Perón's part, but there is no real warrant for this. On the contrary, he faced his difficulties during the succeeding eighteen years with quiet courage, as he had the tragedies in his domestic life. He was not Hotspur and, however much he might have regretted it, he was not Alexander the Great. But that was more a matter of temperament than of courage.[6]

Among Perón's motivations in the confusions of mid-September there is no reason to exclude the consideration that he himself citied in his account written some years later. "In case of bombardment, given the absolute lack of active defense, there would have been veritable ruin among the populace. The spectre of the dead on June 16 was visible to the eyes of all and was a reminder not to insist on operations that would have brought inestimable damage. In my heart I feared the destruction of the Eva Perón refinery for the construction of which we had had to face immense sacrifices. The advice that came to me from all sides was to open the gates of the arsenals and arm the *descamisados*. I could have done it, but that would have meant the beginning of a slaughter. I always had the conviction that my mission was to protect the interests of the nation . . ."[7]

He summed it up in an anecdote from the last hours before the fall. At a meeting of generals, all of whom favored a fight to the finish, one of them said to Perón,

"If I were the President I wouldn't surrender. I would insist on fighting."

To which Perón replied immediately, "I would do it too if I were only a general."[8]

If Perón's temperament and values turned him toward moderation in the September crisis, so did the real balance of external forces, favorable though they may have appeared. However firmly the army had been molded into the Peronist configuration during recent years, there was obviously dissension within it now, dissension that had much to do with the broadly felt private and familial concern over the conflict with the Church. The quick sense of independence shown by the army junta in the last days is itself a sign of the latent readiness of some to break with Perón, whose intuition certainly did not desert him overnight. The navy was clearly gone for good, embarked on a mission of desperation from which there could be neither retreat nor compromise, and it possessed the terrible weapon of offshore bombardment, capable of reducing the entire economy to wreckage within hours. Even if the purely military aspects of the revolt could in some miraculous manner be contained without fatal damage, rebellion had corroded so deeply that the longer prospect was bleak and sullen at best.

Finally, Perón's rapport with the public mood, his sensitivity to currents of opinion, must have alerted him to the great differences that separated the present circumstances from those of October 17, 1945. Those differences provide the answer to the second question, why was there no public uprising, indeed no public cry, when Perón fell?

Ten years had passed since the magic night. The power of the regime, impressive enough to the eye, had faded in its core. Some inner essence had gone out of it, perhaps because it was no longer sustained by the spontaneity and the freshness of hope that had brought it to life. The CGT was in a somber mood, having just buried its dead from June 16, and after ten years of comforting prosperity and repeated calls to the Plaza de Mayo, its members were not quite so anxious to heed the old pledge, "Our lives for Perón!" The errors and controversies of the last year had not detached the *descamisados* from

Perón, but they had undoubtedly diminished somewhat the old fervor of the workers and had assisted in the revival of an attitude that was traditionally never far below the surface of Argentine public life, the attitude that whispered, "Let's not get involved." Nor was anyone available to inspire the ranks of the CGT, to do for them what they could or would no longer do for themselves, for the leadership around Perón had faded as well, and men of the stamp of Mercante had long since given way to mediocrities and hacks whose loyalty was as much to employment and influence as to Peronism. Instead, the sole advice of the CGT leadership to the members, given on September 19 by radio, reflected the uncertainty and confusion prevailing in the highest circles—it urged everyone to remain calm. As one of Perón's closest associates put it, ". . . the Argentine people reacted at this moment like an adolescent who had been spoiled by its parents, and suddenly the father died."[9]

But also, one suspects, on an even deeper level one of the qualities of the Argentine civilization was at work. During the last forty years, the tendency to the extreme, which had always characterized individual opinion and action, had become affixed to mass politics in Argentina. This had begun with Yrigoyen, for the simple reason that before his time public life had been the province of the select few who had managed affairs one way or another. But in the election of 1916, with the admission of the middle classes to the electoral process, the violent flux and reflux of public opinion became a feature of life. Yrigoyen was elected, and reelected in 1924, with mass adoration. Six years later, the faintest blast of General Uriburu's trumpet leveled the walls around Yrigoyen and he departed amidst odium, or indifference at best. Similar adoration attended Perón in 1946, and indifference was his lot in 1955 on the part of those who did not go so far as to hate him. It would happen again and again. In 1958, Arturo Frondizi would be elected with acclaim and devotion, and he would fall in 1962, bereft of defenders. Dr. Arturo Illia would be elected in 1963 with rejoicing and in 1966 he would be deposed, abandoned by everyone in sight. Over the years, the pattern thus became embedded in the ethos because it was congenial to both the social and the individual psychologies that prevailed. This seems to be related to an unsettling national tendency to hedge, quickly, against political failure, doubtless because so much is at stake in a country dominated by government, and the last man to leave the sinking leader has much to lose.[10]

With Yrigoyen, the tide that had flowed and ebbed had flowed again, at the time of his death. With Perón, too, the departing tide would turn once more, for he was not wholly abandoned and events mostly beyond his control came to his rescue and restarted the cycle of the tides. But that day was eighteen years below the horizon and quite inconceivable to almost everyone but Perón as he began his exile.

A Time of Wandering

From the embassy Perón was driven through empty streets still darkened in the strange gloom to a Paraguayan gunboat then docked in the harbor. He was received aboard the ship with full military honors, for a generous act of his from 1954 now returned its bread to him in true Biblical fashion. With his sure sense of Latin dignity and style, he had delivered to Paraguay some war trophies captured by Argentine forces in the long war of 1865–70 and held ever since. The response of President Alfredo Stroessner of Paraguay had been to confer upon Perón honorary citizenship and the honorary rank of general in the Paraguayan army. The warmth of his reception aboard the gunboat and in Asunción was now one of Perón's very few consolations.

He marked time now for almost two weeks while details of his safe-conduct and his transportation to Asunción were worked out. He also wrote two letters to Nelly Rivas, who had been summarily lifted up, carried out of the presidential residence, and driven home by two members of the custodial staff. Both letters were intercepted en route to Nelly and subsequently published. In one of them Perón addressed her as "Dear little girl," and concluded with "A big kiss from your daddy," He urged her to be calm and assured her that she could live for a long time on what he had given her. He spoke of her going to Asunción with his two pet poodles. "You are all I have, and the only beloved thing left for me," he wrote. "You can imagine I think of you all day long." And then he continued with a very interesting juxtaposition: "Take care of the poodles for me, and when you come to Asunción, bring both of them to me. I love those rascals a lot."[11]

It was a difficult time for Nelly. The bewildered adolescent was now committed to a reformatory for eight months while her parents went into exile in Montevideo, where they soon lost the thousands that Perón had given them. They eventually returned, destitute, and Nelly's mother took in laundry to support her ailing husband. The three of them, with the poodles in tow, made an attempt later to reach Perón in exile, through Asunción, but they were turned back at the border. In 1958, Nelly married a former Argentine employee of the American embassy and turned to a quiet life in a provincial town, now a bit disillusioned: "His attitude was stupid, and I don't understand it

Perón at his desk in the Casa Rosada, outlining his economic message in a radio address, March 1952. Credit: AP/Wide World Photos.

Perón and his third wife, Isabel Martínez de Perón ("Isabelita"), in Madrid, March 1962. Credit: AP/Wide World Photos.

Left to right: Isabel Perón; Vicente Solano Lima, subsequently Perón's vice-president; Perón; Delia Parodi, head of the Peronist Coordinating and Supervision Council and Peronist Women's leader; and Augusto Vandor, prominent labor leader, August 1964. Credit: AP/Wide World Photos.

Perón, with one of his poodles, Madrid, 1965. Credit: AP/Wide World Photos.

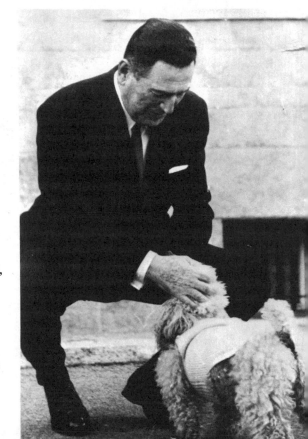

Perón in Madrid, 1965. Credit: AP/Wide World Photos.

Perón and Isabel, Madrid, 1965. Credit: AP/Wide World Photos.

Isabel Perón being greeted at the Madrid airport by Perón (left) and Jorge Antonio (right), 1966. Credit: AP/Wide World Photos.

Perón greeting Ricardo Balbín, leader of the Radical Party, Buenos Aires, July 1973. Credit: AP/Wide World Photos.

Perón being interviewed during a convalescence from an illness, Buenos Aires, November 1973. At the right, José López Rega. Credit: AP/Wide World Photos.

Rare photograph of Isabel kneeling by Perón's casket at a high mass in the metropolitan cathedral, July 1974. Credit: AP/Wide World Photos.

yet. He should have informed me about our situation, so I would know how we were. It was his obligation."[12]

Early in October, a lumbering seaplane flew in from Paraguay and landed on very choppy seas, near the gunboat. Perón was transferred from the one to the other, once almost plunging into the water, and the plane took off as best it could, dragged down by the pitching waves. It must have been an ordeal for Perón, who intensely disliked air travel, for the plane barely made it into the air. At the border, the seaplane was met by a Paraguayan plane whose copilot was President Stroessner himself, to escort Perón to the airport in Asunción as a courtesy.

Perón spent a month in the little-known, landlocked nation whose relations with Argentina had not infrequently been fearful and wary. He liked both the country and President Stroessner. The people welcomed him with flowers and music, delighting him into high praise: ". . . they seemed more Peronist than the ones in Argentina."[13] But he was in almost immediate trouble through his violation of the usual strict rules restraining political activity by exiles, even as he denied any such thing. He gave an interview, in his folksy vein, to the United Press the day after his arrival. "They say that one day the Devil was walking on the street, and there came a tremendous downpour. He couldn't find anything open to shelter him, and he took refuge in a church that had its doors open. They say that while the Devil was in the church he behaved himself well. I am going to do like the Devil, and while I'm in Paraguay I'll honor its noble hospitality. If some day it occurs to me to turn to politics, I'll go to my own country and become active there."[14] A few minutes later he was all politics, roundly abusing the Argentine government as false and illegal, a creature of parasites.

He also referred to the rumors of his wealth, rumors destined never to abate. He had taken a bit of cash when he left, and his aide managed to lay his hands on another sum, which he delivered to Perón on the gunboat, amounting to $50,000 after conversion into U.S currency. Aside from this, Perón had, as he insisted, the house in Buenos Aires that had belonged to Evita, the small country place in San Vicente, the royalties from Evita's *La Razón de mi Vida*, a legacy that Alberto Dodero left to Evita, and numerous gifts from his friends and from the public. That was it. "If anyone finds anything that I didn't mention, he can keep it."[15] There is nothing in Perón's conduct, then or thereafter, to indicate that this account was an exaggeration or a cover-up, or that he was anything more than what he claimed to be, that is, considering the requirements of exile, a relatively poor man.

Perón realized that Argentine pressures would increase and that it was time to move on.[16] He left Asunción on November 2, for Panama. The next day there was a disappointment. A brief visit to Para-maribo, in Surinam, was scheduled, and Perón knew that Prince Bernhard of the Neitherlands was then visiting there. He sent a tele-graphic greeting to Bernhard before his arrival, saying he would like to see him. Perón had treated him well in Argentina when Bernhard had visited there in support of Dutch business interests, giving him a horse and other gifts. But now the telegram was not answered. Perón was highly indignant. He liked everyone he met during his short stop-over (describing them as Peronists) except the Dutch, whom he had never liked from the first; he termed them hybrids. But Bernhard was the worst: "Who is Prince Bernhard? As we say, a shit!"[17]

When Perón reached Panama on November 6, President Arnulfo Arias unofficially asked him to call upon him. Perón had already begun to speak of permanent exile there, and the conversation of the two men must have been favorable to this new plan, for on the 8th Perón signed in at the old Washington Hotel in Colón, on the other side of the Isthmus. This was a gracious, antique, and relatively economical edifice, surrounded by seaside palms, and lightly inhabited. The United States government owned it but was not the operator. Here Perón stayed for a "literary hibernation" while he worked on a new book, an apologia that appeared before long under the title *La Fuerza es el dere-cho de las bestias,* Force is the Law of the Beasts, the title coming from Cicero.

But the question of residence remained troublesome. The United States government was concerned that its ownership of the hotel would be construed as support of Perón and his cause and would complicate relationships with Argentina. Pressures were therefore brought to induce a move on his part, and Perón eventually rented a small house in Colón.[18] He also acquired a small Opel automobile; his Argentine chauffer, Isaac Gilaberte, had come to share the exile as aide and driver. Otherwise, Perón continued to live in the simplest possible manner, a familiar figure walking in the evening in his *guayabera* along the waterfront of Manzanillo Bay, mingling with the town folk, attending boxing matches at the Colón arena.

Speculation began to grow as to Perón's continuing connection with Argentine events. His secretary-courier was apprehended trying to cross the Paraguayan border into Argentina. And his natural caustic hostility to the successor government in Buenos Aires, installed by the military officers who had overthrown him the year before, had appeared in some interview statements published in *Bohemia* in Havana soon after his arrival in Panama. These utterances were an eloquent demonstration, if any were needed, of his undiminished powers of colorful invective: "I already said before that the military dictatorship will vanish like the fish that begin to decompose at the head. These people that have such bad heads are beginning to smell of rot . . . None of them has two fingers of forehead . . . I repeat that a bad person is preferable to a dummy. The bad one at least has a possibility of regeneration, but the dummy is irredeemable."[19]

The impressions that Perón made upon others during his stay in Panama varied considerably. Some found him in good health and spirits, and others had a different impression. One visitor, a Latin American academic and journalistic of wide experience and sensitive intuition, interviewed him after his return to Colón in May: 'He received me in his pyjamas. I found him rather a pathetic figure, almost a Graham Greeneish caricature of a South American politician who has lost power." The impression he made was one of ". . . dejection and rather seedy decline—being down at heel with a vengeance . . . He felt let down, there was no doubt about this in my mind, but the explanation of his downfall was, not surprisingly, distorted by intense bitterness . . . he had great hopes for the political actions of the CGT and appeared to be confident that he would return to Argentina before too long. He attributed his downfall almost solely to international conspiracies to which treacherous elements in the armed forces had lent themselves, and believed that the sorry state of the Argentine economy was almost exclusively the result of American and British machinations." The reference in this interview to a foreign element in his overthrow provides an interesting evidence of the unevenness and almost erratic variability of Perón's views during this period; in the *Bohemia* interview several months before, he had emphasized very explicitly that the United States as such had played no part in his fall.

The interviewer continued with a comment on basic personality. "Although when I saw him he was a pretty dilapidated version of his old self, one could still understand how he could have charmed audiences from a position of power . . . Now that I think about it, Allende [the president of Chile who was deposed in 1973] had a bit of this charm, but while in the case of the Chilean it was a wiry, staccato frankness that won the day, in the case of Perón it was a soft surrendering, cajoling tactic that appeared to produce results. He smiled too much, and perhaps because of the proximity of his downfall was too prone to exaggerated gestures and mannerisms which detracted from whatever it was that he was saying: he lacked *gravitas.*"[20]

There was much about Panama that Perón did not like, beginning with the insufferable heat. As he saw it, the country had ". . . three mother-industries: gambling, prostitution, and contraband."[21] His relations with the Panamanian politicians brought bickerings and complaints. And he suffered a disadvantage in the form of crazy rumors that had preceded him, identifying him as the possessor, literally or through access, of huge sums of money—$700 million was a typical estimate—and thus in a position to assure the destiny of whomever got to him first.[22] It was difficult to persuade those who importuned that he was scraping along with a dwindling small reserve, bits and drabs from occasional articles, and the gifts of well-wishers. It was time to be on the move.

But Panama made a memorable contribution to the history of Perón and of Argentina, in the form of his encounter there with the woman who would become his third wife. María Estela Martínez, usually known as Isabel or Isabelita, was a young Argentine woman of comfortable middle class parentage in little-developed La Rioja in the northwest, between Córdoba and the Chilean border. Her father, a bank official, died during her childhood and the loss left its imprint. Her mother was preoccupied with a possible remarriage and the young girl went, by her own choice, to the home of friends who took her in as their own and did well by her. She aspired to a career and studied music and dance. Her forte was folk dancing, and she eventually joined a touring group sponsored by the Eva Perón Foundation. The group toured Latin America and the September events in Argentina found them in Guatemala, from where they drifted down to Panama. Just before Christmas 1955, the group attended a small party for Perón in the Washington Hotel at his invitation, and Isabel met him. She was twenty-four years old, slim, with light brown, wavy hair and eyes wide-set in a beautifully rounded face.

Someone in the group asked Perón for a letter of introduction to a friend in Argentina, and Perón sat down to type it then and there. Isabel said to him,

"You don't have a secretary, General?"

"No, girl, I don't have a secretary because I can't pay for one. I can barely pay my hotel bill."

"Why don't you make me your secretary?"

"Fine, but I can't pay you any salary, or anything like that."[23]

This was not much assurance, but it sufficed. She moved in and began to fill the empty spaces, as Nelly Rivas had done. She sang and danced a bit, cooked, took charge of the modest domestic administration that was called for, and provided a female presence. In Argentina in the best of times, with a thousand contacts and activities available to him, Perón had feared solitude. Now, in the least fortunate of times with solitude a real possibility, his need for constant companionship had become imperative. Isabel would provide this for the rest of his life, now as his companion and later as his wife, an attractive woman of routine skills and modest social and intellectual attainments, untouched by fire or by Perón's favorite Oil of Samuel. Observing her as she poured maté and prepared Argentine delicacies for Perón and walked with him in twilight by the sea, any political prognosticator would have offered odds in the millions against her becoming the first female president of a nation in the Western Hemisphere.

The Venezuelan government was, on balance, responsive to Perón's desire for a change of locale. The president, Marcos Pérez Jiménez, was an army strongman. Short, corpulent, moon-faced, with heavy and dark tortoiseshell glasses, "PJ" had somewhat the appearance of an owl. He was basically sympathetic to Perón, but he would not overdo it.[24]

Perón and Isabel arrived in Caracas on August 8, and were met by an Argentine residing there who would serve as an aide. He typified a problem that Perón could never solve adequately or permanently during his exile, that is, the selection of close aides and emissaries to the Peronista faithful who could combine competence and loyalty. It was not an easy assignment and there were few takers. Such a man as Jorge Antonio, soon to appear at Perón's side, who had brains, money, fervent loyalty and the willingness to disrupt his own life, was obviously almost one of a kind. For the rest, young men of an adventuresome tendency might appear, but they would be, almost by necessity, either long-shot gamblers with the restlessness of that breed, or misfits looking for an anchor, or ideologues willing to suffer for the faith, but unwilling to compromise and follow Perón's twisting course.

It was the latter orientation that marked the most notable of these early colleagues of the exile years, John William Cooke. He was only thirty-six when he began corresponding with Perón in May 1956, but his career in politics was a decade old. He had served as a Peronist deputy in the first Congress under the Peronato. He became Perón's principal deputy in Argentina while he was still in prison in Patagonia, following Perón's fall, and he was with Jorge Antonio, Héctor Cámpora, and others in a spectacular escape to Chile in 1957. In the late 1950s, a flood of correspondence flowed between Perón and Cooke, subsequently published in two volumes, and in these letters Perón at times encouraged Cooke to believe that he was Perón's successor, by the laying on of hands. "It's undeniable that I am a bit old, and that makes me think that you should be preparing yourself to take over the direction. Men like you, who have been molded by all the ordeals, are the ones the Movement needs in this new stage . . ."[25] He later confirmed in a written direction to his followers that Cooke would succeed him, if and when. A man who would take this literally was too naive to serve as Perón's delegate, let alone his successor, but Cooke seems to have cherished his illusions. His true vocation was that of the ideologue, and he drifted steadily to the left, aided and prodded by a woman friend, later his wife, whose insurrectionary preferences were fierce and rigid.[26] He tried to bring off a revolutionary strike in 1959, failed, and was relieved of his delegate's position by Perón. He died in Cuba in 1968, still preaching a revolutionary Peronism based on labor. By then he was isolated on the far extreme, a lonely precursor of the violent Peronist left.[27]

Perón was never really at ease in Caracas. He resented the distant pose of Pérez Jiménez, he considered the regime deficient in the human sense, he disliked the climate and the sanitation, and he deplored the economy: "They live well in the center of Caracas, but if you go out ten kilometers the kids are naked."[28] And perhaps worst of all, he was becoming the embodiment of discord. The Argentine government believed firmly that Perón was directing from a distance a campaign of sabotage and insurrection within Argentina and it responded in two ways. The first and more direct was to attempt the liquidation of Perón. In the spring, an attempt was made, through a Yugoslav gunman, but the hireling thought better of it at the last minute, gave up the project, and went to see Perón, who took a liking to him: "A good man . . . and, considering his profession, a gentleman."[29] On May 25, a time bomb blew up Perón's Opel. By this time Perón had taken to carrying a revolver in the waistband of his trousers and an Argentine aide was carrying a folding automatic pistol in a little briefcase. An interviewing journalist to whom the guns were displayed sensed fear in both men. He also found Perón's apartment to be small and unattractive, with a hall, living–dining room, kitchen, bedroom, and two bathrooms, all poorly furnished and not too clean. The sole adornment in the living room was a small painting on glass of Evita. The interviewer went to look at it, and when Perón asked if he knew whose portrait it was, he said, "Yes."

Perón put the fingers of his right hand to his mouth, kissed them in a gesture to the portrait, and exclaimed,

"What a woman!"

The impression given by Perón on this occasion was unfavorable. He appeared to the journalist (contrary to the latter's expectation) to be glib and superficial, and soft, evasive, yielding rather than strong and virile. There was nothing particularly virile about his income, either, as he described it: the local equivalent of $900 a month, of which almost a quarter went for rent.[30]

The second kind of response by the Argentine government was intense diplomatic pressure against Venezuela, backed by secondary and quieter pressure on the United States to nudge Venezuela to expel Perón. By midsummer the dispute was intense. The Argentines accused Venezuela of permitting Perón to plot against Argentina, contrary to the rules of exile; Venezuela accused Argentina of fomenting assassination plots from its embassy in Caracas; and the United States was in the middle, with the Argentines now thinking that Big Oil, Venezuela, and the United States were synonymous, and that somehow it all tied in with Perón's unpopular attempt to sign the petroleum contract with Standard Oil of California in 1955. If the United States tilted toward Venezuela and applied no pressure, it jeopardized relations with Argentina and would appear to support Perón and Big Oil; if the United States tilted toward Argentina and applied pressure to move Perón on his way, it would have to change its whole policy on political exile and would no longer have any reason to continue giving shelter in Puerto Rico to the exiled leader of the Venezuelan democratic forces, Romulo Betancourt, who was very popular in the United States. In the midst of the hubbub, in midsummer, Argentina and Venezuela severed diplomatic relations.[31]

All three countries remained at an impasse. What was really needed was some external act that would knock over the checkerboard so that the game could start afresh. As luck would have it, such an event now occurred: Pérez Jiménez and his government fell. The army rose, and on January 23, 1958, while gunfire reverberated over Caracas, he fled to the Dominican Republic. Four days later, Perón, too, arrived in Ciudad Trujillo, then the name of the ancient city of Santo Domingo. Isabel followed, accompanied by John William Cooke and Americo Barrios, an Argentine journalist, who was the most recent in the continuing line of private secretaries, and the poodles came soon after, escorted by a friend.

Perón and Isabel lived briefly in the Jaragua Hotel across George Washington Boulevard from the Caribbean shore. The Jaragua was then the second-ranked hotel on the luxury list, a place for tourists, and Perón found it unsuitable and too costly. He moved very soon to the Hotel Paz, a simple establishment downtown that sufficed for a year. He also lived for a time in the Hotel Montaña, at Jarabacoa, high in the interior mountains, and he had access later to the beach home of Ramfis Trujillo, the dictator's son, at Boca Chica.[32] Perón, however, was not a beach type. He could praise the seaside scenery, but in the

vacationer's dilemma of the mountains or the shore he firmly preferred the mountains.

Perón liked the Dominican Republic and felt quite at ease. The
rigid police state maintained by Rafael Trujillo, who had run the
country like a private estate for almost three decades and who owned
a surprising amount of it, took care of security concerns. Perón was
relatively inactive politically during his two years in the Dominican
Republic, although he continued to plan, and messengers and representatives went back and forth quietly to Argentina. He and Isabel
lived very unobtrusively, rarely visiting the homes of Dominicans. They
would be seen in town frequently, merging into the scene, having
dinner at Vesuvio's, the open-air restaurant on the boulevard alongside the Caribbean breakers, he the amiable big man with the easy
smile and she the rather delicate beauty with the fair complexion and
the wide-set eyes. Dominicans noted, mostly with surprise, the economy of his ways and his bourgeois faithfulness to Isabel, for the local
tradition ran to politicians who were free spenders and even more
free womanizers. His only indulgence seemed to be an adolescent
devotion to his motorbike, which he used constantly with obvious glee.
Those who knew him personally were stuck by his thoughtfulness and
his human empathy, and by his simple naturalness: he was "sen-
cillo."[33]

The essential ingredient in Perón's well-being in the Dominican
Republic was his relationship with Trujillo, the factor that was almost
the sole reality for everyone and everything in the nation. That austere, remote, and distrustful man was not easy to know or to enjoy,
but Perón appears to have done both. Superficially, one would expect
little compatibility between the leader who had been elected by labor
and the dictator who had suppressed it; between the plain general for
whom the formal clothing of protocol was a torture and who received
interviewers in slacks and casual sweaters, and the perfumed and gor-
geously attired general who wore his decorations; between the athlete
and sportsman and the man whose physical exertion was limited to
an occasional canter on horseback; between the man who happily limited himself to one woman and a domestic setting, and the man who
compulsively bedded every attractive female in sight; between the
strongman who sometimes threatened violence but did not spill blood
and the strongman who rarely mentioned violence but perpetrated it
daily; between the reader, writer, and incessant communicator and
the man of no books and few words; between the exile who could
barely scrape up the rent and the possessor of hundreds of millions.
What they did have in common was mostly their ages (Trujillo was

the older by four years), their general international orientation, their views of themselves as creators of new national societies, and a hatred of Spruille Braden.

In any case, they got along well. They met on many occasions, occasionally had meals together, and talked for hours, if Perón did not exaggerate.[34] He thought Trujillo would be a good leader to put in charge of a unified Inter-American body if one were to be formed.[35] Trujillo contributed $25,000 to help Perón's finances, so a measure of gratitude would be a natural response. But so unmixed was Perón's praise for his host, and so surprising was the account of the Dominican Republic that appeared in his dictated memoirs some years later, that one must wonder what psychological factors were at work. The tapes were made late in Perón's exile, when Trujillo and his son, Ramfis, were both dead. No apparent motivation is discernible for the gross distortions and mistakes that make the account useless as a description of Trujillo and his country but significant as a revelation of Perón's own psychology.

One reads in these extraordinary paragraphs all manner of perverse nonsense that is directly contrary to undisputed facts.[36] Perón's approval extended even to Ramfis, a troubled and undisciplined young man who devoted his life to frivolity, polo, orgies and debauch, and the avoidance of work. It would have been hard to find his equal among the dissipated sons of the Argentine oligarchy, and if any had existed, Perón would certainly have kicked him from Misiones to the tip of Patagonia. But because Ramfis was the son of his friend, it was different.[37] Perón had no selfish motive for fudging history as he did. He could have balanced his account, or, if that were too painful, he could have remained discreetly silent. Why would he indulge in such aberrations?

The only possible explanation seems to be an emotional blockage of some kind, governing his perception, blinding his vision. It is a powerful demonstration of his very emotional nature. In any political context he could summon the discipline necessary to control this emotionality in the interest of tactics and larger ends. But now, dictating in Madrid long after, the restraints fell away and the emotions remained. They remained, moreover, faithful to the civilization: they remained extreme. Loyalty was a prized value, loyalty to a friend, to the enemy of your own enemies. But what is loyalty if it is not extreme? In the tradition, loyalty is akin to political power in that if it is shared or diluted it is no longer itself. It thus becomes one of the doorways through which unreality and mythology enter the civilization.

Perón's released emotions also stand forth in his references to North

Americans in his taped memoirs. Tactics no longer required conceal-
ment of his dislike. He left the Hotel Jaragua, he noted, because he
did not have the money and because it was full of Americans, and he
was allergic to them. He reported that Trujillo burst into guffaws when
Perón said to him that he could not stand the gringos at the Jaragua
and wanted to be with Dominicans instead. And he quoted approvingly, as his own sentiment, a hardly complimentary remark of the
Spanish poet, Augustín de Foxa. Perón had said to the poet, "I realize
that you don't like the Americans, but I suppose you like their dollars." And de Foxa had replied, "Yes, true enough, but I also like
ham, and that's no reason for me to go and bring the pigs into my
house to live."[38]

Dominican cordiality notwithstanding, the problem that had pursued Perón since his fall rose again, the issue of his plotting against
the Liberating Revolution. He was, of course, doing what he could in
that direction, within the limits of the discretion imposed on all Latin
American exiles; it was much less than he would have desired, but
much more than the Argentine government was prepared to accept,
since, doubtless, not even his complete silence and inactivity would
have allayed the suspicions and paranoia rampant in Buenos Aires.
As early as March 1958, the Argentine government was protesting to
Trujillo. Diplomatic relations were severed for several months and by
late summer of 1959, Argentine agitation was as lively as it had been
in the days of Caracas.

But again events intervened, not as dramatically as they had when
President Jiménez fell, but implacably. Nineteen fifty-nine brought
increasingly serious troubles for Trujillo in Venezuela, in Cuba, in the
United States, and at home. Perón could read the signs. He made his
moves, and on December 29, the Argentine Foreign Office could
inform the American embassy in Buenos Aires that the Franco government in Spain had agreed to admit the controversial exile, who
would depart shortly for Madrid. Trujillo paid all costs.[39]

Turmoil in Argentina

Perón's wanderings were no more restless than was life in the
Argentina that had rejected him. There, a succession of leaders, some
well-intentioned and others more typical of their caste, attempted to
implement the Liberating Revolution, grappling with tasks that were
beyond solution, given the perversities of the moment and the force
of the civilization that pressed all about.

The first to attempt the impossible was General Lonardi, who was inaugurated as president on September 23, 1955 in the wake of Perón's departure. An ocean of people murmured before him in the Plaza San Martín in another of those immense gatherings peculiar to Argentina and made familiar by Peronist usage. It was almost his last moment of comfort. Lonardi, a devout Catholic, was a man of unusual purity of purpose. Although he was seriously handicapped by political inexperience, his instincts and his intelligence were sound and they directed him to the theme he announced on the 23rd: "Neither victors nor vanquished." But reality had its way. There *were* victors, many of them; and there *were* the vanquished, very many, indeed. And there was no agreement, no bond of common interest or loyalty, between them. Although its modern-day symbol was far distant, the Great Rift seemed wider than ever.

President Lonardi did his best in the brief time that was his lot before he fell on November 13, ill and near death. But a great tidal force of anti-Peronism prevailed. The Congress was dissolved. The provinces and the universities were intervened. The members of the Supreme Court were dismissed. Leading Peronists went into refuge or exile or into prison. A national investigating commission charged Perón and all Peronista members of Congress since 1946 with treason on the ground that they had used their power illegitimately. The army's special tribunal of honor found Perón guilty of incitement to crime and violence, of sowing hate within the nation, of violation of the constitution, of disloyalty to the army, of failure to discharge responsibility, and of an improper way of life, including cohabitation with a minor, and it recommended that Perón be deprived of his title and grade in the army and the use of its uniform.[40] Yet all this zeal by the government and by the army was seen by many of Perón's bitter opponents as faintness of heart; nothing but the utter extinction of every Peronist trace would satisfy.

General Pedro Aramburu succeeded Lonardi as provisional president, working with a military council. Peronist Party leaders were forbidden to participate in politics and the Party itself was dissolved and its assets appropriated. The Peronist name and its symbols were banished from public print. The social legislation of the Peronato was respected in accordance with pledges that Lonardi had given, but the CGT was intervened. Unions lost their power to run their internal affairs in the accustomed manner, which had generally been democratic and effective, and were forbidden to intrude into politics. Plural unions were authorized.[41] In 1956–58, real wages for manufacturing workers were higher than in any three-year period except 1948–50, but it was all lost in high-handed, insensitive tactics. President Aramburu realized this, but much too late, admitting in 1968 that his labor policy had been a total failure, and that his choice of Labor Minister was unfortunate, and that other approaches would have been better, had he only known at the time.[42]

The gathering pressures coalesced in a military uprising in June 1956, led by a retired Peronist general, Juan José Valle. It was a brief and inept affair, but in the aftermath, twenty-seven men, nine of them civilian, were executed by firing squads. This was quite without precedent in Argentina and it was to cast a very long and evil shadow.[43]

Political discussion with wide participation, dormant under the Peronato, was now strikingly evident. Out of the babble of voices a new leader began to emerge, Arturo Frondizi, the leader of the Radicals' intransigent wing, the UCRI. A striking figure, lean and tall and dominated by a great hawk's beak of a nose, Frondizi was rather more cool and intellectual than the run of Argentine politicians, given to concepts rather than to the warm *abrazo,* but rich, nevertheless, in the basic skills of maneuver that assured survival in Argentine politics, if anything could. Although he was firmly anti-Peronist, he was also a realist and he began to take a soft line on the big issue of Peronism. He was allied with a successful businessman, Rogelio Frigerio, who preached a doctrine of industrial development that required social and industrial peace and some accommodation with the Peronist masses.

These policies smacked too much of Peronism for the Aramburu government and for the other centers of Radical power, and the latter now came together in a new party, the Radical Civic Union of the People, the UCRP, headed by Ricardo Balbín. On July 27, 1957, elections were held for a constitutional convention that would formulate a new order. Many parties participated, but only three groupings were decisive: the UCRP, the UCRI, and the blank votes that represented Peronism, for Perón had done the best he could, given the confused channels of communication and the tenuous links to his followers, to urge them to abstain or to spoil their ballots or to hand in blank ballots.[44] The results were subject to various interpretations. The UCRP received 24.2 percent of the vote, the UCRI percent 21.2 percent, and the blank votes amounted to 24.3 percent. Perón saw good auguries in the blanks plus the spoiled votes plus presumed abstainers plus many who were doubtless confused. And Frondizi saw the shape of the future when he added the UCRI votes and the blanks, an exercise that pointed with great clarity to the logic of an alliance with Perón, strange as such might seem to those who saw history as stereotype rather than as opportunity.[45]

The constitutional convention managed to reinstate the constitution of 1953 before it fizzled out, lacking even a quorum. It was high time for elections, and these were scheduled for February 23, 1958. Ricardo Balbín would represent the UCRP on a ticket that was closer to the themes of the Liberating Revolution, and Arturo Frondizi would lead the UCRI in a campaign directed to amnesty, development, and outreach across class lines.

President Aramburu did the best he could to dilute Frondizi's appeal by authorizing the participation of three "neo-Peronist" parties, designed to draw off some of the Peronist votes. The time was thus appropriate for Frondizi's imaginative effort to reach a working alliance with Perón. At first Perón was not interested,[46] but that was before the neo-Peronist groups had been legitimized. Their presence on various ballots would be a temptation to resist any orders he might give to abstain or to vote in blank. By the end of 1957, he had persuaded himself of the virtues of a Frondizi alliance. He extended an invitation, and on January 3, 1958, Rogelio Frigerio appeared in Caracas to negotiate.

From that moment, the evolution of the alliance, and, in fact, its very nature, becomes murky. Frigerio has referred to a single trip to Caracas, but there were almost certainly two trips, both in January.[47] The second session in Caracas was cut short by the fall of Pérez Jiménez on the 21st and the quick disappearance of Perón into the Dominican embassy. Frigerio completed the document in Buenos Aires, signed it, and sent it up on February 5 to Perón, who was now in Santo Domingo. On February 10, the latter's messenger arrived in Buenos Aires carrying Perón's hand-written letter of instructions to his followers to vote for Frondizi, thus overriding earlier ambiguous instructions merely to vote against the continuation of the Liberating Revolution. The working alliance of Perón and Frondizi was now a fact, but its nature and extent are still a mystery.

Perón released what he claimed was the text of the agreement in June 1959, after he and Frondizi had parted ways. This text is similar to a document given to the American ambassador in Santo Domingo by Generalissimo Trujillo.[48] It was dated "In February, 1958." This agreement is a slightly watered-down version of another text dated January 20–21, 1958, and given to the American embassy in Santo Domingo by a journalist. The commitments of the parties vary slightly in the two versions, but in both of them, in exchange for Peronist support in the election, Frondizi pledged himself to "reestablish the conquest achieved by *Justicialismo* in the social, economic and political orders," and he adopted various specific policies including the annulment of judicial measures of the Liberating Revolution, the revision of its economic programs, restitution of confiscated properties, including those of the Eva Perón Foundation, repeal of union restrictions, recognition of the Peronista Party and return of its property, replacement of the Supreme Court, and, finally, a constitutional convention within two years, to reform the constitution completely and to call for new general elections.

But this was not the end of the matter. Frigerio has contended that the document he and Frondizi had signed and that he had caused to be delivered to Perón in Santo Domingo was merely an agreement to combine against Balbín's candidacy and against the neo-Peronists, and it contained no concrete measures. This version of the agreement has never been produced in written form. To complete the mystification, Frondizi insisted from first to last that he never signed any agreement whatsoever.[49]

Whatever the truth of the documents may be, the pact did exist in some form and it was highly effective. The elections were held without incident on February 23, 1958, and Frondizi won by a large margin—he received more than 4,000,000 votes to 2,415,000 for Balbín, plus a strong majority in the Chamber of Deputies. The UCRI's increase over its showing in the July elections was the result of the massive shift of blank ballots to Frondizi. It was also a spectacular verification of Peronist loyalty and of Perón's ability to exert control through feeble channels over enormous distance.

But questions about the pact remain, on a deeper level than that of documentary verification. Why did the two leaders enter into such an agreement, and what were their plans and psychologies in regard to it?

On Perón's side, the answers are relatively clear. His heart was with his 1957 stance of going it alone and abstaining from all involvement in the election, but there were difficulties with this. Perhaps unexpectedly, the government had authorized the neo-Peronist parties and it would be awkward to request the faithful to forego a vote for these in favor of a non-vote. He had already ordered a blank vote in the July elections—how would another such request be received by impatient followers? The justifications for a blank vote were difficult to explain with primitive means of communication. And there were affirmative reasons, as Perón explained to Jorge Antonio, the associate who had just joined him the night before the Frondizi pact was signed. It was an instruction in *realpolitik* for the new recruit. We know, Perón began, that Frondizi wants to help himself through us. But Perón would support him because of his formal promises and because this would avoid a greater evil. "To repeat, Jorge, I don't believe that he will comply with any of it. But . . . we can't do anything else. To a great extent, we've lost the power of decision. We have to hope, until we can regain our strength and freely recover our initiative. If, on the other hand, Frondizi complies with the pact, the next elections will have to include us. If he doesn't, he will stay in power a very short time: two or three years in any case and, fatally, he will fall by his own doing." One shot would account for two birds, Perón insisted. One bird was Balbín, who would lose, and the other was Frondizi, who would be pulled down.[50]

On Frondizi's side, the motivation was apparent: he wanted to win, and with an evident mandate. If he had won while the Peronists were casting blank votes, the victory would have been hollow and dubious. But after victory, what was Frondizi thinking about? If the agreement released by Perón was authentic, Frondizi's promises were impossibilities, even absurdities. His undertakings amounted to the overthrow of the Liberating Revolution and the restoration of Peronism, a program that would obviously result in his displacement by the military at some early moment. Why would he wish victory through means that would make it impossible to govern from the day of his inauguration? How could he have accepted, in effect, a voluntary limitation of two years on the six-year presidential term he had spent his life pursuing? The obvious answer is that he did not, and could not, have intended to implement these wild commitments, so unreal that the government at first refused to believe in them and Frondizi himself had to deny them. Equally, Perón was too astute a realist to have expected implementation from Frondizi, beyond perhaps a token gesture here and there. It surely was a cynical bond arranged by two masters of guile, too impermanent to qualify as a marriage of convenience, really a passionless one-night stand in which both parties bought and sold.

Particularly in the case of Frondizi, the compact leads to questions about the Argentine political process in general. It has been suggested, persuasively, that his candidacy and its theme of developmentalism were premature, and that it might have been better for Frondizi to let grievances subside under some more gradual regime before he made his move.[51] But having made it, he compounded his difficulties by the pact with Perón that was sure to involve him in direct confrontation with a disappointed Peronism inflamed by what would be considered bad faith. Both of these major steps by Frondizi were matters of broad judgment, calling less for shrewdness than for wisdom. Although Frondizi was intelligent and well-intentioned and the possessor of unusual political skills, they ran more to tactics than to grand strategy. Like many another Argentine politician, he enjoyed concepts and promoted broad themes, but excelled at the details of intense jockeying. The more narrow and immediate the issue, the more astutely leaders of this mold handled it. The more profound the issue became and the wider the implications it raised, and the more it depended upon patience and restraint and the careful balancing of factors, the less successful they were. This was, of course, not true of all, but the panorama of Argentine politics in the twentieth century does suggest such a tendency.

There is in this an echo of the ethos, the echo of *viveza criolla,* the propensity to trickiness and the sly coup, and the public acceptance of such sleight of hand. There is an echo also of the love of display and drama in the almost romantic quick cut and thrust of tactical exchanges, an element totally lacking in solemn reflections about long-term factors. And the tendency comports well with the familiar expressions of individualism, quick, personalized tactics in the *caudillo* tradition. But a politics of tactical finesse, divorced from the wisdom that could give it meaning and permanence, becomes a hollow politics; and a hollow politics breeds cynicism and estrangement; and cynicism and estrangement produce, at their best, leaders such as Perón and Frondizi who prevail because they are at one with the civilization that calls them forth and sooner or later casts them down.

General Aramburu behaved responsibly in the transfer of power, but Frondizi had to contend with the extremisms of Peronism and anti-Peronism, as much a conflict of emotional attitudes as of politics.[52] Nor would the general public psychology assist him in a time of need, for it maintained, as always, one of the mental sets of the civilization: the outlining of a solution or the first step in a process disposes of the entire problem then and there. A good speech is a program accomplished. The unveiling of a plan amounts to its consummation. And in the present case, the assumption of power by a determined man is itself a solution of everything, and quick results will flow.

Some results certainly did appear. There was considerable industrial development. Within three months, in an extraordinary display of brass, the Frondizi who had been in the front lines of the "petroleum nationalists" awarded production contracts to foreign producers, with brilliant success.[53] Foreign financing was obtained, and new industries and public works were inaugurated.[54] But the advances came with fearful difficulty. Everything that pleased this person or group displeased that one. Controversy and distrust were everywhere. In November 1958, in the face of a politically motivated strike against his petroleum policy, Frondizi invoked a State of Siege, and it remained in force until he fell. The step has been construed as a tactic admission that the collaboration with Perón could no longer be sustained,[55] and, in fact, Perón was now trying to bring him down.[56] The seal upon their break was firmly affixed by Perón in June 1959, with his release of his version of the Perón–Frondizi Pact.

Several blunders now doomed Frondizi. The military objected to his Cuban policies. And his decision to permit neo-Peronist parties, now banded together in a Justicialist Front, to participate in congressional and gubernatorial elections in March 1962 resulted in substantial victories for them and corresponding losses for Radical candidates. It was the end for the Florentine. In the dark, early hours of the morning of March 29, Frondizi, still resisting resignation, agreed to his own detention at Martín García Island, among the shades of Yrigoyen and Perón. It was all done gently and quietly, and with a touch of dignity.[57]

> To speak of Spain is to speak of one's mother. It is
> the land of nobility.
>
> — Juan Perón, *Yo, Juan Domingo Perón*

11. The Spanish Exile
1961–1973

Life in the Motherland

WHEN PERÓN'S FLIGHT into deeper exile landed him at
Seville on January 5, 1961, he had the comfort of knowing that to
some extent a way had been prepared for him by one of his most
faithful followers and advisors, Jorge Antonio. From the beginning,
Antonio was unique within the ranks of Peronism. Tall, dark, brooding in expression, courtly, he came, in his later years, to reflect a kind
of avuncular wisdom, touched with glints of mystery. If he had been
a canine instead of a man, he would have been one of those appealing,
sad-eyed, and sagacious basset hounds that seem to sense the universal dilemmas. He was born in 1917 to parents of Syrian and Lebanese
heritage in the raw vibrancy of the Boca section of Buenos Aires. Before
long, he developed the true talent for business, the entrepreneurial
vocation, that was more characteristic of the new immigrant stock (and
of the Levant) than of the old Creole society. By the 1950s, he was
well established as one of the most successful of the new breed of
Argentine industrialists, with investments and enterprises in several
fields and his base in an important factory for the manufacture of
Mercedes Benz trucks.

These activities brought him into contact with the government,
and Antonio came to be seen as a Peronist sympathizer. When the

regime fell, he was jailed for two and a half years, most of the time at Ushuaia, in farthest Patagonia. He and several other high level prisoners, including the future president, Héctor Cámpora, made a spectacular escape to Chile, masterminded and financed by Antonio. By the time the letter from Perón reached him in Santiago in May 1957, he was a confirmed and dedicated Peronist. The letter was long and thoughtful, sixteen pages of it in its reprinted form, and in it Perón outlined his thoughts for the future and his hope that Antonio would join him. He pointed out the sacrifices involved. "Our struggle is not a short-term matter and one who enters into it will possibly do so for life. The worst fate is that of those who repent. Therefore, before entering into this, one should think it through. There are great possibilities, but as generally happens in life, the dangers are directly proportional to the risks, and those in turn to the possibilities." It was time, Perón wrote, to form a team that would lead the movement whose enormous potential would soon fall into the hands of the younger leaders. "I am an old politcian who is reaching the end of his road. You, a young man who could be beginning it."[1]

Somewhat later, Antonio turned up in Caracas to announce that he would be at Perón's side. He remained there until the end of the Peronato, providing immense financial support and disinterested advice, to the deteriment of his business affairs and his family life. Although he became involved in the deepest core of the Peronist movement as Perón's confidant and personal agent, he was always more the man of business than the politician. He approached politics from its idealistic side, never becoming fully adjusted to such maneuvers as Perón's support of Frondizi in 1958. He was one of that rare breed, a Quixote who knows how to meet a payroll, and his attachment to Perón, as follower to leader and son to father, attests vividly Perón's power to summon a loyalty almost fanatical. A single instance of that power moved Antonio deeply. Perón, visiting in Antonio's home on one occasion, addressed himself to Antonio's four young sons, saying, "Your father has been for me what I have never had, a son. And he has the good fortune to have several. I am sure that you will come to understand him well, and to serve him as he will serve you. The only thing I've not been able to do with anyone is to have my own son, and now I've done that with your father."[2]

It soon became apparent that Perón's visa had been granted without the knowledge of Generalissimo Franco, who was not slow to take umbrage. He would not rescind the visa or refuse asylum, but neither would he cause his bureaucracy to cut through its haze of permits and procedures. Perón had to live in Málaga, on the southern coast, for several months while the formalities for residence in Madrid were addressed. He was then permitted to live a short distance outside the capital, and only after a year did he go to Madrid itself[3], settling into an apartment directly beneath the living quarters of Ava Gardner, whom he judged to be "the most beautiful animal on earth."[4]

No more was heard now of an earlier attempt by Perón to obtain a residence visa from the Swiss government. That such an application was made and rejected appears from a disclosure by the Swiss embassy in Washington. This may have been the source of Perón's ferocious dislike of Switzerland and everything connected with it. The style and personality of the Swiss were certainly almost as different from those of the Argentines as they could be, but something more personal was surely involved. "Switzerland is a country I don't like . . . one of the few places in the world that I don't know or have any interest in knowing. I know some Swiss, and that's enough for me . . . a country where all the bandits come together . . . the place where they hide everything they rob from the others."[5]

A great many other things that Perón didn't like were enumerated in a very long and very turgid letter that he directed to President John F. Kennedy in July 1961. It was an astonishing document whose purpose was obscure, unless it was to influence the United States against Argentina at a forthcoming hemispheric conference in Punta del Este, Uruguay, and its technique was even more obscure, for it was blunt and hostile to the point of counterproductivity. The United States and England together had caused his fall; America and its people were much disliked and its news services were evil; Frondizi was the most discredited president in Argentine history and a stooge of the United States; assistance to Argentina should be channeled through the unions; the Argentine government was "a swarm of bandits and another swarm of ignoramuses."[6] It was a bewildering performance, and the author's judgement was more than suspect.

The Caribbean countries had turned an indulgent eye on Perón's relationship with Isabel, but that was not the Spanish style. The austerity and morality of Castile had not dimished with time or with the Franco regime, and an early marriage was indicated. It took place in Madrid in a private home on November 15, 1961, after friends had intervened with a bishop to authorize a "marriage of convenience" for the sake of Isabel, since the ambiguity created by the alleged excommunication of Perón in 1955 had not been dissipated.[7]

In 1962, Perón built what would be his permanent home in Madrid, in the section known as Puerta de Hierro, the Iron Gate. The house was paid for by Jorge Antonio, who refused the credit for his assistance and presented it to Perón as the gift of various friends in Madrid.[8] Perón designed the house with the aid of an architect and supervised its construction closely, even to the point of taking coffee and cognac to the bricklayers on cold mornings. It was as a fine toy to a deprived child, although it was relatively modest, a typical middle-class house with a living room and a den or office downstairs and three bedrooms above. The garden was Perón's particular pride, for he selected the trees and plants and watched over them with an unsuspected dedication to gardening.

Settled in with the dogs and the roses, Perón began to attain a bit of comfort and his days a degree of routine. He still arose early, at half past six, breakfasted on coffee and two pieces of toast, and went walking in the garden with José Cresto, the old friend of Isabel's family who had served *in loco parente* for her in Argentina and who had now come to live with the Peróns. They would examine the plants, handle minor chores, and conduct warfare against the ants. Each tree had to be inspected: "I talked to them a bit, you know? A tree is a very important thing." At nine, Perón would return to the office on the first floor and attend to correspondence and reading for two hours. At eleven, there would be, without fail, an hour of fencing with Isabel, to whom he had taught this art at which she had become very proficient. At twelve, he would go back to the garden again, and then to lunch at half past one. Soup, a main dish that could be a small steak or some paella, fruit, and coffee. Than a short walk and a nap until four, followed often by a trip downtown or to some nearby place, returning by seven. At half past eight, they would watch television, with dinner at half past nine. An hour later, Perón would be in bed, reading for perhaps three hours: "An old custom. Perhaps this would be the most meaningful hour of the day for me."[9] Except for summer trips to Irun and an occasional excursion to Biarritz, these simple routines were his life in Spain.

The hours of reading at night were meaningful in another sense as well, for they were part of a process, noted particularly by those closest to Perón, that changed him significantly and prepared the way for the Perón who attempted in his last years to unite rather than to separate, at least in the sense of his basic strategy. His reading and study had slacked off, under pressure of events, during the 1950s and in the time of the Caribbean exile, and now they resumed, more profound than before,[10] and contributed an important element to the new process, which was one of Europeanization. Although Spain is quite untypical of Europe, Perón was now in contact with people and experiences that represented a continental civilization different from what he had known before. He had new sources of information and new examples, and his absorptive mind and personality took it all in. An Argentine who was among the most intimate of his collaborators has defined the process: ". . . to read, to live, to know, to associate with Europeans, changed him. It made him more moderate, more comprehensive, more human . . . the all-powerful man I knew in 1950, 1952, 1954, 1955, changed. He was more humanistic, more respectful of others, perhaps because he had felt the force of misfortune. I noted the change each time that I saw him, more, more."[11]

The problem of finances continued to be troublesome. Most of Perón's expenses while he was living in Caracas and Santo Domingo had been paid by Jorge Antonio, for Perón seemed to need everything, down to the barest necessities. Now Antonio was still providing most of the living expenses and also general funds which, in part, were channeled to Argentina in support of Peronist activity.[12] Things got a bit better as time went on, but not much. Frondizi sent a contribution of $85,000 shortly after his election, and toward the end of the decade the unions in Argentina began to contribute something, perhaps $1,000 a month. The Argentine lawyer who represented Perón during the exile did not charge for his services, nor was he reimbursed for the transportation and other costs of his various trips to Spain.[13] There were no hidden bank accounts in Switzerland or elsewhere, as persistent rumors insisted.[14] Perón made the point in his typical way: "I sometimes think that if I had the fortune that my enemies attribute to me, I could have bought them all."[15]

One problem was solved, however, in 1963. Perón's relationship with the Church was clarified. The excommunication that dated from 1955 did not, technically, apply to him, for it failed to comply with certain requirements of canon law. But the shadow of the document had to be dispelled sooner or later. Jorge Antonio and Raúl Matera, Perón's current representative in Argentina, delivered to the Vatican a letter from Perón in which he sought the restoration of his good standing, and they returned to Madrid with a document certifying that he, and the Argentine government, had merely been threatened with excommunication. Subsequently, according to Antonio, who was present, one of the bishops whom Perón had expelled in June 1955, called on him in Madrid and expressed regrets.[16]

As the 1960s advanced, a new difficulty arose, and to this there was no answer: Perón's health began slowly to deteriorate. In 1964, he had an operation for prostatic tumors, which were found to be

nonmalignant. But they were recurring, and several similar operations were necessary in the following years, each at a shorter time
interval. What worried Perón most, however, was the presence of a
large cyst in his liver. It was quiescent but Perón feared its irruption
at any moment. More serious, in fact, was a third ailment, arterioscle-
rosis, that was creeping up. Its effects were irregular and the loss of
memory was quite evident at some times and not at all at others. Perón
was aware of this. Once, while visiting Antonio, he had a request.
"Look, Jorge, strange things are happening to me that are disagreeable. I lose my memory too easily. There are times when I don't respond
accurately. Please, if you see signs of this in me at any time during a
meeting, let me know and cut off the conversation immediately."[17] It
was a dilemma that would steadily deepen, for he was increasingly
conscious of the element of time that had entered his life. By the end
of the decade, when he had attained the age of seventy-five, he knew
by instinct and by medical advice that in all probability only three or
four more years remained. This became clear in 1970 when the
American ambassador to Spain asked Perón's physician, Dr. Antonio
Puigvert, for an opinion concerning Perón's physical prospects. The
doctor replied in writing, and then told Perón what he had said:

"I told him that you will live three or four years if you take sufficient care, but if you don't you'll die before that. Now, remember I'm
Spanish, and more than that, I'm your friend. I want you to take care
of yourself because I don't want to give bad information to the United
States ambassador."[18]

Only once in the years of the sixties was his relatively quiet routine
broken. In response to requests by important supporters (including
Augusto Vandor, a top labor leader, and Delia Parodi, the head of
the Peronist Women's Movement), Perón had committed himself to a
return to Argentina by the end of 1964, and it would be necessary to
honor this pledge by attempting its fulfillment. It was not known how
the Argentine government would react, for some of the signals were
positive and some implications were negative. The destination of the
trip was to be Montevideo, and Perón hoped that there would be some
grand gesture of reconciliation and unity by the government, after
which further steps with the president, Dr. Illia, could follow the
breakthrough.[19] Perón's first prostate operation intervened, and by
autumn, when he was physically on his feet again, specific plans were
notably absent. The whole problem of arrangements was bucked over
to Jorge Antonio, who obtained a first-class cabin for the group on an
Iberia flight to Montevideo on December 2. Great secrecy and deception attended all the plans, to discourage journalists and others through

whom Buenos Aires would be alerted in time to prepare a counter-offensive. So extreme was this security that Antonio himself drove his Mercedes to the airport with Perón hidden in the trunk for the first part of the trip.[20]

Just as the group was boarding the plane, an official of Iberia appeared with the demand that Jorge Antonio sign a document commiting himself to indemnify the company for all losses that might occur on account of Perón's passage. "Naturally, I signed without reading it."[21] There spoke the civilization, the primacy of dignity, the instinct for the grand and romantic gesture, the feeling for the noble and the extreme.

As the plane began to descend over Río de Janeiro for its scheduled stop en route, Perón said to Antonio, sitting next to him, "Now we'll see how they're going to behave; I wouldn't be surprised if they do something nasty to us." His instinct was political and sure, while Antonio spoke of the law and of the papers that were in order and of the obvious arbitrariness of any interference. Perón winked an eye and replied,

"Yes, you're right, Jorge, but we're going to see what they'll say down there."[22]

They found out soon enough. The landing area was filled with a mass of troops with guns at the ready. "I confess," said Antonio, "that my heart stopped beating for a moment." Officers came aboard and invited the group to leave the plane. They refused. The Brazilians persisted. "I don't accept invitations or orders from Brazilians," Perón replied. "Therefore I don't intend to leave the plane." The Brazilians made it clear that if the Argentines persisted, they would be detained, as would the crew of the plane and the aircraft itself. Perón gave in, of necessity, and the group was held in a waiting room for seventeen hours. During that time Perón refused all refreshment, including water, and such was his vexation and resentment that when one of the Brazilians asked if he wanted to reset his watch with the correct time, he replied, "No, I don't want anything from this country, not even the time of day."[23] The plane continued on to Montevideo and Buenos Aires without them, and on its return trip the Argentines were put aboard, destined for Madrid.

The Brazilians had responded to intense pressure from the Argentine government, generated by the armed forces. The Brazilians had their own motives as well. "We blocked the passage of Perón not only at the request of the Argentine government," stated the foreign minister some months later, "but also in defense of legitimate Brazilian interests, since the presence of that one in Argentina would constitute a danger to our national security."[24]

Jorge Antonio was in anguish at the setback: ". . . the pain burrowed into me, very deeply, as if to plant its roots in my soul . . ." The others were crushed, and Perón was sobered. Outwardly he remained confident. "My obligation is to bring it [the movement] to a safe port. If we have been good, we will return. If not, it is better that we never return."[25] Sometimes a note of modesty intruded, as in the example of Perón's comment in 1968, so often quoted, "It's not that we've been all that good, but rather that our successors were so bad."[26] The unofficial Perón was talking, not the one who proclaimed optimism to the world.

But Perón had to accept new and strict limits on his political activity.[27] Antonio was exiled from Spain, went briefly to Paris, and at the end of 1964 settled in Asunción where the ever-cooperative General Stroessner granted him a degree of political latitude.

Perplexity and Frustration in Argentina

The fall of Arturo Frondizi in March 1962 was the immediate prelude to a period of almost disastrous confusion in Argentina. The next eighteen months were as bitter and chaotic a time as the country had ever experienced, a time of economic decline and hardship and political divisiveness so extreme that it seemed as if no Argentine could agree with any other on anything.

The constitutional successor to Frondizi (the vicepresidency was vacant) was the president of the Senate, Dr. José María Guido, who assumed office on March 30. The armed forces that sustained him were fearfully split, the CGT was divided into two factions, and every political party was in shreds. For a time, the hardest of hard lines prevailed, as Guido was carried along by the army *Colorados*, anti-Peronist without limit and known to their detractors as the "gorillas," who were opposed by a moderately anti-Peronist faction called the *Azules*. The cabinet disintegrated. The suspended Congress was dissolved. Tanks and sandbags appeared in the streets. New decrees banning the remotest hints of Peronism flowered like leaves. A cartoon caught the mood, picturing the hapless president, sitting at a table with his hand raised in schoolboy fashion, opposite four fearsome generals, including the war minister, General Poggi; the caption read, "May I go to the toilet, General Poggi?"[28]

Abruptly, in September, the *Azules* rose against the chiefs in the war ministry. Several days of fighting followed and the smoke and shudder of battle came to Buenos Aires and to Rosario. Civil war was not far distant. The *Azules* were effective, both in battle under their leader, General Juan Onganía, and in political maneuvers. They issued the document known as Communiqué No. 150, on September 22, a brief and cogent call for elections with the participation of all sectors of opinion, combined with insistence upon "the impossibility of a return to the past." President Guido supported the *Azules*, General Onganía became interim commander in chief of the army, and the day was won for moderation.[29]

But it was a moderation that became less moderate as elections approached. These were rescheduled for July 7, under a system of proportional representation designed to dilute the Peronist mass.[30] Given the obsession with Peronism, this made sense, but a larger vision would have discerned danger in so open an invitation to the perpetual splintering and division. Although the old Sáenz Peña system of two-thirds to the leading party and one-third to the runner-up distorted the verdict of the balloting, it gave definition and permanence to the party system. But the blocs and coalitions that would be inevitable under proportional representation were doubtless less offensive to the political leaders than they would be to the national interest.

The miserable year 1962 staggered to a close, and the national profile still reflected one great central reality, islandlike, surrounded by an ocean of endless and shifting currents, cross currents, and reverse currents. That central reality, despite superficial alterations, had not changed since its first appearance in 1944: the nation still had not come to grips with Peronism, which continued to command all fears and divide all loyalties. Communiqué No. 150 of the military *Azules*, enlightened as it was, suffered from the same overriding ambivalence of calling for elections with full participation but forbidding a return to the past. The agenda for the first half of 1963 would be dominated by these two irreconcilable objectives as leaders of every group and faction twisted and writhed in an effort to prevent or insure the return of the past through full and free elections.

In this obscurantism and mad jumble that made the first half of 1963 a byword for chaos, the tactics of Perón and the lesser Peronist leaders played a full part. They evolved along at least two lines, parallel but dissimilar, either of which could be elevated or diminished as requirements of the moment dictated, all in accordance with a well-known saying of Perón that dated from this period: "I have a right hand and a left hand, and I know how to use them both." The first line was based in the CGT, now split into the "62" grouping, which was firmly Peronist, and the independent unions known as the "32." The "62" was much the larger, and its discipline and firmness of purpose made it a formidable political instrument. For Perón, however, the issues of leadership within the "62" was a continual concern. He wanted it to be effective, but not so effective that it might create a separate power center within labor that could learn to operate independently of advice from Madrid. The solution, entirely typical of Perón, was to encourage a divided leadership guided and balanced by the left and the right hand, sometimes successively, sometimes simultaneously. The left hand worked with the head of the "62," Andrés Framini, an experienced labor leader whose instinct generally led him to the more aggressive side of a strategy.

The right hand worked with Augusto Vandor, known as "El Lobo," the wolf. Vandor was also a lifelong labor official, but despite the menace of his sobriquet he was the most moderate of the prominent CGT leaders, seeking alliances and adaptation rather than confrontation. He was competent and well-respected and a pillar of support for Peronism, but he was also the source of a nagging suspicion that called for careful monitoring from the house in Madrid, for of all the leaders, it was Vandor who would most naturally gravitate toward the concept that Perón feared and mistrusted, the concept of "Peronism without Perón." He had not struggled and waited for so many years with the thought of applauding anyone else on center stage. To the small extent that personal ambition and disinterested public service can be separated as strands of motivation, they both appeared to reinforce this attitude. High political ambition had become solidified by time and newly reinforced by blows to his pride and by the hope of vindication; and he believed quite sincerely that his policies were in the national interest and that no one else could implement them with the prestige and skill he commanded. Many, of course, disagreed with the first part of that proposition, far fewer with the second.

The other line of Peronist response was founded in such inchoate political organization as was available in the interstices of the repressive decrees in force, or as could be jerry-built by semi-clandestine means. A thirty-member coordinating council was now functioning, handling day-to-day business and presenting a moderate image. It was headed by Dr. Raúl Matera, a prominent neurosurgeon of matinee-idol appearance and charm, whose pronouncements linked Peronist doctrine to the Catholic social themes, with a stress on "community" and political unification.[31] So much for strategy. Tactics were a different matter, gyrating wildly, a call for prudence one day, an appeal for pitiless violence the next.

For a tantalizing moment early in 1963, a rough consensus appeared possible as all major parties spoke of a common approach to eventual elections. But a reaction soon followed, with anarchy. Andrés Framini chose this juncture to attack with impartial fervor the armed forces and Communiqué No. 150 and to announce that the Peronists would call for revolution if they were excluded from the elections; and he was arrested for his pains. The navy rose in a futile four-day revolt. And on May 24, Raúl Matera resigned as head of the Peronist coordinating council, pushed out by Perón and convinced, according to the medical conclusions he confided to a United States embassy official, that he had been representing a paranoiac, an abnormal man, but one who remained a hero to the Argentine masses.[32]

Given such immense disorder, it was remarkable that the elections were even held. The concept of a National Front linking the Peronists and several other parties hovered about briefly, wraithlike, and then dissolved. Then a final dramatic gesture changed everything: forty-eight hours before the balloting, Perón ordered his followers to boycott the elections by abstention or by casting blank ballots for all offices.

July 7 arrived. Rarely has so much been expected of an election so battered. All 21,139 elective offices in Argentina from the presidency down to school boards, had to be filled. Sixty-nine parties offered candidates for various positions. There were ten presidential candidates.[33] The winner was Dr. Arturo Illia, the candidate of the UCRP, the anti-Frondizi Radicals, who would be a minority president with just over 25 percent of the vote. The blank and null votes amounted to a little over 20 percent, a Peronist testimonial that was neither spectacular nor seriously disappointing.

The new president was an obscure small-town physician from the province of Córdoba. He knew little of national life, and neither he nor his party and associates had expected his victory. At sixty-three years of age, with his white hair, benign expression, and mellow ways, he seemed a figure of reassurance in an environment largely devoid of that quality. But it was soon apparent that Dr. Illia was the wrong president at the wrong time. He was seen to be quite out of touch with the problems of the time, unsophisticated, parochial, and "sure of himself with the frightening certainty of the simple minded."[34] And the cartoonists soon went to work on him as a doddering old healer trying to cure an ill nation with an assortment of potions and herbal remedies out of rural folklore. No one doubted his honesty and decency and goodwill, but neither did most of those outside his UCRP circle doubt his lack of capacity, or share his primitive optimism that a good harvest would redeem all deficiencies.

In general, the administration was passive and unimaginative in its programs, or in its lack thereof, and failed to assert its authority with emphasis. Its image was further reduced by the results of partial congressional elections held in March of 1965, when Peronist candididats won 36 percent of the vote, outpolling UCRP candidates by 3,400,000 to 2,600,000. It was black news for the Illia government, since further balloting was scheduled for March 1967, with half of the Congress up for election as well as important governorships, and there were few who doubted that the armed forces would move before that date to cut off the possibility of further Peronist successes. It was, therefore, the very worst of times in which to alienate the military further, but President Illia did just that when, at the end of 1965, he nudged General Onganía, the commander in chief of the army, out of office. That rigid and remote officer had been the bastion of legalism among the *Azules* and he had remained the strongest supporter of civilian government. As such, he was Illia's best protection against the coup that was likely in any case, and to move him aside was both a portent and a symbol of the government's sense of unreality.

The coming of the revolution in those last months was unique in its manner. It did not, like the famous fog, arrive on little cat feet, silently. Neither did it come with a bang and a blare of trumpet. Rather, it came almost like a funeral procession down the middle of a street, slowly, solidly, heralded in the press and known to all. It was so thoroughly discussed that it almost took on the aspect of *fait accompli* before its details were even addressed by its planners. And there was an inimitable touch of Feydeau: just before the event, a weekly publication, *Primera Plana*, conducted a straw poll among leading citizens to see how many favored a revolution and how many were opposed. Sedition had risen, or fallen, to the level of marketing analysis.

It was all very simple and straightforward. On the afternoon of June 28, in a high-level dispute concerning personnel, the army commander in chief refused to recognize the authority of the war minister, who spoke for Illia. At dawn on the 29th, military personnel peacefully occupied the presidential chambers. There had been no shots, no prisoners, no exiles, no arrests. Dr. Illia, again the country physician, returned to Córdoba Province.[35]

So much for what happened. But why? What did it all signify? In the answer there is much that bears upon the phoenixlike return of Juan Perón several years later, and upon the workings of the Argentine civilization that made that return possible, perhaps almost inevitable.

Many of the reasons for the overthrow of the Illia government are apparent and have been alluded to. It was torpid and passive and, above all, lacked authority. This latter failing seems to have been particularly offensive to the psychological preferences of the public, immersed in the long tradition of executive strength. More specifically, there were fears in military and political circles alike of a Peronist resurgence in 1967. The military also felt strongly that national defense was related to economic development, and that progress in that field was impossible with a government that imaged a tortoise.

But even granting the validity of all this, something more remains. After all, the Illia government was legitimate in its inception, and the faults to be found with it hardly seem strong enough to explain or to justify the unanimity of the sentiment against it; the only elements that supported President Illia to the end were his own faction of the Radicals and the university and youth sectors of the populace. Almost everyone else sighed with relief and looked forward. There must have been strong tuggings of the subconscious to have alienated so many despite the absence of drastic provocation. And the state of the general morale in the 1960s indeed suggests that this was the case.

There seemed to be a general malaise of spirit during the decade, as there had been in the thirties. "Today large numbers of young people want nothing so much as to emigrate," an observer living in Buenos Aires wrote in May 1962. "Banker and chairwoman alike will tell you there is no community; your cab driver most probably will offer an unsolicited comment such as *'Pero qué país'* in a tone that leaves little doubt that he means 'what a lousy country.' "[36] One of the little literary reviews of that period caught the tone precisely in an article entitled "Argentina Doesn't Exist." Referring to the collective rancor that seemed to possess the country, it noted:[37]

"It is not directed against one disagreeable factor, defined if changing. It is not pointed at public transportation, salaries, the cost of living, nor . . . the misgovernment of Guido nor the Armed Forces. The Argentine's is a profound disgust; he is displeased with Argentina; he resents the country. The gentleman who waits in an interminable queue does not protest the lack of attendants; he who travels crushed in the depth of the omnibus does not rebel against *Transportes Buenos Aires;* the industrialist who has to bribe officials to obtain a credit does not complain about the Government; the laborer who has to work in three separate jobs to survive doesn't concentrate his invective against the enterprise which pays him so little. No, each one of them will generalize in his turn, saying, 'This is a country of . . .' "

Whatever the description, the phenomenon was the same and it was more or less uniform as between Buenos Aires and the rest of the country. In the middle sixties, an in-depth study was made of life in the city of Paraná, a middle-size regional center. The conclusions were instructive and included much evidence of the social fragmentation and discontent that marked the time and that were often reflected in the direct words of citizens who offered their views:

From the beginning of our independence we have continuously been searching for a savior—somebody to come from Mount Sinai to bring salvation . . . we remain an amorphous mass of people seeking for a savior.—The concept of neighborliness . . . has not been translated into social reality. There is a strong anomie in the situation. It is difficult for the middle class to form groups of a secondary nature. This may have something to do with the way people judge each other. There are always two opposite poles; left or right, good or bad, for or against. People look at each other in these terms and react to such distinctions.—There is a manifest lack of group action in the city to cope with the social problems and a high degree of disunity . . . — . . . It is difficult to understand this nation and this people. We have everything that is necessary to be an excellent nation, but I believe we lack spiritual fortitude . . . The majority agrees that it is necessary to live in a democracy, but they do not understand this deeply, I think . . . We want a democratic tyrant who will take us on the road to salvation. It is all very amorphous nowadays . . . We have a constitution copied from democratic nations, but it seems strange to our mentality and does not function well here.[38]

It was as if these residents of Paraná were anticipating the remark that Perón would make in 1973: "We are a politicized country, but without a political culture."[39]

The final comment of the last of the quoted citizens of Paraná seems prescient as well as representative—the formal political system seen as a strange and unworkable thing—for by the time the Illia administration fluttered to the ground this view had become implicit in the thought of many. Everything was beginning to be seen as unworkable: the juridical framework, the bombastic parties, the leaders themselves. Democracy itself as an ideal (however the conceptions of it might vary) was not under challenge, but the post-1955 variants of it were seen as deficient, as irresponsible, and as not even participatory, since the largest single grouping in the country, the Peronists, were excluded. But that merely pointed to the dilemma, for the Peronists were still a clear minority, and so was every other grouping in the country. The combined anti-Peronists, who were 60 to 70 percent of the populace, could agree at times on short-term negative objectives, but their divisions were so deep that their various separate minorities could achieve no governing majority.

Thus, although the incorporation of Peronism in the legitimate political process remained the single overriding operational issue, as unresolved as ever, the concerns of some had now begun to go beyond,

envisioning total impasse as the national problem, an impasse that
would still exist even if Peronism were allowed full participation. This
fear of total immobility under the existing system was the hidden
imperative that gave the new Onganía regime its distinctive quality.[40]

The government that succeeded Illia so easily and gently was, in
fact, quite different from anything that had gone before. It called
itself, rather impressively, the Argentine Revolution, and the claims
that it advanced for itself were not marked by abnegation. Forgoing
the usual cant about temporary and de facto measures and a "bridging role" and the expectation of early elections and so on, the Argentine Revolution asserted its constituent powers for the creation of a
new order. On its second day, the military junta that had designed
the coup issued a Statute of the Revolution that claimed and exercised
sweeping powers, a document paramount to the constitution that was
left in place. The statute announced that the new order would be "of
long duration," and what Onganía and his colleagues had in mind
with that term was perhaps fifteen to twenty years.[41] The statute also
announced that the Congress, the provincial legislatures, and all political parties were dissolved and that legislative powers had devolved
upon the president. The edicts he would promulgate were to have the
status not of the familiar decrees but of laws. All members of the
Supreme Court were soon replaced. The executives sent to rule the
provinces were no longer "interventors" but "governors," just as if
they had been elected. The military junta, having wrought these
astonishing changes, "elected" a president to preside over them, and
the choice, as everyone knew it would be, was General Juan Carlos
Onganía. But then there was a genuine surprise: contrary to all custom, the junta thereupon dissolved itself within twenty-four hours, in
reflection of Onganía's strong feelings against military involvement in
government.[42]

These developments brought General Onganía to the forefront of
attention for the first time in his fifty-two years. The successful leader
of the army *Azules,* and retired at the ill-advised insistence of President Illia, he remained the only officer with anything like unanimous
prestige, a status he had won by ability and professionalism.

In a personal sense, President Onganía was as different from the
usual run as was the Argentine Revolution among insurrectionary
movements. He was a man of very few words and he had left no trail
of utterance to trip him up. Not since Yrigoyen had so silent a leader
risen in the loquacious and histrionic world of Argentine politics. He
was aloof, austere, private. He came from a modest family and he had
none of the social and vocational connections that weigh so heavily in

the intertwined circles of his country. Without links to industry or the oligarchy or labor or the intellectuals, he was exclusively a man of the army, a soldier's soldier. He was a devout and practicing Catholic in a land where most men accepted the faith as a natural element of the Argentine environment, as something that did not require heavy thought. He was given to weekend spiritual retreats, known as *cursillos,* which stressed prayer and meditation. His honesty was unquestioned, for his morality took its strict lineaments from his piety. In the army, his guiding stars had been legality, hierarchy, vertical command, and abhorrence of political contamination. He fervently desired the departure of the armed forces from politics, and politics from the armed forces, and although he had accepted the overthrown of Illia because it was inevitable, he had done nothing to instigate it. On the contrary, he had refused to reach for power in the time of President Guido when he could have had it for the asking. His appearance now in the presidency, in response to the unanimous backing of his colleagues and a vacuum everywhere else, was a one-time exception mandated by circumstances. More typical of the man was his concept of the junta that dissolved itself in twenty-four hours.

Most typical of all, however, was a single anecdote that could stand as a portrait of General (and President) Onganía. Soon after he had assumed the presidency, he received a visit from a close associate, General Alejandro Lanusse. The two men had collaborated in the *Azules* movement; Lanusse had supported the Argentine Revolution and was now a senior commander on active duty. As he entered the presidential office, Onganía rose to greet his friend, inquiring at the same time whether the visit had been cleared with the commander in chief of the army (according to regulations). No, replied General Lanusse, the visit was purely personal, a social call. Onganía terminated the visit with three words: "Good afternoon, General."[43]

General Onganía entered the presidency with certain advantages and some distinct handicaps. His good fortune lay in the mood of the time, for he was welcomed on almost all sides. His silence had contributed to a mystique that hung about him. So little was known of this strong and mysterious man of so few words. In their eagerness to believe, many attributed to him sensibilities that he did not have and a modernizing mission foreign to him, and they were happy to ignore his authoritarian tendencies, his pre-Conciliar Catholic fundamentalism, and the fact that his political ideology was a blank page. Thus much of the public assumed that matters had finally been arranged on Mount Sinai, that all Argentine people and all Argentine hopes could now be united, and that the savior who had descended to do these things was now in the Casa Rosada. The intensity of this faith was directly proportional to the seriousness of the national crisis over the preceding decade. Therefore, Onganía began his term as president with a boundless mandate perhaps without national precedent. Certainly he had more freedom of action, more unfettered opportunity to work his will, than Perón had had in 1946.

Onganía's disadvantages were the obverse side of the qualities that made him attractive. If he had few enemies, neither did he have friends and associates. If there were no political blunders and hostilities on his record, neither was there political experience or skill. If morality was meaningful to him, so was righteous rigidity. His had usually been a lonely voice, but in politics the lonely voice lacks a chorus of supporting interests.

It followed that his administraton was strangely detached and that its evolution was in the direction of isolation. He could have built upon one or more of three important groups: labor, or the politicians, or the armed forces. But he counted upon none of these. Labor was not hostile to him at the outset, but he had no ghost of a relationship with the CGT or with the ranks of labor as individuals. It was clear from the Statute of the Revolution that all the works and the forms of the politicians had been swept aside. And as for the armed forces, after the military junta had been dissolved on June 29, 1966, President Onganía did not have a single meeting with any significant military group until May 1970, and his contacts with the armed forces leadership were held to the necessary minimum.[44] It was almost as if a circus acrobat were to attempt a difficult balancing act on a high wire but without benefit of the wire.

It is not surprising, therefore, that the initial euphoria faded into a general realization that the last word in saviors had not yet been pronounced. The administration's measures were not generally popular. The earliest among them was the intervention of all of the national universities, provoking mass resignations of faculty members and continuing student agitation. The reason was the belief of the government, shared widely by many social elements, including most of the Peronist movement, that the universities were cradles of subversion.[45] The economic measures of the government were likewise unpopular. An economic stabilization plan of the controversial Minister of Economy, Adalbert Krieger Vasena, looked to devaluation of the peso, monetary stability, and reductions in the inflation rate and the budget. The objectives were laudable but in practice the neoliberal programs seemed to favor capital rather than labor, industry rather than agriculture, and foreign rather than local ownership. Krieger Vasena's immense prestige abroad had only a faint echo at home.

The government's relations with labor were, on the whole, muted. The Peronists were so split between the Vandor faction that was inching toward independence and the loyalist faction now under José Alonso that there was little vitality left for a coordinated position respecting the administration.

In the social field, Onganía had in mind reorganizations that would emphasize community relationships, for he was concerned with the *desencuentro,* the dissociation among people that had preoccupied the citizens of Paraná in their appraisals of the nation. But time did not permit.

One of the problems of the government, general rather than specific, was its flavor and tone. The ascetic and almost monastic quality that was one aspect of President Onganía was multiplied in his administration, many of whose leaders were also men of the *cursillos.* Their common characteristics were probity, lack of political experience, a technological bent, a certain otherworldliness, and fertility, for they were Catholic family men in every sense. The question was, could purists so remote from Argentine reality govern such a difficult nation? The doubt was not dissipated by an early campaign, fortunately short-lived, aimed at stamping out miniskirts and kissing in public. The problems that can arise from unleavened virtue were in the mind of one of the leading bishops of the Church when he viewed a gathering of these appointees at a governmental function. With a sigh, he murmured, "When are they going to select some sinner?"[46]

It seems odd to fault an Argentine government on this score, but it was so much of a good thing that it contributed to the regime's image of anachronism. Avant garde manifestations and excesses were in vogue in much of the rest of the world, while in Argentina there was a medieval tinge, less the Renaissance that the nation had wanted than a throwback to Savonarola. The sinners who were everywhere except in the government were not pleased.

But all such problems, whether social or economic or political, were overshadowed in the third year of the Onganía government by a development that crystalized in 1969, brought down the administration in 1970, and changed the course of Argentine history for a decade: political violence had come to Argentina.

The Peronist Left and the Descent into Violence

The growth of Peronist left-wing tendencies had begun, rather modestly, as far back as the late 1950s. It was not a conversion of the

old non-Peronist leftists, but rather a radicalization of younger Peronists and the incorporation of various nationalists who thirsted for action.
Diverse in their origins and former loyalties, they had drifted into a
common belief in socialism, often Marxist in character, with emphasis
also on extreme populist orientations and a strongly anti-United States
nationalism. The progress of this leftism was jerky rather than continuous for the next decade, impeded by the hostility that the traditional
left had always felt for Peronism and by the failure of workers to
develop any militancy that went beyond their trade union demands
and the return of Perón. Then in the late 1960s, hardened in place
like some Maginot Line erected to prevent any middle-of-the-road
solution of the national ills, it settled into a general revolutionary
aspiration that soon found expression in urban guerrilla operations.[47]

Several developments favored the growth of a revolutionary leftist
cause at this time. The failure of the shotgun marriage between Perón
and Frondizi in 1958 and the early divorce of their parties had left
greater disillusionment among hopeful Peronists than one would have
anticipated, and some now saw salvation in a turn to direct action.
Many hard-edged Peronists were alarmed at the rise of Vandor and
his rejection of confrontation in favor of conciliation with Peronism-
without-Perón. Vandor gradually began to prevail within Peronist ranks
during the 1960s, although he never reached the point of cutting the
apron strings, but the very thought of such "apostasy" was enough to
edge some toward the barricades. The influence of Castro's revolution in Cuba could not really prevail against the anticommunism that
was basic in Peronism, but it could and did affect individual Peronists
who were innately of the left, such as John William Cooke.

The most significant impetus for a revolutionary movement, however, came from recent changes in Catholic doctrine and practice.
This was the era of Vatican II, of Pope John XXIII's *Pacem in terris*,
of Pope Paul VI's *Populorum progressio*, of the Colombian priest, Cam-
ilo Torres, who became a martyr to the guerrilla cause, of worker-
priests and the Third World Priests Movement, of dialogue with
Marxists and of churchly attacks on the profit motive, inequality, and
the sins of the rich nations. Beliefs of this kind, strongly supported by
the lower orders of the Church, cast a redeeming glow about actions
that would previously have been seen as the work of lawless ruffians.
The whole mood of the times was softened and prepared for the revolutionary stroke by this about-face of the Church, and the efforts of
the hierarchy to balance the trend by more moderate formulations
seemed to fade away in the excitement.

There was one more factor working in favor of the revolutionary option, and that was the statements of support that Perón made from time to time. He was too Creole and too linked to Argentine traditions and psychology to relate to leftist faiths of foreign origin. But in the 1960s, he was operating from a great distance in a political melee that seemed infinitely complex. Much juggling was necessary. This held visceral appeal for him, and no source of support would be turned away. He needed the loyalist CGT, the Vandorist CGT, the political Peronists and the neo-Peronists, the Peronist youth, and now that extreme left-wing Peronists had appeared with their talk of class struggle and violent encounter, he needed them, too.

In the early days of his exile, when life was less complicated, Perón had at times advocated violence but in a manner rather abstract. Tapes would come from some Caribbean place of exile suggesting the resort to force, or he would write in that vein to Cooke in their interminable correspondence. "The more violent we are the better," he had commented in a letter in November 1956.[48] But Perón could not develop a policy toward the revolutionary left in a vacuum, for the other elements of his perpetual balancing would not stand still. Everything interacted with everything else, and when the first test came, it was apparent that the revolutionary Perón had much less stamina than the Machiavellian political Perón. The test involved something called the Revolutionary Peronist Movement, the MRP.

This was an alliance of revolutionaries and less extreme reformists. Two thousand delegates assembled in Buenos Aires at its founding in August 1964 to hear a message of support from Perón. It seemed unequivocal, and it was. But it was also unreal. Perón had been alarmed at recent gains of the Vandor faction in the CGT and wanted to use the MRP as a warning shot across Vandor's bow. Vandor and his group rushed to Madrid and returned a couple of weeks later, having made their peace. They were back in line and they had their reward: written instructions from Perón appointing a Vandor colleague as Perón's delegate in Argentina, confirming the Justicialist Party as the only Peronist political organization, and expressly repudiating the MRP and his own delegate who had delivered his message to it, expelling him from the Peronist movement. The MRP dried up and died within days.[49]

But the far left would have its uses, and it would need encouragement. Perón's stimulus was equal to the task. He began to talk and write approvingly of "national socialism," a term that meant one thing to the old ultraright, which remembered the ideology of the Second World War, and quite another to young leftists already persuaded that Perón was a socialist at heart, waiting only for the strategic moment to reveal the faith that was his and theirs. Sometimes Perón's references were to "Christian national socialism," but this was not defined either. His language veered to the left in other respects that were persuasive to the already persuaded: ". . . the history of the world has been the history of the peoples against the imperialisms. From the Phoenicians to our times, the land has never been liberated from the rule of the imperialists. But neither have the peoples ceased to fight against them."[50] He was also expressing the strongest of his anti-United States views: "I believe completely the opposite of those who claim that we can't live without the United States . . . I am convinced that the worst scourge of our peoples is precisely the economic, political and social intervention of the United States in our countries."[51]

Much of this came to a head in a book written by Perón and first published in 1968, *La hora de los pueblos,* a volume that carried over, literally, some of the views expressed in his *Latina América: Ahora o Nunca.* Neither of these was among Peron's better performances. Filled with loose talk and silly history, they raised the question of his declining powers. The reader is informed that the British have met modern revolutionary requirements by a "directed evolution" that produced two main parties, of the left and of the right, "both managed from the Masonic central office; in other words, a single party divided into two wings." The reader also learns that the North Americans have met this requirement by organizing two parties of the right, "which permits them to maintain their plutocratic system and sustain theoretically a democratic simulation to deceive the fools, so abundant in politics, or to stimulate the scoundrels, who also abound."[52] Foolish though they be, these remarks are a commentary on Perón's cultural formation, yet another display of his belief that political creativity is necessarily born in the central power source.

But the significance of these works in the immediate context lay partly in their tilt toward the left-wing viewpoint, both in language and in concept. The oligarchy as the universal object of disdain was now joined by the bourgeoisie, a word and a group high on the leftist hate list. "The reign of the bourgeoisie has terminated throughout the world. The government of the peoples begins. With that, demi-liberalism and its consequence, capitalism, has ended its cycle; the future belongs to the peoples."[53] There was much support also for the Third World cause, then a favorite of the extreme left, and for *Justicialismo* as an example for its development and integration.[54]

In the year of *La Hora*'s publication, other events, not directly related to it, were preparing the way for the radical and guerrilla violence that would emerge full blown in 1970. A militant group known as the

Peronist Armed Forces, FAP, was formed for the original purpose of pursuing rural warfare. A small group known as the Descamisado Command appeared about the same time, as did the split in the Trotskyist ranks that would soon give birth to the People's Revolutionary Army, ERP, one of the most bitterly violent of the bands of the 1970s. And a tiny group of militants, a dozen in all, came together in Buenos Aires and Córdoba to form what would in time be known as the Montoneros, and to begin the two years of training and planning that would precede their spectacular entry into the national consciousness in 1970.[55]

The violence itself, apart from scattered instances in previous years, began in 1969, although its full blast coincided with the decade of the 1970s. In June 1969, fifteen supermarkets in Buenos Aires owned by a Rockefeller company were fire-bombed in protest against Nelson Rockefeller's visit to the city. The terrorists who did it were members of a group called the Revolutionary Armed Forces, FAR, founded in 1966 to support Che Guevara's Bolivian exploits, but not "Peronized" until 1971.[56] On the last day of the month came a dramatic stroke, the assassination of Augusto Vandor by members of the ENR, a shadowy "hit squad" that was probably a front for the Descamisado Command. The motive was punitive and purgative. The ERP held to its primitive conviction that Vandor's conciliatory labor policies constituted treason, and that traitors should be punished, and the movement purged, by execution.[57]

The events of June were sensational, but the most momentous development, the one that gave the year its character of a turning point, had already occurred in May. It involved violent protest, but it was of a different kind, with different motivations. It reflected popular discontent rather than the more specialized and esoteric grudges of the ideological and clandestine left.

Popular discontent was indeed a greater menace for the government and the nation than the more lurid capers of the guerrilla left. The activity of the latter, however harmful it might become in the short run, was an aberration, for it was alien to the society and commanded no wide allegiance or sympathy. Argentina, turbulent and ungovernable since 1930, was nevertheless not a country of violence, and the endless squabbles and coups had rarely been stained by blood. But if popular, as opposed to ideological, agitation were to take a violent turn, that would be an immediate threat to the government. And popular agitation there was, based on the unpopularity of the government as it revealed its true colors in action. The unpopularity was particularly severe among the few elements that had opposed

Onganía from the beginning, that is, the students and intellectuals who had suffered the brunt of the prompt and brutal interventions of the universities. It was this sector that now lighted a bonfire of civil strife.

It began in mid-May in total obscurity in Corrientes, one of the most obscure areas of the country, over the most obscure of causes, the price of food at the canteen of the local university. There was a student demonstration. Twenty-four were injured and one was killed. Sympathy strikes erupted in other universities, and a huge demonstration in Rosario brought another death. The army occupied Rosario and the local CGT called for a general strike. This developed into a larger strike in Córdoba on May 29 that exploded into two days of street violence, with shooting, barricades, the occupation of the central city by hot-headed protesters, and an orgy of looting, destruction, and chaos. The army occupied the city. Fourteen were dead and hundreds injured. This was the famous *cordobazo*.[58]

The government responded as best it could, which was not very well. The killing of Vandor a month later was followed immediately by imposition of a State of Siege. Krieger Vasena was replaced as minister of economy. In November, Onganía solemnly consecrated the Argentine nation to "the protection and divine invocation of the immaculate heart of Mary" at an elaborate ceremony in the Shrine of the Virgin of Luján. But the *cordobazo* had decided the fate of his administration. It struggled on for another eleven months, and then another dramatic event delivered the coup de grace.

On May 29, 1970, two young men called on ex-president Pedro Aramburu in his apartment in Buenos Aires and kidnapped him. They were dressed in military uniforms and told the retired general that they had come to serve as a bodyguard. Aramburu was an important national figure. President from 1955 to 1958, he had remained an influential power in the highest political circles and had polled a respectable vote in the 1963 elections for the presidency. The abduction of so prominent a leader, and his execution on June 1, was quite without precedent and was certain to reverberate from one end of the country to the other. Credit for the brazen stroke was claimed by a group that introduced itself to the public as the Montoneros: "Our organization is a union of men and women who are profoundly Argentine and Peronist, ready to fight with gun in hand for the seizure of power for Perón and his People, and the construction of a Free, Just, and Sovereign Fatherland." Their communiqué also referred to Justicialist doctrine and to Christian and nationalist inspiration.[59]

The Montoneros had selected the ex-president as their victim for several reasons. Partly because of his prominence; partly because he had been president at the time of the illegal executions after the Del Valle revolt in 1956; partly because it was he who had launched Evita's corpse on its mysterious travels; and partly because for more than a year he had been working behind the scenes for an end to the Onganía government and for resort to an electoral solution that would entail the splitting of the Peronist movement through enticement of the more moderate and flexible leaders into a broad electoral alliance. But that would be the end of Peronism as the revolutionary force that the Montoneros believed it to be, and for them any conciliatory solution was death itself.

But who were the Montoneros? Unknown as individuals, they still numbered in June 1970 only the original twelve, now hardened by their two years of preparation. Of the founders, few had come to maturity as Peronists and there had been little or no leftist influence on their development. Their political origins were in conservative and traditional Catholicism, and in the organization known as the Tacuara, an action-oriented right-wing organization of the firmest persuasion, colored by Falangist principles. But ideology in a pure sense was secondary in the development of these militants. Nationalism was a more potent driving force, and so was the psychological commitment to violent and direct action. These were the two constants in their evolution, and it was a coincidence of the times, in the form of their encounter with radical Catholicism and the indoctrination offered by left-wing priests, that gave precise contours to those two forces. Nationalism and direct action were now blended with radical Catholic notions of social justice, and the progression to revolutionary Peronism came naturally.[60]

That transition was immeasurably facilitated by the Creole personality that the early Montoneros cultivated, doubtless sincerely: ". . . a union of men and women who are profoundly Argentine and Peronist . . . ," in the words of the early Montonero communiqué. Resistant to Marxism, as others of the extremists were not, the Montoneros drew upon historic imagery and legend. Their very name revived old deeds now embellished with myth, for the original Montoneros were the bands of rough gaucho horsemen who had fought behind their *caudillos* in the era of independence. In their field operations that were soon to come against banks, military posts, and similar targets, the reborn Montoneros were sometimes garbed in the blue of the national flag. Their interviews and pronouncements invoked the metaphors and symbols of the national past. Their motto was itself an affirmation of the extremism and the resistance to compromise that was so striking a feature of the civilization: All or Nothing.

In the uproar that followed the abduction of Aramburu, 22,000 men were mobilized to find his body and apprehend his kidnappers. The body was found in mid-July, buried beneath the cellar of an *estancia* in Buenos Aires Province[61] where he had been held, but the kidnappers eluded capture and next surfaced on July 1, in La Calera, in Córdoba Province, where they took over the bank, the police station, and the town hall before retreating. Early in September came another remarkable bank robbery, again an operation of almost military scope and precision. But by this time there had been heavy losses to the security apparatus and recruitment was slow, so that by the end of 1970 there were still only about twenty members. They had been less consistently active than the FAP, the best entrenched of the urban guerrilla operations, but they had dramatized the revolutionary struggle and caught the public imagination.[62]

The Onganía government could not survive these wild doings, and the president was brought down by military pressure on June 8.[63] The succession went to an inconspicuous general, Roberto Levingston, so little known to the public that the announcement of his selection as president was accompanied by a curriculum vitae and a photograph, as if a corporation were issuing a press release about the appointment of a new Marketing Director for a regional subsidiary. It must be said that during the nine months he held office the new president did little to efface the anonymity in which he had arrived. Violence continued, with the assassination in August of José Alonso, the prominent Peronist CGT leader who was considered by the ENR as blemished, like Vandor, by a conciliatory taint. For a time, Montonero activity took the form of robberies and raids with few fatalities. The new minister of economy had sound ideas but they were lost in the inflation, in the political tossing and turning that negated all plans, and in the labor strikes and militancy. The common assumption that the regime would quickly open the path to new elections drooped as Levingston began to talk in terms of four or five years.[64]

Broad public unrest was obvious, and the Montoneros seemed to awaken a sympathetic response among many, particularly Third World enthusiasts, youth, and some Peronists. At the funeral of two slain Montonero founders in September 1970, one of whom had been an abductor of ex-president Aramburu, one of the presiding priests was Father Hernán Benítez, Evita's confessor, who now thanked the Lord for the two young men, accusing the nation of having murdered them. Leading Peronists attended, and Perón himself sent a wreath.[65] Catholic Action groups were beginning to weave an aura of martyrdom around dead militants. Things were not going well.

Again it was Córdoba that sealed the fate of a government. In March 1971 came the "little *Cordobazo,*" the *Cordobacito,* not a guerrilla insurrection but another popular uprising that was the visible surface of very deep discontents. Again there were barricades and chaos in the streets and a general strike, millions of dollars in burned and destroyed property, and occupation by army troops, 3,500 of them.[66] General Lanusse, the dominant member of the chiefs of staff, who more than any other military leader desired a prompt electoral solution along tolerant lines, recognized a hopeless position and decided to intervene, outlining a policy contrary to Levingston's. The president went peacefully, and on March 23, General Lanusse assumed the presidency.[67]

The way was thus prepared for negotiations between the government of the Argentine Revolution and Perón for the restoration of a constitutional order. It was realized now on all sides that Peronism would have a place in that order, and that the admission of Peronism into the public system would help to inoculate both of these against the infections of the far left. It would be a Peronism with or without Perón, depending on how the balance of forces and skills came to rest. The agonies of time present were assuaged a little by the hint of time past, for the central theme of the admission of the prodigal recalled the legitimization of Radicalism in the days of Roque Sáenz Peña and Yrigoyen.[68]

And since ours is a charismatic movement, what will
be left after me will be a mere political party, it won't
be good for anything. It will be destroyed within
hours of my burial . . .

Concerning my eventual heir, it's a question that I've
been arranging for years through the institutionali-
zation of the movement.

— Juan D. Perón in Enrique Pavon Pereyra, *Conversaciónes
con Juan Domingo Perón*

12. The Return of the Phoenix

The End of Exile

THE ESTABLISHED ROUTINES of daily life in Madrid continued unchanged into the early 1970s, although there were now more
and more guests and delegations and continuous writing and correspondence. Despite the rather erratic waning of Peron's health, there
were intervals of travel or other activity in which the old undiminished Perón stood forth. His interest in sports, fencing and boxing in
particular, never left him. Indeed, the social essence of the man, consisting in part of an amiable and gregarious informality, never changed
with age, appearing in its undiluted form in an episode late in the
1960s. An Argentine business man named Ronald Crosby had found
himself, through an improbable sequence of events, in a charity boxing exhibition, matched against an over-the-hill pugilist named Peralta. Crosby survived, with some broken ribs, and Peralta invited him
to a return match in Madrid, where the latter was going to live, saying
that he would get "the old man" to referee the fight. The match was
scheduled, and Perón was in his element, bounding around the ring
in obvious happiness. He liked the way Crosby was willing to take a
hammering for charity, and told him that he was "my kind of man,"
adding an invitation back to the house for a drink. The drink led to
repeated visits by Crosby and his wife for get-acquainted talks that
lasted for most of a week.[1]

Nevertheless, in the last years of exile two changes were at work whose effects on Perón, on Peronism, and on Argentina would be great. The first was in the role and personality of Isabel. She began to move beyond the horizons of the hostess, the greeter, the walking companion, the household sprite who appeared at teatime. Jorge Antonio, attempting to direct from Paraguay the forthcoming congressional elections in Argentina, began to feel the efforts of the Argentine government to extradite him. Perón decided to bolster General Stroessner's resolution with a letter and a personal plea for Antonio's continued welcome in Asunción, and delivered both of them through Isabel. She arrived in Paraguay toward the end of April 1965, intending to remain three days. But Antonio urged her to stay on, and she did so happily, devoting herself to the hundreds of visitors who poured across the border to talk, to view, to touch. She preached the political messages of Perón, sought to align the Peronist troops, and lobbied President Stroessner. She stayed in his country for about two months in this political baptism.[2]

Soon after her return to Spain, Antonio received a letter from Perón referring to changes in Isabel that he described as ". . . of great importance." And indeed they were, for they marked the beginning of a political ambition that would change her view of Perón and of herself. She would not become another Evita, probably not even in her own imagination, but she would see herself as a woman who had a mission as the wife of a remarkable political leader and as a political actor of some importance in her own right.

The Peronists had shown unexpected strength in the March elections of 1965, and an important provincial election was scheduled for April 1966 in Mendoza, where the Vandor elements were promoting a schism. Isabel arrived in Buenos Aires in October 1965 for a major intervention, armed with a letter and a casette from Perón. This time she remained for nine months, during which the Peronista loyalists got the better of the Vandorists in Mendoza. She was continuously immersed in the give-and-take and her ambition expanded, not dramatically but surely. Perón gave her high praise.[3]

The vistas now opening changed the relationship of Isabel and Perón. Her sentiments at first had been those of respect and consideration, while Perón's had been almost paternal. The extreme difference in their ages and Perón's preference for unions based upon comfort and company rather than upon passion almost assured this. But after 1965 there was a difference. Isabel, without abandoning her admiration, now began to see herself as allied in a political crusade with Perón, from whom she had learned much but to whom she was no longer subordinated by natural destiny. It does not appear that their mutual affection had ever been set aglow,[4] but the marriage worked—most of the time, that is, for on occasion there were hard disputes between them, less dramatic, but much better authenticated, than those attributed by idle rumor to Evita's marriage. Isabel at least once left Perón and the house for a brief period and went to stay with friends.[5]

One of the most poignant moments in the marriage tells of the lack of deep emotional commitment. As Perón was about to be wheeled to the operating room for one of his prostate operations in the late 1960s, he asked that Jorge Antonio be allowed to accompany him. Permission was granted and Antonio was present throughout. After the period in the recovery room, Perón was returned to his own room, where Isabel waited. The anesthetic began to wear off, and Perón, still in deep lethargy, murmured, "Eva, please don't leave me alone, don't go, stay with me, I need you, I need you more than ever." And struggling to move his hand a bit, he touched Isabel's hand on the edge of the bed, murmuring again, "Evita, don't leave me."[6]

The second change that left its mark upon the decade was one of the curiosities of Argentine history, the coming of José López Rega. He appeared from nowhere. Nine years later he returned to nowhere. During much of the period in between, his power and influence, always unofficial and, at times, official as well, were probably second to those of no other Argentine, Perón alone excepted. And in the year following Perón's death, he was supreme. Strange men had appeared in the Argentine political scene before; Yrigoyen was unusual to the point of strangeness, But López Rega went beyond all that. He was weird.[7]

Rarely has so much political power emerged from a base of so little substance. López Rega had once been a corporal in the Buenos Aires police force, a rank near the bottom, and he had served in dull and routine assignments. He was a failed singer of immodest dreams and modest ability. And he had taken to spiritualism and the occult as a career, writing several unintelligible tomes that he printed with his own small press. The title of the largest, *Astrología esoterica: Secretos develados,* Esoteric Astrology: Secrets Unveiled, suggests the nature of these works. The surprised reader is told that the material came from God, who wished to share it with the author, and that, in another case, the book was written in conjunction with the Archangel Gabriel, who descended to commune with López Rega in his sleep. The writings are thick with "forces" and "patterns" and "signs" and provided the basis for the man's early venture into business, a brief fling (together with an impressionable army officer) at a "beauty institute," where women could learn how to relate their grooming to the astrological forces governing them.[8]

This was the unheralded dark power who turned the gaze of his cold blue eyes upon Isabel when they were introduced during her 1965–66 stay in Argentina, a meeting he had contrived through an intermediary of disputed identity. She responded not to the physical image of this rather routine-appearing man of forty-nine but to the otherworldly aura that those of similar bent sensed about him. Isabel, like Perón, was open to the phenomena of the occult, not in an extreme sense but in the style of interested toleration. López Rega wormed his way into her confidence, a confidence that would later become dependency. He persuaded her to take him back with her to Madrid as her secretary, abandoning his wife and daughter. When he got there he happily accepted every menial task. He did anything to make himself useful and necessary. But not for very long, for the day was not distant when he would acquire over Isabel the strange dominance that Rasputin achieved over the Tsarina Alexandra, or that Du Maurier's Svengali held over Trilby. It was the kind of dominance that many Argentines attributed to witchcraft, and López Rega came to acquire the sobriquet *El Brujo,* the male witch, or warlock.

Jorge Antonio became aware of this new development in the summer of 1966, soon after Isabel and the bizarre secretary had returned. Perón appeared in Antonio's office in a rage.

"Isabel has come back with a secretary named López Rega. I don't want him in the house for anything."

But Jorge Antonio was soon to learn about the matter on his own. López Rega turned up in his office one day, bringing a gift, a proposition, and a threat.

"Look, Jorge Antonio," he began. "I know that you're the person who has the most influence over Perón. I've come to tell you that it's going to work out well for everyone. Because look," and he produced the gift, a shopworn copy of his *Astrología esoterica,* which he proceeded to inscribe to Antonio, "It's all written here. Everything you have to know to succeed. We're going to make a kind of council: Isabel, you and I. Because nobody has influence over Isabel like I have. And there's another thing. If you don't accept this, I'll screw you."

"To hell with you!" Antonio replied, precipitating the warlock's departure. As López Rega left, Antonio aimed a kick at him and threw *Astrología esoterica* at his head, the heavy volume breaking in two. Undaunted, the extraordinary warlock paused for a final word as he passed the threshold: "You're going to go along with me, eh?"[9]

For a year or more, López Rega lived in a tiny apartment by himself, and then one day Isabel left her house, saying to Perón "Either he comes or I go."[10] It was not long before López Rega came to live in the small home of the man who disliked him, achieving the title of Perón's private secretary. He was the source of infinite mischief between Perón and Isabel and within the entire inner circle of Peronism, for no one except Isabel liked him or could manage even a minor degree of trust in him. On the side he dabbled in business ventures that were invariably unsuccessful. Perón was furious to discover in 1967 that López Rega had been marketing in Brazil a restorative tonic that featured a drawing of Perón on the label, with the notation that he retained his youth by drinking this product. He ordered López Rega from the house and thereby brought on a difficult confrontation with Isabel, who finally managed to reverse the decision.[11] Another sour business involved the exportation of wigs, and López Rega attributed its failure to the machinations of rival warlocks. But he remained at the center of Peronism, doing odd jobs, intruding into political decisions, preparing astrological charts on leading army officers,[12] diverting those he thought should not get to see Peron, creating with the impressionable and probably well-meaning Isabel an invisible but powerful cordon around the most popular leader Argentina had ever known, fulfilling the boast he had made in Jorge Antonio's office.

It was a sorrowful time for Antonio because it also brought a parting of the ways with Isabel. In 1970, he acted as an intermediary on Perón's behalf with an Argentine army officer. Isabel learned of it and became distrustful, fearing a plot of some kind. She berated Antonio furiously when he next visited, shouting that he was not to have any more meeting with military men. He took deep offense.

"Calm yourself, Señora, please . . . I'm not going to suggest meetings again . . . but it's finished here. I will not set foot in your house again, Señora."

Perón was afflicted, pleading "Jorge, please . . . please . . ." He accompanied Antonio as the latter left, saying, "Please, Jorge, nothing has happened. Tomorrow Isabelita will have forgotten about it." A little later he again attempted a reconciliation.

"Day after tomorrow, Jorge, five in the afternoon, a few friends are coming to the house . . . come and have tea, because Isabelita is sorry."

"Never again in my life, General," Antonio replied. He was true to his word, for the dignity so prized by his tradition demanded no less. Thereafter he telephoned Perón at his home only during certain hours agreed upon, when Perón would be there.[13]

Most of these personal problems originated with López Rega and his devious ways and purposes. They deepened Perón's dependency on the structure gradually being built up around him, while at the same time distracting and fragmenting those who had been his intimates. It was the worst of times for such a development because the political process in Argentina was quickening. And the determination of President Lanusse to achieve a prompt electoral solution meant that the critical hour for a possible Peronist restoration was at hand.

The complications facing Perón were increasing. He was still preoccupied with the balance between the conciliatory and the militant wings of the labor movement, and in July 1970, the CGT was reunited under the leadership of a firm Peronist, José Rucci of the Metalworkers' Union. It did not bring much comfort to José Alonso, the pro-Peronist leader who had vied with Vandor, for the extreme left found him likewise insufficiently militant and the ENR in August disposed of him as it had Vandor—with bullets. By 1970, Peronism was rooted more completely than ever before in the labor movement, since middle-class and professional elements that had once adhered out of conviction or opportunism had by now slipped away, and this meant a certain loss of maneuvering room for Perón.[14] This would change again in 1971 and 1972 as many Argentines began to feel that the nation had run out of alternatives and that perhaps only Perón and his new emphasis on national unity could bring salvation. So the monolithic reliance on labor and an attempt to reach out to others, particularly students and intellectuals, would henceforth have to be balanced.[15]

Above all, however, an equilibrium would have to be maintained between the forces of right and far left. As violence swelled, the juggling of left, center, and right became more imperative and increasingly difficult. The complexity and the ever-varying ideologies of the left complicated matters even more, as some were Trotskyist in derivation and program, while others were Guevarist in orientation, or devotees of urban guerrilla warfare.[16] The Montoneros, who came to occupy a leading position in the confusing ranks of the left, were Socialist but not Marxist, anti-imperialist, and full of Third World consciousness that exalted national liberation over class struggle.[17]

One quality that many of these groups held in common, however, although it was strongest among the Montoneros and absent within the ERP, was a certain naiveté concerning Perón. This was often accompanied by a serious misreading of Argentine history. They insisted that Perón was a revolutionary, a national socialist in their own image, and that everything that pointed in a different direction was a tactic on his part. Thus obsessed, they easily forgot that Perón's record was one of electoral solutions, class-conciliation in the interests of an organized community, and firm opposition to socialism as well as communism.[18]

Perón's opponent in the political cut and thrust and parry of the early seventies was the new president, General Lanusse. Unlike Onganía, he had a strong class connection in that his family was old and established, well-to-do, and identified with the landowning elite of the ancient Liberal System. His anti-Peronist credentials were unquestioned, since he had spent four years in prison after the failed military uprising against Perón in 1951. But he had a broader and more realistic vision than most, and a less tenacious grip on personal grudges.[19] His concept of a Great National Accord was generous and advanced: an alliance that would unite moderate Peronists with the traditional anti-Peronists, isolating the militant left; the return of Perón, who would participate in the process; and elections, open to Peronists other than Perón himself, which would deprive the extreme left of legitimacy.[20] Actions calculated to implement this design followed quickly.

In July 1971, political activity and the party organizations were restored. President Lanusse had already indicated in an interview with C. L. Sulzberger of the *New York Times* that he was willing to negotiate with Perón directly, and the Justicialist Party was given legal recognition in January 1972.[21]

With these steps came various gestures designed to reinforce them through the removal of sticking points that had acquired a life of their own. Perón's presidential pension was revived in July, with payment of the amounts accrued since his fall in 1955, and the statutory rape charge involving Nelly Rivas, pending since the days of Illia, was dropped. But the most important of the gestures was as sensitive and profound in its symbolism as imagination could conceive. This was the return of the coffin and the corpse of Evita.

Since the day the corpse disappeared so mysteriously, in 1956, its recovery had been at the top of the agenda of the radical left. The Montoneros, in particular, had elevated Evita into a cult. The Argentine preoccupation with the rituals and symbols of death was itself a sensitizing factor in the loss of the corpse. Inevitably, a scrambled undergrowth of rumor and legend grew almost immediately around the only fact known with certainty, that the body had disappeared. There was talk of midnight showings of the coffin, of candles and flowers that followed its alleged movements, of false coffins filled with ballast to confuse the trail, of enemies who urinated upon the corpse, of an envelope, delivered to Aramburu and to be opened after his death, which contained the name of a dead priest and a cemetery in Milan, of Aramburu's alleged confession to the Montoneros that the body was in Rome, and much else that was spectacularly romantic.

In fact, the coffin had been buried in a cemetery in Milan under the name of María Maggi de Magistris. When the time for its reappearance came in 1971, it was exhumed and transported across Europe by hearse and van. On the night of September 23, it arrived at Perón's house in Madrid with an escort of police jeeps. It was carried into the living room where Perón, Isabel, Jorge Paladino (Perón's current top representative in Argentina), López Rega, Jorge Rojas Silveyra (the Argentine ambassador to Spain), and a pair of monks were assembled. The top was pried off. There was a bit of dampness inside, minor disturbances, and a flattened nose on the mummified body, but the state of preservation testified to the meticulous and macabre work of Dr. Ara in the hours following Evita's death. They gazed in silence upon the legendary being thus strangely restored to those who lived and remembered.

"It's Evita," Perón said. Isabel fingered the blonde tresses, removing the rusted and broken hairpins.[22]

Lanusse took the plunge in October 1971, announcing that elections would be held in March 1973. In a sense, this was the culmination of a line of action that Perón had inaugurated in November 1970, when he had sponsored an alliance called the "Hour of the People," a coalition of Peronists, the Radicals associated with Ricardo Balbín, the Popular Conservative Party, and several lesser groupings.[23]

The Hour of the People was viewed dimly by Peronists who were of leftist faith. But, oddly, Perón's reputation for slippery tactics, which would normally be a cause for distrust, was henceforth to serve as a source of trust for the Montoneros and others. Their reasoning was simple, but quite erroneous: here was Perón dealing with moderate elements and traditional forces; but they knew in their hearts that Perón was really a revolutionary; surely, therefore, the Hour of the People was a large tactic calculated to confuse and to gain time for the revolution. Mistaken though it was, this view was not an absurdity, for Perón kept stoking it with plausibility. Almost as if to confirm the distorted vision of the left, Perón appeared to support it soon after the announcement of elections, when he replaced a moderate personal representative, Jorge Paladino, with Héctor Cámpora, one of the most malleable men ever to hold high office.

Cámpora, a dentist, had dabbled in Peronism for years. He was one of the group that had been jailed in Patagonia in 1957, the group that had included Jorge Antonio and John William Cooke. He had prayed much in jail, promising God never to return to political activity,[24] and when he escaped it was due to the efforts of others more determined and competent than he. Without a political base in the labor movement or in Peronist politics, and having no other place to lean, he inclined toward the left. But his appointment by Perón at this juncture probably represented less a gesture to the left than Perón's conviction that Paladino had concentrated on negotiation and conciliation to the exclusion of the hard-line alternatives that Perón also wished to stress at the same time, following his double-barrelled approach, the so-called integral strategy. Nothing else, he thought, would preserve all options and maintain maximum pressure on the Lanusse government. As for the leftists who hailed Cámpora's appointment as the harbinger of the new and true Perón, they failed to note and evaluate the appointment by Perón, in the same month, of a military and political advisor, Lieutenant Colonel Jorge Osinde, a man of the hard right with whom their destiny would rendezvous in blood and recrimination two years later.[25]

Meanwhile, in Madrid, Perón was presiding over other initiatives for reconciliation. His rhetoric revealed the change. In the time of the Peronato, one of the standard maxims had been, "For a Peronist there is nothing better than another Peronist." Now the word "Argentine" was substituted for "Peronist" in each case.[26] More significantly, Perón turned to his tradition, to his deep preference, and invoked the shades of the organized community in the form of the social pact. This was an agreement, research for which was begun in 1971, between the CGT and the CGE, the organization representing various employers. Its purpose was to settle wage and price policies for a new administration, with freezes and controls so adjusted that both labor and capital could live with them. The social pact was to prove more than a campaign exercise, and it came to life in the third Perón administration and thereafter.[27]

A shorter-lived vehicle was the Civic Front of National Liberation, FRECILINA, which appeared in July 1972. This was another coalition that included, of all people, ex-president Arturo Frondizi, who apparently had not lost his appetite for election agreements with Perón.[28]

All this evidence of fraternity, however, was disturbing to the hard-nosed among the military, whom Lanusse had to balance and appease. Murmurs grew that Perón was about to take a yard rather than an inch, and Lanusse had to insure that his concept of an invitation to

Peronism would not benefit the man who personified it. An outright restriction on Perón would be too drastic for the mood of the moment, and Lanusse found a more subtle way. On July 7, in a speech to an armed forces banquet, he announced a government decision: any candidate for the 1973 presidential elections would have to be residing in Argentina by August 25, 1972, a time interval that he knew was too short for Perón to comply with.[29] Perón rejected the condition almost immediately, for reasons of image and prestige.

But negotiations continued. There was even a brief attempt by Perón and Lanusse to negotiate directly, through the channel of a government minister. A "plan for reconciliation" emerged from this, presented to the government by Cámpora on behalf of Perón on October 4. It would seem that a proposal thus jointly sponsored and that was immediately praised by both sides would have excellent prospects, but this would underestimate the possibilities for discord in the Argentine politics of the 1970s. Of course, the plan had to be discussed, and that became the problem: who would discuss it, and with whom? On this they could not agree, and the idea languished and died in the universal distrust and confusion.[30]

Although the air was filled with projects and promises of conciliation and alliance, Perón would not lessen his support for the violent left, which was doing its best to disrupt conciliation and alliance. Nothing seemed too extreme for him to say in defense of the revolutionary option. In February 1971, replying to a Montonero letter that assumed his electoral strategy was a mere tactic, he stated, ". . . As to the electoral option, I don't believe in it either."[31] In the summer of the same year, Perón released a filmed interview in which he approved violence, dismissed elections as a tactic, saluted fallen and jailed leftists, and quoted Mao Tse-tung.[32] At the end of the year, he wrote to Montonero sources, telling their activists to hit the regime until it fell.[33] In March and April 1972, the nation was shocked by the useless and brutal kidnapping and killing of a FIAT executive, but Perón expressly refused, when requested by Lanusse's representative, to condemn the affair, even though the guerrillas who did it, the ERP, were not Peronists. At the end of 1972, he told a news conference in Madrid that if he were fifty years younger he, too, would go around "planting bombs and taking justice into my own hands."[34] To the day of his inauguration he continued unvaryingly to insist that these murderous excesses were the natural reaction of the people to the government's violence, and that when the government changed, the bloodletting would cease.

How to account for this taste for violence on the part of one who had never used it? There are a number of explanations. Whether they also serve as justifications raises interesting moral issues. First, Perón was engaged in a struggle against a military regime that he deeply distrusted, attempting by every available leverage to force it into elections he was sure Peronism would win. The left was a substantial and blindly devoted element. Can one reject such a potent and useful ally before the balloting? Second, the left, and particulaly the Montonero left, with its spectacular dramas of violence and its colorful capers that echoed Robin Hood, had found a sympathetic response in parts of the public who obscrved with fascination. Third, the left was useful in moderating what might otherwise have become unrestrained and monolithic labor union power.[35] Fourth, Perón realized what the left did not: the left could never come to power because it lacked a genuine base. It had no foothold, much less a foundation, in the labor movement. Its numbers, he knew, were limited—he estimated its extent as no more than 10 percent of the total Peronist vote.[36] To him it was a condiment rather than a staple of political diet: "The left is like the vinegar in the salad. You have to put a little in so you can eat it."[37] Fifth, it is apparent that Perón overestimated his ability to control the left at such time as he might return to power.

This is attested by Perón's comments in a discussion with Jorge Antonio, a little before Perón's return to Argentina. He had been recording one of his hard-line statements calling for a revolutionary solution, and Antonio remarked,

"And these young people, General, at the proper time are you going to be able to control them?"

Perón was confident. "When I'm in the country, Jorge, I'll say four words to them, and they'll fall in line."

"I'm not so sure about that," Jorge Antonio replied. "Things have changed, and they are still changing."

"You're going to see it, you'll see it."[38]

But the tactic of unwavering support for violent solutions raises questions that go beyond brass-knuckle politics. Even if one grants that Perón's strategy contradicted his tactics, that his ultimate intentions were sound, that only he commanded the following and the prestige necessary to heal the country, and that he could do no healing unless he could first get elected, a hard reality remains: the warfare initiated by the left in the late 1960s and 1970s, and the counterwarfare that it inevitably provoked, introduced immeasurable sorrow and devastation and contamination into Argentine life. The consequences resonate even today, and they will remain until the last of the generation that lived through so much blood and terror has passed away. Is any potential healer morally entitled to take upon himself the responsibility of an infallible destiny and mission? And if so, may he stand by while the patient sinks into a coma (and even help to accelerate the decline) because he is confident that when conditions are sufficiently desperate he will be called in to practice his arts? There are endless shadings and complexities here, and the questions are not easy. But one may ask them.[39]

Perón decided to visit Argentina in November 1972, to prepare his forces for the 1973 elections and to construct the electoral front that he had been negotiating. He flew first to Rome, where he was met by about 130 enthusiastic Peronists headed by Héctor Cámpora, who had flown in on a chartered plane so they could accompany Perón on the flight to Argentina.[40] On November 17, the huge entourage landed in Buenos Aires, where preparations had been made on a rather fantastic scale. Demonstrations were banned, a paid holiday had been declared to ward off a general strike, radio stations and public utilities had been put under police protection, firearm permits had been revoked, troop deployments were ordered, Ezeiza Airport was guarded by roadblocks and designated a military zone, naval ships were sent on "special maneuvers," and public schools were suspended.[41]

Perón was home for the moment, and none of his neighbors would forget it. On a previous trip, Isabel had acquired a residence, paid for by Perón's followers, in the suburb of Vicente López. It was a three-story house of white brick and cement on a quiet street lined with plane trees and acacias. Now the throngs that had missed Perón at the strictly controlled airport swarmed into the placid neighborhood, a hundred thousand enthusiasts, trampling gardens, mashing a three-foot brick wall with their sheer mass and weight, splintering hedges, and painting slogans such as "Perón: Revolution" on the neighbors' walls. It looked, as a reporter put it, ". . . as though a herd of elephants followed by a wave of locusts had passed through."[42] Perón and Isabel apologized to the neighbors, and a Peronist fund paid for the repairs.

Except for its circuslike beginning, the visit took on a subdued tone. Perón was little in evidence, appearing from time to time at a window in his home, sometimes in pajamas, to wave to followers outside. He held one press conference. He attended a lengthy meeting of assorted political leaders who might be grist for the mill of coalition, but little was achieved. There were twenty-four speakers, beginning with Perón, and one of those present characterized the performances as "a monologue in twenty-four parts."[43] Otherwise, Perón rarely ventured out of his home, preferring to negotiate there at ease. His age and his quickly fading energy were noted and his generally subdued activity was a bewilderment to many, among whom was the not-untypical young student who complained, "The Peronist Youth expected him to lead a Socialist revolution and now we're completely disoriented. But he's just sitting at home and wheeling and dealing like any old politician." Instead of wild calls to action, activists of this stripe heard a very different message from the old leader, speaking from the window of his home: "I want to ask you to stay calm and be prudent."[44]

The political groupings could not agree on a grand alliance. The Balbín Radicals and some others found certain of the Peronists' demands too suffocating and they went their own way. What survived was a lesser alliance dominated by the Peronist Justicialist Party and including Frondizi's group and fourteen minor aggregations. This coalition, which proceeded to nominate Perón in spite of the legal prohibition, was known as the Justicialist Front of National Liberation, FREJULI.[45] There were no discussions or negotiations during this trip between Perón and representatives of President Lanusse.

On December 14, Perón returned to Madrid by way of Paraguay and Peru. He left behind a statement, conciliatory in tone, calling for continued peace and declining, with thanks, the FREJULI presidential nomination, which he could not have accepted in any case. Two days later, the Justicialist Party and FREJULI held their nominating conventions, and Perón's decision on the candidate who would be substituted for him was revealed.[46] It was Héctor Cámpora, and it produced reactions ranging from incredulity to anger to resignation. But habit prevailed, as did the authoritarian principles of Peronism. Cámpora was nominated, as was Perón's selection for vice president, Vicente Solano Lima, a former Conservative who now worked closely with the Peronists. The Justicialist Party action automatically mandated similar action by FREJULI. In the aftermath, however, Perón's unexpected designation of Cámpora aroused much speculation. Theories and variations of theories abounded. Some saw it as some kind of power play by López Rega. Others suggested that it was part of an intricate plot by Perón to bring about cancellation of the elections so that he could profit from further confusion. None of these gossamer spinnings had substance. The reality was more direct and simple, however astonishing it may have been in its cynical manipulation of a weak reed. And it had all been decided before Perón arrived in Argentina in November.

One day in Madrid, late in 1972, Perón had appeared at the office of Jorge Antonio. He picked up three ashtrays on Antonio's desk, sat down, and started to talk.

"Look, Jorge, we have to choose a presidential candidate. If you were in the country, maybe it would be easier, but the two of us are here. We have three candidates among the possibilities—there are others, but we have three candidates who are in Madrid now. One of them is Cámpora." And he placed an ashtray alongside on the desk. "Another is Dr. Benítez [Antonio Benítez, a leading Peronist, who had once headed the Chamber of Deputies]." And he placed another ashtray alongside the first. "And the third is Dr. Taiana [an eminent surgeon, a moderate Peronist and once a physician for Evita]." And the third ashtry was added to the line on the desk. "Which would you choose?"

"General," Jorge Antonio said, "why are you involving me in this business when you've already decided?"

"Okay, but I want your opinion."

"I'm not going to give my opinion. I know that you've already chosen the candidate."

"All right, look," Perón continued. "The most competent one is Dr. Taiana, but he has an in-law who is a general, and the pressure of the generals might mean he couldn't impose Peronism the way it needs to be in Argentina. The second one is Dr. Benítez. He's from Corrientes, he's a Peronist, he's brilliant, but he's very political. I'm not sure, if he came to power, that we could control the situation with him. The third one is Cámpora, who's going to do what I say, but I'm always going to tell him to do what the country needs. What do you think?"

"I know that you've already decided, and that's why I'm not going to give you my opinion."

"If it works out, when he complies with his agreement with me, he'll have fifteen days in power. Then we'll call for new elections, and the people will elect whom they want. If I'm it, then it will be me, and it it's not me, God will say. But I'm sure it's going to be me."

"Very well, General, but if it's all decided, why this conversation?"

"Out of respect to you. You're my friend and I also want your opinion and I want you to know about it."

They continued the talk, now about Solano Lima. "Invite him to Madrid," Perón requested, "and we'll propose to him that he be the vice president—because he's a gentleman, he's our friend. He was a political enemy, but he's a gentleman who has fine qualities and he'll do for this. He'll be the brake on Cámpora."

Later, when Perón was preparing to leave for Buenos Aires, Jorge Antonio reverted to the subject of Cámpora, voicing a concern to Perón.

"General, what if Cámpora later on feels that he really is the president?"

"Don't worry," Perón replied, "he's not going to feel that he's the president. If he complies with what I'm going to plan, he'll have to hand in his resignation in fifteen days, and we'll call an election in thirty days. If he doesn't comply, in two months we'll throw him out."[47] Perón used rather more tactful language when he communicated with Cámpora, but the substance was clear enough: if, in Perón's opinion, things did not go satisfactorily in the anticipated Cámpora administration, Cámpora would be called upon to resign. He accepted the nomination with that understanding.[48] History would soon record how well Perón had judged his man.

The campaign for the March elections was anticlimactic. Cámpora as the Justicialist and FREJULI candidate, and Ricardo Balbín as the candidate of the Radicals who had refused to join FREJULI, had the election pretty much to themselves. The Peronist Youth produced a campaign slogan that provided both a rationale and an insight into reality, a slogan that appeared everywhere, on walls and fences, in print, in posters: *Cámpora al gobierno, Perón al poder,* Cámpora to the Government, Perón to Power. Under the regulations established for the election, a runoff, second election would be required if no candidate received 50 percent of the vote in the first round. Cámpora, on the crest of the Peronist wave that combined disenchantment and hope, won 49.56 percent. But his lead over Balbín, with 21.29 percent, was so great that no one had the stomach for further contention based on .44 percent, and Lanusse did the sensible thing by declaring, without objections from any source, that Cámpora was the national choice. Peronism had returned. Could Perón be far behind?

The Strangest Interlude—Perón and Cámpora

Peronism took formal command of the government on May 25, 1973, with the inauguration of Héctor Cámpora. It was a memorable day, the high-water mark of the Peronist left, and of the willing, weak president whose sympathies responded to it through the intercession of family and associates.

Control of the streets on days of high political drama had been among the first priorities of the principal public men since the coming of Perón. It was directly related to that very Argentine political pheonomenon, the massing of thousands and hundreds of thousands in streets and plazas to participate in great events. This May 25 was no exception, and the streets were in the possession of the left, and particularly the left of the Peronist Youth. Banners and streamers bore the colors and insignia of the Montoneros and the FAR, whose stewards controlled access to critical points with a mandate that superceded that of the police and the armed forces. The latter suffered an opprobrium that was almost palpable and were fortunate if they were not threatened and spat upon. The rhymed chant rolled over the multitude like the call of doom: "They're going, they're going, they'll never return." ("Se van, se van, y nunca volverán.")

A crude, visceral joy possessed the immense throng. More than half a million Peronists found themselves happily reborn in the plaza in front of the Congress building where Cámpora was sworn in, and in the Plaza de Mayo in front of the Casa Rosada to which he was transferred by helicopter, and in the fourteen blocks of the immense *Avenida de Mayo*, which connects the two centers of government. On the ground, only those could pass who were certified by the street commanders of the militant faithful, and thus the American secretary of state, William Rogers, could not get through and had to retire to the embassy. The only foreign representatives permitted free passage were President Salvador Allende of Chile and the Cuban president, Osvaldo Dorticos, both of whose leftist credentials were beyond dispute. In the evening, some 10,000 demonstrators converged on the prison in which more than 200 political prisoners were held. Although an amnesty proceeding was already under way, that was too formal for the mood of the moment, and Cámpora was happy to respond to the street pressure by issuing a pardon almost on the instant, after Congress, summoned for an emergency session, concurred.[49]

But the signs of a contrary tendency were not absent, even now in the surging carnival of triumph. The labor bureaucracy was long accustomed to dominating the public turf in these great displays and was not about to yield political primacy. The festivities of May 25 included instances of physical combat between labor and the left, and the latter's cry of *Patria Socialista* was answered resoundingly with shouts for the *Patria Peronista*.

Cámpora, always impressionable, began to show clear signs of a leftward evolution, but Perón himself did not. One of the leading youth delegates in the Peronist ranks was Rodolfo Galimberti, a hard leftist; in an unguarded moment, he suggested, between the election and the inauguration, the creation of a people's "militia," to be composed of students and workers. In April, he was summoned to Madrid. He had already recanted on the issue of arms for such a group, but Perón forced his resignation and disgrace. The JP (Juventud Peronista) leadership had to support Perón and condemn one of its own.[50]

Violence had continued from the guerrilla left during the interim after the election. The ERP, bound by no ties to Perón, still saw a bloodbath as the solution, and its kidnappings and assassinations did not slacken. The Montoneros, on the other hand, concentrated at this stage more on political than on insurrectionary activity, in the name of unconditional support for Perón. But the Peronist movement in its first days was as fractured in power as it had been in opposition, with right and left butting heads in the form of work stoppages, demonstrations, and general disorder. The Montoneros, however, continued serene in their misconceptions of Perón, believing, still, that he, like them, was engaged in a phase of national reconstruction and liberation that would be the prelude to the inevitable "national construction of socialism."[51] If they had been more sensitive to nuance, or more apprehensive, they might have felt just the beginnings of a turn of the wind when Cámpora's cabinet appointments were announced. The minister of interior and the foreign minister were congenial to the Montonero influence, but the labor and the economy ministries were in the hands of traditional Peronist types, and the minister of social welfare, the far-right López Rega, was a dark sign, indeed.

The Montonero influence in the government, while clear enough, was limited for the most part to middle and lower ranks of leadership. The Montoneros were now clearly the most significant force on the political left, but they held only eight seats in the FREJULI bloc of 145 deputies in the chamber, and their representation in provincial governments was clearly secondary. Only in the universities, and the University of Buenos Aires in particular, were Montonero or leftist elements in control.[52]

But Cámpora had little opportunity to reflect upon any of these matters, or upon the economy that was again in crisis with inflation and deficit. He did implement the social pact between labor and employers, on June 8, which the Montonero leadership endorsed, perhaps because they did not grasp its implications for the management of labor relations. But in his brief time as president, Cámpora was preoccupied with the issue of Perón. The old leader had not returned to Argentina for the inauguration, nor had Isabel, but he was planning to fly to Buenos Aires in the latter part of June. Cámpora flew to Madrid to escort him home and was soundly snubbed and rebuffed for his pains. Perón did not greet him at the airport, or attend a reception in Cámpora's honor that Generalissimo Franco arranged, or participate in any of the ceremonies that resulted from the visit of a head of state.[53] He was certainly piqued at Franco, who had ignored him during the years in Madrid, and he believed that the Spanish government was ill-repaying the support that Peronist Argentina had given to Spain in the postwar years of Iberian diplomatic isolation. But Perón's tactic was also aimed at distancing himself from his surrogate, perhaps to lessen the embarrassment of replacing him in the short interval that was likely.

But everything was soon overtaken by the famous event that marked Perón's return to Argentina, on June 20: the "Ezeiza Massacre." Perón and Cámpora flew together, along with a full load of the high-spirited faithful, in a chartered plane. Meanwhile, preparations were under way in Buenos Aires for the greatest public gathering in the nation's history. The reception would be held at an overpass on a public highway leading to the airport, since the facilities at Ezeiza itself were insufficient for so mammoth a gathering. A holiday was declared. Free transportation was provided for anyone in the country. Shelters were erected and wood was collected on the approaches and stacked for a thousand campfires.

But such a mighty assemblage would necessarily be a political event of the first magnitude and the government planned accordingly in a manner that would demonstrate its superiority to the leftist organizations in the art of controlling the streets. The man in charge was Perón's security advisor, Colonel Jorge Osinde, an inhabitant of the far right who now operated out of López Rega's social welfare ministry as under-secretary for sports. Government and rightist forces and labor representatives would dominate the committees and the planning as well as the area of the overpass itself. The day came, and the marching columns of the left, banners high in bright sunshine, approached the area through seas of humanity, for it was in fact the largest mobilization ever heard of in Argentina. The estimates of attendance have gone as high as four million, and the lowest have been in the range of one and a half million.[54]

Perón's plane was to land at Ezeiza at three in the afternoon, and Perón was to reach the overpass by helicopter. But hours before that moment, the gravitation of events took over, and the naive joy and festive happiness curdled. In the area of the overpass, there was jostling for position between the official forces that had arrived early and the approaching advance guard of the hugely mobilized left. Shouts and chants and insults began to reverberate back and forth. At about two-thirty, the pressures exploded. There were bursts of gunfire from the overpass directly into the leftists trying to occupy the area facing the speakers' platform. A few of the leftists retaliated with lesser weaponry, the press corps and everyone else who could find shelter dived for protection, and in a moment chaos and blood prevailed. Perón's plane was already over southern Brazil, and Vice President Solano Lima, establishing radio contact, diverted it to a military airport near Buenos Aires, where Perón landed before his transfer to the city by helicopter. The indications were that he was less than pleased. It was a far cry from the spirit of his concluding words in his message of June 3 to the nation: "A big and warm embrace for all my friends, and an affectionate and respectful greeting to all other Argentines."[55]

No accurate count of the carnage at Ezeiza was ever given. It continued sporadically after the first shootout, with pursuit even of the wounded. Twenty-five persons were known dead, but so inaccurate was the news coverage and the subsequent information that the number could have ascended into the hundreds. More than 400 injuries were recorded, again, very probably an understatement. The Buenos Aires press corps reached a consensus estimate of two hundred dead and more than a thousand injured.[56] But more was involved than the casualities, for the Ezeiza massacre was a landmark in the early stage of official rightist reaction to leftist violence and intimidation, a reaction that would swiftly grow into one of the great forces of the decade.

Perón's first comments to the nation, on the next day, reflected a somber and responsible urgency. Turning to the center and to moderation, he spoke of order and discipline and hard work. There was no comfort for the Peronist left. Still seeking a healing formula, he now developed his relationship with Ricardo Balbín, the leading voice in the Radical chorus at this time. The two men visited and found more ground for agreement than could have been imagined in the old days. But before such initiatives could be developed, fate intervened in the form of a health crisis for Perón. On June 26 came warnings of a heart attack. Dr. Pedro Cossio, a heart specialist, was called in, and on the 28th, the attack struck. Peron weathered it and was able to sit up in about a week. He was in this situation when the final crisis of the brief Cámpora administration was played out.

The circumstances and the motivations have been warmly disputed. It is certain that an unscheduled cabinet meeting was summoned by Isabel on July 6 at the presidential residence in Olivos, and that those attending included the president, the vice president, Isabel, and the ministers, including López Rega and Dr. Taiana, the latter then serving as minister of education and as a physician for Perón, who was upstairs, sitting in a chair and still recuperating from his heart attack. Those who attended have differed in certain details of their recollections. Dr. Taiana recalls that both López Rega and Isabel spoke, bringing events to a head. The vice president believes that López Rega placed the problem of Cámpora's resignation before the group and that Isabel said nothing. The criticisms, from whichever source, were based on dissatisfaction with the infiltration of leftist influences in the government and in society, and took account of the fact that Perón had now returned and should exercise the power that really resided in him. President Cámpora defended himself, stressed that he was occupying the presidency at the request of Perón, and indicated that he would give it up without difficulty if Perón so wished.[57] There was a general recognition, noted by Cámpora himself, that opinion in the country favored the return of Perón to direct power. Solano Lima and Cámpora then submitted their resignations.

Cámpora, Isabel, López Rega, and Dr. Taiana then went upstairs to announce the resignations to Perón. The scene was intensely emotional. Perón rose from his chair and stood up. He and Cámpora embraced, tears running down their faces. Alarmed by the evident stress, Dr. Taiana moved in to check Perón's pulse and blood pressure.[58]

There has been much speculation concerning the true course of these events. In his memoirs, Cámpora in effect supports the interpretation given here, which is based on Jorge Antonio's account of the "ashtray" conference: that is, Cámpora's designation and election was a temporary device, almost a subterfuge to get around the August 25 residency requirement that eliminated Perón as a candidate, and that Cámpora held the presidency at Perón's will.[59] Perón subsequently echoed this version,[60] the logical consequence of which was the inevitable call for Cámpora to step down soon after Perón returned to take charge. But there is a second version, with variations. The vice president, Solano Lima, has claimed that Cámpora had no intention of resigning, that he never mentioned such a thing during the campaign, and that Perón told him, Solano Lima, that, because of his health, he definitely did not plan to become the president. He would be an elder statesman while Cámpora administered.[61] For these reasons, and from their assessment of the broad factors involved, several authorities have concluded that Perón did not intend from the beginning to discard Cámpora and take the office himself, and that he was compelled to this extreme by the failure of the Cámpora administration. In this view, references later to an original design being carried out were mere face-saving.[62]

There are two principal difficulties with this second version and its variants. First, the belief that Perón was sincere in his original designation of Cámpora as president and of himself as elder statesman is based on the recollections of those who were involved only second-hand. Only Perón and Jorge Antonio, according to the latter's account, were privy to the decision from the beginning. Second, the conclusion that Perón nominated Cámpora with a full term in mind does not seem tenable in the light of Perón's psychology. For eighteen years, he had worked for the survival of his movement and for his own return to power; he hungered for full vindication, for the reconstruction of the country, and for the verdict of history; he knew he had little time left for so much rebirth. Now, after a thousand perils and frustrations, he stood in 1972 and 1973 on the threshold of an almost miraculous return. Is it reasonable to suppose that after all this he would deliberately hand everything over to a frail successor who had no merits except loyalty and no skills beyond pliability? If he had wanted a true successor, he would have designated Taiana or Benítez or someone else. If he had wanted a life on the sidelines as elder statesman or otherwise he could have had it years ago, and in well-paid comfort. His health, which was assumed to impede his ambition, as it might have done in the case of someone less possessed by power, was, on the contrary, more likely to spur him to the quickest possible return to the presidency, and the shortest route lay through Cámpora.

In any case, events quickly unfolded. Cámpora restored Perón's army rank of lieutenant general on July 11, and his and Solano Lima's resignations were transmitted to Congress on the 13th. The interim executive power was transmitted, by manipulative means, to Raúl Lastiri, president of the chamber of deputies and son-in-law of López Rega. New presidential elections were announced for September 23. The question of Perón's vice-presidential running mate now rose, and given his health, the matter was important. There was some talk of enlisting Ricardo Balbín, just as there had always been talk of alliance between Peronists and some wing of the Radicals, but the suggestion lacked both plausibility and time.[63] The selection would be revealed on August 4, at a party congress in which the political and labor elements of the Peronists would predominate, for the Peronist Youth and their colleagues on the left were now in retreat.

The gathering on August 4 performed its business with unanimity and dispatch. Perón's nomination was a formality. Then came the surprise: the vicepresidential nominee would be Isabel. For the left, this was a wicked blow as well as an amazement, but they took it with resignation and discipline and in the delusive belief that soon Perón would find himself and make everything right.[64] For the others, it was something of a bewilderment. Again, there has been much speculation about the strange choice that was so pregnant with significance for the Argentine future.

There is general agreement that one of the reasons was pressure applied by Isabel and those around her, particularly López Rega, who saw in her a ticket to the top. A leading Radical reported Perón's remark to him: "At this late stage in my life, I simply could not resist the pressure from within my own bedroom."[65] Jorge Antonio has concurred in this assessment of inner-circle pressure and has also suggested that Perón felt he owed something to Isabel for her years with him, and that he regarded his designation of her as a kind of vindication for his failure when Evita had wanted the same honor.[66] And there were practical reasons based in politics. By selecting Isabel, Perón could avoid tipping the scale of party power too heavily to left or right, or to one faction as opposed to another; and he could avoid the creation of a power center around someone who might slip out of control.

The Third Presidency—Ashes and Death

Perón was the man of the hour, the only hope, strangely reborn in the esteem of those who once felt only fear, distrust or dislike. In Washington, the State Department shared the faith inspired by this unique resurrection. As a policy-making official put it, "I think this is the moment for Perón. He alone can bring cohesion to Argentina. There is no one else left, so he has come to represent opportunity."[67]

The campaign for the elections on September 23 was devoid of surprise or incident. There was much stress on consensus and harmony of interests, particularly in a speech by Perón to the members of Congress on August 30. On the following day came the highlight of the campaign, and, indeed, a highlight of the entire process of reconciliation, in the form of a gigantic labor and youth rally in front of the CGT headquarters. Estimates of attendance reached almost a million. For eight hours, Perón, enjoying a moment of comparative vitality, was in public view on the balcony of the building, much of the time standing in review as the marching columns paraded past. The youth elements, representing every possible tendency, combined with the labor ranks of the CGT without incident, and in that heady hour it seemed as if Perón might indeed be able to thrust the Ezeisa massacre out of the public mind and replace it with the elusive accord.[68]

The election seemed familiar. The principal opponent was again Ricardo Balbín, and the the only real issue was the size of the Perón victory. As before, voting was orderly and free of fraud. Perón's winning percentage was 61.85. Balbín and his Radicals, with 24.3 percent of the vote, and several lesser parties immediately pledged their support. Almost 90 percent of the electorate was thus represented in a display of unity unknown in the nation's history.[69] But it would fade on the morrow of its coalescence, for the heart of it was Peronism and Peronism's many mansions were no longer a house.

The full force of this was evident almost immediately. José Rucci, the secretary-general of the CGT and a strong ally of Perón, had incurred the hostility of the left, which found his militancy inadequate and deduced treason accordingly, its assassins pumping a stream of bullets into Rucci a scant two days after the healing election of Perón. The responsibility is generally attributed to the Montoneros, although the facts are obscure.[70]

The election was over and, upon his inauguration on October 12, Perón was free to move as he thought best. He would have preferred to retain the support of the left if he could have domesticated it and brought it under his control. But the Montoneros and the FAR, who had announced their unification with glad words at the time of the inauguration and who had written then "Today, Perón is Argentina . . . He is Fatherland,"[71] were an indigestible mass. Even in their growing disillusionment, however, they could not break with Perón because they still believed in his ultimate revolutionary purpose and because without him they were little more than violent gangs with a talent for metaphysical theorizing.

If Perón could not live with the left on his own terms, he was prepared to cut it adrift. He was disheartened by the unreasoning lawlessness whose full impact began to dawn upon him now that the responsibility for order was his own. The essential thing was labor, the CGT.[72] If support or acquiescence were forthcoming from that quarter, the left could be isolated into a police problem. So the liquidation of Rucci was followed almost at once by a "reserved document" issued by the Peronist leadership, which made no bones about the fact that the government was now at war with "terrorist and Marxist groups" who were said to have infiltrated Peronism. For some time, the Montoneros refused to believe it, although Perón himself had announced the document, and his signature was clearly appended to it. On November 8, Perón followed up with a speech at the CGT in which he compared the infiltrating radical left to "germs" engaged in contamination.[73]

In mid-January, an attack by ERP units on an army garrison in the city of Azul led to broad consequences. The governor of Buenos Aires

Province, who had an affinity for the left, was forced out after Perón spoke critically of him. An insurrection led by the police overturned the provincial government in Córdoba and ejected the left-leaning governor and a leftist labor leader allied to him, before the province was intervened in March. Three other provinces were also intervened. Penal legislation was introduced in congress, tightening the criminal code, and Perón told a group of FREJULI deputies who had raised questions about the bill that they could support it or resign. They resigned.[74] There was a simultaneous evolution of rightist counter force. Small armed groups, para-military in nature, appeared on the trail of the left. During a two-week period at the beginning of 1974, twelve leftist militants were killed and twenty-five leftist Peronist headquarters were demolished. Perón would not speak out against these excesses, and others like them, and when a left-wing journalist, a Peronist, asked him during a press conference if the government were investigating such matters, he ordered that she be prosecuted for slander.[75]

Perón's natural response to the problem of channeling dangerously volatile youthful energies and psychologies was to think of a General Confederation of Youth, which would unite everything within its jurisdiction. But in January 1974, the Montoneros refused to attend an important meeting on the subject called by Perón, on the ground that ultra-rightist representatives would also be present.[76] The disagreements among the young, no less bitter than those among their elders, were simply too fervent, and the concept of a youth confederation never matured.

In one area of significance to youth, that of university reform, the Peronist restoration found constructive solutions. In a departure from his earlier approach, Perón now adopted a relatively nonpolitical policy that was consistent with the broader and more open character of his new administration. In 1954, Perón had dictated a Bonapartist approach to university rule, sponsoring a congressional law that made the universities into appendages of the national government. In 1973, in contrast, Perón made the wise move of appointing Dr. Jorge Taiana, still one of his personal physicians, as minister of education. Taiana, an enlightened and open-mined man, favored autonomy and said so to Perón. The latter agreed enthusiastically: "Look, Taiana, put some distance between the executive power and the president of the republic on the one hand and the university on the other. Because if you name a rector for them, they'll always raise questions and objections even if it was Jesus Christ himself. Let them organize their affairs and elect their own authorities."[77] The result was a new and liberalizing

university law in 1974, the first legislation in this controversial field
that had ever achieved unanimous approval in Congress.

But there was no dearth of other and less tractable problems in
the months that followed Perón's return. The economy, as usual, was
in trouble. Inflation was running free at more than 6 percent a month
and in July 1974, the EEC banned all imports of Argentine beef, with
drastic results for the trade balance. But the economy necessarily
received short shrift from Perón in his third presidency. Politics were
too volatile and violent, and his health was becoming another significant problem in itself.

It was not that he lacked care and concern. Isabel had inherited
from Evita the vocation of tending his health and she persisted, despite
all his sneaking evasions. She denied him desserts not on his diet, but
he ate them on the sly. She was adamance itself on the subject of his
smoking, and he was reduced to begging an occasional cigarette during walks in the gardens of the official residence. Sometimes she would
appear in the garden when he was thus breaking rules, and he would
instantly flick the cigarette into the shrubbery and pop a mint candy
into his mouth from the supply he always carried with him for such
an emergency.[78] She did what she could, but it would not suffice.

The winter weather, raw and damp, had been an affliction for
Perón after his June 1973 return and it coincided with the heart attack
that followed in July. His recovery during the next month or two
seemed encouraging, but perhaps Perón knew otherwise in some secret
corner of his consciousness. His friend, Enrique Pavón Pereyra, raised
the question of health late in September.

"I had a bad cold that I'm recovering from," Perón answered. "I
took to bed for a while and then I stayed at home convalescing. I had
a viral pericarditis. The matter of the heart can't be taken lightly, but
I'm recovering perfectly, in spite of the ups and downs that come with
that kind of illness."

His summary was succinct: "I'm not as bad as some of the journalists say, but neither am I as well as I say I am."[79] He was equally direct
with Dr. Taiana when the latter told him in October that he looked
well: "Only the coachwork, doctor, because the engine is running
badly."[80] In August, in a speech to the governors of the provinces, he
had been very explicit: "I'm old now, and . . . my end is approaching . . ."[81]

A bit of military ceremony soon after these private comments
accentuated his physical frailty. He flew by helicopter to the aircraft
carrier Argentina had by now acquired, almost a hundred miles at
sea, to inspect and visit. The weather was severe, the winds of late

winter gusted furiously, and Perón suffered from exposure as he clambered about the ship, up and down, in and out.

In November came another crisis that in its way reinforced the lesson taught by bread cast upon the water. One of Perón's neighbors, Julio Luqui Lagleyze, was a doctor. He came to the attention of the Perón household during the summer of 1973, when his young daughter slipped and fell beneath one of the presidential automobiles, which, fortunately, was moving very slowly. She was taken to the hospital and soon recovered, but Isabel heard of the matter and was very concerned. She kept in touch, and sent López Rega to the child's bedside to offer assistance. "If you don't tell the vicepresident that the little girl is well, she's not going to have a quiet moment," he told the doctor. "I must bother you to go and see the Señora."

Dr. Lagleyze thereupon visited Isabel to report, and thus came to be known to the presidential staff. When Perón suffered a bad attack of pulmonary edema in the early morning hours of November 21, and no doctor was at hand, Dr. Lagleyze came to mind immediately. Rushing to his house, staff members roused him and brought him back to Perón's room. Perón was in great difficulty, breathing heavily and fighting off asphyxiation from the liquids collecting in his lungs. López Rega, who seemed to perform the strangest diversity of functions in this unusual household, was administering oxygen to Perón through a tube. Isabel rummaged about frantically and came running in with a medicine chest. Fortunately it contained a solution of aminofiline, and Dr. Lagleyze rapidly injected it. Between this and other measures, the patient rallied, and by the time Dr. Cossio was located and brought to the house an hour later, the crisis had passed. But death had been held off by the narrowest of margins.[82]

What could not be held off, however, was the political conflict that seemed as impervious to resolution as ever. The left, and the Montoneros, still clutched their necessary lifeline to Perón, although their awareness of what was happening grew daily more acute. Early in February, they heard Perón, in an address to right-wing youth, assail them in still stronger language as "idiots" and "deceivers."[83] In March, the Montoneros held a mass rally, the last they would sponsor before their clandestine future closed in upon them, and their complaints were loud. But they were directed against their opponents, particularly the trade union leaders and their political colleagues whom they thought had betrayed the Peronist movement. For Perón himself there were no hard words.[84]

The situation, however, was essentially unstable. Something had to break. It happened on May Day, that time of great meetings and addresses. The government scheduled a traditional jamboree in the Plaza de Mayo. Isabel would crown the Queen of Labor, Perón would speak, and festivity would reign in the old style. But the Montonero left had other ideas and determined on a great splurge of popular might during which they would break through the cordon that they believed separated Perón from his people and address the president directly, reviving the revolutionary camaraderie that surely united them still. About 100,000 persons were in the plaza, the left having mobilized perhaps 60,000; labor accounted for the rest. The organizers of the event, all proper government types, had forbidden banners and flags other than those of the nation and of the unions, but the Montoneros got around this by bringing in cans of spray paint and redoing the labor banners on the spot in revolutionary prose. They were feisty and psychologically keyed to a fine, high pitch, quivering for action and release.

By the time Perón arrived by helicopter and appeared on the balcony of the Casa Rosada a little after five, that scene of so many memories and triumphs was already resounding with chants and cries. Back and forth, between left and right, they echoed and reechoed, dying away in the swell of murmurous new sound. Isabel was greeted by "There's only one Evita" and "If Evita lived, she would be a Montonero." Rough jeers disdained the crowning of the Queen of Labor. Then, for a moment, the Plaza stood silent in tribute to Evita and to all Peronists who had died, but only for a moment: the quiet was shattered at once by the slow dirgelike beat of a JP drum, and the name of a fallen Montonero, called out in a great voice, with the massed response from the Montonero ranks . . . "Present!" And another name . . . "Present!" And another and another and another . . . "Present!" . . . "Present!" . . . "Present!" . . .

Perón rose to speak, and a wave of chanting greeted him, the chanting of the question recently adopted by the Montonero faithful: "What's going on, General? Why is the popular government full of 'gorrilas'?" Perón responded in fury, casting aside much of his speech that praised unity and the trade union movement, and verbally assaulted the left. "Stupid idiots," "Beardless wonders," and other epithets came rolling forth. The Montonero ranks broke out in a particularly offensive chanted slogan that rhymes in Spanish and referred to the two famous labor leaders assassinated by the left: "Rucci, traitor, say hello to Vandor!" Perón responded with ominous references to ". . . punishment not having been inflicted yet," "infiltrators," "mercenaries in the service of foreign money" and "pernicious elements" and invoked warfare on them if they persisted. But they left, marching out of the plaza, chanting and shouting as he still spoke. The plaza was soon more than half empty, and the union and rightist forces swarmed after the departing leftists, attacking them with stones and poles.[85]

The four words of which Perón had spoken to Jorge Antonio had failed, as had four thousand. Antonio, watching Perón, understood that he had suffered a terrible blow, and that he would die in disillusion, tired of politics and all the rest. "And there, at that moment, I had the *absolute* certainty that Perón said, silently, 'Here I want to die.' That is to say, he wanted to die in the grandeur of duty performed."[86]

But it was not quite time. Perón attacked the left again in mid-May, after its leadership had announced its continuing loyalty on the 6th with the stoicism that had now become habit.[87] The running conflict with the left was suspended in June long enough for Perón to make a quick but tiring trip to Paraguay, a last gesture to the country he had found so congenial. The Paraguayans had a gesture of their own, a twenty-one gun salute from the gunboat that had been his first refuge after his fall in 1955. But Perón was tired, more than ever. He met with Ricardo Balbín soon after he returned from Paraguay, and Balbín quoted him in a somber vein: "I'm dying," Perón had said.

On the morning of May 12, he spoke on television in support of the social pact and denounced its opponents in the ranks of business and labor. He also hinted at the possibility of his resignation, as he had done not infrequently before, and, as before, he got the response he wanted—the CGT declared an immediate strike and ordered its workers to the Plaza de Mayo. There, in the late afternoon, Perón delivered what would be his last words to the Argentine nation, and his final sentence was infused with the spirit of November twilight: "To conclude, I hope that God will grant you all the happiness and felicity you deserve. I appreciate profoundly your coming here to this historic Plaza de Mayo. I carry in my ears what for me is the most marvelous of music, the words of the Argentine people."[88]

At the end of the week, Isabel and López Rega left for Geneva, where she was scheduled to speak to the International Labor organization. Perón developed another cold, or the grippe as it was annouced. On the advice of Dr. Cossio he remained at home, working as best he could. On May 19, Dr. Taiana noted a decline in Perón and summoned López Rega from Rome, where he had gone. The warlock arrived the next day, and on the 28th, with Perón worsening, Isabel cut short her trip and flew home.

Perón's bronchial complication was developing into pneumonia. Confined to his bed, and weakening, he signed his last decree, on

Saturday, July 29, delegating the powers of the presidency to Isabel, In the privacy of his chamber he had been talking during these last few days with an army chaplain, Father Ponzo, as if engrossed in things beyond this world. On the 30th, he received communion and the sacrament of penance from the priest. And in the hours after midnight his heart began to falter in its rhythm, intimating the cardiac arrest that would follow the dawn.

There was a brief improvement in the morning, and Perón was visited by Isabel and López Rega and one of the cabinet ministers. At half past eleven, the physical signs indicated a sharp deterioration. Dr. Taiana was summoned urgently from a nearby room. Hastening to Perón's side, he found him propped in bed, his face turning blue, his breath labored, his voice a whisper. His last words were, "Taiana, I'm leaving this world . . . my people . . . my people . . . " and then he lay still.[89]

Several hours before, he had said to Father Ponzo, "You have made me so familiar with the idea of death that, truly, I will receive it as a benediction."[90]

> I know that they're anxious for the succession, but
> they should understand that my only successor is the
> Argentine nation. I have no heirs.
>
> — Juan Perón in Enrique Pavón Pereyra, *Conversaciónes con
> Juan Domingo Perón*

Postscript: Peronism as Memory and Legend

THE DEATH OF Juan Perón was attended by lesser obsequies than the immense rites that had preempted all Argentina at the passing of Evita. He had requested that his body not be embalmed, and the public had to be content with a funeral mass at the Buenos Aires cathedral and two days of wake when the coffin was exhibited in the Congress. The casket was eventually transferred to a tomb containing the bodies of his grandfather and his mother. He left no immediate family, except Isabel, and, as he had foreseen, his true heirs were the Argentine people.

In the public sense, however, the death of Perón wrought immeasurable consequences. With him died the last hope for some degree of social reconciliation. If the earlier portions of his career had brought division and harsh conflict as he worked to bring the forgotten and the marginal into national life, the last years were clearly aimed at bringing together what he and the old habits of the civilization had forced apart. The chances that Perón in his prime could have done something so monumental would probably have been less than even. That he could have done so in his seventies, even with unimpaired health, was still less likely. But that any other individual or any group could have done so in the conditions prevailing in 1970 and thereafter was the most unlikely of all, unlikely to the point of impossibility.

Events were to make clear immediately that no keeper of the legend had survived Perón as he had survived Evita, and that if Peronist myth and memory were to persist, they would have to do so by the endless regeneration of their own internal dynamics, not by new accretions.

Isabel assumed the presidency with dignity and good intentions. A pious Roman Catholic, she began each day with her devotions in chapel.[1] But faith could not invent political competence, and the presence of López Rega, confirmed as her secretary, was all about her as if she were mantled in some great penumbra. He determined her policies, reinforced her will, and mouthed her very words after her as he stood nearby while she spoke in public. His domination of the government was an absolute assurance of fatal conflict.

It came soon. The left had been forced out of power in the Peronist movement, in the Congress, in the provinces, and in the universities. Its press media were banned in August and September. And so the Montoneros went underground again, declaring war on the government. "Within the next twelve months they were to establish themselves as the mightiest urban guerrilla force ever seen in the whole of Latin America."[2] So much for the pious hope that a legitimate government, by reason of its existence, would deprive subversion of its raison d'être and therefore of its vitality. By this time, the Montoneros had militarized their organization, and by 1975, they had become wealthy through kidnappings, had mobilized an estimated 5,000 people, and had developed a taste for the assassination of police officials.[3] The government declared a State of Siege on November 6, 1974, and it remained in effect into the next decade.[4]

In all of this, the Montoneros held fast to the legends of Peronism, sustained in part by the delusions that never left them and in part by the absence of anything else to cling to. Their dilemma now was what it always had been: they were far too militant and radical to find a home in the main house of Peronism, and too closely bound to Peronist mythology to erect one elsewhere.[5] In this spirit, the left was immediately locked in combat with the right, which also spoke out of memory and legend, the right that claimed the true inheritance through the direct laying-on-of-hands by Perón and that dominated the commanding heights of the state. The instincts of the civilization were transmuted almost explosively as the extremism of civil disagreement passed into bloodshed on a scale never know before in the country.

The instrumentality of the right in this savage encounter was the Argentine Anti-Communist Alliance, known as the Triple A death squad. Its founder and patron was López Rega, who was not making a crude jest when he remarked somewhat later that the violent left had such hard heads that hammers should be used on them.[6] The strange warlock fell in July 1975, forced out by the army and by labor opposition, and he disappeared as abruptly as he had arrived. But, by now, multitudes who were mere political activists or stood innocently in the line of fire had begun to suffer and die.[7]

By 1976, the political death rate had increased to a killing every five hours, with a bomb explosion every three.[8] The Peronist myth notwithstanding, it was apparent that the armed forces would intervene. Everyone knew it, and almost everyone either accepted or welcomed the thought. It happened on March 25. A junta headed by General Jorge Videla took over; the economic side was entrusted to a minister, José Martínez de Hoz, whose social ties and views were reminiscent of the old Liberal System, and whose measures were soon desperately unpopular in all but oligarchic and foreign circles. Isabel was sent to the far south, to a chalet in the Andean lake country, where she remained under house arrest. She was subsequently transferred to Perón's country home at San Vicente and charged with the embezzlement of funds belonging to the Eva Perón Foundation. She was finally released in July 1981 and took up residence in Madrid, where she has remained ever since, returning to Buenos Aires infrequently and only for ceremonial occasions involving her symbolism as the bearer of the Peronist legend.

But the army's real interest was the matter of subversion. The Guevarist ERP was quickly disposed of. It had retreated to remote Tucumán province, and the army went in and completely exterminated it, root and stem. The Montoneros were another matter, and urban guerrilla warfare required other countertactics, or so the army thought, including a definition of subversion that extended to sympathizers and fellow travelers, to the disseminators of ideas the army found uncongenial, and to foreign refugees and political activists who might be suspect. The army understood that the net of repression, cast so wide, would certainly bring in many who were marginal or entirely innocent; it did not welcome this prospect, but it accepted it, deeming it inevitable since the state had to be preserved and there was insufficient time and manpower (and in some cases, desire) to fine-tune the process.

In this spirit the hard days began. There was no proscription of Peronism as such, only a state of total war against the violent left as very broadly defined. Toward the end of 1976, the death squads were accounting for an average of fifteen abductions every day,[9] and a new word had come into common usage: the *desaparecidos*, the "disappeareds," who had been hauled away to oblivion in the black Ford Falcons of the Triple A.

This was more than the Montoneros had expected. The army had written entirely new rules for this unprecedented confrontation and these paid no heed to the traditional public accountability and legalization of detention. Now the repression was clandestine in all aspects. As the foremost student of the Montonero phenomenon aptly puts it, "Under the new regime, not only was torture more savage: the detainee was now at the disposal of captors who had all the time in the world, were unmolested by judicial interference, could totally isolate the prisoner from society, and had no need to produce a living person at the end."[10]

By these unprecedentedly Draconian means, the military government soon decimated the Montoneros. Two thousand casualties were recorded within the first year of the new regime.[11] By this time, the Montonero left had become further radicalized and had come to have a less charitable evaluation of Perón. He had failed to do the many things he should have done and what he had done was in important respects incorrect: "Peronism is finished and the people are orphans."[12] By the end of 1977, most of the survivors had fled Argentina. Some of them attempted a return in 1979, under the delusion that the masses were likely to rise in the streets. But the workers held to their Peronist faith and their workplaces, and the Montonero remnants that survived again fled Argentina. Guerrilla subversion of the left was not quite dead, but the traces of life that remained were merely a very feeble testimony to a very minor nuisance.

But the cost of the military government's victory had been incalculable. In terms of casualties alone, the figures are breathtaking. In 1984, the Argentine civil rights organizations placed the total of the known dead and "disappeareds" at about 9,000. Mass graves filled with bones, newly revealed torture chambers from which the screams still seemed to reverberate, and the organized mothers of the "disappeareds" milling about daily in the Plaza de Mayo, were only a few of the scars that hinted at the social and psychic destruction wrought at deeper levels.

Political unrest was a factor in the demise of the juntas headed by General Videla and General Roberto Viola. A coup organized by General Leopoldo Galtieri ushered in the third junta in December 1981. But the state of the economy was probably an even more important factor, for the juntas could do nothing with it, and the austerity demanded by the economists in charge would have required more force than the juntas were willing to commit.

Events seemed to call for an abrupt change, and General Galtieri and his junta found the justification for one in their invasion of the Islas Malvinas, or Falkland Islands, on April 2, 1982.[13] The assertion of sovereignty over the islands was as old as the Argentine Republic, and so was the failure to make headway in negotiations with the British. Hints of a military move had been given in private to journalists, and the latter had done their part. In January, the Buenos Aires press began to point the way: Conditions favored an aggressive move against the Malvinas; the foreign minister and the president were competent and decisive; Argentina would regain its vigor and its place in the world.

But the foreign minister was mistaken in almost every judgement and recommendation he had been called upon to make, and the president was quite unable to conduct a victorious war, and the forces that had invaded on April 2 surrendered on June 14. Crowds in the Plaza de Mayo looked up at the famous balcony of the Casa Rosada, now empty, screaming "Galtieri, son of a whore!" The junta fell and its successor, with everything lost on all sides, had no choice: It called for new elections and a return to constitutional government.

The elections were held in October 1983 as a direct competition between the Peronist Party and the reworked Radicals. The Peronists nominated a rather ineffective candidate and mounted an inept campaign, and they lost, with 40 percent of the vote, as against 52 percent for the Radical candidate, Dr. Raúl Alfonsín. It was the first electoral loss for Peronism in a presidential campaign.

Whether President Alfonsín can maintain unity remains an open question. Several factors favor him strongly, including the lost war and the utter weariness of the nation after years of violence and crisis. The depth of the disrepute into which the armed forces have fallen makes the possibility of their being enlisted by enemies of the government less likely for some time to come. On the other hand, Peronism remains a lively faith, capable even in the new president's moment of triumph of denying him the labor legislation he had sought. As it did on former occasions, Peronism has retreated into the formidable redoubt of the labor movement, and its capacity for opposition will certainly multiply as austerity and time inevitably erode the lustre of the administration. But Peronism has already suffered a major split, and its prospects must therefore be included among the enigmas.

Above all, perhaps, the future of Argentina and of Peronism will depend on certain qualities of the civilization that have retained a remarkable identity even as they have changed over time. Among those qualities are the distinctive values and psychologies of the people and the social divisions that have separated them. Most of these were already familiar in the days of May and they persisted while the men of Rosas rode the pampas, persisted in the noontime of the Liberal System, persisted in the voice of *Martín Fierro,* persisted in the homage paid to Yrigoyen, persisted in the sweet and bitter sorrows of the tango in the time of the *Concordancia,* persisted until Perón and Evita gave new form to them in the works of the Peronato. And persisted after the Peronato. And probably persist today, for such is the way of time past and of memory and legend.

Because Juan Perón interpreted these changing and yet changeless themes with an intuition born of his identification with them, his successes and his failures and his memory and his legend will certainly figure prominently in time future as well, thus remaining a part of the eternal Argentine present.

APPENDIX
NOTES
SOURCES
BIBLIOGRAPHY
INDEX

Appendix: *PRESIDENTS OF ARGENTINA*

PRESIDENT	DATES OF INCUMBENCY	METHOD OF SELECTION
Justo José de Urquiza	1854–1860	Coup d'etat
Santiago Derquí	1860–1861	Election
Bartolomé Mitre	1862–1868	Congressional designation
Domingo Faustino Sarmiento	1868–1874	Election
Nicolás Avellaneda	1874–1880	Election
Julio A. Roca	1880–1886	Election
Miguel Juárez Celman	1886–1890	Election
Carlos Pellegrini	1890–1892	Constitutional succession
Luis Sáenz Peña	1892–1895	Election
José Evaristo Uriburu	1895–1898	Constitutional succession
Julio A. Roca	1898–1904	Election
Manuel Quintana	1904–1906	Election
José Figueroa Alcorta	1906–1910	Constitutional succession
Roque Sáenz Peña	1910–1914	Election
Victorino de la Plaza	1914–1916	Constitutional succession
Hipólito Yrigoyen	1916–1922	Election
Marcelo T. de Alvear	1922–1928	Election
Hipólito Yrigoyen	1928–1930	Election
José Felix Uriburu	1930–1932	Coup d'etat
Agustín P. Justo	1932–1938	Election
Roberto M. Ortiz	1938–1942	Election
Ramón S. Castillo	1942–1943	Constitutional succession

PRESIDENT	DATES OF INCUMBENCY	METHOD OF SELECTION
Arturo Rawson	Jun. 1943 (two days)	Coup d'etat
Pedro P. Ramírez	1943–1944	Army designation
Edelmiro Farrell	1944–1946	Army designation
Juan Domingo Perón	1946–1955	Election
Eduardo A. Lonardi	Sep.–Nov. 1955	Coup d'etat
Pedro E. Aramburu	1955–1958	Coup d'etat
Arturo Frondizi	1958–1962	Election
José María Guido	1962–1963	Coup d'etat
Arturo Illia	1963–1966	Election
Juan Carlos Onganía	1966–1970	Coup d'etat
Roberto Marcelo Levingston	1970–1971	Coup d'etat
Alejandro Lanusse	1971–1973	Coup d'etat
Héctor José Cámpora	May–Jul. 1973	Election
Raúl Lastiri (acting president)	Jul.–Oct. 1973	Constitutional succession
Juan Domingo Perón	1973–1974	Election
María (Isabel) Martínez de Perón	1974–1976	Constitutional succession
Jorge R. Videla	1976–1981	Coup d'etat
Roberto E. Viola	Mar.–Dec. 1981	Army designation
Leopoldo F. Galtieri	Dec.–Jun. 1981–1982	Army designation
Reynaldo B. Bignoni	1982–1983	Army designation
Raúl Alfonsín	1983–	Election

Notes

Prologue

1. The symbolism of this song as a key to the appeals of Peronism is noted in the perceptive first chapter in Frederick C. Turner and José Enrique Miguens, eds., *Juan Perón and the Reshaping of Argentina*, p. 12.
2. Tommy Sue Montgomery, ed., *Mexico Today*, pp. 4–5. Octavio Paz's introduction to this book, from which the quotations are taken, contains many acute insights into the Hispanic civilization and its contrasts with the Anglo-Saxon ethos.

The Enigmas of Argentina

1. James Bryce, *South America: Observations and Impressions*, p. 315. See also Carlos F. Díaz Alejandro, *Essays on the Economic History of the Argentine Republic*, p. 1.
2. Cecil Jane, *Liberty and Despotism in Spanish America*, p. 173.
3. Howard J. Wiarda, *Corporatism and National Development in Latin America*, pp. 11–20. For an interesting discussion of the extent to which Latin America is "democratic," or wishes to be, see Howard J. Wiarda, ed., *The Continuing Struggle for Democracy in Latin America*, ch. 1, and Glen Dealy, "Prolegomena on the Spanish-American Political Tradition," in *Hispanic American Historical Review*, February 1968, pp. 37ff. Wiarda, *Corporatism*, p. 153, notes the tendency of countries outside of the North American and European areas to define themselves in terms of the Western "world culture," however inappropriate it may be historically and culturally.

The Enigmas of Perón

1. This thought has been expressed by several observers, including Nicholas Fraser and Marysa Navarro, *Eva Perón*, p. 35.

2. Enrique Pavón Pereyra, *Conversaciónes con Juan D. Perón,* p. 187.
3. William Ascher, *Scheming for the Poor:*

The Politics of Redistribution in Latin America, p. 58.

1. The Land

1. Ezequiel Martínez Estrada, *X-Ray of the Pampa,* p. 7.
2. John W. White, *Argentina: The Life Story of a Nation,* pp. 3–5; Ysabel Rennie, *The Argentine Republic,* pp. 3–4.
3. Preston E. James, *Latin America,* p. 296. For good general geographic descriptions of Argentina, see ch. 9 of this work, and ch. 9 of Harold Blakemore and Clifford T. Smith, eds., *Latin*

America: Geographical Perspectives.
4. James, *Latin America,* pp. 301–2 provides an interesting account of the role of the mule, and of the mule trade with Peru, as the economic foundation of the region in early colonial times.
5. Glyn Williams, *The Desert and the Dream: A Study of Welsh Colonization in Chubut, 1865–1915,* p. 113.

2. From Colony to Modern Nation, 1516–1880

1. Mariano Picón-Salas, *A Cultural History of Spanish America: From Conquest to Independence,* p. 43.
2. See Samuel Eliot Morison, *The European Discovery of America: The Southern Voyages A.D. 1492–1616,* p. 581, for a description of the route from Spain to the Rió de la Plata, and some aspects of the North American comparison sketched in the following paragraph of the text.
3. Wiarda, *Corporatism,* pp. 100–1 traces briefly some of the elements of the complicated heritage. For the theme of the primacy of public over private values, see Glen Caudill Dealy, *The Public Man: An Interpretation of Latin American and Other Catholic Countries;* and for the public aspect of personal honor, Bartolomé Bennassar, *The Spanish Character: Attitudes and Mentalities from the Sixteenth to the Nineteenth Century,* p. 223. Paul Horgan has written of the Roman origins of Spain, and has included references, in his *Great River,* Vol. I.
4. Jorge Mañach, *Frontiers in the Americas: A Global Perspective,* p. 51.
5. Picón-Salas, *Cultural,* pp. 39–40. See also Wiarda, *Corporatism,* p. 54; O. Carlos Stoetzer, *El Pensamiento Político en la america española durante el período de la emancipación (1789–1825),* Vol. I, pp. 15ff.; Bernice Hamilton, *Political Thought in Sixteenth Century*

Spain, pp. 4ff.; Harold Eugene Davis, *Latin American Social Thought,* p. 37.
6. Wiarda, *Corporatism,* p. 97.
7. For good general discussions, see Claudio Véliz, *The Centralist Tradition of Latin America,* pp. 3–15; and James A. Scobie, *Buenos Aires: Plaza to Suburb, 1870–1910,* pp. 218ff. Bennassar, *Spanish Character,* ch. V, considers attitudes toward power, work, and wealth.
8. Octavio Paz in Montgomery, *Mexico,* p. 10. For the stress on honor, Bennassar, *Spanish Character,* pp. 213ff.; and for values concerning economic activity, Frederick B. Pike, *Spanish America, 1900–1970: Tradition and Social Innovation,* pp. 35–8.
9. Mañach, *Frontiers,* p. 50. See also Scobie, *Buenos Aires,* pp. 227–28; and José Luis Romero, *A History of Argentine Political Thought,* p. x.
10. Salvador de Madariaga, *The Fall of the Spanish-American Empire,* p. 28.
11. Mañach, *Frontiers,* p. 52.
12. Martínez Estrada, *X-Ray,* p. 26.
13. Ibid., p. 35.
14. Ysabel Rennie, *The Argentine Republic,* p. 19.
15. Romero, *A History,* p. 45.
16. Scobie, *Buenos Aires,* pp. 227–28.
17. Alistair Hennessy, *The Frontier in Latin American History,* p. 25.
18. Jonathan C. Brown, *A Socioeconomic History of Argentina, 1776–1860,* p. 65.

19. James R. Scobie, *Revolution on the Pampas: A Social History of Argentine Wheat, 1860–1910*, p. 115.
20. James, *Latin America*, p. 352.
21. For a general view of the British invasions, see H. S. Ferns, *Britain and Argentina in the Nineteenth Century*, ch. 1.
22. Ibid., p. 30.
23. Ibid., pp. 69–70.
24. Wiarda, *Corporatism*, pp. 147, 153; Lars Schoultz, *The Populist Challenge: Argentine Electoral Behavior in the Postwar Era*, pp. 13 and 94; Richard D. Mallon, with Juan V. Sourrouille, *Economic Policy Making in a Conflict Society: The Argentine Case*, p. 5; Ricardo del Barco, "Del gobierno militar al regimen peronista (1943–1955), in *Criterio*, December 24, 1982, p. 698.
25. In this aspect, the essence of the Rift is well described in Peter Winn, "From *Martín Fierro* to Peronism: A Century of Argentine Social Protest", in *The Americas*, July 1978, pp. 89ff.
26. Romero, *A History*, p. 47.
27. For a good account of the nature of values and opinions in the interior, see Romero, *A History*, pp. 96–116.

28. George Reid Andrews, *The Afro-Argentines of Buenos Aires, 1800–1900*, p. 97. For an interesting account of the career of Rosas and reference to his success in repelling the efforts of England and France to intervene in Argentina, see Ferns, *Britain*.
29. Andrews, *Afro-Argentines*, p. 97.
30. For a description of Rosas's techniques and policies at this stage, see Ferns, *Britain*, pp. 209ff.
31. Quoted in Hubert Herring, *A History of Latin America: From the Beginnings to the Present*, p. 601. This work contains a good account of the era of Rosas, pp. 594–606.
32. John Frank Cady, *Foreign Investment in the Río de la Plata 1838–1850: A Study of French, British and American Policy in Relation to the Dictator Juan Manuel Rosas*, pp. 10–14. This work contains a balanced judgment of Rosas, seeking to understand him rather than merely to condemn him.
33. Herring, *A History*, pp. 609–12, for a view of this period.
34. Frances C. Crowley, *Domingo Faustino Sarmiento*, p. 110.
35. Hennessy, *The Frontier*, p. 90.

3.   Argentina in the Years of Triumph, 1880–1930

1. Donna J. Guy, *Argentine Sugar Politics: Tucumán and the Generation of Eighty*, pp. 3–4. An authoritative review of Argentine economic history is contained in Díaz Alejandro, *Essays*, pp. 1–66.
2. Arthur P. Whitaker, *Argentina*, pp. 20–21, 42.
3. James, *Latin America*, p. 337.
4. Nicolás Sánchez–Albornoz, *The Population of Latin America: A History*, p. 155.
5. Blakemore and Smith, *Latin America*, pp. 417–18.
6. White, *Argentina*, p. 231; see also Andrew Graham-Yooll, *The Forgotten Colony*, p. 17, which makes the further point that since there was no British colonial administration or army to coalesce these areas of influence into institutional domination, the British influence, although widespread, was uneven. For a summary account of the

Argentine railroad system, its origins and its development, see Laura Randall, *An Economic History of Argentina in the Twentieth Century*, pp. 171–79.
7. Hennessy, *The Frontier*, p. 84.
8. Rennie, *The Argentine*, p. 140; Hennessy, *The Frontier*, p. 112.
9. Herring, *A History*, p. 624.
10. Graham-Yooll, *The Forgotten*, pp. 216–19.
11. Scobie, *Revolution*, p. 121; for a good description of rural life in these times, and the wasting of the interior in favor of the capital, see Carl C. Taylor, *Rural Life in Argentina*. One consequence was the absence of a middle class (with its customary values) rooted in land ownership; see Gino Germani, *Authoritarianism, Fascism and National Populism*, p. 136.
12. Scobie, *Revolution*, pp. 53ff.
13. James, *Latin America*, p. 341.
14. See Hennessy, *The Frontier*, pp. 7ff for

observations on the Turner Thesis in relation to Argentina.

15. Guy, *Argentine Sugar*, pp. 4–5.
16. H. S. Ferns, *The Argentine Republic, 1516–1971*, p. 187.
17. Rennie, *The Argentine*, p. 162.
18. Tomás R. Filol, *Social Factors in Economic Development: The Argentine Case*, p. 30; for the statistics of immigrant ownership, see Solberg, *Immigration*, pp. 42ff. The sociological effects of the immigration are analyzed in Germani, *Authoritarianism*, pp. 136ff.
19. Reactions to immigration from 1900 to 1920 are described in Pike, *Spanish America*, pp. 117–19. See Solberg, *Immigration*, p. 141.
20. Solberg, *Immigration*, pp. 154–56.
21. Ibid., p. 155.
22. James R. Scobie, *Argentina: A City and a Nation*, p. 133.
23. For a good, extended treatment of this subject, see Scobie, *Buenos Aires.*
24. Ibid., pp. 126, 135.
25. Ibid., pp. 201, 204, 253.
26. Ibid., p. 234; for the creative and innovating qualities of the old elite, see José Luis de Imaz, *Los Que Mandan*, pp. 121ff.
27. Rennie, *The Argentine*, p. 150; see also Bryce, *South America*, p. 318; the traditional Hispanic stress on visible public ostentation is described in Bennassar, *Spanish Character*, ch. 7.
28. Scobie, *Buenos Aires*, p. 232ff; for the prevalence of upward mobility, see Germani, *Authoritarianism*, p. 145. Lower-to-middle class mobility is noted in Filol, *Social Factors*, p. 30.
29. David Rock, *Politics in Argentina, 1890–1930*, pp. 17–20; see also Romero, *A History*, pp. 183ff., and Filol, *Social Factors*, p. 30.
30. For a view emphasizing social alteration in Buenos Aires and the littoral, but not in the interior, see Germani, *Authoritarianism*, p. 140.
31. Ronald C. Newton, *German Buenos Aires, 1900–1933: Social Change and Cultural Crisis*, p. 96; for a particularly interesting account of the interaction between German immigrants and the Argentine environment, see p. 93 ff. in particular.
32. Scobie, *Buenos Aires*, pp. 231–32.
33. Solberg, *Immigration*, p. 170.

34. See Herring, *A History*, p. 629; Romero, *A History*, p. 217.
35. Solberg, *Immigration*, pp. 108–14.
36. Richard J. Walter, *The Socialist Party of Argentina, 1890–1930*, p. 76.
37. For the early history of the Party, see Robert J. Alexander, *Latin American Political Parties*, pp. 109ff.; see also Rock, *Politics*, pp. 71ff.
38. Rennie, *The Argentine*, p. 194.
39. Ibid., p. 206.
40. Rock, *Politics*, pp. 51, 55.
41. Rennie, *The Argentine*, p. 199; Romero, *A History*, p. 217.
42. Rock, *Politics*, pp. 34, 38.
43. Ibid., pp. 39–40.
44. For an interesting account of Yrigoyen and of his election in 1916, see White, *Argentina*, chs. 14 and 15.
45. Rock, *Politics*, p. 99; Rennie, *The Argentine*, p. 206.
46. Rennie, *The Argentine*, p. 192.
47. Rock, *Politics*, pp. 178–79.
48. Torcuato Luca de Tena, ed. *Yo, Juan Domingo Perón*, p. 19.
49. See *El Hombre del Destino*, No. 1, pp. 1–20, for an account of the Perón family and of Juan Perón's infancy. Also, *La Nación*, June 23, 1983, article entitled "De nombres 'y apellidos"; *Diario de Sesiónes de la Camera de Diputados*, May 17, 1951, pp. 204ff.; Enrique Pavón Pereyra, *Perón: Preparación de una vida para el mando, 1895–1942*, chs. 1 and 12.
50. Photocopy of Declaration of Birth, made by Mario Perón on October 8, 1895, in the Office of Civil Registry in Lobos, in the possession of the author.
51. *El Hombre*, No. 1, p. 7; see Joseph A. Page, *Perón: A Biography*, pp. 19ff. for descriptions of Lobos, Perón's house, and the family background.
52. *El Hombre*, No. 1, p. 20.
53. Ibid., No. 1, p. 4; in the opinion of Perón's close friend, Jorge Antonio, it was such experiences that led Perón to his populist convictions: "He lived the terrible differences between his family and the peons . . . [the latter] sleeping in the shed, without bed sheets, with only one or two blankets, sometimes without even a bed." (Interview with Jorge Antonio.)
54. Juan Perón, "Memorias de Juan Perón, 1895–1945," p. 2.

55. *El Hombre,* No. 1, p. 18.
56. Ibid., No. 1, p. 20.
57. Ibid., No. 2, pp. 21ff.
58. Luca de Tena, ed., *Yo,* p. 100.
59. *El Hombre,* No. 2, p. 21. For Perón's strongly critical views on the teaching of Argentine history at the *Colegio,* see the same source, p. 33.
60. Ibid., No. 2, p. 33.
61. A different, and rather more British, view of the *Letters* was expressed by

Lord Macaulay: "Lord Chesterfield stands much lower in the estimation of posterity than he would have done if his letters had never been published." (Essay on Horace Walpole). A description of Perón's love of classical reading and of the impact of Plutarch upon his life is contained in Enrique Pavón Pereyra, *Perón tal como es,* p. 81.
62. Perón, *Memorias,* p. 5.
63. *El Hombre,* No. 3, p. 41.

4. The Conservative Restoration, 1930–1943

1. For the best and most broad treatment of the military in general during this period, see Robert Potash, *The Army and Politics in Argentina, 1928–1945: Yrigoyen to Perón.*
2. Ibid., pp. 42ff; Alberto Ciria, *Parties and Power in Modern Argentina (1930–1946),* pp. 6ff.
3. Mark Falcoff and Ronald H. Dolkart, eds., *Prologue to Peron: Argentina in Depression and War, 1930–1943,* p. 37.
4. Ciria, *Parties,* pp. 11–12; Potash, *Army, 1928–1945,* pp. 43, 64.
5. Potash, *Army, 1928–1945,* pp. 44ff.
6. Whitaker, *Argentina,* p. 85; Romero, *A History,* p. 218.
7. Whitaker, *Argentina,* p. 84.
8. Ciria, *Parties,* p. 8.
9. Potash, *Army, 1928–1945,* p. 60.
10. For a contrary view, to the effect that the military intervention was less a new departure than a culmination of previous trends, see Ciria, *Parties,* p. 18.
11. Potash, *Army, 1928–1945,* pp. 52ff.
12. Ibid., pp. 53–54.
13. Ibid., p. 78.
14. Rennie, *The Argentines,* pp. 227–28.
15. Potash, *Army, 1928–1945,* ch. 4; Ciria, *Parties,* pp. 19–53.
16. For a general view of the period, see Potash, *Army, 1928–1945,* ch. 5; for the fraudulent election, see Whitaker, *Argentina,* p. 90.
17. Ciria, *Parties,* pp. 64–74 for details of the Castillo administration.
18. Ibid., p. 123ff.; Rock, *Politics,* p. 272.
19. Rennie, *The Argentine,* p. 342.
20. Walter, *The Socialist,* pp. 227–28.
21. Rennie, *The Argentine,* p. 262. On this topic in general, see Ciria, *Parties,* pp. 112–28.
22. Falcoff and Dolkart, eds., *Prologue,* p. 193.
23. Solberg, *Immigration,* p. 28.
24. Ysabel Fisk and Robert A. Rennie, *Argentina in Crisis,* p. 40.
25. Ciria, *Parties,* pp. 20–21.
26. Falcoff and Dolkart, *Prologue,* p. 86; Whitaker, *Argentina,* pp. 92–93. The continuing debate about the extent and effects of foreign "imperialist" influence on Argentina ranges from Laura Randall's contention that Argentina has been essentially independent economically for half a century (*Economic History,* pp. 5, 257) to the view of Carlos Escude that malign foreign influences have been the paramount cause of Argentine decline (*Gran Bretaña, Estados Unidos y la declinación argentina, 1942–1949*).
27. H. S. Ferns, *The Argentine Republic,* p. 123.
28. Falcoff and Dolkart, *Prologue,* pp. 103, 106ff.
29. Ibid., p. 103ff.
30. Rennie, *The Argentine,* pp. 220, 340–41; for the continuing role of the elite classes in finance and in intellectual activity, see Imaz, *Los Que,* pp. 125ff.
31. Whitaker, *Argentina,* pp. 93–94.
32. Falcoff and Dolkart, *Prologue,* pp. 67–68; Randall, *Economic History,* pp. 5 and 14; Díaz Alejandro, *Essays,* pp. 103–4. For a good general account, see Gary W. Wynia, *Argentina in the Postwar Era: Politics and Economic Policy-Making in a Divided Society,* pp. 28ff.
33. For the effects of the new industrialization upon trade ties with Britain, see Falcoff and Dolkart, *Prologue,* p. 98.

34. Ibid., p. 9.
35. On this theme generally, see Ciria, *Parties,* pp. 148ff. The origins of the intensified nationalism in the revulsion against the changes wrought by immigration, at the time of the first World War, were noted above, ch. 3, n. 20.
36. Romero, *A History,* pp. 237ff.
37. Ciria, *Parties,* pp. 17–18.
38. Ibid., pp. 144ff.
39. Rennie, *The Argentine,* pp. 272–73; for a description of nationalism that does not observe the distinction between the old and the new, see Fisk and Rennie, *Argentina,* p. 39; see also George Pendle, *Argentina,* p. x. Samuel L. Baily, in *Labor, Nationalism and Politics in Argentina,* chs. 4 and 5, and pp. 187ff., provides a history and analysis of the varieties of nationalism in the labor movement, identifying "Criollo nationalism," based in immigrant workers from the interior, as a basic support for Peronism.
40. Carl E. Solberg, *Oil and Nationalism in Argentina,* pp. 112–13. Chs. 3,4, and 5 of this work are a good general authority on the history of petroleum in Argentina.
41. Potash, *Army, 1928–1945,* pp. 23–24.
42. Graham-Yooll, *The Forgotten,* p. 20.
43. Potash, *Army, 1928–1945,* pp. 117–19.
44. Falcoff and Dolkart, *Prologue,* pp. 118ff.
45. Falcoff and Dolkart, *Prologue,* pp. 136–37.
46. Ibid., pp. 138ff.
47. Ibid., pp. 150–51.
48. Martínez Estrada, *X-Ray,* p. 258.
49. Falcoff and Dolkart, *Prologue,* p. 145.
50. Juan D. Perón, *Tres revoluciónes militares,* pp. 13–20.
51. Ibid., p. 53.
52. Ibid., pp. 15–17.
53. Page, *Perón,* p. 32.
54. Interview, source withheld by request.
55. The book is *Perón: Preparación de una vida para el mando, 1895–1942,* by Enrique Pavón Pereyra, a writer very close to Perón. This work covers Perón's life in detail up to 1942; the first edition was published in 1952, and the second, which added a chronology of Perón's life up to 1953, was published in the latter year. The chronology notes the birth and death of Evita, but both chronology and text omit even a mention of Potota.
56. Arthur Whitaker, *The United States and the Southern Cone: Argentina, Uruguay, and Chile,* pp. 34–35; Herring, *A History,* pp. 557–58; Pavón Pereyra, *Perón,* p. 182.
57. Page, *Perón,* pp. 34–35; for Perón's self-serving denial of spying, see Luca de Tena, ed., *Yo,* p. 189.
58. Luca de Tena, ed., *Yo,* p. 26; Pavón Pereyra, *Perón,* pp. 197–98.
59. Pavón Pereyra, *Perón,* p. 200.
60. Ibid. p. 204.
61. Luca de Tena, ed., *Yo,* pp. 26–27.
62. Ibid., p. 26.
63. Pavón Pereyra, *Perón,* pp. 208–12.
64. For Perón's version of the episode, see Luca de Tena, ed, *Yo,* pp. 101–2: for the Pavón Pereyra account, see his *Perón,* p. 209; the discrepancies between these versions are dissected in "La Historia que Conto Perón," *Redacción,* No. 62, April 1978 (Supplement); the information concerning Perón's emissary and his search for the woman comes from a reliable interview source with first-hand knowledge (name of source withheld).
65. Pavón Pereyra, *Perón,* pp. 209–10.
66. Luca de Tena, ed., *Yo,* p. 28.
67. Pavón Pereyra, *Perón,* p. 214; the most complete account of *Lencinismo* and *Bloquismo* is in Celso Rodríguez, *Lencinas y Cantoni: El Populismo Cuyano en Tiempos de Yrigoyen.*
68. Pavón Pereyra, *Perón,* pp. 222–23.
69. Whitaker, *Argentina,* p. 34.
70. See note 32 above.
71. Fisk and Rennie, *Argentina,* p. 41.
72. Ibid., p. 38; Randall, *Economic History,* p. 228.
73. Filol, *Social Factors,* p. 37; Ferns, *Britain,* p. 85. Interesting examples of the phenomenon are easy to find. The Anchorena family, probably the richest in Argentina in the mid-nineteenth century, invested a mere £200 in the British railways then being constructed, and never increased the holding. Around 1940, the Buenos Aires stock exchange did not list industrial or commercial securities, limiting itself to government issues. For the view that cultural characteristics of Argentine society were criti-

cal in determining the nature of Argentine economic development and limiting it, see Filol, *Social Factors*, pp. 38 and 40. In Robert Alexander's interview in November 1952 with the Argentine sociologist, Torcuato Di Tella, the latter saw technology and industrialization as foreign processes, root causes of social instability.

74. Fisk and Rennie, *Argentina*, pp. 37–38.
75. Ibid., p. 38.
76. Rennie, *The Argentine*, pp. 313–37.
77. Ibid., pp. 336, 315.
78. Taylor, *Rural Life*, pp. 381–82, 395.
79. Ibid., p. 272; Robert Alexander interview with Torcuato Di Tella, November 1952.
80. Ciria, *Parties*, pp. 55–57.
81. Lars Schoultz, *The Populist Challenge: Argentine Electoral Behavior in the Postwar Era*, p. 21, including the quotation from Peter Smith, "Social Mobilization, Political Participation, and the Rise of Juan Perón," *Political Science Quarterly*, March 1969.
82. Francis Herron, *Letters from the Argentine*, p. 128; for an account of the history of organized labor in Argentina, see Baily, *Labor*, ch. 1.
83. Whitaker, *Southern Cone*, p. 171.
84. White, *Argentina*, pp. 19–20.
85. Herron, *Letters*, p. 251. The quoted words were written in 1943. See also, Mark Jefferson, *Peopling the Argentine Pampas*, p. 7.
86. James Oliver Robertson, *American Myth, American Reality*, p. 216.
87. Falcoff and Dolkart, *Prologue*, pp. 29–30.

5. Perón's Rise to Power, 1943–1945

1. Potash, *Army, 1928–1945*, p. 183.
2. Luca de Tena, ed., *Yo*, p. 34.
3. Potash, *Army, 1928–1945*, pp. 184–185.
4. Felix Luna, *El 45*, pp. 57–58.
5. Potash, *Army, 1928–1945*, p. 186, n. 11.
6. This was a tendency, even a preference, that Perón manifested very early in his career, and it was notable for its rarity among Latin American strongmen. He would often approach an "establishment" of some kind, and then, in the face of early difficulty, veer off and begin again with the lower ranks. It was doubtless related to his affinity for the young and to his early military success in working with the disadvantaged.
7. Potash, *Army, 1928–1945*, pp. 194ff.
8. Ibid., p. 193.
9. Perón, *Tres*, p. 112.
10. For Potash's interesting, and convincing, theory of guilt on the part of Colonel Avalos, arising out of a violent incident in the 1943 revolution, see his *Army, 1928–1945*, pp. 281–82.
11. Luca de Tena, ed., *Yo*, p. 36; see also Potash, *Army, 1928–1945*, p. 196, n. 31.
12. Ciria, *Parties*, p. 76.
13. Potash, *Army, 1928–1945*, pp. 196–197.
14. Ibid., p. 192, n. 22.
15. The origins of this spectacular document are discussed in Embassy BA despatch 1813, Jan. 17, 1946, 835.00 / 1–1746, which attributes it to an army group other than the GOU; Potash, *Army, 1928–1945*, p. 196, n. 33. For an example of its earlier acceptance by some serious historians, see Harold F. Peterson, *Argentina and the U.S. 1810–1960*, p. 431.
16. Luca de Tena, ed., *Yo*, p. 36.
17. Ibid., p. 37.
18. Alejandro Magnet, *Neustros vecinos justicialistas*, p. 38; for a very different account of Perón's entry into the June 4, 1943, plot, and his relation to it, see Pavón Pereyra, *Conversaciónes*, p. 34, in which Perón appears to be exercising his considerable powers of historical exaggeration and imagination.
19. Potash, *Army, 1928–1945*, pp. 211–212.
20. Ibid., p. 212.
21. Ibid., p. 22.
22. Luna, *45*, p. 22.
23. See Sumner Welles, *Seven Decisions that Shaped History*, pp. 206–7, 229, 238.
24. Peterson, *Argentina*, pp. 390–93.
25. Ibid., pp. 404ff.
26. See Randall Bennett Woods, *The Roosevelt Foreign-Policy Establishment and the "Good Neighbor": The United States and*

Argentina 1941–1945, ch. 2, for a good account of the bureaucratic rivalry.

27. See *Foreign Relations of the United States,* 1943, vol. 5, pp. 447–51 and 454–60; *Department of State Bulletin,* IX, Sept. 11, 1943, p. 160ff.

28. Potash, *Army, 1928–1945,* p. 222; Luna, *45,* p. 24.

29. Luna, *45,* p. 24.

30. Potash, *Army, 1928–1945,* p. 224, n. 55.

31. Ciria, *Parties,* p. 85.

32. Peterson, *Argentina,* p. 434.

33. Potash, *Army, 1928–1945,* p. 230.

34. Ibid., p. 235.

35. Ibid.

36. Luca de Tena, ed., *Yo,* p. 37. Juan Bramuglia claimed credit for the Peronist social policies, asserting that he had inculcated specific views in Perón, whose ideas were vague (Robert Alexander interview, July 1956). Bramuglia's friend and collaborator, Mercante, claimed, on the contrary, that Perón had "very clear views concerning the social revolution" long before June 1943 ("La Historia del Peronismo—XI," *Primera Plana,* August 24, 1965, p. 42). Perón's views were eclectic and many advisers may have had a share in them, but his general orientation seeems to have been developed internally.

37. Ciria, *Parties,* p. 82.

38. Jorge Newton, *Perón el visionario,* p. 60.

39. Ibid.

40. Ibid., p. 61.

41. Luca de Tena, ed., *Yo,* p. 38.

42. Ibid.

43. Newton, *Perón,* p. 62.

44. "El Peronismo, (1)," *Todo es Historia,* pp. 150–51; Luca de Tena, ed., *Yo,* pp. 38–40; "La Historia del Peronismo—VIII", *Primera Plana,* August 3, 1965, pp. 43–44.

45. Luca de Tena, ed., *Yo,* p. 41.

46. Potash, *Army, 1928–1945,* p. 227

47. Ibid., p. 228.

48. For Perón's techniques with regard to his talks to groups, see "Historia del Peronismo—III," *Primera Plana,* June 29, 1965, p. 42.

49. Robert J. Alexander, *Juan Domingo Perón: A History,* p. 37. Baily, *Labor,* p. 75, notes that Perón's purpose extended beyond bread and butter

benefits, and aimed at a new status for labor in the national life.

50. Luca de Tena, ed., *Yo,* p. 40.

51. Ibid., p. 41.

52. Peter H. Smith, *Politics and Beef in Argentina: Patterns of Conflict and Change,* pp. 236ff.

53. Schoultz, *The Populist,* p. 38; Alexander, *Juan Domingo,* p. 38.

54. Union democracy at the local level is described in Alexander's interview, May 1956, with Luis Cerrutti Costa, Minister of Labor in 1955 under Lonardi.

55. Alexander, *Juan Domingo,* p. 12. The party statutes from 1919 to 1945 banned political activity by the party in unions (see Alexander's interview, October 1946, with Angel Di Giorgio, a union official).

56. Schoultz, *The Populist,* p. 38.

57. Luca de Tena, ed., *Yo,* pp. 44–45.

58. Schoultz, *The Populist,* p. 39. The awareness of labor leaders that Perón had now taken over their followers is exemplified in Robert Alexander's interview, October 1946, with José Argana, a union official.

59. Bonifacio del Carril, *Crónica interna de la Revolución Libertadora,* pp. 32ff.; del Carril, *Memorias,* pp. 16–17; Potash, *Army, 1928–1945,* p. 239.

60. Potash, *Army, 1928–1945,* pp. 216ff.

61. Ibid., p. 242.

62. Ibid., p. 240.

63. Ibid., p. 248.

64. Ibid.

65. Del Carril, *Memorias,* pp. 34–35.

66. Embassy BA Telegram 2489, March 2, 1944, 835.00 / 3-244.

67. F.R.U.S., 1944, Vol. 7, pp. 260–62.

68. Embassy BA despatch 2848, May 9, 1944, 835.00 / 5-944.

69. Ibid.

70. The speech is printed in Juan D. Perón, *El Pueblo quiere saber de qué se trata,* pp. 72ff.

71. *New York Times,* July 4, 1944.

72. Potash, *Army, 1928–1945,* p. 247.

73. Ibid., pp. 251–52; Randall, *Economic History,* pp. 141–43.

74. Peterson, *Argentina,* p. 437.

75. See Otelo Borroni and Roberto Vacca, *La Vida de Eva Perón,* for a good account of Evita's early years. This work, and *Eva Perón* by Nicolas Fraser and Marysa Navarro, provide a gen-

76. Luca de Tena, ed., *Yo*, pp. 49ff.
77. Perón, *Del Poder al Exilio*, pp. 68–69.
78. Fraser and Navarro, *Eva*, p. 33
79. Ibid. p. 8.
80. Ibid., p. 10.
81. For a description of these years, see Borroni and Vacca, *La Vida*, pp. 15–29; "La Historia del Peronismo—II," *Primera Plana*, June 22, 1965, p. 48.
82. Fraser and Navarro, *Eva*, p. 22.
83. Ibid., p. 47.
84. Ibid., p. 34.
85. Luca de Tena, ed., *Yo*, p. 54; Perón, *Del Poder*, p. 69.

86. Luca de Tena, ed., *Yo*, p. 55.
87. Borroni and Vacca, *La Vida*, p. 35.
88. Pavón Pereyra, *Conversaciónes*, p. 31.
89. Fraser and Navarro, *Eva*, p. 44, from which the translation of the quoted words is taken; Borroni and Vacca, *La Vida*, p. 85.
90. Luna, *45*, pp. 137–38. For the views of Avalos concerning Perón and Evita, see "La Historia del Peronismo—III," *Primera Plana*, June 29, 1965, p. 42.
91. Fraser and Navarro, *Eva*, p. 44.
92. Borroni and Vacca, p. 86.
93. Luca de Tena, ed., *Yo*, pp. 54–55.

6. Peronism Ascendant, 1945–1946

1. See Woods, *Roosevelt*, pp. 209–14 for a brief overview of the period.
2. F.R.U.S., *1944*, Vol. 7, pp. 287ff.
3. Woods, *Roosevelt*, p. 176, and source cited in n. 41.
4. Ibid., pp. 180–81.
5. Sumner Welles, *Where Are We Heading?*, p. 206; note comments in Potash, *Army, 1928–1945*, p. 254, and n. 254. Welles described an agreement reached during the secret talks: military aid and abandonment of economic restrictions in exchange for implementation of hemispheric commitments under the Rió Pact and Argentine reentry into the hemispheric fold after the Mexico City conference.
6. Peterson, *Argentina*, p. 144.
7. Embassy BA despatch 17663, March 29, 1945, 835.00/3–2945. See also Luna, *45*, pp. 26, 17, and 27; del Carril, *Memorias*, p. 64.
8. Embassy BA despatch 17401, March 2, 1945, 835.00/3–245. References to Perón's policies during this brief period are contained in F.R.U.S. 1945, IX:388.
9. Potash, *Army, 1928–1945*, pp. 256–58.
10. Ibid., p. 257.
11. Embassy BA telegram 792, April 23, 1945, 835.00/4–2345; Luna, *45*, pp. 140–41.
12. *New York Times*, April 18–21, 1945; Woods, *Roosevelt*, pp. 194–95.
13. Embassy BA despatch 17663, March 29, 1945, 835.00/3–2945; see also

Mecham, *United States*, p. 267.
14. F.R.U.S. 1945, Vol. 9: 380ff. and 507ff.; Potash, *Army, 1928–1945*, p. 259; Spruille Braden, *Diplomats and Demagogues: The Memoirs of Spruille Braden*, p. 333; Gary Frank, *Juan Perón vs. Spruille Braden: The Story Behind the Blue Book*, Chapter VII.
15. For some of the political consequences, see Potash, *Army, 1928–1945*, p. 259, n. 71.
16. Embassy BA telegram 1565, July 17, 1945, 835.00/7–1745.
17. Embassy BA monthly summary, Feb. 24, 1954, 735.00/2–2454.
18. Embassy Caracas despatch 8399, Feb. 8, 1946, 835.00/2–846.
19. Embassy BA telegram 1416, July 3, 1945, 835.00/7–345.
20. Embassy BA despatch 579, Aug. 18, 1945, 835.00/8–1845, contains an appraisal of the significance, or lack of significance, of this development.
21. Luna, *45*, pp. 147–48, 175; see also Potash, *Army, 1928–1945*, p. 260.
22. Embassy BA despatch 433, July 31, 1945, 835.00/7–3145; Luna, *45*, pp. 157–58.
23. Embassy BA despatch 655, undated but believed to be Aug. 29, 1945, 835.00/9–1045; see also Embassy BA despatch 579, Aug. 18, 1945, 835.00/8–1845; Luna, *45*, p. 167.
24. Embassy BA despatch 579, Aug. 18, 1945. 835.00/8–1845; see also Embassy BA despatch 653, Aug. 29, 1945, 835.00/8–2945.

25. Luna, *45*, p. 97. A full account of the event, as described in *La Prensa*, and the text of the speech, are quoted by Luna beginning on page 130; For Braden's perception of the event, see his *Diplomats*, pp. 333–34.

26. Braden, *Diplomats*, p. 333.

27. Enclosure to Embassy BA despatch 653, Aug. 29, 1945, 835.00 / 8–2945.

28. Embassy BA despatch 655, Aug. 29 (?), 1945, 835.00 / 9–1045.

29. Embassy BA despatch 689, Sept. 1, 1945, 835.00 / 9–145; Embassy BA despatch 727, Sept. 6, 1945, 835.00 / 9–645; Luna, *45*, p. 174.

30. Embassy BA despatch 655, Aug. 29 (?), 1945, 835.00 / 9–1045; Luna *45*, p. 97 for the role of the courts in regard to the political agitation of the moment; pp. 186–87 for a summary of the contending forces; and pp. 94–95 for general remarks.

31. Luna, *45*, pp. 180–82. The *Times* of London, given to sober reporting, estimated 500,000; the police estimate was 65,000; other accounts suggest 250,000. See Luna, *45*, p. 199, and Potash *Army, 1928–1945*, pp. 264–65.

32. Luna, *45*, pp. 207–8. Rawson's arrival was incorrectly reported by the embassy as September 24; see Embassy BA, despatch 1040, Oct. 10, 1945, 835.00 / 10–2045.

33. Embassy BA despatch 1040, October 10, 1945, 835.00 / 10–2045.

34. Luna, *45*, p. 209; Embassy BA despatch 1040, Oct. 10, 1945, 835.00 / 10–2045.

35. Embassy BA despatch 1040, October 10, 1945, 835.00 / 10–2045.

36. Potash, *Army, 1928–1945*, pp. 269–70.

37. Ibid.; for a different version, in which the plans were signed, see Page, *Perón*, p. 115.

38. Potash, *Army, 1928–1945*, p. 270.

39. P. Nuñez Arca, *Perón, Man of America*, pp. 102–3; Luna, *45*, pp. 226–27. For Perón's desire to avoid violence, see "La Historia del Peronismo—XVII," *Primera Plana*, October 5, 1965, p. 51.

40. Nuñez Arca, *Perón*, pp. 103–4.

41. "La Historia del Peronismo—XVI," *Primera Plana*, September 28, 1965, p. 42; Potash, *Army, 1928–1945*, p. 268.

42. Luna, *45*, pp. 227–28.

43. Nuñez Arca, *Perón*, p. 104. His permission for the speech has been characterized as the worst error of Avalos during these critical days; see "La Historia del Peronismo—XVII," *Primera Plana*, October 5, 1965, p. 52.

44. Embassy BA despatch 1241, Nov. 3, 1945, 835.00 / 11–345. This document contains a detailed account of the events during the period October 10–25. See also Luna, *45*, pp. 232–34.

45. Fraser and Navarro, *Eva*, p. 58.

46. Luna, *45*, pp. 246–7.

47. Page, *Perón*, p. 122; on the effect of the delay in forming a cabinet, see Potash, *Army, 1928–1945*, p. 273–74.

48. The letters that Perón wrote from Martín Garciá are reproduced in Luna, *45*, pp. 334ff. The letter to Evita is also contained in Borroni and Vacca, *La Vida*, pp. 108–9.

49. Luca de Tena, ed., *Yo*, p. 64.

50. Fraser and Navarro, *Eva*, p. 55. Juan Bramuglia, among other insiders, denied that Evita had anything to do with October 17, regarding it as spontaneous (his interview with Robert Alexander, July 1956). Cipriano Reyes believed that he deserved much of the credit and that neither Evita nor Mercante deserved any ("La Historia del Peronismo—XII," *Primera Plana*, August 31, 1965, p. 46).

51. It seems clear that the gigantic labor demonstration on the 17th was to a considerable extent spontaneous and impromptu in origin (see Luna, *45*, pp. 310ff. and 272–74), although the organizational push of the CGT was also a factor. For a view stressing the latter aspect, see del Carril, *Memorias*, pp. 75–78; for an opinion that discounts the effect of the CGT almost completely, see Gino Germani, *Authoritarianism, Fascism, and National Populism*, pp. 186ff. The spontaneous aspect is stressed in Robert Alexander's interview in the late 1940s with Alcides Monteil, a Peronist labor official and deputy, who also stressed that the most significant among the benefits of Peronism was the new feeling of status, of belonging, that it gave to many.

52. Luna, *45*, p. 258; Germani, *Authoritarianism*, p. 185.
53. Luna, *45*, p. 283.
54. Luna, *45*, p. 288.
55. A hour-by-hour chronology of the day's climax is provided in "La Historia del Peronismo—XIX," *Primera Plana*, October 19, 1965, pp. 43ff.; see Luna, *45*, pp. 293–97, for a description of the setting for Perón's speech, and its delivery. The quotations from the speech as reproduced in the text are from the version printed in Juan Perón, *El pueblo ya sabe de qué se trata*, pp. 185–87.
56. For observations on the absence of a single official text of Perón's speech on the 17th, see Luna, *45*, p. 339, n. 79. A description of the 17th is contained in "La Historia del Peronismo—XVIII," *Primera Plana*, October 12, 1965; and in XIX, October 19, 1965, pp. 41ff.
57. Fraser and Navarro, *Eva*, pp. 69–70, and n. 4.
58. Ibid., p. 70.
59. Luca de Tena, ed., *Yo*, p. 80.
60. Fraser and Navarro, *Eva*, p. 71.
61. Embassy BA despatch 1161, Oct. 24, 1945, 835.00 / 10–2445.
62. Embassy BA despatch 1590, Dec. 15, 1945, 835.00 / 12–1545.
63. Embassy BA despatch 1590, Dec. 15, 1945, 835.00 / 12–1545.
64. Luna, *45*, pp. 395ff.; Embassy BA despatch 1161, Oct. 24, 1945, 835.00 / 10–2445.
65. Embassy BA despatch 1747, Jan. 9, 1946, 835.00 / 1–946; Luna, *45*, p. 344ff.
66. Embassy BA despatch 1747, Jan. 9, 1946, 835.00 / 1–946. A description of the UD and its preelectoral activity can be found in "La Historia del Peronismo—XV," *Primera Plana*, September 21, 1965, pp. 38ff.
67. Luna, *45*, p. 364.
68. Embassy BA despatch 1161, Oct. 24, 1945, 835.00 / 10–2445.
69. Embassy BA despatch 1161, Oct. 24,

1945, 835.00 / 10–2445; for the army's role, see Potash, *Army, 1945–1962*, pp. 7–11, 16–19.
70. Enclosure No. 2 to Embassy Havana despatch 918, Jan. 17, 1945, 835.00 / 1–1745. See also Enclosure to Embassy Havana despatch 883, Jan. 11, 1945, 835.00 / 1–1145.
71. Luna, *45*, pp. 319–20.
72. Embassy BA despatch 1591, Dec. 15, 1945, 835.00 / 12–1545; Mañach interview, Enclosure 2 to Embassy Havana despatch 918, Jan. 17, 1946, 835.00 / 1–1746.
73. Page, *Perón*, pp. 136–7; Luna, *45*, pp. 412–23.
74. Embassy BA despatch 1747, Jan. 9, 1946, 835.00 / 1–946; for a description of the campaign, see also Luna, *45*, pp. 415–27.
75. Luna, *45*, pp. 439–40.
76. Ibid., pp. 356ff.
77. Embassy BA telegram 2940, Nov. 23, 1945, 835.00 / 11–2345; Luna, *45*, pp. 407–10.
78. DOS telegram 1488 to Embassy BA, Oct. 23, 1945, 835.00 / 10–1945; see also Embassy BA telegram 2598, Oct. 19, 1945, 835.00 / 10–1945.
79. Embassy BA despatch 1241, Nov. 3, 1945, 835.00 / 11–345; Embassy BA despatch 1747, Jan. 9, 1946, 835.00 / 1–946.
80. Embassy BA despatch 1747, Jan. 9, 1946, 835.00 / 1–946.
81. *New York Times*, Feb. 13, 1946, p. 1.
82. Braden, *Diplomats*, p. 356; Frank, *Perón vs. Braden*, p. 104.
83. Luna, *45*, pp. 429–31.
84. Enclosure 1 to Embassy BA despatch 2056, Feb. 15, 1946, 835.00 / 2–1546; Embassy BA despatch 1747, Jan. 9, 1946, 835.00 / 1–946.
85. Embassy BA telegram 564, Feb. 22, 1946, 835.00 / 2–2246.
86. Embassy BA telegram 583, Feb. 25, 1946, 835.00 / 2–2546.
87. Potash, *Army, 1945–1962*, p. 45, n. 70; Luna, *45*, pp. 464ff.
88. Luna, *45*, pp. 476ff.

7. Peronism in Power, 1946–1950

1. Pavón Pereyra, *Conversaciónes*, p. 202.
2. Ibid., p. 24.
3. Embassy Santiago despatch 12,576, Aug. 7, 1945, 835.00 / 8–745.

4. Interview with Jorge Taiana.
5. Page, *Perón*, pp. 157–58.
6. Pavón Pereyra, *Conversaciónes*, p. 187.
7. Luna de Tena, ed., *Yo*, p. 173, 103.
8. Interview with Jorge Antonio. The controlled, analytical side of Perón was perhaps best expressed in his remarks to U.S. Ambassador Bruce in August, 1947: "President Perón . . . remarked that to his mind it was not so much a question of friendship between the two countries as a matter of self-interest. He added that there was really no such thing as friendship between two countries and that friendship usually lasted only as long as there was no direct conflict of interests." (Enclosure No. 1 to Embassy BA despatch 2924, August 27, 1947, 711.35 / 8– 2747.
9. Pavón Pereyra, *Conversaciónes*, p. 210.
10. Interview with Isidoro Ventura Mayoral, Perón's personal attorney.
11. Luca de Tena, ed., *Yo*, pp. 95–107; for Perón's views on painting, pp. 273–74; various interview sources.
12. Luna, *45*, p. 475; Enclosure 2 to Embassy BA despatch 19, May 28, 1946, 835.00 / 5–2846.
13. DOS office memorandum, June 10, 1946, 835.00 / 6–746.
14. Guido Di Tella, *Argentina under Perón 1973–1976*, p. 22.
15. Perón, *Ya Sabe*, p. 212. The speech is also reproduced in part in Perón, *Habla Perón*, pp. 196–97.
16. Embassy BA despatch 388, June 3, 1948, 835.00 / 6–348; Potash, *Army, 1945–1962*, pp. 48–50.
17. Potash, *Army, 1945–1962*, pp. 50–51.
18. Embassy BA despatch 356, July 16, 1946, 835.00 / 7–1646.
19. Embassy BA despatch 860, Aug. 17, 1946, 835.00 / 8–1746.
20. Enclosure to Embassy BA despatch 1053, Oct. 22, 1946, 835.00 / 10–2246.
21. Embassy BA despatch 1807, Feb. 7, 1947, 835.00 / 2–747.
22. Embassy BA despatch 3289, Dec. 4, 1947, 835.00 / 12–447. For a review of the parties and the political struggles of this period, see "La Primera Presidencia—III," *Primera Plana*, May 17, 1966, p. 36.
23. Potash, *Army, 1945–1962*, p. 91; Page, *Perón*, p. 176.
24. Felix Luna, *Argentina: De Perón a Lanusse—1943–1973*, pp. 45–46; the impeachment process is described in some detail in Page, *Perón*, pp. 164– 67, and in "La Primera presidencia— VIII," July 5, 1966, pp. 36ff.
25. Interview with Jorge Antonio. A revealing insight is afforded in Robert Alexander's interview in April 1958 with Dr. Valdovinas, a UCR National Committee member, who conceded that Perón had used "only the necessary minimum of violence," and that he "had kept only the absolutely essential number of politicians in prison."
26. Embassy BA despatch 37, Jan. 15, 1948, 835.00 / 1-1548; Potash, *Army, 1945–1962*, p. 90.
27. Embassy BA despatch 1316, Nov. 26, 1946, 835.00 / 11–2646.
28. Embassy BA despatch 609, Oct. 1, 1948, 835.00 / 10–148.
29. Embassy BA airgram 37, Jan. 21, 1949, 835.00 / 1–2149; Embassy Montevideo telegram 30, Feb. 17, 1949, 835.00 / 2–1749.
30. DOS Memorandum, Nov. 10, 1948, 835.00 / 11–1045.
31. Page, *Perón*, p. 200.
32. "La Primera Presidencia—XLVIII." *Primera Plana*, July 13, 1967, in which Evita depicts Perón as having spent a sleepless night tossing in bed, complaining about Mercante's failure to understand his (Perón's) real desire to be overruled; Luna, *De Perón*, p. 57; see also Page, *Perón*, pp. 203–4.
33. See F.R.U.S. 1949, Vol. 2, pp. 485ff., for an account of the enactment of the amendment. The entire project of the new constitution is described in "La Primera Presidencia," *Primera Plana*, June 13, 1967 pp. 38ff.
34. The inherent conflict and ill-will between the two diplomats, rooted in personality, temperament, and perception, is almost palpable in Braden's memoirs and in Messersmith's reporting from Buenos Aires. Their candor is unusual in a diplomatic context.
35. Braden, *Diplomats*, p. 363.
36. Letter, Messersmith to Dean Acheson, Aug. 16, 1946, 835.00 / 8–1646.
37. Peterson, *Argentina*, pp. 471–71.

38. Embassy BA despatch 3146, Oct. 29, 1947, 835.00 / 10–2947; Embassy BA despatch 312, April 15, 1948, 835.00 / 4–1548.
39. Peterson, *Argentina,* pp. 470–73.
40. Di Tella, *Argentina,* pp. 18–21, 207; Wynia, *Argentina,* pp. 75, 80.
41. The remarks of Assistant Secretary Miller were made in a study group meeting on Argentina at the Council on Foreign Relations, Feb. 15, 1951, the minutes of which are in DOS File 611.35 / 2–1551.
42. Wynia, *Argentina,* p. 80. Juan Bramuglia, in his inverview with Robert Alexander in July 1956, attributed the phenomenon to Perón's military formation, but this narrow view is not convincing.
43. Embassy BA despatch 782, Nov. 30, 1950, 735.00 / 11–3050; Potash, *Army, 1945–1962,* pp. 103–4.
44. Embassy BA despatch 891, Aug. 14, 1947, 835.00 / 8–1447; "La Primera Presidencia—XXXII," February 21, 1967, pp. 34ff.; and XXXIII, February 28, 1967, pp. 36ff.
45. Page, *Perón,* p. 211.
46. Enclosure No. 1 to Embassy BA despatch 1531, April 4, 1951, 735.00 / 4–451.
47. Embassy BA despatch 1320, March 6, 1951, 611.35 / 3–651.
48. Potash, *Army, 1945–1962,* p. 104, and diplomatic sources cited.
49. A good general review of the La Prensa case and related matters is contained in Embassy BA Memorandum dated May 3, 1951, Mallory to the ambassador, 611.35 / 5–351.
50. For further information on the La Prensa case and the press, see Embassy BA Monthly Summary No. 31, April 20, 1951, 735.00 / 4–2051; Monthly Summary No. 32, May 10, 1951, 735.00 / 5–1051; Embassy BA Report, May 1, 1951, 735.00 / Mayday 5–251. The texture and grit of the government's campaign is colorfully recounted in Robert Alexander's interview with María Constanza, a *La Prensa* editorial staff member, in October 1955, including the establishment by the government of an "oral newspaper" across the street, whose amplified and continuous bel-

lowing of the news was designed to distract the *La Prensa* workers.
51. William Munger, "Academic Freedom Under Perón", *Antioch Review,* Summer 1947, p. 275.
52. Whitaker, *Argentina,* pp. 127–28.
53. Embassy BA despatch 388, Sept. 14, 1950, 735.00 / 9–1450.
54. Gene H. Bell-Villada, *Borges and His Fiction: A Guide to His Mind and Art,* pp. 262ff.
55. The story is included in Jorge Luis Borges, *Ficciones.*
56. Jorge Luis Borges, *The Aleph and Other Stories 1933–1969,* p. 218.
57. Pavón Pereyra, *Perón tal,* p. 373.
58. Borges, *The Aleph,* p. 241.
59. Jorge Abelardo Ramos, *La era del peronismo,* p. 140.
60. Emir Rodriguez Monegal, *Jorge Luis Borges: A Literary Biography,* pp. 395–98, 401.
61. Fraser and Navarro, *Eva,* pp. 75–77.
62. Ibid., pp. 82–83.
63. Borroni and Vacca, *La Vida,* ch. 5.
64. Fraser and Navarro, *Eva,* pp. 92; details of the trip are provided in "La Primera Presidencia—XXIII," December 6, 1966, pp. 36ff.
65. Fraser and Navarro, p. 82.
66. Embassy BA despatch 2969, Sept. 9, 1947, 835.00 / 9–947.
67. For examples of the Embassy's reports and comments, see Embassy BA despatch 2871, Aug. 14, 1947, 835.00 / 8–1447; despatch 2969, Sept. 9, 1947, 835.00 / 9–947; despatch 388, June 3, 1948, 835.00 / 6–348.
68. *Time,* July 14, 1947.
69. Fraser and Navarro, *Eva,* pp. 116–17.
70. Ibid., pp. 117–18.
71. Ibid., pp. 118–21.
72. "Eva Perón and Her Social Work," Subsecretariat of Information of the Presidency, 1950. This government office published many such pamphlets and releases, as well as large annual reviews, profusely illustrated, covering all aspects of national life during the years in question. Evita's social work is thus covered in detail in the volume for 1949, "Doce Meses de Gobierno de Perón."
73. Interview with Jorge Antonio, in which Evita's passion for service is described as "an imperious necessity."

74. Fraser and Navarro, *Eva*, p. 111.
75. "Yadarola Judges Perón: Defense of the Rights of Man,", privately printed by Mauricio L. Yadarola, a Radical deputy, 1950.
76. Embassy BA despatch 760, May 5, 1950, 735.00 / 5–550.
77. Fraser and Navarro, *Eva*, pp. 107–8.
78. Argentine Policy Review paper, enclosed with DOS memorandum dated Oct. 4, 1951, 611.35 / 10–451; DOS Policy Statement, October 26, 1951, 611.35 / 10–2651. The embassy once remarked, in April 1949, "She probably has more intestinal fortitude and energy than all the so-called good members of the Cabinet put together, and she knows how to throw her weight around." (Embassy BA despatch 322, April 28, 1949, 835.00 / 4–2849).
79. The luncheon at Campo de Mayo is described in Potash, *Army, 1945–1962*, pp. 94–98; the Miller incident is referred to in Embassy BA despatch 1319, March 6, 1951, 735.00 / 3–651; see also minutes of meeting at Council on Foreign Relations, February 15, 1951, DOS File 611.35 / 2–1551; for a general review of Evita's role, see Alberto Ciria, *Perón y el justicialismo*, pp. 109–21.
80. Luca de Tena, ed., *Yo*, pp. 99–100.
81. Ibid., p. 145.
82. Embassy BA despatch 744, May 3, 1950, 735.00 May Day / 5–350.
83. Embassy BA despatch 486, March 22, 1950, 735.00 / 3–2250.
84. Embassy BA despatch 486, March 22, 1950, 735.00 / 3–2250.
85. Quoted in Fraser and Navarro, *Eva*, pp. 90–91; see n. 2, p. 90.
86. Eva Perón, *Historia del Peronismo*, pp. 12, 20, 38, 57, 75, 124, 138, 168.
87. Ibid., p. 41, 139, 145, 148, 155.
88. Embassy BA May Day despatch 744, May 3, 1950, 735.00 / May Day 5–350.
89. Ferns, *The Argentine*, pp. 145–46; Díaz Alejandro, in *Essays*, values net reserves of gold and foreign exchange at $1,687 million.
90. Díaz Alejandro, *Essays*, p. 266; Ferns, *The Argentine*, pp. 143ff.
91. Page, *Perón*, pp. 169–70.
92. Di Tella, *Argentina*, p. 18; Wynia, *Argentina*, pp. 49ff.; Ferns, *The Argentine*, p. 148; "El Peronismo (I)," *Todo es Historia, 5*, pp. 138–41. Raul Prebisch, the famous Argentine economist, who preceded Miranda as general manager of the Central Bank, termed Miranda "a real fool." (interview with Robert Alexander, May 1971).
93. Ferns, *The Argentine*, p. 157; see Díaz Alejandro, *Essays*, p. 135. Details of the losses are given in "La Primera Presidencia—X," *Primera Plana*, July 26, 1966, p. 35.
94. Wright, *British*, p. 273. Those who defend the railroad purchases often do so in large part on the basis of unavailability of capital goods in Britian in the immediate post-war period and the erosion of the value of the blocked sterling through inflation, so that Argentina presumably had little alternative. See Randall, *Economic History*, pp. 188–89. But it has not been demonstrated that the entire sterling area was barren of all useful goods and services or that inflation over a short term would dilute the balances sufficiently to make them less productive than the railroad purchases.
95. Ferns, *The Argentine*, p. 150.
96. Ferns, *The Argentine*, p. 153. Generally, see James, *Latin America*, p. 360; Blakemore and Smith, *Latin America*, pp. 444–45.
97. Ascher, *Scheming*, pp. 62, 64; Randall, *Economic History*, p. 99. For references to growth rates, see Randall, *Economic History*, pp. 80–81 and 158. See also Luna, *De Perón*, p. 48. For the expansion and success during 1945–48, see Díaz Alejandro, *Essays*, p. 110. The critical view of Peronist economic performance is set forth in Díaz Alejandro, *Essays*, pp. 106–26, summarized as follows (p. 126): "Peronist policies present a picture of a government interested not so much in industrialization as in a nationalistic and populist policy of increasing the real consumption, employment and economic security of the masses—and of the new entrepreneurs. It chose those goals even at the expense of capital formation and of the economy's capacity to transform. The favorable external conditions of 1946–48 helped to mask the conflict between

nationalist and populist goals and long-run economic development, a conflict that became clearer after 1948. A final irony is that greater attention to exportables during 1943–55 would

have resulted in more, rather than less, industrialization, as the examples of Canada and Australia suggest . . ."
98. Ferns, *The Argentine*, pp. 157–58.

8. Peronism at High Tide

1. A. E. Van Niekerk, *Populism and Political Development in Latin America*, pp. 151–55, 257; Ciria, *Peronism*, pp. 4–5 and n. 14; Petras and Zeitlin, eds., *Latin America*, p. 257; for a contrary view, see Romero, *A History*, pp. 238ff.
2. Whitaker, *Argentina*, p. 105.
3. Embassy BA letter, Messersmith to Lyon, May 21, 1947, 835.00 / 5–2147. For Perón's views concerning Jews and Arabs, as referred to in this paragraph, see Luca de Tena, ed., *Yo*, pp. 88–91.
4. Embassy Caracas despatch 8468, March 3, 1946, 835.00 / 3–546 (Mañach interview). For Peronism as a movement for class conciliation, see Ciria, *Perón*, p. 181. This work has a good general description of Peronism, pp. 122–31.
5. See Van Niekerk, *Populism*, pp. 148–49. See also James Petras and Maurice Zeitlin, eds., *Latin America: Reform or Revolution?*, pp. 258–59.
6. Van Niekerk, *Populism*, pp. 158–59; Pavón Pereyra, *Perón tal*, p. 23; Pavón Pereyra, *Conversaciónes*, p. 28.
7. Turner and Miguens, *Juan Perón*, p. 182; see also pp. 163–65.
8. Embassy BA despatch 312, April 15, 1948, 835.00 / 4–1548; the Policy Statement is in DOS File 611.35 / 3–2150.
9. For a contrary view, see del Carril, *Memorias*, pp. 81–84. Some others use the term "dictator" and "dictatorship" almost casually. Juan Bramuglia believed that Perón's government was less totalitarian than the Liberating Revolution that replaced it in 1955, and that it was more personalistic than authoritarian (his interview with Robert Alexander, July 1956).
10. Petras and Zeitlin, eds., *Latin America*, p. 174, n. 33; p. 166.
11. Turner and Miguens, eds., *Juan Perón*, pp. 174–75; Richard Gillespie, *Sol-*

diers of Perón: Argentina's Montoneros, p. 23.
12. Gillespie, *Soldiers*, pp. 21ff. The difficulty of definition is seen in the remarkable diversity of opinion among the almost forty scholars and assorted authorities cited in Carlos S. Fayt, *La naturaleza del peronismo*, pp. 161–221. See also Van Niekerk, *Populism*, pp. 148–49.
13. Whitaker, *Southern Cone*, pp. 157–59; Kalman H. Silvert, *Essays in Understanding Latin America*, pp. 27, 161–62, 194.
14. Ciria, *Perón*, pp. 20–27; Claudio Véliz, ed., *Obstacles to Change in Latin America*, pp. 70ff.; Petras and Zeitlin, eds.; *Latin America*, p. 257.
15. Véliz, *Conformity*, p. 100. For description and analysis of Latin American populism in general, see Van Niekerk, *Populism*.
16. London *Times*, December 4, 1945. For the view that *caudillo* politics are a form of populism, see Germani, *Authoritarianism*, p. 135.
17. Ascher, *Scheming*, p. 17.
18. Perón, *Tres*, p. 122.
19. Ascher, *Scheming*, pp. 63–64.
20. Turner and Miguens, eds., *Juan Perón*, pp. 174–75.
21. Ibid., p. 186. For the sources of Peronism, see Peter H. Smith, "The Social Base of Peronism" in *Hispanic American Historical Review*, Feb. 1972; Turner and Miguens, eds., *Juan Perón*, chs. 7 and 8; Petras and Zeitlin, eds., *Latin America*, pp. 256–57, 260–62; Ciria, *Peronismo*, pp. 6–12 for ten sources of Perón's political power.
22. Gillespie, *Soldiers*, p. 2.
23. Celso Rodriguez, *Lencinas y Cantoni: El Populismo Cuyano en Tiempos de Yrigoyen*, pp. 337–38. For an appraisal of Radicalism as a form of populism, see Germani, *Authoritariansm*, p. 142.
24. Pavón Pereyra, *Conversaciónes*, p. 28.
25. Whitaker, *Argentina*, p. 94.

26. Ibid., pp. 94, 71.
27. Ibid., p. 103.
28. See Embassy BA despatch 1609, Dec. 19, 1945, 835.00 / 12–1845; Enclosure 2 to Embassy Havana despatch 934, Jan. 22, 1946, 835.00 / 1–2246; Embassy BA despatch 1559, Dec. 12, 1945, 835.00 / 12–1245; and Embassy BA despatch 1609, Dec. 18, 1945, 835.00 / 12–1845; Pavón Pereyra, *Perón tal,* pp. 211–16.
29. Imaz, *Los Que,* pp. 36–37; see Whitaker, *Argentina,* pp. 132–34, for a description of *Justicialismo* and the Third Position.
30. Raúl A. Mende, *Justicialism: The Peronist Doctrine and Reality,* p. 66. This small work, endorsed by Perón, is the best source on *Justicialismo.* See also Gillespie, *Soldiers,* pp. 17–18; Van Niekerk, *Populism,* pp. 149ff. For the balance between individualism and collectivism, see Frederick B. Pike and Thomas Stritch, eds., *The New Corporatism: Social-Political Structures in the Iberian World,* pp. 162–63 and n. 24.
31. Del Carril, *Memorias,* pp. 21–23, 50; as to Argentine Action, see Whitaker, *Argentina,* p. 103.
32. See Embassy BA despatch 349, Sept. 6, 1950, 735.00 / 9–650; Embassy BA despatch 891, Dec. 21, 1950, 735.00 / 12–2150.
33. Ascher, *Scheming,* pp. 113–14.
34. Van Niekerk, *Populism,* p. 149.
35. Juan Perón, *La comunidad organizada,* pp. 86–88, 92, 109, 108.
36. Speech, "La C.G.T. escucha a Perón," given by Juan Perón to the Central Committee and regional delegates of the C.G.T., Aug. 9, 1950, a copy of which is in the files of the author.
37. Wynia, *Argentina,* pp. 54–59, 248.
38. Perón, *Conducción,* p. 235.
39. Ibid., p. 31.
40. Perón, *Ya sabe,* p. 209.
41. Interview with Jorge Antonio.
42. Rodriguez, *Lencinas,* p. 299.
43. Interview with Jorge Antonio.
44. Perón, *Ya sabe,* p. 185; Van Niekerk, *Populism,* pp. 154, 207.
45. Enclosure to Embassy Caracas despatch 8468, March 5, 1946, 835.00 / 3–546; Embassy BA despatch 1609, Dec. 18, 1945, 835.00 / 12–1845; Enclosure No. 2 (Jorge Mañach interview) to Embassy Havana despatch 934, Jan. 22, 1946, 835.00 / 1–2246.
46. Perón, *Ya sabe,* p. 207.
47. Perón, *Orientación Política,* p. 10.
48. The Huntington statement is in George N. Atiyeh, ed., *Arab and American Cultures,* pp. 147ff. The Secret DOS Policy Statement is in File 611.35 / 3–2150. The other three sources of basic conflict were seen as Argentine aspirations for dominance in South America, its competition with the U.S. for agricultural markets, and its "intense national pride."
49. Perón, *Orientación,* p. 15.
50. Pavón Pereyra, *Perón tal,* pp. 41, 45.
51. Speech, "Discurso Pronunciado en la Academia Argentina de Letras con Motivo del Día de la Raza . . . ," given by Juan Perón, Oct. 12, 1947, a copy of which is in the files of the author.
52. Van Niekerk, *Populism,* p. 155.

9. The Ebb Tide of Peronism, 1950–1955

1. Wynia, *Argentina,* pp. 66–67; for a reference to Perón's public silence, pp. 69–70.
2. Luca de Tena, ed., *Yo,* p. 189.
3. Embassy BA despatch 617, Oct. 24, 1950, 735.00 / 10–2450; for Perón's reference to the Congress, see Pavón Pereyra, *Perón tal,* pp. 67–68.
4. Embassy BA Monthly Summary 35, Aug. 10, 1951, 735.00 / 8–1051.
5. Interview with Jorge Antonio; Luca de Tena, ed., *Yo,* pp. 116–17.
6. Embassy BA despatch 112, July 25, 1950, 735.00 / 7–2550. Bramuglia claimed that he broke with Perón because of labor and newspaper policy differences, although he admitted Evita's hostility (Robert Alexander interview, July 1956). For Miranda's account of his early days with Perón, see "La Primera Presidencia—XI," *Primera Plana,* August 24, 1965, pp. 42ff.
7. Luna, *De Perón,* pp. 69–70.

8. Perón, *Del poder al exilio,* p. 77; Page, *Perón,* p. 236.
9. Borroni and Vacca, *La Vida,* p. 237.
10. Embassy BA despatch 53, Jan. 10, 1950, 735.00 / 1–1050.
11. Page, *Perón,* p. 235; Fraser and Navarro, *Eva,* p. 134; "La Primera Presidencia—XXVII," January 3, 1967, p. 38.
12. Embassy BA despatch 53, Jan. 10, 1950, 735.00 / 1–1050.
13. Page, *Perón,* p. 235; but see Fraser and Navarro, p. 135. The resignation may have been because of offense at Evita's rejection of the advice and her mistrust of the doctor's motives: see Borroni and Vacca, *La Vida,* p. 242.
14. Embassy BA despatch 693, April 24, 1950, 735.00 / 4–2450.
15. Enclosure No. 1 to Embassy BA despatch 51, July 11, 1951, 735.00 / 7–2451.
16. Embassy BA Monthly Summary 32, May 10, 1951, 735.00 / 5–1051.
17. Embassy BA despatch 282, Aug. 24, 1951, 735.00 / 8–2451; Fraser and Navarro, *Eva,* pp. 143–47; Borroni and Vacca, *La Vida,* pp. 261–64 for details of the assembly.
18. Embassy BA despatch 379, Sept. 12, 1951, 735.00 / 9–1251, Fraser and Navarro, *Eva,* p. 146.
19. Embassy BA despatch 379, Sept. 12, 1951, 735.00 / 9–1251.
20. Embassy BA Security Report (March 1952), 735.00 / 3–2452.
21. For a general account, see Fraser and Navarro, *Eva,* ch. 10.
22. Ibid., p. 153.
23. Ibid., p. 155.
24. Embassy BA despatch 1468, March 31, 1952, 735.00 / 3–3152.
25. Interview with Jorge Antonio.
26. Embassy BA despatch 1628, May 2, 1952, 735.00 May Day 5–252; Borroni and Vacca, *La Vida,* p. 278.
27. Perón, *Del Poder,* p. 79.
28. Borroni and Vacca, *La Vida,* p. 298.
29. Fraser and Navarro, *Eva,* p. 157; see n. 12, p. 157 for a psychological analysis.
30. Borroni and Vacca, *La Vida,* p. 290.
31. Fraser and Navarro, *Eva,* pp. 163–67.
32. Pedro Ara, *El Caso Eva Perón.*
33. For the stories concerning the disappearance of Evita's corpse, see Fraser and Navarro, pp. 175–78; Perón's account of Evita's death and the embalming of her body is contained in his *Del poder al exilio,* pp. 77–84.
34. Embassy BA despatch 477, Oct. 20, 1952, 735.00 / 10–2052.
35. Embassy BA despatch 282, Aug. 24, 1951, 735.00 / 8–2451.
36. Interview with Jorge Antonio.
37. Interview with Jorge Taiana.
38. Interview with Jorge Antonio.
39. Interview with Jorge Antonio.
40. Embassy BA despatch 228, Aug. 26, 1952, 735.00 / 8–2652.
41. New York Times, Feb. 4–5 and 8–9, 1952; Potash, *Army, 1945–1962,* pp. 140–41.
42. Potash, *Army, 1945–1962,* pp. 141–42.
43. Ibid., pp. 143–44.
44. Petras and Zeitlin, eds., *Latin America,* p. 174, n. 33.
45. Ascher, *Scheming,* pp. 52–53.
46. Ibid., pp. 57–59.
47. Embassy BA despatch 783, Dec. 18, 1952, 735.00 / 12–1852.
48. Ferns, *The Argentine,* pp. 159–61; Wynia, *Argentina,* pp. 71–73.
49. Ferns, *The Argentine,* p. 161.
50. Embassy BA despatch 826, Dec. 30, 1952, 735.00 / 12–3052.
51. Embassy BA despatch 826, Dec. 30, 1952, 735.00 / 12–3052.
52. Embassy BA despatch 1025, Feb. 11, 1953, 735.00 / 2–1153.
53. Embassy BA despatch 1295, April 8, 1953, 735.00 / 4–853.
54. Embassy BA despatch 1297, April 10, 1953, 735.00 / 4–1053.
55. Luca de Tena, ed., *Yo,* pp. 190–91 for Perón's references to Duarte; for his emotional reactions to the investigation, see Potash, *Army, 1945–1962,* pp. 147–48. Background and details of Duarte's death are in "La Segunda Presidencia—IX," *Primera Plana,* July 2, 1968, pp. 46ff.; and X, July 9, 1968, pp. 46ff. Efforts were made after Duarte's death and burial to respond to the rumors of suicide; his decomposing corpse was secretly exhumed and the head was cut off for analysis, but the results were inconclusive (interview with Dr. Jorge Taiana).
56. Interview with Jorge Antonio. Corroboration is found in the statement of a witness who observed Duarte

being carried into his apartment by two men who held him suspended in the air "as if he were unconscious." ("La Segunda Presidencia—X," *Primera Plana,* July 9, 1968, p. 48.)

57. Embassy BA despatch 1336, April 20, 1953, 735.00 / 4–2053; see also Embassy BA despatch 1443, May 13, 1953, 735.00/5–1353.

58. Embassy BA despatch 1493, May 27, 1953, 735.00 / 5–2753; for a description of the destruction of the Jockey Club and the party properties, see "La Segunda Presidencia—XX," *Primera Plana,* October 8, 1968, pp. 48ff.

59. Embassy BA despatch 1493, May 27, 1953, 735.00 / 5–2753.

60. Embassy BA despatch 164, Aug. 20, 1953, 735.00 / 8–2053.

61. Embassy BA despatch 197, Aug. 31, 1953, 735.00 / 8–3153.

62. Embassy BA despatch 487, Nov. 9, 1953, 735.00 / 11–953.

63. Potash, *Army, 1945–1962,* p. 156; for implementation of the conciliation policy, see Embassy BA despatch 1103, May 28, 1954, 735.00 / 5–2854. See also Embassy BA despatch 323, Oct. 1, 1953, 735.00 / 10–153.

64. Potash, *Army, 1945–1962,* pp. 153–54.

65. Embassy BA despatch 159, Aug. 25, 1954, 735.00 / 8–2554.

66. Ascher, *Scheming,* p. 113.

67. Wynia, *Argentina,* p. 76.

68. Embassy BA despatch 349, Oct. 20, 1954, 735.00 / 10–2054.

69. Luna, *De Perón,* p. 82.

70. Peterson, *Argentina,* p. 486.

71. Potash, *Army, 1945–1962,* pp. 163–64; for references to the revival of foreign investment, see Peterson, *Argentina,* p. 489.

72. Embassy BA despatch 13, July 7, 1953, 611.00 / 7–753.

73. For a summary of Perón's petroleum policies, see Carl E. Solberg, *Oil and Nationalism,* pp. 163–64; see also Randall, *Economic History,* pp. 195ff. for the history of Argentine petroleum policy; Potash, *Army, 1945–1962,* pp. 178–80. The political setting for the petroleum policy disputes is described in "La Segunda Presidencia—XVI," *Primera Plana,* September 10, 1968, pp. 49ff.

74. Embassy BA Secret Security Report, March 24, 1952, 735.00 / 3–2452.

75. Article by "Descartes," *Democracia,* April 24, 1952.

76. Article by "Descartes," *Democracia,* April 30, 1952.

77. Article by "Descartes," *Democracia,* May 8, 1952.

78. Embassy BA despatch 1165, March 16, 1953, 611.35 / 3–1653.

79. Peterson, *Argentina,* p. 487.

80. Embassy BA despatch 93, July 31, 1953, 611.35 / 7–3153. The letters exchanged between President Eisenhower, Perón, and Milton Eisenhower in July and August 1953 (Perón's was in his own handwriting) are brought together under cover of DOS Memorandum dated November 6, 1962, File 735.11 / 11–662.

81. DOS Memorandum for the President, Nov. 19, 1953, 735.00 / 11–1953.

82. Embassy BA letter, Griffis to Miller, Aug. 25, 1950, 611.35 / 8–2550. Ambassador Nufer was having the same problem almost three years later—see Embassy BA despatch 1190, March 19, 1953, 611.35 / 3–1953.

83. DOS, Letter dated May 2, 1950, Potofsky to Miller, 611.35 / 5–250. Miller, in his private comments, went so far as to say, in April 1951, that "The principal obstacle to cooperation between the U. S. and Argentina is the extremely adverse opinion toward Argentina in this country, rather than adverse opinion in Argentina toward the U. S." (DOS Memorandum, Miller to OAS, File 611.35 / 4–3051.

84. Embassy BA Monthly Summary, Feb. 24, 1954, 735.00 / 2–2454; letter, Woodward (DOS) to Zengotita (US Embassy Havana), April 19, 1954, 611.35 / 4–1954.

85. Article by "Descartes," *Democracia,* Jan. 24, 1952; see also Embassy BA despatch 1283, Feb. 20, 1952, 735.00 / 2–2052.

86. Embassy BA despatch 1283, February 20, 1952, 735.00 / 2–2052.

87. Magnet, *Justicialistas,* p. 191. The trip that followed is described in "La Segunda Presidencia—XXIII," *Primera Plana,* October 29, 1968, pp. 44ff.

88. Juan Perón, *Latinoamerica: Ahora o nunca,* pp. 77ff.

89. The information in the text concerning Vargas and the Brazilian response

in general was provided by Maria Cecilia Ribas Carneiro, a Brazilian scholar, authority on Vargas, and vice-director of the Centro do Memória Social Brasileira (R.J.), in correspondence with the author.

90. Magnet, *Justicialistas,* p. 193. Perón went so far as to repeat to Ambassador Nufer the wild story of President Vargas's authorization to Perón to speak for him in Chile (Embassy BA despatch 1464, May 15, 1953, 611.35 / 5–1853). See Donald W. Bray, "Peronism in Chile," *Hispanic American Historical Review,* February 1962, p. 42. This article has a good account of Argentine–Chilean relations during the Peronato.

91. Thomas E. Skidmore, *Politics in Brazil, 1930–1964: An Experiment in Democracy,* pp. 132–33.

92. Arthur P. Whitaker, *Argentine Upheaval: Perón's Fall and the New Regime,* pp. viii–ix; *New York Times,* April 10, 1955.

93. Luca de Tena, ed., *Yo,* p. 175.

94. "Perón y La Iglesia", in *Todo es Historia,* October 1984, p. 24.

95. Embassy BA despatch 349, Oct. 20, 1954, 735.00 / 10–2054.

96. "Perón y La Iglesia", in *Todo es,* p. 35; for Perón's version, see Pavón Pereyra, *Perón tal,* pp. 70ff. For the conflict in general, see John J. Kennedy, *Catholicism, Nationalism, and Democracy in Argentina,* pp. 207–13; "La Segunda Presidencia—XXX," *Primera Plana,* December 24, 1968, pp. 59ff.; XXXI, December 31, 1968, pp. 61ff.; XXXIII, January 14, 1969, pp. 41ff. Kennedy, *Catholicism,* refers to the absence of any real challenge to Perón from a Christian Democratic party, p. 210.

97. Embassy BA despatch 203, Sept. 9, 1955, 735.00 / 9–955.

98. "Perón y La Iglesia", in *Todo es,* p. 37; Kennedy, *Catholicism,* p. 209. For details of *Acción Catholica,* see Kennedy, *Catholicism,* pp. 180ff.

99. "Perón y La Iglesia", in *Todo es,* pp. 39–40.

100. Whitaker, *Argentina,* p. 142. Msgr. D'Andrea, a liberal, anti-Peronist cleric, believed that Perón broke with the hierarchy because he was "all-absorbing." (Interview with Robert Alexander, date unknown).

101. Luna, *De Perón,* pp. 82–84; Potash, *Army, 1945–1962,* pp. 171–6; see also "Perón y La Iglesia," in *Todo es,* pp. 42ff.

102. Whitaker, *Argentina,* pp. 145–46.

103. Peterson, *Argentina,* pp. 494–95 for a short summary of reasons; see also Whitaker, *Argentine Upheaval,* pp. 72–76; Kennedy, *Catholicism,* pp. 208–10.

104. Magnet, *Justicialistas,* p. 195.

105. "La Segunda Presidencia—VII," June 18, pp. 46–48. This history of the UES is delineated in "La Segunda Presidencia—VI," *Primera Plana,* June 11, 1968, pp. 48ff.

106. A somewhat related explanation has been advanced by Bonifacio del Carril, suggesting an excess of arrogance as the cause, and comparing it to Perón's error of judgment in forcing the appointment of Nicolini in 1945; see del Carril, *Memorias,* p. 69.

107. Page, *Perón,* pp. 304–5; Potash, *Army, 1945–1962,* p. 186.

108. "Perón y La Iglesia," in *Todo es,* pp. 54–55; for Perón's commentary on the expulsion of the bishops, see Pavón Pereyra, *Perón tal,* pp. 71–77.

109. Embassy BA despatch 1184, June 24, 1955, 735.00 / 6–2455; Page, *Perón,* p. 309.

110. For an account of the June 16 revolt, see the *New York Times,* June 18, 1955, with the reprint of the army communiqué; Whitaker, *Argentine Upheaval,* pp. 8–11.

111. "Perón y La Iglesia," in *Todo es,* p. 58.

112. Jorge Antonio, *Y Ahora Qué?,* p. 345; for Perón's condemnation of the rioting, see Embassy BA telegram 130, Aug. 9, 1955, 735.00 / 8–955.

113. Luca de Tena, ed., *Yo,* pp. 216–17.

114. Interview with Jorge Antonio.

115. "Perón y La Iglesia," in *Todo es,* p. 60. A general description of June 16 is contained in "La Segunda Presidencia—XXXII," *Primera Plana,* January 7, 1969, pp. 32ff.

116. Embassy BA despatch 24, July 7, 1955, 735.00 / 7–755.

117. Embassy BA despatch 24, July 7, 1955, 735.00 / 7–755.

118. Embassy BA despatch 1184, June 24, 1955, 735.00 / 6–2455; Embassy BA despatch 24, July 7, 1955, 735.00 / 7–755.

119. "Perón y La Iglesia," in *Todo es*, pp. 60–61.
120. Embassy BA telegram 45, July 16, 1955, 735.00 / 7–1655; for the full text of the speech, see Embassy BA despatch 51, July 19, 1955, 735.00 / 7–1955; see also Embassy BA telegram 46, July 18, 1955, 735.00 / 7–1855, and "Perón y La Iglesia," in *Todo es*, pp. 61–62.
121. Embassy BA despatch 24, July 7, 1955, 735.00 / 7–755.
122. Embassy BA despatch 24, July 7, 1955, 735.00 / 7–755.
123. Embassy BA despatch 160, August 26, 1955, 735.00 / 8–2655.
124. Embassy BA telegram 218, August 31, 1955, 735.11 / 8–3155; Embassy BA despatch 177, Sept. 2, 1955, 735.11 / 9–255; Potash, *Army, 1945–1962*, pp. 193–94.
125. The speech is printed in *La Nación*, Sept. 1, 1955, and in the Black Book,

pp. 263–64; see also Embassy BA despatch 177, Sept. 2, 1955, 735.11 / 9–255.
126. Page, *Perón*, p. 315, and n. 38. For a general description of the speech and the events of July–August, see "La Segunda Presidencia—XXXV," *Primera Plana*, January 20, 1969, p. 20ff.
127. Embassy BA Telegram 234, September 2, 1955, 735.00 / 9–255.
128. Potash, *Army, 1945–1962*, pp. 195–96.
129. The letter is reproduced in Embassy BA despatch 228, Sept. 26, 1955, 735.00 / 9–2655.
130. Potash, *Army, 1945–1962*, pp. 202–4.
131. Pavón Pereyra, *Perón tal*, p. 158.
132. Perón, *Del Poder*, pp. 54–55; for a detailed treatment of Perón's fall, covering the period from early September to the 23rd, see Embassy BA despatch 228, Sept. 26, 1955, 735.00 / 9–2655.

10.   The Caribbean Exile, 1955–1960

1. Interview with Jorge Antonio, who saw Perón's failure to mount a military counter effort as one of the few weaknesses in the leader he so admired.
2. Potash, *Army, 1945–1962*, pp. 201, 205.
3. Pavón Pereyra, *Perón tal*, p. 92, where Perón is quoted as saying "I believe that no man has sufficient attributes of power to justify his taking the life of a single man," and pointing out that under the Peronato violence did not extend to the taking of life.
4. Pavón Pereyra, *Convesaciónes*, p. 115.
5. Pavón Pereyra, *Perón tal*, p. 20.
6. Pavón Pereyra, *Convesaciónes*, p. 188.
7. Perón, *Del Poder*, p. 24.
8. Ibid. For the view that Perón's motivation was the preservation of the equilibrium of the state, see Ciria, *Perón*, pp. 129–30.
9. Interview with Jorge Antonio.
10. Gary Wynia, "Argentina: The Frustration of Ungovernability," in *Politics, Policies, and Economic Development in Latin America*, p. 34.
11. "La Segunda Presidencia—VII", *Primera Plana*, June 16, 1968, p. 48;

Perón has described his stay on the Paraguayan gunboat in his *Del Poder*, pp. 64–66.
12. "La Segunda Presidencia—VII", *Primera Plana*, June 16, 1968, p. 48.
13. Luca de Tena, ed., *Yo*, pp. 235–37; Perón, *Del Poder*, pp. 64–66. Perón's stay is described in "La Caida y El Exilio—XIII," *Primera Plana*, August 5, 1969, pp. 50ff.
14. Embassy BA despatch 298, Oct. 19, 1955, 735.00 / 10–1955, for the text of the interview.
15. Embassy BA despatch 298, Oct. 19, 1955, 735.00 / 10–1955.
16. Embassy Asunción telegram 58, Oct. 3, 1955, 735.00 / 10–355; see also Embassy BA despatch 272, Oct. 7, 1955, 735.00 / 10–755; Embassy Asunción despatch 124, Oct. 11, 1955, 735.00 / 10–1155; and Embassy BA despatch 289, Oct. 17, 1955, 735.00 / 10–1755.
17. Luca de Tena, ed., *Yo*, pp. 238–39.
18. DOS Memorandum of Conversation, Feb. 20, 1956, 735.00 / 0–2056; DOS Memorandum for the Files, Feb. 24, 1956, 735.00 / 2–2456; DOS Memorandum for the Files, Feb. 24, 1956,

735.00 / 2–2456; DOS Memorandum of Conversation, Feb. 24, 1956, 735.00 / 2–2456.
19. *Bohemia,* Nov. 20, 1955.
20. Correspondence between Claudio Véliz, who conducted the interview, and the author.
21. Pavón Pereyra, *Perón tal,* p. 194.
22. Luca de Tena, ed., *Yo,* p. 242.
23. Interview with Jorge Antonio; Luca de Tena, ed., *Yo,* p. 241; Page, *Perón,* pp. 339–40.
24. Judith Ewell, *The Indictment of a Dictator: The Extradition and Trial of Marcos Pérez Jiménez,* pp. 28ff., for a description of "PJ."
25. Juan Perón and John William Cooke, *Correspondencia,* Vol. 1, p. 9.
26. Interview with Jorge Antonio.
27. Gillespie, *Soldiers,* pp. 35–38, 44–45.
28. Luca de Tena, ed., *Yo,* p. 247.
29. Ibid., p. 250.
30. Embassy Caracas despatch 644, April 18, 1957, 735.00 / 4–1857.
31. Embassy BA telegram 50, July 8, 1957, 735.00 / 7–857; Embassy BA telegram 67, July 10, 1957, 735.00 / 7–1057; Embassy BA telegram 73, July 11, 1957, 735.00 / 7–1157; DOS telegram to Embassy BA, July 11, 1957, 735.00 / 7–1157; Embassy Caracas telegram 31, July 12, 1957, 735.00 / 7–1257.
32. Interview sources in the Dominican Republic, names withheld.
33. Interview sources in the Dominican Republic, names withheld; Luca de Tena, ed., *Yo,* pp. 259ff.
34. Ibid., p. 264; interview sources, names withheld.
35. Interview source in the Dominican Republic, name withheld.
36. Luca de Tena, ed., *Yo,* pp. 264–65.
37. Ibid., pp. 263–64.
38. Ibid., pp. 260–61.
39. Embassy BA despatch 974, Dec. 30, 1959, 735.00 / 12–3059; for the role of Trujillo, see Pavón Pereyra, *Conversaciónes,* p. 112.
40. Embassy BA despatch 336, Nov. 1, 1955, 735.00 / 11–155.
41. Potash, *Army, 1945–1962,* pp. 228–29.
42. For the situation of labor in general, see Baily, *Labor,* ch. 8; Ascher, *Scheming,* pp. 65–68. The views of ex-President Aramburu are contained in Robert Alexander's interview with him, June 7, 1968. To the effect that the Aramburu policies made the workers more fanatically Peronist than they had been under the Peronato, see Robert Alexander's interviews with Victor Agusto Alcorta, a labor ministry official (May 1956) and Raúl Alonso, a union official (April 1955) The insensitivity of the government interventors is noted in the Alexander interview with Martín Fuchs, a UCR official (June 1956). See also Luna, *De Perón,* pp. 105–8.
43. Potash, *Army, 1945–1962,* pp. 230–35.
44. Perón and Cooke, *Correspondencia,* Vol. I, pp. 210ff.
45. Potash, *Army, 1945–1962,* pp. 255–56, and n. 52.
46. Perón and Cooke, *Correspondencia,* Vol. II, p. 46, for reference to Perón's views on the virtues of "intransigence."
47. Potash, *Army, 1945–1962,* pp. 266ff., which contains an account of the evolution of the alliance. A brief overview is found in Luna, *De Perón,* pp. 115–16.
48. Embassy Ciudad Trujillo despatch 434, Feb. 26, 158, 735.00 / 2–2658.
49. Potash, *Army, 1945–1962,* pp. 267–70; Luna, *De Perón,* p. 117.
50. Antonio, *Y Ahora,* pp. 359–60.
51. The suggestion was made in Potash, *Army, 1945–1962,* p. 377.
52. Luna, *De Perón,* pp. 121–23.
53. DOS Bulletin, XL, Jan. 19, 1952, pp. 100–106; Peterson, *Argentina,* pp. 511–12; Whitaker, *Argentina,* p. 161.
54. Luna, *De Perón,* pp. 126–29; Wynia, *Argentina,* p. 91.
55. Potash, *Army, 1945–1962,* p. 297.
56. For a good description of Frondizi's impossible situation, see Gillespie, *Soldiers,* pp. 32–34. See also Potash, *Army, 1945–1962,* p. 313.
57. Luna, *De Perón,* pp. 137–43.

11. The Spanish Exile, 1961–1973

1. The letter is reprinted in Antonio, *Y Ahora,* pp. 336–52. The text quotations are at pp. 341, 349, and 350.
2. Interview with Jorge Antonio.
3. Interview with Jorge Antonio.
4. Pavón Pereyra, *Conversaciónes,* p. 218.
5. Luca de Tena, ed., *Yo,* p. 107; for the action of the Swiss government, see DOS Office Memorandum, Feb. 2, 1960, 735.00 / 2–260.
6. A copy of the letter was enclosed with Embassy BA despatch 165, Aug. 4, 1961, 735.00 / 8–861. The letter itself was dated "July 1961." See also communication dated July 12, 1961 from the Executive Secretariat, DOS, to ARA—Romano, enclosing a copy of the letter, 735.00 / 7–1261.
7. Page, *Perón,* p. 373.
8. Interview with Jorge Antonio.
9. Luca de Tena, ed., *Yo,* pp. 272–73.
10. Interview with Jorge Antonio.
11. Interview with Jorge Taiana.
12. Interview with Jorge Antonio; Pavón Pereyra, *Conversaciónes,* p. 111.
13. Interview with Isidoro Ventura Mayoral, Perón's personal attorney.
14. Interview with Jorge Antonio.
15. Pavón Pereyra, *Conversaciónes,* p. 222.
16. Interview with Jorge Antonio.
17. Interview with Jorge Antonio.
18. Interview with Jorge Antonio.
19. Correspondence between Jorge Antonio and the author.
20. Correspondence between Jorge Antonio and the author.
21. Antonio, *Y Ahora,* p. 390.
22. Antonio, *Y Ahora,* p. 392.
23. Interview with Jorge Antonio.
24. Antonio, *Y Ahora,* pp. 394–95; for the entire episode, pp. 384–97.
25. Pavón Pereyra, *Conversaciónes,* p. 95.
26. Pavón Pereyra, *Conversaciónes,* p. 206.
27. Pavón Pereyra, *Perón tal,* pp. 199–206, for Perón's views concerning the return and his version of the events.
28. Institute of Current World Affairs (ICWA) Report JR-10, May 30, 1962; Luna, *De Perón,* p. 148; ICWA Report JR-10, May 30, 1962, for a good review of the early Guido period; the military showdown is described in the

New York Times, April 22, 1962.
29. Luna, *De Perón,* pp. 153–56; *New York Times,* Sept. 19, 20, 21, and 23, 1962; ICWA Report JR-17, Dec. 30, 1962.
30. *New York Times,* Nov. 20, 1962.
31. *New York Times,* Nov. 20, 1962; June 28, 1962; July 8, 1962; June 28, 1962. The ups and downs of the Coordinating Council are described in Embassy BA despatch 1312, April 18, 1962, 735.00 / 4–2562.
32. Embassy BA telegram 1357, Nov. 29, 1962, 735.00 / 11–2962.
33. ICWA Report JR–23, June 30, 1963; for a general view and assessment, see American Universities Field Staff (AUFS) East Coast South America Series, Feb. 1964, (JWR-1-64).
34. Luna, *De Perón,* p. 171.
35. Luna, *De Perón,* pp. 183–84; AUFS, Nov. 1966, (JWR-7-66).
36. ICWA Report JR–10, May 30, 1962.
37. ICWA Report JR–10, May 30, 1962.
38. Ruben E. Reina, *Paraná: Social Boundaries in an Argentine City,* pp. 341–42, 344, 349–50, 365, 353, 344–46.
39. Juan Perón, "Message to the Governors of the Provinces," Feb. 8, 1973, a copy of which is in the author's files; for the contention that Argentines are a " 'conglomeration' of people rather than an 'organic' community," see Filol, *Social Factors,* pp. 3, 22.
40. AUFS, Nov. 1966, (JWR-7-66).
41. Luna, *De Perón,* p. 205. For a general description of Onganía and the Argentine Revolution, see Peter G. Snow. *Political Forces in Argentina,* pp. 136–40.
42. AUFS, Nov. 1966, (JWR-7-66).
43. AUFS, Nov. 1966, (JWR-8-66); Luna, *De Perón,* p. 187.
44. AUFS, Nov. 1966, (JWR-7-66); on the military aspect, see Luna, *De Perón,* pp. 198–99.
45. AUFS, Nov. 1966, (JWR-8-66).
46. Luna, *De Perón,* p. 197.
47. Gillespie, *Soldiers,* pp. 29ff. This is the most recent, thorough, and authoritative work on the Argentine revolutionary left in the 1960s and 1970s.

48. Perón and Cooke, *Correspóndencia,* Vol. I, p. 35, cited in Gillespie, *Soldiers,* p. 41.
49. Gillespie, *Soldiers,* pp. 30, 42–43.
50. Pavón Pereyra, *Perón tal,* p. 223.
51. Ibid., p. 51, 178.
52. Perón, *La Hora,* pp. 19–20.
53. Ibid., p. 20, 171.
54. Ibid., p. 171; see also pp. 167, 170.
55. Gillespie, *Soldiers,* pp. 60, 106–8.
56. Ibid., pp. 107–8, 66.
57. Ibid., pp. 108, 170–71.
58. Luna, *De Perón,* pp. 202–4; Gillespie, *Soldiers,* pp. 65–66.
59. Gillespie, *Soldiers,* pp. 89–91.
60. Ibid., pp. 47ff.
61. Ibid., p. 94.
62. Ibid., pp. 97, 99.
63. Luna, *De Perón,* pp. 204–6.
64. Ibid., pp. 209–11.
65. Gillespie, *Soldiers,* p. 98.
66. Ibid., p. 113.
67. Luna, *De Perón,* p. 213.
68. Di Tella, *Argentina,* p. 43.

12. The Return of the Phoenix

1. Robert Alexander, interview with Ronald Crosby, October 1971.
2. An account of Isabel's political activity is contained in Antonio, *Y Ahora,* pp. 403–4; interview and correspondence with Jorge Antonio.
3. For Perón's tribute to Isabel's powers of *conducción,* see Pavón Pereyra, *Perón tal,* pp. 274–75.
4. Interview with Jorge Antonio.
5. Any Ventura, *Jorge Antonio: El hombre que sabe demasiado,* p. 129.
6. Interview with Jorge Antonio.
7. Ventura, *Jorge Antonio,* pp. 125ff.; *New York Times,* July 6, 1974; Page, *Perón,* ch. 44.
8. Page, *Perón,* p. 399.
9. Ventura, *Jorge Antonio,* pp. 125–26.
10. Ibid., p. 106.
11. Correspondence with Jorge Antonio.
12. Page, *Perón,* p. 400.
13. Interview with Jorge Antonio.
14. Gillespie, *Soldiers,* p. 100.
15. Luna, *De Perón,* p. 215.
16. Gillespie, *Soldiers,* pp. 106–7.
17. Ibid., pp. 109, 101–3.
18. Ibid., pp. 42, 104.
19. Lanusse and his record are described in a long article in the *New York Times,* Aug. 20, 1972; see also Luna, *De Perón,* p. 213.
20. Di Tella, *Argentina,* p. 43; Gillespie, *Soldiers,* pp. 92, 114–15.
21. Gillespie, *Soldiers,* p. 114.
22. Fraser and Navarro, *Eva,* pp. 175–78, 182–83, 187–89; Page, *Perón,* pp. 424–25.
23. Gillespie, *Soldiers,* p. 104; Page, *Perón,* p. 415.
24. Perón and Cooke, *Correspóndencia,* Vol. 1, p. 72.
25. Gillespie, *Soldiers,* pp. 105–6.
26. Pavón Pereyra, *Conversaciónes,* p. 171.
27. Di Tella, *Argentina,* pp. 56–57, 122ff.; for analysis of its implementation, see Wynia, *Argentina,* pp. 212–35.
28. Gillespie, *Soldiers,* p. 104, n. 23; Page, *Perón,* p. 429.
29. *New York Times,* July 9, 1972.
30. Turner and Miguens, eds., *Juan Perón,* pp. 111–12.
31. Gillespie, *Soldiers,* pp. 104–5.
32. Page, *Perón,* p. 422.
33. Gillespie, *Soldiers,* p. 74.
34. Page, *Perón,* p. 448.
35. Di Tella, *Argentina,* p. 46.
36. Gillespie, *Soldiers,* p. 207.
37. Pavón Pereyra, *Conversaciónes,* p. 170.
38. Interview with Jorge Antonio.
39. For the view that Perón's policy was tactically correct, see Page, *Perón,* p. 420.
40. *New York Times,,* Nov. 16, 1972.
41. *New York Times,* Nov. 16, 1972.
42. *New York Times,* Nov. 21, 1972.
43. *New York Times,* Nov. 26, 1972.
44. *New York Times,* Nov. 20 and Dec. 15, 1972.
45. Gillespie, *Soldiers,* pp. 104, 115.
46. *New York Times,* Dec. 15 and Dec. 19, 1972; for more on Perón's visit, see Nov. 19 and Dec. 7, 1972, as well as the *Christian Science Monitor,* Dec. 16, 1972.
47. Interview with Jorge Antonio.
48. Interview and correspondence with Jorge Antonio.
49. Di Tella, *Argentina,* p. 52, 54–55; Gillespie, *Soldiers,* pp. 123–26.
50. Gillespie, *Soldiers,* pp. 140–41.
51. Ibid., pp. 127–28.
52. Ibid., pp. 131–34.

53. Page, *Perón,* pp. 460–61.
54. For a general view, see Page, *Perón,* pp. 463–66.
55. The message was reprinted in the Buenos Aires press, June 22, 1973. A copy in pamphlet form is in the files of the author.
56. Turner and Miguens, eds., *Juan Perón,* p. 129; Gillespie, *Soldiers,* pp. 152–53.
57. Interviews with Jorge Taiana and Vicente Solano Lima.
58. Interview with Jorge Taiana.
59. Héctor Cámpora, *El Mandato de Perón,* pp. 83ff.
60. Page, *Perón,* p. 468, and n. 26. Arturo Frondizi also believed this (interview with Robert Alexander, August 1974).
61. Turner and Miguens, eds., *Juan Perón,* p. 131, for the Solano Lima interview.
62. Ibid., pp. 129–31.
63. See ibid., pp. 133–34, for the view that Perón was sincere in this, but was deterred by serious difficulties.
64. Gillespie, *Soldiers,* pp. 143–44.
65. Interview with Jorge Antonio; Turner and Miguens, eds., *Juan Perón,* p. 134, where the same remark is quoted from another source.
66. Interview with Jorge Antonio.
67. *New York Times,* July 29, 1973.
68. Turner and Miguens, eds., *Juan Perón,* pp. 134–35; Gillespie, *Soldiers,* 139–40.
69. Turner and Miguens, eds., *Juan Perón,*

pp. 135–36. For the Washington view, see the *New York Times,* July 29, 1973.
70. Gillespie, *Soldiers,* pp. 165ff., and n. 4, p. 165.
71. Ibid., p. 144.
72. Ibid., p. 136.
73. Ibid., p. 144.
74. Di Tella, *Argentina,* pp. 62–63; Page, *Perón,* pp. 480–82.
75. Gillespie, *Soldiers,* p. 156.
76. Ibid., p. 147.
77. Interview with Jorge Taiana.
78. Interview with Julio Cesar Varela, *Director General de Ceremonial y Audencias* in the Casa Rosada, 1973–1976.
79. Pavón Pereyra, *Conversaciónes,* p. 182.
80. Interview with Jorge Taiana.
81. Speech of August 2, 1973, given at the residence in Olivos, a copy of which is in the author's files.
82. Julio A. Luqui Lagleyze, "Yo salvé la vida a Perón," in *Todo Es Historia,* No. 104, Jan. 1976, p. 71.
83. Juan Perón, *Juan Perón, 1973–1974: Todos sus discursos, mensajes y conferencias completos,* Vol. 2, pp. 69ff.
84. Gillespie, *Soldiers,* p. 148.
85. Ibid., pp. 148–50.
86. Interview with Jorge Antonio.
87. *New York Times,* May 7, 1974.
88. *La Prensa,* July 14, 1974.
89. Correspondence between Dr. Taiana and the author.
90. Pavón Pereyra, *Conversaciónes,* p. 191.

Postscript: Peronism as Memory and Legend

1. Interview with Julio Cesar Varela.
2. Gillespie, *Soldiers,* pp. 163–64.
3. Ibid., p. 180 for Bunge y Born; pp. 174ff. for a general account.
4. Ibid., p. 184.
5. Ibid., p. 143.
6. Ibid., p. 186.
7. Ibid., pp. 155, 216.
8. Ibid., p. 223.
9. Ibid., pp. 235ff.
10. Ibid., p. 245.
11. Ibid., p. 238.
12. Ibid., p. 240.
13. *Sunday Times* of London Insight Team, *War in the Falklands: The Full Story,* p. 27.

Sources

Diplomatic Materials

This study has made much use of the unpublished diplomatic documentary records available in the National Archives in Washington, D.C. These include the U.S. Department of State Decimal File 835, covering Argentine Internal Affairs, which was renumbered to 735 as of January 1, 1950; and Decimal File 711.35, covering United States–Argentine Relations, likewise renumbered as of January 1, 1950, to 611.36; and similarly numbered decimal files for various other hemispheric nations. The Argentine Blue Book Files were also consulted.

For the period beginning January 1, 1955, it has been necessary to rely upon diplomatic records obtained from the Department of State pursuant to the Freedom of Information Act. These have been extensive and include materials from various Decimal Files and geographic points of origin, including Argentina, Paraguay, Panama, Venezuela, the Dominican Republic, Cuba, and Spain.

The published diplomatic records contained in the annual series edited by the Department of State, *Foreign Relations of the United States* (F.R.U.S.) have been consulted, as have relevant issues of *The Department of State Bulletin*.

Interview Sources

Various interviews were conducted in Buenos Aires and in New York. Since many of the events concerned, and sometimes the persons involved, are still politically sensitive, requests for privacy were occasionally made. The names of interviewees who have not requested privacy are indicated in footnotes at the appropriate point, if such citation has been deemed helpful.

I have also drawn upon the extensive Argentine interview materials accumulated over many years by Professor Robert J. Alexander of Rutgers University. Sincere appreciation is hereby expressed to Professor Alexander for his generous and helpful sharing of these substantial files and for his permission to quote therefrom, with attribution if desired. I have drawn upon 113 of these Alexander interviews, including nine with ex-President Arturo Frondizi, twelve with Ricardo Rojas, and others with ex-Presidents Aramburu and Illia and a wide variety of men and women active in Argentine public and private life. One of these interviews, with Juan D. Perón in September 1960, appears as Appendix B in Professor Alexander's book, *Juan Domingo Perón: A History.*

Compilations

There is no single compilation that does or probably could assemble Juan Perón's vast output of speeches, messages, articles, and correspondence, formal and informal. Many individual speeches have been printed in pamphlet form, and a collection of these is contained in the author's files.

Various compilations do exist, however, bringing together some of Juan Perón's more important utterances and writings in these rather confused categories. The following are the most notable:

El pueblo quiere saber de qué se trata, published in Buenos Aires in 1944 and reprinted in that city by Editorial Freeland in 1973 (a collection from 1943 and 1944); *El pueblo ya sabe de qué se trata,* published in Buenos Aires (no date) and reprinted there by Editorial Freeland in 1973 (containing speeches from late 1944 into 1946); *Perón expone su doctrina: teoria y doctrina del Peronismo,* published in Buenos Aires by Editorial "Nueva Argentina" in 1948 (excerpts from speeches during the period 1943–1947, arranged by subject matter); *Orientación Política,* published in Buenos Aires in 1982 by Ediciónes Sintesis S.R.L. (bringing together six articles on a variety of topics written in June 1948); *Habla Perón,* published in Buenos Aires in 1950 by the Subsecretaria de Informaciones de la Presidencia (a collection of 474 excerpts from Perón's speeches at seminars, meetings, etc., from 1946–1950); *Política y estrategia,* published in Buenos Aires in 1952 under the name "Descartes" (the complete collection of weekly articles that appeared in *Democracia* under Perón's pseudonym between 1951 and 1952); *Perón–Cooke correspondencia,* 2 vols., published in Buenos Aires by Granica Editor in 1973 (the letters exchanged by Perón and John William Cooke beginning in mid–1956); *Conceptos Políticos,* published in Buenos Aires in 1982 by Editora Volver (excerpts from speeches and writings in the 1940s and 1950s); and *Juan Perón, 1973–1974: Todos sus discursos, mensajes y conferencias completos,* 2 vols., published in Buenos Aires by Editorial de la Reconstrucción in 1974 (speeches and messages during the years indicated).

Compilations of Evita's speeches and writings include: *La palabra, el pensamiento y la acción de Eva Perón,* published in Buenos Aires in 1973 by Editorial Freeland; and *Escribe Eva Perón,* published in Buenos Aires in 1973 by Ediciónes Argentinas. Also of interest is Evita's last will and testament, published in Buenos Aires by Servicio Internacional de Publicaciones Argentinas in 1952 under the title of *La ultima voluntad de Eva Perón.*

Newspapers and Periodicals

NEWSPAPERS: *The New York Times; The Christian Science Monitor; The New York Herald Tribune; The Washington Post; The Times* (London); *The Manchester Guardian Weekly; La Nación* (Buenos Aires); *La Prensa* (Buenos Aires).

PERIODICALS: *Primera Plana* (Buenos Aires); *Esto Es* (Buenos Aires); *Time; Todo Es Historia* (Buenos Aires); *Foreign Affairs; The Economist; The Nation; Redacción* (Buenos Aires); *Criterio* (Buenos Aires); *Bohemia* (Havana).

Miscellaneous

The official Army Dossier of Juan Perón, compiled by the *Direccíon General del Personal, Ejercito Argentino.* Copy in the possession of the author.

Libro Negro de la Segunda Tirania, the so-called Black Book, published by the Argentine Government in 1958.

The reports published by American Universities Field Staff in its East Coast South

America Series, written by representatives residing in Buenos Aires: Kalman Silvert in the late 1950s and James W. Rowe in 1964.

The reports published by the Institute of Current World Affairs, written from Buenos Aires by James W. Rowe in the 1960s.

El Hombre del Destino, a weekly publication consisting of forty-five numbers, published in Buenos Aires in 1973.

Bibliography

The Writings of Juan Perón and Eva Perón

Perón, Juan Domingo. *Apuntes de historia militar*. Buenos Aires: Republica Argentina, 1951.
———. *Conducción política*. Buenos Aires: Ediciónes Mundo Peronista, 1952.
———. *Del poder al exilio. Como y quienes me derrocaron*. Buenos Aires, no date. Republished by Ediciónes Sintesis S.R.L., 1982.
———. *Doctrina Peronista*. Buenos Aires: Republica Argentina, 1952. Republished by Editora Volver, 1982.
———. *El frente oriental de la Guerra Mundial en 1914*. Buenos Aires: Instituto Geografico Militar, 1931.
———. *La comunidad organizada*. Buenos Aires: Secretaria Política de la Presidencia de la Nacion, 1984.
———. *La fuerza es el derecho de las bestias*. Montevideo: 1959. Republished in Buenos Aires by Ediciónes Sintesis S.R.L., 1974.
———. *La hora de los pueblos*. Madrid: 1968. Republished in Buenos Aires by Editorial Pleamar in 1973 and by Editora Volver in 1982.
———. *Latinoamérica: Ahora o nunca*. Madrid: 1967. Republished in Buenos Aires by Ediciónes Sintesis in 1973.
———. *Los vendepatria*. Caracas: Editorial Atlas, 1957. Republished in Buenos Aires by Editorial Freeland in 1974.
———. "Memorias de Juan Perón (1895–1945)." *Panorama*. Buenos Aires, April 14, 1970.
———. *El Proyecto Nacional*. Buenos Aires: El Cid Editor, 1981.
———. *Toponimia Patagónica de Etimología Araucana*. Buenos Aires: Ministerio de Agricultura, 1935.
———. *Tres revoluciónes militares*. Buenos Aires: Ediciónes Corac S.R.L., 1972.
———. *Yo, Juan Domingo Perón: Relato autobiografico*. Luca de Tena, Torcuato, Luis Calvo and Estaban Peicovich, eds. Barcelona: Editorial Planeta, 1976.
Perón, Eva. *La Razón de mi Vida*. Buenos Aires: Ediciones Peuser, 1951. English translation: *My Mission in Life*. New York: Vantage Press, 1952.
———. *Historia del Peronismo*. Buenos Aires: Subsecretaria de Informaciones, 1951.

Books

Aizcorbe, Roberto. *Argentina: The Peronist Myth.* Hicksville, N.Y.: Exposition Press, 1975.
Alberto Astiz, Carlos, ed. *Latin American International Politics.* Notre Dame, Ind.: University of Notre Dame Press, 1969.
Alexander, Robert J. *An Introduction to Argentina.* New York: Praeger, 1969.
———. *The Perón Era.* New York: Columbia University Press, 1951.
———. *Organized Labor in Latin America.* New York: Free Press, 1965.
———. *Juan Domingo Perón: A History.* Boulder, Col. Westview Press, 1979.
———. *Latin American Political Parties.* New York: Praeger, 1973.
———. *Trotskyism in Latin America.* Stanford: Hoover Institution Press, 1973.
———. *Today's Latin America.* New York: Praeger, 1968.
———. *Labor Relations in Argentina, Brazil, and Chile.* New York: McGraw-Hill, 1962.
———. *Prophets of the Revolution.* New York: Macmillan, 1962.
Amadeo, Mario. *Ayer, hoy, manaña.* Buenos Aires: Ediciones Gure, 1956.
Andrews, George Reid. *The Afro-Argentines of Buenos Aires, 1800–1900.* Madison: University of Wisconsin Press, 1980.
Antonio, Jorge. *Y Ahora Qué?* Buenos Aires: Ediciónes Verum et Militia, 1966.
———. *Ahora o nunca.* Buenos Aires: private printing, 1975.
Ara, Pedro. *El caso Eva Perón.* Madrid: CVS Ediciónes, 1974.
Areilza, Jose María de. *Así los he visto.* Barcelona: Editorial Planeta, 1970.
Arenas Luque, Fermín V. *Como era Buenos Aires.* Buenos Aires: Editorial Plus Ultra, 1979.
Ascher, William. *Scheming for the Poor: The Politics of Redistribution in Latin America.* Cambridge, Mass.: Harvard University Press, 1984.
Atiyeh, George N., ed. *Arab and American Cultures.* Washington: American Enterprise Institute for Public Policy Research, 1977.
Atkins, G. Pope. *Latin America in the International Political System.* New York: The Free Press, 1977.
Baily, Samuel L., ed. *Nationalism in Latin America.* New York: Alfred A. Knopf, 1971.
———. *Labor, Nationalism, and Politics in Argentina.* New Brunswick, N.J.: Rutgers University Press, 1967.
Barager, Joseph R., ed. *Why Perón Came to Power: The Background to Peronism in Argentina.* New York: Alfred A. Knopf, 1968.
Barba, Enrique M. *Quiroga y Rosas.* Buenos Aires: Editorial Pleamar, 1974.
Barco, Ricardo del. *El Regimen Peronista, 1946–1955.* Buenos Aires: Editorial de Belgrano, 1983.
Barnes, John. *Evita, First Lady: a Biography of Eva Perón.* New York: Grove Press, 1978.
Barrios, Américo. *Con Perón en el exilio.* Buenos Aires: Editorial Treinta Dias, 1964.
Beaulac, Willard I. *The Fractured Continent: Latin America in Close-up.* Stanford: Hoover Institution Press, 1980.
Bell-Villeda, Gene H. *Borges and His Fiction: A Guide to His Mind and Art.* Chapel Hill: University of North Carolina Press, 1981.
Bennassar, Bartolomé. *The Spanish Character: Attitudes and Mentalities from the Sixteenth to the Nineteenth Century.* Berkeley, Calif.: University of California Press, 1979.
Beveraggi Allende, Walter. *El partido laborista, el fracaso de Perón y el problema argentino.* Montevideo: private printing, 1954.
Blakemore, Harold, and Clifford T. Smith, eds. *Latin America: Geographical Perspectives.* London: Methuen, 1971.
Blanksten, George J. *Perón's Argentina.* Chicago: University of Chicago Press, 1953.
Borges, Jorge Luis. *Ficciones.* New York: Grove Press, 1962.
———. *Dreamtigers.* Austin, Texas: University of Texas Press, 1964.
———. *The Aleph and Other Stories, 1933–1969.* New York: Bantam Books, 1970.
Borroni, Otelo, and Roberto Vacca. *La Vida de Eva Perón.* Buenos Aires: Editorial Galerna, 1970.
Bourne, Richard. *Political Leaders of Latin America.* London: Pelican, 1969.

Braden, Spruille. *Diplomats and Demagogues: The Memoirs of Spruille Braden.* New Rochelle, N.Y.: Arlington House, 1971.
Bradford, Saxton E. *The Battle for Buenos Aires.* New York: Harcourt, Brace, 1943.
Brown, Jonathan C. *A Socioeconomic History of Argentina, 1776–1860.* New York: Cambridge University Press, 1979.
Bruce, James. *Those Perplexing Argentines.* New York: Longmans, Green, 1953.
Bruno, Cayetano. *Historia Argentina.* Buenos Aires: Editorial del Bosco, 1977.
Bryce, James. *South America: Observations and Impressions.* New York: Macmillan, 1920.
Burnett, Ben G., and Kenneth F. Johnson. *Latin America: Dimensions of the Quest for Stability.* Belmont, Calif.: Wadsworth Publishing Company, 1968.
Bustos Fierro, Raúl. *Desde Perón hasta Onganía.* Buenos Aires: Ediciónes Octubre, 1969.
Cabot, John Moors. *Toward Our Common American Destiny.* Freeport, N.Y.: Books for Libraries Press, 1955.
Cady, John Frank. *Foreign Investment in the Río de la Plata 1838–1850: A Study of French, British and American Policy in Relation to the Dictator Juan Manuel Rosas.* Philadelphia: University of Pennsylvania Press, 1929.
Campobassi, José S. *Sarmiento y su epoca.* 2 vols. Buenos Aires: Editorial Losada, 1975.
Cámpora, Héctor J. *La revolución peronista.* Buenos Aires: Editorial Universitaria de Buenos Aires, 1973.
———. *El mandato de Perón.* Buenos Aires: Ediciónes Quehacer National, 1975.
Canchini, Santiago. *Los Evangelicos en el tiempo de Perón. Memorias de un pastor bautista sobre la libertad religiosa en la Argentina.* Buenos Aires: Editorial Mundo Hispano, 1972.
Canton, Dario. *Elecciónes y partidos en la Argentina. Historia, interpretación y balance: 1910–1966.* Buenos Aires: Siglo XXI Argentina Editores, 1973.
———. *El parlamento argentino en epoca de cambio: 1890, 1916, y 1946.* Buenos Aires: Instituto Torcuato Di Tella, 1946.
———. *Military Interventions in Argentina: 1900–1966.* Buenos Aires: Torcuato Di Tella Institute, 1967.
Cardenas, Gonzalo H. *Las luchas nacionales contra la dependencia.* Buenos Aires: Editorial Galerna, 1969.
———. *El Peronismo.* Buenos Aires: Carlos Perez, 1969.
Carreno, Virginia. *Estancias y estancieros.* Buenos Aires: Editorial y Libreria Goncourt, 1968.
Carril, Bonifacio del. *Crónica interna de la Revolución Libertadora.* Buenos Aires: Emece Editores, 1959.
———. *Memorias Dispersas: El Coronel Perón.* Buenos Aires: Emece Editores, 1984.
Celesia, Ernesto H. *Rosas: Aportes para su historia.* 2 vols. Buenos Aires: Editorial y Libreria Goncourt, 1968–69.
Ciria, Alberto. *Perón y el justicialismo.* Buenos Aires: Siglo Veintiuno Editores, 1971.
———. *Peronismo—Mythology or Ideology?* Berkeley: University of California Press, 1967.
———. *Parties and Power in Modern Argentina (1930–1946).* Translated by Carlos A. Astiz with Mary F. McCarthy. Albany: State University of New York Press, 1974.
———. *Estados Unidos nos mira.* Buenos Aires: Ediciónes La Bastilla, 1973.
———, et al. *La decada infame.* Buenos Aires, 1969.
———, et al. *New Perspectives on Modern Argentina.* Bloomington: Indiana University Press, 1972.
Cochran, Thomas F., and Ruben Reina. *Entrepreneurship in Argentine Culture: Torcuato di Tella and S.I.A.M.* Philadelphia, 1962.
Collier, David, Ed. *The New Authoritarianism in Latin America.* Princeton: Princeton University Press, 1980.
Colom, Eduardo. *17 de octubre: La revolución de los descamisados.* Buenos Aires: La Epoca, 1946.
Confalonieri, Orestes D. *Perón contra Perón.* Buenos Aires: Editorial Antygua Press, 1956.
Conil Paz, Alberto A., and Gustavo E. Ferrari. *Argentina's Foreign Policy, 1930–1962.*

Notre Dame, Ind.: University of Notre Dame Press, 1963.
Connell-Smith, Gordon. *The United States and Latin America: An Historical Analysis of Inter-American Relations.* New York: Halsted Press, 1974.
Corbett, Charles D. *The Latin American Military as a Socio-Political Force: Case Studies of Bolivia and Argentina.* Coral Gables, Fla.: University of Miami Press, 1972.
Córdoba, Tomás. *La Argentina: Perón y después.* Caracas: Ediciones Cidal, 1975.
Cortes Conde, Roberto, and Ezequiel Gallo. *La formación de la Argentina moderna.* Buenos Aires: Paidos, 1972.
Cowles, Fleur. *Bloody Precedent.* New York: Random House, 1952.
Crawford W. Rex. *A Century of Latin American Thought.* Cambridge, Mass.: Harvard University Press, 1961.
Crowley, Frances C. *Domingo Faustino Sarmiento.* New York: Twayne Publishers, 1972.
Davis, Harold Eugene. *Latin American Social Thought.* Washington: University Press of Washington, 1961.
———, Larman C. Wilson, et al. *Latin American Foreign Policies: An Analysis.* Baltimore: The Johns Hopkins University Press, 1975.
———, John J. Finan, and F. Taylor Peak, eds. *Latin American Diplomatic History.* Baton Rouge: Louisiana State University Press, 1977.
———, et al. *Revolutionaries, Traditionalists, and Dictators in Latin America.* New York: Cooper Square Publishers, 1973.
———. *Latin American Thought.* Baton Rouge: Louisiana State University Press, 1972.
Dealy, Glen Caudill. *The Public Man: An Interpretation of Latin American and Other Catholic Countries.* Amherst: University of Massachusetts Press, 1977.
Díaz, Fanor. *Conversaciónes con Rogelio Frigerio.* Buenos Aires: Hachette, 1977.
Díaz Alejandro, Carlos F. *Essays on the Economic History of the Argentine Republic.* New Haven: Yale University Press, 1970.
Di Tella, Guido. *Argentina Under Perón 1973–1976.* London: Macmillan, 1983. Translated as *Perón-Perón 1973–1976.* Buenos Aires: Editorial Sudamericana, 1983.
Di Tella, Torcuato S. *El Sistema Político Argentino y la Clase Obrera.* Buenos Aires: Editorial Universitaria de Buenos Aires, 1964.
———, Gino Germani, Jorge Graciarena, et al. *Argentina, sociedad de masas.* Buenos Aires: Editorial Universidad de Buenos Aires, 1965.
Duff, Ernest A., and John F. McCamant, with Waltraud Q. Morales. *Violence and Repression in Latin America: A Quantitative and Historical Analysis.* New York: Free Press, 1976.
Duggan, Laurence. *The Americas: The Search for Hemisphere Security.* New York: Henry Holt and Co., 1949.
Eidt, Robert C. *Pioneer Settlements in Northeast Argentina.* Madison: University of Wisconsin Press, 1971.
Eisenhower, Milton. *The Wine is Bitter: The United States and Latin America.* New York: Doubleday, 1963.
Elliott, J. H. *Imperial Spain—1469–1716.* New York: St. Martin's Press, 1963.
Escude, Carlos. *Gran Bretaña, Estados Unidos y la declinación argentina, 1942–1949.* Buenos Aires: Belgrano, 1983.
Ewell, Judith. *The Indictment of a Dictator: The Extradition and Trial of Marcos Pérez Jiménez.* College Station, Texas: Texas A & M University Press, 1981.
Falcoff, Mark, and Ronald H. Dolkart, eds. *Prologue to Perón: Argentina in Depression and War, 1930–1943.* Berkeley: University of California Press, 1975.
Fayt, Carlos S. *La naturaleza del peronismo.* Buenos Aires: Viracocha, 1967.
———. *El político armado: dinámico del proceso político argentino: 1960–1971.* Buenos Aires: Ediciónes Pannedille, 1971.
Fernández, Julio A. *The Political Elite in Argentina.* New York: New York University Press, 1970.
Ferns, H. S. *Argentina.* New York: Praeger, 1969.
———. *Britain and Argentina in the Nineteenth Century.* Oxford: Oxford University Press, 1960.
———. *The Argentine Republic, 1516–1971.* New York: Barnes & Noble Books, 1973.

Ferrer, Aldo. *The Argentine Economy*. Berkeley: University of California Press, 1967.
Fienup, Darrell F., et al. *The Agricultural Development of Argentina*. New York: Praeger, 1969.
Filol, Tomás R. *Social Factors in Economic Development: The Argentine Case*. Cambridge, Mass.: MIT Press, 1961.
Firpo, M. Eduardo. *Perón y los peronistas*. Buenos Aires: Alberdi, 1965.
Fisk, Ysabel, and Robert A. Rennie. *Argentina in Crisis*. New York: Foreign Policy Association, 1944.
Foxley, Alejandro, ed. *Income Distribution in Latin America*. New York: Cambridge University Press, 1976.
Francis, Michael J. *The Limits of Hegemony: United States Relations with Argentina and Chile during World War II*. Notre Dame, Ind.: University of Notre Dame Press, 1977.
Frank, Gary. *Struggle for Hegemony in South America: Argentina, Brazil, and the United States During the Second World War*. Coral Gables, Fla.: Center for Advanced Studies, University of Miami, 1979.
———. *Juan Perón vs. Spruille Braden: The Story Behind the Blue Book*. Lanham, Maryland: University Press of America, 1980.
Frank, Waldo. *South American Journey*. New York: Duell, Sloan and Pearce, 1943.
Fraser, Nicholas, and Marysa Navarro. *Eva Perón*. New York: W. W. Norton & Company, 1980.
Gallo, Ezequiel. *Farmers in Revolt: The Revolution of 1893 in the Province of Santa Fe, Argentina*. London: The Athlone Press, 1976.
Gálvez, Manuel. *Vida de Hipólito Yrigoyen*. Buenos Aires: Tor, 1959.
Gambini, Hugo. *El 17 de Octubre, 1945*. Buenos Aires: Editorial Brujula, 1969.
———. *El primer gobierno peronista*. Buenos Aires: Centro Editor de America Latina, 1971.
———. *El peronismo y la iglesia*. Buenos Aires: Centro Editor de America Latina, 1971.
Gazzera, Miguel, and Norberto Ceresole. *Peronismo: Autocritica y perspectivas*. Buenos Aires: Editorial Descartes, 1970.
Gellman, Irwin F. *Good Neighbor Diplomacy: United States Policies in Latin America*. Baltimore: The Johns Hopkins University Press, 1979.
Germani, Gino. *Authoritarianism, Fascism and National Populism*. New Brunswick N.J.: Transaction Books, 1978.
———. *Estructura social de la Argentina*. Buenos Aires: Editorial Raigal, 1955.
———. *Política y sociedad en una epoca de transicíon*. Buenos Aires: Editorial Paidos, 1962.
Gillespie, Richard. *Soldiers of Perón: Argentina's Montoneros*. Oxford: Clarendon Press, 1982.
Godio, Julio. *La caida de Perón: de junio a setiembre*. Buenos Aires: Granica Editor, 1973.
Goldwert, Marvin. *Democracy, Militarism, and Nationalism in Argentina, 1930–1966: An Interpretation*. Austin: University of Texas Press, 1972.
González, Ernesto. *Que fué y que es el peronismo*. Buenos Aires: Ediciones Pluma, 1974.
Graham, Richard, and Peter H. Smith, eds. *New Approaches to Latin American History*. Austin: University of Texas Press, 1974.
Graham-Yooll, Andrew. *The Forgotten Colony*. London: Hutchinson, 1981.
———. *Tiempo de tragedia: Cronología de la revolución argentina*. Buenos Aires: Ediciones de la Flor, 1972.
Greenup, Ruth, and Leonard Greenup. *Revolution Before Breakfast: Argentina, 1941–46*. Chapel Hill: University of North Carolina Press, 1947.
Griffis, Stanton. *Lying in State*. Garden City, N.Y.: Doubleday & Company, 1953.
Guardo, Ricardo C. *Horas difíciles*. Buenos Aires: Ediciónes A. Peña Lillo, 1963.
Guy, Donna J. *Argentine Sugar Politics: Tucumán and the Generation of Eighty*. Tempe: The Center for Latin American Studies, Arizona State University, 1980.
Halperín Donghi, Tulio. *Guerra y finanza en los orígenes del estado argentino (1790–1850)*. Buenos Aires: Belgrano, 1983.
———. and Torcuato S. Di Tella, Eds. *Los fragmentos del poder*. Buenos Aires: 1970.
———. *Argentina: La democracia de masas*. Buenos Aires: Editorial Paidos, 1972.

Hamill, Hugh M., Jr., ed. *Dictatorship in Spanish America*. New York: Alfred A. Knopf, 1965.
Hamilton, Bernice. *Political Thought in Sixteenth-Century Spain*. Oxford: Clarendon Press, 1963.
Harbison, W. A. *Evita, A Legend for the Seventies*. London: Star Books, 1977.
Haring, Clarence H. *The Spanish Empire in America*. New York: Harcourt, Brace and World, 1963.
Hartz, Louis, et al. *The Founding of New Societies*. New York: Harcourt, Brace and World, 1964.
Hennessy, Alistair. *The Frontier in Latin American History*. London: Edward Arnold, 1978.
Hernández, José. *The Gaucho Martín Fierro*. Translated by Frank Carrino, Alberto J. Carlos, and Norman Mangouni. Albany: State University of New York Press, 1974.
Hernández Arregui, Juan José. *La formación de la conciencia nacional: 1930–1960*. Buenos Aires: Ediciónes Hachea, 1960.
———. *Peronismo y socialismo*. Buenos Aires: Ediciónes Corregidor, 1973.
Herring, Hubert, *A History of Latin America: From the Beginnings to the Present*. London: Jonathan Cape, 1954.
Herron, Francis. *Letters from the Argentine*. New York: G. P. Putnam's Sons, 1943.
Hodges, Donald C. *Argentina, 1943–1976: The National Revolution and Resistance*. Albuquerque: University of New Mexico Press, 1976.
Holmes, Olive. *Perón's Greater Argentina and the United States*. New York: Foreign Policy Association, 1948.
Horgan, Paul. *Great River: The Rio Grande in North American History*. New York and Toronto: Rinehart & Company, 1954.
Horowitz, Irving Louis, ed. *Masses in Latin America*. New York: Oxford University Press, 1970.
Hull, Cordell. *The Memoirs of Cordell Hull*. Vol. 2. New York: Macmillan, 1948.
Humphreys, R. A. *Tradition and Revolt in Latin America and Other Esssays*. New York: Columbia University Press, 1969.
Ianni, Octavio. *La Formación del Estado populista en America Latina*. Mexico City: Ediciónes Era, 1975.
Ibarguren, Carlos. *La Historia que he vivido*. Buenos Aires: Peuser, 1955.
Imaz, José Luis de. *Estructura social de una ciudad pampeana*. 2 vols. La Plata: Instituto de Historia de la Filosofía y el Pensamento Argentino, Universidad Nacional de la Plata, 1965.
———. *Los Que Mandan*. Translated by Carlos A. Astiz. Albany: State University of New York Press, 1970.
Ionescu, G., and E. Gellner, eds. *Populism: Its Meanings and National Characteristics*. New York: Macmillan, 1969.
Irazusta, Julio. *Perón y la crisis argentina*. Buenos Aires: La Voz del Plata, 1956.
———. *Balance de siglo y medio*. Buenos Aires: Ediciónes Theoria, 1966.
James, Preston E. *Latin America*. New York: Odyssey Press, 1950.
Jane, Cecil. *Liberty and Despotism in Spanish America*. New York: Cooper Square Publishers, 1966.
Jauretche, Arturo. *F.O.R.J.A. y la decada infame*. Buenos Aires: Coyoacan, 1962.
———. *Los profetas del odio*. Buenos Aires: A. Peña Lillo, 1967.
———. *El medio pelo en la sociedad argentina. (Apuntes para una sociología nacional)*. Buenos Aires: A. Peña Lillo, 1967.
Jefferson, Mark. *Peopling the Argentine Pampas*. New York: American Geographical Society, 1926.
Jorrin, Miguel, and John D. Martz. *Latin-American Political Thought and Ideology*. Chapel Hill: University of North Carolina Press, 1970.
Josephs, Ray. *Argentine Diary: The Inside Story of the Coming of Fascism*. New York: Random House, 1944.

Kelly, Sir David Victor. *The Ruling Few, or the Human Background to Diplomacy.* London: Hollis and Carter, 1952.

Kennedy, John J. *Catholicism, Nationalism, and Democracy in Argentina.* Notre Dame, Ind.: University of Notre Dame Press, 1958.

Kirkpatrick, Jeane. *Leader and Vanguard in Mass Society: A Study of Peronist Argentina.* Cambridge: MIT Press, 1971.

Knight, Thomas J. *Latin America Comes of Age.* Metuchen, N.J.: Scarecrow Press, 1979.

Kohl, James, and John Litt. *Urban Guerrilla Warfare in Latin America.* Cambridge, Mass.: MIT Press, 1974.

Landsberger, Henry A., ed. *The Church and Social Change in Latin America.* Notre Dame, Ind.: University of Notre Dame Press, 1970.

Lanusse, Alejandro A. *Mi testimonio.* Buenos Aires: Lasserre Editores, 1977.

Lascano, Luis C. Alen. *La Argentina ilusionada: 1922–1930.* Buenos Aires: Ediciónes La Bastilla, 1975.

Levine, Ricardo. *A History of Argentina.* Chapel Hill: University of North Carolina Press, 1937.

Lewis, A. R., and Thomas F. McGann, eds. *The New World Looks at its History.* Austin: University of Texas Press, 1963.

Lowenthal, Abraham F., ed. *Armies and Politics in Latin America.* New York: Holmes & Meier, 1976.

Lucero, Franklin. *El precio de la lealdad.* Buenos Aires: Editorial Propulsion, 1959.

Luna, Felix. *El 45: Crónica de un año decisivo.* Buenos Aires: Editorial Jorge Alvarez, 1969.

———. *Los caudillos.* Buenos Aires: Editorial Jorge Alvarez, 1966.

———. *Argentina de Perón a Lanusse—1943–1973.* Buenos Aires: Editorial Planeta, 1972.

———. *Yrigoyen.* Buenos Aires: Editorial Desarrollo, 1964.

———. *Diálogos con Frondizi.* Buenos Aires: Editorial Desarrollo, 1963.

Lux-Wurm, Pierre. *Le Peronisme.* Paris: Librairie Générale de Droit et de Jurisprudence, 1965.

Madariaga, Salvador de. *The Fall of the Spanish-American Empire.* New York: Collier Books, 1963.

Mafud, Julio. *Psicología de la viveza criolla.* Buenos Aires: Editorial Américale, 1965.

———. *Sociología del peronismo.* Buenos Aires: Editorial Américale, 1972.

Maggi, Ginna. *Patria y traición: Confabulacion Ibáñez–Perón.* Buenos Aires: Ediciónes Gure, 1957.

Magnet, Alejandro. *Nuestros vecinos justicialistas.* Santiago: Editorial del Pacifico S. A., 1953.

———. *Nuestros vecinos argentinos.* Santiago: Editorial del Pacifico, S. A., 1956.

Maier, Joseph, and Richard W. Weatherhead. *The Latin American University.* Albuquerque: University of New Mexico Press, 1979.

Main, Mary (María Flores). *The Woman with the Whip.* Garden City: Doubleday, 1952.

Mallon, Richard D., in collaboration with Juan V. Sourrouille. *Economic Policy-Making in a Conflict Society: The Argentine Case.* Cambridge, Mass.: Harvard University Press, 1975.

Malloy, James M., ed. *Authoritarianism and Corporatism in Latin America.* Pittsburgh: University of Pittsburgh Press, 1977.

Mañach, Jorge. *Frontiers in the Americas: A Global Perspective.* New York: Teachers College Press, 1975.

Mander, John. *The Unrevolutionary Society: The Power of Latin American Conservatism in a Changing World.* New York: Alfred A. Knopf, 1969.

Marsal S., Pablo. *Perón y la iglesia.* Buenos Aires: Ediciónes Rex, 1955.

Martínez, Alberto B., and Maurice Lewandowski. *The Argentine in the Twentieth Century.* London: T. Fisher and Unwin, 1911.

Martínez, Pedro Santos. *La nueva Argentina.* 2 vols. Buenos Aires: Edictiónes La Bastilla, 1976.

Martínez de Hoz, José Alfredo. *La agricultura y la ganadería en el periodo 1930–1960.* Buenos Aires: Editorial Sudamericana, 1967.

Martínez Estrada, Ezequiel. *X-Ray of the Pampa.* Translated by Alain Swietlicki. Austin: University of Texas Press, 1971.
Martz, John D., and Lars Schoultz, eds. *Latin America, the United States, and the Inter-American System.* Boulder, Col.: Westview Press, 1980.
Masur, Gerhard. *Nationalism in Latin America: Diversity and Unity.* New York: Macmillan, 1966.
Matsushita, Hiroshi. *Movimiento obrero argtentino 1930 / 1945: Sus proyecciónes en los orígines del peronismo.* Buenos Aires: Siglo Veinte, 1983.
McGann, Thomas F. *Argentina: The Divided Land.* Princeton: D. Van Nostrand Company, 1966.
———. *Argentina, the United States and the Inter-American System.* Cambridge, Mass.: Harvard University Press, 1957.
Mecham, J. Lloyd. *The United States and Inter-American Security, 1889–1960.* Austin: University of Texas Press, 1963.
Melo, Carlos R. *Los partidos políticos argentinos.* Córdoba: Universidad Nacional de Córdoba, 1964.
Mende, Raúl A. *El Justicialismo: Doctrina y Realidad Peronista.* Buenos Aires: ALEA, 1950. English translation published by Imprenta Lopez in Buenos Aires, 1952.
Mendes, Candido. *Beyond Populism.* Albany: State University of New York Press, 1977.
Milensky, Edward S. *Argentina's Foreign Policies.* Boulder, Col.: Westview Press, 1978.
Montgomery, Tommie Sue, ed., *Mexico Today.* Philadelphia: Institute for the Study of Human Issues, 1982.
Monzalvo, Luis. *Testigo de la primera hora del peronismo.* Buenos Aires: Editorial Pleamar, 1974.
Mora y Araujo, Manuel, and Ignacio Llorente. *El Voto Peronista: Ensayos de sociología electoral argentina.* Buenos Aires: Editorial Sudamericana, 1980.
Morison, Samuel Eliot. *The European Discovery of America: The Southern Voyages, 1492–1619.* New York: Oxford University Press, 1974.
Mosconi, Enrique. *YPF y las empresas extranjeras.* Buenos Aires: 1957.
Mujica, Carlos. *Peronismo y cristianismo.* Buenos Aires: Editorial Merlin, 1973.
Murmis, Miguel, and Juan Carlos Portantiero. *Estudios sobre los orígines del peronismo.* Vol. 1. Buenos Aires: Siglo Veintiuno, 1971.
Naipaul, V. S. *The Return of Eva Perón.* New York: Alfred A. Knopf, 1980.
Navarro, Marysa. *Evita.* Buenos Aires: Ediciónes Corregidor, 1981.
Navarro Gerassi, Marysa. *Los nacionalistas.* Buenos Aires: Editorial Jorge Alvarez, 1968.
Newton, Jorge. *Perón el visionario.* Buenos Aires: Guillermo Kraft, 1955.
Newton, Ronald C. *German Buenos Aires, 1900–1933: Social Change and Cultural Crisis.* Austin: University of Texas Press, 1977.
Nicolls, M. W. *The Gaucho: Cattle Hunter, Cavalryman, Ideal of Romance.* Durham, N.C.: Duke University Press, 1941.
Nuñez Arca. P. *Perón, Man of America.* Buenos Aires: privately printed, 1950.
Odell, Peter R., and David A. Preston. *Economies and Societies in Latin America: A Geographical Interpretation.* New York: Wiley, 1973.
O'Donnell, Guillermo. *Modernization and Bureaucratic Authoritarianism: Studies in South American Politics.* Berkeley: Institute of International Studies, University of California, 1973.
Ortega y Gasset, José. *Invertebrate Spain.* New York: W. W. Norton & Company, 1937.
Oszlak, Oscar. *La Formacíon del estado argentino.* Buenos Aires: Belgrano, 1983.
Owen, Frank. *Perón: His Rise and Fall.* London: Cresset Press, 1957.
Page, Joseph A., *Peron: a Biography.* New York: Random House, 1983.
Panaia, Marta, Ricardo Lesser, and Pedro Skupch. *Estudios sobre los orígines del peronismo.* Vol. 2. Buenos Aires: Siglo Veintiuno. 1973.
Parera, Riccardo Gregorio. *Democracia cristiana en la argentina: Los hechos y las ideas.* Buenos Aires: Editorial Nahuel, 1967.
Pastor, Reynaldo. *Frente al totalitarianismo peronista.* Buenos Aires: Bases Editorial, 1959.
Pavón Pereyra, Enrique. *Perón: Preparacíon de una vida para el mando, 1895–1942.* Buenos Aires: Ediciónes Espino, 1952.

————. *Conversaciónes con Perón*. Buenos Aires: Colihue / Hachette, 1978.
————. *Coloquios con Perón*. Madrid: Editores Internacionales Tecnicos Reunidos, 1973.
————. *Perón tal como es*. Buenos Aires: Editorial Macacha Guemes, 1973.
————. *Vida de Perón*. Buenos Aires: Editorial Justicialista, 1965.
————. *Los ultimos dias de Perón*. Buenos Aires: Ediciónes La Campana, 1981.
Pendle, George. *Argentina*. London: Royal Institute of International Affairs, 1963.
Peña, Milciades. *Masas, caudillos y elites. La dependencia argentina de Yrigoyen a Perón*. Buenos Aires: Ediciónes Fichas, 1973.
————. *El peronismo: Seleccíon de documentos para la historia*. Buenos Aires: Ediciónes Fichas, 1972.
Perelman, Angel. *Como hicimos el 17 de octubre*. Buenos Aires: Editorial Coyocan, 1961.
Pérez Amuchastegui, A. J. *Mentalidades Argentinas*. Buenos Aires, 1965.
Peterson, Harold F. *Argentina and the U. S. 1810–1960*. Albany: State University of New York Press, 1964.
Petras, James, and Maurice Zeitlin, eds. *Latin America: Reform or Revolution?* Greenwich, Conn.: Fawcett Publications, 1968.
Picón-Salas, Mariano. *A Cultural History of Spanish America: From Conquest to Independence*. Translated by Irving A. Leonard. Berkeley: University of California Press, 1962.
Pike, Frederick B. *Spanish America, 1900–1970: Tradition and Social Innovation*. New York: W. W. Norton & Company, 1973.
————, ed. *Latin American History: Select Problems*. New York: Harcourt, Brace and World, 1969.
————, and Thomas Stritch, eds. *The New Corporatism: Social-Political Structures in the Iberian World*. Notre Dame, Ind.: University of Notre Dame Press, 1974.
Platt, D.C.M., ed. *Business Imperialism 1840–1930: An Inquiry Based on British Exerience in Latin America*. New York: Oxford University Press, 1977.
Portes, Alejandro, and John Walton. *Urban Latin America: The Political Condition from Above and Below*. Austin: University of Texas Press, 1976.
Potash, Robert A. *The Army and Politics in Argentina, 1928–1945: Yrigoyen to Perón*. Stanford: Stanford University Press, 1969.
————. *The Army and Politics in Argentina, 1945–1962: Perón to Frondizi*. Stanford: Stanford University Press, 1980.
Prebisch, Raul. *Change and Development—Latin America's Great Task. Report Submitted to the Inter-American Development Bank*. New York: Praeger, 1971.
Prieto, Ramon. *De Perón a Perón: De 1946 a 1973*. Buenos Aires: Ediciónes Macacha Guemes, 1974.
————. *Correspondencia Perón–Frigerio, 1958–1973*. Buenos Aires: Ediciónes Macacha Guemes, 1975.
Puig, Manuel. *Betrayed by Rita Hayworth*. New York: E. P. Dutton & Co., 1971.
————. *Heartbreak Tango*. New York: E. P. Dutton & Co., 1973.
Puiggros, Rodolfo. *El Peronismo, sus causas*. Buenos Aires: Editorial Jorge Alvarez, 1969.
————. *Historia crítica de los partidos políticos argentinos*. Buenos Aires: Argumentos, 1956.
Quinterno, Carlos A. *Militares y populismo: La crisis argentina de 1966 a 1976*. Buenos Aires: Editorial Temas Contemporaneos, 1978.
Ramos, Jorge Abelardo. *La era del peronismo*. Buenos Aires: Ediciónes del Mar Dulce, 1982.
————. *Perón. Historia de su triunfo y su derrota*. Buenos Aires: Ediciónes Amerindia, 1959.
————. *De octubre a setiembre*. Buenos Aires: A. Peña Lillo, 1959.
————. *Revolución y contrarevolución en la Argentina: Nueva historia de los argentinos*. Buenos Aires: La Reja, 1961.
Randall, Laura. *An Economic History of Argentina in the Twentieth Century*. New York: Columbia University Press, 1978.
Rangel, Carlos. *The Latin Americans: Their Love-Hate Relationship with the United States*. New York: Harcourt Brace Jovanovich, 1977.

Real, Juan José. *30 años de historia argentina*. Buenos Aires: Actualidad, 1962.
Recchini de Lattes, Zulma L., and Alfredo E. Lattes. *Migraciónes en la Argentina*. Buenos Aires: 1969.
Reina, Ruben E. *Paraná: Social Boundaries in an Argentine City*. Austin: University of Texas Press, 1973.
Remmer, Karen L. *Party Competition in Argentina and Chile; Political Recruitment and Political Policy, 1890–1930*. Lincoln, Neb.: University of Nebraska Press, 1984.
Rennie, Ysabel. *The Argentine Republic*. New York: The Macmillan Company, 1945.
Reyes, Cipriano. *Yo hice el 17 de octubre: Memorias*. Buenos Aires: GS Editorial, 1973.
———. *Que es el laborismo*. Buenos Aires: Ediciónes R. A., 1946.
Rippy, J. Fred. *British Investments in Latin America, 1822–1949*. Minneapolis: University of Minnesota Press, 1959.
Rivera, Enrique. *Peronismo y frondizismo*. Buenos Aires: Editorial Patria Grande, 1958.
Rivera, Julius. *Latin America: A Sociocultural Interpretation*. New York: Irvington-Halsted, 1978.
Robertson, James Oliver. *American Myth, American Reality*. New York: Hill and Wang, 1980.
Rock, David. *Politics in Argentina, 1890–1930: The Rise and Fall of Radicalism*. New York: Cambridge University Press, 1975.
———, ed. *Argentina in the Twentieth Century*. Pittsburgh: University of Pittsburgh Press, 1975.
Rodríguez, Celso. *Lencinas y Cantoni: El populismo cuyano en tiempos de Yrigoren*. Buenos Aires: Editorial del Belgrano, 1977.
Rodríguez Molas, Ricardo. *Historia social del gaucho*. Buenos Aires: Ediciónes Maru, 1968.
Rodríguez Monegal, Emir. *Jorge Luis Borges: A Literary Biography*. New York: E. P. Dutton, 1978.
Rom, Eugenio R. *Así hablaba Juan Perón*. Buenos Aires: A. Peña Lillo, 1980.
Romero, José Luis. *A History of Argentine Political Thought*. Translated by Thomas F. McGann. Stanford University Press, 1963.
———. *La experienca Argentina y otro ensayos*. Buenos Aires: Editorial del Belgrano, 1980.
———. *El desarrollo de las ideas en la sociedad Argentina del siglo XX*. Mexico: Fondo de Cultura Economico, 1965.
Rouquie, Alain. *Poder militar y sociedad política en la Argentina*. 2 vols. Translated by Arturo Iglesias Echegaray. Buenos Aires: Emece Editores, 1981.
Sábato, Ernesto. *El otro rostro del peronismo: Carta abierta a Mario Amadeo*. Buenos Aires: Gure, 1957.
Saldias, Adolfo. *Historia de la confederación Argentina*. 3 vols. Buenos Aires: Editorial Universitaria de Buenos Aires: 1968.
Sammartino, Ernesto E. *La verdad sobre la situación argentina*. Montevideo: privately printed, 1951.
Sánchez-Albornoz, Nicolás. *The Population of Latin America: A History*. Berkeley: University of California Press, 1974.
Sanguinetti, Horacio. *La democracia ficta: 1930–1938*. Buenos Aires: Ediciónes La Bastilla, 1975.
Santander, Silvano. *Técnica de una traición: Juan Domingo Perón y Eva Duarte, agentes del nazismo en la Argentina*. Buenos Aires: Editorial Antygua, 1955.
Santillan, Diego Abad de. *Historia institucional argentina*. Buenos Aires, 1966.
Sargent, Charles S. *The Spacial Evolution of Greater Buenos Aires, Argentina, 1870–1930*. Tempe: Center for Latin American Studies, Arizona State University, 1974.
Schaedel, Richard E., ed. *Social Change in Latin America*. Austin: University of Texas Press, 1967.
Schmitter, Philippe C., ed. *Military Rule in Latin America: Function, Consequences and Perspectives*. Beverly Hills: Sage Publications, 1973.
Schoultz, Lars. *The Populist Challenge: Argentine Electoral Behavior in the Postwar Era*. Chapel Hill: University of North Carolina Press, 1983.

Scobie, James R. *Argentina: A City and a Nation*. New York: Oxford University Press, 1964.
———. *Revolution on the Pampas: A Social History of Argentine Wheat, 1860–1910*. Austin: University of Texas Press, 1964.
———. *Buenos Aires: Plaza to Suburb: 1870–1910*. New York: Oxford University Press, 1964.
Sebrelli, Juan José. *Buenos Aires, vida cotidiana y alienación*. Buenos Aires: Ediciónes Siglo Veinte, 1965.
———. *Eva Perón: Aventurera o militante?* Buenos Aires: Editorial La Pleyade, 1982.
Silvert, Kalman H. *Essays in Understanding Latin America*. Philadelphia: Institute for the Study of Human Issues, 1977.
———. *The Conflict Society: Reaction and Revolution in Latin America*. New Orleans: Hauser Press, 1961.
———, ed. *Expectant Peoples: Nationalism and Development*. New York: Vintage, 1967.
———, et al. *The Americas in a Changing World*. New York: Quadrangle / The New York Times Book Company, 1975.
Skidmore, Thomas E. *Politics in Brazil, 1930–1964: An Experiment in Democracy*. New York: Oxford University Press, 1967.
Smith, Oscar E. *Yankee Diplomacy: U. S. Intervention in Argentina*. Dallas: Southern Methodist University Press, 1953.
Smith, Peter H. *Argentina and the Failure of Democracy: Conflict Among Political Elites, 1904–1955*. Madison: University of Wisconsin Press, 1974.
———. *Politics and Beef in Argentina: Patterns of Conflict and Change*. New York: Columbia University Press, 1969.
Snow, Peter G. *Political Forces in Argentina*. New York: Praeger, 1979.
Sobel, Lester A., ed. *Argentina and Perón, 1970–1975*. New York: Facts on File, 1975.
Solberg, Carl E. *Immigration and Nationalism: Argentina and Chile, 1890–1914*. Austin: University of Texas Press, 1970.
———. *Oil and Nationalism in Argentina: A History*. Stanford: Stanford University Press, 1979.
Stein, Stanley J. and Barbara H. *The Colonial Heritage of Latin America: Essays on Economic Dependence in Perspective*. New York: Oxford University Press, 1970.
Steward, Dick. *Trade and Hemisphere: The Good Neighbor Policy and Reciprocal Trade*. Columbia: University of Missouri Press, 1975.
Stoetzer, O. Carlos. *El pensamiento político en la america española durante el período de la emancipación (1789–1825)*. 2 vols, Mardrid: Instituto de Estudios Políticos, 1966.
———. *Two Studies on Contemporary Argentine History*. New York: Argentina Independent Review, 1980.
Sunday Times of London Insight Team. *War in the Falklands: The Full Story*. New York: Harper & Row, 1982.
Tamarin, David. *Argentine Labor in an Age of Transition, 1930–1945: A Study in the Origins of Peronism*. Albuquerque: University of New Mexico Press, 1985.
Taylor, Carl C. *Rural Life in Argentina*. Baton Rouge: Louisiana State University Press, 1948.
Taylor, J. M. *Eva Perón: The Myths of a Woman*. Chicago: University of Chicago Press, 1979.
Theroux, Paul. *The Old Patagonian Express: By Train Through the Americas*. Boston: Houghton Mifflin Company, 1979.
Tulchin, Joseph S., ed. *Problems in Latin America*. New York: Harper & Row, 1973.
Turner, Frederick C. *Catholicism and Political Development in Latin America*. Chapel Hill: University of North Carolina Press, 1971.
Turner, Frederick C., and José Enrique Miguens, eds. *Juan Perón and the Reshaping of Argentina*. Pittsburgh: University of Pittsburgh Press, 1983.
Van Niekerk, A. E. *Populism and Political Development in Latin America*. Rotterdam: Rotterdam University Press, 1974.
Véliz, Claudio. *The Centralist Tradition of Latin America*. Princeton: Princeton University Press, 1980.

————, ed. *The Politics of Conformity in Latin America.* New York: Oxford University Press, 1967.
————, ed. *Obstacles to Change in Latin America.* New York: Oxford University Press, 1965.
Ventura, Any. *Jorge Antonio: el hombre que sabe demasiado.* Buenos Aires: A. Peña Lillo, 1982.
Vigo, Juan M. *Crónicas de la resistencia. La Vida por Perón.* Buenos Aires: A. Peña Lillo, 1973.
Villanueva, Javier. *The Inflationary Process in Argentina, 1943–1960.* Buenos Aires: Instituto Torcuato Di Tella, 1966.
Wagley, Charles. *The Latin American Tradition.* New York: Columbia University Press, 1968.
Walker, John, ed. *The South American Sketches of R. B. Cunningham Graham.* Norman: University of Oklahoma Press, 1978.
Walter, Richard J. *Student Politics in Argentina: The University Reform and Its Effects, 1918–1964.* New York: Basic Books, 1968.
————. *The Socialist Party of Argentina, 1890–1930.* Austin: Institute of Latin American Studies, 1977.
————. *The Province of Buenos Aires and Argentine Politics, 1912–1943.* Cambridge: Cambridge University Press, 1985.
Weil, Felix J. *Argentine Riddle.* New York: John Day, 1944.
Weisbrot, Robert. *The Jews of Argentina: From the Inquisition to Perón.* Philadelphia: The Jewish Publishing Society of America, 1979.
Welles, Sumner. *The Time for Decision.* New York: Harper & Brothers, 1944.
————. *Seven Decisions that Shaped History* New York: Harper & Brothers, 1951.
————. *Where Are We Heading?.* New York: Free Press, 1966.
Wesson, Robert, ed. *Politics, Policies, and Economic Development in Latin America.* Stanford: Hoover Institution Press, 1984.
Whitaker, Arthur P. *The United States and Argentina.* Cambridge, Mass.: Harvard University Press, 1954.
————. *Argentina.* Englewood Cliffs, N.J.: Prentice-Hall, 1964.
————. *Argentine Upheaval: Perón's Fall and the New Regime.* New York: Praeger, 1956.
————. *The United States and the Southern Cone: Argentina, Uruguay, and Chile.* Cambridge, Mass.: Harvard University Press, 1977.
————. *The Western Hemisphere Idea: Its Rise and Decline.* Ithaca: Cornell University Press, 1954.
————, and David C. Jordan. *Nationalism in Contemporary Latin America.* New York: 1966.
White, John W. *Argentina: The Life Story of a Nation.* New York: Viking Press, 1942.
Wiarda, Howard J. *Corporatism and National Development in Latin America.* Boulder, Col.: Westview Press, 1981.
————, ed. *Politics and Social Change in Latin America: The Distinct Tradition.* Amherst: University of Massachusetts Press, 1974.
————, ed. *The Continuing Struggle for Democracy in Latin America.* Boulder, Colorado: Westview Press, 1980.
————, and H. F. Klein, eds. *Latin American Politics and Development.* Boston: Houghton-Mifflin, 1979.
Williams, E. J. *Latin American Political Thought: A Developmental Perspective.* Tucson: University of Arizona Press, 1974.
Williams, Glyn. *The Desert and the Dream: A Study of Welsh Colonization in Chubut, 1865–1915.* Cardiff: University of Wales Press, 1975.
Woods, Randall Bennett. *The Roosevelt Foreign-Policy Establishment and the "Good Neighbor": The United States and Argentina 1941–1945.* Lawrence: Regents Press of Kansas, 1979.
Worcester, Donald E., and Wendell G. Schaeffer. *The Growth and Culture of Latin America.* New York: Oxford University Press, 1971.
Wright, Ione S., and Lisa M. Nekhom. *Historical Dictionary of Argentina.* Metuchen, N.J.: Scarecrow Press, 1978.

Wright, Winthrop R. *British-Owned Railways in Argentina: Their Effect on Economic Nationalism 1854–1948*. Austin: University of Texas Press, 1974.
Wynia, Gary W. *Argentina in the Postwar Era: Political and Economic Policy-Making in a Divided Society*. Albuquerque: University of New Mexico Press, 1978.
———. *The Politics of Latin American Development*. New York: Cambridge University Press, 1978.
Zea, Leopoldo. *The Latin American Mind*. Translated by James H. Abbott and Lowell Dunham. Norman: University of Oklahoma Press, 1963.
Zinn, Ricardo. *Argentina: A Nation at the Crossroads of Myth and Reality*. New York: Speller, 1979.

Articles and Essays

Alexander, Robert J. "Peronism and Argentina's Quest for Leadership in Latin America." *Journal of International Affairs,* Vol. 9, No. 1 (1955)
Baily, Samuel L. "Marriage Patterns and Immigrant Assimilation in Buenos Aires, 1882–1923." *Hispanic American Historical Review,* February 1981.
Beezley, W. H. "Caudillismo: An Interpretive Note." *Journal of Inter-American Studies,* 11 (July 1969)
Bishko, C. J. "The Iberian Background of Latin American History." *Hispanic American Historical Review,* February, 1956,
Bray, Donald W. "Peronism in Chile." *Hispanic American Historical Review,* January 1962.
Butler, David. "Charisma, Migration and Elite Coalescence: An Interpretation of Peronism." *Comparative Politics,* April 1969.
Dealy, Glen. "Prolegomena on the Spanish-American Political Tradition." *Hispanic American Historical Review,* February 1968.
Di Tella, Torcuato S. "Stalemate or Coexistence in Argentina." In *Latin America: Reform or Revolution?,* edited by James Petras and Maurice Zeitlin. Greenwich, Conn.: Fawcett Publications, 1968.
Falcoff, Mark, and Raúl Scalabrini Ortiz. "The Making of an Argentine Nationalist." *Hispanic American Historical Review,* February 1972.
Gillen, John. "Ethos Components in Modern Latin American Culture." *American Anthropologist,* 57, p. 491.
Goldwert, Marvin. "The Rise of Modern Militarism in Argentina." *Hispanic American Historical Review,* May 1968.
Gomez, Rosendo A. "Intervention in Argentina, 1860–1930." *Inter-American Economic Affairs,* I, December, 1947.
Goodrich, C. "Argentina as a New Country." *Comparative Studies in Society and History,* Vol. VII (1964).
Goodwin, Paul B., Jr. "Anglo-Argentine Commerical Relations: A Private Sector View." *Hispanic American Historical Review,* February 1981.
Haigh, R. M. "The Creation and Control of a Caudillo." *Hispanic American Historical Review,* November, 1964.
Hoffman, Fritz L. "Perón and After." Part I: *Hispanic American Historical Review,* November 1956; Part II: May 1959.
Ilsley, Lucretia L. "The Argentine Constitutional Revision of 1949." *The Journal of Politics,* May 1952.
Jordan, David C. "Argentina's Bureaucratic Oligarchies." *Current History,* February 1972.
———. "Perón's Return, Allende's Fall, and Communism in Latin America." *Orbis,* Fall 1973.
Kennedy, John J. "Accountable Government in Argentina." *Foreign Affairs,* April 1959.
Kenworthy, Eldon. "Argentina: The Politics of Late Industrialization." *Foreign Affairs,* April, 1967.
———. "The Foundation of the Little-Known Case in Theory Formation, or What Peronism Wasn't." *Comparative Politics,* October 1973.

————. "Peronism: Argentina's Experiment with Populism." In *Problems in Latin America*, edited by Joseph S. Tulchin. New York: Harper & Row, 1973.

Lafaye, J. "The Spanish Diaspora: The Enduring Unity of Hispanic Culture." Washington: Wilson Center, Latin American Program, 1977.

Little, Walter. "Party and State in Peronist Argentina, 1945–1955." *Hispanic American Historical Review*, November 1973.

————. "Electoral Aspects of Peronism, 1946–1954." *Journal of Inter-American Studies*, August 1973.

Merks, Gilbert W. "Recessions and Rebellions in Argentina, 1870–1970." *Hispanic American Historical Review*, May 1973.

Morse, Richard M. "A Prolegomenon to Latin American Urban History." *Hispanic American Historical Review*, August 1972.

————. "Some Characteristics of Latin American Urban History." *American Historical Review*. January 1962.

————. "The Heritage of Latin America." In *The Founding of New Societies*, edited by Louis Hartz. New York: Harcourt, Brace and World, 1964.

Munger, William L. "Academic Freedom Under Perón." *Antioch Review*, Summer 1947.

Murmis, Miguel, and Juan Carlos Portantiero. "Estudios sobre los orígenes del peronismo." *Siglo XXI*, 1971 (Buenos Aires).

Nun, José. "A Latin American Phenomenon. The Middle Class Military Coup." In *Latin America: Reform or Revolution?*, edited by James Petras and Maurice Zeitlin.

Polit, Gustavo. "The Argentine Industrialists." In *Latin America: Reform or Revolution?*, edited by James Petras and Maurice Zeitlin.

Potash, Robert A. "Argentine Political Parties 1957–58." *Journal of Inter-American Studies*, October 1959.

Ranis, Peter. "Peronismo Without Perón." *Journal of Inter-American Studies*, January 1966.

Silverman, Bertram. "Labor Ideology and Economic Development in the Peronist Epoch." *Washington University Studies in Comparative International Development*, Vol. 4, No. 11 (1968–69)

Silvert, Kalman. "Nationalism in Latin America." *The Annals*, March 1961.

————. "Peronism in Argentina: A Rightist Reaction to the Social Problem of Latin America." In *Latin American History: Select Problems*, edited by Frederick B. Pike. New York: Harcourt, Brace and World, 1969.

Smith, Peter H. "The Social Base of Peronism." *Hispanic American Historical Review*, February 1972.

————. "Social Mobilization, Political Participation, and the Rise of Juan Perón." *Political Science Quarterly*, March 1969.

Snow, Peter G. "The Class Basis of Argentine Political Parties." *American Political Science Review*, No. 63, 1969.

Solberg, Carl. "Immigration and Urban Social Problems in Argentina and Chile, 1890–1914." *Hispanic American Historical Review*, May 1969.

————. "Agrarian Unrest and Agrarian Policy in Argentina, 1912–1930." *Journal of Interamerican Studies and World Affairs*, January 1971.

Stabb, Martin S. "Argentine Letters and the Peronato: An Overview." *Journal of Inter-American Studies and World Affairs*, Vol. XIII, (1971)

Tannenbaum, Frank. "The Political Dilemma in Latin America." *Foreign Affairs*, April 1960.

Walter, Richard J. "Elections in the City of Buenos Aires during the First Yrigoyen Administration: Social Class and Political Preference." *Hispanic American Historical Review*, November 1978.

————. "The Intellectual Background of the 1918 University Reform in Argentina." *Hispanic American Historical Review*, May 1969.

Whitaker, Arthur. "The Argentine Paradox." *Annals*, March 1961,

Winn, Peter. "From Martín Fierro to Peronism: A Century of Argentine Social Protest." *The Americas*, July 1978.

Wolff, Eric, and Edward Hansen. "Caudillo Politics: A Structural Analysis." *Comparative*

International Development, Vol. IX, (1966–67)
Worcester, Donald E. "The Spanish American Past—Enemy of Change." *Journal of
    Inter-American Studies,* January 1969.
Wynia, Gary W. "Argentina: The Frustration of Ungovernability." In *Politics, Policies,
    and Economic Development in Latin America,* edited by Robert Wesson. Stanford:
    Hoover Institution Press, 1984.
Zuvekas, Clarence, Jr. "Economic Growth and Income Distribution in Postwar Argen-
    tina." *Inter-American Economic Affairs,* Winter 1966.

Index

Acheson, Dean, 154, 196–97
agriculture, 31, 44, 46, 48–49
Air Force, Argentine, 126
Aldrey, Oscar, 69
Alea S.A., 200
Alem, Leandro N., 56, 57, 225
Alfonsín, Raúl, 373
Allende, Salvador, 355
Aloe, Carlos, 200
Alonso, José, 338
Alvarez, Juan, 164, 168
Alvear, Marcelo T. de, 62, 72, 75,
    208
anarchy and anarchists, 30, 34–35,
    56, 60, 182
Anaya, Elbio, 101
Antonio, Jorge, 88, 236, 249, 301,
    310, 314–15, 317, 318, 319–21,
    341, 342, 343, 344–45, 350,
    353–54, 359, 360, 361, 367
Apold, Raúl, 273
Apuntes de historia militar (Perón), 83,
    125
Ara, Pedro, 246–47
Aramburu, General Pedro, 307–8,
    309, 336–38, 347

Araucanian Indians, 83, 85
Argentina:
    admission to United Nations, 139
    Castilian heritage, 22–27
    civilization, 2–3
    colonial period, 23–24, 27–33
    cultural heritage, 2–3
    economy, 7, 8, 19, 45, 71–72, 76–
        77, 91–92
    geography of, 17–21, 30, 36
    Great Rift, 35–37
    historical overview, 7–9
    immigrants and immigration, *see*
        immigrants and immigration
    independence, 33–35
    industrialization, 225
    internal migrations, 77
    land policy, 31, 34, 47
    Liberal System, 40, 45, 49, 50–51,
        76
    national unity, period of, 39–44
    and Paraguay, 41, 42
    popular culture, 80–81
    population, 19, 42, 46
    social orders in, 27–29, 30–31,
        35–36, 49–50, 80

Argentina (*continued*)
  and worldwide depression, 70–71
Argentina, government of, 7–8
  centralization of, 90–91
  Chamber of Deputies, 57, 191
  Congress, 75, 307, 328
  conservative control of, 74–78
  corruption in, 63
  declaration of war (1945), 137–38
  Department of Labor and Wel-
    fare, 116, 175
  and foreign policy, 74, 79, 262–69
  "Fourth Reich" rumor, 151
  Liberating Revolution, 306–13
  Ministry of Agriculture, 46
  National Archives, 70
  National Labor Department, 114–
    15
  neutrality policy (World War II),
    106, 112, 225
  and Perón in exile, 303, 310
  Senate, 191
  Supreme Court, 155, 156, 162,
    190–91, 198, 307, 310, 328
  and United States, *see* United
    States; U.S. State Department
  War Ministry, 158–59
Argentine Action, 226, 228
Argentine-American Cultural Insti-
    tute, 153
Argentine Anti-Communist Alliance
    (Triple A death squad), 370,
    371–72
Argentine Revolution, 328–31, 339
Argentine Socialist Party, 57
Arias, Arnulfo, 298
Arlt, Roberto, 80
army, Argentine, 73
  and Perón, 175, 235, 249, 260
  revolution of 1930, 73–74
  and Yrigoyen, 60, 62, 72
Associated Press, 199
Asunción, 23
Avalos, Eduardo, 101, 105, 110,
    158, 161, 162, 163, 164, 168

Avellaneda, Nicolás, 42, 43
Azules, 321–22, 325, 328, 329

Balbín, Ricardo, 199, 239, 242, 256,
    308, 310, 347, 352, 354, 358,
    360, 361–62, 367
Banco de Buenos Aires, 50
Banco de Crédito Industrial, 127–28
barrio, 52–53
Barrio Norte, 52, 245
Barrio Presidente Perón, 210
Barrios, Americo, 303
Beagle Channel, 20, 84
Bengoa, General Leon, 253
Benítez, Antonio, 353, 360
Benítez, Father Hernán, 246, 338
Berle, Adolf, 137
Bernhard, Prince (Netherlands), 298
Bertolini, Orlando, 253
Betancourt, Romulo, 151, 303
Beveridge, Lord, 89
Beveridge Report, 89
blacks, 28, 38
Bloquismo, 89, 224
Bolivia, 17, 23, 111, 265, 267
Bonafacio del Carril, 121, 228
Bonaparte, Joseph, 33
Bonaparte, Napoleon, 33
Borges, Jorge Luis, 10, 80, 203–5
Borlenghi, Angel, 188, 257, 266,
    274, 276–77
Bormann, Martin, 151
Braden, Spruille, 140-42, 151–54,
    179, 180, 195–97, 263
Bramuglia, Juan, 188, 207, 236
Brazil, 17, 19, 76, 267–69, 320–21
Bruce, James, 197
Bryce, Viscount James, 7
Buchanan, James, 39
Buenos Aires (city):
  colonial trade route to, 23–24, 32
  Creole government, 33, 35–36
  federalization of, 41, 45
  first founding of, 22–23

geography of, 18
and the Great Rift, 35–36
invasion by England, 32–33
population, 32, 42, 51
and Rosas, 38
second founding of, 23
social order in, 51–53
viceroyalty of Río de la Plata, 32, 33
Buenos Aires (province), 18–19
post-independence, 34
Bunge, Alejandro, 225
Bunge, Carlos, 51
Byrnes, James, 154

Cabildo Abierto, 238–42, 248
Cabot, John Moors, 154–55, 179–80
Campo de Mayo, 69, 102, 105, 142, 157, 158–59, 167–68, 212
Cámpora, Héctor, 301, 315, 347–48, 351, 352, 353, 354–61
Cantoni, Frederico, 89, 231
carreta, 29, 30
Casa Rosada, 52, 61, 62, 73
bombing of, 277–78
Castile, 24–27
Castillo, Ramón, 75, 93, 97, 100, 101–2
Catholic Kings, 24, 32
cattle, 18, 31, 45, 47–48
caudillos tradition, 30, 37–38, 39, 40, 42, 89, 93, 312
and Peronism, 171, 223, 225
Chapultepec, Act of, 137, 141, 196
Charles V (king of Spain), 24, 32
Chile, 23
and Perón, 265–67
Perón in, 84–85
Christian Democratic Party, 271
Church, Roman Catholic:
in Argentina, 30
in Castile, 25–26
and Great Rift, 35
and Perón, 178–79, 194–95, 269–76, 277–78, 289, 318

CIO Committee on Latin American Affairs, 264–65
Circulo Militar, 162, 163
Civic Front of National Liberation (FRECILINA), 348
Clarin, 200
Cold War, 196, 197
Colegio Militar de la Nación, 67–68
Coleridge, Samuel Taylor, 21
Colorados, 321
Commonwealth Conference (Ottawa), 76
communications, colonial, 23–24
Comunidad Organizada, La (Perón), 229
communism, 117, 118, 221
Communist Party, 118, 119, 174, 178, 182, 193, 224, 257, 261, 271
Concordancia, 77
Conducción política (Perón), 70, 215, 230
Confederación General del Trabajo (CGT), 119, 166, 192, 202, 210, 229, 236, 238–39, 243, 244, 246–47, 249–50, 255, 257, 258, 260, 266, 272, 277, 281, 289–90, 307, 321, 322–23, 329, 333, 336, 345, 348, 361, 362, 367
Confederación General Professional (CGP), 260
Confederation of Intellectuals, 228
Conservatives, 174, 255, 257, 271, 352
constitutions, 34
constitutional convention, 193–95, 236
of 1853, 40, 46
of 1949, 195, 225
Cooke, John William, 301–2, 303, 332, 333
Cooke, Juan I., 99, 153
Córdoba, 19, 23
cordobazo, 336
Cossio, Pedro, 358, 365, 367

coups:
  Menéndez's, 242, 243, 250, 276
  September 24, 1945, 157
  Suárez, 250, 276
  Toranzo Calderón's, 276–78
  Valle, 308
Creoles:
  in colonial Argentina, 28
  culture, 2–3, 9
  and the Great Rift, 35–36
  and immigrants, 49–54
  values, 39, 228–33
Cresto, José, 317
Crosby, Ronald, 340–41
cuadra, 52–53

death squads, 370, 371–72
Dellepaine, General, 62
Democracia, 200, 206, 207, 262
Democratic Party, 256–57, 259
Desacato, 199, 239, 242
Descalzo, Bartolomé, 82
Descamisado Command, 335
"Descartes," 11, 262–63, 265, 273–
  74
Día de la Raza, 162–63, 164–65
Discépolo, Enrique Santos, 81
Dodero, Alberto, 200, 238, 297
Dominican Republic, Perón in exile
  in, 303–6
Dorticos, Osvaldo, 355
Duarte, Juan (Evita's father), 129–
  30, 131, 172
Duarte, Juan (Evita's brother), 162,
  171, 176, 194, 253–55
Dulles, John Foster, 264, 265
Dutey, Dominga, 63–64, 67

Economic Plan for 1952, 251
economy:
  agriculture, 46, 48–49
  export, 49–50, 71, 76–77, 91–92
  and Latin American states, 265–
    69
  livestock, 43, 45–46

stabilization plan, 330–31
  under Perón, 217–19, 225, 251–
    53, 260–61, 364
Eisenhower, Dwight D., 263–64
Eisenhower, Milton, 264
elections:
  fraud, 42–43, 74–75, 97
  and Perón, 175, 176–78, 242,
    361–362
  and Perón in exile, 308–9
  and Radical Party, 59, 60–61
  and revolution of June 4, 1943,
    106, 152
  universal male suffrage, 60, 75
  women's suffrage, 94
Encarnación, Doña, 38, 226
ENR, 335, 338, 345
Escuela de Suboficiales, 69
Escuela Superior de Guerra, 70
Escuela Superior Peronista, 215
Espejo, José, 236, 240, 244, 249–50
Espindola, Adolfo, 138–39, 140
estancias, 18, 42, 48, 54
estancieros, 30, 32, 38
Esta pueblo necesita (Gálvez), 226
Eva Perón City (La Plata), 19, 210
Eva Perón Day, 241
Eva Perón Foundation, 209–11,
  243, 249, 270, 272, 281, 300,
  310, 371
Everything and Nothing (Borges), 10
Evita (musical), 1, 12, 130
Export-Import Bank, 261, 265
Ezeiza Massacre, 357–58

Facundo (Sarmiento), 41–42
Falkland Islands war, 373
Farago, Ladislas, 151
Farrell, Edlemiro, 89–90, 104, 105,
  110, 113–14, 116, 117, 120–24,
  152, 156, 161, 163, 164, 167,
  168
federalism, 37, 39, 40, 75–76
Ferdinand (king of Spain), 24
Ferdinand VII (king of Spain), 33
Ferns, David, 252

Figueres, Pepe, 151
Figuerola, José, 116, 117–18, 188,
  217, 227, 235–36
Five-year Plan:
  first, 217–18
  second, 251–52, 260
Force is the Law of the Beasts (Perón),
  298
FORJA, 78, 174, 225
Framani, Andrés, 323, 324
Franco, Francisco, 74, 206, 315–16,
  356–57
Fraternidad, La, 117
*Frente Oriental de la Guerra Mundial
  en 1914* (Perón), 83
Freude, Ludwig, 162, 163
Frigerio, Rogelio, 308, 309, 310
Frondizi, Arturo, 259, 280, 290,
  308–13, 321, 348, 352
Fuerza es el derecho de las bestias, La
  (Perón), 298

Galimberti, Rodolfo, 355–56
Galtieri, General Leopoldo, 372–73
Gálvez, Manuel, 51, 80, 203, 226
Garay, Juan de, 23
Gardel, Carlos, 80–81
gauchos, 28–29, 34, 42, 51, 92
Gay, Luis, 173, 236
General Confederation of Youth,
  363
General Economic Confederation
  (CGE), 260, 348
Generation of '80, 45
gente decente, 51–52
gente de pueblo, 51, 52–53
Germany, 79, 109–10, 111–13
Gilaberte, Isaac, 298
Gilbert, Alberto, General, 112
Gonzáles, Enrique P. (Gonzalito), 99,
  100, 101, 102, 103–4, 105, 109,
  110–11, 112, 117
Good Neighbor Policy (U.S.), 106,
  114, 136, 196
Goulart, João, 268

Great Britain:
  and Argentine economy, 49–50,
    71, 76–77, 90–91
  immigrants from, 46–47, 79
  invasion of Buenos Aires, 32–33
  investments in Argentina, 43, 45,
    46–48, 79
  wars with Spain, 32
Great Rift, the, 35–37, 38, 40, 45,
  56, 76, 93–94, 122, 127, 176,
  203–4, 307
Griffis, Stanton, 264
Griffiths, John, 192–93
Guardo, Liliane, 205–6
Guardo, Ricardo, 205
Guido, José María, 321–22, 329
Grupo de Oficiales Unidos (GOU), 98,
  100, 101, 102, 103–5, 109, 110–
  12, 113

Harnisch, Johann, 110
Havana Resolutions, 107
Helmuth, Osmar, 110, 111
Hernández, José, 51, 68
Hispanic culture, 2–3, 9, 24–27
  and Perónism, 170
Historia del Peronismo (Evita Perón),
  215
Historia de una pasión argentina (Mal-
  lea), 80, 93
Hitler, Adolf, 74, 110
Hoover, J. Edgar, 193
hora de los pueblos, La (Perón), 334
Hour of the People, 347
Hughes, Ana (great grandmother),
  63
Hull, Cordell, 107, 108, 109, 114,
  126, 127, 136

Ibáñez, Carlos, 226, 266–67
Ibarguren, Carlos, 80, 225, 226
Ibarguren, Juana, 129–30, 172, 235
Illia, Arturo, 290, 319, 324–26, 328
Imbert, Aníbal, 129
immigrants and immigration, 31, 45,
  46–47

immigrants and immigration (*cont.*)
 and Argentine social orders, 49–
  50, 53–55
 call for, 46
Indians, 28, 30, 31, 42, 45, 47–48
individualism, Hispanic, 26–27, 30,
  31
 in Argentina, 52–53, 57, 94
 and Perón, 68
*Instituto Argentina de Promoción del
  Intercambio* (IAPI), 218, 225
intellectuals, Argentine, 78–81,
  202–5
International Monetary Fund, 252
Isabella (queen of Spain), 24
Italy, Perón in, 86–88
Ivanissevich, Oscar, 237–38

Jackson, Robert, 193
Jauretche, Arturo, 133, 134–35, 225
Jews, in Argentina, 221
Jones, Jesse, 107
Juan Perón Children's Library, 211
Jujuy, 19–20, 23, 93
Junín, 130
Justicialismo, 226–28, 229, 235, 252–
  53, 272, 309, 334
Justicialist Front, 313
Justicialist Front of National Libera-
  tion (FREJULI), 352, 354, 356,
  363
Justicialist Party, 346, 352, 354
Justo, Juan B., 57, 72, 77, 82, 97,
  225

Kennedy, John F., 316
Keyserling, Count, 80
Krause, Karl Christian Friedrich, 58
Krieger Vasena, Adalbert, 330–31,
  336

labor:
 under Perón, 188–90, 235, 264
 pre-Peronato, 94, 166
 after Perón's fall, 307–8, 331

and social revolution, 114–20
 strikes, 56, 62
labor laws, 117–18
Labor Party, 172–74, 177, 186,
  188–89, 192, 199
land policy and ownership, 31, 34,
  47–48
Lanusse, General Alejandro, 329,
  339, 345, 346, 348–49, 354
Laski, Harold, 89
Latino América: Ahora o Nunca
  (Perón), 269, 334
Laws of the Indies, 23
legislation, social, 115–16
Lencinas, Carlos Washington, 89
Lencinas, José Nestor, 89
Lencinismo, 89, 224
Levingston, Roberto, 338
liberalism:
 and the Great Rift, 35, 41–42
Liberal System, 40, 45, 49, 51, 53,
  54, 76
*Life in the Argentine Republic in the
  Days of the Tyrants* (Sarmiento),
  41–42
Lima, Admiral Vernengo, 164
Lives (Plutarch), 68
Lobos, 64–65
logia, *see Grupo de Oficiales Unidos*
  (GOU)
Lonardi, Eduardo, 85, 282, 307
López Rega, José, 342–45, 347, 352,
  356, 358–59, 361, 365, 367,
  368, 370, 370–71
Los Toldos, 129, 171, 172
Lucero, General Franklin, 283, 287
Lugones, Leopoldo, 51, 78, 226
Luna, Felix, 194
Luqui Lagleyze, Julio, 365
Luzardo, Baptista, 268

Magaldi, Agustín, 130
Magellan, Ferdinand, 17, 21
Magallanes, Sixto, 65
Mallea, Eduardo, 80, 92–93

Mañach, Jorge, 175, 226–27
Manual del Aspirante, 70
"March of the Constitution and Liberty," 156
Matera, Raúl, 318, 323, 324
Martín, General Osvoldo, 157–58
Martínez de Hoz, José, 371
Martínez Estrada, Ezequiel, 80, 81
Martínez, María, Estela (Isabel), 300–301, 303, 304, 316
   see also Perón, Isabel
Martín Fierro (Hernández), 51, 68, 182, 203
Martín García Island, 163, 164, 288, 313
Matthews, Herbert, 269
Maurras, Charles, 74
Mazorca, the, 56
Mazza, Captain, 166, 167
Memorias (Perón), 87
Mende, Raúl, 227, 266, 274
Méndez San Martín, Armando, 271
Mendoza, Pedro de, 22
Mendoza, 20, 28, 89, 119, 229
Menéndez, Benjamín, 242, 243, 250, 282
Men of May, 36–37, 40
Mercante, Domingo, 90, 98, 104, 117, 160, 161, 162, 163, 164, 165, 168, 171, 175, 177, 193–94, 236
Messersmith, George, 195–97, 201, 221
mestizos, 28, 30, 31, 35, 51
Mexico City conference, 137
Miller, Edward, 198, 212–13, 265
Miranda, Miguel, 218, 219
Mitre, Bartolomé, 41, 42, 43, 46, 56
Mittlebach, Aristóbulo, Colonel, 163
Montes, Miguel, 98, 101, 102, 104
Montoneros, 336–38, 345, 346–47, 349, 355, 356, 362, 365, 366–67, 370, 371, 372
Morgentheau, Henry, 107
Mosconi, General Enrique, 79, 225

Mussolini, Benito, 74, 87
My Message (Evita Perón), 246
My Mission in Life (Evita Perón), 243, 346

Nación, La, 200
nationalism:
   anti-United States, 332
   cultural and intellectual, 50–51, 78–80
   economic, 78–79, 225, 261
   and the Great Rift, 35
   and Montoneros, 337
   and neutrality, 106, 120–21
   after revolution of 1930, 74, 80, 93
Nationalist Liberation Alliance (ALN), 174, 221, 255
navy, Argentine, 282, 289
Neves da Fontoura, João, 267, 269
New York Times, 113, 264, 269, 346
Nicolini, Oscar, 158
Nufer, Albert, 263, 282

Ocampo, Victoria, 94
O Globo, 241
Ongania, General Juan Carlos, 322, 325, 328–31
Organization of American States (OAS), 197, 265
Orientación política (Perón), 232–33
Ortiz, Roberto, 74, 97
Osinde, Jorge, 348, 357

Pack, George, 244, 249
Paladino, Jorge, 347
pampas, 18–19, 23, 28–29, 30–32, 55, 93
Panama, Perón in exile in, 298–301
Paraguay, 17, 19, 265, 267
   Perón in exile, 291, 297
   war with Argentina, 41, 42
Paraná (city), 19
   Perón in, 69
   study of, 326–27, 331

Paraná (river), 17–18, 19, 22, 24
Parodi, Delia, 319
Partido Unico de la Revolución, 187,
     188–90
pastoralism, 30–31, 44, 46, 48
     Castilian roots, 27
     and Perón, 68
Patagonia, 20–21, 42, 47, 84
     Perón family in, 65–66
Patrón Costas, Robustiano, 97–98,
     99, 100
Pavón Pereyra, Enrique, 86–87, 364
Paz, Alberto Gainza, 201–2
Paz, Octavio, 2
"Peludo, The," 58
     see also Yrigoyen, Hipólito
People's Revolutionary Army (ERP),
     335, 349, 356, 362–63, 371
Peralta, 340
Perlinger, General Luis, 110, 112,
     121, 122, 125, 126
Pérez Jiménez, Marcos, 301, 302,
     303
Perón, Evita, 52, 128–35
     cancer, 237–38, 242–46
     coffin and corpse, 346–47
     death of, 246–48
     devotion to Perón, 207, 214–15
     Foundation, 209–11
     and events of October 12–17,
        1945, 163, 164, 165, 167
     marriage to Perón, 171–72
     Nazi connections, rumored, 142,
        151
     and Perón's political career, 159,
        177
     resentment of, 158, 201
     in Spain, 206–8
     transformation to public figure,
        132–33, 205–17
     vice-presidential nomination,
        239–41
     Women's Party, 212
Perón, Isabel, 300–301, 303, 304,
     316, 341–42, 344, 347, 351,
     358–59, 360–61, 365, 366,

     367–68, 370, 371
Perón, Juana (mother), 64–65
Perón, Juan Domingo, 2–3, 10–13
     abortive return to Argentina,
        319–321
     and armed forces, 120–21, 126–
        27, 156–57
     army career, 67–70, 84–90
     and Borges, 203–5
     and Braden, 141–42, 151–54, 180
     cabinet, 188
     campaign (1945–46), 176–81
     campaign (1972–73), 351–52, 361
     and Cámpora, 354–61
     childhood and family life, 64–67
     and Church, 178–79, 194–95,
        269–76, 277–78, 289, 318
     and CGT, 119
     credibility of biographies and
        accounts, 86–87
     Creole values, 228–33
     Cue interview, 151–52
     death of, 368, 369
     and death of Evita, 248–50
     "Descartes," 11, 262–63, 265,
        273–74
     education, 66–69
     election of, 181–82
     era of conciliation, 256–60
     in Europe, 85–89
     events of October 12–17, 1945,
        162–71
     and Evita, 131–35, 171–72, 301
     exile in Latin America, 297–306
     exile in Spain, 314–21, 340–54,
        361–62
     and Farrell, 89–90, 120, 121
     and Frondizi, 309–13
     GOU, 99, 101, 102, 103–4, 104–
        5, 110–11
     health, 318–19, 358, 364–65,
        367–68
     inauguration of, 187
     and Isabel, 300–301, 316, 364,
        365
     and labor, 114–15, 160, 166

La Plata speech, 125–26, 137
leaderships style, 183–86
and the left, 333
and López Rega, 344–45
marriages, 11, 83–84, 171–72, 316, 341
and Mercante, 90, 160
Military Attaché (Chile), 84–85
Nazi connections, rumored, 142, 151
and Nelly Rivas, 274–76, 291, 297
opposition to, 155–59, 160, 174–76, 230, 276–83
paranoia, 273–74
personality and techniques, 102, 115, 183–86
presidential ambitions (1943–45), 122–23, 139, 152–53
and Ramírez administration, 103–14
reelection of, 238–42
repression under, 197–205, 248
resigns all positions in Farrell government, 159–62
return to Argentina, 357–58
and revolution of June 4, 1943, 98
social revolution, 114–20
support for, 174, 175–76
teacher, 11–12, 69–70, 81–84, 229
third presidency, 362–68
and women, 68, 275
writings, 81–82, 83
vice-presidency, 122–28
visits Argentina (1972), 351–52
Yrigoyen's influence on, 57
Perón, Mario Avelino (brother), 64
Perón, Mario Tomás (father), 64, 68, 70
Perón, Tomás Liberato (grandfather), 63–64
Perón, Tomás Mario (great-grandfather), 63
Peronism and Peronists, 8, 322, 324, 327–28, 339, 347, 360, 362

left, 331–39
literature on, 12
nature of, 220–26
see also Perón, Juan Domingo
Peronist Armed Forces (FAP), 335, 338
Peronista Party, 190, 214, 281, 307, 309, 310
Peronist Women's Party, 212, 238, 319
Peronist Youth, 354, 355
Peru, 23, 76
viceroyalty of, 31
petroleum industry, nationalization of, 10, 79, 261
Philip II (king of Spain), 24, 25, 32
Piraña, 131, 134
Pistarini, General Juan, 159
Poggi, General, 321
polarization, Hispanic, 27
and the Great Rift, 37
political parties, 55–56
Ponzo, Father, 368
Popular Conservative Party, 347
porteños, 36–37
Potash, Robert, 73
Potofsky, Jacob, 264–65
Potosí, 23
Prada, Alfredo, 236–37
Prebisch, Raul, 225
Prensa, La, 178, 199–202, 248, 264
press, the, 199–203, 237, 242
Progressive Democratic Party, 174
provinces, backwardness of, 92–93
Puigvert, Antonio, 319
Punta del Este conference, 316

Quijano, J. Hortensio, 153, 159, 160–61, 173, 177, 258, 268
Quiroga, Facundo, 41

race:
colonial, 28, 30, 31
and the Great Rift, 35–36
Radical Civil Union of the People (UCRP), 308–9, 324–25

Radical Orientation Force of Young
Argentina (FORJA), 78, 174,
225
Radical Party, 55–56, 57, 59–60, 74,
75, 79
election of 1916, 60–61
and Perón, 123, 124–25, 153,
155–156, 174, 193, 226, 238,
239, 255, 256, 257, 261–62, 271
spoils system, 71
wings and factions of, 62, 74, 89,
224–25, 258–59, 347, 352, 360
radio, Perón and, 116, 120, 155
Radio Belgrano, 132, 166
Radio El Mundo, 131
Radiografía de la Pampa (Estrada), 80
railroads, 46, 48
strikes by workers, 69
Ramírez, Emilio, 110
Ramírez, Pedro, 99–100
administration of, 103–14, 115–
16, 123
Rawson, General Arturo, 100–101,
102, 103–4, 123, 140–41, 157–
58
Razón de mi Vida, La (Evita Perón),
243, 297
Reconquest, Spanish, 24–25
reforma constitucional, La (Ibarguren),
225
Rega Molina, Horacio, 203
Renovation Movement (1941), 228
Revolutionary Armed Forces (FAR),
335, 355, 362
Revolutionary Peronist Movement
(MRP), 33
revolutions and revolts:
of June 4, 1943, 97–103
of 1890, 55
of 1893, 55
of 1895, 55, 56
of 1905, 60
of 1930, 72–73
social, 114–20
Reyes, Cipriano, 116–17, 118, 166,
173, 184, 188–89, 192, 199, 236

Río Conference:
of 1942, 107–8
of 1947, 197
Río Declaration, 108
Río de la Plata, 17–18, 22
viceroyalty of, 32, 33
Río Gallagos, 65
Río Grande, 20
Río Negro, 42
Río Treaty, 197, 207
Rivadavia, Bernardino, 34–35
Rivas, Nelly, 274–76, 291, 297
Robertson, James Oliver, 94
Roca, General Julio, 42, 45, 47
Rocha, Gerardo, 269
Rockefeller, Nelson, 136, 140, 154,
335
Rogers, William, 355
Rojas, Admiral Isaac, 282
Rojas, Ricardo, 51, 226
Rojas Silveyra, Jorge, 347
Roosevelt administration, 106–9,
127, 137
see also United States; U.S. State
Department
Rosas, Juan Manuel de, 37–39, 57,
58, 80
Rossi, General Santos, 105–6, 110
Rucci, José, 345, 362

Sabattini, Amadeo, 259
Sábato, Ernesto, 167
Sáenz Peña, Roque, 60, 74
Sáenz Peña law of 1912, 60, 75
Sampay, Arturo, 193–94
San Cristóbal, 69
San Juan, 20, 23, 28, 89
earthquake, 131
San Martín, José de, 18–19, 85
Santa Fe, 23
Perón in, 69
Sarmiento, Domingo Faustino, 41–
43, 46, 51
sauvages argentins, les, 53
Scalabrini Ortiz, Raúl, 80

Scholasticism, Renaissance: in Spain, 26
Semana Tragica, 62
Silveyra, Jorge Rojas, 347
slaves, Black, 28, 30
socialism, 221
Socialist Party, 57, 75, 115, 119, 174, 178, 182, 193, 200, 224, 255, 257
social policies, 114–20, 225, 307
Sociedad Rural, 48
Solano Lima, Vicente, 352, 353, 358, 359, 360
Solari, Angel, 81
Sosa Molina, General José Humberto, 188, 212
Spain:
    Castile, 22–27
    Hispanic culture, 2–3, 22–27
    Perón in exile in, 314–21, 340–54, 361–62
    wars with France and Britain, 32–33
Spencer, Herbert, 50–51
Spengler, Oswald, 80
spiritualism, 334–35
Standard Oil Company of California, 10, 92, 261–62, 273, 303
"State of Internal Warfare," 242, 280
States of Seige:
    under Frondizi, 313
    June 4, 1943, 106, 137, 152
    September 26, 1945, 157, 176, 187
    November 6, 1974, 370
    see also revolutions
Statute of the Peon, 119
Statute of the Revolution, 328, 329
Stettinius, Edward, 136, 154
Storni, Segundo, Admiral, 109, 110
Strait of Magellan, 20, 84
strikes, 56, 62, 336
    and Perón, 69, 192, 235, 367
Stroessner, Alfredo, 291, 297, 321
students, *see* universities

Suárez, Francisco, 26
Suárez, José Francisco, 250, 273
Sueyro, Sabá, Admiral, 110
sugar cultivation, 20, 28, 49
    and labor unions, 119
Sulzberger, C.L., 346
Switzerland, Perón seeks exile in, 316

Taiana, Jorge, 353, 358–59, 360, 363–64, 367, 368
Tamborini, José, 174–75, 181
tango, 80–81
Tehuelche Indians, 21
Teisaire, Admiral Alberto, 121–22, 176, 258–59
Third World, 334, 345
Tierra del Fuego, 17, 20, 84
Times (London), 223
Tizón, Aurelia (Potota), 83–84, 85
Toledo, Juana Sosa, 64
Toranzo Calderon, Admiral Samuel, 276–78
Torre, Lisandro de la, 57–58, 59–61
trade:
    colonial routes, 22–24, 32
Tragic Week (1919), 62
transportation:
    colonial, 29, 32
    post-independence, 43, 45
    road building, 77
Tres revoluciónes militares (Perón), 81–82
Trujillo, Rafael, 151, 304–6
Trujillo, Ramfis, 303–5
Tucumán, 20, 23, 28, 33, 49, 119
Turner, Frederick Jackson, 48–49

UCRI, 308–10
Unión Cívica Radical, 55–56
    see also Radical Party
Unión Cívica Radical Junta Reorganizadora (UCRJR), 173–74, 177, 181, 186, 188
Unión Democrática (UD), 174–75, 178–79, 180–81, 182, 199

Union of Secondary School Students (UES), 271–72, 274
unions, labor, 117–20, 307–8
Unitarios, 37, 39
United Nations, 136, 137, 139
United Press, 199–200, 201
United Provinces of South America, 33, 34
United States, 40, 77, 79
  and Argentine neutrality (World War II), 106–9, 112, 123–24
  and Farrell, 113–14, 123
  Good Neighbor Policy, 106, 136
  investments in Argentina, 92
  nonrecognition of Argentina, 114, 123
  and Peronist left, 332
  recognition of Argentina, 136–38
  relations with Argentina, 99, 232, 262–65
U.S. State Department:
  under Acheson, 154, 198–99
  and Argentine policy in World War II, 124
  and Braden, 140–42, 151–54, 197–99
  and Byrnes, 154–55
  and Eisenhower administration, 263–65
  embassy in Argentina, 173, 177–78, 179–80, 192–93, 208
  and Evita Perón, 212–13, 248
  on fall of Perón, 279–80
  and Perón's exile, 303
  and Perón's plans to achieve presidency (1943–44), 123–24, 125–26, 155
  Secret Policy Statement of March 21, 1950, 222, 232
  under Stettinius, 136–37

universities, 157, 202–3, 330, 356, 363–64
University Law of 1947, 203
Uriburu, General José, 72, 73, 74, 78, 81, 82, 290
Urquiza, General Justo José de, 39, 43
Uruguay, 76, 265, 267
Uruguay river, 17–18, 19

Valle, Juan José, 308
Vandor, Augusto, 323, 332, 335, 336, 345
Vanguardia, 200
Vargas, Getulio, 226, 267–69, 274
Velazco, General Juan, 188
Venezuela, Perón in exile in, 301–3
Videla, Jorge, General, 372
Viola, General Roberto, 372
Vitoria, Francisco de, 26, 273
viveza, 52
viveza criolla, 27, 55, 312
Von der Golz, Marshall, 83, 125
Vuletich, Eduardo, 249–50, 266, 272

Wallace, Henry, 107
War Academy, Perón teaches at, 11, 82–83
War of the Desert, 45
Warren Mission, 140, 141
Welles, Sumner, 107, 108
World War II, Argentine policy during, 106–9

YPF, 79, 225, 261, 282–83
Yrigoyen, Hipólito, 56, 57–63, 70, 259, 290
  fall of, 70–73
  legacy to Perón, 224–25